D0102079

To access your free official Microsoft online course:

1. Go to www.cblearning.com/mstrial
2. Input your unique activation code, found below
3. Choose the 2-hour course you would like – choose from Hyper-V™, Exchange Server 2007, SharePoint® Server 2007, LINQ, VSTO or WCF
4. Fill in your details and required receipt information
5. Your login details will be emailed to you with instructions how to begin your Microsoft Online Learning course
6. You will have 30 days from activation to complete 2-hour course
7. Free course offer ends 31st December 2009

2268 20676 3881

You will need your receipt to access the course

* £25.99 value correct at time of print

Exam 70-293: *Planning and Maintaining a Microsoft Windows Server 2003 Network Infrastructure*

Objective	Pages
Planning and Implementing Server Roles and Server Security (1.0)	
Configure security for servers that are assigned specific roles.	9-31 to 9-37, 14-6 to 14-9
Plan a secure baseline installation.	8-19 to 8-34, 9-2 to 9-18, 10-2 to 10-26, 14-10 to 14-15
■ Plan a strategy to enforce system default security settings on new systems.	8-19 to 8-34, 10-2 to 10-26
■ Identify client operating system default security settings.	8-19 to 8-34, 10-10 to 10-18
■ Identify all server operating system default security settings.	8-19 to 8-34, 9-2 to 9-18, 10-10 to 10-18
Plan security for servers that are assigned specific roles. Roles might include domain controllers, Web servers, database servers, and mail servers.	9-19 to 9-39, 10-2 to 10-26, 14-16 to 14-21
■ Deploy the security configuration for servers that are assigned specific roles.	9-32 to 9-39, 10-19 to 10-26
■ Create custom security templates based on server roles.	9-19 to 9-31, 10-2 to 10-18
Evaluate and select the operating system to install on computers in an enterprise.	8-3 to 8-12, 8-19 to 8-34, 14-22 to 14-25
■ Identify the minimum configuration to satisfy security requirements.	8-3 to 8-12, 8-19 to 8-34
Planning, Implementing, and Maintaining a Network Infrastructure (2.0)	
Install and configure server hardware devices.	2-3 to 2-34, 15-6 to 15-11
■ Configure driver signing options.	2-3 to 2-13
■ Configure resource settings for a device.	2-14 to 2-24
■ Configure device properties and settings.	2-25 to 2-34
Plan and modify a network topology.	1-12 to 1-37, 15-12 to 15-16
■ Plan the physical placement of network resources.	1-31 to 1-37
■ Identify network protocols to be used.	1-12 to 1-30
Plan an Internet connectivity strategy.	3-3 to 3-23, 15-12 to 15-23
Plan network traffic monitoring. Tools might include Network Monitor and System Monitor.	6-2 to 6-15, 15-24 to 15-29
Troubleshoot connectivity to the Internet.	3-24 to 3-33, 15-30 to 15-35
■ Diagnose and resolve issues related to Network Address Translation (NAT).	3-24 to 3-33
■ Diagnose and resolve issues related to name resolution cache information.	3-24 to 3-33
■ Diagnose and resolve issues related to client configuration.	3-24 to 3-33
Troubleshoot TCP/IP addressing.	2-42 to 2-50, 15-36 to 15-40
■ Diagnose and resolve issues related to client computer configuration.	2-42 to 2-50
■ Diagnose and resolve issues related to DHCP server address assignment.	2-42 to 2-50
Plan a host name resolution strategy.	4-3 to 4-41, 4-50 to 4-57, 15-41 to 15-46
■ Plan a DNS namespace design.	4-3 to 4-27
■ Plan zone replication requirements.	4-28 to 4-41
■ Plan a forwarding configuration.	4-28 to 4-41
■ Plan for DNS security.	4-50 to 4-57
■ Examine the interoperability of DNS with third-party DNS solutions.	4-3 to 4-17
Plan a NetBIOS name resolution strategy.	4-3 to 4-17, 4-28 to 4-49, 15-47 to 15-52
■ Plan a WINS replication strategy.	4-3 to 4-17, 4-42 to 4-49
■ Plan NetBIOS name resolution by using the Lmhosts file.	4-3 to 4-17, 4-42 to 4-49
Troubleshoot host name resolution.	4-56 to 4-65, 15-53 to 15-57
■ Diagnose and resolve issues related to DNS services.	4-58 to 4-65
■ Diagnose and resolve issues related to client computer configuration.	4-58 to 4-65

Note: Exam objectives are subject to change at any time without prior notice and at Microsoft's sole discretion. Please visit the Microsoft Learning Certification Web site (*www.microsoft.com/learning/mcp/*) for the most current listing of exam objectives.

MCSE Self-Paced Training Kit (Exam 70-293):

Planning and Maintaining a Microsoft® Windows Server™ 2003 Network Infrastructure, Second Edition

Craig Zacker with
Anthony Steven of
Content Master

PUBLISHED BY
Microsoft Press
A Division of Microsoft Corporation
One Microsoft Way
Redmond, Washington 98052-6399

Library of Congress Control Number 2006922558

Printed and bound in the United States of America.

1 2 3 4 5 6 7 8 9   QWT   1 0 9 8 7 6

Distributed in Canada by H.B. Fenn and Company Ltd.

A CIP catalogue record for this book is available from the British Library.
Microsoft Press books are available through booksellers and distributors worldwide. For further information about international editions, contact your local Microsoft Corporation office or contact Microsoft Press International directly at fax (425) 936-7329. Visit our Web site at www.microsoft.com/mspress. Send comments to *tkinput@microsoft.com*.

Microsoft, Active Directory, ActiveX, Authenticode, BizTalk, FrontPage, IntelliMirror, Microsoft Press, NetMeeting, Tahoma, Verdana, Visual Basic, Visual Studio, Windows, Windows NT, and Windows Server are either registered trademarks or trademarks of Microsoft Corporation in the United States and/or other countries. Other product and company names mentioned herein may be the trademarks of their respective owners.

The example companies, organizations, products, domain names, e-mail addresses, logos, people, places, and events depicted herein are fictitious. No association with any real company, organization, product, domain name, e-mail address, logo, person, place, or event is intended or should be inferred.

This book expresses the author's views and opinions. The information contained in this book is provided without any express, statutory, or implied warranties. Neither the authors, Microsoft Corporation, nor its resellers, or distributors will be held liable for any damages caused or alleged to be caused either directly or indirectly by this book.

Product Planner: Ken Jones
Content Development Manager: Maureen Zimmerman
Project Manager: Maria Gargiulo, Karen Szall

Body Part No. X12-21288

About the Authors

Craig Zacker

Craig is a writer, editor, and networker whose computing experience began in the days of teletypes and paper tape. After making the move from minicomputers to PCs, he worked as an administrator of Novell NetWare networks and as a PC support technician while operating a freelance desktop publishing business. After earning a Master's Degree in English and American Literature from New York University, Craig worked extensively on the integration of Microsoft Windows NT into existing internetworks, supported fleets of Windows workstations, and was employed as a technical writer, content provider, and Webmaster for the online services group of a large software company. Since devoting himself to writing and editing full time, Craig has authored or contributed to many books on networking topics, operating systems, and PC hardware, including *MCSA/MCSE Self-Paced Training Kit (Exam 70-216): Microsoft Windows 2000 Network Infrastructure Administration*, Second Edition, and *MCSA/MCSE Self-Paced Training Kit (Exam 70-218): Managing a Microsoft Windows 2000 Network Environment*. He has also developed educational texts for college courses, online training courses for the Web, and has published articles with top industry publications. For more information on Craig's books and other works, see *http://www.zacker.com*.

Content Master

Anthony Steven is a technology manager with Content Master, a division of CM Group Ltd. Content Master is a Microsoft Gold Certified Partner that specializes in developing technical content. Anthony is a trainer and consultant, and has worked with the Windows Server family of products for many years, specializing in messaging and management technologies. He has authored many technical articles for Microsoft, including the "Security Monitoring and Attack Detection Guide" and the "Identity and Access Management Series." Anthony is married with two children and lives in Nidderdale, Yorkshire, in the United Kingdom.

Steve Ryan is a senior technologist with Content Master. He was one of the first Microsoft Certified Trainers to achieve Windows Server 2003 MCSE status and has authored courseware for Microsoft Learning. He has also written technical documentation, including white papers, and recently authored the "Administrator Accounts Security Planning Guide" and "Services and Service Accounts Security Planning Guide" for Microsoft. Steve is married with three children and lives in East Yorkshire in the United Kingdom.

Paul Roddick is an associate writer for Content Master and has worked with PC networks for more than 21 years, initially as a networking software developer in the 1980s. Today, Paul is actively involved in writing, training, and consulting on Microsoft Windows Server 2003 network infrastructure. He is a Microsoft Certified Trainer and was one of the first UK-based Microsoft Certified Professionals, gaining his certification in 1991. When not working with computers, Paul is a keen thespian and is a member of a local dramatic society.

Contents at a Glance

Practices

Tables

Troubleshooting Labs

Case Scenario Exercises

Contents

What do you think of this book? We want to hear from you!	Microsoft is interested in hearing your feedback about this publication so we can continually improve our books and learning resources for you. To participate in a brief online survey, please visit: *www.microsoft.com/learning/booksurvey/*

2   Planning a TCP/IP Network Infrastructure

4   Planning a Name Resolution Strategy

8   Planning a Secure Baseline Installation

9   Hardening Servers

10   Deploying Security Configurations

Part 2 Prepare for the Exam

14 Planning and Implementing Server Roles and Server Security (1.0)

About This Book

Welcome to *MCSE Self-Paced Training Kit (Exam 70-293): Planning and Maintaining a Microsoft Windows Server 2003 Network Infrastructure*, Second Edition. In this book, you study some of the more advanced applications, protocols, and services included with Windows Server 2003 with Service Pack 1 (SP1) and learn how to use them to create a network that is both efficient and secure. For many of these applications, protocols, and services, implementing them on a network consists of a good deal more than just running an installation program or configuring a few parameters; many of them require careful planning and continual maintenance once you have completed the initial implementation. This book covers all these phases of the implementation process, so you learn all the relevant information about each network infrastructure component.

Planning The 70-293 exam includes simulation questions. Simulating a computer running the Windows Server 2003 operating system, these challenging questions provide you with a virtual computer interface through which you need to perform a number of administrative procedures. A simulation question presents a scenario with a list of requirements that you must translate into a set of procedures to perform. For a demonstration of a simulation, see the "Answering Simulation Questions" demo on the companion CD.

Intended Audience

This book was developed for information technology (IT) professionals who plan to take the related Microsoft Certified Professional (MCP) exam 70-293, *Planning and Maintaining a Microsoft Windows Server 2003 Network Infrastructure*, as well as IT professionals who design, implement, and maintain networks based on Microsoft Windows Server 2003 SP1 and its related technologies.

Note Exam skills are subject to change without prior notice and at the sole discretion of Microsoft.

Prerequisites

The MCSE 70-293 exam and this training kit do not have any official prerequisites, but students should have the following:

- At least one year of experience implementing and administering a Microsoft Windows network with the following characteristics: 250 to 5,000 or more users, at least three physical locations, a minimum of three Active Directory domain controllers, and a variety of network services and resources, such as file and print servers, client/server applications, Internet access, and remote access

- At least one year of experience implementing and maintaining desktop operating systems

- Experience planning and designing networks

About the CD-ROM

For your use, this book includes a companion CD-ROM. This CD-ROM contains a variety of informational aids to complement the book content:

- The Microsoft Press Readiness Review Suite Powered by MeasureUp. This suite of practice tests and objective reviews contains questions of varying degrees of complexity and offers multiple testing modes. You can assess your understanding of the concepts presented in this book and use the results to develop a learning plan that meets your needs.

- An electronic version of this book (eBook). For information about using the eBook, see the section "The eBook" later in this introduction.

- Lab files that you use to complete exercises in this training kit.

- Sample chapters from several Microsoft Press books that give you additional information about Windows Server 2003 and introduce you to other resources that are available from Microsoft Press.

- An overview of Windows Server 2003 Service Pack 1 and Windows Server 2003 R2.

- A free demo: "Answering Simulation Questions."

- A demo and a simulation that introduce you to Shadow Copies.

- Bonus material including white papers and links to a free e-learning course and clinic.

Two additional CD-ROMs contain a 180-day Evaluation Edition of Microsoft Windows Server 2003 with SP1 and R2, Enterprise Edition. You will use SP1 to complete this training kit. R2 is for your reference only; do not install R2 until you have completed the training kit exercises.

Important   The 180-day Evaluation Edition provided with this training kit is not the full retail product and is provided only for the purposes of training and evaluation. Microsoft Technical Support does not support this Evaluation Edition.

For additional support information regarding this book and the CD-ROM (including answers to commonly asked questions about installation and use), visit the Microsoft Press Technical Support Web site at *http://www.microsoft.com/learning/support/books/*. You can also e-mail *tkinput@microsoft.com* or send a letter to Microsoft Press, Attention: Microsoft Press Technical Support, One Microsoft Way, Redmond, WA 98052-6399.

Features of This Book

This book has two parts. Use Part 1 to learn at your own pace and practice what you've learned with practical exercises. Part 2 contains questions and answers that you can use to test yourself on what you've learned.

Part 1: Learn at Your Own Pace

Each chapter identifies the exam objectives that are covered in the chapter, provides an overview of why the topics matter by explaining how the information applies in the real world, and lists any prerequisites that must be met to complete the lessons presented in the chapter.

The chapters contain a set of lessons. Lessons contain practices that include one or more hands-on exercises. These exercises give you an opportunity to use the skills being presented or explore the part of the application being described. Each lesson also has a set of review questions to test your knowledge of the material covered in that lesson.

After the lessons, you are given an opportunity to apply what you've learned in a case scenario exercise. In this exercise, you work through a multistep solution for a realistic case scenario. You are also given an opportunity to work through a troubleshooting lab that explores difficulties you might encounter when applying what you've learned on the job.

Each chapter ends with a summary of key concepts and a short section listing key topics and terms that you need to know before taking the exam, summarizing the key learning points with a focus on the exam.

Real World   Helpful Information

You will find sidebars like this one, which contain related information you might find helpful. "Real World" sidebars contain specific information gained through the experience of IT professionals just like you.

Part 2: Prepare for the Exam

Part 2 helps to familiarize you with the types of questions that you will encounter on the MCP exam. By reviewing the objectives and the sample questions, you can focus on the specific skills that you need to improve before taking the exam.

See Also　For a complete list of Microsoft certification exams and their related objectives, go to *http://www.microsoft.com/learning/mcp/default.asp*.

Part 2 is organized by the exam's objectives. Each chapter covers one of the primary groups of objectives, called *Objective Domains*. Each chapter lists the tested skills you must master to answer the exam questions and includes a list of further reading to help you improve your ability to perform the tasks or use the skills specified by the objectives.

Within each Objective Domain, you will find the related objectives that are covered on the exam. Each objective provides you with several practice exam questions. The answers are accompanied by explanations of each correct and incorrect answer.

On the CD　These questions are also available on the companion CD as a practice test.

Informational Notes

Several types of reader aids appear throughout the training kit.

- **Tip** contains methods of performing a task more quickly or in a not-so-obvious way.
- **Important** contains information that is essential to completing a task.
- **Note** contains supplemental information.
- **Caution** contains valuable information about possible loss of data; be sure to read this information carefully.
- **Warning** contains critical information about possible physical injury; be sure to read this information carefully.
- **See Also** contains references to other sources of information.
- **Planning** contains hints and useful information that should help you plan the implementation.
- **Security Alert** highlights information you need to know to maximize security in your work environment.
- **Exam Tip** flags information you should know before taking the certification exam.
- **Off the Record** contains practical advice about the real-world implications of information presented in the lesson.

Notational Conventions

The following conventions are used throughout this book.

- Characters or commands that you type appear in **bold** type.

- *Italic* in syntax statements indicates placeholders for variable information. Italic is also used for newly introduced terms and book titles.

- Names of files and folders appear in Title caps, except when you are to type them directly. Unless otherwise indicated, you can use all lowercase letters when you type a file name in a dialog box or at a command prompt.

- File name extensions appear in all lowercase.

- Acronyms appear in all uppercase.

- Monospace type represents code samples, examples of screen text, or entries that you might type at a command prompt or in initialization files.

- Square brackets [ ] are used in syntax statements to enclose optional items. For example, [*filename*] in command syntax indicates that you can choose to type a file name with the command. Type only the information within the brackets, not the brackets themselves.

- Braces { } are used in syntax statements to enclose required items. Type only the information within the braces, not the braces themselves.

Keyboard Conventions

- A plus sign (+) between two key names means that you must press those keys at the same time. For example, "Press ALT+TAB" means that you hold down ALT while you press TAB.

- A comma (,) between two or more key names means that you must press each of the keys consecutively, not together. For example, "Press ALT, F, X" means that you press and release each key in sequence. "Press ALT+W, L" means that you first press ALT and W at the same time, and then release them and press L.

Getting Started

This training kit contains hands-on exercises to help you learn about the networking features of Windows Server 2003 with SP1, Enterprise Edition. Use this section to prepare your self-paced training environment. Your environment should meet the system requirements listed at *http://www.microsoft.com/windowsserver2003/evaluation/sysreqs/default .mspx*.

Caution Several exercises require you to make changes to the computer running Windows Server 2003 SP1, which can have undesirable results if the system is used for other purposes or is connected to a production network. It is strongly recommended that you create a new Windows Server 2003 SP1 installation on your computer using the 180-day Evaluation Edition of the operating system provided on the CD-ROM (CD1 only). If the computer is connected to a network, check with your network administrator before attempting these exercises.

Hardware Requirements

Each computer must have the following minimum hardware configuration.

- Minimum CPU: 133 MHz processor (550 MHz is recommended)
- Minimum RAM: 128 MB (256 MB is recommended)
- Hard disk space for setup: 1.5 GB to 2.0 GB
- Display monitor capable of 800 × 600 resolution or higher
- CD-ROM or DVD-ROM drive
- Microsoft Mouse or compatible pointing device
- Network interface adapter (optional)

Software Requirements

The following software is required to complete the procedures in this training kit:

- Windows Server 2003 SP1, Enterprise Edition (A 180-day Evaluation Edition of Windows Server 2003 with SP1 and R2, Enterprise Edition, is included with this training kit.)

Caution The 180-day Evaluation Edition provided with this training kit is not the full retail product and is provided only for the purposes of training and evaluation. Microsoft Technical Support does not support these Evaluation Editions. For additional support information regarding this book and the CD-ROMs (including answers to commonly asked questions about installation and use), visit the Microsoft Press Technical Support Web site at *http: //www .microsoft.com/learning/support/books*. You can also e-mail *tkinput@microsoft.com* or send a letter to Microsoft Press, Attn: Microsoft Press Technical Support, One Microsoft Way, Redmond, WA 98502-6399.

Setup Instructions

Set up your computer according to the manufacturer's instructions. Then install Windows Server 2003 SP1, Enterprise Edition, according to the instructions provided on the installation CD-ROM.

> **Important**   The Evaluation Edition software provided with this training includes Service Pack 1. Install Service Pack 1 (CD1) to complete the exercises in this training kit. Do not install R2 (CD2) until you have completed the exercises. This version of R2 is for your reference only. It is not covered in the 70-293 exam and, therefore, is not covered in this training kit.

Use the following table during installation to help you configure the Windows Setup parameters.

Windows Setup Wizard page	Settings
Regional And Language Options	Default (English)
Personalize Your Software	Enter your name and organization.
Your Product Key	Enter the product key provided with the Windows Server 2003 SP1 CD-ROM.
Licensing Modes	Default
Computer Name And Administrator Password	Computer Name: Server01 Administrator Password: (enter a strong password of your choice)
Modem Dialing Information	Default
Date And Time Settings	Your date, time, and time zone
Networking Settings	Custom Settings IP Address: 10.0.0.1 Subnet Mask: 255.0.0.0 Preferred DNS Server: 10.0.0.1
Workgroup Or Computer Domain	Default (Workgroup named "WORKGROUP")

> **Caution**   If your computers are connected to a larger network, you *must* verify with your network administrator that the computer names, domain name, and other information used in setting up your system as described in this section does not conflict with network operations. If it does conflict, ask your network administrator to provide alternative values and use those values throughout the exercises in this book.

Setup for Practice Exercises

After you complete the Windows Server 2003 SP1 installation, complete the following configuration steps to prepare your computer for the practice exercises in the lessons.

1. Create a folder called Windist on your computer's system drive. Then, copy the contents of the I386 folder on the Windows Server 2003 SP1 CD-ROM to the Windist folder.

2. Use the Manage Your Server page (which appears by default after you log on to the computer for the first time) to add the domain controller role to the server. This installs the Active Directory, DHCP, and DNS services on the computer. The procedure is as follows:

   a. On the Manage Your Server page, click the Add Or Remove A Role hyperlink. The Preliminary Steps page appears.

   b. Click Next. The Configure Your Server Wizard analyzes the computer. When the analysis completes, the Configuration Options page appears.

   c. Click the Typical Configuration For A First Server option button, and then click Next. The Active Directory Domain Name page appears.

   d. In the Active Directory Domain Name text box, type **contoso.com**, and then click Next. The NetBIOS Name page appears.

   e. Click Next to accept the default DNS and NetBIOS domain names. The Forwarding DNS Queries page appears.

   f. Click No, Do Not Forward Queries, and then click Next. The Summary Of Selections page appears.

   g. Click Next to accept your selections. A Configure Your Server Wizard message box appears.

   h. Click OK to begin the installation process. After a few minutes, the computer restarts.

   i. Log on as Administrator. The Server Configuration Progress page appears to continue the installation process.

   j. When the installation is complete, click Next, and then click Finish in the This Server Is Now Configured page.

   k. Close the Manage Your Server window.

3. Install the Microsoft Loopback Adapter (a virtual network interface adapter) using the following procedure:

   a. From Control Panel, display the Add Hardware Wizard.

   b. Click Next to begin the search for new hardware. The Is The Hardware Connected? page appears.

c. Click Yes, I Have Already Connected The Hardware, and then click Next. The Following Hardware Is Already Installed On Your Computer page appears.

d. Scroll down in the Installed Hardware list, select Add A New Hardware Device, and then click Next. The Wizard Can Help You Install Other Hardware page appears.

e. Select the Install The Hardware That I Manually Select From A List (Advanced) option button, and then click Next. The From The List Below, Select The Type Of Hardware You Are Installing page appears.

f. Scroll down in the Common Hardware Types list, click Select Network Adapters, and then click Next. The Select Network Adapter page appears.

g. Select Microsoft in the Manufacturer list and Microsoft Loopback Adapter in the Network Adapter list, and then click Next. The Wizard Is Ready To Install Your Hardware page appears.

h. Click Next again to install the adapter driver.

i. When the Completing The Add Hardware Wizard page appears, click Finish to complete the installation.

4. Rename the icons in the Network Connections window, using the following procedure:

a. Right-click the Local Area Connection icon (corresponding to the network interface adapter in the computer), select Rename from the shortcut menu, and rename it **LAN Connection**.

b. Right-click the Local Area Connection 2 icon (corresponding to the Microsoft Loopback Adapter you just installed), select Rename from the shortcut menu, and rename it **WAN Connection**.

See Also   If you do not have a network interface adapter installed in your computer, you can repeat the procedure in Step 3 twice to install two Microsoft Loopback Adapters, and then rename the two Local Area Connection icons as described here.

The Microsoft Press Readiness Review Suite

The CD-ROM includes a practice test consisting of 300 sample exam questions and an objective review with an additional 125 questions. Use these tools to reinforce your learning and identify any areas where you need to gain more experience before taking the exam.

▶ **To install the practice test and objective review**

1. Insert the companion CD-ROM into your CD-ROM drive.

> **Note** If AutoRun is disabled on your machine, refer to the Readme.txt file on the CD-ROM.

   2. Click Readiness Review Suite on the user interface menu and follow the prompts.

The eBook

The companion CD includes an electronic version of this training kit, as well as bonus material, including sample chapters from several Microsoft Press books and relevant white papers. The eBook and bonus materials are in Portable Document Format (PDF) and can be viewed using Adobe Reader (*http://www.adobe.com*).

▶ **To use the eBook**

   1. Insert the companion CD into your CD-ROM drive.

> **Note** If AutoRun is disabled on your computer, refer to the Readme.txt file on the CD.

   2. Click eBook on the user interface menu and follow the prompts. You can also review any of the other PDF files that are provided for your use.

The Microsoft Certified Professional Program

The Microsoft certifications provide the best method for proving your command of current Microsoft products and technologies. The exams and corresponding certifications are developed to validate your mastery of critical competencies as you design and develop, or implement and support, solutions with Microsoft products and technologies. Computer professionals who become Microsoft certified are recognized as experts and are sought after industry-wide. Certification brings a variety of benefits to the individual and to employers and organizations.

> **See Also** For a full list of Microsoft certifications, go to *http://www.microsoft.com/learning/itpro/default.asp*.

Technical Support

Every effort has been made to ensure the accuracy of this book and the contents of the companion CD. If you have comments, questions, or ideas regarding this book or the companion disc, please send them to Microsoft Press using either of the following methods:

E-mail: *tkinput@microsoft.com*

Postal Mail: Microsoft Press
                 Attn: *MCSE Self-Paced Training Kit (Exam 70-293): Planning and
                 Maintaining a Microsoft Windows Server 2003 Network Infrastructure,*
                 Second Edition, Editor
                 One Microsoft Way
                 Redmond, WA 98052-6399

For additional support information regarding this book and the CD-ROM (including answers to commonly asked questions about installation and use), visit the Microsoft Press Technical Support Web site at *http://www.microsoft.com/learning/support/books/*. To connect directly to the Microsoft Press Knowledge Base and enter a query, visit *http://www.microsoft.com/mspress/support/search.asp*. For support information regarding Microsoft software, please connect to *http://support.microsoft.com/*.

Evaluation Edition Software Support

The 180-day Evaluation Edition provided with this training is not the full retail product and is provided only for the purposes of training and evaluation. Microsoft and Microsoft Technical Support do not support this Evaluation Edition.

> **Caution**   The Evaluation Edition of Windows Server 2003 with SP1 and R2, Enterprise Edition, that is included with this book should not be used on a primary work computer. The Evaluation Edition is unsupported. For online support information relating to the full version of Windows Server 2003 R2, Enterprise Edition, that *might* also apply to the Evaluation Edition, you can connect to *http://support.microsoft.com/*.

Information about any issues relating to the use of this Evaluation Edition with this training kit is posted to the Support section of the Microsoft Press Web site (*http://www.microsoft.com/learning/support/books/*). For information about ordering the full version of any Microsoft software, please call Microsoft Sales at (800) 426-9400 or visit *http://www.microsoft.com*.

Part 1
Learn at Your Own Pace

1 Planning a Network Topology

Exam Objectives in this Chapter:

- Plan and modify a network topology.
- Plan the physical placement of network resources.
- Identify network protocols to be used.

Why This Chapter Matters

This chapter introduces some of the most basic decisions you must make when designing a network for a particular organization at a particular site. As a network designer, you are responsible for determining the requirements of the network's users, administrators, and owners, and then for creating a network plan that attempts to fulfill them all. This chapter is by no means a complete survey of the network design process, but it does demonstrate how certain design decisions have profound repercussions for network planning, implementation, and maintenance.

For example, understanding the properties of the various network media in use today, as summarized in this chapter, helps you understand which medium is best suited to a particular network installation. The choice of medium can be based on the physical nature of the site where the network will be installed, or on the requirements of the network users, or more likely both.

When creating a network design, comprehensive documentation is vital, both for the benefit of the people who will install the network and for those who will maintain it later. This chapter specifies some of the most important information you should include in a network blueprint and indicates how the networking components you choose affect what information you should provide.

Lessons in this Chapter:

Before You Begin

Although it contains some introductory information, this chapter assumes at least a perfunctory knowledge of computer networking, such as the basic physical components of a network and how protocols such as Ethernet and Transmission Control Protocol/Internet Protocol (TCP/IP) contribute to network communications.

Lesson 1: Windows Server 2003 and the Network Infrastructure

A *network infrastructure* is a set of physical and logical components that provide connectivity, security, routing, management, access, and other integral features on a network. During a network's planning phase, engineers select the hardware and software components that will compose the network infrastructure and specify the particular location, installation, and configuration of those components.

After this lesson, you will be able to

- Understand the difference between a network's physical infrastructure and its logical infrastructure
- Describe the network infrastructure planning process
- Understand the process of implementing a network infrastructure plan
- List the tasks involved in maintaining a network infrastructure

Estimated lesson time: 15 minutes

What Is a Network Infrastructure?

In most cases, the elements of a network infrastructure are both inherited and designed. If you are building a network that will be connected to the Internet, for example, certain aspects of the network, such as the use of the TCP/IP protocol suite, are inherited from the Internet. Other network elements, such as the physical layout of basic network components, are chosen by design when the network is first conceived and are then inherited by later versions of the network as it evolves. It is rare for an engineer to have the opportunity to design a network from scratch, with no pre-existing influences. Nearly always, the engineer must incorporate some existing elements into the network design, such as specific applications, operating systems, protocols, or hardware components.

Implementing a network infrastructure is the process of evaluating, purchasing, and assembling the specified components, and installing them in the manner prescribed by the design plan. The implementation process begins with engineers installing the network's hardware infrastructure, including computers, cables, and connectivity devices such as hubs, switches, and routers, as well as printers and other peripherals. After the hardware is in place, the engineers install and configure the operating systems, applications, and other software.

The operating systems running on the computers are the primary software components in the network infrastructure, because they incorporate the protocols and other routines that make network communications possible. In addition to the standard communication protocols common to all network operating systems, the Microsoft Windows Server 2003 family also includes a collection of applications and services that implement important security and special communications capabilities on the network.

The significance of the network infrastructure does not end when the construction of the network is complete, however. The personnel responsible for maintaining the network must have an intimate knowledge of the network's infrastructure to expand the network, perform upgrades, and troubleshoot problems. The 70-293 exam tests your knowledge of how the infrastructure affects the planning, implementation, and maintenance of a medium-to-large network, and of how Windows Server 2003 functions as a part of that infrastructure.

Physical Infrastructure

A network's *physical infrastructure* is its topology—the physical design of the network—along with hardware components such as cabling, routers, switches, hubs, servers, and workstations. The hardware you select when planning the network's physical infrastructure is frequently dependent on elements of the network's logical infrastructure. For example, if you decide to use Ethernet for your network's data-link layer protocol, you are limited to certain specific cable types supported by Ethernet, and the network's connectivity components—hubs, routers, and switches—must be designed for use with Ethernet as well.

For a small network, the physical infrastructure can be very simple—computers, a hub, and a few cables are generally all you need. For medium-to-large networks, however, the physical infrastructure can be extraordinarily complex. In addition to a large fleet of computers, a vast system of cables, and multiple interconnected hubs, the network might require routers or switches to connect segments, plus the additional components needed to support Internet connections, remote client access, wide area connections to other sites, or wireless connectivity.

The hardware used to implement these additional technologies is various and always relates to the network's logical infrastructure. For example, to connect the Ethernet local area network (LAN) in the company headquarters to the Ethernet LAN in a branch office, you must choose a different data-link layer protocol for the wide area network (WAN) connection (such as Point-to-Point Protocol), as well as a different network medium (such as a dial-up or a T-1 connection), and you must be sure that the hardware and software on both LANs support the WAN technology you choose.

 See Also For more information on WAN connections, see Lesson 1 in Chapter 3, "Planning Internet Connectivity," and Lesson 1 in Chapter 5, "Using Routing and Remote Access."

Exam Tip   Familiarity with the physical infrastructure of a network is prerequisite knowledge for the 70-293 exam. You should be familiar with the functions of all the basic hardware components and how to connect them to construct a network.

Logical Infrastructure

A network's *logical infrastructure* comprises the many software elements that connect, manage, and secure hosts on the network. The logical infrastructure allows communication between computers over the pathways described in the physical topology. The logical infrastructure of a network consists of both abstract software elements, such as networking protocols, and concrete elements, such as specific software products.

For example, when designing the infrastructure for a medium-to-large network, you will probably decide to use the TCP/IP protocols for network and transport-layer communications. At this stage of planning, TCP/IP is considered to be an abstract element because you can implement the protocols using any one of several software products. After deciding on the abstract element, you must also select the concrete element you will use to implement that abstract element. After deciding to use TCP/IP, for example, you might then select the TCP/IP implementation found in the Microsoft Windows operating systems.

In addition to basic communication protocols such as TCP/IP, the abstract elements of the logical infrastructure can include security technologies such as digital certificates and the IP Security (IPSec) protocols. Various types of concrete elements can implement these abstract elements.

Planning   For a network based on Windows Server 2003, most concrete elements needed in a typical infrastructure are realized in the operating system itself. In other cases, you might need to implement protocols and abstract security components as separate software products.

Windows Server 2003 includes a large number of optional protocols and services, and deciding which of those protocols and services you want to use is also part of the logical infrastructure design process. In some cases, you might decide to use a third-party product rather than an operating system component. For example, Windows Server 2003 includes a backup software program of its own, but you might decide one of the other network backup software products on the market offers additional features that you need.

Planning a Network Infrastructure

Planning the infrastructure is by far the most complicated part of building a network because during this phase you create the blueprint you will use to implement the network and maintain it later. A complete network infrastructure plan consists of a great deal more than a physical infrastructure layout and a list of hardware and software products. To plan the infrastructure properly, a network designer must consider the requirements of the network's users, its owners, and its hardware and software components.

A basic question the network designer has to ask is: What tasks do the network users have to accomplish? Answering this question requires the designer to define the types of communications the users need and the software they need to accomplish their tasks. However, the process is not as simple as selecting an application. The users' needs can affect many aspects of the network infrastructure.

For example, if the network has users who must be able to view video streamed from the Internet in real time, the ramifications for the network infrastructure design go well beyond the selection of an application that can display a video stream. The designer must also consider other elements, such as the bandwidth that streaming video consumes on the local network and the speed of the Internet connection needed to support the application.

In addition to selecting applications, a network designer must also be conscious of the services the network's users need for their computers to function properly.

> **Exam Tip** A large part of the 70-293 exam is devoted to the planning, implementation, and maintenance of Windows Server 2003 services, such as the DHCP Server service, the DNS Server service, and the Windows Internet Name Service (WINS) service. The planning process for services like these involves not only determining whether to use them, but also designing an IP addressing strategy and a Domain Name System (DNS) namespace, both of which are complex issues covered in depth in Chapter 2, "Planning a TCP/IP Network Infrastructure," and Chapter 4, "Planning a Name Resolution Strategy," respectively.

Security is also an omnipresent consideration in planning a network infrastructure. The designer must attempt to anticipate all possible dangers to the network and plan a suitable security infrastructure to protect it from those dangers. The security infrastructure might include advanced configuration of the operating systems, services, and applications, as well as the use of additional components, such as IPSec and digital certificates. Many of the lessons in this book are devoted to the determination of security requirements and the implementation of security mechanisms on a Windows Server 2003 network.

Implementing a Network Infrastructure

The process of implementing the technologies outlined in a network infrastructure plan typically involves a number of disciplines. Tasks such as the installation of network cables, for example, are frequently delegated to outside contractors that specialize in that type of work. The installation of operating systems and other software components is also part of the implementation process, but this is not a primary focus of the 70-293 exam.

The elements of the implementation process that are covered in the 70-293 exam focus largely on the selection of protocols, operating systems, applications, and security mechanisms that satisfy the requirements of a network's owners, administrators, and users, as determined in the planning process. The exam also covers the process of deploying technologies such as the TCP/IP protocols, the DNS and WINS name-resolution mechanisms, and the IPSec protocol extensions. These deployments include tasks such as selecting the IP addresses and subnet mask that the computers on a network will use, designing a DNS namespace, and creating IPsec policies that ensure the security of communications between specific users or systems.

As a rule, the 70-293 exam focuses on the deployment of these technologies on a medium-to-large network, and it concentrates more on the organizational elements of the deployment than on the process of configuring an individual computer. For example, the exam is more concerned with the process of creating a DNS namespace suitable for a large organization than the installation and configuration of the DNS server application on a single computer running Windows Server 2003.

Maintaining a Network Infrastructure

The completion of the network planning and implementation processes is not the end of the professional's concern for the network infrastructure. To maintain the network properly, administrators must have an intimate knowledge of the infrastructure and the technologies used to implement it. Network infrastructure maintenance includes such tasks as updating operating systems and applications, monitoring ongoing processes, and troubleshooting problems.

Keeping the network's operating systems and applications updated is more complicated than simply downloading the latest patch releases and installing them on all the computers. For a large and complex network infrastructure, you must be careful to test each release before deploying it on the production network. This entails using a lab network to develop an update-release test plan so that you can run the updates in a protected environment before installing them throughout the enterprise. To build a lab network that adequately duplicates the real network, familiarity with the network's infrastructure is essential.

Administrators must monitor many services that are essential to a large network at regular intervals to ensure they are operating properly. This monitoring can include regular examination of logs, function testing, and network traffic analysis. The network administrator must be capable of configuring these services to log the appropriate information and of using Windows Server 2003 tools such as Network Monitor and the Performance console. However, an administrator who is familiar with the use of these tools does not necessarily know what elements to monitor, what performance levels to expect, and how to interpret the log entries. To know how to do these things, the administrator must be familiar with the network infrastructure and with the normal operations of the network so that any deviation from the baseline is apparent.

Troubleshooting is one of the primary maintenance functions of a network administrator. Although much of the infrastructure design and implementation process revolves around the creation of a robust network, problems do occur, and in a large organization, network failures can mean reduced productivity and loss of revenue. To determine the location of a problem and decide on a course of action to remedy it, an administrator must be closely acquainted with the network infrastructure.

Lesson Review

The following questions are intended to reinforce key information presented in this lesson. If you are unable to answer a question, review the lesson materials and try the question again. You can find answers to the questions in the "Questions and Answers" section at the end of this chapter.

1. Which of the following statements about a network's infrastructure is true?

   a. A network infrastructure includes hardware products only.

   b. A network infrastructure includes software products only.

   c. A network infrastructure includes both hardware and software products.

   d. A network infrastructure is a design that does not include specific hardware or software products.

2. Which type of network infrastructure includes the selection of the network and transport layer protocols that are to be used on the network?

   _____

   _____

3. Maintaining a network infrastructure includes which of the following processes? (Choose three.)

    a. Updating the network

    b. Troubleshooting the network

    c. Implementing the network

    d. Monitoring the network

Lesson Summary

- A network infrastructure is a set of components that provide connectivity, security, routing, management, access, and other integral features on a network. A network's physical infrastructure is the physical design of the network, consisting of hardware components such as cabling, routers, switches, hubs, servers, and workstations.

- A network's logical infrastructure comprises the many software elements that connect, manage, and secure hosts on the network.

- When planning a network infrastructure, you must determine the requirements of the network's users, administrators, and owners, and then design a configuration of selected physical and logical components that satisfies those requirements.

- When implementing a network infrastructure, it is important to understand the organizational aspects of the product deployment, such as the allocation of IP addresses and designing a DNS namespace.

- The maintenance of a network infrastructure includes tasks such as deploying software updates, monitoring network performance and processes, and troubleshooting problems.

Lesson 2: Selecting Data-Link Layer Protocols

Connecting a group of computers to the same physical network gives them a medium for communication, but unless the computers can speak the same language, no meaningful exchanges are possible. The languages the computers speak are called protocols; if the computers on a network are to interact, every computer must be configured to use the same protocols. Selecting the appropriate protocols for the network is an important part of the network infrastructure planning process.

After this lesson, you will be able to

- List the seven layers of the Open Systems Interconnection (OSI) reference model and their functions
- List the types of media typically used to construct data networks
- Understand the differences between the various data-link layer protocols and their variants
- Select the appropriate data-link layer protocol for a given environment

Estimated lesson time: 30 minutes

Understanding the OSI Reference Model

In 1984, the International Organization for Standardization (ISO) and what is now the Telecommunication Standardization Sector of the International Telecommunications Union (ITU-T) published a document that divides the functions of a data network into seven layers, as shown in Figure 1-1. "The Basic Reference Model for Open Systems Interconnection," now commonly known as the OSI reference model (ISO/IEC 7498-1:1994 and ITU-T Recommendation X.200), has become an industry standard for teaching and referring to networking functions.

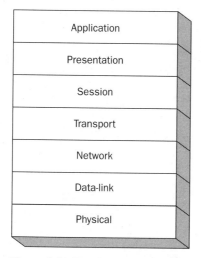

| Application |
| Presentation |
| Session |
| Transport |
| Network |
| Data-link |
| Physical |

Figure 1-1   The OSI reference model

The seven layers of the OSI model define functions that are implemented in various networking protocols, such as Ethernet and TCP/IP. The functions corresponding to the layers are as follows:

- **Physical**   The physical layer defines the nature of the network medium—the actual fabric of the network that joins all the computers together—and the nature of the signals transmitted over the medium. In most cases, the network medium is a form of copper cable that uses electric currents for signaling, but fiber-optic and wireless media are becoming increasingly prevalent.

- **Data-Link**   The data-link layer defines the interface between the network medium and the software running on the computer. Among the data-link layer functions are packet addressing (which allows computers to direct traffic to specific destinations on the local network); media access control (which allows multiple computers to share a single network medium without conflicting); and formatting the frame used to encapsulate data for transmission over the network. The data-link layer divides into two sublayers. The logical link control (LLC) sublayer controls elements such as error checking from node to node on the same LAN, frame synchronization, and flow control. The media access control (MAC) sublayer controls the movement of data packets to and from one network interface card (NIC) to another across a shared channel.

- **Network**   The network layer defines the functions that provide end-to-end communications between computers on different networks. Chief among these functions is routing, which enables computers to relay traffic through intermediate networks to a destination on a remote network any distance away. Other functions include packet sequencing, end-to-end error detection from the sender to the recipient, congestion control, and addressing. While the data-link layer is responsible for local traffic on a single network, the network layer is responsible for directing traffic to its ultimate destination.

- **Transport**   The transport layer provides functions that complement those of the network layer, including guaranteed delivery (which uses packet acknowledgments to ensure data is received), flow control (which regulates transmission speed to avoid dropped packets), and end-to-end error detection (which enables the receiving system to detect damaged packets).

- **Session**   The session layer provides many functions involved in the regulation of the dialog between two computers communicating over the network. For example, the session layer sets up, regulates, and terminates exchanges between the applications at each end of the communication.

- **Presentation**   The presentation layer (sometimes referred to as the syntax layer) is responsible for translating each computer's native syntax into a common transfer syntax readable by the other computers on the network. In some cases, the transfer syntax can provide functions such as data compression and encryption.

- **Application**   The application layer provides the interface between the networking protocol stack and the software running on the computer. For example, this layer provides the interface for e-mail, file transfers, Telnet and File Transfer Protocol (FTP) applications. Applications use the services provided by application-layer protocols, which in turn use the services provided by the other layers beneath them.

It is important to understand that the protocols that implement the functions of the OSI model do not correspond exactly to the individual layers. A computer on a network does not necessarily run seven different protocols, with one corresponding to each layer. Generally speaking, the designer of a network infrastructure selects a data-link layer protocol, such as Ethernet or Token Ring, which actually encompasses both the physical and data-link layers in its functions, and a protocol suite, such as TCP/IP, which implements the functions of the network and transport layers. The session, presentation, and application-layer functions are sometimes provided by a protocol in the suite or by a separate application-layer protocol.

Selecting a Data-Link Layer Protocol

The selection of a data-link layer protocol is the most important decision in the design of the network's physical infrastructure. The data-link layer protocol is not only responsible for strictly data-link layer functions, such as media access control, but also for the network's physical layer implementation. Currently, the most commonly used data-link layer protocol on networks is Ethernet, with Token Ring running a distant second. However, there are several Ethernet variations that provide various levels of performance, and selecting the correct one is crucial.

You need to consider a number of criteria when selecting the data-link layer protocol for use on a network. Because the data-link layer protocol dictates the nature of the network's physical infrastructure, you must consider design elements such as the distance between workstations and the transmission speed you require. You must also consider the nature of the traffic the network will carry and its amount. Additionally, your budget is always an important consideration.

Selecting a Media Type

Although there have been other types of media used in the past, most LANs constructed today use either unshielded twisted pair (UTP) cable or fiber-optic cable. In most cases, UTP cable is sufficient and much less expensive, but fiber-optic cable provides a viable alternative when you have special performance requirements. Network media that consist of cables are called *bounded media*. Recent developments in wireless LAN technologies have also made *unbounded media* (networks that don't use cables) a viable and practical solution.

Unshielded Twisted Pair   UTP is a type of copper cable that consists of four pairs of wires, each of which is twisted together and contained inside a protective sheath. The quality of a particular UTP cable is specified by its category rating. Category 5 (or CAT5) UTP is the most commonly used today, although there are higher grades available for special applications (such as 1000Base-T Gigabit Ethernet networks). The connectors on UTP cables are called RJ-45 and are similar in appearance to telephone cable connectors, except that they have eight pins instead of four.

UTP is one of the cable types supported by all forms of Ethernet and by Token Ring as well. As a network medium, it is the most cost-efficient selection because it is the same type of cable used by telephone networks. In new construction, it is common for the same contractor to install both the telephone and data network cables at the same time.

You install UTP cable using a *star topology*, in which you connect each workstation on the network to a central hub (or repeater), as shown in Figure 1-2. You can then connect hubs to create a larger and more complex network. On an Ethernet network, UTP cable supports distances of up to 100 meters between each workstation and the hub. For most LAN installations, this is more than enough. If greater distances are required, you can modify the location of the hub in your network design or consider using fiber-optic cable, which can span longer distances.

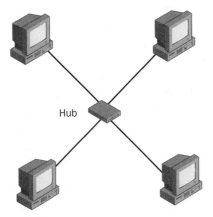

Hub

Figure 1-2   A star topology

Each form of Ethernet that supports UTP cable has its own limitations regarding the number of hubs you can connect. This is one of the main reasons why you must select the data-link layer protocol you intend to use before you start designing the layout of your network infrastructure. For example, if you plan to use standard Ethernet running at 10 megabits per second (Mbps), you can connect up to four hubs on a single LAN, as shown in Figure 1-3. If you use Fast Ethernet (running at 100 Mbps), the Ethernet guidelines dictate that you can use no more than two connected hubs.

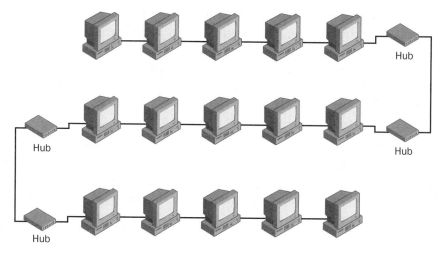

Figure 1-3   A four-hub Ethernet network

> **Off the Record**   When designing an Ethernet network, most network engineers use a basic set of cabling guidelines specified by the Ethernet standards. For example, the 10 Mbps Ethernet standard uses the 5-4-3 rule, which says that a network can consist of no more than five network segments, connected by four repeaters, with no more than three of those segments being populated with devices such as workstations and servers. There are, however, more exacting formulae in the Ethernet standards that add the lengths of the individual cable segments and a coefficient for each hub to arrive at a more precise configuration for the network. In other words, using the more complex formula, you might discover that you are able to exceed the number of hubs specified in the basic Ethernet guidelines if the lengths of your cables are short enough. When designing a complex Ethernet network, you should consult the Ethernet standards and use the more precise formula to ensure that your design falls within the specified requirements.

Fiber Optic   Although it can use the same topology and many of the same data-link layer protocols support it, fiber-optic cable operates on a different principle than UTP and all other copper-based cables. The actual network medium in a fiber-optic cable is a strand of plastic or glass that carries signals in the form of light pulses. Because the signals are not electric, they are immune to electromagnetic interference. In an environment where interference levels are high, such as a factory floor, fiber-optic cable can eliminate the performance degradation that the interference causes on copper cable. Even in a normal office environment, you can install fiber-optic cable near fluorescent light fixtures or electric motors without any difficulties. When using UTP, your network design should keep the copper cables a safe distance away from these possible sources of interference.

Fiber-optic cables are also much less susceptible to attenuation than copper cables. *Attenuation* is the tendency of a signal to weaken as it travels along a medium. This signal weakening is one of the main reasons for the 100-meter UTP-cable length limit. All fiber-optic cables can exceed UTP cables in length, but there are several different types of fiber-optic cable, each with different length limitations. The multimode fiber-optic cable typically used on LANs can span distances ranging from 400 to 2,000 meters, while single-mode fiber can support cable runs as long as 100 kilometers.

In performance and flexibility, fiber-optic cable is superior to UTP in almost every way. Fiber-optic cable is inherently more secure than copper cables because unauthorized people cannot easily tap into the cable and intercept its signals as they can with copper. The drawback of the medium is its additional cost and the special skills required to install and maintain it. Virtually all the tools used to install and test fiber-optic cable are different from those for copper-based cables. Installers must glue the connectors onto a fiber-optic cable—typically using a heat-cured glue and a small oven—while UTP connectors are crimped onto the cable. Also, because of the way light pulses are transferred through the cable, fiber-optic installers must be careful not to bend the cable too sharply.

The raw materials for a fiber-optic installation are far more expensive than their UTP counterparts. There are also far fewer fiber-optic installation contractors than UTP experts, and their skills come at a premium. In addition, many network administrators who have the ability to make minor repairs on UTP cables would be lost when faced with a malfunctioning fiber-optic connection.

> **Planning**   Generally speaking, network designs call for fiber-optic cable only when there are specific reasons for it, such as the need for extra-long cable runs or an environment with a lot of interference.

Wireless Networking   Although wireless network technologies of various types have been around for many years, only recently have they become a viable medium for the average network installation. The older wireless LAN technologies were notoriously slow and unreliable, but a new standard published by the Institute of Electrical and Electronic Engineers (IEEE), called 802.11b, has boosted wireless LAN transmission speeds to 11 Mbps (faster than standard cabled Ethernet) and greatly increased their reliability.

IEEE 802.11b networks can function using two different topologies. The *ad hoc topology*, illustrated in Figure 1-4, consists of two or more computers equipped with wireless network-interface adapters that can communicate with each other interchangeably.

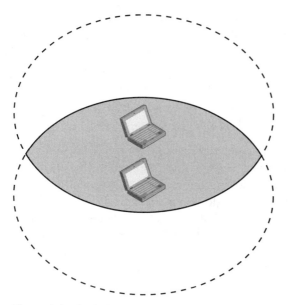

Figure 1-4 A wireless network using the ad hoc topology

The *infrastructure topology* design, as shown in Figure 1-5, enables wireless computers to interact with a standard cabled network. In this topology, you connect a wireless transceiver called an *access point* to the cabled network, and the wireless computers can then interact with the rest of the network through the access point.

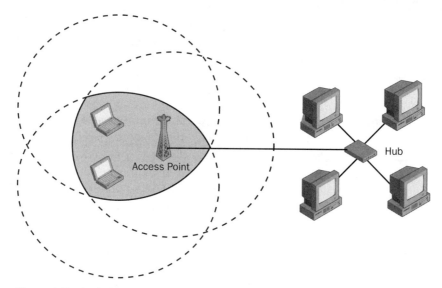

Figure 1-5 A wireless network using the infrastructure topology

Wireless local area networking is becoming increasingly popular now that the products are less expensive and more plentiful, but it is still a technology that is recommended only for installations where a cabled topology is impractical. If you plan on having computers on your network that are frequently moved to different locations, such as laptops or mobile kiosks, wireless can be an excellent solution. Wireless is also a good alternative in locations where running cables would be impractical, such as a lobby or plaza where cable would clash with the décor.

Before incorporating any wireless networking technology into your network infrastructure plan, however, it is strongly recommended that you test the proposed technology thoroughly in the actual locations where it will be used. Wireless transmissions are subject to interference from a wide range of environmental factors, including the number and composition of walls between the transceivers, proximity to machinery and other electrical equipment, and even climatic conditions. The effective transmission range of a wireless device can vary from location to location and even from minute to minute. You should always be sure that the medium you propose to use for your network be viable in the intended location before you invest time and money in the network infrastructure.

Security Alert   Because of recent developments in the wireless networking standards, the popularity of wireless LAN technologies is growing quickly. However, the development of a security infrastructure for these networks has not been growing quite as fast. By definition, any wireless transceiver that comes into the effective transmission range of another transceiver of the same type has the potential to join that network. This creates a serious security hazard because unauthorized users with wireless terminals can conceivably access network resources from outside the organization. For more information on securing a wireless network, see Chapter 13, "Designing a Security Infrastructure."

Selecting a Transmission Speed

Another important factor in the selection of a data-link layer protocol for your network infrastructure is the speed at which the network can transmit data. As with most data-processing technologies, Ethernet networks have gotten faster over the years, and the cutting edge of the technology is a trade-off between high transmission speeds and high equipment prices. Selecting a transmission speed for your network is a matter of determining your users' current and future requirements and balancing them against your budget.

Ethernet offers the most flexibility in terms of transmission speed. The original Ethernet standard called for a 10 Mbps transmission speed. Fast Ethernet, introduced in the mid-1990s, increased the maximum transmission speed to 100 Mbps, and Gigabit Ethernet—the current state of the art—runs at 1,000 Mbps, or 1 gigabit per second (Gbps).

Work is also proceeding on a 10-Gbps Ethernet standard, products for which will surely appear on the market within a few years.

Fast Ethernet Equipment

Although 10-Mbps Ethernet equipment is still widely available, 100-Mbps Fast Ethernet is currently the industry standard. All Fast Ethernet network interface adapters are dual-speed devices, capable of automatically detecting the current speed of a network and adjusting themselves to operate at either 10 or 100 Mbps. Single-speed hubs are still available that run at either 10 or 100 Mbps, but there are also dual-speed hubs on the market with the same automatic speed adjustment capability as a dual-speed network adapter.

A Fast Ethernet network requires Category 5 UTP or better, or fiber-optic cable, but standard Ethernet requires only Category 3. This is not a major impediment, however, because virtually all UTP cable installed today is at least Category 5.

For a typical business LAN, 10 Mbps is usually sufficiently fast to read and write data files stored on network servers. However, a heavily trafficked network or one supporting high-bandwidth applications such as streaming audio or video can benefit from the 100-Mbps Fast Ethernet transmission speed. Despite the fact that many networks don't need the additional bandwidth, Fast Ethernet is the recommended technology for new LAN installations today. Fast Ethernet equipment is almost the same price as standard Ethernet, and the additional speed provides room for growth in the type of applications your network uses.

> **Tip**   Remember that the transmission speed of the LAN usually has little or no effect on the users' Internet access performance. Even the slowest Ethernet LAN, running at 10 Mbps, is six times faster than the 1.544-Mbps T-1 connection large organizations typically use to connect to the Internet.

Gigabit Ethernet is still a relatively new technology, and as a result, it is still quite expensive when compared to Fast Ethernet. You use Gigabit Ethernet primarily for backbone networks and other applications that require its high speed. Although virtually no networks run Gigabit Ethernet to the desktop, it is likely to occur in the future.

Apart from the cost of the equipment, these different Ethernet speeds also vary in their cabling guidelines. Although all forms of Ethernet can still support the 100-meter maximum cable length, there are different limitations on the number of hubs permitted on a LAN, which is a factor you must consider when designing your network. As mentioned earlier in this lesson, a standard Ethernet LAN can have up to four hubs, while a typical Fast Ethernet LAN can have only two. Gigabit Ethernet supports only a single hub on a network.

Selecting an Ethernet Variant

Choosing a variant of the Ethernet protocol for your network is primarily a matter of selecting a cable type and a transmission speed. Table 1-1 lists the Ethernet variants that are currently in common use.

Table 1-1   Ethernet Variants

Ethernet Type	Designation	Cable Type	Speed	Maximum Segment Length
Standard Ethernet	10Base-T	Category 3 UTP	10 Mbps	100 meters
Fast Ethernet	100Base-TX	Category 5 UTP	100 Mbps	100 meters
Fast Ethernet	100Base-FX	62.5/125 multimode fiber optic	100 Mbps	412 meters at half duplex and 2,000 meters at full duplex
Gigabit Ethernet	1000Base-LX	9/125 single-mode fiber optic	1000 Mbps	3 kilometers
Gigabit Ethernet	1000Base-LX	50/125 or 62.5/125 multimode fiber optic	1000 Mbps	550 meters
Gigabit Ethernet	1000Base-SX	50/125 multimode fiber optic (400 MHz)	1000 Mbps	500 meters
Gigabit Ethernet	1000Base-SX	62.5/125 multimode fiber optic (160 MHz)	1000 Mbps	220 meters
Gigabit Ethernet	1000Base-T	Category 5 (or 5E) UTP	1000 Mbps	100 meters

Using Token Ring

Token Ring is a data-link layer protocol that doesn't support as many media types as Ethernet, and at 16 Mbps it does not run as fast, either. However, there is one advantage to Token Ring that makes it a popular solution for some network engineers. The primary difference between Token Ring and Ethernet is that they use different media access control mechanisms. Media access control (MAC) is a sublayer of the data-link layer and is the method the computers on a LAN use to indicate they want to use the network to transmit data. If two computers transmit data at the same time, a conflict occurs called a *collision*, and both transmissions are lost. To prevent collisions, data-link layer protocols have a procedure that enables one computer at a time to take possession of the network so that it can transmit its data without difficulty.

The Ethernet MAC mechanism is called Carrier Sense Multiple Access with Collision Detection (CSMA/CD). With this mechanism, a computer that has data to transmit listens to the network to see whether any other computer is transmitting. If the network is free, the computer proceeds to transmit its data. During the transmission, the computer continues to monitor the incoming signals from the network. If the transmitting computer detects a signal from another computer during its transmission (indicating that the two computers started sending data at nearly the same moment), a collision is said to have occurred. Both systems stop transmitting, pause for a randomly determined period of time, and then begin the entire transmission process over again. If one (or both) of the systems is involved in another collision, it waits twice as long before attempting to transmit again. This introduces a measure of waste, as the computers end up transmitting the same data more than once. With CSMA/CD, a certain number of collisions are normal and expected. As the traffic level on the network increases, so does the number of collisions. For this reason, Ethernet becomes a less effective protocol on a heavily trafficked network.

Token Ring, on the other hand, uses a MAC mechanism called *token passing*. With this method, a computer on the network generates a tiny packet called a token, which circulates endlessly around the network. Only the computer in possession of the token is permitted to transmit its data. When a system wants to transmit data, it waits until the token passes by, grabs the token, and then proceeds to transmit its data. After completing the transmission, the computer then sends out the token again so that another system can use it. The protocol specifications determine how long the system can keep the token, how long it can circulate the token, and how it can generate a new token if one isn't currently in circulation. The advantage of token passing is that there are no collisions whatsoever on a properly functioning network. Consequently, there are also no retransmissions, so no bandwidth is wasted. This also means that a token-passing network functions just as well under heavy traffic conditions as it does in light traffic.

Off the Record   The limited speed of Token Ring networks and the higher hardware prices have kept the protocol a distant second choice to Ethernet, but there are enough Token Ring advocates to keep the products on the market.

Mixing Media

When designing a network for a medium-to-large enterprise, it is not necessary to choose a single data-link layer protocol for the entire internetwork. A router can connect any type of network to any other, so it is possible to select a different data-link layer protocol for each LAN. However, for simplicity of construction and ease of maintenance, it is recommended that you use the same protocol wherever practical. You should use different protocols only when circumstances force you to do so.

> For example, a typical network infrastructure design might call for 100Base-TX Fast Ethernet on all the standard workstation LANs. For the backbone network that connects all the LANs, a faster network with a longer cable span might be necessary. This is a good place for Gigabit Ethernet using fiber-optic cable. For a group of portable computers that are frequently moved to different locations, IEEE 802.11b can provide the flexibility needed.

Practice: Choosing an Ethernet Variant

For each of the following situations, specify which Ethernet variation you would recommend and provide a reason for your selection. You can find answers to the questions in the "Questions and Answers" section at the end of this chapter.

1. A legacy Category 3 UTP cable installation.

   _____

   _____

2. A high-bandwidth backbone network 1,000 meters long.

   _____

   _____

3. A Fast Ethernet LAN connecting 50 workstations in a factory environment with large amounts of electromagnetic interference.

   _____

   _____

Lesson Review

The following questions are intended to reinforce key information presented in this lesson. If you are unable to answer a question, review the lesson materials and try the question again. You can find answers to the questions in the "Questions and Answers" section at the end of this chapter.

1. Data-link layer protocols used on LANs, such as Ethernet, include functions associated with which two layers of the OSI reference model?

   _____

   _____

2. What phenomenon never occurs on a properly functioning Token Ring network but is a normal occurrence on an Ethernet network?

_____

_____

3. List two advantages and two disadvantages of using fiber-optic cable to build a network.

_____

_____

Lesson Summary

- The OSI reference model splits the network communications process into seven layers—physical, data-link, network, transport, session, presentation, and application—which isolate the various functions performed by the networking protocols.

- Selecting a data-link layer protocol is primarily a matter of choosing an appropriate network medium. Unshielded twisted pair, fiber-optic, and wireless media all have benefits and drawbacks making them suitable for some installations and unsuitable for others.

- Transmission speed is an important criterion in selecting the data-link layer protocol. There are various types of Ethernet that run at 10, 100, and 1,000 Mbps.

Lesson 3: Selecting Network/Transport Layer Protocols

Once you have selected a data-link layer protocol for your network, your concerns for the physical infrastructure are finished. It is now time to move upward in the OSI reference model and select the protocols for the network and transport layers and above. There is no need to be concerned about protocol compatibility at this point, because all the data-link layer protocols in current use can function with any network/transport layer protocol combination.

After this lesson, you will be able to

- Describe the circumstances under which you should use the three network/transport layer protocol options supported by Microsoft Windows operating systems

Estimated lesson time: 15 minutes

Windows Server 2003 (like all current Windows operating systems) includes support for three network/transport layer protocol combinations: TCP/IP, Internetwork Packet Exchange (IPX), and the NetBIOS Extended User Interface (NetBEUI). The operating systems can function with any or all of these protocols installed at the same time. TCP/IP and IPX are both collections of protocols (called protocol suites) that function together to provide services that span several layers of the OSI reference model. Both TCP/IP and IPX include network and transport layer protocols, and depending on the functions a computer is performing, the services provided by the protocol suite can at times run all the way up to the application layer. NetBEUI is a monolithic protocol that provides basic network functionality but is not nearly as flexible as TCP/IP or IPX.

Using TCP/IP

TCP/IP is a large collection of protocols that provides a comprehensive array of networking services in addition to basic Windows file sharing. For most network designers, the process of selecting protocols for the network and transport layers is a brief one, because TCP/IP is the only logical selection. Only TCP/IP provides the flexibility, expandability, and Internet compatibility that most networks require. The TCP/IP protocols were designed in the 1970s to support the experimental packet-switching network that eventually became the Internet. Because this network consisted of many different types of computers, the protocols were designed to be completely hardware-independent. This is why the TCP/IP protocols have their own independent addressing system.

The two primary protocols in the TCP/IP suite are the Internet Protocol (IP), which operates at the network layer, and the Transmission Control Protocol (TCP), which operates at the transport layer. There is a second transport-layer protocol called the User Datagram Protocol (UDP). Virtually all TCP/IP communications use the IP protocol at the network layer and either TCP or UDP at the transport layer (see Figure 1-6). In fact, the TCP/IP suite is named for the most commonly used combination of protocols.

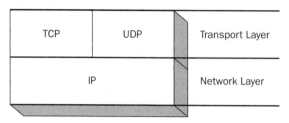

Figure 1-6   TCP/IP network and transport layer protocols

IP is the key protocol of the TCP/IP suite. Almost all TCP/IP traffic is carried using IP packets called datagrams. An IP *datagram* is something like the envelope you use to mail a letter. The datagram has the address of the intended recipient and the address of the sender. As the packet travels across the network, computers read the recipient's address and pass the packet along toward its intended destination. IP is also responsible for routing packets across an internetwork.

Whether a network communication process uses IP with TCP or IP with UDP depends on the requirements of the application generating the network traffic. TCP is a *connection-oriented* protocol, which means that before two computers can communicate, they exchange a series of messages that establish a connection between them. In addition, the computers acknowledge the data packets they receive from each other, ensuring that the transmitted data arrives intact. Computers use TCP when they have to transmit relatively large amounts of data that must arrive intact at the destination. The drawback to using TCP is the additional traffic generated by the connection establishment and acknowledgment messages.

UDP is a *connectionless* protocol, which means that two computers can communicate without establishing a connection first, and they do not transmit dedicated acknowledgment messages. Computers typically use UDP for brief exchanges of data, such as request and response messages, or for data transmissions that can survive the loss of an occasional packet, such as streaming audio or video. The advantage of using UDP is that its overhead is much lower than that of TCP.

In addition to these three primary protocols, the TCP/IP suite includes many others, spanning the OSI reference model from the data-link to the application layer, and providing a number of different administrative functions. When you configure a computer to use TCP/IP, you install the entire suite of protocols at once. In the Windows Server 2003 operating system, the TCP/IP protocol suite takes the form of a single module that you install in the Network Connections tool. The process is similar in other versions of the Windows operating system.

TCP/IP is unquestionably the industry standard in network/transport layer protocols, and it provides all the functionality that any network design could require. When designing a network, the primary drawback to selecting TCP/IP is the individual configuration required for each computer. On a TCP/IP network, every computer must have a unique IP address in addition to other configuration parameters. Originally, administrators had to individually configure each computer by hand, but today, technologies such as the Dynamic Host Configuration Protocol (DHCP) can automate the TCP/IP configuration process.

Note   There have been several enhancements to TCP/IP in Windows Server 2003 Service Pack 1. These include turning on SYN attack protection by default, new SYN attack notifications, and a new TCP port allocation algorithm. However, these enhancements are not covered in the exam and therefore are not covered in this training kit.

See Also   See Chapter 2, "Planning a TCP/IP Network Infrastructure," for more information about IP addressing and TCP/IP configuration.

Using IPX

IPX is also a suite of protocols that provides some of the same basic communications features as TCP/IP. The IPX protocols were developed by Novell for use with their NetWare operating system. Until the release of NetWare version 5 in 1998, computers had to use IPX to communicate with NetWare servers. However, NetWare 5 included support for TCP/IP, and it is now possible to eliminate IPX from a NetWare network.

Unlike the TCP/IP standards, which are in the public domain, the IPX standards are privately owned by Novell, who does not make them available to outside software developers. As a result, Microsoft developed its own version of the IPX protocols, called NWLink, to provide the Windows operating systems with NetWare connectivity. Windows Server 2003 still includes support for NWLink, in the form of a protocol module called NWLink IPX/ SPX/NetBIOS Compatible Transport Protocol, as do the other Windows operating systems.

The IPX suite, like TCP/IP, consists of several different protocols. IPX itself is the network layer protocol that carries most of the suite's traffic. Sequenced Packet Exchange (SPX) is a connection-oriented transport layer protocol that is the IPX equivalent of TCP, and the NetWare Core Protocol (NCP) is roughly the equivalent of UDP.

The primary difference between the IPX protocol suite and TCP/IP is that IPX is designed for use on personal computer LANs only, while TCP/IP can support a network of any type and any size. One reason is that IPX does not have a self-contained addressing system, as TCP/IP does. IPX uses the hardware address coded into each computer's network interface adapter to identify that system on the network.

Although it is possible to use the IPX protocols alone for Windows file sharing, few network administrators do this. IPX does not provide the Internet connectivity that most networks need. In most cases, administrators use IPX only for NetWare connectivity in cases where all NetWare servers are not and cannot be configured to use TCP/IP. For example, if a network still has a few old NetWare version 3.*x* servers that users need to access occasionally, the design might call for the installation of the IPX protocols on the workstations, but in most cases the computers will have TCP/IP or NetBEUI installed as well for native Windows communications.

Using NetBEUI

NetBEUI was the default networking protocol of the Windows NT 3.1 and Windows for Workgroups operating systems when these systems were first released in 1993. At the time, PC networking was in its infancy; networks were relatively small and centrally located. NetBEUI uses the NetBIOS namespace to identify the computers on a network, a practice that Windows retained until the release of Windows 2000, which switched to the DNS namespace. Windows Server 2003 still includes support for NetBIOS naming, but the operating system no longer includes the NetBEUI protocol module.

> **Tip**   Although Windows Server 2003 does not include NetBEUI, there are still occasions when you might want to install the protocol, such as for testing whether a network communications problem is being caused by a TCP/IP configuration error or a network hardware fault. You can still install the NetBEUI module on a Windows Server 2003 computer, using the installation files included with Windows XP Professional or Windows XP Home Edition. These files are located in the \Valueadd\Msft\Net\Netbeui folder on the Windows XP distribution CD-ROM.

NetBEUI is a relatively simple networking protocol that provides basic file sharing services for Windows computers. NetBEUI is a single protocol—not a suite—and does not require any individual configuration, as TCP/IP does. This is because NetBEUI uses the NetBIOS name specified by the installer during the Windows Setup procedure as the computer's identifier on the network. NetBEUI also cannot provide Internet connectivity as TCP/IP can.

NetBEUI is intended for use on small LANs and is not suitable for a large enterprise network. This is because the NetBEUI protocol cannot route traffic between networks and therefore cannot support internetwork traffic. Both TCP/IP and IPX use separate identifiers for the network and for the individual computers on the network. A single IP address contains both a network and a host identifier. IPX uses the hardware address to identify the computer, and the NetWare installer assigns another address to each individual network. Therefore, both TCP/IP and IPX traffic can be addressed to a specific computer on a specific network anywhere in the enterprise.

The only identifier that NetBEUI uses is the computer's NetBIOS name. This name identifies the computer on the network, but there is no identifier for the network itself. NetBEUI therefore cannot address traffic to a specific computer on another network.

Planning   If you are designing a network that consists of a single LAN, such as for a home or a small business, NetBEUI is a suitable choice. However, if you are designing an internetwork, or if your computers need access to the Internet, you should not use NetBEUI.

Tip   Although it might not be a suitable full-time protocol for your network, NetBEUI also has value as a troubleshooting tool. If you have computers on the same TCP/IP LAN that cannot communicate, and you suspect there might be a TCP/IP configuration problem, you can install NetBEUI on the computers as a test. If the computers can successfully communicate using NetBEUI, you know that the networking hardware is functioning properly and the problem lies somewhere in the TCP/IP installation or configuration.

Lesson Review

The following questions are intended to reinforce key information presented in this lesson. If you are unable to answer a question, review the lesson materials and try the question again. You can find answers to the questions in the "Questions and Answers" section at the end of this chapter.

1. Which of the following network/transport layer protocols can you use for Windows file sharing when installed alone?

   a. TCP/IP only

   b. TCP/IP and NetBEUI only

   c. TCP/IP and IPX only

   d. TCP/IP, IPX, and NetBEUI

2. Under what conditions would a network designer be obliged to install the IPX protocol suite on workstations using Windows operating systems?

   _____

   _____

3. Which of the following are connection-oriented protocols? (Choose all that apply.)

   a. NetWare Core Protocol (NCP)

   b. Transmission Control Protocol (TCP)

   c. Sequenced Packet Exchange (SPX)

   d. User Datagram Protocol (UDP)

Lesson Summary

- TCP/IP is the industry standard protocol suite at the network and transport layers. Because it has a self-contained addressing system, TCP/IP can support any type of computer network and is expandable to almost any size.

- The IPX protocol suite is designed for use with the Novell NetWare operating system, but Windows can also use it for its own file sharing.

- NetBEUI is a relatively simple protocol that supports Windows file sharing on small networks, but it is not routable and is therefore unsuitable for internetwork installations.

Lesson 4: Locating Network Resources

One important part of the network infrastructure design process is creating a blueprint that specifies the locations of network components. After you have selected the protocols that the network will use, you have a lot of the information needed to plot the locations of network resources, such as the maximum lengths for your cables and the number of hubs you can use on each LAN. To complete the blueprint, you need a diagram of the site where the network is to be installed, as well as some idea where the furniture and other fixtures will be located.

After this lesson, you will be able to

- Understand the criteria used to determine network component locations
- Plan locations for workstations, peripherals, cables, connectivity devices, and servers on your network

Estimated lesson time: 20 minutes

Determining Location Criteria

Creating a network blueprint is not the concern of the IT department alone. Although certain technical aspects of the network design would be lost on most people—such as the locations of servers and routers—the network blueprint also determines where the workstations for the network's users will be located, and this obviously concerns the people responsible for the office floor plan.

The criteria you must consider when planning the locations for network components are various. Chief among these is access by users to the equipment they need to perform their jobs. This means that users must have convenient access to workstations that are appropriate to their tasks, as well as access to peripheral devices such as printers and scanners. However, although user convenience is important, equipment must also be easily accessed by technical support and maintenance staff. For network infrastructure equipment, such as servers, hubs, and routers, the physical security of the devices is another vital factor when creating the blueprint. Finally, there are the requirements of the business and its owners, such as cost, appearance, portability, and expandability.

Locating Workstations

Assuming that a floor plan for the site already exists that includes the location of users' desks and other furniture, it may seem as though locating workstations is simply a matter of putting a computer on each desk. Actually, there is a good deal more to it than that. Planning also includes determining what type of computer is needed and exactly where the equipment should be located in relation to the desk.

Most users in a typical office are well served by a standard desktop computer as a workstation, but you still must choose the type of case the computer will have. Mini-tower cases are ideal if the computer will be located under the desk, and they usually provide sufficient room inside the case for adding new drives and other components. However, you should take into account that having the computers on the floor makes access more difficult for technical support personnel and might require extra-long cables for the monitor, mouse, and keyboard. The horizontal cases in small form are better suited for placement on the user's desks and generally provide easier mainte-nance access, but they tend to take up more room than most users would like.

> **Tip**   One development in PC hardware that is useful in saving desktop space is inexpensive LCD (liquid crystal display) flat panel monitors. These monitors take up far less space than traditional CRT (cathode ray tube) models and, being lighter, are much easier to move around the desk as needed.

In some offices, every user has a desk and every desk has a computer. However, this is not always the case. For example, your network might require kiosk-style worksta-tions that different people use throughout the day. In this case, the network blueprint should specify a location for the kiosk that is convenient for users and provides other resources they need, such as desktop space and printer access.

Some users do not need standard desktop workstations, and you should note these in the blueprint as well. People who use laptops or other portables as their primary com-puters might need docking stations on their desks, or they might only need access to a cable jack providing a network connection.

Locating Peripherals

The locations of printers and other shared components are an important element of the network blueprint. In this case, the primary concern is ergonomics. Select locations for printers that provide convenient access for the users but are far enough away to avoid interference and discomfort. Some types of printers release ozone and other gases dur-ing their operation that can be irritating or even toxic to some people. However, plac-ing all printers in a closed room at the far end of the hall is likely to be inconvenient to everyone.

When considering printer locations, you should take into account maintenance access to the machine and also proximity to expendable supplies, such as paper, toner, and ink. In some cases, you might also have to consider the physical security of the printer. For example, you might want to make sure that an expensive color printer with a high per-page printing cost be kept in a locked room so that only authorized personnel can use it.

Locating Cables

The cable diagram is an important part of the network blueprint, because this part of the network is likely to be invisible once the construction of the network is completed. To maintain and troubleshoot the network infrastructure, technicians must know where the cables are located and how they are arranged. In addition to the cable runs themselves, the blueprint should also specify the locations of obstacles that cables must detour around and the location of each cable terminus, either at a wall plate or a patch panel.

Part of selecting a network medium involves determining how the cables will be installed, based on the physical characteristics of the site. Typically, the cable installation for a medium-to-large office network is internal, meaning that the cables run inside walls and drop ceilings or sometimes under raised floors. In this type of installation, you should know the exact layout and construction of the site. If it is necessary to run cables down from the ceiling in the center of a room, the plan should note the exact location of a utility pole that will contain the cables.

Creating the cabling diagram requires more than a simple floor plan of the site. To route the cables properly, the network designers must be aware of any obstacles that can interfere with the cable's installation or performance, and these obstacles often do not appear on standard floor plans. For example, when using copper-based cable such as UTP, you must know the locations of fluorescent light fixtures and other possible sources of electromagnetic interference so that the installer knows to route the cables around them. You should also document the locations of heating and air conditioning ducts, plenums, firewalls, and other obstacles that the installer might have to route cables around or through. In most cases, this requires the network designer to carefully examine the site.

Another factor you should consider is that wiring diagrams are typically two-dimensional overviews of the site while cables often have to travel in three dimensions. For example, when you install cable runs in a drop ceiling and terminate them at wall plates, the diagram should specify exactly where the cable goes down from the ceiling space into the wall. The diagram should also specify how high the wall plate should be off the floor and note whether the vertical wall itself contains any barriers that installers might have to work around. If the installation should include telephone as well as data cables, the plan should differentiate between the two and contain the codes that the installers will use to mark the cables so that they can be located later.

A diagram for an external cable installation requires other details, particularly where the cables are to be secured and how—such as using staples, raceways, or cable ties.

Furniture location can also be significant, as can the cable color if you are attempting to match it to the walls.

Finally, the diagram should contain a sufficient number of additional cable runs to provide for future expansion of the network.

Locating Connectivity Devices

Before you can create a diagram of your network's cable runs, you must decide where your hubs and patch panels will be located. A patch panel is a cabling nexus, a terminus for multiple cable runs that enables you to connect each cable to a hub port, which joins the cables to a network. The number of patch panels and hubs you need and their locations depend on the size of your network and of the installation site.

The main limiting factor in the patch panel and hub locations is the maximum allowable length of your network cables. UTP cable runs can be up to 100 meters long, meaning that you have to choose a location for your patch panel that is no more than 100 meters from your most distant workstation. In most office sites, this is not a big problem. However, don't forget that the maximum cable length includes the lengths of all patch cables (which are the individual cables running from the wall plate to the computer and from the patch panel to the hub). In addition, cable runs are frequently longer than they appear because of the need to run around obstacles and up and down inside walls. For this reason, network plans should always specify ceiling heights and exact locations of wall plates.

If the building in which the network will be installed is small enough, you can run all the cables to patch panels in a single location. However, this might require you to run large numbers of cables between floors. If the building does not have conduits between floors that provide sufficient space for the cables, this alternative might not be practical.

A common configuration in buildings with several floors is to have all the cable runs for each floor terminate in a single location, such as a utility closet. You can then connect the individual floors using relatively few cables. Depending on the size and configuration of the network and the protocols you decide to use, you can connect the floors using hubs or switches, creating one single LAN, or using routers, creating an internetwork. In the latter case, the individual LANs on each floor are called *horizontal networks*, and the LAN running between the floors and connecting the horizontal networks is called a *backbone network*, as shown in Figure 1-7.

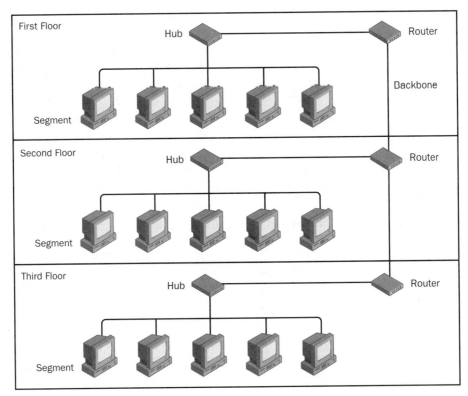

Figure 1-7   Three horizontal networks connected by a backbone network

Locating Servers

Servers are among the most important components of a business network, and the locations you select for them depend on who will be responsible for their daily operation and maintenance. In any case, servers should be more physically secure than workstations, and they should have protection against power spikes and interruptions.

Some networks have departmental servers, and administrators prefer to physically place them in the individual departments, leaving each group of workers responsible for its own server. This policy generally affords less physical security for the server and creates a greater risk of unauthorized access to the computer itself. Whenever possible, you should locate departmental servers in locked closets, with appropriate power protection and environmental controls. In some cases, the utility closet on each floor of a building, containing the hubs and patch panels, also functions as a server closet.

Other organizations prefer to place all their servers in a single data center, where professional administrators can maintain them. This is often a preferable solution because the data center is usually easier to secure physically and typically has sufficient power and environmental controls already.

On internetworks, the location of a server can also depend on the locations of the users who need to access it. Departmental servers can be preferable in situations where the users in the department are the only people accessing that server. This keeps all the server traffic local to the departmental LAN. For servers that users all over the enterprise must access, such as mail and database servers, it is preferable to place the servers where you can connect them directly to the backbone network. This practice minimizes the amount of internetwork traffic. If you were to connect a company mail server to a horizontal LAN, mail traffic from the entire enterprise would be shunted to that individual LAN, possibly flooding it. By connecting the server directly to the backbone, the mail traffic from all the horizontal LANs travels no farther than the backbone network, which is designed to support those traffic levels.

Practice: Blueprinting a Network Infrastructure

For each of the following pieces of information, give a reason why a network infrastructure blueprint would contain that information. You can find answers to the questions in the "Questions and Answers" section at the end of this chapter.

1. Locations of fluorescent light fixtures

   _____

   _____

2. Cable color

   _____

   _____

3. Ceiling height

   _____

   _____

4. Size of cable conduits running between floors

   _____

   _____

5. Locations of locked rooms and closets

   _____

   _____

Lesson Review

The following questions are intended to reinforce key information presented in this lesson. If you are unable to answer a question, review the lesson materials and try the question again. You can find answers to the questions in the "Questions and Answers" section at the end of this chapter.

1. List one piece of information that a diagram of an external cable installation needs that an internal installation diagram does not need.

   _____

   _____

2. Which of the following is the term for a LAN that connects all the computers on a single floor of a building?

   a. Backbone network

   b. Horizontal network

   c. Internetwork

   d. Patch panel

3. What negative result can occur when you connect an enterprise server to a horizontal network?

   _____

   _____

Lesson Summary

- Creating a blueprint containing the locations of all network components is a critical part of the network infrastructure planning process.

- The network blueprint should contain the exact locations of all network workstations and peripherals and their types.

- Planning the cable layout for a network requires understanding the limitations imposed by the protocols you've selected and a familiarity with the network site.

- Many internetworks consist of multiple horizontal networks connected by a backbone network.

- Server locations depend on who must access the server, where the server traffic originates, and who will be responsible for maintaining the server.

Case Scenario Exercise

Litware Inc., a manufacturer of specialized scientific software products, is expanding its operation into a new city and has purchased an office building there. The building will house the inside and outside sales forces for the city and the surrounding area, as well as the company's primary research and development facility. You have been assigned the task of designing the data network for the new office.

The office building is a three-story brick structure built in the late 1940s. The heating plant is original to the building, although central air conditioning was added in the 1970s. Before being purchased by Litware, each floor of the building was leased to a series of different tenants, many of whom restructured the internal floor plan to suit their own needs. As a result, the layout of each floor is substantially different from the others, and the existing cabling systems are completely separate from each other. The previous tenants have left their cables in place, along with the wall plates and the patch panels, but they have taken all other networking equipment with them.

The Realtor showing the building was able to provide a basic floor plan for each of the three stories. The current state of the three floors is as follows:

- **First floor**   This floor recently housed an accounting firm, and consists of ten individual offices. These offices are currently wired with Category 5 UTP cable for telephone and data connections.

- **Second floor**   At the time of the building's sale, this floor housed a telemarketing firm. The floor consists of a single large room filled with cubicles, which are wired with Category 3 UTP cable for both telephone and data connections.

- **Third floor**   This floor housed the offices of a graphic design company and, to accommodate its high bandwidth needs, has been wired with multimode fiber-optic cable.

Your task is to design a network for the building that can support the following facilities:

- An inside sales department that is basically a call center, where employees receive telephone calls from potential customers. These employees use their workstations to enter caller information into a customer database, take orders for merchandise, and provide product information, both over the phone and by mail.

- An outside sales department, which consists of personnel who travel to the sites of potential customers in the area to provide product information, negotiate terms, and furnish pre-sales technical support. These salespeople also need access to facilities where they can meet with potential customers visiting the Litware building. The computing needs of the outside sales staff include access to the company's customer database, the ability to run presentation software in the office and at customer sites, and the ability to demonstrate the operation of the company's software products. The salespeople are therefore equipped with notebook computers, which they use in the office and while traveling.

■ A research and development laboratory where scientists and programmers can work together to explore new ideas and create new products. The people in this department need powerful computers and large amounts of network bandwidth for their software testing procedures, but above all, they require a secure network so that there is no possibility of competitors learning about products in development.

Taking these requirements into account, answer the following questions about the design of this network:

1. Specify which floor of the building is best suited for each of the three departments listed and give your reasons why.

   _____

   _____

2. Which of the three departments to be housed in the new building could best make use of a wireless network medium? Why?

   _____

   _____

3. Which of the three floors has the most secure cable installation at the present time? Why?

   _____

   _____

4. Assuming that you plan to use Ethernet throughout the building, which variant would you use on each floor? Why?

   _____

   _____

5. Apart from the computers themselves, what connectivity components must Litware install on each of the three networks in the building to make it a functioning Ethernet network?

   _____

   _____

6. What components would you have to add to the plan to connect the LANs on each of the three floors to a single 1000Base-T Gigabit Ethernet backbone network?

_____

_____

7. Assuming that all three networks are connected to a single backbone, on which network would it make the most sense to connect the server hosting the company's customer database? Explain your answer.

   a. The first floor network

   b. The second floor network

   c. The third floor network

   d. The backbone network

_____

_____

8. Assuming that all three networks are connected to a single backbone, which would be the best network/transport layer protocol to use for the entire internetwork? Why are the other available protocols less suitable?

_____

_____

Chapter Summary

- A network infrastructure is a set of physical and logical components that provide connectivity, security, routing, management, access, and other integral features on a network.

- The OSI reference model splits a network's functionality into seven layers: application, presentation, session, transport, network, data-link, and physical.

- UTP cables are inexpensive and relatively easy to install, but they are subject to electromagnetic interference and can span only limited distances.

- Fiber-optic cables are more resistant to electromagnetic interference and attenuation than copper cables, but they are more expensive and difficult to install and maintain.

- Ethernet is the most popular data-link layer protocol on LANs worldwide. Ethernet can use many different types of network media and run at several different speeds.

- TCP/IP is the industry standard protocol suite for the network and transport layers and is suitable for most network installations. Other protocols, such as IPX and NetBEUI, are useful only in special situations.

- Creating a blueprint of a network's infrastructure is an essential part of the planning process. The blueprint should specify the locations of all major network components, including cables, hubs and other connection devices, computers, and peripherals.

Exam Highlights

Before taking the exam, review the key points and terms that are presented below to help you identify topics you need to review. Return to the lessons for additional practice, and review the "Further Reading" sections in Part 2 for pointers to more information about topics covering the exam objectives.

Key Points

- The OSI reference model is a standard tool for network planning, implementation, and troubleshooting. You must understand the functions of each of the model's seven layers.

- A network's infrastructure consists of physical and logical components, categorized as hardware and software. You should be familiar with the standard components of data networks, how they function, and how they connect.

- Planning a network topology consists of selecting an appropriate network medium, deciding on the speed at which the network should run, selecting a data-link layer protocol, and then blueprinting the locations of all the network's components.

- Planning the physical placement of network resources consists of selecting locations for workstations and servers, diagramming cable locations, and creating secured facilities for routers, hubs, and other connection devices.

- Selecting the protocols for a network is a matter of evaluating the needs of the network users and balancing them against the requirements specified by the management.

Key Terms

Attenuation   The tendency of a signal to weaken as it travels along a medium. The longer the distance traveled, the more the signal attenuates. All signals attenuate as they travel along a network medium, but different media are subject to different degrees of attenuation. Signals on copper-based cables such as UTP attenuate relatively quickly, while signals can travel longer distances over fiber-optic cable because they attenuate less.

Ad hoc topology   A wireless networking topology in which two or more wireless devices communicate directly with each other, as long as they remain within their respective transmission ranges.

Infrastructure topology   A wireless networking topology in which a transceiver called an access point is connected to a standard cabled network, and several wireless devices communicate with the cabled network by transmitting signals to, and receiving them from, the access point.

Media access control (MAC)   The mechanism used by a data-link layer protocol to regulate transmissions by several computers on a shared network medium. MAC mechanisms are designed to prevent computers on the same medium from sending data simultaneously, causing a collision that damages both transmissions.

Questions and Answers

Page
1-10

Lesson 1 Review

1. Which of the following statements about a network's infrastructure is true?

    a. A network infrastructure includes hardware products only.

    b. A network infrastructure includes software products only.

    c. A network infrastructure includes both hardware and software products.

    d. A network infrastructure is a design that does not include specific hardware or software products.

    c

2. Which type of network infrastructure includes the selection of the network and transport layer protocols that are to be used on the network?

    The logical infrastructure.

3. Maintaining a network infrastructure includes which of the following processes? (Choose three.)

    a. Updating the network

    b. Troubleshooting the network

    c. Implementing the network

    d. Monitoring the network

    a, b, and d

Page
1-23

Lesson 2 Practice

For each of the following situations, specify which Ethernet variation you would recommend and provide a reason for your selection.

1. A legacy Category 3 UTP cable installation.

    10Base-T, because this is the only Ethernet variation that can use Category 3 UTP cable.

2. A high-bandwidth backbone network 1,000 meters long.

    1000Base-LX Gigabit Ethernet with single-mode fiber-optic cable, because this is the only high-bandwidth Ethernet variation that supports a 1,000-meter cable length.

3. A Fast Ethernet LAN connecting 50 workstations in a factory environment with large amounts of electromagnetic interference.

    100Base-FX, because only a fiber-optic network is resistant to electromagnetic interference.

Page
1-23

Lesson 2 Review

1. Data-link layer protocols used on LANs, such as Ethernet, include functions associated with which two layers of the OSI reference model?

The physical and data-link layers.

2. What phenomenon never occurs on a properly functioning Token Ring network but is a normal occurrence on an Ethernet network?

Collisions.

3. List two advantages and two disadvantages of using fiber-optic cable to build a network.

Advantages: Fiber-optic cables are immune to electromagnetic interference, can span longer distances, and are inherently more secure than copper cables. Disadvantages: Fiber-optic cables are more expensive than copper, more difficult to install, and require specialized tools.

Page
1-29

Lesson 3 Review

1. Which of the following network/transport layer protocols can you use for Windows file sharing when installed alone?

   a. TCP/IP only

   b. TCP/IP and NetBEUI only

   c. TCP/IP and IPX only

   d. TCP/IP, IPX, and NetBEUI

d

2. Under what conditions would a network designer be obliged to install the IPX protocol suite on workstations using Windows operating systems?

The IPX protocols are required on workstations using Windows operating systems only when it is necessary to connect with NetWare servers earlier than version 5 or running IPX only.

3. Which of the following are connection-oriented protocols? (Choose all that apply.)

   a. NetWare Core Protocol (NCP)

   b. Transmission Control Protocol (TCP)

   c. Sequenced Packet Exchange (SPX)

   d. User Datagram Protocol (UDP)

b and c

Page
1-36
Lesson 4 Practice

For each of the following pieces of information, give a reason why a network infrastructure blueprint would contain that information.

1. Locations of fluorescent light fixtures

For a network that uses copper-based cables, fluorescent light fixtures can be a significant source of electromagnetic interference. A network blueprint should contain the locations of these fixtures so that the network designer can route cables around them.

2. Cable color

For a network using an external cable installation, matching the cable color to the wall color can help make the cables less visible.

3. Ceiling height

Cable length measurements must include vertical as well as horizontal distances. Specifying ceiling height enables the network designer to account for vertical cable runs from the ceiling down to the wall plate.

4. Size of cable conduits running between floors

The configuration of a large network in a building with several floors can be partially dependent on the amount of space available to run cables between floors. If this space is limited, it might not be practical to run a large number of cables to centrally located hubs in a data center. The designer might have to locate individual hubs on each floor instead.

5. Locations of locked rooms and closets

In most cases, it is best to place servers, hubs, routers, and other critical or expensive devices in physically secure locations. A network blueprint should specify these secure locations.

Page
1-37
Lesson 4 Review

1. List one piece of information that a diagram of an external cable installation needs that an internal installation diagram does not need.

The diagram should specify where and how the cables are to be secured.

2. Which of the following is the term for a LAN that connects all the computers on a single floor of a building?

    a. Backbone network

    b. Horizontal network

    c. Internetwork

    d. Patch panel

b

3. What negative result can occur when you connect an enterprise server to a horizontal network?

The horizontal network on which the server is located can be overloaded with traffic from all the other horizontal networks.

Page
1-39

Case Scenario Exercise

1. Specify which floor of the building is best suited for each of the three departments listed and give your reasons why.

The first floor is best suited to the outside sales department, because it provides individual offices for the salespeople's meetings, and because it is wired with Category 5 cable, providing the potential for more bandwidth to support more elaborate applications required by the users. The second floor is best suited to the inside sales call center, because it already has cubicles in place that are wired with Category 3 UTP. This cable supports a 10Base-T network, which is sufficient for the users' needs. The third floor is best suited to the research and development department, because the fiber-optic cable provides the combination of high bandwidth and security that these users need.

2. Which of the three departments to be housed in the new building could best make use of a wireless network medium? Why?

The outside sales department could best make use of a wireless network medium, because the salespeople use portable computers. A wireless network would enable them to access network resources from any location in their department.

3. Which of the three floors has the most secure cable installation at the present time? Why?

The third floor is currently the most secure, because it uses fiber-optic cable, which cannot easily be tapped.

4. Assuming that you plan to use Ethernet throughout the building, which variant would you use on each floor? Why?

The Category 5 UTP cable on the first floor supports 100Base-TX Fast Ethernet, which is the current standard for horizontal Ethernet networks. The Category 3 UTP cable installed on the second floor network can't support Fast Ethernet, so you must use 10Base-T Ethernet. The fiber-optic cable on the third floor supports 100Base-FX Fast Ethernet, providing sufficient bandwidth for the R&D users.

5. Apart from the computers themselves, what connectivity components must Litware install on each of the three networks in the building to make it a functioning Ethernet network?

Each network requires installation of a hub to make it a functioning Ethernet LAN.

6. What components would you have to add to the plan to connect the LANs on each of the three floors to a single 1000Base-T Gigabit Ethernet backbone network?

   To connect the three horizontal networks to a 1000Base-T backbone, you must install a router on each of the three networks and connect each of the three routers to a 1000Base-T hub using a length of UTP cable rated at least Category 5.

7. Assuming that all three networks are connected to a single backbone, on which network would it make the most sense to connect the server hosting the company's customer database? Explain your answer.

   a. The first floor network

   b. The second floor network

   c. The third floor network

   d. The backbone network

   d, because users on the first and second floor networks have to access the customer database, and connecting the server to the backbone prevents any one of the horizontal networks from being flooded with database traffic from the other networks.

8. Assuming that all three networks are connected to a single backbone, which would be the best network/transport layer protocol to use for the entire internetwork? Why are the other available protocols less suitable?

   TCP/IP is the best protocol suite to use for the internetwork. IPX is less suitable because it is designed for use with Novell NetWare servers. NetBEUI is less suitable because it does not support routing traffic between networks.

2 Planning a TCP/IP Network Infrastructure

Exam Objectives in this Chapter:

- Plan a TCP/IP network infrastructure strategy.
    - ❑ Analyze IP addressing requirements.
    - ❑ Plan an IP routing solution.
    - ❑ Create an IP subnet scheme.
- Troubleshoot TCP/IP addressing.
    - ❑ Diagnose and resolve issues related to client computer configuration.
    - ❑ Diagnose and resolve issues related to DHCP server address assignment.

Why This Chapter Matters

Assigning appropriate IP addresses to individual computers is an essential part of the network design process. Using unregistered IP addresses is the most effective means of preventing unauthorized access to your network from the Internet, but you must also understand when using registered IP addresses is required. Learning how to subnet a network address and calculate IP addresses and subnet masks not only prepares you to design a network, it also helps you troubleshoot problems related to IP addressing and TCP/IP configuration.

Routing is another TCP/IP function that is essential to network design. Understanding the functions of routers and switches helps you choose the correct components for a network, learn how the Internet functions, and deal with problems involving internetwork communications.

Lessons in this Chapter:

Before You Begin

This chapter includes basic information on IP addressing, routing, and subnetting, but also assumes a working knowledge of TCP/IP protocols, the structure of an IP address, and how routers connect networks and forward IP traffic to its destination. You should also read and complete the case scenario in Chapter 1, "Planning a Network Topology," before proceeding with this chapter.

Lesson 1: Determining IP Addressing Requirements

TCP/IP is the most popular protocol suite for data network installations, but not because it is the easiest to set up. When, during network infrastructure planning, you decide to use TCP/IP, you must be aware of the additional effort this decision implies. Network administrators must configure every TCP/IP computer with a unique IP address, as well as with other configuration parameters. Before administrators can do this, however, they must determine what types of IP addresses to use, based on the communication requirements of the network.

After this lesson, you will be able to

- Understand the difference between public and private IP addresses
- List the IP address ranges designated by the Internet Assigned Numbers Authority (IANA) for private use
- Describe how computers with private IP addresses are able to access the Internet
- Understand the differences between a network address translation (NAT) router and a proxy server
- Specify which computers on a network should use public addresses and which should use private addresses

Estimated lesson time: 20 minutes

Using Public and Private Addresses

The TCP/IP protocols use IP addresses to identify the computers on a network. Every packet that a TCP/IP computer transmits contains the IP address of the computer that is the packet's intended recipient, and routers use that address to forward the packet to the appropriate destination. For this system to function properly, every computer must have a unique IP address. If duplicate addresses were to exist on the network, routers would contain incorrect information and packets would end up in the wrong place.

On a private network, network administrators are responsible for ensuring that the address assigned to every computer is unique. As long as the address assigned to each computer is different, it doesn't matter what addresses the administrators use, as long as they subnet them properly. On a public network such as the Internet, however, IP address assignments are more complicated because the Internet consists of thousands of connected networks, each with its own administrators. If the administrators of each network were to select their own IP addresses at random, duplication and chaos would result.

IP Addresses and Subnet Masks

IP addresses are typically expressed using *dotted decimal notation*, in which an address consists of four integers—often called *quads*, *octets*, or *bytes*—between 0 and 255, separated by periods. Like an IP address, a subnet mask consists of 32 bits. In decimal form, the subnet mask appears much like an IP address. In binary form, each of the 32 bits has a value of 0 or 1. When you compare a subnet mask with an IP address, the address bits that correspond to the 1 bits in the mask are the network identifier bits. The address bits that correspond with the 0 bits in the mask are the host identifier bits. For example, a typical IP address and subnet mask, expressed in the decimal notation used when configuring a TCP/IP computer, appears as follows:

```
IP address:   192.168.32.114
Subnet mask:  255.255.255.0
```

When you convert the address and mask into binary notation, they appear as follows:

```
IP address:   11000000 10101000 00100000 01110010
Subnet mask:  11111111 11111111 11111111 00000000
```

Because the first 24 bits in the subnet mask have the value 1, this indicates that the first 24 bits in the IP address make up the network identifier. The final eight bits in the mask have the value 0, which means that the final eight bits in the address are the host identifier. If the subnet mask value were 255.255.0.0 instead, this would indicate that the network identifier and host identifier each consists of 16 bits. The division between the 1 and 0 bits can occur almost anywhere in the subnet mask, as long as both the network and host identifiers are each at least two bits long.

Using Registered Addresses

To prevent IP address duplication on the Internet, an administrative body called the IANA functions as the official IP address registrar. To connect computers directly to the Internet, you must obtain a network address from the IANA. A network address is just a network identifier. The administrators of the network using that identifier are responsible for assigning unique host identifiers to the individual computers and other devices on the network. By combining the network identifier assigned by the IANA with a unique host identifier, the administrators are able to calculate the IP addresses for the computers on that network.

Off the Record   Although the IANA ultimately assigns all Internet network addresses, network administrators today do not deal with the address registrar directly. Instead, they obtain a network address from an Internet service provider (ISP). The ISP might have obtained the network address from a local (LIR), national (NIR), or regional Internet registry (RIR) (which is assigned pools of addresses by the IANA directly), but it is also likely that the ISP obtained the address from its own service provider. Internet addresses often pass through several layers of service providers in this way before they get to the organization that actually uses them.

Why Use Registered Addresses?   If you have computers on your network that you want to be accessible from the Internet (such as Web servers), you must configure them with IP addresses that the IANA has registered. This is because only registered addresses are visible from the Internet. For a user on the Internet to access your company Web server, a client application, such as a Web browser, must initiate communication by sending a request to the server. The browser can't do that if it doesn't have the server's address. (Users on your network who want to access Internet services do not require registered addresses; this matter is covered later in this lesson.)

Why Not Use Registered Addresses?   Theoretically, you can use registered IP addresses for all the computers on your network, but this practice has two serious drawbacks:

■ It depletes the IP address space. If every device with an IP address today (which includes a great many mobile telephones, automobiles, and other devices, in addition to computers) had a registered IP address, the pool of available addresses would be well on its way to depletion. Even now, a program to expand the IP address space from 32 (called Internet Protocol Version 4 or IPv4) to 128 bits, called IPv6, is currently under way to prevent the possibility of depleting the entire IP address space in the future.

See Also   For more information about IPv6, see *Understanding IPv6* (Microsoft Press, 2003). Additionally, the Internet Engineering Task Force (IETF) has published a number of proposed Requests for Comments (RFC) standards that you can consult, such as RFC 2464, "Transmission of IPv6 Packets over Ethernet Networks."

■ Using registered IP addresses on a private network presents a serious security hazard. Not only can a computer with a registered IP address access systems on the Internet, the systems on the Internet can also access the computer.

Security Alert   You must set up some sort of firewall to protect Web servers and other computers that must have registered addresses. For example, you can use packet filtering to permit only Hypertext Transfer Protocol (HTTP) traffic using port 80 to reach your Web server from the Internet. This means that Internet users can access the Web server using only standard browser requests. Other types of traffic—such as those used by Internet predators to plant viruses, steal data, and cause mayhem—are blocked. Without some protection, an intruder will eventually target a registered system, and the results can range from irritating to catastrophic.

Protecting computers with registered addresses is a complex process that requires constant vigilance from the network's administrators. If you configure all your computers with registered addresses, you compound this protection process unnecessarily. You can use several methods to assign unregistered IP addresses to your network's computers while still enabling them to access the Internet.

General practice in network design calls for using registered IP addresses only on computers that must be accessible from the Internet, such as Web and mail servers. You can obtain the addresses you need from your ISP. In most cases, designers place these computers on a *perimeter network* that is separate from the servers and workstations needed by the organization's internal users, as shown in Figure 2-1. This perimeter network is sometimes referred to colloquially as a demilitarized zone (DMZ) because these registered computers are not as fully protected as the internal systems. Although the registered computers are still behind a firewall, they are able to receive more traffic from the Internet than the internal computers can.

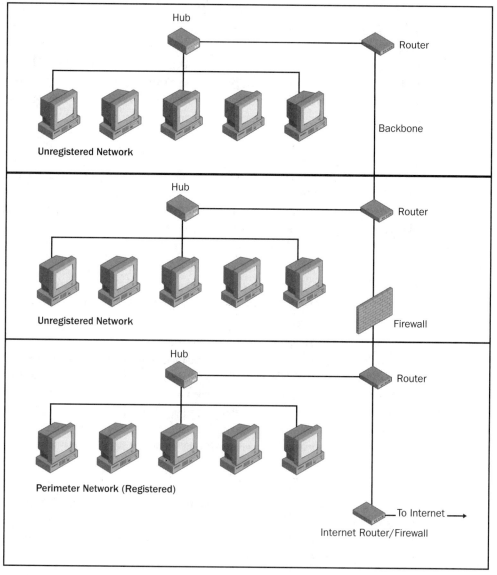

Figure 2-1   Computers with registered IP addresses located in a perimeter network

Using Unregistered Addresses

Most TCP/IP networks use unregistered IP addresses (also called private network addresses) for the servers and workstations that only internal users need to access. These are addresses that are not registered with the IANA, and as a result, they are invisible to the Internet. Because they are invisible, Internet criminals cannot specifically target them for virus distribution or other types of compromise (although they are still vulnerable in other ways). As described in RFC 1918, "Address Allocation for Private Internets," the IANA has set aside three IP address ranges for use by private networks. These addresses are not registered to any single network, so anyone can use them for computers and other devices on a private network.

The private IP address ranges designated by the IANA are as follows:

- 10.0.0.0 through 10.255.255.255
- 172.16.0.0 through 172.31.255.255
- 192.168.0.0 through 192.168.255.255

Tip   On a private network that is not connected to the Internet in any way, you can use any IP addresses you want to, registered or not, because there is no way for them to conflict with the registered users of those addresses on the Internet. However, if your network users access the Internet in any way, you should always use the designated private address ranges to prevent conflicts with Internet computers.

Accessing the Internet from a Private Network

The logical question that remains, however, when you elect to use unregistered IP addresses on your network, is how your users can access the Internet. If unregistered addresses are invisible to the Internet, how is an Internet Web server supposed to respond to a request from a browser on an unregistered network? The answer is that the network designer incorporates a mechanism into the network infrastructure that enables unregistered clients to access Internet services. The two most common mechanisms of this type are NAT and proxy servers.

Using Network Address Translation

Network address translation is an application built into a router that functions as an intermediary between unregistered clients on a private network and registered Internet servers. Client computers can use NAT to send requests to Internet servers and receive replies, despite the fact that the clients have unregistered network addresses. This provides the unregistered computers with Internet access, without compromising their protection from Internet intrusion.

> ### Connecting to the Internet with Routers
>
> A *router* is a network layer device that connects two networks and permits traffic to pass between them. Routers therefore have two network interfaces and two IP addresses, one for each network. If you want to give your network users access to the Internet, you must have a router connecting your network with that of an ISP. A router can be a software application running on a normal computer, or it can be a dedicated hardware device costing anywhere from under one hundred to many thousands of dollars. For more information on routers and TCP/IP routing, see Lesson 3 of this chapter.

When a client application generates a request for information from a server on the Internet, the client computer generates a request message and packages it in an IP datagram. The *datagram* is essentially the envelope that carries the message to its destination. Like a postal envelope, the datagram includes the address of the destination system and the address of the sender; the only difference is that these are IP, not postal, addresses.

Understanding Routing   To get the request to the destination server, the client computer sends it to a nearby router, which receives the datagram, evaluates the destination address, and forwards the packet to the appropriate location, either the specified server or another router. The datagram might pass through a dozen or more routers on its journey. Eventually, the destination server receives the datagram, processes the request contained inside, and generates a reply using the sender's address from the original datagram as the destination. The routing process then occurs in reverse, with the reply datagram eventually finding its way back to the client computer.

If the sender's IP address in the request datagram is unregistered, however, the reply can never make it back to the client computer because routers cannot process unregistered addresses properly. When you use NAT, the first router that receives the request datagram from the client makes some slight modifications to it. A NAT router connects both to a private network, using unregistered addresses, and to an ISP's registered network. This means that the NAT router has one unregistered address and one registered address.

Understanding NAT Routing   Under normal conditions, routers do not modify datagrams any more than the postal service modifies envelopes. A NAT router, however, modifies each datagram it receives from an unregistered client computer by changing the sender's IP address. When a client sends a request message in a datagram to a NAT router, NAT substitutes its own registered IP address for the client computer's unregistered address in the datagram and then forwards it to the destination in the normal manner. The NAT router also maintains a table of unregistered addresses on the private network so that it can keep track of the datagrams it has processed.

When the destination server receives the request, it processes it in the normal manner and generates its reply datagram. However, because the sender's address in the request datagram contained the NAT router's registered address, the destination server addresses the reply datagram to the NAT router, and routers can forward it in the normal manner. When the NAT router receives the reply from the server, it modifies the datagram again, substituting the client's unregistered address for the destination address in the datagram, and forwards the packet to the client on the private network.

The NAT router's processes are invisible to the client and the server. The client has generated a request and sent it to a server, and it eventually receives a reply from that server. The server receives a request from the NAT router and transmits its reply to the same router. Both the client and the server have functioned normally, unaware of the NAT router's intervention. More importantly, the client computer remains invisible to the Internet and is protected from most types of unauthorized access.

Microsoft Windows Server 2003 can function as a router, and it contains a NAT implementation as part of the Routing and Remote Access service (RRAS). Because the NAT router functions are invisible to the unregistered computer, users can access the Internet with any client application. The one thing you can't do with a standard NAT implementation is run an Internet server. This is because the client must initiate the client/server transaction, and a client computer on the Internet has no way of contacting the server running on an unregistered computer first.

> **Tip**   Some NAT implementations enable you to assign registered IP addresses to specific unregistered computers on the private network. This ability allows you to use an unregistered computer to establish a presence on the Internet without compromising the security of the unregistered computer. All the incoming client traffic is actually going to the NAT router, which relays it to the server on the unregistered network.

Using Proxy Servers

A *proxy server* is similar to a NAT router in that it functions as an intermediary between client computers on a private network and servers on the Internet. Unlike NAT, however, a proxy server is an independent software product that runs at the application layer and is not incorporated into a router. When an unregistered client wants to send a request to an Internet server, the computer forwards the request datagram to a proxy server instead. The proxy server sends an identical request to the destination server, receives a reply, and relays the results back to the client. For the proxy server to communicate with Internet servers, it must have a registered IP address.

Unlike NAT routers, proxy servers do not process all TCP/IP traffic. Proxy servers only work with specific client applications, and you must configure the clients themselves to send their messages to the proxy server instead of to the actual destination, using an interface like the one shown in Figure 2-2. At one time, the need to configure individual clients was the primary drawback of proxy servers, but some client applications can now detect the presence of a proxy server on the network and configure themselves to use the server automatically.

Figure 2-2   The Internet Explorer proxy server configuration interface

Proxy servers also differ from NAT routers in that they enable the network administrator to exercise more control over users' access to the Internet. For example, administrators running a proxy server that gives clients access to Internet Web servers can, in most cases, create a list of specific Web sites that users are not permitted to access, as well as restrict times that users are permitted to access the Web. Proxy servers can also log users' activity, enabling administrators to examine users' access patterns and maintain a record of specific Internet activities. In addition, proxy servers are usually able to cache information from frequently visited sites. When a user requests a Web page that the proxy server has recently downloaded for another user, the server can send a reply to the client immediately using cached information. This speeds up the user's response time and reduces traffic on the network's Internet connection.

Proxy servers provide client computers with the same degree of security as NAT routers. Because only the proxy server communicates directly with the Internet, the actual clients on the unregistered network remain invisible to potential intruders. However, despite the protection that both NAT and proxy servers provide for unregistered computers on a private network, they cannot always overcome the shortsightedness of the network's users. As mentioned earlier, there is no way for an Internet predator to access a computer on an unregistered network directly, because with NAT and proxy servers, the client must initiate communications. However, if the client computer does initiate communications with the wrong computers on the Internet (whether intentionally or not), it is vulnerable to all kinds of attacks.

Security Alert   One of the most common ploys used by Internet criminals today is to dupe an unsuspecting user into downloading and running a program that is essentially a special-purpose server application. The intruders may camouflage these programs, called Trojan horses or just Trojans, as image files or other innocent applications, which are typically delivered through e-mail or downloaded from a Web site. When the user runs the program, it broadcasts the computer's availability to the Internet, enabling unauthorized users to take control of it at will. Private addressing therefore provides a distinct advantage over using public addresses, but it is not a panacea.

Planning IP Addresses

A first step in creating an IP addressing plan for your network is determining what types of Internet access each computer requires, if any. Most organizations today give their network computers some access to the Internet, and in these cases, you should know the circumstances in which you must use registered IP addresses. For computers that are strictly Internet clients, that is, for users who need access to the Web and similar services, unregistered IP addresses are the best solution, along with either a NAT router or a proxy server. Whether you use NAT or a proxy server depends on how much Internet freedom you want to grant your users and what types of client applications they will use.

For computers that must function as Internet servers, registered IP addresses are required. Most networks need only a few registered IP addresses, and they lease them from their ISP for a nominal fee. For organizations with a large Internet presence requiring many addresses, you might have to acquire a network address of your own and assign host addresses as needed.

Using registered IP addresses affects the network infrastructure design in other ways as well. As mentioned earlier, most organizations put Web servers and other registered computers on a network of their own. This also means that you should not use these same computers to run important internal services. For example, you should not use the same computer to host your Web server and your company's private customer database. A registered computer is inevitably more vulnerable to attack than an unregistered one, and it should contain only the information needed to perform its primary function.

Practice: Using Registered and Unregistered IP Addresses

For each of the following types of computers, specify whether it should have a registered or an unregistered IP address, or both, and why. You can find answers to the questions in the "Questions and Answers" section at the end of this chapter.

1. A corporate Web server providing product information to Internet clients around the world

    _____

    _____

2. A NAT router enabling clients on a private network to access Internet servers

    _____

    _____

3. An intranet Web server on a private network used to provide human resources information to employees

    _____

    _____

4. A client computer that accesses Web servers on the Internet using a NAT router

    _____

    _____

5. A proxy server providing Internet Web access to clients on a private network

    _____

    _____

Lesson Review

The following questions are intended to reinforce key information presented in this lesson. If you are unable to answer a question, review the lesson materials and try the question again. You can find answers to the questions in the "Questions and Answers" section at the end of this chapter.

1. Which of the following statements about NAT routers and proxy servers are true? Choose all answers that are correct.

   a. NAT routers and proxy servers must have two IP addresses.

   b. A NAT router can provide Internet access to any client application on the private network.

   c. Proxy servers can cache information they receive from Internet servers.

   d. The Windows Server 2003 operating system includes a proxy server.

2. What are the two primary reasons why you should use unregistered IP addresses for Internet client computers?

   _____

   _____

3. Which of the following best describes the function of a subnet mask?

   a. A subnet mask indicates whether an IP address is registered or unregistered.

   b. A subnet mask specifies the sizes of the network and host identifiers in an IP address.

   c. A subnet mask is a value assigned by the IANA to uniquely identify a specific network on the Internet.

   d. A subnet mask enables an IP address to be visible from the Internet.

Lesson Summary

- Every computer on a TCP/IP network must have a unique IP address.

- Computers that are visible from the Internet must have IP addresses that are registered with the IANA.

- For security, a network designer often places computers with registered IP addresses on a separate network.

- Computers on private networks typically use unregistered IP addresses to protect them from unauthorized access and to conserve the IP address space.

- Computers with unregistered IP addresses can access the Internet as clients using a NAT router or a proxy server.

Lesson 2: Planning an IP Routing Solution

An IP router is a hardware or software device that connects two local area networks (LANs), relaying traffic between them as needed. Part of designing a network infrastructure is determining how many LANs you will create and how you will connect them. When you are designing a small network, routing is not a major consideration because you can put all your computers on a single LAN. For medium-to-large networks, this is not a practical solution. You have to create several LANs and then connect them so that any computer on the network can communicate with any other computer.

Your IP routing plan can be simple or complex, depending on the size of the network installation, the number of LANs you decide to create, and how you choose to connect the LANs. A small network might have a single router connecting the LAN to an ISP to provide network users with Internet access. A large network installation might consist of many different LANs, all connected with routers. The ultimate IP routing scenario is the Internet itself, which is composed of thousands of networks connected by thousands of routers.

Typically, an IP routing plan specifies how many LANs there will be in your network installation and how you will connect the LANs. The plan should also specify the types of routers the network will use, and how the routers will get the information they need to forward packets to their destinations.

After this lesson, you will be able to

- Understand router functions
- Use routers to connect LANs and wide area networks (WANs)
- Understand the difference between routing and switching

Estimated lesson time: 20 minutes

Understanding IP Routing

When a computer on a TCP/IP network transmits a packet, the datagram in the packet contains the IP address of the destination computer, as well as the address of the sender. If the destination address is on the same LAN as the sender, the packet travels directly to that destination. If the destination is on a different network, the sender transmits a packet to a router instead. This router is known as the computer's *default gateway*. (In TCP/IP parlance, the term gateway is synonymous with router.) You specify the default gateway address for your computers along with their IP addresses and subnet mask during the TCP/IP configuration process.

The default gateway is the interface between the sender's own network and all the other connected networks. When the router receives a packet, it reads the destination address and compares the address to the entries in its routing table. A *routing table* is a list of destination addresses, with the information needed to forward traffic to those destinations. Using the information in its routing table, the router determines where to send the packet next. The router might be able to transmit the packet directly to its destination (if the router has an interface on the destination network), or it might send the packet to another router, where the entire process begins again. On a private network, packets might travel through several routers on the way to a given destination. On the Internet, packets commonly pass through a dozen routers or more.

Tip   To see a list of the routers between your computer and a specific destination address, you can use the traceroute utility that is provided with most TCP/IP implementations. On computers running the Microsoft Windows operating systems, the traceroute utility is called Tracert.exe. To use it, display a Command Prompt window and type **tracert *address***, where *address* is the IP address of a destination computer.

Routers obtain the information in their routing tables in one of two ways. Either an administrator manually enters the information, which is called *static routing*, or the router receives the information automatically from another router using a specialized routing protocol. This is called *dynamic routing*. On Internet routers, the routing tables can be long and complex, but the tables on private network routers are simple.

Creating LANs

Ethernet LANs are typically defined in terms of broadcast domains and collision domains.

■ A *broadcast domain* is a group of computers, all of which receive broadcasts transmitted by any one of the computers in a group. For example, when you connect 100 computers using only Ethernet hubs, any one of those computers can generate a broadcast and all the other computers will receive it.

■ A *collision domain* is a group of computers that are connected in such a way that when any two computers transmit packets at exactly the same time a collision occurs. The collision destroys both packets and forces the computers to retransmit them.

When you create two LANs and join them using a router, you are creating two separate broadcast domains, because routers do not forward broadcast transmissions from one network to another, and two separate collision domains, because packets transmitted on the same network may collide, but packets on different networks do not.

Planning   The reason to split a private network into multiple LANs is to create different broadcast domains and collision domains.

If you were to have thousands of computers all connected to the same LAN, each computer would have to devote an inordinate amount of time to processing broadcast messages. In addition, there would be a high collision rate because so many computers would be contending for the network medium at the same time. More collisions mean more packet retransmissions. The result would be a slow, inefficient network. By splitting that network into multiple LANs, you create individual broadcast and collision domains, reducing the number of broadcasts each system has to process and the number of collisions that occur.

Routing and Network Topology Design

In Lesson 3 of Chapter 1, "Planning a Network Topology," you learned that network designers often split the network into a series of horizontal networks, each of which is connected to a backbone network using a router. This design provides an efficient routing solution. No matter how many horizontal networks you have in your installation, a transmitted packet never has to travel through more than two routers to get to any destination on the network (as shown in Figure 1-7). Each packet passes through one router to get from its origin network to the backbone and through a second router to get from the backbone to the destination network. Connecting the horizontal networks in series would require packets to pass through a separate router for each network they traverse.

The number of LANs you create and the number of computers in each LAN depend on the data-link layer protocol you select for your network. Some protocols have specific limitations on the number of computers they support on a single LAN while others have implied limits based on other factors, such as the maximum number of hubs you can use. In many cases, however, a network's LAN configuration is based on geographical or political factors. For example, if you are designing a network for a multi-story office building, creating a separate LAN for each floor might be the most convenient solution. In other cases, designers create a separate LAN for each department or division in the organization.

Another advantage of routers is that they can connect networks running completely different protocols at the data-link layer. Whenever a packet arrives at a router, it travels up through the protocol stack only as high as the network layer (see Figure 2-3). The router strips off the data-link layer frame from the packet and processes the IP datagram contained inside. When the router has determined how to forward the datagram to its next destination, it repackages the datagram in a new data-link layer frame prior to transmission. This new frame can be the same as, or different from, the original frame on the packet when it arrived on the router. So if your network infrastructure design calls for different data-link layer protocols or different network media to satisfy the requirements of different users, you can connect those different networks using routers. You can connect two different types of Ethernet, such as connecting a 100Base-TX Fast Ethernet horizontal LAN (using Category 5 unshielded twisted pair cable) to a 1000Base-SX Gigabit Ethernet backbone (using fiber-optic cable), or even connecting an Ethernet LAN to a Token Ring LAN.

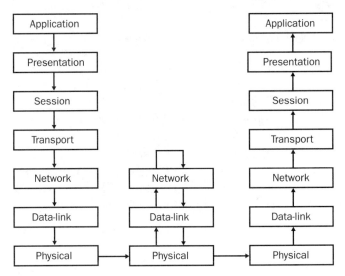

Figure 2-3   A router processing network traffic

Creating WANs

In addition to connecting LANs, routers can also connect a LAN to a WAN connection, enabling you to join networks at different locations. This is the most common application for routers today. Every network connected to the Internet uses a router to connect the private network to an ISP's network. The ISP in turn has its own routers that provide the connection to the Internet. Even a simple Windows computer using the Internet Connection Sharing (ICS) feature is functioning as a router.

Some network installations also use routers and WAN connections to join distant offices. For example, a branch office might be connected to corporate headquarters using a T-1 line, which is a permanent, digital telephone connection between the two sites. To connect the networks at those sites, each one has a router connecting it to one end of the T-1, as shown in Figure 2-4. The T-1 itself then becomes a two-node network, connecting the two remote LANs. A computer at one site that has to send traffic to a computer at the other site sends its packets to the router on the local network. The router then forwards the packets over the T-1 to the router at the other site. The second router then forwards the packets to the LAN in the other office.

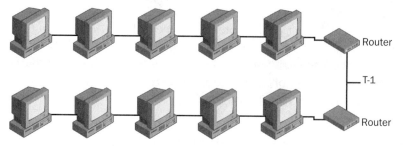

Figure 2-4   Two remote networks connected using routers and a WAN

You will learn later in this chapter that there are alternatives to routers for connecting LANs at the same site. However, routers are essential for connecting networks using a WAN. This is because WANs use different data-link layer protocols than LANs. A typical WAN connection uses a TCP/IP protocol called the Point-to-Point Protocol (PPP) at the data-link layer. PPP is designed solely for connections between two nodes. With PPP, unlike Ethernet, there is no contention for the network medium and no need for packet addressing. The control overhead of the PPP is therefore much lower than that of Ethernet or Token Ring. The routers not only provide the interface to the WAN, they also repackage the datagrams for transmission over a different type of network.

Using Routers

The routers you use to connect your LANs can take many different forms. Some routers are software products. A Windows Server 2003 computer is capable of functioning as a router, providing you install two network interface adapters in the computer and configure RRAS to function as a LAN router. Windows Server 2003 can also function as a router connecting a LAN to the Internet. The only differences between the two router functions are the RRAS configuration and the fact that one of the network interfaces is a modem or other device providing a WAN connection to an ISP.

On most networks, routers are more likely to be separate hardware devices than standard computers. Stand-alone routers are available in many sizes and price ranges. The smallest and most inexpensive routers are devices the size of an external modem that are designed to connect a home or small business LAN to the Internet. More elaborate Internet access routers are designed to support larger networks. Most of these routers can use NAT so that the clients on the private network can use unregistered IP addresses.

> **Planning**   Routers for connecting LANs tend to be high-end devices and are frequently modular. This type of device consists of a router frame, which you typically install in a data center and populate with modules that provide interfaces to your various networks. The advantage of this design is that you can connect LANs (or WANs) of any type by purchasing the appropriate modules and inserting them into the frame.

Using Switches

While routers are necessary for connecting distant networks with WANs, today's networks do not use them for connecting LANs together as often as they used to. Switches have largely replaced routers on internal networks. A *switch* is a network connection device similar in appearance to a hub but with different internal functions.

A typical Ethernet hub is strictly a physical layer device. Electrical (or fiber-optic) signals generated by devices on the network enter the hub through one of its ports. The hub then amplifies the signals and transmits them through all the other ports simultaneously. The hub does not read the contents of the data packets it forwards or even recognize that they are data packets. The hub's function is strictly electrical (or photonic). It has no intelligence.

Switches receive signals from network devices in the same way as a hub, but the switch is intelligent and can read the contents of the data packets it receives. The switch reads the destination address in each incoming packet, amplifies the signals like a hub, and then forwards the packet, but only through the port providing the connection to the packet's destination.

When you connect a group of computers to a hub, every packet transmitted by every computer is forwarded to every other computer. This means that the network interfaces in the computers spend a significant amount of time reading the addresses of incoming packets and discarding them because they are intended for another destination. Connect the same group of computers to a switch, and the amount of traffic on the network is reduced substantially because packets travel directly from the source only to their destinations and nowhere else. Each pair of computers on the network has, in effect, a dedicated connection between them, using the full bandwidth of the network medium. There is less contention for the network medium, and therefore there are fewer collisions.

You can use switches in place of hubs on your individual horizontal networks. These are called *workgroup switches* or *switching hubs*. As a replacement for routers, however, you can also use a single high-performance switch in place of a backbone network. By using switching hubs on your horizontal networks and connecting them to a single backbone switch, you create a network infrastructure in which every computer can open a dedicated connection to any other computer. For larger networks, you can add a third level of switches, connecting your workgroup switches to a departmental switch and your departmental switches to a backbone switch.

Off the Record   You can connect standard hubs to departmental or backbone switches, providing each horizontal network with a dedicated connection to every other horizontal network. This is not as efficient as a fully switched network, but it provides a performance improvement over routers and a backbone that all computers in the enterprise share.

Real World   **Switches, Routers, and Performance**

Because they are more intelligent, switches are more expensive than standard Ethernet hubs, but they are less expensive than comparable routers. Routing is a more complicated task than switching because a router has to strip off each packet's data-link layer frame, process the information in the IP datagram, and then package the datagram in a new frame before transmitting it. A basic switch, in contrast, only has to read the data-link layer address in each packet and forward it to the appropriate port. For this reason, switching is also far faster than routing.

Replacing the routers on an existing network with switches usually results in an increase in performance. Designing a network from the outset to use switches enables you to achieve peak performance from the network equipment you select. Even a standard 10-megabit-per-second (Mbps) Ethernet network can yield exceptional performance when each workstation has a dedicated, full-bandwidth connection to every other workstation.

Combining Routing and Switching

Unlike routers, which operate at the network layer, switches are data-link layer devices, and this presents a new problem. By connecting LANs with switches, you are essentially creating one huge LAN. Although switching eliminates the problem of having one huge collision domain, all computers on the network are still in the same broadcast domain. When a computer on the network transmits a broadcast message, every computer on the entire network receives it. This type of setup can consume large amounts of bandwidth unnecessarily.

The solution to this problem lies in a switch's ability to create virtual LANs, or VLANs. A virtual LAN is a group of computers on a switched network that functions as a subnet. When one computer in a VLAN generates a broadcast transmission, only the other computers in the same VLAN receive it. Network administrators create VLANs in the switch by specifying the addresses of the computers in each subnet.

Planning   One big advantage to creating subnets with VLANs is that the computers in a subnet can have physical locations anywhere in the enterprise. With VLANs, you can create subnets based on criteria other than physical proximity, such as membership in a workgroup or department.

VLANs are logical constructions that form an overlay to the switched network. The computers are still switched, but the VLANs enable them to behave as though they are routed. Further difficulty arises, however, when computers on different VLANs have to communicate with each other. In this case, some element of actual routing is necessary, and various types of switches treat this requirement in different ways. Switches that are strictly layer 2 (that is, data-link layer) devices sometimes have a port for a connection to a router. This type of device operates under a "switch where you can, route where you must" philosophy. The device switches all traffic between computers on the same VLAN, but it sends all traffic between computers on different VLANs to the router for processing.

Another solution to this problem is most commonly called *layer 3 switching*, although specific switching hardware manufacturers have other names for the technique, including *multilayer routing* and *cut-through routing*. A layer 3 switch has the capabilities of a switch and a router built into a single device. Rather than examine the datagram information for every packet, a layer 3 switch examines the first packet in each series to determine its final destination, and then uses standard layer 2 switching for the subsequent packets sent to the same destination. The philosophy for this type of device is "route once, and switch afterwards."

Workgroup and departmental switches are relatively simple devices. Some manufacturers have lines of hubs and switches that are outwardly identical, differing only in their internal construction. Layer 3 switches are much more complex, typically taking modular form, like high-end routers. Installing this type of switch enables you to connect different types of horizontal networks, providing essentially the same functions as a router, but with greater speed and efficiency.

Practice: Designing an Internetwork

In the following exercises, the diagrams represent a network installation that consists of four independent LANs. Working directly on the diagrams, add the components necessary to fulfill the requirements given in each exercise. Be sure to add all the necessary cables, hubs, routers, or switches, and label them accordingly. Don't forget to label the device connecting the computers in each LAN as well. You can find answers to the exercises in the "Questions and Answers" section at the end of this chapter.

Exercise 1: Internetwork Design with a Single Broadcast Domain and Multiple Collision Domains

In the following diagram, add the components needed to connect the LANs to an internetwork that consists of a single broadcast domain and several collision domains.

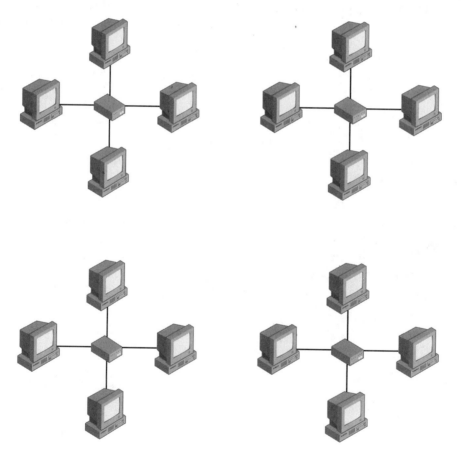

Exercise 2: Internetwork Design with Multiple Broadcast and Collision Domains

In the following diagram, add the components needed to connect the LANs in an internetwork that consists of five broadcast domains and five collision domains.

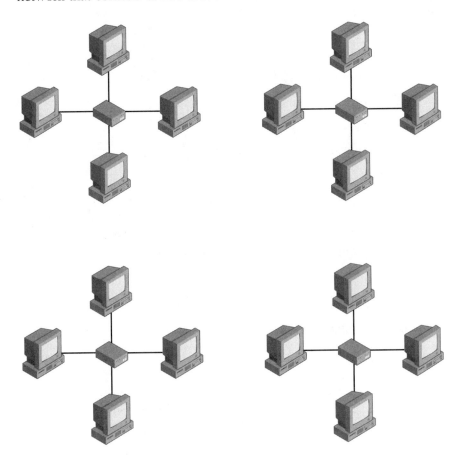

Lesson Review

The following questions are intended to reinforce key information presented in this lesson. If you are unable to answer a question, review the lesson materials and try the question again. You can find answers to the questions in the "Questions and Answers" section at the end of this chapter.

1. Replacing the hubs and routers on an internetwork with switches creates a network that has which of the following?

   a. One broadcast domain and one collision domain

   b. One broadcast domain and multiple collision domains

   c. One collision domain and multiple broadcast domains

   d. Several collision domains and several broadcast domains

2. Specify the OSI reference model layer at which each of the following devices operates.

   a. A switch

   b. A router

   c. A hub

3. Which of the following Windows Server 2003 TCP/IP configuration parameters specifies the address of a router?

   a. Preferred DNS server

   b. Subnet mask

   c. Default gateway

   d. IP address

4. When you replace the routers on an internetwork with switches that include no VLAN or layer 3 capabilities, which of the following is a possible reason for poor network performance?

   a. Excessive collisions

   b. Excessive broadcast traffic

   c. Excessive number of workstations on the LAN

   d. Excessive number of collision domains

Lesson Summary

- Large networks typically consist of multiple LANs connected by routers. Routers are network layer devices that enable communication between the networks while maintaining separate broadcast and collision domains.

- Routers can take the form of software or hardware, and range from Routing and Remote Access in Windows Server 2003 to inexpensive Internet access devices to expensive modular installations that support large networks.

- A typical network design consists of several horizontal networks, all connected to a single backbone network.

- A switch is a data-link layer device that intelligently forwards traffic to specified destinations. Switches can replace many routers in your network infrastructure design, creating a network that is more efficient and economical.

- Replacing routers with switches creates a network with a single broadcast domain. Virtual LANs are logical subnets that exist inside switches, enabling you to limit the propagation of broadcasts throughout the network.

Lesson 3: Planning an IP Addressing and Subnetting Strategy

Once you have determined what types of IP addresses your network will use and have decided how many LANs you are going to create and how you're going to connect them, you can begin the process of calculating the network's IP addresses, subnet masks, and default gateway addresses. You can also plan how the network administrators are actually going to perform the TCP/IP configuration tasks.

After this lesson, you will be able to

- Understand how to subnet a network
- Calculate a subnet mask
- Calculate IP addresses on subnetted networks

Estimated lesson time: 30 minutes

Obtaining Network Addresses

In Lesson 1 of this chapter, you learned about the circumstances under which to use registered and unregistered IP addresses, and you have presumably used this information to design a network infrastructure in which the computers use the appropriate address types. If some or all of your computers require registered IP addresses, you can obtain them in one of two forms, depending on how many addresses you need.

Planning   If you need only a few registered addresses, you can obtain them singly from your ISP along with an appropriate subnet mask, although you will almost certainly have to pay an extra monthly fee for them. If the computers requiring the registered address are all on the same LAN and must communicate with each other, be sure that you obtain addresses in the same subnet. If you need a large number of registered IP addresses, you can obtain a network address from the ISP and use it to create as many host addresses as you need.

A network address is the network identifier portion of an IP address plus a subnet mask. For example, if your ISP were to assign you the network address 192.168.65.0, with a subnet mask of 255.255.255.0, you can assign IP addresses ranging from 192.168.65.1 to 192.168.65.254 to your computers. The network address you receive from the ISP depends on the class of the address and on the number of computers you have requiring registered addresses.

Off the Record   In practice, the network address your ISP assigns you will not be part of the private address range used in this example. Also, it will probably be more complex than the address shown here, because the ISP will be assigning you only a small portion of the addresses assigned to them.

Understanding IP Address Classes

The IANA divides the IP address space into three basic classes. Each class provides a different number of possible network and host identifiers, and therefore, each is suitable for installations of a specific size. The three classes, and the relative sizes of the network and host identifiers, are shown in Figure 2-5.

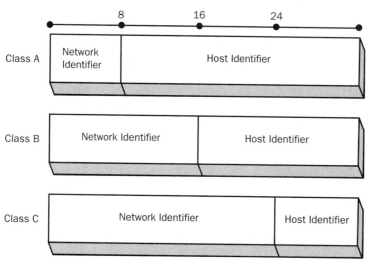

Figure 2-5   IP address classes

Table 2-1 provides additional information about each of the address classes, including the value of the first binary bits and the first decimal byte in each class. The value of the first bits and first byte are what you use to determine the class of a particular network address. The table also specifies the number of bits in the network and host identifiers for each class, as well as the number of possible addresses you can create with each identifier.

Table 2-1   IP Address Classes

IP Address Class	Class A	Class B	Class C
First bit values (binary)	0	10	110
First byte value (decimal)	1–127	128–191	192–223
Number of network identifier bits	8	16	24
Number of host identifier bits	24	16	8
Number of possible networks	126	16,384	2,097,152
Number of possible hosts	16,777,214	65,534	254
Subnet mask	255.0.0.0	255.255.0.0	255.255.255.0

To compute the number of possible addresses you can create with a given number of bits, you use the formula 2^x-2, where x is the number of bits. You subtract two because the original IP addressing standard states that you cannot use the values consisting of all zeros and all ones for network or host addresses. Most routers and operating systems, including Windows Server 2003, now enable you to use all zeros for a network or subnet identifier, but you must be sure that all your equipment supports these values before you decide to use them.

Exam Tip   Be sure to familiarize yourself with the information in Table 2-1, especially the number of possible networks and hosts available for the three IP address classes, and with the formula for computing the number of possible addresses. It is common for the exam to contain questions requiring you to know how many network or host identifier bits are required for a given installation.

In Lesson 1, you learned about the IP address ranges designated by the IANA for use by private networks. Each of the three ranges corresponds to one of the IP address classes, as follows:

- Class A: 10.0.0.0 through 10.25.255.255

- Class B: 172.16.0.0 through 172.31.255.255

- Class C: 192.168.0.0 through 192.168.255.255

Off the Record   In addition to Classes A through C, there are two additional address classes, Class D and Class E. The IANA has allocated Class D addresses for use as multicast identifiers. A *multicast address* identifies a group of computers on a network, all of which possess a similar trait. Multicast addresses enable TCP/IP applications to send traffic to computers that perform specific functions (such as all the routers on the network), even if they are located on different subnets. Class E addresses are defined as experimental and are as yet unused.

Understanding Subnetting

Whether you obtain a registered network address from your ISP or you use one of the private IP address ranges designated by the IANA, you are free to subnet that address as needed. Subnetting is the process of creating individual network addresses out of a larger network address. To create a subnet, you borrow some host identifier bits from a network address and use them to create a subnet identifier. You can then increment the value of the subnet identifier to create multiple subnets, and increment what's left of the host identifier to create individual hosts on each subnet.

Subnetting is an essential part of the IP addressing process, as you can probably tell when you study the table of IP address classes shown earlier in this lesson. There are only 126 Class A network addresses available in the entire IP address space, for example, and each one of those addresses supports more than 16 million hosts. There are some very large network installations in this world, but none of them have as many as 16 million computers. Assigning an entire Class A network address to a particular organization for its exclusive use would therefore be extremely wasteful if subnetting was not involved.

In a standard Class A address, the network address is the first 8 bits, which in decimal form translates to the first quad in the address. For example, 10.0.0.0 is an example of a Class A address, and it would use a subnet mask value of 255.0.0.0. Because a Class A address has 24 host identifier bits, far more than are needed for any single network, it is no problem to borrow some of those bits to create a subnet identifier. If you decide to borrow 8 bits for the subnet identifier, the breakdown of the address changes as shown in Figure 2-6. You also change the subnet mask of the address to 255.255.0.0 because the primary function of the mask is to specify where in the IP address the host identifier begins.

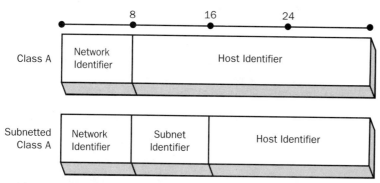

Figure 2-6   Subnetting a Class A address

To use the subnetted Class A address, you increment the subnet identifier and the host identifier separately. For example, to create your first subnet, you give the subnet identifier a value of one. This means that the network address for this subnet is 10.1.0.0. You now have 16 bits left for the host identifier, which means you can create up to 65,534 host addresses in that one subnet ($2^{16}-2=65,534$). The first host address in this subnet is therefore 10.1.0.1. This is the IP address value you use to configure the first computer in the subnet, along with the subnet mask value of 255.255.0.0. The second address in the subnet is 10.1.0.2, and the next addresses can proceed from 10.1.0.3 all the way to 10.1.255.254, utilizing all 16 bits of the host identifier.

To create the second subnet, you simply increment the subnet identifier value again, giving you a network address of 10.2.0.0 and IP addresses ranging from 10.2.0.1 to 10.2.255.254. Because you have allocated 8 bits to the subnet identifier, you can create up to 254 subnets on this network ($2^8-2=254$). The network address for the last subnet would be 10.254.0.0, with the IP addresses in that subnet ranging from 10.254.0.1 to 10.254.255.254.

Subnetting Between Bytes

When the boundaries between your network, subnet, and host identifiers fall between the bytes of your IP address, subnetting is quite easy. However, you can use any number of bytes for a subnet identifier, and sometimes you are forced to create subnets that don't work out so evenly. For example, if you have a Class C network address you want to subnet, you obviously can't create an 8-bit subnet identifier because there would be no bits left for the host identifier. Therefore, you have to use fewer than 8 bits, which means your subnet identifier and host identifier values must be combined in the IP address into a single decimal number.

> **Tip**   A number of software tools are available that can simplify the process of calculating IP addresses and subnet masks for complex subnetted networks. One of these, available as freeware, is Wild Packets' IP Subnet Calculator, available for download at *http://www.wildpackets .com/products/free_utilities/ipsubnetcalc/overview*. However, you should be aware that tools like these are not permitted when taking Microsoft Certified Professional (MCP) exams, so you must be capable of performing the calculations manually.

For example, we can assume you have access to the entire 192.168.42.0 Class C network address, and you have to create five subnets containing 25 computers each. Because this is a Class C address, you have 8 bits for the host identifier, some of which you must borrow for the subnet identifier. Using the 2^x-2 formula, you determine that a 3-bit subnet identifier enables you to create up to six subnets ($2^3-2=6$), leaving you a 5-bit host identifier, with which you can create up to 30 hosts ($2^5-2=30$) on each subnet. At this point, the subnetting process becomes more difficult. You still have to increment the subnet and host identifiers separately, as you did earlier with the Class A address, but you also must combine the subnet and host identifier values into a single decimal number that forms the fourth quad of the IP address.

Calculating IP Addresses Using the Binary Method

To understand the problem more clearly, it helps to view the IP address in binary form, as follows:

```
  192       168       42        0
11000000 10101000 00101010 00000000
```

The first three quads of the IP address (192.168.42) are the network identifier, and these remain the same for all IP addresses on the network; only the fourth and final quad will change. To create your first subnet, you assign the subnet identifier a value of 1, which appears as follows in binary form:

```
001 00000
```

You then increment the host identifier, using a value of 1 for the first IP address in the first subnet, resulting in the following binary value:

```
001 00001
```

To express these binary subnet and host identifier values as a single 8-bit decimal number, you combine them before converting them, as follows:

```
000100001=33
```

The IP address of the first computer on the first subnet is therefore 192.168.42.33. To compute the address of the second computer on the same network, you increment the host identifier only and convert the result to a decimal. A 5-bit host identifier value of 2, in binary form, is 00010, which results in the following conversion:

```
00100010=34
```

The IP address of the second computer on the first subnet is therefore 192.168.42.34. You can then continue to increment the host identifier until you reach the maximum value for a 5-bit identifier, as follows:

```
00111110=62
```

The IP address of the last computer on the first subnet is therefore 192.168.42.62.

To create the second subnet, you increment the 3-bit subnet identifier from 001 to 010, and then you increment the host identifier in the same way as before. The first and last addresses on the second subnet are as follows:

```
01000001=65
01011110=94
```

The result is that the IP addresses for the second subnet range from 192.168.42.65 to 192.168.42.94. You can then continue incrementing the subnet identifier until you reach the sixth and last subnet, which provides the following first and last host values:

```
11000001=193
11011110=222
```

The range of addresses for the final subnet is therefore 192.168.42.193 to 192.168.42.222.

Calculating a Subnet Mask

In addition to calculating the IP addresses, you also have to calculate the subnet mask value for your subnetted network. Once again, this task is easier to understand if you express the values in binary form. The combined network and subnet identifiers for the Class C network in this example total 27 bits, as follows:

```
11111111 11111111 11111111 11100000
```

Because the first three quads are all ones, they all have the value 255, as in any Class C network. The binary value of the fourth quad (11100000), when converted to decimal form, is 224. The resulting subnet mask for all the computers on this Class C network is therefore 255.255.255.224.

Exam Tip   In some publications, and particularly in the MCP exams, you are likely to see IP address assignments notated in the form of a network address, followed by a slash and the number of 1-bits in the subnet mask. For example, the address 192.168.42.32/27 refers to a network address of 192.168.42.32 with a subnet mask of 255.255.255.224.

Converting Binaries to Decimals

The easiest way to convert binary values to decimals is, of course, to use a calculator. The Windows Calculator in Scientific mode does this easily. However, when taking the MCSE exam, the version of Windows Calculator that you are permitted to use has standard mode only, which cannot perform binary-to-decimal conversions (or exponent calculations). Therefore, you should know how to do these calculations by hand. To convert a binary number to a decimal, you assign a numerical value to each bit, starting from the right with 1 and proceeding to the left, doubling the value each time. The values for an 8-bit number are therefore as follows:

```
128   64    32    16    8    4    2    1
```

You then line up the values of your 8-bit binary number with the eight conversion values, as follows:

```
1     1     1     0     0    0    0    0
128   64    32    16    8    4    2    1
```

Finally, you add together the conversion values for the 1-bits only:

```
1      1     1     0     0    0    0    0
128   +64   +32   +0    +0   +0   +0   +0   =224
```

Therefore, the decimal equivalent to the binary value 11100000 is 224.

Calculating IP Addresses Using the Subtraction Method

Manually calculating IP addresses using binary values can be a slow and tedious task, especially if you are going to have hundreds or thousands of computers on your network. However, when you have the subnet mask for the network and you understand the relationship between subnet and host identifier values, you can calculate IP addresses without having to convert them from binary to decimal values.

To calculate the network address of the first subnet, begin by taking the decimal value of the quad in the subnet mask that contains both subnet and host identifier bits and subtracting it from 256. Using the previous example of the Class C network with the subnet mask of 255.255.255.224, the result of 256 minus 224 is 32. The network address of the first subnet is therefore 192.168.42.32. To calculate the network addresses of the other subnets, you repeatedly increment the result of your previous subtraction by itself. For example, if the network address of the first subnet is 192.168.42.32, the addresses of the remaining five subnets are as follows:

```
192.168.42.64
192.168.42.96
192.168.42.128
192.168.42.160
192.168.42.192
```

To calculate the IP addresses in each subnet, you repeatedly increment the host identifier by one. The IP addresses in the first subnet are therefore 192.168.42.33 to 192.168.42.62. The 192.168.42.63 address is omitted because this address would have a binary host identifier value of 11111, which is a broadcast address. The IP address ranges for the subsequent subnets are as follows:

```
192.168.42.65 to 192.168.42.94
192.168.42.97 to 192.168.42.126
192.168.42.129 to 192.168.42.158
192.168.42.161 to 192.168.42.190
192.168.42.193 to 192.168.42.222
```

Practice: Subnetting IP Addresses

For each of the following IP address assignments, specify the number of bits in the subnet identifier, the number of possible IP addresses in each subnet, the subnet mask for the IP addresses, and the IP address ranges for the first and last subnet.

10.0.0.0/19

   1. Number of bits in subnet identifier: _____

   2. Number of possible IP addresses in each subnet: _____

   3. Subnet mask: _____

   4. First subnet: _____

   5. Last subnet: _____

192.168.214.0/29

1. Number of bits in subnet identifier: _____

2. Number of possible IP addresses in each subnet: _____

3. Subnet mask: _____

4. First subnet: _____

5. Last subnet: _____

172.28.0.0/20

1. Number of bits in subnet identifier: _____

2. Number of possible IP addresses in each subnet: _____

3. Subnet mask: _____

4. First subnet: _____

5. Last subnet: _____

Lesson Review

The following questions are intended to reinforce key information presented in this lesson. If you are unable to answer a question, review the lesson materials and try the question again. You can find answers to the questions in the "Questions and Answers" section at the end of this chapter.

1. Which of the following is the correct formula for calculating the number of subnets or hosts you can create with a given number of bits represented by x?

    a. x^2+2

    b. 2^x+2

    c. 2^x-2

    d. x^2-2

2. What is the correct subnet mask to use on a Class B network with a 10-bit subnet identifier?

    a. 255.192.255.255

    b. 255.255.255.192

    c. 255.255.192.0

    d. 255.192.0.0

3. How many hosts can you create on a subnet with 9 bits available for the host identifier?

_____

_____

4. In the IP address assignment 10.54.113.0/24, what does the number 24 represent?

   a. The number of bits in the subnet identifier

   b. The number of bits in the host identifier

   c. The number of bits in the combined subnet and host identifiers

   d. The number of bits in the combined network and subnet identifiers

5. Which IP address class provides the largest number of hosts per subnet?

_____

_____

Lesson Summary

- If you require registered IP addresses for your network, you must obtain them from your ISP. For an unregistered network, you can use any of the addresses in the private address ranges designated by the IANA.

- You can create subnets using any network address by using some of the host identifier bits to create a subnet identifier.

- You use the formula 2^x-2 to calculate how many hosts or subnets you can create using a given number of bits.

- You can calculate subnet masks and IP addresses by using the binary values of the numbers, incrementing them as needed, and then converting the results back into decimals.

Lesson 4: Assigning IP Addresses

Once you have calculated the IP addresses and subnet mask for the computers on your network, you should include in your plan just how the actual TCP/IP configuration process for each of the computers is going to proceed. There are two basic alternatives from which to choose. You can manually configure each computer, or you can use DHCP, an automated TCP/IP configuration service included with Windows Server 2003 and many other operating systems.

After this lesson, you will be able to

- List the drawbacks of manual TCP/IP client configuration
- Understand how DHCP automatically configures TCP/IP clients

Estimated lesson time: 15 minutes

Manually Configuring TCP/IP Clients

Configuring the TCP/IP client on a Windows computer by hand is a relatively simple task, but when compounded by hundreds or thousands of computers, it can become an administrative nightmare. Not only does an administrator have to travel to each computer to configure its settings, but the administrator must also take steps to ensure that each computer is assigned an IP address that is appropriate for the subnet on which the computer is located and that does not duplicate the IP address of any other computer in the enterprise. For a large network installation in which time is at a premium, you might have to bring in temporary personnel to help with the TCP/IP configuration chores.

Planning   Keep in mind that in addition to the time and staff needed to perform the initial TCP/IP configurations, you will also need to spend time to manually reconfigure a computer if you later decide to move it to a different subnet.

Off the Record   For a large network installation, manually configuring TCP/IP clients is time-consuming, inefficient, and prone to errors. DHCP enables you to automatically configure your computers and reconfigure them each time they start up. If you decide to move a computer to a different subnet, DHCP assigns it a new address and reclaims the old one for assignment to another computer.

Installing a DHCP Server

DHCP consists of an application layer protocol and a service running on one or more of your network servers. Windows Server 2003 includes a DHCP implementation, as do most other network server operating systems. All current Windows operating systems also include DHCP client capabilities, which activate by default. If you install Windows XP on a new computer, for example, and connect it to a network, during the computer's first boot sequence it transmits messages requesting an IP address assignment to any DHCP servers on the network. DHCP servers can assign IP addresses and subnet masks, and they can also provide other configuration settings, including default gateway addresses and Domain Name System (DNS) server addresses.

To set up a Windows Server 2003 DHCP server:

1. Install the service on the computer.

2. Configure it by specifying a range of IP addresses for the DHCP server to assign, called a *scope*.

3. Optionally, configure a variety of DHCP options that provide the other TCP/IP configuration parameters your computers need, such as the list of DNS servers available to the client.

4. Activate the scope and, if you are using the Active Directory directory service on your network, authorize the DHCP server in the Active Directory database.

Understanding DHCP Allocation Methods

The Windows Server 2003 DHCP server can assign IP addresses using three different allocation methods, which are as follows:

- **Dynamic allocation**   Assigns an IP address to a client computer from a scope, for a specified length of time. DHCP servers using dynamic allocation only lease addresses to clients. Each client must periodically renew the lease to continue using the address. If the client allows the lease to expire, the address is returned to the scope for reassignment to another client.

> **Note**   Dynamic allocation is the default method for the Windows Server 2003 DHCP server, and it is particularly suitable for networks where IP addresses are in short supply or for networks on which you frequently move computers from one subnet to another.

- **Automatic allocation**   Permanently assigns an IP address to a client computer from a scope. Once the DHCP server assigns the address to the client, the only way to change it is to manually reconfigure the computer. Automatic allocation is suitable for networks where you do not often move computers to different subnets. It reduces network traffic by eliminating the periodic lease renewal messages needed for dynamic allocation. In the Windows Server 2003 DHCP server, automatic allocation is essentially dynamic allocation with an indefinite lease.

■ **Manual allocation**   Permanently assigns a specific IP address to a specific computer on the network. In the Windows Server 2003 DHCP server, manually allocated addresses are called *reservations*. You use manually allocated addresses for computers that must have the same IP address at all times, such as Internet Web servers that have their IP addresses associated with their host names in the DNS namespace. Although you can just as easily configure such computers manually, DHCP reservations prevent the accidental duplication of permanently assigned IP addresses.

Planning a DHCP Deployment

To configure the TCP/IP clients on your computers using DHCP, you must specify in your network infrastructure plan how many DHCP servers you intend to deploy and where to locate them. DHCP clients rely on broadcast transmissions to locate and contact DHCP servers. This means that a DHCP client can only communicate directly with a DHCP server on the same LAN. Fortunately, this does not mean you have to install a DHCP server on every one of your LANs. Most routers are equipped with DHCP relay-agent capabilities you can use to support multiple networks with one DHCP server.

A *DHCP relay agent* is a module you configure with the IP addresses of DHCP servers on other networks. The relay agent listens for broadcast transmissions from DHCP clients, and when it receives them, it forwards the messages to the DHCP servers on another network. The relay agent then functions as the intermediary between the DHCP client and server during the entire configuration process.

Although one DHCP server can configure thousands of clients, most network designers deploy several servers for fault tolerance purposes. However, when you have multiple Windows Server 2003 DHCP servers on your network, you must configure them with separate IP address scopes. DHCP servers do not work together. Each server has its own scopes, from which it allocates IP addresses. If you configure two DHCP servers with scopes that contain the same IP address ranges, you will end up with duplicate IP addresses on your network.

You can configure two DHCP servers with scopes to service the same subnet, however. Microsoft recommends that you distribute the IP addresses for a subnet in an 80:20 ratio. Configure one server with a scope containing 80 percent of the addresses available for the subnet, and then configure a second server with the remaining 20 percent of the addresses for that subnet. This provides a fault-tolerance mechanism in case one of the servers fails for an extended length of time.

Practice: Installing and Configuring the DHCP Service

In this practice, you install, authorize, and configure the DHCP service on Server01. You also create a scope and configure a range of addresses for the scope.

Caution   For this exercise, ensure that Server01 is on an isolated network (or no network at all) so that it doesn't conflict with IP addressing strategy already in place.

Exercise 1: Installing and Authorizing the DHCP Server

In this exercise, you install and authorize the DHCP Server service on Server01.

1. Log on to Server01 as Administrator.

2. Click the Start menu, point to Control Panel, and then click Add Or Remove Programs. The Add Or Remove Programs window appears.

3. In the left frame, click Add/Remove Windows Components. The Windows Components Wizard appears.

4. In the Components box, scroll down and click Networking Services, but do not click or change the status of the check box to the left of this option.

Note   Windows Server 2003 has already selected the Networking Services check box because you've already installed some networking services on Server01.

5. Click Details. The Networking Services dialog box appears.

   In the Subcomponents Of Networking Services box, select the Dynamic Host Configuration Protocol (DHCP) check box.

6. Click OK. The Windows Components page reappears.

7. Click Next. The Configuring Components page shows a progress indicator as the changes you requested are made. The Completing The Windows Components Wizard page appears.

8. Click Finish.

9. Close the Add Or Remove Programs window.

10. Click the Start menu, point to All Programs, point to Administrative Tools, and then click DHCP. The DHCP console appears and Server01.contoso.com [10.0.0.1] is listed in the console tree.

11. In the console tree, expand Server01.contoso.com [10.0.0.1]. A red down-arrow appears to the left of Server01.contoso.com [10.0.0.1].

12. Click Server01.contoso.com [10.0.0.1] and, from the Action menu, select Authorize. The red down-arrow remains until you create at least one scope. Leave the DHCP console open to complete the next exercise.

Exercise 2: Creating and Configuring a DHCP Scope

In this exercise, you create and configure a DHCP scope on Server01.

1. Verify that Server01.contoso.com [10.0.0.1] is highlighted, and then from the Action menu, select New Scope. The New Scope Wizard appears.

2. Click Next. The Scope Name page appears.

3. In the Name text box, type **Scope01**.

4. In the Description text box, type **Training network**, and then click Next. The IP Address Range page appears.

5. Type **10.0.0.1** in the Start IP Address text box, and type **10.0.0.254** in the End IP Address text box.

6. In the Subnet Mask text box, notice that the server automatically changes the mask to 255.0.0.0.

7. Check the value in the Length spin box. Notice that the server automatically enters 24 for the subnet mask length. This means that 24 bits of the IP address are allocated to the network address. Eight bits remain for allocating host addresses on the network.

8. Click Next. The Add Exclusions page appears.

9. In the Start IP Address text box, type **10.0.0.1**.

10. In the End Address text box, type **10.0.0.1**.

11. Click Add.

12. Notice that 10.0.0.1 To 10.0.0.11 appears in the Excluded Address Range box.

13. Click Next. The Lease Duration page appears. Read the information on this page, and notice that the default lease duration is 8 days.

14. Click Next to accept the default lease duration. The Configure DHCP Options page appears, asking if you would like to configure the most common DHCP options now.

15. Select the No, I Will Configure These Options Later option button, and then click Next. The Completing The New Scope Wizard page appears.

16. Read the instructions on this screen, and then click Finish. An icon representing the new scope appears in the DHCP console.

Notice that Server01.contoso.com now contains a green up-arrow. This is because you have authorized the server and created a scope. The red down-arrow to the left of the scope indicates you have not yet activated the scope. You will activate the scope in a later procedure.

Leave the DHCP console open to complete the next exercise.

Exercise 3: Configuring Scope Options

In this exercise, you configure DHCP so that it sends the preferred DNS and DNS domain name to the DHCP client upon registration. This procedure is similar to setting server options, which apply to all DHCP clients using this server, and setting individual client options.

1. In the console tree, expand Scope01, click Scope Options, and then from the Action menu, click Configure Options. The Scope Options dialog box appears.

2. In the General tab, scroll down and select the 006 DNS Servers check box, which enables the options in the Data Entry group box.

3. In the Server Name text box, type **server01** and then click Resolve. The IP address 10.0.0.1 appears in the IP Address text box.

4. Click Add.

5. Scroll down in the Available Options box, and select the 015 DNS Domain Name checkbox.

6. In the String Value text box, type **contoso.com** and then click OK. The DHCP server will now deliver the DNS data to DHCP client computers within this scope along with their IP addresses.

7. Select Server01.contoso.com [10.0.0.1] and, from the Action menu, select Activate. The scope is now activated.

8. Close the DHCP console.

Lesson Review

The following questions are intended to reinforce key information presented in this lesson. If you are unable to answer a question, review the lesson materials and try the question again. You can find answers to the questions in the "Questions and Answers" section at the end of this chapter.

1. Which type of DHCP address allocation would you typically use for an Internet Web server? Why?

   _____

   _____

2. What configuration tasks must you perform on a newly installed Windows XP workstation to activate the DHCP client?

_____

_____

3. What is the function of a DHCP relay agent?

_____

_____

Lesson Summary

■ You can configure the TCP/IP clients on your network manually, or you can use DHCP servers to automatically allocate IP addresses and other configuration parameters to your computers as needed.

■ A DHCP server using manual allocation assigns specific IP addresses to specific clients permanently. Administrators typically use manual allocation for Internet servers and other computers that require static IP addresses.

■ A DHCP server using permanent allocation assigns IP addresses from a pool to DHCP clients, which retain them until an administrator manually reconfigures them.

■ A DHCP server using dynamic allocation assigns IP addresses to DHCP clients from a pool, and then reclaims them when a specified lease period expires.

■ DHCP relay agents forward the DHCP broadcast messages generated by clients to DHCP servers on other networks. This enables a single DHCP server to furnish IP addresses for an entire internetwork.

Lesson 5: Troubleshooting TCP/IP Addressing

Using the TCP/IP protocol suite on your network tends to be more problematic than using other protocols, in large part because of the need to individually configure each computer. Most isolated TCP/IP communications problems are related to the client configuration process in some way, and a large part of the TCP/IP troubleshooting process is recognizing the effects of various configuration errors.

After this lesson, you will be able to

- Determine whether a network communications problem is related to TCP/IP
- Understand how TCP/IP client configuration problems can affect computer performance
- List the reasons why a DHCP client might fail to obtain an IP address from a DHCP server

Estimated lesson time: 20 minutes

Isolating TCP/IP Problems

When a computer experiences a network communications problem, there are obviously many possible sources of error. The difficulty could lie in the TCP/IP protocol stack, it could be a problem with the data-link layer protocol, or it could even be a hardware problem such as a broken cable or a faulty network interface adapter. Before you begin troubleshooting possible TCP/IP problems, you should make sure the trouble is in fact related to the TCP/IP stack.

One sure way to test whether a network communications problem is related to TCP/IP is to try using a different protocol on the computer. NetBIOS Extended User Interface (NetBEUI) is the best choice for this type of test because it is a single, monolithic protocol and requires no configuration. However, Windows Server 2003 no longer includes the NetBEUI protocol, so you can use the IPX protocols for testing, in the form of the NWLink IPX/SPX/NetBIOS Compatible Transport Protocol module, instead.

To do this, you install the NetBEUI or IPX protocol module in the Network Connections tool and then unbind the Internet Protocol (TCP/IP) module in the Advanced Settings dialog box. (To access the Advanced Settings dialog box, right-click Network Connections in the Control Panel menu, click Open to display the Network Connections window, and then select Advanced Settings from the Advanced menu in the Network Connections window, as shown in Figure 2-7.) At this point, you've activated the alternative protocol and deactivated the TCP/IP module. If the computer is still unable to communicate with the other computers on the network, you know the problem is not related to TCP/IP. You should start looking at the networking hardware and the computer's data-link layer protocol drivers. If the computer can communicate using the alternative protocol but it can't by using TCP/IP, you know there is a TCP/IP-related problem, most likely related to the protocol's configuration.

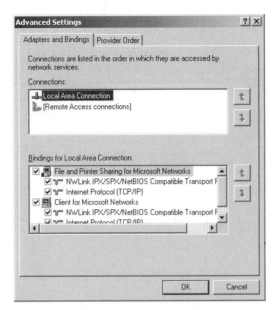

Figure 2-7   The Network Connections control panel's Advanced Settings dialog box

Troubleshooting Client Configuration Problems

The most obvious source of problems on a TCP/IP network is the existence of duplicate IP addresses. When two computers have the same IP address, packets end up in the wrong place and message transactions are interrupted. Fortunately, the Windows operating systems check for the existence of a duplicate address each time the computer starts. If Windows detects a duplicate IP address, it disables the TCP/IP protocol stack on the newly started computer and displays an error message specifying the hardware address of the system with which the computer is in conflict. The computer that is the original owner of the duplicate address continues to function normally. When you reconfigure the other computer with a different, nonconflicting IP address, the TCP/IP stack becomes active again on that computer.

Incorrect Subnet Masks

As you learned earlier in this chapter, the function of the subnet mask is to let the computer know which bits of the computer's IP address identify the host and which bits identify the network on which the host is located. If two computers have different subnet masks, their network addresses are different, and the computers see them as being on different subnets even if they have correct IP addresses. Computers that are on different subnets cannot communicate with each other except through a router, so if you have a computer that can't communicate with the other systems on the network, the problem might be that the computer's subnet mask is incorrect.

To view the subnet mask and all the other TCP/IP configuration settings at once on a computer running Windows 2000, Windows XP, or Windows Server 2003, you can use the Ipconfig.exe program. Display a Command Prompt window, type **IPCONFIG /all** on the command line, and press Enter to generate a display like the following:

```
Windows IP Configuration
        Host Name . . . . . . . . . . . . .: CZ7
        Primary DNS Suffix  . . . . . . . .: adatum.com
        Node Type . . . . . . . . . . . . .: Hybrid
        IP Routing Enabled. . . . . . . . .: No
        WINS Proxy Enabled. . . . . . . . .: No
        DNS Suffix Search List. . . . . . .: adatum.com
Ethernet adapter Local Area Connection:
        Connection-specific DNS Suffix  .:
        Description . . . . . . . . . . . .: Intel(R) PRO/100 VE Network Connection
        Physical Address. . . . . . . . . .: 00-D0-59-83-B1-52
        DHCP Enabled. . . . . . . . . . . .: No
        IP Address. . . . . . . . . . . . .: 192.168.2.7
        Subnet Mask . . . . . . . . . . . .: 255.255.255.0
        Default Gateway . . . . . . . . . .: 192.168.2.99
        DNS Servers . . . . . . . . . . . .: 192.168.2.10
                                             192.168.86.15
        Primary WINS Server . . . . . . . .: 192.168.2.10
```

Incorrect Default Gateway Addresses

If a TCP/IP computer is able to communicate with other systems on the same LAN but is unable to communicate with systems on other LANs, there is likely a problem with the computer's default gateway. The default gateway is the router that a computer uses whenever it has to communicate with a computer on another network. The routing table of a TCP/IP computer contains specific network addresses and information on how to reach them. If the computer must send traffic to a system on one of the networks listed in the table, the computer uses that table entry to route the packets properly. If the computer has traffic to send to a system on a network that is not listed in the table, the computer sends the traffic to the default gateway.

If a TCP/IP computer does not have a default gateway address in its configuration, it can communicate with the other systems on the LAN (because no router is needed), but it can't communicate with other networks. In the same way, if the default gateway address is incorrect and doesn't point to a router, or points to a router that is not functioning properly, no internetwork communication can occur. If you find that one of your computers is impaired in this way, you should check the Default Gateway setting in the Internet Protocol (TCP/IP) Properties dialog box if your computer uses a static IP address (see Figure 2-8), or by using the IPCONFIG /all command if the computer has obtained its address from a DHCP server. If the default gateway address is correct, you should check the functionality of the default gateway itself to make sure that it is running and routing traffic.

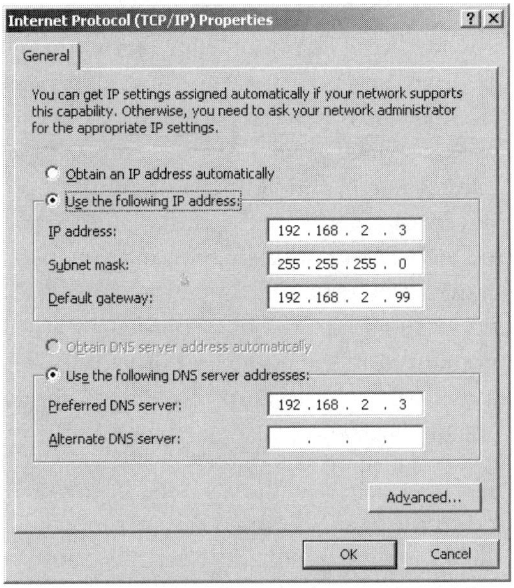

Figure 2-8   The Internet Protocol (TCP/IP) Properties dialog box

Name Resolution Failures

A common cause of TCP/IP communication problems is a failure to successfully resolve names into IP addresses. TCP/IP network communication is based on IP addresses. Every message packet generated by a TCP/IP computer contains a destination IP address and a source IP address. IP addresses are difficult for human beings to use and remember, however. As a result, the TCP/IP developers devised services like DNS and the Windows Internet Name Service (WINS), which enable people to use friendly names for computers instead of IP addresses.

Name resolution is the process by which a computer converts a name into an IP address. In the case of DNS names, for example, the computer sends the name to a DNS server, which replies with the IP address associated with the name. The computer can then initiate communications using the IP address rather than the name.

If a TCP/IP computer fails to communicate with another computer, it might be because the name resolution has failed. This means that the two computers are both functioning properly; they just don't have the IP addresses they need to communicate. To test for a name resolution failure, try to communicate with the destination computer using its IP address instead of its name. For example, if you are trying to contact a Web server using the uniform resource locator (URL) *http://www.adatum.com/home.html* and you cannot connect, try using the server's IP address instead of its name, as in the URL *http://10.112.65.34/home.html*. If the connection succeeds, the problem lies in the name resolution.

Windows computers can use either DNS or WINS for name resolution. If your network uses the Active Directory directory service, it relies on DNS for name resolution. DNS name resolution is also required for Internet connectivity. To resolve DNS names into IP addresses, the computer must have the IP address of a functioning DNS server as part of its TCP/IP configuration. If the DNS server address is incorrect, or if the DNS server itself is malfunctioning, name resolution cannot occur and TCP/IP communication attempts that use names will fail. The Internet Protocol (TCP/IP) Properties dialog box (see Figure 2-8) enables you to specify a preferred DNS server address and an alternate DNS server address. The latter provides fault tolerance if the preferred server is unreachable or malfunctioning. You can check the validity of the addresses in a computer's TCP/IP configuration by using the Nslookup.exe program from the command prompt to send a name resolution request to those specific servers. If the Nslookup test fails, either the address does not point to a valid DNS server or the DNS server itself is malfunctioning.

If you are running WINS on your network, your computers must have the IP address of one or more WINS servers specified in the WINS tab of the Advanced TCP/IP Settings dialog box (see Figure 2-9). WINS is one of several NetBIOS name resolution mechanisms that Windows computers can use, so an incorrect WINS server address or even the failure of a WINS server to resolve names might not be as immediately evident as a DNS problem. Windows computers can resolve the NetBIOS names of systems on the local LAN even without WINS (by using broadcast transmissions as a fallback). However, if the WINS server addresses are incorrect or the servers are not functioning, the computer cannot resolve the NetBIOS names of computers on other LANs (because broadcasts are limited to the local network).

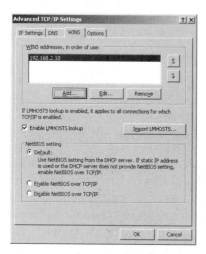

Figure 2-9   The WINS tab of the Advanced TCP/IP Settings dialog box

> **Note**   Name resolution is an important issue on a Windows network, and an important part of network infrastructure planning. For more information on name resolution, see Chapter 4, "Planning a Name Resolution Strategy."

Troubleshooting DHCP Problems

If you are using DHCP servers to automatically configure the TCP/IP clients in your network's computers, there are still problems that can arise with the DHCP clients and the DHCP server. Some of these problems and their solutions are described in the following sections.

Failure to Contact a DHCP Server

When you configure your Windows computers to obtain their IP addresses and other TCP/IP configuration settings from a DHCP server, you may sometimes find that the DHCP server has apparently assigned an incorrect IP address to a computer. No matter what address scope you have configured the DHCP server to use, a client might have an address that begins with 169.254. This is not an address that the DHCP server has assigned. Rather, the computer has failed to contact the DHCP server on the network and has assigned itself an IP address using a Windows feature called Automatic Private IP Addressing (APIPA).

APIPA is designed to enable Windows computers on a small LAN to configure their own IP addresses. For example, if you connect a few computers to build a home network, there is no need to manually configure the IP addresses because APIPA automatically assigns a unique address in the same Class B subnet to each computer on the network. This is fine for a home or small business network, but it is not acceptable on your carefully planned large network installation.

When a DHCP client resorts to using APIPA to obtain an IP address, it is because the DHCP messages the computer has broadcasted on the network have gone unanswered. There are several reasons why this might happen. First, the computer might be unable to communicate with the network at all because of a hardware or data-link layer protocol problem. You can test that theory by installing another network/transport layer protocol on the computer. If no network communications are possible with the alternative protocol, it is time to start looking at the computer's networking hardware and data-link layer protocol drivers.

> **Tip**   After you determine that the problem is due to the client hardware or software configuration and then correct the problem, you must delete the APIPA-supplied address from the system's TCP/IP configuration before it can send another request to the DHCP server.

The client's failure to obtain an IP address from the DHCP server might also result from a problem at the server end of the connection. If this is the case, you will see the same problem on multiple client computers. The DHCP server might be experiencing a hardware or software problem of its own, preventing it from communicating with the network. You can use the same alternative protocol test to determine if this is the case.

The DHCP requests that clients transmit to servers are broadcast messages; they must be because the client does not yet have the IP address needed to send a unicast message. Broadcasts are limited to the local network, so if the DHCP server is not on the same LAN as the client, it cannot receive the request directly. You must use a DHCP relay agent for a DHCP server to support clients on other networks, and this introduces another potential source of communication problems. DHCP relay agents are built into the routers that connect networks or are supplied by the RRAS service in Windows Server 2003, and you must configure them with the addresses of the DHCP servers on the other networks. This is so that the relay agent can receive the broadcasts from DHCP clients and send them to the DHCP servers on the other networks as unicasts. If you have forgotten to configure the relay agent, or if you have configured it with an incorrect DHCP server address, the clients' attempts to contact the DHCP server will fail.

Failure to Obtain an IP Address

In some cases, DHCP clients might be able to communicate with the network but are still failing to obtain IP address assignments from DHCP servers. This could be because of an incorrect scope on the server or because of an error in the server's own TCP/IP configuration. You should check the scope itself first, to be sure that you have created it correctly and that you have activated it. Also be sure that the DHCP Server service is running on the server computer and that the DHCP server is authorized by Active Directory (if you are using Active Directory on your network).

Using regular scopes, a DHCP server can only supply IP addresses to subnets of which the server itself is a member. For example, if you create a scope to supply your DHCP clients with IP addresses on the 192.168.67.0/24 subnet, the DHCP server must have an IP address in that subnet itself.

> **Note**   DHCP servers must have manually configured IP addresses. They cannot obtain their addresses from another DHCP server or supply one to themselves.

When the DHCP server is servicing clients on the local network, having an IP address on the same subnet is usually not a problem. However, if you have multiple IP subnets on a single physical network, or if the DHCP server is providing addresses to distant networks using relay agents, you must create scopes for networks other than the one to which the DHCP server is connected. To enable the server to supply addresses to the clients on other subnets, you can either configure the DHCP server with multiple IP addresses, one in each subnet for which you have created a scope, or you can combine the scopes for the various subnets into a superscope. A *superscope* is an administrative grouping of existing scopes supporting multiple IP subnets on the same physical network, which you can activate and deactivate collectively.

Failure to Obtain Correct DHCP Options

When you configure a DHCP server, creating a scope enables the server to assign IP addresses to clients and supply them with a correct subnet mask. For all other TCP/IP configuration parameters, such as default gateway and DNS server addresses, you must configure the server to deliver DHCP options along with the IP address. *DHCP options* are specific configuration parameter settings that the server can deliver along with the IP address and subnet mask. The DHCP server in Windows Server 2003 enables you to configure DHCP options for specific scopes or for the entire server. For example, if you want all your DHCP clients, no matter what subnet they are on, to use the same DNS server, you should create a server option. For the default gateway address (called the 003 Router option by DHCP), you should use scope options because the computers on each scope need a different gateway address.

If your DHCP clients are receiving IP addresses but are not receiving their DHCP options properly, you should first check to see whether you have mistakenly created a scope option instead of a server option, or whether you have created a scope option for the wrong scope. It is also possible the client does not support a particular option that you have configured the server to provide. Microsoft's DHCP server is designed to support clients running many different operating systems and contains many options that are exclusive to non-Windows clients.

Lesson Review

The following questions are intended to reinforce key information presented in this lesson. If you are unable to answer a question, review the lesson materials and try the question again. You can find answers to the questions in the "Questions and Answers" section at the end of this chapter.

1. When a TCP/IP computer can communicate with the local network but not with computers on other networks, which of the following configuration parameters is probably incorrect?

   a. IP address

   b. Subnet mask

   c. Default gateway

   d. Preferred DNS server

2. How do you determine whether name resolution failure is the cause of a network communication problem?

_____

_____

3. Why must a DHCP client use broadcast transmissions to request an IP address from a DHCP server?

   a. Because the DHCP server can only receive broadcasts

   b. Because the DHCP client does not yet have an IP address

   c. Because the DHCP server can service requests only from computers on the same LAN

   d. Because the DHCP client must inform all the other clients on the network of its intention to request an IP address

Lesson Summary

- An incorrect subnet mask makes the computer appear to be on a different network, preventing LAN communications.

- A missing or incorrect default gateway address prevents communication with other networks.

- A missing or incorrect DNS or WINS server address can prevent the computer from resolving other systems' names.

- When a Windows Server 2003 DHCP client fails to make contact with a DHCP server, the client computer uses APIPA to assign itself an IP address.

- Most DHCP communication problems that are not the result of hardware or driver errors are caused by incorrect configuration of the DHCP client, server, or relay agent.

Case Scenario Exercise

You are the network infrastructure design specialist for Litware Inc., a manufacturer of specialized scientific software products, and you have already created a basic network design for their new office building, as described in the Case Scenario Exercise in Chapter 1. The office building is a three-story brick structure built in the late 1940s, which has since been retrofitted with several different types of network cabling by various tenants. In your original design, each floor of the building has a separate Ethernet LAN, as follows:

- **First Floor**   Ten individual offices, each with a single computer using 100Base-TX Fast Ethernet

- **Second Floor**   Fifty-five cubicles, each with a single computer using 10Base-T Ethernet

- **Third Floor**   A laboratory setting with network connections for up to 100 computers using 100Base-FX Fast Ethernet

The three LANs are all connected to a backbone network that is running 1000Base-T Gigabit Ethernet and using dedicated computers running Windows Server 2003 as routers. In addition to connecting the LANs, the backbone network is connected to the corporate headquarters network in another city using a hardware router and a T-1 line. A second T-1 line to the corporation's ISP is connected to the backbone using an Internet access router.

The Litware home office has also recently notified you that you must modify the network design because they have now decided to use the new facility to house the corporation's Internet Web servers. To accommodate this addition, you add another LAN to the design, located in the building's locked basement. The basement LAN consists of six Web servers running Windows Server 2003, connected by 100Base-TX Fast Ethernet and running on Category 5 unshielded twisted pair (UTP) cable. One of the computers running Windows Server 2003 also has a 1000Base-T Gigabit Ethernet adapter installed in it, enabling it to route traffic to the backbone.

Because the Web servers must be visible from the Internet so that potential customers can access them, they must have IP addresses that are registered with the IANA. The home office has informed you that the corporation has obtained the registered Class C network address 207.46.230.0 from its ISP. The company has already subnetted the address using a 3-bit subnet identifier. All the subnets are already in use by other company offices except for the last one, which is available for your use.

For the three remaining LANs, you have decided to use unregistered IP addresses. The computers on these networks will be able to access the Internet using the NAT capabilities of the Internet access router on the backbone. Your IP addressing plan calls for using a single private network address, 172.19.0.0/22, with one (and only one) subnet allocated to each of the four unregistered LANs.

Given this information, answer the following questions about your IP addressing plan:

1. What subnet mask should you use for the Web server computers on the basement LAN?

   _____

   _____

2. How many subnets are there on the 207.46.230.0/27 network in total, and how many hosts can there be on each subnet?

   _____

   _____

3. What is the range of registered IP addresses available for your use?

_____

_____

4. How many routers are there on the building's networks? How many of the routers are computers running Windows Server 2003, and how many are hardware devices?

_____

_____

5. Which of the following IP address classes can you not use when selecting a network address for your unregistered LANs? (Choose all that apply.)

    a. Class A

    b. Class B

    c. Class C

    d. Class D

6. For each answer you selected in question 5, explain why you cannot use an address in that class for your unregistered LANs.

_____

_____

7. Assuming that you will use a network address in the Class B private address range designated by the IANA, what is the maximum number of subnet identifier bits you can use and still have a sufficient number of host identifier bits to support the computers on each of your networks?

_____

_____

8. Using the network address specified earlier, how many subnet identifier bits are you using for your unregistered network address?

_____

_____

9. What subnet mask must you use for the unregistered LANs on your network?

_____

_____

10. List the IP address ranges for the first four subnets created from your unregistered network address.

Troubleshooting Lab

You are deploying DHCP on a newly constructed network consisting of four horizontal LANs connected to a backbone network. Each of the five LANs is a separate IP subnet. You have installed the Microsoft DHCP Server service on one Windows Server 2003 computer that is connected to the backbone network, and you have installed and configured a DHCP relay agent on each of the four routers connecting the backbone to the horizontal LANs. After configuring the DHCP server by creating the appropriate scopes and options, you start the client computers.

For each of the problem scenarios below, specify which listed conditions (a, b, c, or d) could be the cause of the difficulty.

a. One of the DHCP relay agents is improperly configured.

b. One of the scopes on the DHCP server has not been activated.

c. One of the cables connecting a client to its hub has been accidentally cut.

d. The Router (default gateway) option on the DHCP server is configured as a server option, not a scope option.

1. All of the computers successfully obtain IP addresses from the DHCP server except one, which has an IP address of 169.254.0.1.

2. All of the computers on one of the five horizontal LANs fail to obtain IP addresses from the DHCP server.

3. All of the computers on the backbone LAN fail to obtain IP addresses from the DHCP server.

4. The computers on four of the five LANs are able to communicate with the local network only.

Chapter Summary

■ Computers that are visible from the Internet must have IP addresses that are registered with the IANA.

■ Computers on private networks typically use unregistered IP addresses to protect them from unauthorized access and to conserve the IP address space.

■ Computers with unregistered IP addresses can access the Internet as clients using a NAT router or a proxy server.

■ Large networks typically consist of multiple LANs connected by routers, network layer devices that enable communication between the networks while maintaining separate broadcast and collision domains.

■ A switch is a data-link layer device that intelligently forwards traffic to specified destinations. Switches can replace many routers in your network infrastructure design, creating a more efficient and economical network.

■ If you require registered IP addresses for your network, you must obtain them from your ISP. For an unregistered network, you can use any addresses in the private address ranges designated by the IANA.

■ You can create subnets using any network address by using some host identifier bits to create a subnet identifier. You can calculate subnet masks and IP addresses by using the binary values of the numbers, incrementing them as needed, and then converting the results back into decimals.

■ You can configure the TCP/IP clients on your network manually, or you can use DHCP servers to automatically allocate IP addresses and other configuration parameters to your computers as needed.

■ Most DHCP communication problems that are not the result of hardware or driver errors are caused by incorrect configuration of the DHCP client, server, or relay agent.

Exam Highlights

Before taking the exam, review the following key topics and terms to help you identify topics you need to review. Return to the lessons for additional practice, and review the "Further Reading" sections in Part 2 for pointers to more information about topics covering the exam objectives.

Key Points

- Every computer on a TCP/IP network must have a unique IP address. Computers visible to the Internet must have registered addresses. Computers accessing the Internet through NAT routers or proxy servers can use unregistered addresses.

- Routers are network layer devices that connect networks into an internetwork while keeping their collision domains and broadcast domains separate.

- Switches are data-link layer devices that connect networks into one large network. Although switching all but eliminates collisions from an Ethernet installation, the network still consists of one large broadcast domain.

- To subnet a network, you borrow some bits from the host identifier and use them to create a subnet identifier. You can then split a network address into separate subnets, each of which is a separate entity on a TCP/IP network.

- Most TCP/IP communications problems are the result of incorrect configuration settings on the TCP/IP client. The problems can result from typographical errors during a manual client configuration or from incorrect configuration of a DHCP server or relay agent.

Key Terms

Network address translation (NAT)   A router function that enables client computers on a private network with unregistered IP addresses to access Internet resources without exposing themselves to possible intrusion from the Internet.

Proxy server   An application layer software component that relays transmissions between unregistered client computers on a private network and the Internet. Proxy servers can also regulate client access to specific Internet resources and cache Internet information for rapid access by other clients.

Collision domain   A group of computers connected so that any two systems transmitting packets at the same time will cause a collision. Computers connected to a shared Ethernet hub, for example, are said to be in the same collision domain. Connecting two LANs with a router creates an internetwork with two separate collision domains.

Broadcast domain   A group of computers connected so that a broadcast message transmitted by any system will reach all other connected computers. Computers connected by hubs or switches form a single broadcast domain. Connecting two LANs with a router creates an internetwork with two separate broadcast domains.

Questions and Answers

Page
2-12

Lesson 1 Practice

For each of the following types of computers, specify whether it should have a registered or an unregistered IP address, or both, and why.

1. A corporate Web server providing product information to Internet clients around the world

Registered, because for clients on the Internet to send requests to the server, the server must have a registered IP address

2. A NAT router enabling clients on a private network to access Internet servers

Both, because the NAT router must be connected to the private network to communicate with the clients, and it must connect to the Internet so that it can communicate with the Web servers

3. An intranet Web server on a private network used to provide human resources information to employees

Unregistered, because although the computer is a Web server, the clients are also located on the private network and the server does not have to be visible to the Internet

4. A client computer that accesses Web servers on the Internet using a NAT router

Unregistered, because the NAT router is responsible for communicating with the Internet servers requested by the client

5. A proxy server providing Internet Web access to clients on a private network

Registered, because the proxy server is responsible for sending the clients' requests to the Web servers on the Internet

Page
2-12

Lesson 1 Review

1. Which of the following statements about NAT routers and proxy servers are true? Choose all answers that are correct.

   a. NAT routers and proxy servers must have two IP addresses.

   b. A NAT router can provide Internet access to any client application on the private network.

   c. Proxy servers can cache information they receive from Internet servers.

   d. The Windows Server 2003 operating system includes a proxy server.

   b and c

2. What are the two primary reasons why you should use unregistered IP addresses for Internet client computers?

To conserve the public IP address space and to protect the private network from unauthorized access by Internet predators.

3. Which of the following best describes the function of a subnet mask?

   a. A subnet mask indicates whether an IP address is registered or unregistered.

   b. A subnet mask specifies the sizes of the network and host identifiers in an IP address.

   c. A subnet mask is a value assigned by the IANA to uniquely identify a specific network on the Internet.

   d. A subnet mask enables an IP address to be visible from the Internet.

   b

Page
2-22
Lesson 2 Practice

Exercise 1: Internetwork Design with a Single Broadcast Domain and Multiple Collision Domains

In the following diagram, add the components needed to connect the LANs to an internetwork that consists of a single broadcast domain and several collision domains.

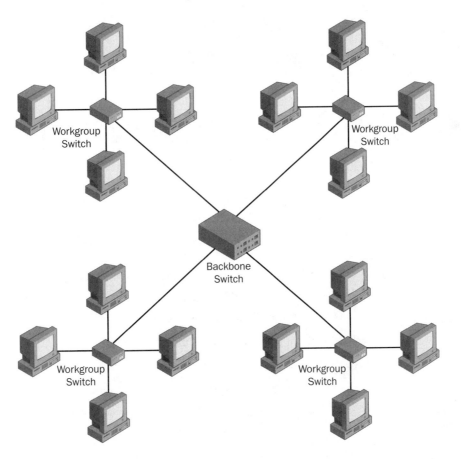

Exercise 2: Internetwork Design with Multiple Broadcast and Collision Domains

In the following diagram, add the components needed to connect the LANs in an internetwork that consists of five broadcast domains and five collision domains.

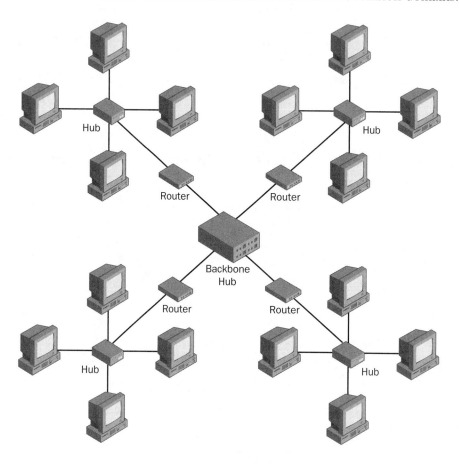

Lesson 2 Review

1. Replacing the hubs and routers on an internetwork with switches creates a network that has which of the following?

   a. One broadcast domain and one collision domain

   b. One broadcast domain and multiple collision domains

   c. One collision domain and multiple broadcast domains

   d. Several collision domains and several broadcast domains

b

2. Specify the OSI reference model layer at which each of the following devices operates.

   a. A switch

   b. A router

   c. A hub

   a. Data-link, b. Network, c. Physical

3. Which of the following Windows Server 2003 TCP/IP configuration parameters specifies the address of a router?

   a. Preferred DNS server

   b. Subnet mask

   c. Default gateway

   d. IP address

   c

4. When you replace the routers on an internetwork with switches that include no VLAN or layer 3 capabilities, which of the following is a possible reason for poor network performance?

   a. Excessive collisions

   b. Excessive broadcast traffic

   c. Excessive number of workstations on the LAN

   d. Excessive number of collision domains

   b

Page 2-32 **Lesson 3 Practice**

For each of the following IP address assignments, specify the number of bits in the subnet identifier, the number of possible IP addresses in each subnet, the subnet mask for the IP addresses, and the IP address ranges for the first and last subnet.

10.0.0.0/19

1. Number of bits in subnet identifier: 11

2. Number of possible IP addresses in each subnet: 8,190

3. Subnet mask: 255.255.224.0

4. First subnet: 10.0.32.1 to 10.0.63.254

5. Last subnet: 10.255.224.1 to 10.255.255.254

192.168.214.0/29

1. Number of bits in subnet identifier: 5

2. Number of possible IP addresses in each subnet: 6

3. Subnet mask: 255.255.255.248

4. First subnet: 192.168.214.9 to 192.168.214.14

5. Last subnet: 192.168.214.249 to 10.255.214.254

172.28.0.0/20

1. Number of bits in subnet identifier: 4

2. Number of possible IP addresses in each subnet: 4,094

3. Subnet mask: 255.255.240.0

4. First subnet: 172.28.16.1 to 172.28.31.254

5. Last subnet: 172.28.240.1 to 172.28.255.254

Page
2-33
Lesson 3 Review

1. Which of the following is the correct formula for calculating the number of subnets or hosts you can create with a given number of bits represented by x?

   a. x^2+2

   b. 2^x+2

   c. 2^x-2

   d. x^2-2

   c

2. What is the correct subnet mask to use on a Class B network with a 10-bit subnet identifier?

   a. 255.192.255.255

   b. 255.255.255.192

   c. 255.255.192.0

   d. 255.192.0.0

   b

3. How many hosts can you create on a subnet with 9 bits available for the host identifier?

   510

4. In the IP address assignment 10.54.113.0/24, what does the number 24 represent?

   a. The number of bits in the subnet identifier

   b. The number of bits in the host identifier

   c. The number of bits in the combined subnet and host identifiers

   d. The number of bits in the combined network and subnet identifiers

   d

5. Which IP address class provides the largest number of hosts per subnet?

   Class A

Page
2-40

Lesson 4 Review

1. Which type of DHCP address allocation would you typically use for an Internet Web server? Why?

   Manual allocation because the Web server must be permanently assigned a specific IP address.

2. What configuration tasks must you perform on a newly installed Windows XP workstation to activate the DHCP client?

   None. The DHCP client on a Windows computer is activated by default.

3. What is the function of a DHCP relay agent?

   A DHCP relay agent enables DHCP clients to obtain IP address assignments from DHCP servers located on other networks by relaying the clients' broadcast transmissions to specific server addresses.

Page
2-49

Lesson 5 Review

1. When a TCP/IP computer can communicate with the local network but not with computers on other networks, which of the following configuration parameters is probably incorrect?

   a. IP address

   b. Subnet mask

   c. Default gateway

   d. Preferred DNS server

   c

2. How do you determine whether name resolution failure is the cause of a network communication problem?

   By using an IP address to establish the connection instead of a name.

3. Why must a DHCP client use broadcast transmissions to request an IP address from a DHCP server?

    a. Because the DHCP server can only receive broadcasts

    b. Because the DHCP client does not yet have an IP address

    c. Because the DHCP server can service requests only from computers on the same LAN

    d. Because the DHCP client must inform all the other clients on the network of its intention to request an IP address

    b

Page
2-51

Case Scenario Exercise

Based on the information provided in the Case Scenario Exercise, answer the following questions:

1. What subnet mask should you use for the Web server computers on the basement LAN?

    255.255.255.224

2. How many subnets are there on the 207.46.230.0/27 network in total, and how many hosts can there be on each subnet?

    6 subnets, with 30 hosts on each

3. What is the range of registered IP addresses available for your use?

    207.46.230.193 to 207.46.230.222

4. How many routers are there on the building's networks? How many of the routers are computers running Windows Server 2003, and how many are hardware devices?

    There are six routers in total: two are hardware devices and four are computers running Windows Server 2003.

5. Which of the following IP address classes can you not use when selecting a network address for your unregistered LANs? (Choose all that apply.)

    a. Class A

    b. Class B

    c. Class C

    d. Class D

    c and d

6. For each answer you selected in question 5, explain why you cannot use an address in that class for your unregistered LANs.

   You cannot use a Class C address because there is no way for a subnetted Class C address to support the 100 computers required on the third floor with a single subnet. You cannot use a Class D address because this address class is reserved for multicast addresses.

7. Assuming that you will use a network address in the Class B private address range designated by the IANA, what is the maximum number of subnet identifier bits you can use and still have a sufficient number of host identifier bits to support the computers on each of your networks?

   9

8. Using the network address specified earlier, how many subnet identifier bits are you using for your unregistered network address?

   6

9. What subnet mask must you use for the unregistered LANs on your network?

   255.255.252.0

10. List the IP address ranges for the first four subnets created from your unregistered network address.

    172.19.4.1 to 172.19.7.254

    172.19.8.1 to 172.19.11.254

    172.19.12.1 to 172.19.15.254

    172.19.16.1 to 172.19.19.254

Troubleshooting Lab

For each of the problem scenarios below, specify which listed conditions (a, b, c, or d) could be the cause of the difficulty, based on the information provided in the Troubleshooting Lab.

a. One of the DHCP relay agents is improperly configured.

b. One of the scopes on the DHCP server has not been activated.

c. One of the cables connecting a client to its hub has been accidentally cut.

d. The Router (default gateway) option on the DHCP server is configured as a server option, not a scope option.

1. All the computers successfully obtain IP addresses from the DHCP server except one, which has an IP address of 169.254.0.1.

c

2. All the computers on one of the five horizontal LANs fail to obtain IP addresses from the DHCP server.

a

3. All the computers on the backbone LAN fail to obtain IP addresses from the DHCP server.

b

4. The computers on four of the five LANs are able to communicate with the local network only.

d

3 Planning Internet Connectivity

Exam Objectives in this Chapter:

- Plan an Internet connectivity strategy.

- Troubleshoot connectivity to the Internet.

  - ❏ Diagnose and resolve issues related to Network Address Translation (NAT).

  - ❏ Diagnose and resolve issues related to name resolution cache information.

  - ❏ Diagnose and resolve issues related to client configuration.

Why This Chapter Matters

In this chapter, you learn about developing an Internet access strategy that enables your network users to access the services they need efficiently and securely. To connect a network to the Internet, you must select an appropriate connection type based on the network's requirements, determine what IP addresses you will use on your client computers, and decide how you will protect the network from Internet intruders.

Although it is easy to connect a network to the Internet, doing so with appropriate security complicates the process considerably. This chapter examines the various types of shared Internet connections you can use for a network, describes how to evaluate a network's Internet access needs, and describes the methods you can use to protect the network from Internet predators. When planning an Internet access solution for your network, you might think that the security hazards in your situation are minimal and that the potential for abuse of the Internet connection by your own users is not an issue. Many network administrators feel this way at first and subsequently change their minds, usually when something bad happens. It is a good idea to consider these factors at the start so that you can implement an Internet access solution that is sufficient and secure, before you lose any money or data.

Lessons in this Chapter:

Before You Begin

This chapter requires an understanding of basic TCP/IP communications, IP addressing, and network infrastructure, as covered in Chapter 1, "Planning a Network Topology," and Chapter 2, "Planning a TCP/IP Network Infrastructure." You should also complete the Case Scenario Exercises in Chapters 1 and 2 before you perform the Case Scenario Exercise in this chapter.

Lesson 1: Planning an Internet Connectivity Infrastructure

Virtually every organization that runs a data network wants to provide its users with some type of access to the Internet. E-mail and Web sites have become essential business tools in recent years, and supplying these tools has become a standard requirement of IT professionals. The questions of how you will provide the network with Internet access, how much Internet access you will provide, and how you will secure your private network against unauthorized access from the Internet are essential parts of a network designer's infrastructure plan.

After this lesson, you will be able to

■ List the criteria for determining how much Internet bandwidth a network needs

Estimated lesson time: 30 minutes

It wasn't that long ago that even businesses relied primarily on modems and telephone lines to provide users with Internet access. For this solution, each user required a modem, a dedicated phone line, and an account with an Internet service provider (ISP). An administrator also had to install the hardware, configure the computer to use it, and support it when something went wrong. This solution rapidly became expensive and impractical for businesses with many users requiring Internet access.

Today, the most common Internet access solution for businesses is to install a wide area network (WAN) connection running from the organization's private network to an ISP and share it among all the users on the network. The WAN connection can use any technology, ranging from a standard dial-up modem to a high-speed leased telephone line. You connect the private network to the WAN using a router, which forwards all traffic not destined for an address on the private network over the connection to the ISP. The ISP's network then relays the traffic to the Internet.

Determining Internet Connectivity Requirements

Sharing an Internet connection has become an increasingly complex undertaking in recent years. Not only do you have to provide users with sufficient Internet bandwidth to support their needs, but you must also consider the possibility of users abusing the Internet access you give them and be concerned with the dangers of having your private network connected to the Internet. Your Internet access strategy must take all these factors into account before you even begin to implement it.

How Much Bandwidth?

One basic question a network designer must ask when devising an Internet access strategy is how much bandwidth the users will need to perform their jobs. The answer dictates what type of WAN connection the network will need, what kind of ISP account is required, and how high the monthly fees will be. To answer this question, you must estimate how many users will require Internet access at one time, what applications they will use, what activities they will perform, and when.

How Many Users?

Calculating the number of users is not as easy as it might first appear. Of course, you can find out how many employees there are in the organization and how many of them use computers connected to the network. However, you must also determine how many users are working at any one time and how much of that time they spend accessing the Internet.

Planning   You might find out that a maximum of 250 users work on the network at one time, but then you have to determine how much time they spend actually accessing the Internet. An executive who sends an occasional e-mail and checks a fact on a Web site once in a while is distinct from a shipping clerk who spends the whole day using the Web to print shipping labels and track package deliveries.

What Applications Do the Users Need?

Another concern is the Internet applications that the network users run and how they use them. A single e-mail user, for example, consumes little bandwidth, unless the user is attaching huge files to e-mail messages, in which case the bandwidth requirements can be high. Web browsing can vary from simple text pages to File Transfer Protocol (FTP) downloads and elaborate streaming audio and video applications that also consume substantial bandwidth. You must attempt to estimate the Internet use patterns of the network's users and provide them with sufficient bandwidth to satisfy their needs.

Planning   Estimating the appropriate amount of Internet client bandwidth that you should supply for a network also depends on whether you intend to give the users full Internet access or whether you intend to limit them to certain applications, sites, or times of day. For more information about regulating client Internet access, see Lesson 2 of this chapter.

Another factor to consider is that client applications need not generate all your network's Internet activity. You might have to supply bandwidth for the organization's Internet servers as well, and estimating the amount of bandwidth these servers need can be even more difficult than estimating client consumption. Unlike the bandwidth for client Internet access, which network administrators often try to keep to a minimum, in most organizations the object is to draw as much traffic as possible to their Internet Web servers.

Real World   Web Servers and Internet Bandwidth

Web servers provide product information and customer support that inside sales and customer service personnel would otherwise provide. As a result, factors such as new product release schedules and unforeseen technical support issues, as well as the overall growth (or reduction) of the company, can affect the amount of bandwidth consumed by Web servers. When estimating the bandwidth needs of Web servers, you should always provide a greater margin for growth than when you are estimating client bandwidth needs. A temporary slowdown due to a shortage of bandwidth can be an annoyance to company employees, but when customers experience problems, it can mean lost business.

Another important consumer of Internet bandwidth these days is virtual private network (VPN) connections. A VPN is a type of WAN connection between network sites, or between a computer and a network, that uses the Internet as a network medium. Rather than use an expensive dedicated connection, such as a long-distance telephone call or a leased line, both parties in a VPN use a local ISP to establish a low-cost connection to the Internet. The systems then use a special protocol to create a secured channel across the Internet (called a *tunnel*) between them. Some organizations use VPNs to connect branch offices, and others use them to enable traveling or telecommuting employees to connect to the company network without incurring long-distance telephone charges. VPNs can consume a great deal of Internet bandwidth, depending on the type and amount of data passing between the connected systems.

When Is Internet Bandwidth Needed?

When estimating the amount of Internet bandwidth an organization needs, you should plan to provide sufficient support for the network's peak usage times. An understanding of an organization's timetable can help you ascertain the network's Internet bandwidth needs in several ways. First, the organization's daily schedule is a factor. A company that works only from 9 A.M. to 5 P.M. typically requires most of its client bandwidth only during that period, while a company that operates around the clock needs bandwidth at all times.

Web servers and some other applications, such as off-site backups, might require large amounts of bandwidth during non-business hours. Knowing the company's business model can help you estimate these types of bandwidth needs. For example, a company on the East Coast of the United States that does business in Europe might need a large amount of bandwidth for its Web servers during the early morning hours when the company is closed but its European customers are awake and doing business.

Planning A company's annual schedule can also affect its bandwidth needs dramatically. Retailers that do lots of business during the holidays, accountants during tax season, and travel and tourism businesses that thrive in the warm weather are just three examples of seasonal businesses. It would not do to estimate their Internet bandwidth needs during a slow time of year, only to find that you've grossly underestimated their needs during the busy season.

Understanding how an organization's operating schedule relates to its Internet bandwidth needs is particularly important when you are selecting the technology that the network will use to connect to its ISP. Some types of WAN connections provide a specified amount of bandwidth at all times while others can accommodate variances in bandwidth or can even be shut down entirely when not needed.

Planning For a company that completely shuts down and requires no bandwidth at all outside of business hours, an Internet connection with a per-minute fee that they can disconnect at night might be an economical solution while the same type of connection would be impractical for a company that requires bandwidth around the clock.

Where Are the Users Located?

In addition to estimating the Internet bandwidth the network will require, you should also consider the locations of the computers that have to access the Internet. Knowing these locations can help you determine where you should place the router and Internet connection equipment. In many cases, organizations provide Internet access to all of their users, so it is best to connect the router to the backbone network or to another central point. If the computers needing Internet access are all located in one area, such as a group of Web servers that are the only Internet computers on the network, you should locate the Internet connection in the same area to prevent the traffic from congesting the rest of the network.

Internet Access and IP Addressing

Knowing the locations of Internet users can also help you design your IP addressing strategy for the network. In many cases, the type of Internet access a particular computer needs is the deciding factor in determining whether to assign it a registered or an unregistered IP address. If you choose to use NAT to provide unregistered computers with Internet access, bear in mind that the presence of Internet clients on multiple subnets affects NAT implementation.

See Also   For more information on using NAT to provide secure Internet access to unregistered computers, see Lesson 3 of this chapter.

Choosing an Internet Connection Type

The hardware for a shared Internet connection, at minimum, consists of a router and a WAN connection. The various types of WAN technologies that Internet connections use are summarized in Table 3-1.

Table 3-1   Internet Access WAN Technologies

Connection Type	Transmission Speed	Applications
Dial-up modem	Up to 53 Kbps	■ E-mail for up to 10 simultaneous users ■ Web browsing for 2 to 3 simultaneous users ■ Large FTP downloads for 1 or 2 simultaneous users
Integrated Services Digital Network (ISDN) Basic Rate Interface (BRI)	Up to 128 Kbps	■ E-mail for up to 20 simultaneous users ■ Web browsing for 6 to 8 simultaneous users ■ Large FTP downloads for 3 or 4 simultaneous users
Integrated Services Digital Network (ISDN) Primary Rate Interface (PRI)	Up To 1.544 Mbps	■ E-mail for 120 or more simultaneous users ■ Web browsing for 75 to 100 simultaneous users ■ Large FTP downloads for 40 to 50 simultaneous users
Cable television networks (CATV)	Up to 512 Kbps downstream; up to 128 Kbps upstream	■ E-mail for 50 or more simultaneous users ■ Web browsing for 25 to 30 simultaneous users ■ Large FTP downloads for 12 to 15 simultaneous users
Asymmetrical Digital Subscriber Line (ADSL)	Up to 640 Kbps downstream; up to 160 Kbps upstream	■ E-mail for 60 or more simultaneous users ■ Web browsing for 30 to 35 simultaneous users ■ Large FTP downloads for 15 to 18 simultaneous users

Table 3-1 Internet Access WAN Technologies

Connection Type	Transmission Speed	Applications
T-1	1.544 Mbps	■ E-mail for 120 or more simultaneous users ■ Web browsing for 75 to 100 simultaneous users ■ Large FTP downloads for 40 to 50 simultaneous users
Fractional T-1	Up to 1.544 Mbps, in 64 Kbps increments	■ Variable, depending on bandwidth
T-3	44.736 Mbps	■ E-mail for 3,000 or more simultaneous users ■ Web browsing for 2,000 to 3,000 simultaneous users ■ Large FTP downloads for 1,000 to 1,500 simultaneous users
Frame relay	Variable	■ Variable, depending on bandwidth

Dial-Up Modem Connections

It is possible to share dial-up modem connections with a network. However, a single dial-up modem connection reaching a maximum of 53 kilobits per second (Kbps) can satisfy the Internet bandwidth requirements of only a handful of users and only as long as they don't run high-bandwidth applications and don't expect stellar performance. If your network has users who need only occasional access to the Internet, you can install one or more modems and share them using Internet Connection Sharing (ICS) on a Windows computer or an inexpensive stand-alone router that provides NAT services.

ISDN

Integrated Services Digital Network (ISDN) is a digital dial-up service that uses the standard cabling provided by the telephone company plus special equipment at your network site. There are two ISDN services; Basic Rate Interface (BRI, also known as 2B+D) provides up to 128 Kbps of bandwidth, and Primary Rate Interface (PRI) up to 1.544 Mbps, which is the same speed as a T-1. PRI is common overseas but is rarely seen in the U.S. BRI service is available from many telephone companies, but it doesn't provide much more bandwidth than a standard dial-up modem connection. You can service a small network with a BRI connection or use it to provide limited Internet access to a larger network. For example, if you want to provide the users of a medium-sized network with Internet e-mail capabilities only, ISDN might be an effective solution.

The main advantage of ISDN is that it is a dial-up service, like a standard telephone connection. To access the Internet and establish a connection, you use your equipment to dial the ISDN number of your ISP. You can disconnect from the ISP's network when you don't need Internet access, such as after business hours, and if you want to change ISPs, all you have to do is dial a different number.

This ability to disconnect is what makes ISDN an economically viable Internet access solution. In most cases, you must pay a per-minute charge to the telephone company providing the service (in addition to a monthly fee, plus whatever your ISP charges for the connection), so remaining connected around the clock can be expensive. In some cases, using dial-on-demand technology to connect to the ISP only when your users need Internet access can keep the cost lower than a dedicated connection using another technology can.

The disadvantages of ISDN are its relatively high cost per kilobit of bandwidth, and the fact that the end-user equipment must be located within a specified distance (usually 18,000 feet) of the telephone company's nearest point of presence (POP).

CATV and DSL

CATV networks and *Digital Subscriber Line (DSL)* are Internet access solutions targeted primarily at home users, but they can be effective for a business network as well. Many CATV providers take advantage of their extensive private fiber optic networks by using them to provide Internet access as well as television signals. The Internet bandwidth that CATV networks provide can vary, depending on the number of subscribers in the local area, but is often as high as 512 Kbps. Cable television companies operate what is essentially a metropolitan area network (MAN), in which neighboring subscribers share a network medium and the bandwidth it provides. This means that your available bandwidth can be reduced when other subscribers in your area are transferring a lot of data.

DSL is a telephone company service that provides high-speed, digital transmissions using standard telephone cables. A DSL connection is a dedicated link between two sites that provides a predetermined amount of bandwidth at all times. There are many different types of DSL connections, all of which have slightly different names, such as ADSL and High-bit-rate Digital Subscriber Line (HDSL). This is why the technology is sometimes called by the generic name xDSL. ADSL is the most popular DSL variant for Internet access and can provide transmission rates of up to 8 Mbps, although transmission rates between 256 and 512 Kbps are more common. Telephone companies and other large data carriers frequently use HDSL over fiber optic cables.

Both CATV and ADSL Internet connections suffer from what some network designers would consider a fatal flaw: they are asymmetrical. An *asymmetrical* connection is one that runs at different speeds in each direction. In these cases, the downstream transmission rate (that is, from the service provider to the subscriber) is much higher than the upstream rate. CATV networks are designed to carry signals from the provider to the subscriber; there is very little upstream bandwidth available, and the provider typically sets a maximum upstream transmission rate ranging from 56 to 128 Kbps. Asymmetrical DSL connections have an upstream transmission rate that is fixed at a lower speed than the downstream rate.

For network access to the Internet, an asymmetrical connection might not be a major drawback, as long as the majority of network users are running Internet client applications, such as Web browsers. In normal use, client applications send only brief requests upstream and receive larger amounts of data from the downstream connection. Web servers and other Internet server applications, however, frequently send large amounts of traffic upstream, which is why consumer CATV and DSL connections are often unsuitable for shared network Internet connections. There are DSL technologies that are symmetrical, however. You must check with your local telephone carrier to find out what is available in your area. As with ISDN, DSL service is limited in its maximum distance from the nearest POP, so DSL might not be an alternative for you.

Internet access through a CATV network is generally inexpensive (about $40 per month, in most cases) and is a viable alternative for a small-to-medium-sized network that does not require a huge amount of bandwidth. However, because CATV providers usually target their Internet service to home users, you should check your local provider's policy about using the connection for network access. DSL is far more flexible than CATV. Some DSL providers have packages intended for business use that provide sufficient bandwidth for larger networks.

Leased Lines

A leased line (sometimes called a dedicated line) is a permanent, usually digital telephone connection between two points that provides a fixed amount of bandwidth at all times. The most common type of leased line used for connecting a medium or large network to the Internet is the T-1, running at 1.544 Mbps. A T-1 provides a great deal of bandwidth between your network and that of your ISP, in both directions, 24 hours a day. Although you can use a T-1 as a single data pipe, the connection actually consists of 24 separate channels running at 64 Kbps each. Most service providers enable you to purchase one or more of these separate channels. This is called *fractional T-1* service, and it enables you to purchase just about any amount of bandwidth you need.

The next step up from a T-1 connection is a T-3, which is the equivalent of 672 channels running at 64 Kbps each, or 28 T-1s, for a total of 44.736 Mbps. The Internet uses T-3 connections for backbones, and ISPs often use them to obtain their own Internet access, but a T-3 is usually far more bandwidth than a single network installation needs and is also too expensive.

To install a leased line, you must make arrangements with a telephone carrier for the installation and then buy or lease a piece of equipment called a *Channel Service Unit /Data Service Unit (CSU/DSU)* (see Figure 3-1). You must also arrange with an ISP for the installation of the connection's other end at their site and negotiate a contract for Internet access at the line's rate of speed. The price of a leased line is typically a monthly fee based on its transmission rate and on the distance between the two connected sites. Using a local ISP can be a major financial benefit for this reason. Some

nection between two points, you install a leased line at each site, running to a service provider. The service provider maintains a frame relay network called a *cloud*, which provides the connection between the two leased lines, as shown in Figure 3-2. You contract with the service provider for a certain amount of bandwidth through the cloud, called a *committed information rate (CIR)*, which is guaranteed at all times. When your bandwidth needs drop below the CIR, you pay a rate based on the bandwidth you use. Your bandwidth can also exceed the CIR during periods of high traffic, called *burst periods*, for an additional fee specified in the contract. The service provider is able to do this because it can reclaim any bandwidth you are not using and sell it to other customers.

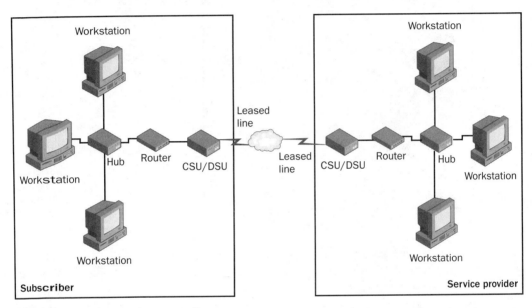

Figure 3-2   A frame relay connection

To use frame relay for Internet access, you must locate an ISP that provides this service, and you still must install a leased line between your site and that of the ISP. The bandwidth of the leased line you install should be slightly more than you actually need for Internet access. You then contract for a CIR that is somewhat lower than the bandwidth of the leased line. For example, for a company that shuts down after business hours, you might design an Internet access strategy consisting of a T-1 line connecting the network site to an ISP, with a frame relay contract containing a CIR of 1 Mbps. When the company is closed, it won't pay any ISP fees, and when it's opened, it has a guaranteed 1 Mbps of bandwidth, plus the ability to exceed the CIR during high-traffic periods.

Frame relay in no way diminishes the cost of installing and maintaining the leased line connecting the network to the ISP, but it can reduce the network's ISP costs by 20 to 40 percent in cases in which the company does not make full use of the T-1's bandwidth at all times.

telephone companies can provide the Internet access as well as the leased l
nating the need to involve a third party in the negotiations. These providers c
package deals available that provide an array of Internet access services at an
price.

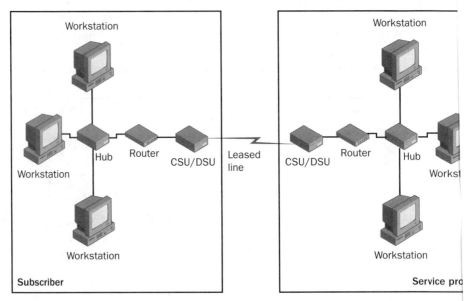

Figure 3-1   A leased line connection

When creating an Internet access plan, you must understand that leased lines
a different world from most of the low-end Internet access solutions describe
in this lesson. Installing a leased line for Internet access represents a significal
ment in time and money. In addition to the monthly fees for the leased line i
for the ISP's services, the cost of the installation and the CSU/DSU at both end
stantial, and once the line is in place, it is permanent. You cannot change ISPs
having another line installed to the new destination. Before actually installing
line, you should discuss your needs with several telephone carriers and ISPs
feel for their services and obtain competitive bids.

As an Internet access solution, leased lines are best suited to networks that requ
amounts of bandwidth around the clock. When you install a leased line, you are p
a given amount of bandwidth 24 hours a day. An organization that completely shu
and requires no Internet access for a portion of the day is wasting a lot of money. H
for some organizations, the money lost in this way more than offsets the cost of o
the bandwidth they need during business hours by some other means.

Frame Relay

Frame relay is a WAN technology designed to provide a variable amount of bar
and enable you to pay only for the bandwidth you use. To set up a frame relay W

Practice: Understanding WAN Speeds

Using the information provided in this lesson, place the following Internet connection technologies in order from lowest to highest, based on the amount of bandwidth they provide.

1. T-3
2. CATV
3. ISDN Basic Rate Interface
4. ADSL
5. Dial-up modem
6. T-1

Lesson Review

The following questions are intended to reinforce key information presented in this lesson. If you are unable to answer a question, review the lesson materials and try the question again. You can find the answers to the questions in the "Questions and Answers" section at the end of this chapter.

1. Which of the following servers does *not* require a computer with a registered IP address?

   a. Internet Web servers

   b. Internet e-mail servers

   c. DNS servers used for Internet domain hosting

   d. DNS servers used for Internet name resolution

2. Which of the following WAN technologies are asymmetrical? (Choose all answers that are correct.)

   a. CATV

   b. ISDN

   c. ADSL

   d. T-1

3. Which of the following Internet connection types enables you to save money when the network is not using any Internet bandwidth? (Choose all answers that are correct.)

   a. ISDN

   b. DSL

   c. Fractional T-1

    d. Frame relay

Lesson Summary

- When creating an Internet access strategy for a network, the first step is estimating how much Internet bandwidth the network needs.

- The Internet bandwidth needed by a network is based on the number of users and the types of applications they run.

- WAN technologies such as dial-up modems, ISDN, CATV, DSL, leased lines, and frame relay provide varying amounts of bandwidth and operational characteristics, which you must evaluate before selecting one for an Internet connection.

- Asymmetrical Internet connections are suitable for use by clients, but not by servers.

Lesson 2: Selecting Routers and ISPs

Once you have decided what type of WAN technology you will use to connect the network to the Internet, you can then select the components that will connect to each end of the WAN link. At your private network site, you must install a router. The other end of the WAN link must be connected to a router as well, which the ISP furnishes.

After this lesson, you will be able to

- Describe the various WAN technologies used for Internet connections
- Understand the criteria used to select an ISP for a network Internet connection

Estimated lesson time: 15 minutes

Choosing a Router Type

You learned in Lesson 2 of Chapter 2, "Planning a TCP/IP Network Infrastructure," that routers, especially Internet access routers, can have many forms and sizes. A computer running Microsoft Windows Server 2003 can function as a router for the Internet access technologies described in Lesson 1 of this chapter. You can configure the Routing and Remote Access Service (RRAS) module to route traffic between a local area network (LAN) and any type of WAN link that you can connect to the computer. RRAS also includes support for NAT, so you can configure the computers on the LAN with unregistered IP addresses and have them access the Internet using NAT.

Real World   Internet Connection Sharing

A simple Microsoft Windows XP workstation using a dial-up modem and telephone line to connect to the Internet can function as a router if you activate the ICS feature. ICS can supply the other computers on a small LAN with IP addresses and subnet masks and configure them to use the ICS computer as the default gateway. The modem provides the connection to an ISP, which is no less a WAN connection than more expensive and complicated technologies.

Stand-alone Internet routers are hardware devices that connect to your network and to the WAN providing access to the Internet. At the lower end of the price range, these routers tend to be all-in-one devices that provide services such as NAT and the Dynamic Host Configuration Protocol (DHCP), in addition to basic routing. You can get routers like this that enable you to share a dial-up modem, ISDN, CATV, or DSL connection with your network by connecting the device directly to the WAN. Because these routers use NAT to provide Internet access to the LAN, the service provider is aware only of the single connection. Smaller devices like these are therefore not suitable for larger networks or for networks that require using registered IP addresses on some of their computers.

As you move up the price range towards more expensive routers, you tend to see fewer all-in-one units, and you are more likely to want comprehensive routing solutions for the entire enterprise network. High-end modular routers enable you to add modules supporting many different types of WAN as well as LAN connections, enabling you to connect a network to an ISP using almost any type of link.

Planning   With a high-end modular router, you are more likely to have to supply services such as NAT and DHCP separately, using a dedicated firewall product or a Microsoft Windows server.

No matter what type of WAN technology you use to connect to the Internet, you must connect one end of the link to a router at your site, and your ISP must do the same. Most WAN technologies described in this lesson require some piece of equipment at each end of the connection. For a dial-up connection, that piece of equipment is a modem. For leased lines, the CSU/DSU functions as the terminus of the connection.

Off the Record   ISDN, CATV, and DSL connections also require devices that are colloquially referred to as modems, even though they are digital components that do not perform the modulation/demodulation functions that define a true modem.

Dial-up modems connect to a computer's serial port, and most other WAN devices can connect to a standard Ethernet network interface adapter installed in a computer, or they can connect directly to a stand-alone router, as shown in Figure 3-3. The router functions as the network's default gateway for all IP addresses other than those on the private network.

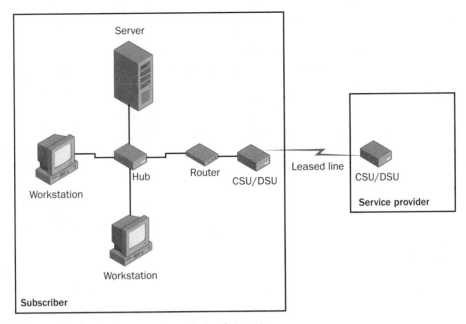

Figure 3-3   A network connection to the Internet

Choosing an ISP

When you design an Internet access strategy for a medium or large network, selecting an ISP is an important part of the plan. The primary function of an ISP is, of course, to provide access to the Internet. The ISP maintains its own network, which is connected to the Internet, to which you can connect using various WAN technologies. ISPs can function at various levels of the Internet food chain. Those that are higher up in the chain have networks connected directly to Internet backbones, while others are just intermediaries that obtain bandwidth from another ISP and resell it to their customers. In addition, some ISPs target home users as their primary customer base while others seek business clients.

Off the Record   ISP selection is particularly important when you use a high-bandwidth connection that is expensive to install, such as a leased line. You don't want to find out a month after the installation that the ISP you selected provides bad service, cannot furnish the bandwidth you need, or is going out of business.

Both high-level and low-level ISPs have their advantages and disadvantages. A large ISP near the top of the food chain has more bandwidth available, as well better in-house servers, routers, and other equipment. Many ISPs of this type maintain redundant Internet backbone connections and have fault-tolerant hardware installations, which together minimize the chances of a service outage. These providers often support more WAN connection options and offer more diverse services as well. The disadvantage of this type of ISP is that you have to pay top dollar for these benefits. In many cases, they are worth it, especially for a large network that relies on Internet communications.

Smaller ISPs frequently offer substantial monetary savings compared to the larger providers, and they might be able to provide more personal service. The disadvantage is that the ISP might not really be equipped to provide for your needs and probably has less money invested in its own network infrastructure. This means that the smaller ISP probably provides fewer service options than the larger ones and that the chances of an extended service outage are greater.

Off the Record   In addition to these disadvantages, it's possible that the small ISP will go out of business. This is a danger with a larger ISP too, although a lesser one.

In addition to providing Internet access, ISPs also provide a variety of other services. When a home user dials in to an ISP from a stand-alone computer, the ISP not only provides Internet access, but also furnishes the user with a registered IP address, Domain Name System (DNS) services, and an e-mail account. To provide these services, the ISP must maintain its own application servers.

Part of planning for a network's Internet access is deciding which application services the ISP should provide and which ones you will provide in-house. Home users typically get all the essential services they need in a package deal, but businesses usually negotiate for these services individually. This is because businesses often provide some services themselves while contracting with the ISP to supply others.

Some application services that are typically available from ISPs catering to business customers are as follows:

Multiple WAN Support

ISPs oriented towards residential users might support only dial-up modem connections, but business-oriented ISPs typically can support a variety of WAN connection types, such as ISDN, DSL, and leased lines, and they can provide Internet access at a wide range of bandwidth levels.

Exam Tip   Be sure you understand the functions of the various servers involved in providing a network with Internet connectivity, such as DNS and NAT servers.

IP Addresses

Every Internet access solution requires one IP address at minimum. Even if you plan to use unregistered IP addresses on your network, you need one registered address to connect your NAT router or proxy server to the Internet. In most cases, ISPs provide one dynamically assigned, registered address as part of the Internet access service. If you plan on hosting Web or other Internet servers, you might need to obtain additional registered IP addresses from the ISP and pay an additional fee for them.

Off the Record   Most ISPs also differentiate between dynamically assigned IP addresses and static ones. A NAT router, for example, can use a different registered IP address every day and still function properly. An Internet Web server must have the same registered IP address all the time so that clients on the Internet can locate it using its DNS name. You usually must pay extra to obtain static IP addresses from an ISP.

DNS Servers

Internet clients require the services of a DNS server to resolve the names of sites and users into IP addresses. DNS is one of the easiest services to host yourself, and many business customers do not need to use their ISP's DNS servers. Windows Server 2003 includes a DNS server implementation, which you might have to install anyway (to support Active Directory, for example), so you can use it to provide name resolution services to your Internet clients at the same time. A Windows server can provide this basic name resolution capability even if it has an unregistered IP address itself. Other DNS services, such as domain hosting, require that the DNS server have a registered IP address.

See Also   For more information about DNS and name resolution, see Chapter 4, "Planning a Name Resolution Strategy."

E-Mail Services

For a stand-alone computer, the e-mail services an ISP provides include one e-mail account (or possibly several, in the case of a family plan) and access to the ISP's e-mail servers. Once the ISP creates the account, no further interaction with the customer is required unless a problem arises. In most cases, the e-mail requirements for businesses are more substantial A company e-mail solution for a medium-to large-network requires a lot of accounts and consequently a lot of account maintenance. An ISP has to factor in the cost of paying someone to service the business customer by continually creating and revoking accounts, changing passwords, and performing other maintenance chores when charging for e-mail services at this level.

Off the Record Some ISPs provide corporate e-mail services without providing the maintenance services. You can contract with an ISP to host your e-mail servers while you perform the maintenance tasks yourself, using a Web-based interface over the Internet.

Most medium-to-large organizations prefer to run their own mail servers, because it is cheaper in the long run and easier for network administrators to perform routine maintenance chores themselves directly on the server rather than wait for the ISP to do it or use a Web interface. To run an e-mail server that supports Internet e-mail, however, the computer must have a registered IP address so that other mail servers on the Internet can send messages to it, and you must have a domain registered in the DNS.

Web Hosting

Some organizations maintain a presence on the Internet by running their own Web servers, but many others rely on ISPs to host their Web sites for them. Running Internet Web servers requires that the computers have registered IP addresses, and as with e-mail servers, the Web servers' addresses must be registered in the DNS so that Internet users can access them. Web servers also present a security risk because they are as liable to attract the wrong kind of users as the right kind.

When running Web servers in-house, you have to take steps to secure them, such as by creating a perimeter network and installing a firewall. Outsourcing the Web servers with an ISP eliminates the danger to the private network and prevents you from having to worry about furnishing the servers with sufficient Internet bandwidth. ISPs often price Web hosting services based on the amount of bandwidth the servers use, but the ISP has all the bandwidth the Web servers need readily available. If the traffic to the Web servers increases significantly, you might end up paying a higher monthly fee for the hosting service, but you won't have to spend a fortune to install a faster connection at your site.

Internet Domain Hosting

To host an Internet domain, you must register the domain name with one of the many Internet registries by paying a fee and supplying the IP addresses of the DNS servers that are to be the authoritative sources for information about that domain. You can pay an ISP to use their DNS servers for this purpose, or you can run your own DNS servers, but whichever you choose, those servers must be available to the Internet at all times. If the authoritative DNS servers for your domain are not available, then Internet users cannot access your Web servers and cannot send you e-mail.

Planning If you already plan on running your own DNS servers to provide name resolution services for your Internet clients, you can use the same ones to host your domain. Although you don't need registered IP address for internal name resolution, the DNS servers must have registered IP addresses to host the domain.

Practice: Configuring a Windows Server 2003 Router

In this practice, you configure the Routing And Remote Access tool on Server01 to route traffic between the two network interface adapters installed in the computer. For this exercise, the Microsoft Loopback Adapter is presumed to be connected to a WAN device providing a connection to an ISP. The other adapter (which is the actual network interface card in the computer) is connected to the local private network. After configuring RRAS, you then disable it to prepare for later practice.

 Note   The Microsoft Loopback Adapter is a software component included with Windows Server 2003 that you install as part of the server Setup procedure documented in the "About This Book" chapter.

Exercise 1: Configuring Routing and Remote Access

In this procedure, you perform a manual configuration that leaves RRAS with only basic routing functions.

1. Log on to Server01 as Administrator.

2. Click Start, point to All Programs, point to Administrative Tools, and then click Routing And Remote Access. The Routing And Remote Access console appears, and SERVER01 (local) is listed in the console tree.

3. Click SERVER01 (local), and from the Action menu, select Configure And Enable Routing And Remote Access. The Routing And Remote Access Server Setup Wizard appears.

4. Click Next. The Configuration page appears.

   Notice that there are five options that you can select to create different RRAS configurations.

5. Select the Custom Configuration. Select Any Combination Of The Features Available In Routing And Remote Access option button, and then click Next. The Custom Configuration page appears.

6. Select the LAN Routing check box, and then click Next. The Completing The Routing And Remote Access Server Setup Wizard page appears.

7. Click Finish. A Routing And Remote Access message box appears, asking if you want to start the service.

8. Click Yes. The Routing and Remote Access service starts, and new entries appear in the console tree.

   Notice that the IP Routing icon contains only three subheadings: General, Static Routes, and NAT/Basic Firewall.

9. Click the NAT/Basic Firewall subheading. Leave the Routing And Remote Access console open for the next procedure.

   Notice that no interfaces appear in the detail pane for this subheading, indicating that the NAT and firewall functions are not in use.

> **Security Alert**   RRAS is now configured to route traffic between the local network and the ISP's network, which is in turn connected to the Internet. You should understand that this is a basic router configuration, with no security mechanisms of any kind. You must also configure the server with a default gateway address that will send all external traffic to the ISP's router. You use this configuration only when you want to connect computers with registered IP addresses directly to the Internet, and when you intend to manually configure the firewall features in RRAS or use a third-party firewall product to protect your computers from unauthorized access by Internet intruders.

Exercise 2: Disabling Routing and Remote Access

In this procedure, you disable RRAS, removing the configuration you just created. This leaves RRAS in its original state so that you can create a different configuration later in this chapter.

1. Click SERVER01 (local), and from the Action menu, select Disable Routing And Remote Access. A Routing And Remote Access message box appears, warning you that you are disabling the router.

2. Click Yes. The Routing and Remote Access service is stopped, and the subheadings beneath the SERVER01 (local) icon disappear.

3. Close the Routing And Remote Access console.

Lesson Review

The following questions are intended to reinforce key information presented in this lesson. If you are unable to answer a question, review the lesson materials and try the question again. You can find the answers to the questions in the "Questions and Answers" section at the end of this chapter.

1. Which of the following components must you have for your network to run its own Internet e-mail server? (Choose all answers that are correct.)

   a. A DNS server to host the domain

   b. A registered IP address

   c. A Web-based administration interface

   d. A registered domain name

2. Internet access routers marketed as all-in-one devices typically include which additional services?

_____

_____

3. List three advantages of using a larger, high-level ISP compared to a smaller one.

_____

_____

Lesson Summary

- ISPs can provide a variety of services to business clients in addition to simple Internet access.

- ISPs typically charge extra for additional IP addresses, and they differentiate between dynamic and static address assignments.

- ISPs can provide access to application servers, such as Web, e-mail, and DNS servers.

- Part of Internet access strategy is determining which services you should implement in-house and which you should obtain from the ISP.

Lesson 3: Securing and Regulating Internet Access

In addition to specifying what type of Internet connection to install and what services to obtain from the ISP, an Internet access plan should specify how you will protect the network from unauthorized intrusions by Internet predators and what restrictions you will impose on the network users' Internet access. An Internet connection is a door to the outside world that can operate in both directions, and it is vital to minimize the risk of your network being compromised from outside. However, not all security threats come from outside. Your own users can jeopardize your network by running unauthorized applications, monopolizing Internet bandwidth, and exposing your systems to viruses and other damaging software.

After this lesson, you will be able to

- Determine the Internet access security requirements for a network
- Understand the security ramifications of using NAT
- Understand the security capabilities of a proxy server

Estimated lesson time: 20 minutes

Determining Internet Security Requirements

Providing network users with Internet access is a balance between functionality and security. In Chapter 2, "Planning a TCP/IP Network Infrastructure," you learned how the difference between using registered and unregistered addresses is important to your network's security. Deciding which computers will use these address types is the first step in providing secure Internet access.

You can choose to grant your users complete access to the Internet by assigning registered IP addresses to their computers. This solution enables the users to run any Internet client or server application, using all the bandwidth available to them. However, using registered IP addresses also exposes your network to many kinds of abuse.

 Security Alert   Not only can outside users on the Internet access your computers using the registered addresses, your internal users can also abuse their privileges by running their own Web servers and other unauthorized applications.

It is possible to secure a registered network by installing a firewall between the computers and the Internet connection. You must do this if you have Web servers or other computers on your network that require registered IP addresses. However, using unregistered IP addresses is a simpler method of securing your Internet clients and also enables you to implement more comprehensive security and access control mechanisms.

Deciding how secure your network needs to be and how you are going to implement that security is important in designing an Internet access strategy. Once you have selected a type of Internet connection for your network and have developed an IP addressing strategy, it is time to think about how much Internet access you want to give your users. Determining the security requirements for the network helps you to determine what additional hardware and software you need to install.

Limiting Applications

One way of securing your network's Internet access is to limit the Internet applications that users are permitted to run. You implement a basic application restriction by using unregistered IP addresses. When an unregistered computer is not visible from the Internet, Internet systems cannot initiate contact with it. Therefore, the computer is restricted to running Internet client applications, which by definition initiate communications with a server on the Internet.

Tip   Restricting users to client applications means they cannot run their own Internet servers, such as Web and FTP servers.

Another method of restricting the applications that people can use to access the Internet is to filter the packets passing over the Internet connection based on their ports. Every TCP/IP packet contains a source port number that identifies the application that generated it and contains a destination port number that identifies the receiving application. The port numbers are included in the packet's transport layer protocol header.

Real World   Port Filtering

Web servers communicate with clients using the Hypertext Transfer Protocol (HTTP), and HTTP uses port number 80. If you create a port filter on your network stopping all traffic addressed to port 80, your computers can't send HTTP requests to Web servers and therefore can't access Web sites. Port filtering does not prevent the user from actually running the Web browser, but it does prevent the browser from communicating with servers on the Internet.

To create packet filters, you use a firewall or a router with packet filtering capabilities. If you use a computer running Windows Server 2003 as the router connecting your network to your ISP, you can create packet filters in the RRAS module.

Limiting Users

In most organizations with Internet connections, there are different types of users who require varying degrees of Internet access to perform their jobs. In your own Internet access plan, you might want to provide all the network's users with e-mail capabilities but restrict Web browsing to a certain group of users and FTP capabilities to still another group.

There are two methods you can use to provide different levels of Internet access for individual users. The first is to use packet filtering. In addition to filtering packets based on port numbers, you can filter them based on IP addresses. By combining these two filter types, you can specify the ports that each computer on the network is permitted to use.

> **Tip**   Regulating Internet access using packet filtering can be time consuming for network administrators.

The second method is to use a software product that recognizes users and enables you to grant them access to specific Internet services. Proxy server products, such as Microsoft Internet Security and Acceleration (ISA) Server 2004, include features like these as well as other capabilities.

Regulating Internet Access

As mentioned earlier, network security hazards can originate from internal sources as well as external ones. Your own network users might not cause as much damage as Internet intruders can, by introducing viruses or wantonly deleting files, but they can still hamper network operations by monopolizing Internet bandwidth or lower productivity by spending too much time on personal Internet activities.

For these reasons, many network administrators impose restrictions on Internet use, such as specifying sites that users can access, limiting the hours during which users can access the Internet, and limiting the amount of bandwidth they can use. These features are also included in proxy server products.

Using NAT

NAT is a primary method enabling computers with unregistered IP addresses to access the Internet. As described in Chapter 2, "Planning a TCP/IP Network Infrastructure," NAT functions as an intermediary between a client computer on an unregistered network and the Internet. For each packet generated by a client, the NAT implementation substitutes a registered address for the client's unregistered address.

Following are three basic types of NAT:

- **Static NAT**   Static NAT translates a number of unregistered IP addresses to an equal number of registered addresses (see Figure 3-4) so that each client always uses the same registered address. This type of NAT does not conserve the IP address space because you need the same number of registered addresses as unregistered addresses. Static NAT is also not as secure as the other NAT types because each computer is permanently associated with a particular registered address, which makes it more possible for Internet intruders to direct traffic to a particular computer on your network using that registered address.

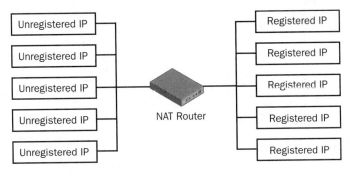

Figure 3-4   Static NAT

■ **Dynamic NAT**   Dynamic NAT is intended for circumstances in which you have fewer registered IP addresses than unregistered computers (see Figure 3-5). Dynamic NAT translates each unregistered computer to one of the registered addresses. Intruders on the Internet are less able to associate a registered address with a particular computer (as in static NAT) because the registered address assigned to each client changes frequently. The main drawback of dynamic NAT is that it can support only the same number of simultaneous users as you have registered IP addresses available. If all the registered addresses are in use, a client attempting to access the Internet receives an error message.

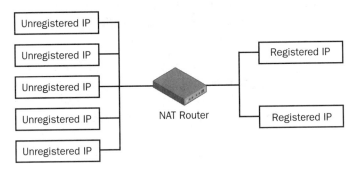

Figure 3-5   Dynamic NAT

■ **Masquerading**   Masquerading translates all the unregistered IP addresses on your network using a single registered IP address (see Figure 3-6). To enable multiple clients to access the Internet simultaneously, the NAT router uses port numbers to differentiate between packets generated by and destined to different computers. Masquerading provides the best security of the NAT types because the association between the unregistered client and the registered IP address/ port number combination in the NAT router lasts only for the duration of a single connection.

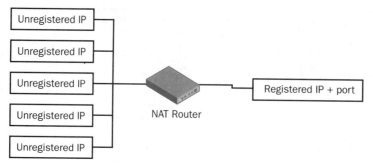

Figure 3-6   Masquerading NAT

NAT Security

Most NAT implementations today rely on the masquerading technique because it minimizes the number of registered IP addresses needed and it maximizes the security provided by NAT. Note, however, that NAT by itself, even using masquerading, is not a true firewall and does not provide ironclad security for high-risk situations. NAT effectively blocks unsolicited requests and other probes from the Internet, meaning that it thwarts intruders searching for unprotected file shares and private Web or FTP servers. However, NAT does not prevent users on the Internet from launching directed denial of service attacks against specific computers on the private network or from using other, more complex tactics to compromise your network.

Off the Record   Under normal conditions, client computers are not often subject to threats like these, so a NAT server and a good anti-virus program (kept current with frequent virus signature updates) are usually sufficient. However, Internet servers and other high-traffic computers are more likely to be targeted by intruders and generally require more comprehensive firewall protection.

NAT and Stateful Packet Inspection

Some NAT implementations include additional security capabilities, typically a technique called *stateful packet inspection*. Stateful packet inspection is a generic term for a process in which the NAT router examines the incoming packets from the Internet more carefully than usual. In a typical NAT implementation, the router is concerned only with the IP addresses and port numbers of the packets passing through it. A NAT router that supports stateful packet inspection examines other network and transport layer header fields as well, looking for patterns in various damaging behaviors, such as IP spoofing, SYN floods, and teardrop attacks. Various manufacturers implement stateful packet inspection in different ways, so not all NAT routers with this capability offer the same degree of protection.

Port Forwarding

Although Internet computers cannot initiate transactions with a computer on a NAT-protected network under normal conditions, it is possible to host a Web or other server on an unregistered system using a technique called *port forwarding*. Port forwarding occurs when the NAT router creates a mapping between a specific registered IP address and port number and a specific unregistered address on the private network. This mapping enables traffic that the NAT router would ordinarily block to get through to its destination.

Real World   Port Forwarding

An additional benefit of port forwarding is that the router can manipulate translation to provide additional functionality, such as load balancing. A NAT server can receive requests destined for one particular registered address and distribute them among several unregistered addresses. This means that if you have a Web site that receives high levels of traffic, you can deploy multiple, identical Web server computers and split the load between them.

Using a Proxy Server

NAT provides some security for unregistered computers while giving them access to the Internet, but because it operates at the network layer, it permits clients to use any application. NAT also provides little true firewall protection, except in the case of those NAT routers that support stateful packet inspection. For network administrators who want more protection, and who want more control over their users' Internet activities, another option, called a proxy server, is available.

A *proxy server* is an intermediary between clients and the Internet, like a NAT router, except that it functions at the application layer. Unregistered clients send their Internet access requests to the proxy server, which generates its own identical requests and sends them to the server on the Internet. When the proxy server receives a response, it relays the information back to the client on the unregistered network.

Early proxy servers were relatively simple software programs that supported only a few client applications, such as Web browsers and e-mail clients. The administrator or user also had to configure each client to send its requests to the proxy server's IP address, rather than try to send them directly to the Internet. Today, proxy servers have evolved into comprehensive Internet access solutions that provide support for all major applications and enable administrators to exercise significant control over users' Internet activities.

Exam Tip Be sure you understand how NAT routers and proxy servers work and the differences between the two.

Using Microsoft Internet Security and Acceleration Server 2004

ISA Server 2004 is a proxy server product that provides extensive firewall capabilities, including filtering at the packet, circuit, and application levels. These capabilities enable the proxy server to block most types of attacks attempted by Internet intruders, with greater efficiency than a typical NAT implementation. The server can also examine the data arriving from the Internet—whether it is contained in Web pages, e-mail messages, or other forms—to see if the files contain viruses or other potentially damaging code.

In addition to protecting the network from outside intrusion, ISA provides extensive internal security capabilities. Using a policy-based model, you can monitor and regulate user access to the Internet. Using a firewall client provided with the product, you can require users to authenticate to the ISA server before they are granted Internet access and grant them specific levels of access based on their identities. This means you can easily control user access to specific Internet applications and locations as well as maintain logs of Internet activities. You can also limit the time users can spend on the Internet by scheduling the hours when access is available.

Most proxy servers are also capable of accelerating client performance by caching information downloaded from the Internet. Repeated client visits to the same Web site, for example, are satisfied using the files stored on the proxy server, rather than repeating the download from the Internet. Because the proxy server is located on the company network, its response time with the cached information is far faster than that of the Internet server from which it was originally obtained.

Selecting an Internet Access Method

When using unregistered IP addresses for your network clients, deciding whether to use a NAT router or a proxy server to provide Internet access for your users should be based on the amount of security you think your network needs. For average, nontechnical Internet users, a NAT router provides efficient access and is easy to install and configure. For power users who are more likely to abuse their Internet access, a proxy server might be preferable.

Practice: Configuring a NAT Router

In this practice, you configure the RRAS module on Server01 to function as a NAT router connecting the private network with an ISP's network. For this exercise, the Microsoft Loopback Adapter installed in the Server01 computer is presumed to be connected to a WAN device providing a connection to the ISP. The other adapter is connected to the local private network. Afterward, you disable the RRAS configuration to return the service to its original state.

Exercise 1: Configuring Routing And Remote Access as a NAT router

In this procedure, you use a predetermined configuration option supplied with RRAS to create a router that uses NAT and basic firewall techniques to protect the private network from intruders.

1. Log on to Server01 as Administrator.

2. Click Start, point to All Programs, point to Administrative Tools, and then click Routing And Remote Access. The Routing And Remote Access console appears, and SERVER01 (local) is listed in the console tree.

3. Click SERVER01 (local), and from the Action menu, select Configure And Enable Routing And Remote Access. The Routing And Remote Access Server Setup Wizard appears.

4. Click Next. The Configuration page appears.

5. Select the Network Address Translation (NAT). Allow Internal Clients To Connect To The Internet Using One Public IP Address option button, and then click Next. The NAT Internet Connection page appears.

6. With the Use This Public Interface To Connect To The Internet option button selected (as it is by default), select the WAN Connection interface. Note the Enable Security On The Selected Interface By Setting Up Basic Firewall. Basic Firewall Prevents Unauthorized Users From Gaining Access To This Server Through The Internet check box is also selected by default. Click Next. The Completing The Routing And Remote Access Server Setup Wizard page appears.

7. Click Finish. The Routing and Remote Access service starts and subheadings appear under SERVER01 (local).

   Note that the Internet Group Management Protocol (IGMP) has been installed, providing support for IP multicasting.

8. Click the NAT/Basic Firewall subheading.

9. In the details pane, select the interface representing the network interface adapter connecting the computer to the private LAN (typically, the Local Area Connection interface), and from the Action menu, select Properties. The Properties dialog box for the interface appears.

   Note that the Private Interface Connected To Private Network option button is selected.

10. Click Cancel to close the Properties dialog box.

11. In the details pane, select the WAN Connection interface, and from the Action menu, select Properties. The Properties dialog box for the interface appears.

    Note that the Public Interface Connected To The Internet option button is selected by default, along with the Enable NAT On This Interface and Enable A Basic Firewall On This Interface check boxes. These features provide protection for the Internet connection interface by preventing access to the private network by unauthorized users.

12. Click Cancel to close the Properties dialog box.

13. Leave the Routing And Remote Access console open for the next exercise.

Exercise 2: Disabling Routing And Remote Access

In this procedure, you disable RRAS, removing the configuration you just created. This leaves RRAS in its original state so that you can create different configurations in later chapters.

1. Click SERVER01 (local), and from the Action menu, select Disable Routing And Remote Access. A Routing And Remote Access message box appears, warning that you are disabling the router.

2. Click Yes. The Routing and Remote Access service is stopped, and the subheadings beneath the SERVER01 (local) icon disappear.

3. Close the Routing And Remote Access console.

Lesson Review

The following questions are intended to reinforce key information presented in this lesson. If you are unable to answer a question, review the lesson materials and try the question again. You can find the answers to the questions in the "Questions and Answers" section at the end of this chapter.

1. Port filtering can provide which of the following Internet access control capabilities?

   a. Limit the applications users can run

   b. Prevent specific users from accessing the Internet

   c. Limit the applications that can access the Internet

   d. Prevent specific computers from accessing the Internet

2. Specify which of the three types of NAT processing (static, dynamic, or masquerading) provides the best security, and state why this is so.

   _____

   _____

3. How many registered IP addresses does a dynamic NAT router require?

   a. None

   b. One

   c. One for every unregistered IP address

   d. One for each simultaneous connection

Lesson Summary

- Determining a network's Internet security requirements is a major part of developing an effective Internet access strategy.

- An Internet connection is a gateway that can work in both directions, enabling Internet users to access your private network as well as allowing your users Internet access.

- Security problems can also originate on the private network, from users who monopolize or abuse the Internet connection.

- Most NAT implementations today use masquerading, a technique that maps unregistered IP addresses to a single registered IP address, combined with a port number.

- Proxy server products have evolved to now include an array of firewall and access control features that provide a comprehensive Internet security solution for a private network.

Lesson 4: Troubleshooting Internet Connectivity

Network users often report problems connecting to the Internet, and the first job of the troubleshooter is to determine the location of the problem. All Internet communications use the TCP/IP protocols, so any of the TCP/IP problems described in Lesson 5 of Chapter 2, "Planning a TCP/IP Network Infrastructure," can also affect Internet connectivity. However, there are also many other possible causes, ranging from trivial faults affecting a single computer to serious situations that jeopardize the functionality of the entire network.

After this lesson, you will be able to

■ Determine the location of an Internet access problem

■ Understand client configuration problems that can interrupt Internet access

■ Understand router, NAT, and proxy server problems that can interrupt Internet access

Estimated lesson time: 20 minutes

Determining the Scope of the Problem

The first step in troubleshooting an Internet access problem is to determine how widespread the problem is. This can help you isolate the approximate location of the fault. Assuming that the user reporting the problem can reproduce it at will, the simplest way to begin is for the help desk technician to try to reproduce the fault on other computers using the same steps the user did when experiencing the problem. The ideal way is to begin by recreating the fault on a system connected to the same hub as the problem computer, proceed to a system on another hub but on the same LAN, and then repeat the process on another LAN. If you can't reproduce the user's problem on any other computer, you know the problem is in the computer itself or the computer's connection to the network.

> **Note**   A problem that is isolated to the computers on one hub or on one LAN can indicate a fault in the hub or in one of the connections between hubs. A problem that affects all the computers on the network can result from a problem with the Internet access router or with the Internet itself.

The next step of the process is to determine whether the problem is limited to Internet connectivity. To do this, you attempt to access a resource on the local network (such as a file system share) from the computer experiencing the problem, and then you repeat the attempt with resources on other LANs. If the user's computer cannot contact the local network or the Internet, you know the problem is related to the internal network infrastructure and not to the components providing the Internet connection.

Once you have some idea of how widespread the problem is, you can prioritize it and assign it to the appropriate support personnel.

> **Real World   Troubleshooting**
>
> Because an Internet communications fault has so many possible causes, the process of isolating the cause of the problem is critical. It enables support personnel to determine who should be responsible for resolving the problem. In large organizations, technical support people are frequently divided into tiers that are responsible for increasingly complicated problems. For example, failure to access an Internet server could result from a configuration problem on the client computer, in which case a system administrator would handle the problem. The failure could also be due to a cabling problem, which a physical infrastructure specialist or an outside contractor would handle. A problem with a router or a proxy server would be delegated to a networking specialist. Finally, the problem could lie with the ISP or the Internet itself, in which case responsibility would lie outside the organization.

Diagnosing Client Configuration Problems

Internet communication problems that are isolated to a single computer typically result from incorrect client configuration. If the computer cannot connect to local network or Internet resources, you should check the basic TCP/IP configuration parameters, such as the IP address and subnet mask. If the computer can access resources on the local network but not on other networks or the Internet, the default gateway setting is either incorrect or pointing to a malfunctioning router.

Default Gateway Problems

The default gateway address enables the computer to forward all traffic destined for computers not on the private network to the Internet access router, which is connected to the organization's ISP. The router could be a standard router, a NAT router, or a proxy server. However, this does not mean that every computer must have the Internet access router's address as its default gateway. Every computer must have access to a default gateway on the local network, and if the Internet access router is connected to a different network (such as the backbone), the default gateway must be able to forward all Internet traffic to the Internet access router.

If the problematic computer can access internal resources on other networks but cannot access the Internet, the default gateway address in the TCP/IP configuration is pointing to a functional router, but the router might not be configured to forward Internet traffic properly. This would cause other computers using that default gateway to experience the same problems. Check the routing table on the default gateway router to make sure that it contains a path leading (directly or not) to the Internet access router.

Name Resolution Problems

A common cause of Internet connectivity problems is the client computer's failure to resolve DNS names into IP addresses. When name resolution fails, the client computer can't access Internet resources using host and domain names. To determine if name resolution failure caused the problem, you can attempt to access an Internet resource using its IP address instead of its DNS name. If the attempt is successful, you know that either the client computer is configured with an incorrect DNS server address or that the DNS server specified in the computer's TCP/IP configuration is not functioning properly.

See Also For more information on troubleshooting name resolution problems, see Lesson 6 in Chapter 4, "Planning A Name Resolution Strategy."

Diagnosing NAT and Proxy Server Problems

If you determine that the Internet connection problem is reproducible on other computers, or if you receive similar problem reports from other users, you are more likely dealing with a problem that affects one of the components providing Internet access to the entire network. If the network uses an intermediate device, such as a NAT router or a proxy server, the problem might be located in one of these components.

Tip To determine if the NAT router or proxy server is the source of the problem, you can try to access the Internet using a computer that does not go through an intermediate device, such as a Web server or other system with a registered IP address and direct access to the Internet router. If direct Internet communication is possible, but connections going through the NAT router or proxy server fail, start looking for the fault in these components.

Both NAT routers and proxy servers must have an interface that connects directly to the Internet using a registered IP address. This means that these devices can suffer from any of the same TCP/IP configuration problems as a client computer. Check the standard TCP/IP configuration parameters in the device, such as the IP address and subnet mask, the default gateway, and the DNS server addresses.

A NAT router or proxy server can also access the Internet itself but have a problem servicing the client computers on the unregistered network. In the case of a NAT router, make sure that the NAT implementation is configured to work with the unregistered IP addresses you have assigned to the client computers. For a proxy server, troubleshooting can be more complex. The proxy might in fact do the job it was configured to do, yet block access to the Internet because the user's authentication failed or because a policy on the server prohibits access. The user might try to access an unauthorized Internet site or try to access the Internet at an unauthorized time, for example. All technical support personnel that field such problems must be aware of the policies configured on the proxy server so that they do not waste time troubleshooting nonproblems.

Diagnosing Internet Connection Problems

If the individual computer is not at fault, and the NAT router or proxy server is functioning properly, the problem might lie with the Internet access router. You can check the router to make sure that both its network interfaces are configured properly, with one connecting to the internal network and one to the WAN link providing access to the ISP. The router's routing table should have a default gateway entry that sends traffic for all but the internal networks through the WAN interface to the ISP's router.

If the Internet access router is functioning correctly, the problem might be with the Internet connection itself. In most cases, the WAN connection uses a hardware device, such as a CSU/DSU, which you can power cycle or reset. This might solve the problem in some cases, but at other times the difficulty might be in the actual WAN connection. These connections always involve a service provider of some type (which might or might not be the same as your ISP), and they might experience hardware or software problems that interrupt your connection.

> **Tip**   WAN technology problems are a likely cause of a widespread Internet access problem, as many types of WAN connections can experience temporary outages.

Your ISP might also experience a problem that inhibits their own connectivity to the Internet, and if they can't connect, you can't either. You often hear reports (whether genuine or not) of a backhoe operator in some other city accidentally cutting a cable, which causes a service interruption to your ISP, your WAN provider, or a major Internet backbone. In these cases, there is little to do except keep in close contact with your providers to obtain status updates and register your displeasure. This is one occasion when you might regret signing up with a smaller ISP rather than with the large, expensive company that maintains multiple, redundant T-3 connections to various Internet backbones.

Lesson Review

The following questions are intended to reinforce key information presented in this lesson. If you are unable to answer a question, review the lesson materials and try the question again. You can find the answers to the questions in the "Questions and Answers" section at the end of this chapter.

1. A user is unable to access an Internet Web site but can access file system shares on the same LAN. Which of the following might be the problem? (Choose all answers that are correct.)

    a. The user's computer has an incorrect IP address.

    b. The user's computer has an incorrect default gateway address.

    c. The user's hub is malfunctioning.

    d. The router connecting the LAN to the ISP is malfunctioning.

2. What does a troubleshooter do to determine the scope of an Internet connection problem?

    _____

    _____

3. If a Web server with a registered IP address can access the Internet but client computers with unregistered addresses cannot, which of the following components might be the source of the problem?

    a. The CSU/DSU

    b. The Internet access router

    c. The proxy server

    d. The WAN connection

Lesson Summary

- Reproducing the fault on other computers can tell you whether the problem is in the computer itself or in a component that affects other users as well.

- An incorrect default gateway address or a malfunctioning default gateway router can hinder Internet connectivity while leaving local communications intact.

- To determine if an Internet connection problem is caused by a name resolution failure, which could be the result of an incorrect DNS server address or a malfunctioning DNS server, try connecting to the Internet using an IP address instead of a DNS name.

- NAT routers and proxy servers have network interfaces just like client computers, and they must have correct TCP/IP client configuration parameters. The NAT configuration and proxy server functions must also be correct.

- If no other components are at fault, the Internet access router or the WAN connection to the ISP might be the cause of the Internet connection problem. A service provider's equipment, or even the Internet itself might also cause a problem with the Internet connection.

Case Scenario Exercise

You are the network infrastructure design specialist for Litware Inc., a manufacturer of specialized scientific software products. You have already created a network design for their new office building, as described in the Case Scenario Exercise in Chapter 1. The office building is a three-story brick structure built in the late 1940s, which has since been retrofitted with several types of network cabling by various tenants. In your original design, each building floor has a separate Ethernet LAN, as follows:

- **First floor**   Ten individual offices, each with a single computer using 100Base-TX Fast Ethernet.

- **Second floor**   Fifty-five cubicles, each with a single computer using 10Base-T Ethernet.

- **Third floor**   A laboratory setting with network connections for up to 100 computers using 100Base-FX Fast Ethernet.

The three LANs are all connected to a backbone network, running 1000Base-T Gigabit Ethernet and using dedicated computers running Windows Server 2003 as routers.

You are authorized by the home office to install an Internet connection for the entire network, and you are designing an Internet access strategy. The network users have varying needs. The inside sales department numbers 55 people, who need access to Internet e-mail only. The company also has 20 outside salespeople based in this office, all of whom are equipped with laptop computers that they use to access the company network through VPN connections. The salespeople dial into a national ISP account from wherever they happen to be and open a secure connection through the Internet to a remote access server located in the building. The salespeople use the remote network connection to access the company database, download product updates from company servers, and check their e-mail on the company mail server.

The research and development lab on the third floor houses approximately 50 scientists and technicians, but they have special needs. In addition to e-mail and Web access for all workers, these people must frequently upload and download large files to and from Internet servers as well as access real-time video streams from other locations over the Internet.

All users in the building work a single shift, from 9 A.M. to 5 P.M., weekdays only. All client computers are shut down during nonworking hours. However, in addition to these users, the building also houses the company's six Internet Web servers, which receive heavy traffic and must remain connected to the Internet at all times.

Based on this information, answer the following questions about the Internet access strategy for this Litware, Inc. building.

1. For each of the following Internet access solutions, specify why it would or would not be suitable for this installation.

   a. ISDN Basic Rate Interface

   b. ADSL

   c. T-1

   d. Frame relay

2. All computers on the building's three client LANs use unregistered IP addresses, and the router connecting the backbone network to the Internet WAN link has NAT, port forwarding, and packet filtering capabilities. Explain how you would have to modify the Internet access strategy to support each of the following capabilities.

   a. Enable the scientists on the third floor to temporarily activate a server that streams video live over the Internet.

   b. Prevent the inside sales personnel from running any Internet application other than an e-mail client.

   c. Authenticate users before granting them Internet access and limiting Internet access to certain hours of the day.

Troubleshooting Lab

You work the help desk for a large corporation with a T-1 connection to the Internet. All client computers have unregistered IP addresses and access the Internet through a proxy server. An ISP hosts the company's Web servers at a facility that maintains three redundant T-3 connections to the Internet. The ISP guarantees a 98 percent connectivity rate. A call comes in from a user in the Marketing department named Mark, who says, "I can't access the company Web site! Our Internet connection must be down! You have to call our ISP right away and have them fix it!" After calming Mark down somewhat, you begin troubleshooting. Place the following troubleshooting steps in the order you should perform them.

1. Call the ISP, and ask if there is a problem with the company's Internet service.

2. Call a user who is connected to the same hub as Mark, and ask if she can access the Internet.

3. Power cycle the CSU/DSU for the T-1 providing Internet access.

4. Try to access the company Web site using a computer with a separate dial-up modem connection to the Internet.

5. Ask Mark to try to access a different site on the Internet.

6. Call a user on a different LAN from Mark, and ask if he can access the Internet.

7. Ask Mark to repeat his actions and see if he still can't access the company Web site.

8. Try to access the company Web site using a computer on the network with a registered IP address.

9. Check the NAT router logs to see if they are functioning properly.

Chapter Summary

- When creating an Internet access strategy for a network, the first step is estimating how much Internet bandwidth the network needs. The Internet bandwidth needed by a network is based on the number of users and the types of applications they run.

- WAN technologies such as dial-up modems, ISDN, CATV, DSL, leased lines, and frame relay provide varying amounts of bandwidth and operational characteristics, which you must evaluate before selecting one for an Internet connection.

- ISPs can provide a variety of services to business clients in addition to providing simple Internet access. Part of the Internet access strategy is determining which services you should implement in-house and which you should obtain from the ISP.

- An Internet connection is a gateway that can work in both directions, enabling Internet users to access your private network as well as allowing your users Internet access. Security problems can also originate on the private network, from users who monopolize or abuse the Internet connection.

- Most NAT implementations today use masquerading, a technique that maps unregistered IP addresses to a single registered IP address combined with a port number.

- Proxy server products have evolved to now include an array of firewall and access control features that provide comprehensive Internet security for a private network.

- The first step in troubleshooting an Internet connectivity problem is to isolate its location. Reproducing the fault on other computers can tell you whether the problem is in the computer itself or in a component that affects other users as well.

- To determine if an Internet connection problem is caused by a name resolution failure, which could be the result of an incorrect DNS server address or a malfunctioning DNS server, try connecting to the Internet using an IP address instead of a DNS name.

- NAT routers and proxy servers have network interfaces just like client computers, and they must have correct TCP/IP client configuration parameters. The configuration of the NAT and proxy server functions must also be correct.

- If no other components are at fault, the Internet connection problem might be caused by the Internet access router or the WAN connection to the ISP. The problem might also be caused by a service provider's equipment, or even be in the Internet itself.

Exam Highlights

Before taking the exam, review the key points and terms that are presented below to help you identify topics you need to review. Return to the lessons for additional practice, and review the "Further Reading" sections in Part 2 for pointers to more information about topics covering the exam objectives.

Key Points

- The initial steps of Internet connectivity planning are to determine how much bandwidth the network needs and what WAN technology you should use to supply that bandwidth.

- To connect your network to the Internet using the WAN technology you've chosen, you must decide what type of router to use at your site, what ISP you want to use, and what services you want the ISP to provide.

- To provide users with Internet access safely, you should secure your network by using unregistered IP addresses and a NAT router or proxy server.

- The first steps in troubleshooting Internet connectivity problems are to determine the scope of the problem and then isolate its location.

- Internet connectivity problems are frequently caused by TCP/IP configuration errors, NAT router proxy server configuration errors, or malfunctioning WAN connections.

Key Terms

Network address translation (NAT)   A router function that provides client computers with Internet access by substituting the router's registered IP address for the clients' unregistered addresses in individual data packets.

Stateful packet inspection   An optional NAT feature that enables the router to inspect the contents of data packets for potentially damaging code.

Proxy server   An application layer software product that functions as an intermediary between unregistered client computers and the Internet. In addition to providing Internet access, proxy servers can restrict Internet access, log Internet activity, and cache Internet data.

Questions and Answers

Page
3-13
Lesson 1 Practice

Using the information provided in this lesson, place the following Internet connection technologies in order from lowest to highest, based on the amount of bandwidth they provide.

1. T-3

2. CATV

3. ISDN Basic Rate Interface

4. ADSL

5. Dial-up modem

6. T-1

    5, 3, 2, 4, 6, 1

Page
3-13
Lesson 1 Review

1. Which of the following servers does *not* require a computer with a registered IP address?

    a. Internet Web servers

    b. Internet e-mail servers

    c. DNS servers used for Internet domain hosting

    d. DNS servers used for Internet name resolution

    d

2. Which of the following WAN technologies are asymmetrical? (Choose all answers that are correct.)

    a. CATV

    b. ISDN

    c. ADSL

    d. T-1

    a and c

3. Which of the following Internet connection types enables you to save money when the network is not using any Internet bandwidth? (Choose all answers that are correct.)

   a. ISDN

   b. DSL

   c. Fractional T-1

   d. Frame relay

   a and d

Page
3-22

Lesson 2 Review

1. Which of the following components must you have for your network to run its own Internet e-mail server? (Choose all answers that are correct.)

   a. A DNS server to host the domain

   b. A registered IP address

   c. A Web-based administration interface

   d. A registered domain name

   a, b, and d

2. Internet access routers marketed as all-in-one devices typically include which additional services?

   DHCP and NAT

3. List three advantages of using a larger, high-level ISP compared to a smaller one.

   The possible advantages include support for multiple WAN connection technologies, more Internet bandwidth available, redundant Internet backbone connections, fault tolerant hardware, and more diverse services.

Page
3-33

Lesson 3 Review

1. Port filtering can provide which of the following Internet access control capabilities?

   a. Limit the applications users can run

   b. Prevent specific users from accessing the Internet

   c. Limit the applications that can access the Internet

   d. Prevent specific computers from accessing the Internet

   c

2. Specify which of the three types of NAT processing (static, dynamic, or masquerading) provides the best security, and state why this is so.

Masquerading provides the best security because mapping a client's unregistered IP address to the NAT router's registered address lasts only for the duration of the connection.

3. How many registered IP addresses does a dynamic NAT router require?

    a. None

    b. One

    c. One for every unregistered IP address

    d. One for each simultaneous connection

    d

Page
3-38

Lesson 4 Review

1. A user is unable to access an Internet Web site but can access file system shares on the same LAN. Which of the following might be the problem? (Choose all answers that are correct.)

    a. The user's computer has an incorrect IP address.

    b. The user's computer has an incorrect default gateway address.

    c. The user's hub is malfunctioning.

    d. The router connecting the LAN to the ISP is malfunctioning.

    b and d

2. What does a troubleshooter do to determine the scope of an Internet connection problem?

Attempt to reproduce the problem with other computers on the same hub, on the same LAN, and on different LANs.

3. If a Web server with a registered IP address can access the Internet but client computers with unregistered addresses cannot, which of the following components might be the source of the problem?

    a. The CSU/DSU

    b. The Internet access router

    c. The proxy server

    d. The WAN connection

    c

Case Scenario Exercise

Based on the information in the Case Scenario Exercise, answer the following questions about the Internet access strategy for the Litware, Inc. building.

1. For each of the following Internet access solutions, specify why it would or would not be suitable for this installation.

   a. ISDN Basic Rate Interface

   At 128 Kbps, the ISDN BRI service would not provide sufficient bandwidth for the building's users.

   b. ADSL

   ADSL is an asymmetrical service that provides relatively little upstream bandwidth, which would be insufficient for the Internet Web servers in the building.

   c. T-1

   A T-1 leased line would be a suitable connection for this building because it provides sufficient bandwidth both upstream and downstream and operates around the clock.

   d. Frame relay

   Frame relay would be an excellent Internet access solution for this building because it enables the company to pay only for the bandwidth it uses and because it also supports bursts of bandwidth in excess of the contracted transfer rate.

2. All computers on the building's three client LANs use unregistered IP addresses, and the router connecting the backbone network to the Internet WAN link has NAT, port forwarding, and packet filtering capabilities. Explain how you would have to modify the Internet access strategy to support each of the following capabilities.

   a. Enable the scientists on the third floor to temporarily activate a server that streams video live over the Internet.

   To enable a server behind a NAT router to have a presence on the Internet, you must use port forwarding to associate the server's unregistered IP address with a specific registered address and port.

   b. Prevent the inside sales personnel from running any Internet application other than an e-mail client.

   To limit the inside sales users to e-mail access only, you can create IP address and port filters on the NAT router that block all Internet traffic from the IP addresses of the users' computers, except for that containing the port numbers associated with e-mail protocols.

   c. Authenticate users before granting them Internet access and limiting Internet access to certain hours of the day.

   You cannot configure a NAT router to authenticate users and control access based on the time of day. You would have to install a proxy server product that provides these features.

Page
3-40

Troubleshooting Lab

Place the following troubleshooting steps in the order you should perform them.

1. Call the ISP, and ask if there is a problem with the company's Internet service.

2. Call a user who is connected to the same hub as Mark, and ask if she can access the Internet.

3. Power cycle the CSU/DSU for the T-1 providing Internet access.

4. Try to access the company Web site using a computer with a separate dial-up modem connection to the Internet.

5. Ask Mark to try to access a different site on the Internet.

6. Call a user on a different LAN from Mark, and ask if he can access the Internet.

7. Ask Mark to repeat his actions and see if he still can't access the company Web site.

8. Try to access the company Web site using a computer on the network with a registered IP address.

9. Check the NAT router logs to see if they are functioning properly.

7, 5, 2, 6, 8, 4, 9, 3, 1

4 Planning a Name Resolution Strategy

Exam Objectives in this Chapter:

- Plan a host name resolution strategy.
  - ❑ Plan a DNS namespace design.
  - ❑ Plan zone replication requirements.
  - ❑ Plan a forwarding configuration.
  - ❑ Plan for DNS security.
  - ❑ Examine the interoperability of DNS with third-party DNS solutions.
- Plan a NetBIOS name resolution strategy.
  - ❑ Plan a WINS replication strategy.
  - ❑ Plan NetBIOS name resolution by using the Lmhosts file.
- Troubleshoot host name resolution.
  - ❑ Diagnose and resolve issues related to DNS services.
  - ❑ Diagnose and resolve issues related to client computer configuration.

Why This Chapter Matters

Although the process of installing and configuring services such as DNS and the Windows Internet Name Service (WINS) on computers running the Microsoft Windows Server 2003 family is relatively simple, deploying these services on a large enterprise network consists of more than installing software. This chapter is concerned not so much with the mechanics of installation as it is with planning a name resolution strategy. Implementing the Domain Name System (DNS) on a large network requires the careful design of a namespace that insulates the internal network from the Internet and makes it possible to distribute the responsibility for the service among various administrators.

Lessons in this Chapter:

Before You Begin

This chapter requires basic understanding of Transmission Control Protocol/Internet Protocol (TCP/IP) communications, as provided in Chapter 2, "Planning a TCP/IP Network Infrastructure," as well as familiarity with DNS server and client services, as implemented in the Microsoft Windows operating systems.

Lesson 1: Determining Name Resolution Requirements

Name resolution is an essential function on all TCP/IP networks, and the network infrastructure design process includes a determination of what names your computers will use, and how those names will be resolved into Internet Protocol (IP) addresses. As with IP addressing itself, the names you choose for your computers are affected by your network's interaction with the Internet and by the applications the computers are running.

After this lesson, you will be able to

- Understand the construction of DNS names
- Explain the DNS name resolution process
- List the NetBIOS name resolution processes supported by computers running the Microsoft Windows operating system
- Determine what types of name resolution mechanisms you must deploy on your network

Estimated lesson time: 40 minutes

What Is Name Resolution?

TCP/IP communications are based on IP addresses. Every IP datagram transmitted by a TCP/IP computer contains a source IP address, which identifies the computer sending the datagram, and a destination IP address, which identifies the computer that is to receive it. Routers use the network identifiers in the IP addresses to forward the datagrams to the appropriate locations, eventually getting them to their final destinations.

Off the Record   Computers are able to read and process IP addresses easily, but human beings unfortunately cannot. It is not practical to expect people to remember the 32-bit IP addresses associated with Web sites, file system shares, and e-mail addresses, so it has become common practice to assign friendly names to these resources. This is why you use names like www.adatum.com for Internet Web sites, access the computers on your network by browsing among a list of names instead of IP addresses, and address e-mail messages to marklee@adatum.com, rather than to marklee@10.1.54.87.

Friendly names are only for use by people; they do not change the way the TCP/IP computers communicate among themselves. Whenever you use a name instead of an address in an application, the computer must convert the name into the proper IP address before initiating communications with the target computer. This name-to-address conversion is called *name resolution*. When you type the name of an Internet server in your Web browser, the first thing your computer does is resolve that name into an IP address. Once the computer has the address of the Internet server, it can send its first message, requesting access to the resource you specified in the browser.

> **Note**   Although it is possible, in some cases, for computers themselves to resolve names into IP addresses, most of the time the computer sends the name to another system on the network and receives a response containing the IP address associated with the name. The resource that the computer uses to resolve the name depends on the type of name and the application that generates the name resolution request.

What Types of Names Need to Be Resolved?

To design a name resolution strategy for an enterprise network, you must know the types of names that the computers will have to resolve. Networks running Microsoft Windows operating systems use two basic types of names for computers and other resources: DNS names and Network Basic Input/Output System (NetBIOS) names. DNS is the name resolution mechanism that computers use for all Internet communications and for private networks that use the Active Directory directory service provided with Windows Server 2003 and Windows 2000 Server.

All the names that you associate with the Internet, such as the names of Internet servers in Uniform Resource Locators (URLs) and the domain names in e-mail addresses, are part of the DNS namespace and are resolvable by DNS name servers. All Internet service providers (ISPs) have DNS servers, which they make available to their customers, but Windows Server 2003 includes its own DNS server, which you can deploy on your private network.

> **Off the Record**   Active Directory is also based on DNS, and the names you assign to computers on an Active Directory network can also be resolved by DNS servers, but you must deploy a DNS on your own network for this purpose.

Windows operating systems prior to Windows 2000 used NetBIOS names to identify the computers on the network. The NetBIOS name of a Windows system is the computer name that you assign it during the operating system installation. Windows includes several different name resolution mechanisms for NetBIOS names, and chief among these is WINS.

> **Off the Record**   Even though Windows operating system releases starting with Windows 2000 rely on Active Directory instead of NetBIOS names, all Windows operating system versions still include a WINS client, and Windows Server 2003 and Windows 2000 Server still include the WINS server, so that they can interact with computers on the network running the older operating systems.

If all the computers on your network are running Windows 2000 and later versions and you have installed Active Directory, the network is not using NetBIOS names, and you don't have to run WINS servers. You can also disable the NetBIOS Over TCP/IP (NetBT) protocol on your computers using the controls in the NetBIOS Settings box, found in the WINS tab in the computer's Advanced TCP/IP Settings dialog box.

Using Host Tables

In the 1970s, when the Internet was still an experimental network called the ARPANET, system administrators assigned friendly names to their computers, which they called *host names*. A host name is a single word that administrators used to represent the computer's IP address in applications and other references. To resolve host names into IP addresses, every computer had a *host table*, which was simply a text file called hosts that contained a list of host names and their equivalent IP addresses, similar to the following list:

```
172.16.94.97    server1      # source server
10.25.63.10     client23     # x client host
127.0.0.1       localhost
```

The first column of the host table contained IP addresses, the second column contained host names, and the third column (including everything after the # symbol) contained the administrator's comments, which the computer ignored when processing the table. When an application encountered a reference to a host name, it consulted the computer's hosts file, searched for the name, and read the IP address associated with that name. Every TCP/IP computer still contains a host table, although few of them actually use it anymore. On a computer running Windows Server 2003, the host table is called Hosts, and it is located in the %Systemroot%\System32\Drivers\Etc folder.

Because the ARPANET was quite small when the host table was invented, the table was not too large, and the administrators did not have to change it very often. As the ARPANET grew, however, so did the number of computers on the network and so did the size of the host table. Soon, the network grew to the point that host tables became impractical. To address these problems, development began on what came to be known as the DNS.

Using the DNS

At its core, the DNS is still a list of names and their IP addresses, but instead of storing all the information in one place, the DNS distributes it among servers all over the Internet. The DNS consists of a hierarchical namespace, a collection of name servers, and DNS clients called *resolvers*. Each name server is the authoritative source for a small part of the namespace. When DNS servers receive name resolution requests from resolvers, they check their own records for the IP address associated with the requested name. If the server does not have the information needed, it passes the request to other DNS servers until it reaches the authoritative server for that name. That authoritative server is the ultimate source for information about that name, so the IP address it supplies is considered definitive. The authoritative server returns a reply containing the IP address to the requesting server, which in turn relays it back to the resolver, as shown in Figure 4-1.

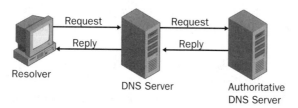

Figure 4-1   DNS servers relay requests and replies to other DNS servers

For the DNS to function in this manner, it was necessary to divide the namespace in a way that would distribute it among many servers. It was also necessary to devise a methodology that would enable a server to systematically locate the authoritative source for a particular name. To accomplish these goals, the developers of the DNS created the concept of the domain. A *domain* is an administrative entity that consists of a group of hosts (which are usually computers). When a DNS server is the authoritative source for a domain, it possesses information about the hosts in that domain, in the form of *resource records*. The most common resource record is the Host (A) resource record, which consists of the host name and its equivalent IP address.

> **Off the Record**   In addition to Host (A) resource records, DNS servers also maintain other types of resource records that contain additional information about the hosts.

Therefore, the full name for a computer in the DNS consists of two basic parts: a host name and a domain name. Note the similarity between the DNS name and an IP address, which also consists of two parts: a network identifier and a host identifier. The host name, as in the days before DNS, is a single word that identifies a specific computer. Unlike host names in the early days, however, current host names do not have to be unique in the entire namespace; a host name only has to be unique in its domain.

Understanding Domains

The domain name part of a DNS name is hierarchical and consists of two or more words, separated by periods. The domain namespace takes the form of a tree that, much like a file system, has its root at the top. Just beneath the root is a series of top-level domains, and beneath each top-level domain is a series of second-level domains.

At minimum, the complete DNS name for a computer on the Internet consists of a host name, a second-level domain name, and a top-level domain name, written in that order and separated by periods. The complete DNS name for a particular computer is called its *fully qualified domain name (FQDN)*.

Understanding FQDN Notation

Unlike an IP address, which places the network identifier first and follows it with the host identifier, the notation for an FQDN places the host name first, followed by the domain name, with the top-level domain name last. For example, in the FQDN www.adatum.com, www is a host (or computer) in the adatum.com domain. In the adatum.com domain name, com is the top-level domain and adatum is the second-level domain. Technically, every FQDN should end with a period, representing the root of the DNS tree, as follows:

```
www.adatum.com.
```

However, the period is rarely included in FQDNs today.

Name Resolution and the Domain Hierarchy

The hierarchical nature of the DNS domain namespace is designed to make it possible for any DNS server on the Internet to use a minimum number of queries to locate the authoritative source for any domain name, as shown in Figure 4-2. This efficiency is possible because the domains at each level are responsible for maintaining information about the domains at the next lower level. For example, if a DNS server receives a name resolution request for www.adatum.com from a client resolver, and the server has no information about the adatum.com domain, it forwards the request to one of the root name servers on the Internet. This is called a *referral*.

> **Note**   The *root name servers* are the highest-level DNS servers in the namespace, and they maintain information about the top-level domains. Software developers preconfigure all DNS server implementations with the IP addresses of multiple root name servers, so they can send referrals to these servers at any time.

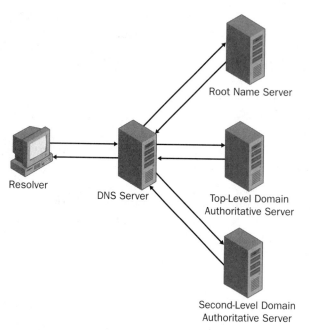

Figure 4-2 The DNS name resolution process

On receiving the request, the root name server reads the top-level domain in the requested name, in this case *com*, and returns a resource record that contains the IP addresses of the authoritative servers for the com domain to the requesting server. With this information, the requesting server can now send a duplicate of the client request to the authoritative server for the top-level, or com, domain. The top-level domain server reads the requested name and replies with a resource record that contains the IP addresses of the authoritative servers for the second-level domain, in this case adatum.

The requesting server can now forward its request to the server that is ultimately responsible for the adatum.com domain. The adatum.com server reads the requested name and replies by sending the resource record for the host called www to the requesting server. The requesting server can now relay the resource record to the client that originally requested the resolution of the www.adatum.com FQDN. The client reads the IP address for www.adatum.com from the resource record and uses it to send packets to that server.

Reverse Name Resolution

The name resolution process described in the previous section is designed to convert DNS names into IP addresses. However, there are occasions when it is necessary for a computer to convert an IP address into a DNS name. This is called a *reverse name resolution*. Because the domain hierarchy is broken down by names, there is no apparent way to resolve an IP address into a name using iterative queries, except by forwarding the reverse name resolution request to every DNS server on the Internet, which is obviously impractical.

To address this problem, the developers of the DNS created a special domain called in-addr.arpa (described in RFC 1035, "Domain Implementation and Specification"), specifically designed for reverse name resolution. The in-addr.arpa second-level domain contains four additional levels of subdomains. Each of the four levels consists of subdomains that are named using the numerals 0 to 255. For example, beneath in-addr.arpa, there are 256 third-level domains, numbered from 0 to 255. Each of those 256 third-level domains has 256 fourth-level domains beneath it, also numbered from 0 to 255. Each fourth-level domain has 256 fifth-level domains and the fifth-level domains have 256 sixth-level domains, as shown in Figure 4-3.

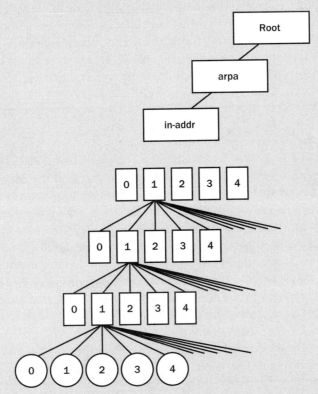

Figure 4-3   The DNS reverse lookup domain

Using this hierarchy, it is possible to express an IP address as a domain name, and to create a resource record in the domain that contains the name associated with the IP address. For example, to resolve the IP address 192.168.89.34 into a name, a DNS server would locate a domain called 34.89.168.192.in-addr.arpa in the usual manner and read the contents of a special type of resource record called a *Pointer (PTR)* resource record to determine the name associated with that IP address. The IP address is reversed in the domain name because in IP addresses, the host identifier is on the right, and in FQDNs, the host name is on the left.

Speeding Up the DNS

Although this might seem like a long and tedious process, the DNS name resolution procedure usually occurs in a few seconds or less. Several DNS elements speed up the process. The first reason for the quick responses is that the most commonly used top-level domains, such as com, org, and net, are actually hosted by the root name servers, eliminating one iteration from the request referral process.

The second reason is that most DNS server implementations maintain a cache of information they receive from other DNS servers. When a server possesses information about a requested FQDN in its cache, it responds directly using the cached information rather than sending another referral to the authoritative server for the FQDN's domain. Therefore, if you have a DNS server on your network that has just successfully resolved the name www.adatum.com by contacting the adatum.com server, a second user trying to access the same host a few minutes later would receive an immediate reply from the local DNS server rather than having to wait for the entire referral process to repeat.

DNS Query Types

DNS servers recognize two types of name resolution requests: *recursive queries* and *iterative queries*. In a recursive query, the DNS server receiving the name resolution request takes full responsibility for resolving the name. If the server possesses information about the requested name, it replies immediately to the requestor. If the server has no information about the name, it sends referrals to other DNS servers until it obtains the information it needs. TCP/IP client computers send recursive queries to their designated DNS servers. In an iterative query, the servers that receive the name resolution request immediately respond with the best information they possess at the time, whether that information is a fully resolved name or a reference to another DNS server. DNS servers use iterative queries when communicating with each other. It is considered impolite to configure one DNS server to send a recursive query to another DNS server, except in the case of a special type of server called a forwarder, which is specifically configured to interact with other servers in this way.

Understanding the Domain Hierarchy Levels

The top two levels of the DNS hierarchy, the root and the top-level domains, exist primarily to respond to queries for information about other domains. The root name servers do nothing but respond to millions of iterative requests by sending out the addresses of the authoritative servers for the top-level domains.

> **Note**   There are seven primary top-level domains: com, net, org, edu, mil, gov, and int, plus two-letter international domain names representing most of the countries in the world, such as fr for France and de for Deutschland (Germany). Recently, a number of newer top-level domains promoted by Internet entrepreneurs, such as biz and info, have been added.

Each top-level domain has its own collection of second-level domains. Individuals and organizations can lease these domains for their own use. For example, the second-level domain adatum.com belongs to a company that purchased the name from one of the many Internet registrars now in the business of selling domain names to consumers. For the payment of an annual fee, you can purchase the rights to a second-level domain.

To use the domain name, you must supply the registrar with the IP addresses of the DNS servers that you want to be the authoritative sources for information about this domain. The administrators of the top-level domain servers then create resource records pointing to these authoritative sources, so that any com server receiving a request to resolve a name in the adatum.com domain can reply with the addresses of the adatum.com servers.

> **Planning**   To create authoritative sources for your domain, you can deploy your own DNS servers using Windows Server 2003 or another operating system, or you can pay to use your ISP's DNS servers.

> **Real World   Domain Naming**
>
> After you purchase the rights to a second-level domain, you can create as many hosts as you want in that domain simply by creating new resource records on the authoritative servers. You can also create as many additional domain levels as you want. For example, you can create the subdomains sales.adatum.com and marketing.adatum.com, and then populate each of these subdomains with hosts. The only limitations to the subdomains and hosts you can create in your second-level domain are that each domain name can be no more than 63 characters long, and that the total FQDN (including the trailing period) can be no more than 255 characters long. For the convenience of users and administrators, most domain names do not even approach these limitations.

Determining DNS Requirements

If you plan to give network users client access to the Internet, they must have direct access to one or more DNS servers. You can run your own DNS servers on your network for this purpose, or you can use your ISP's DNS servers. You do not need to register a domain name. The clients' DNS servers can be *caching-only servers*, meaning that they exist only to process name resolution requests sent by clients, and they can be located on your private network, with unregistered IP addresses.

Hosting an Internet Domain

If you plan to host an Internet domain, you must register a second-level domain name and give the IP addresses of your DNS servers to your domain registrar. These servers must have registered IP addresses and must be available on the Internet at all times. The servers do not have to be on your network, and do not have to be in the domain you have registered. You can use your ISP's DNS servers for this purpose (for a fee), but be aware that you will occasionally have to change the server configuration to create or modify the resource records stored there. If you maintain your own DNS servers, you can manage the resource records yourself and retain full control over their security. If your ISP hosts your domain, you might have to have them make the changes, and they might charge you an additional fee for each modification.

Hosting Internet Servers

If you plan on hosting Internet servers on your network, you must have access to a registered domain on the Internet, with authoritative DNS servers on which you can create resource records that assign host names to your servers. You can either register your own domain (in which case you must meet the requirements described in the previous paragraph, "Hosting an Internet Domain"), or you can use your ISP's DNS servers, in which case they must create the necessary resource records for you.

Using Active Directory

If you plan to run Active Directory on your network, you must have at least one DNS server on the network that supports the *Service Location (SRV)* resource record, such as the DNS Server service in Windows Server 2003. Computers on the network running Windows 2000 and later versions use DNS to locate Active Directory domain controllers. To support Active Directory clients, the DNS server does not have to have a registered IP address or an Internet domain name.

Combining DNS Functions

In many cases, a network requires some or all of these DNS functions, and you must decide which ones you want to implement yourself and which you want to delegate to your ISP. It is possible to use a single DNS server to host both Internet and Active Directory domains, as well as to provide name resolution services for clients. However, when planning a DNS name resolution strategy for a medium or large network, you should run at least two DNS servers, to provide fault tolerance.

> **Important**   If you plan to use your ISP's DNS servers for any functions other than client name resolution, be sure that the DNS server implementation they are using is compatible with the Windows Server 2003 DNS servers you are using, and that they are able to provide the services you need.

You might also want to consider splitting up these functions by using several DNS servers. For example, you can use your ISP's DNS servers for client name resolution even if you are running your own DNS servers for other purposes. The main advantage of using your ISP's servers is to conserve your network's Internet bandwidth. Remember that the Internet name resolution requests that DNS servers receive from client resolvers are recursive queries, giving the first server responsibility for sending iterative queries to other DNS servers on the Internet to resolve the name. When the DNS server receiving the recursive queries is on your private network, all the iterative queries the server generates and their responses go through your Internet access router, using your bandwidth (see Figure 4-4). If your clients use a DNS server on your ISP's network (which is nearly always a free service), only one query and one response go through your router. The ISP's DNS servers generate all the iterative queries, and these queries travel directly to the Internet.

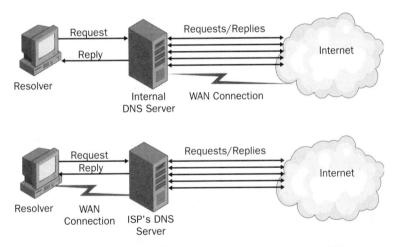

Figure 4-4   Using the ISP's DNS server saves Internet bandwidth

Using NetBIOS Names

If computers on your network are running versions of Microsoft Windows earlier than Windows 2000, they are using NetBIOS names and must have a means of resolving those names into IP addresses. When Microsoft originally incorporated networking capabilities into the Windows operating systems, it relied on NetBIOS names to identify computers and on the NetBEUI protocol for communications. NetBEUI uses these names exclusively; the protocol has no other addressing system. Later, Microsoft adopted TCP/IP as its default protocol, but continued to use NetBIOS to provide friendly names for computers until the release of Active Directory with Windows 2000.

> **Off the Record**   These earlier Windows operating systems are capable of interacting with computers running Windows 2000 and later versions because the computers maintain an equivalent that is compatible with NetBIOS for every Active Directory name.

The NetBIOS namespace is flat, not hierarchical like the DNS namespace. Each computer has a single NetBIOS name up to 16 characters long, which must be unique on the network. In the Windows operating system, the sixteenth character is reserved for a code that identifies the type of resource represented by the name; therefore, the NetBIOS names you assign to computers running Windows operating systems can be no longer than 15 characters. The non-hierarchical nature of the NetBIOS namespace means that it is not as scalable as DNS, and indeed it need not be, because NetBIOS is intended for private networks only, not for huge networks like the Internet.

NetBIOS Name Resolution Mechanisms

Windows has several name resolution mechanisms for NetBIOS names, which are as follows:

- **WINS**   WINS is a NetBIOS name server included with all current server versions of the Windows operating system. WINS registers the names and IP addresses of Windows NetBIOS computers as they start up and compiles its own name resolution database. Every computer running a Windows operating system includes a WINS client that an administrator must configure with the IP address of at least one WINS server on the network. Before the computer running the Windows operating system can communicate with another NetBIOS computer on the network, it sends a message called a NAME QUERY REQUEST as a unicast to its WINS server. The message contains the NetBIOS name of the other computer, and the WINS server responds with the IP address associated with the name. WINS servers are able to provide NetBIOS name resolution services for an entire enterprise network running Windows operating systems.

- **Broadcast transmissions**   When an administrator does not configure a computer running a Windows operating system to use WINS for NetBIOS name resolution, the system attempts to resolve names by broadcasting a NAME QUERY REQUEST message. The computer that possesses the name in the message is responsible for replying to the sender with its IP address. The broadcast transmission method is less efficient than WINS, both because broadcasts generate more network traffic than unicasts and because broadcast transmissions are limited to the local network.

- **Lmhosts**   This text file contains a lookup table that is much like the Hosts file originally used by TCP/IP systems. Lmhosts name resolution is extremely fast, because no network communication is required, but administrators must update the file manually, making the method subject to the same administrative drawbacks as the Hosts file. Computers running Windows operating systems that rely on broadcast name resolution typically use Lmhosts as a backup method for resolving the names of computers that are not on the local network.

- **NetBIOS name cache**   No matter what other NetBIOS name resolutions they use, all computers running Windows operating systems also maintain a cache of recently resolved names and their IP addresses. When a computer needs to resolve a NetBIOS name, it always checks the cache first. This enables the computer to avoid repeatedly resolving the same names.

Windows uses these name resolution mechanisms in combination, depending on the configuration of the computer. When you configure a computer to use WINS, it resolves NetBIOS names by first checking the NetBIOS name cache, then sending messages to its WINS server. If the WINS server fails to resolve a name or is unavailable, the computer reverts to broadcast name resolution, and then to Lmhosts. Computers not configured to use WINS generate broadcast transmissions after checking the cache, then revert to Lmhosts if broadcast transmissions fail to resolve the name.

Determining NetBIOS Name Resolution Requirements

If your network has computers running Windows operating systems that use NetBIOS on multiple local area networks (LANs), running WINS servers is all but essential. Otherwise, your network would be burdened with the additional traffic generated by broadcast name resolution, and you would have to create and update an Lmhosts file for every computer that has to resolve NetBIOS names on other LANs. If all your NetBIOS computers are in the same broadcast domain on a single local area network (LAN), you can do without WINS because the broadcast transmission method is automatic and requires no administration. However, if you have a large number of NetBIOS computers, you might want to use WINS anyway to save network bandwidth.

> **Real World   WINS Deployment**
>
> Deploying a single WINS server is simply a matter of installing the WINS service on a computer running Windows Server 2003 and then configuring the NetBIOS computers with the WINS server's IP address. If your Active Directory systems have to access the NetBIOS computers, you should configure their WINS clients as well. Microsoft recommends that you install at least two WINS servers on your network to provide fault tolerance. You can configure WINS servers to replicate their databases with each other, so that each one has a complete list of all the NetBIOS computers on the network.

Off the Record   Although WINS is generally not a major administrative burden, you might want to consider eliminating NetBIOS and NetBT traffic from your enterprise completely by upgrading all your downlevel computers to Windows 2000 or higher.

Using Local Host Name Resolution

Although network administrators rarely use Hosts and Lmhosts files as primary name resolution methods, these files are useful as fallback mechanisms. If you have computers performing critical functions that would be interrupted by the failure of a name resolution mechanism, you can create a Hosts or Lmhosts file on these computers. The file would contain the names and IP addresses of systems that must be resolvable for the critical functions to proceed.

Practice: Specifying Name Resolution Requirements

For each of the DNS server functions listed below (numbered 1 through 4), specify whether you must have:

    a. A DNS server with a registered IP address

    b. A registered domain name

    c. A DNS server with a connection to the Internet

    d. Administrative access to the DNS server

1. Internet domain hosting

2. Internet client name resolution

3. Web server hosting

4. Active Directory domain hosting

Lesson Review

The following questions are intended to reinforce key information presented in this lesson. If you are unable to answer a question, review the lesson materials and try the question again. You can find answers to the questions in the "Questions and Answers" section at the end of this chapter.

1. What is the technical term for a DNS client implementation?

    _____

    _____

2. In what domain would you find the PTR resource record for a computer with the IP address 10.11.86.4?

    a. 10.11.86.4.in-addr.arpa

    b. in-addr.arpa.4.86.11.10

    c. 4.86.11.10.in-addr.arpa

    d. in-addr.arpa.10.11.86.4

3. What is the maximum length of a single DNS domain name?

    a. 255 characters

    b. 15 characters

    c. 16 characters

    d. 63 characters

4. Which of the following statements are true about the broadcast transmission method of NetBIOS name resolution? (Choose all correct answers.)

    a. The broadcast method generates more network traffic than the WINS method.

    b. Broadcasts can only resolve the names of computers on local networks.

    c. To use the broadcast method, a computer must have an Lmhosts file.

    d. The broadcast method is faster than WINS.

Lesson Summary

- Name resolution is the process of converting the friendly names you assign to computers into the IP addresses that TCP/IP systems need to communicate. The two types of names that Windows computers might have to resolve are DNS names and NetBIOS names.

- DNS is a hierarchical, distributed database of names and IP addresses that is stored on servers all over the Internet. A DNS name consists of a single host name plus a domain name that consists of two or more words, separated by periods.

- Individual users and organizations can lease second-level domain names, giving them the right to create any number of hosts and additional domain levels.

- Depending on the functions required by your network, a DNS server might require a registered IP address, a registered domain name, an Internet connection, or an Internet connection in combination with a registered IP address or registered domain name.

- Microsoft Windows versions prior to Windows 2000 use NetBIOS names to identify network computers. Windows supports a number of NetBIOS name resolution mechanisms, including WINS.

Lesson 2: Designing a DNS Namespace

After you have determined how your network will use the DNS, it is time to begin designing the DNS namespace for your network. The namespace design can include a host-naming pattern for all the computers on your network, as well as the more complex naming of the network's domains and subdomains, both on the Internet and in Active Directory.

After this lesson, you will be able to

- Create an effective DNS domain hierarchy
- Divide domain and host naming rules
- Create a namespace with internal and external domains

Estimated lesson time: 30 minutes

Using an Existing Namespace

If you are designing a new network from scratch, you are creating a new DNS namespace as well, which means that you don't have to work existing domains and hosts into your naming strategy. If the organization for which you are designing the network already has domain names in use, whether internal or external, or has a computer naming strategy already in place, it is probably best to retain those elements and build your new DNS namespace around them.

If the organization already has an Internet presence, they probably already have at least one registered domain name and the use of a DNS server to host the domain. You can continue using the existing domain name, even expanding it to include internal subdomains. You can also continue using the existing DNS server, or migrate the DNS services to a new server on the network you are designing. If you change the DNS server, you must inform the domain registrar so they can alter the IP addresses of the authoritative servers in the top-level domain records. The changes can take a few days to propagate throughout the Internet, so it is a good idea to have an overlap period during which both the old and new DNS servers are operational.

Upgrading NetBIOS to DNS

If you are upgrading a NetBIOS network to Windows Server 2003 and Active Directory, you already have an internal NetBIOS namespace, which you can migrate to DNS, gradually or immediately. For example, if you are currently using WINS for NetBIOS name resolution, you can configure Windows Server 2003 DNS servers to resolve the NetBIOS names by sending queries to your WINS servers. You can also continue to use your existing NetBIOS names by integrating them into your DNS namespace design.

If you are deploying Active Directory on your network for the first time, and you have an existing namespace of any kind, be careful to design your Active Directory hierarchy in coordination with the names you already have.

Creating Internet Domains

Designing a DNS namespace for your organization's Internet presence is usually the easiest part of deploying DNS. Most organizations register a single second-level domain and use it to host all their Internet servers.

Registering a Domain

In most cases, the selection of a second-level domain name depends on what is available. A large portion of the most popular top-level domain, com, is already depleted, and you might find that the name you want to use is already taken. In this case, you have three alternatives: choose a different domain name, register the name in a different top-level domain, or attempt to purchase the domain name from its current owner.

If you are certain that you want to use the second-level domain name you have chosen, for example, when the name is a recognizable brand of your organization, your best bet is usually to register the name in another top-level domain. Although the org and net domains are available to anyone, these domains are associated with non-profit and network infrastructure organizations, respectively, and might not fit your business. As an alternative, a number of countries around the world with attractive top-level domain names have taken to registering second-level domains commercially.

See Also   For a list of the Internet domain name registrars that the Internet Corporation for Assigned Names and Numbers (ICANN) has accredited, see *http://www.icann.org /registrars/accredited-list.html*.

Using Multiple Domains

Some organizations maintain multiple sites on the Internet for various reasons. Your organization might be involved in several separate businesses that warrant individual treatment, or your company might have independent divisions with different sites. You might also want to create different sites for retail customers, wholesale customers, and providers. Whatever the reason, there are two basic ways to implement multiple sites on the Internet:

- **Register a single second-level domain name and then create multiple subdomains beneath it**   For the price of a single domain registration, you can create as many third-level domains as you need, and you can also maintain a single brand across all your sites. For example, a company called Contoso Pharmaceuticals might register the contoso.com domain, and then create separate

Web sites for doctors and patients, in domains called doctors.contoso.com and patients.contoso.com.

- **Register multiple second-level domains**   If your organization consists of multiple completely unrelated brands or operations, this is often the best solution. You must pay a separate registration fee for each domain name you need, however, and you must maintain a separate DNS namespace for each domain. A problem might arise when you try to integrate your Internet domains with your internal network. You can select one of your second-level domains to integrate with your internal namespace, or you can leave your internal and external namespaces completely separate, as discussed later in this lesson.

Creating Internal Domains

Using DNS on an internal Windows Server 2003 network is similar to using DNS on the Internet in many ways. You can create domains and subdomains to support the organizational hierarchy of your network in any way you want. When you are designing a DNS namespace for a network that uses Active Directory, the DNS domain name hierarchy is directly related to the directory service hierarchy. For example, if your organization consists of a headquarters and a series of branch offices, you might choose to create a single Active Directory tree and assign the name adatum.com to the root domain in the tree. Then, for the branch offices, you create subdomains beneath adatum.com with names like miami.adatum.com and chicago.adatum.com. These names correspond directly to the domain hierarchy in your DNS namespace.

When selecting names for your internal domains, you should try to observe these rules:

- **Keep domain names short**   Internal DNS namespaces tend to run to more levels than Internet ones, and using long names for individual domains can result in excessively long FQDNs.

- **Avoid an excessive number of domain levels**   To keep FQDNs a manageable length and to keep administration costs down, limit your DNS namespace to no more than five levels from the root.

- **Create a naming convention and stick to it**   When creating subdomains, establish a rule that enables users to deduce what the name of a domain should be. For example, you can create subdomains based on political divisions, such as department names, or geographical divisions, such as names of cities, but do not mix the two at the same domain level.

- **Avoid obscure abbreviations**   Don't use abbreviations for domain names unless they are immediately recognizable by users. Domains using abbreviations such as NY for New York or HR for Human Resources are acceptable, but avoid creating your own abbreviations just to keep names short.

- **Avoid names that are difficult to spell**   Even though you might have established a domain naming rule that calls for city names, a domain called *albuquerque.adatum.com* will be all but impossible for most people (outside New Mexico) to spell correctly the first time.

When you are designing an internal DNS namespace for a network that connects to the Internet, consider the following rules:

- **Use registered domain names**   Although using a domain name on an internal network that you have not registered is technically not a violation of Internet protocol, this practice can interfere with the client name resolution process on your internal network.

- **Do not use top-level domain names or names of commonly known products or companies**   Naming your internal domains using names found on the Internet can interfere with the name resolution process on your client computers. For example, if you create an internal domain called microsoft.com, you cannot predict whether a query for a name in that domain will be directed to your DNS server or to the authoritative servers for microsoft.com on the Internet.

- **Use only characters that are compliant with the Internet standard**   The DNS server included with Windows Server 2003 supports the use of Unicode characters in UTF-8 format, but the RFC 1123 standard, "Requirements For Internet Hosts—Applications and Support," limits DNS names to the uppercase characters (A–Z), the lowercase characters (a–z), the numerals (0–9), and the hyphen (-). You can configure the Windows Server 2003 DNS server to disallow the use of UTF-8 characters.

See Also   The two primary DNS standards are RFC 1034, "Domain Names: Concepts and Facilities," and RFC 1035, "Domain Names: Implementation and Specification." These and numerous other documents related to the development and operation of the DNS are freely available at *http://www.ietf.org*.

Creating Subdomains

Owning a second-level domain that you have registered gives you the right to create any number of subdomains beneath that domain. The primary reason for creating subdomains is to delegate administrative authority for parts of the namespace. For example, if your organization has offices in different cities, you might want to maintain a single DNS namespace, but grant the administrators at each site autonomous control over the DNS records for their computers. The best way to do this is to create a separate subdomain for each site, locate it on a DNS server at that site, and delegate authority for the server to local network support personnel. This procedure also balances the DNS traffic load among servers at different locations, preventing a bottleneck that could affect name resolution performance.

Combining Internal and External Domains

When you are designing a DNS namespace that includes both internal and external (that is, Internet) domains, there are three possible strategies you can use, which are as follows:

- Use the same domain name internally and externally
- Create separate and unrelated internal and external domains
- Make the internal domain a subdomain of the external domain

Using the Same Domain Name

Using the same domain name for your internal and external namespaces is a practice that Microsoft strongly discourages. When you create an internal domain and an external domain with the same name, you make it possible for a computer in the internal network to have the same DNS name as a computer on the external network. This duplication wreaks havoc with the name resolution process.

> **Important**   It is possible to make this arrangement work, by copying all the zone data from your external DNS servers to your internal DNS servers, but the extra administrative difficulties make this a less than ideal solution.

Using Separate Domain Names

When you use different domain names for your internal and external networks, you eliminate the potential name resolution conflicts that come with using the same domain name for both networks. However, using this solution requires you to maintain two separate DNS namespaces. The different domain names can also be a potential source of confusion to users who have to distinguish between internal and external resources.

Using a Subdomain

The solution that Microsoft recommends for combining internal and external networks is to register a single Internet domain name and use it for external resources, and then create a subdomain beneath that domain name and use it for your internal network. For example, if you have registered the name adatum.com, you would use that domain for your external servers and create a subdomain such as int.adatum.com for your internal network. If you have to create additional subdomains, you can create fourth-level domains beneath int for the internal network, and additional third-level domains beneath adatum for the external network.

The advantages of this solution are that it makes it impossible to create duplicate FQDNs, and it lets you delegate authority across the internal and external domains, which simplifies the DNS administration process. In addition, you have to register and pay for only one Internet domain name.

> **Exam Tip**   The question of how to create DNS domains for internal and external use is vital to the planning of a name resolution strategy. It is also important to understand the ramifications of using the same domain for internal and external use, of using two second-level domains, and of creating a third-level domain.

Creating an Internal Root

When you use the Windows Server 2003 DNS server with the namespace configurations described thus far, your network's namespace is technically part of the Internet DNS namespace, even if your private network computers are not accessible from the Internet. This is because all your DNS servers use the root of the Internet DNS as the ultimate source for information about any part of the namespace. When a client sends a name resolution request to one of your DNS servers, and the server has no information about the name, it begins the referral process by sending an iterative query to one of the root name servers on the Internet.

If you have a large enterprise network with an extensive namespace, you can create your own internal root. You do this by creating a private root zone on one of your Windows Server 2003 DNS servers. This causes the DNS servers on your network to send their iterative queries to your internal root name server rather than to the Internet root name server. Keeping DNS traffic inside the enterprise speeds up the name resolution process.

> **Planning**   Creating an internal root is recommended when the majority of your clients do not need frequent access to resources outside your private namespace. If your clients access the Internet through a proxy server, you can configure the proxy to perform name resolutions by accessing the Internet DNS namespace instead of the private one. If your clients require access to the Internet, but do not go through a proxy server, you should not create an internal root.

Creating Host Names

After you have created the domain structure for your DNS namespace, it is time to populate these domains with hosts. You should create hosts the same way you create domains, by devising a naming rule and then sticking to it. In many cases, host-naming rules are based on users, geographical locations, or the function of the computer.

For workstations, a common practice is to create host names from some variation on the user's name, such as a first initial followed by the user's surname. For example, the host name for Mark Lee's computer would be Mlee. Many organizations also use similar naming rules to create user account names and e-mail addresses. Following the same pattern for DNS host names enables users to keep track of only one name. For servers, the most common practice is to create host names describing the server's function or the department that uses it, such as Mail1 or Sales1.

Whatever naming rules you decide to use for your namespace, you should adhere to the following basic practices:

- **Create easily remembered names** Users and administrators should be able to figure out the host name assigned to a particular computer using your naming rules alone.

- **Use unique names throughout the organization** Although it is possible to create identical host names as long as they are located in different domains, this practice is strongly discouraged. You might have to move a computer and put it in a new domain that already has a host by that name, causing duplication that interferes with name resolution.

- **Do not use case to distinguish names** Although you can use both uppercase and lowercase characters when creating a computer name on a computer running a Windows operating system, DNS itself is not case-sensitive. Therefore, you should not create host names that are identical except for the case of the letters, nor should you create host names that rely on case to be understandable.

- **Use only characters supported by all of your DNS servers** As with domain names, avoid using characters that are not compliant with the DNS standard, unless all the DNS servers processing the names support these characters. The NetBIOS namespace supports a larger character set than DNS does. When you are upgrading a Windows network that uses NetBIOS names to one that uses DNS names, you might want to use the Unicode (UTF-8) character support in the Windows Server 2003 DNS server to avoid having to rename all your computers. However, you must not do this on computers that are visible from the Internet; these systems must use only the character set specified in RFC 1123.

Practice: Designing a DNS Namespace

Fabrikam, Inc., is constructing a new data network and has registered the Internet domain name fabrikam.com. You are to design a DNS namespace for the network and, in the diagram below, write the fully qualified domain name for each computer in the space provided. Base your design on the following information:

- Fabrikam.com is the only second-level domain name you can use.

- The internal network should be in a different domain from the external network.

- The company consists of three internal divisions: Sales, Human Resources, and Production. Each division is to be represented by a separate subdomain in the namespace.

- Each division has departmental servers performing various roles and serving as many as 200 workstations, only some of which are shown in the diagram. Your host names should identify the function of each computer.

- Three servers on an external perimeter network host the company's Internet services: Web, FTP, and e-mail. These servers must be in the domain fabrikam.com.

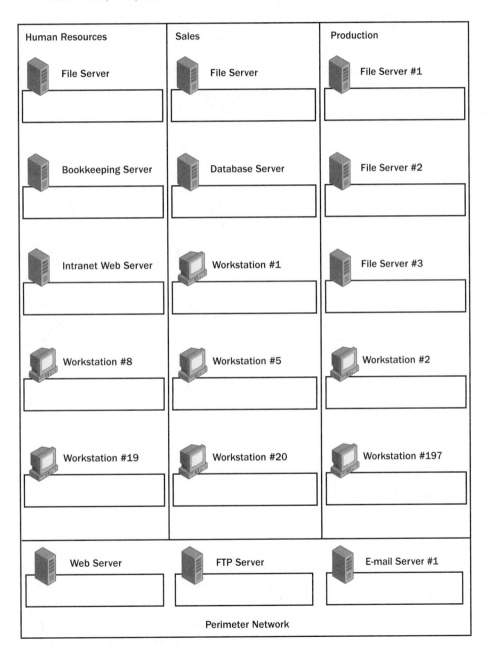

Lesson Review

The following questions are intended to reinforce key information presented in this lesson. If you are unable to answer a question, review the lesson materials and try the question again. You can find answers to the questions in the "Questions and Answers" section at the end of this chapter.

1. Which of the following is the best reason to create subdomains in a DNS namespace?

   a. To speed up the name resolution process

   b. To delegate administrative authority over parts of the namespace

   c. To create identical host names in different domains

   d. To duplicate an existing Internet namespace

2. Why should you never use the same domain name for your internal and external namespaces?

   _____

   _____

3. Which of the following domain naming examples, for an organization with the registered domain adatum.com, conforms to the practices recommended by Microsoft?

   a. An external domain called ext-adatum.com and an internal domain called int-adatum.com

   b. An external domain called ext.adatum.com and an internal domain called adatum.com

   c. An external domain called ext.adatum.com and an internal domain called int.adatum.com

   d. An external domain called adatum.com and an internal domain called int.adatum.com

Lesson Summary

- When creating a DNS namespace, devise naming rules for domains and hosts and stick to them.

- If you require multiple domains for your DNS infrastructure, you can either register several second-level domain names or register one domain name and create additional domain levels beneath it.

- Creating subdomains enables you to delegate authority over parts of the namespace and to balance the DNS traffic load among multiple servers.

■ When combining internal and external domains, the recommended practice is to use a registered domain name for the external network and to create a subdomain beneath it for the internal network.

■ Creating an internal root speeds up the name resolution process by keeping the process wholly inside the enterprise.

Lesson 3: Implementing a DNS Name Resolution Strategy

After you have determined your network's name resolution requirements and designed your DNS namespace, it is time to actually implement the name resolution services by installing and configuring servers. Toward this end, you must first decide how many servers you need and where you are going to locate them, and then determine how you are going to configure the servers.

After this lesson, you will be able to

- Explain the functions of caching-only DNS servers and forwarders
- List the types of zones you can create on a Windows Server 2003 DNS server
- Understand the differences between file-based zones and Active Directory-integrated zones

Estimated lesson time: 15 minutes

How Many DNS Servers?

A Windows Server 2003 DNS server running on a computer with a 700 MHz Pentium III processor can handle up to 10,000 name resolution queries per second, so in most instances, private networks use multiple DNS servers for reasons other than a heavy client load. Some of the other reasons for deploying multiple DNS servers on your network are as follows:

- **Providing redundancy** For a network that relies heavily on DNS name resolution, having a single DNS server means having a single point of failure. You should plan to deploy a sufficient number of DNS servers so that at least two copies of every zone are always online.

- **Improving performance** For a DNS client, the combination of a nearby DNS server and a reduced traffic load on that server means improved name resolution performance.

- **Balancing traffic load** Even when a single server is capable of handling the name resolution requests for your entire network, the network might not be up to the task. Having all the network's DNS traffic converge on a single subnet can overload the LAN and slow down the name resolution process, as well as interfere with the other computers sharing the network. Deploying multiple servers on different subnets enables you to balance the DNS traffic between them and avoid creating bottlenecks.

- **Reducing WAN traffic** When your network consists of LANs at multiple sites, connected by multiple wide area network (WAN) links, it is usually best to have a DNS server at each site. WAN links are relatively slow compared to

LAN connections, and their bandwidth can be quite expensive. Having a DNS server at each site prevents name resolution traffic from monopolizing the WAN connections. This practice also prevents router or WAN connection failures from interrupting name resolution services.

- **Delegating authority**   In a large organization, it might be impractical for a single administrative team to maintain the DNS namespace for the entire enterprise. It is often more efficient to split the namespace into several domains and have the administrative staff in each department or division or office location maintain their own DNS resource records. While it is not essential that you allocate a separate DNS server to each domain, circumstances usually dictate this setup.

- **Supporting Active Directory**   The Active Directory directory service relies heavily on DNS. Active Directory clients use DNS to locate domain controllers and browse the network. You should deploy enough DNS servers to support the needs of Active Directory and its clients.

You should consider all these factors when deciding how many DNS servers you need, and when balancing them against factors such as hardware and software costs and the administrative burden of running multiple servers.

Understanding DNS Server Types

You can deploy Windows Server 2003 DNS servers in a number of different configurations, depending on your infrastructure design and your users' needs.

Using Caching-Only Servers

It is not essential for a DNS server to be the authoritative source for a domain. In its default configuration, a Windows Server 2003 DNS server can resolve Internet DNS names for clients immediately after its installation. A DNS server that contains no zones and is hosting no domains is called a *caching-only server*. If you have Internet clients on your network, but you do not have a registered domain name and are not using Active Directory, you can deploy caching-only servers that simply provide Internet name resolution services for your clients.

> **Off the Record**   The Windows Server 2003 DNS server comes configured with the names and IP addresses of the root name servers on the Internet, so it can resolve any Internet DNS name using the procedure described in Lesson 1 of this chapter. As the server performs client name resolutions, it builds up a cache of DNS information, just like any other DNS server, and begins to satisfy some name resolution requests using information in the cache.

In some instances, you might want to use some caching-only servers on your network even if you are hosting domains. For example, if you want to install a DNS server at a branch office for the purpose of Internet name resolution, you are not required to host a part of your namespace there. You can simply install a caching-only server in the remote location and configure it to forward all name resolution requests for your company domains to a DNS server at the home office, while the caching-only server resolves all Internet DNS names itself.

> **Exam Tip**   Be sure you understand the difference between a caching-only DNS server and one that hosts domains.

Using Forwarders

A *forwarder* is a DNS server that receives queries from other DNS servers that are explicitly configured to send them. With Windows Server 2003 DNS servers, the forwarder requires no special configuration. However, you must configure the other DNS servers to send queries to the forwarder. To do this, from the Action menu in the DNS console, select Properties to display the server's Properties dialog box, click the Forwarders tab, and then supply the IP address of the DNS server that will act as a forwarder (see Figure 4-5). You can also specify multiple forwarder IP addresses, to provide fault tolerance.

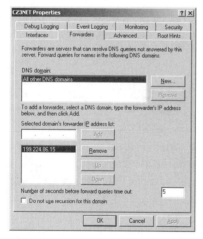

Figure 4-5   The Forwarders tab in a DNS server's Properties dialog box

You can use forwarders in a variety of ways to regulate the flow of DNS traffic on your network. As explained earlier, a DNS server that receives recursive queries from clients frequently has to issue numerous iterative queries to other DNS servers on the Internet to resolve names, generating a significant amount of traffic on the network's Internet connection.

There are several scenarios in which you can use forwarders to redirect this Internet traffic. For example, if a branch office is connected to your corporate headquarters using a T-1 leased line, and the branch office's Internet connection is a much slower shared dial-up modem, you can configure the DNS server at the branch office to use the DNS server at headquarters as a forwarder, as shown in Figure 4-6. The recursive queries generated by the clients at the branch office then travel over the T-1 to the forwarder at the headquarters, which resolves the names in the usual manner and returns the results to the branch office DNS server. The clients at the branch office can then use the resolved names to connect to Internet servers directly, over the dial-up connection. No DNS traffic passes over the branch office's Internet connection.

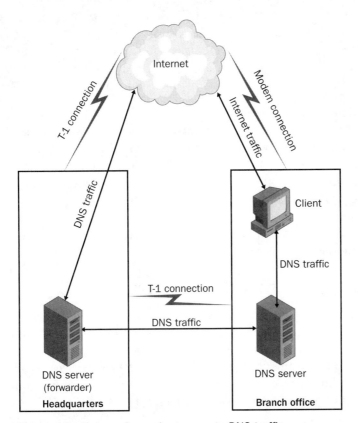

Figure 4-6   Using a forwarder to reroute DNS traffic

You can also use forwarders to limit the number of servers that transmit name resolution queries through the firewall to the Internet. If you have five DNS servers on your network, all of which provide both internal and Internet name resolution services, you have five points where your network is vulnerable to attacks from the Internet. By configuring four of the DNS servers to send all their Internet queries to the fifth server, you create only one point of vulnerability.

Chaining Forwarders

One DNS server that is functioning as a forwarder can also forward its queries to another forwarder. To combine the two scenarios described in the previous section, you can configure your branch office servers to forward name resolution requests to various DNS servers at headquarters, and then have the headquarters servers forward all Internet queries to the one server that transmits through the firewall.

Using Conditional Forwarding

One of the new features in Windows Server 2003 is the ability to configure the DNS server to forward queries conditionally, based on the domain specified in the name resolution request. By default, the forwarder addresses you specify in the Forwarders tab in a DNS server's Properties dialog box apply to all other DNS domains. However, when you click New and specify a different domain, you can supply different forwarder addresses so that requests for names in that domain are sent to different servers.

As an example of conditional forwarding, consider a network that uses a variety of registered domain names, including contoso.com. When a client tries to resolve a name in the contoso.com domain and sends a query to a DNS server that is not an authoritative source for that domain, the server normally must resolve the name in the usual manner, by first querying one of the root name servers on the Internet. However, using conditional forwarding, you can configure the client's DNS server to forward all queries for the comtoso.com domain directly to the authoritative server for that domain, which is on the company network. This keeps all the DNS traffic on the private network, speeding up name resolution and conserving the company's Internet bandwidth.

You can also use conditional forwarding to minimize the network traffic that internal name resolution generates by configuring each of your DNS servers to forward queries directly to the authoritative servers for their respective domains. This practice is an improvement even over creating an internal root, because there is no need for the servers to query the root name server to determine the addresses of the authoritative servers for a particular domain.

Using conditional forwarding extensively on a large enterprise network has two main drawbacks: the amount of administrative effort needed to configure all the DNS servers with forwarder addresses for all the domains in the namespace, and the static nature of the forwarding configuration. If your network is expanding rapidly and you are frequently adding or moving DNS servers, the need to continually reconfigure the forwarder addresses might be more trouble than the savings in network traffic are worth.

Creating Zones

A *zone* is an administrative entity you create on a DNS server to represent a discrete portion of the namespace. Administrators typically divide the DNS namespace into zones to store them on different servers and to delegate their administration to different people. Zones always consist of entire domains or subdomains. You can create a zone that contains multiple domains, as long as those domains are contiguous in the DNS namespace. For example, you can create a zone containing a parent domain and its child, because they are directly connected, but you cannot create a zone containing two child domains without their common parent, because the two children are not directly connected (see Figure 4-7).

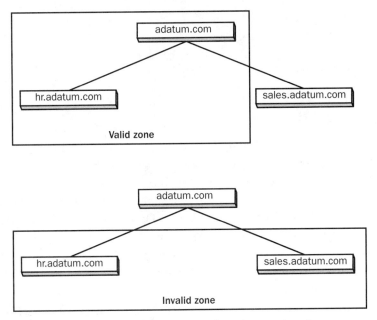

Figure 4-7   Valid zones must consist of contiguous domains

You can divide the DNS namespace into multiple zones and host them on a single DNS server if you want to, although there is usually no persuasive reason to do so. The DNS server in Windows Server 2003 can support as many as 200,000 zones on a single server, although it is hard to imagine what scenario would require this many. In most cases, an administrator creates multiple zones on a server and then delegates most of them to other servers, which then become responsible for hosting them.

Understanding Zone Types

Every zone consists of a zone database, which contains the resource records for the domains in that zone. The DNS server in Windows Server 2003 supports three zone types (see Figure 4-8), which specify where the server stores the zone database and what kind of information it contains. The three zone types are as follows:

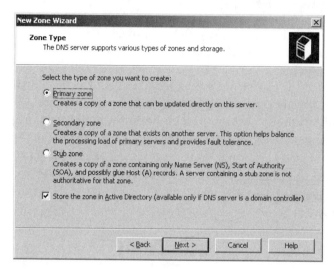

Figure 4-8   The Zone Type page of the New Zone Wizard

- **Primary zone** A primary zone contains the master copy of the zone database, where administrators make all changes to the zone's resource records. By default, if your DNS server is also a domain controller, the primary zone data will be stored in Active Directory to ease administration, improve replication, and increase security. If you clear the Store The Zone In Active Directory (Available Only If DNS Server Is A Domain Controller) check box, the server creates a primary master zone database file on the local drive. This is a simple text file that is compliant with most non-Windows DNS server implementations.

- **Secondary zone** A duplicate of a primary zone on another server, the secondary zone contains a backup copy of the primary master zone database file, stored as an identical text file on the server's local drive. You cannot modify the resource records in a secondary zone manually; you can only update them by replicating the primary master zone database file, using a process called a *zone transfer*. You should always create at least one secondary zone for each primary zone in your namespace, both to provide fault tolerance and to balance the DNS traffic load. You typically create secondary zones only when you decide not to store the primary zone in Active Directory.

- **Stub zone** A copy of a primary zone that contains Start Of Authority (SOA) and Name Server (NS) resource records, plus the Host (A) resource records that identify the authoritative servers for the zone, the stub zone forwards or refers requests. When you create a stub zone, you configure it with the IP address of the server that hosts the zone from which you created the stub. When the server hosting the stub zone receives a query for a name in that zone, it either forwards the request to the host of the zone or replies with a referral to that host, depending on whether the query is recursive or iterative.

You can use each of these zone types to create forward lookup zones or reverse lookup zones. Forward lookup zones contain name-to-address mappings and reverse lookup zones contain address-to-name mappings. If you want a DNS server to perform name and address resolutions for a particular domain, you must create both forward and reverse lookup zones containing that domain.

Practice: Understanding DNS Server Functions

For each of the statements listed below (numbered 1 through 4), specify whether the DNS server being described is an example of:

a. A caching-only server

b. A forwarder

c. Conditional forwarding

d. A server with a stub zone

1. A DNS server that contains only SOA, NS, and A resource records

2. A DNS server that receives all the unresolvable queries from another server, which has been specifically configured to send them

3. A DNS server with no zones that services client name resolution requests

4. A DNS server that sends all name resolution requests for a specific domain to another server

Using File-Based Zones

When you create primary and secondary zones, and do not configure the DNS server to store them in Active Directory, you must configure zone transfers from the primary to the secondaries to keep them updated. In a *zone transfer*, the server hosting the primary zone copies the primary master zone database file to the secondary zone so that their resource records are identical. This enables the secondary zone to perform authoritative name resolutions for the domains in the zone, just as the primary can. You can configure zone transfers to occur when you modify the contents of the primary master zone database file, or at regular intervals.

Originally, the DNS standards defined the zone transfer process as a complete replication of the entire zone database file. At specified times, the DNS server hosting the primary zone transmits the file to all the servers hosting secondary copies of that zone. File-based zone transfers use a relatively simple technique in which the servers transmit the zone database file in its native form, or sometimes with compression. You must manually create secondary zones and configure the servers to perform the zone transfers. A later DNS standard document (RFC 1995, "Incremental Zone Transfer in DNS") defines a new replication method called *incremental zone transfers*. An incremental zone transfer consists of only the data that has changed since the last zone transfer. The Windows Server 2003 DNS server supports incremental zone transfers, but reverts to full transfers when one of the servers does not support the new standard.

> **Planning**   A Windows Server 2003 DNS server can host both primary and secondary zones on the same server, so you don't have to install additional servers just to create secondary zones. You can configure each of your DNS servers to host a primary zone, and then create secondary zones on each server for one or more of the primaries on other servers. Each primary can have multiple secondaries located on servers throughout the network. This provides not only fault tolerance, but also prevents all the traffic for a single zone from flooding a single LAN.

Using Active Directory-Integrated Zones

When you are running the DNS server service on a computer that is an Active Directory domain controller and you select the Store The Zone In Active Directory (Available Only If DNS Server Is A Domain Controller) check box while creating a zone in the New Zone Wizard, the server does not create a zone database file. Instead, the server stores the DNS resource records for the zone in the Active Directory database. Storing the DNS database in Active Directory provides a number of advantages including ease of administration, conservation of network bandwidth, and increased security.

In Active Directory-integrated zones, the zone database is replicated automatically along with all other Active Directory data. Active Directory uses a multiple master replication system so that copies of the database are updated on all domain controllers in the domain. You don't have to create secondary zones or manually configure zone transfers because Active Directory performs the database replication automatically.

By default, Windows Server 2003 replicates the database for a primary zone stored in Active Directory to all the other domain controllers running the DNS server in the Active Directory domain where the primary is located. You can also modify the scope of zone database replication to keep copies on all domain controllers throughout the enterprise, or on all domain controllers in the Active directory domain, whether or not they are running the DNS server. If all your domain controllers are running Windows Server 2003, you can also create a custom replication scope that copies the zone database to the domain controllers you specify. To modify the replication scope for an Active Directory-integrated zone, open the zone's Properties dialog box in the DNS console, and in the General tab, click Change next to Replication: All DNS Servers In the Active Directory Domain to display the Change Zone Replication Scope dialog box. Then, select the replication scope you want to use and click OK.

> **Important**   Both DNS and Active Directory use administrative entities called domains, but the two are not necessarily congruent. For the sake of clarity, you might want to consider creating an Active Directory domain hierarchy that corresponds to your DNS domain hierarchy, but if you don't, be sure that everyone responsible for these two services remembers the distinction between DNS domains and Active Directory domains.

Active Directory conserves network bandwidth by replicating only the DNS data that has changed since the last replication, and by compressing the data before transmitting it over the network. The zone replications also use the full security capabilities of Active Directory, which are considerably more robust than those of file-based zone transfers.

Because Windows Server 2003 automatically replicates the Active Directory database to other domain controllers, creating secondary zones is not a prerequisite for replication. Indeed, you cannot create an Active Directory-integrated secondary zone. However, you can create a file-based secondary zone from an Active Directory-integrated primary zone, and there are occasions when you might want to do this. For example, if no other domain controllers are running DNS in the Active Directory domain, there are no other domain controllers in the domain, or your other DNS servers are not running Windows Server 2003, you might have to create a standard secondary zone instead of relying on Active Directory replication. If you do this, you must manually configure the DNS servers to perform zone transfers in the normal manner.

Practice: Creating a Zone

In this practice, you implement the namespace design you created in the practice for Lesson 2 of this chapter by creating a new DNS zone on your Server01 computer and then populating that zone with subdomains and resource records corresponding to your Fabrikam, Inc., namespace.

Exercise 1: Creating a Zone

In this procedure, you create a new DNS zone on Server01. This zone is for practice purposes only and will not interact or interfere with the existing zones.

1. Log on to Server01 as Administrator.

2. Click Start, point to All Programs, point to Administrative Tools, and then click DNS. The DNS console appears, with SERVER01 (local) listed in the console tree.

3. Expand the Forward Lookup Zones folder.

4. Select the Forward Lookup Zones folder and then, on the Action menu, click New Zone. The New Zone Wizard appears.

5. Click Next. The Zone Type page appears.

6. Leave the (default) Primary Zone, Creates A Copy Of A Zone That Can Be Updated Directly On This Server option button selected and then clear the Store The Zone In Active Directory (Available Only If DNS Server Is A Domain Controller) check box. Click Next. The Zone Name page appears.

7. Type **fabrikam.com** in the Zone Name text box and then click Next. The Zone File page appears.

8. Verify that the default Create A New File With This File Name option is selected and the default file name is supplied (fabrikam.com.dns). Click Next. The Dynamic Update page appears.

9. Click Next to accept the default Do Not Allow Dynamic Updates, Dynamic Updates Of Resource Records Are Not Accepted By This Zone, You Must Update These Records Manually option button. The Completing The New Zone Wizard page appears.

10. Click Finish. A new fabrikam.com zone icon appears in the Forward Lookup Zones folder.

11. Leave the DNS console open for the next exercise.

Exercise 2: Creating Subdomains

In this procedure, you create subdomains corresponding to your namespace design in the fabrikam.com zone. The subdomains enable you to create the resource records for the computers in the subdomains.

1. In the DNS console, select the fabrikam.com zone in the console tree and, from the Action menu, select New Domain. A New DNS Domain dialog box appears.

2. Type the name you selected as the internal third-level domain name for fabrikam.com during your Lesson 2 practice and then click OK. The new subdomain appears in the detail pane.

> **Important** When typing the subdomain name in the New DNS Domain dialog box, type only the third-level domain name. For example, if you chose int.fabrikam.com as the internal domain for your namespace, you would type **int** in the dialog box, not **int.fabrikam.com**. Each domain you create is added to the existing domain structure in the zone.

3. Repeat steps 1 and 2 to create all the other subdomains in your namespace design.

4. For example, to create a subdomain called hr.int.fabrikam.com, you would expand the fabrikam.com zone, select the int domain, and create a new domain within it, giving the new domain the name hr.

5. Leave the DNS console open for the next exercise.

Exercise 3: Creating Resource Records

In this procedure, you populate the zone and subdomains with resource records corresponding to the computers in your Fabrikam, Inc., namespace design.

1. Select the fabrikam.com zone in the console tree.

2. From the Action menu, select New Host (A). The New Host dialog box appears.

3. In the Name (Use Parent Domain Name If Blank) text box, type the host name you selected for the Web server in the perimeter network.

> **Important**   Type only the host name, not the FQDN, in the text box. Notice that in the Fully Qualified Domain Name (FQDN) box, the console automatically appends the domain name to the host name you supply and displays the FQDN for the resource record.

4. Type **10.10.10.1** in the IP Address text box and then click Add Host. A DNS message box appears, stating that the server successfully created the host resource record.

5. Click OK. The New Host dialog box reappears with the Name text box blanked out, ready to create another Host (A) resource record.

6. Repeat steps 3 to 5 to create Host (A) resource records for the FTP and e-mail servers in the perimeter network, using other addresses on the same subnet.

7. Select each of the subdomains you created in the fabrikam.com zone in Procedure 2 and create Host (A) resource records for the computers in the subdomains, using the process outlined in steps 2 to 5.

   When you are finished, all the computers in your namespace design should have Host (A) resource records in the fabrikam.com domain with FQDNs corresponding to those in the diagram you created in your Lesson 2 practice.

8. Close the DNS console.

Lesson Review

The following questions are intended to reinforce key information presented in this lesson. If you are unable to answer a question, review the lesson materials and try the question again. You can find answers to the questions in the "Questions and Answers" section at the end of this chapter.

1. Which of the following DNS zone types cannot be stored in the Active Directory database?

   a. Primary

   b. Secondary

   c. Stub

   d. None of the above

2. Storing DNS resource records in the Active Directory database eliminates the need for which of the following? (Choose all correct answers.)

   a. Stub zones

   b. Secondary zones

   c. Zone transfers

   d. Primary zones

3. The DNS namespace for a company consists of one second-level domain, which has three child subdomains. Each of the three child subdomains also has three subdomains, at the fourth level. What is the maximum number of domains that you can include in a zone that does not contain the second-level domain?

   a. 1

   b. 3

   c. 4

   d. 12

Lesson Summary

■ In addition to supporting clients, administrators deploy multiple DNS servers to provide fault tolerance, balance the client load and the network traffic, delegate authority over specific domains, and support Active Directory.

■ A caching-only server is a DNS server that is not the authority for any domains, but simply provides name resolution services for clients.

- You can configure a DNS server to forward all name resolution requests it cannot resolve itself to a server called a forwarder.

- A zone is an administrative entity on a DNS server that represents a specific portion of the DNS namespace. There are three types of zones: primary, secondary, and stub.

- You can configure a Windows Server 2003 DNS server to store zone databases either in files, requiring a replication process called a zone transfer, or in Active Directory, which replicates them automatically.

Lesson 4: Implementing a NetBIOS Name Resolution Strategy

If you have determined that your network must use NetBIOS names to support computers running versions of Windows earlier than Windows 2000, you have two name resolution alternatives: the broadcast transmission method or WINS.

After this lesson, you will be able to

■ Create and deploy an Lmhosts file

■ Configure WINS servers to replicate their databases

Estimated lesson time: 15 minutes

Using Broadcasts with Lmhosts

The broadcast transmission method of NetBIOS name resolution by itself is suitable only for small, single-segment networks, because broadcast transmissions do not propagate beyond the boundaries of the LAN. However, it is possible to use broadcasts in combination with an Lmhosts file to provide a complete NetBIOS name resolution method for multi-segment networks.

Exam Tip   The broadcast name resolution method requires no manual configuration or administration. NetBIOS computers that you have not configured as WINS clients use broadcasts to resolve names automatically. However, to provide name resolution for NetBIOS computers on other networks, you must create an Lmhosts file and deploy it on each NetBIOS computer.

As described earlier in this chapter, an Lmhosts file is a lookup table containing NetBIOS names and their equivalent IP addresses. Because you have to create the Lmhosts file manually, the easiest way to implement this solution is to create a single file and deploy it on all the NetBIOS computers on your network. To do this, you create the file and store it on a network share that is accessible from all the NetBIOS computers. On each NetBIOS computer, you open the Advanced TCP/IP Settings dialog box in the Internet Protocol (TCP/IP) Properties dialog box, click the WINS tab, and select the Enable Lmhosts Lookup check box (see Figure 4-9). Then you click Import Lmhosts and browse to the file you created, to copy it to the computer.

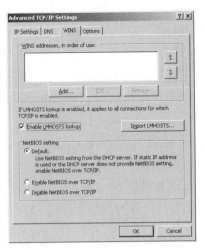

Figure 4-9   The WINS tab in the Advanced TCP/IP Settings dialog box

After you have completed this procedure, the computer will use the broadcast method to resolve NetBIOS names, and if this method fails, it will try to look up the name in the Lmhosts file. If the computer does not find the name in the Lmhosts file, name resolution fails.

Creating an Lmhosts File

Creating an Lmhosts file is largely a matter of typing the NetBIOS names and IP addresses of the computers on your network that clients must be able to access. There are some additional options that increase the efficiency of the file. In most cases, the use of Lmhosts files is practical only when clients require access to a few key servers on other networks. Creating and maintaining an Lmhosts file that contains entries for all the computers on the network can be an administrative nightmare that is easily avoided by installing WINS servers.

Lmhosts is a text file that you can create using Windows Notepad or any text editor and save to the %Systemroot%\System32\Drivers\Etc folder of a computer running Windows. The basic entries of the Lmhosts file consist of an IP address followed by at least one space, and then the NetBIOS name associated with that address. Following the NetBIOS name and separated by at least one more space, you can insert a pound (#) symbol and type a comment. The system ignores everything on that line after the pound symbol when processing the file. Each entry must appear on a separate line, as shown in the following example:

```
192.168.5.65      Hrserver      #Human Resources server
192.168.9.34      Fserve1       #File server 1
192.168.2.110     Smtp          #Internet e-mail server
```

In addition to the standard name-to-address mappings, Lmhosts also supports a number of extensions that can increase the efficiency of name resolution and simplify the deployment of Lmhosts files. These extensions are as follows:

- **#PRE**   Preloads Lmhosts entries into the computer's NetBIOS name cache

- **#DOM:*domain***   Associates the entry with the domain specified by the domain variable

- **#INCLUDE *pathname***   Causes the system to locate and parse an Lmhosts file at a remote location, identified by pathname, as if it were local

- **#BEGIN_ALTERNATE and #END_ALTERNATE**   Surrounds   a   group   of #INCLUDE extensions, causing the system to process each statement in turn until it locates one of the included Lmhosts files successfully

- **\0*nn***   Allows the use of non-printing characters in NetBIOS name entries

Using the #PRE Extension   The most useful of these extensions, as far as the efficiency of NetBIOS name resolution is concerned, is the #PRE tag. When you add this extension to any standard Lmhosts entry, after the NetBIOS name and before any comments (separated by at least one space), the computer reads the entry during system startup and loads it into memory as part of the NetBIOS name cache. As a result, the computer can resolve the name immediately, using the information stored in memory without having to perform a broadcast name resolution or search the Lmhosts file on disk. An example of the #PRE extension follows:

```
192.168.9.34    Fserve1   #PRE   #File server 1
```

Using the #INCLUDE Extension   The #INCLUDE extension can simplify the process of deploying Lmhosts files. Rather than create and maintain a separate file for each NetBIOS computer, you can create a single Lmhosts file and store it on a network share that is accessible to all clients. For each computer, you then create an Lmhosts file that contains an #INCLUDE entry specifying the location of the common Lmhosts file on the network, as follows:

```
#INCLUDE \\Fserve1\Admin\Lmhosts
```

You use standard Universal Naming Convention (UNC) notation for the path name specifying the location of the common Lmhosts file. However, it is important to remember that the computer must have a way to resolve the NetBIOS name of the server hosting the common file (in this case Fserve1). The best way to ensure this is to create a #PRE entry for that server's name in each computer's Lmhosts file. The #PRE entry should precede the #INCLUDE statement so that the name is already in the NetBIOS name cache when the system processes the #INCLUDE. In addition, for the computer to be able to access the common Lmhosts file, you must add the name of the share where the common Lmhosts file is stored (in this case \Admin) to the list of shares in the HKEY_LOCAL_MACHINE\SYSTEM\CurrentControlSet\Services\Lanmanserver \Parameters\Nullsessionshares registry key on the server.

You can also maintain multiple common Lmhosts files on various network shares for fault tolerance, configuring your NetBIOS clients to access each share in turn until it successfully accesses a file. An example of this technique follows:

```
#BEGIN_ALTERNATE
#INCLUDE \\Fserve1\Admin\Lmhosts
#INCLUDE \\Fserve2\Admin\Lmhosts
#END_ALTERNATE
```

Deploying WINS Servers

In most cases, if your network has a continuing commitment to NetBIOS, it is much easier to install WINS servers than it is to create and maintain Lmhosts files. The WINS service on a computer running Windows Server 2003 is capable of registering and resolving NetBIOS names immediately after installation. After you have installed the WINS servers, you configure the WINS clients on your NetBIOS computers to use them. For example, in Windows XP Professional, you configure the WINS client by adding the IP addresses of one or more WINS servers to the WINS tab of the Advanced TCP/IP Settings dialog box, from the Internet Protocol (TCP/IP) Properties page of your network connection.

Off the Record   When a client computer starts, it transmits its NetBIOS name to its designated WINS server along with its IP address, and the server automatically creates a record for that computer in its database. This process is called *name registration*. After the computer has registered its NetBIOS name with WINS, any other WINS client on the network can resolve that name.

A single WINS server can provide name resolution services for up to 10,000 clients. However, as with DNS, you should always install multiple WINS servers to provide fault tolerance and load balancing. Although WINS servers require no configuration to register and resolve names, you do have to configure them manually to replicate their databases. When you have multiple WINS servers on your network, and you divide your NetBIOS clients among them, each server has its own separate database. To enable each WINS server to resolve any NetBIOS name on the network, you must configure all the WINS servers to replicate their databases with each other.

Configuring WINS Replication

WINS servers can replicate their databases by pushing data to or pulling data from other servers, or both. When you configure a WINS server as a *push partner,* the server sends messages to all its pull partners whenever the database changes. The pull partners then respond by requesting an update, and the push partner transmits any new database records. A WINS server that you configure as a *pull partner* issues requests to its push partners for database records with version numbers higher than the last record it received during the previous replication.

> **Planning** The basic difference between push and pull partnerships is that push partners trigger replication events when a specific number of database changes have occurred, while pull partners initiate replication according to a predetermined schedule. Therefore, a push partnership is preferable when you connect the WINS servers by a fast link and don't mind if replication occurs at any time. Pull partnerships are preferable for servers connected by slower links, such as WAN connections, because you can schedule replication to occur during off hours, when traffic is low.

Because the records on any WINS server can change, it is important for each server to replicate its data to all the other WINS servers. This way, every WINS server has a complete listing of the NetBIOS computers on the network. For the replication process to function properly, you must configure each WINS server to be both a push and a pull partner, but the two partnerships don't necessarily have to be with the same server.

Obviously, if you have only two WINS servers on your network, they must be partners with each other. You configure each server to be a push/pull partner with the other in the WINS console. After creating the replication partner, you click the Advanced tab in that partner's Properties dialog box, shown in Figure 4-10. For the pull partnership, you specify when the pull replication should occur and the interval between pull replications. For the push partnership, you specify the number of updates to the WINS database that must occur before the next replication event.

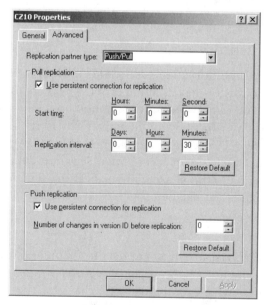

Figure 4-10 The Advanced tab in a WINS replication partner's Properties dialog box

When you have more than two WINS servers on your network, you have greater flexibility in designing your replication topology. When all the WINS servers are connected by fast links, such as LAN connections, one common solution is to configure them in the form of a ring, with each server acting as the push partner to its downstream neighbor and the pull partner to its upstream neighbor, as shown in Figure 4-11. To configure the replication for this topology, you create two partnerships on each WINS server, making one a push partner and one a pull partner.

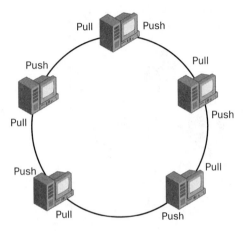

Figure 4-11   A WINS ring replication topology

One problem with this topology is that a failure of any one connection between two WINS servers prevents all the servers from being updated properly. To address this problem, you can create redundant partnerships, traveling in the other direction, to form a double ring topology, as shown in Figure 4-12. The only additional cost is the amount of network traffic generated by the replication process.

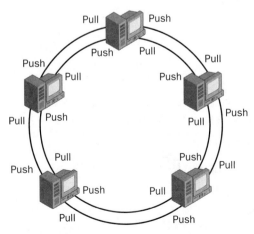

Figure 4-12   A WINS double ring replication topology

If your network consists of multiple sites connected by WAN links, you probably want to minimize the WINS replication traffic passing over those links. The strategy for this is to create only a single push/pull partnership over each link, with replication scheduled to occur during low-traffic hours. For example, in Figure 4-13, the WINS servers at each site all replicate among themselves, using high-speed LAN connections. The administrator then chooses one server at each site to partner a server at the other site. This way, only one connection uses the WAN link, instead of two or more.

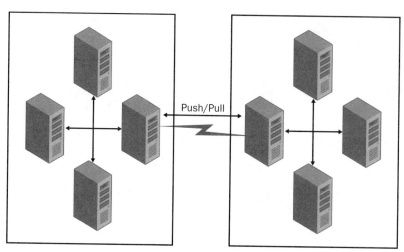

Figure 4-13   Minimizing WINS traffic over WAN links

Practice: Installing a WINS Server

In this practice, you install the WINS service on your Server01 computer.

1. Log on to Server01 as Administrator.

2. Click the Start menu, point to Control Panel, and then select Add Or Remove Programs. The Add Or Remove Programs window appears.

3. In the left frame, click Add/Remove Windows Components. The Windows Components Wizard appears.

4. In the Components box, scroll down and select Networking Services, but do not select or clear the check box to the left of this option.

5. Click Details. The Networking Services dialog box appears.

6. In the Subcomponents Of Networking Services box, select the Windows Internet Name Service (WINS) check box.

7. Click OK. The Windows Components page reappears.

8. Click Next. The Configuring Components page shows a progress indicator as it makes the changes you requested. The Completing The Windows Components Wizard page appears.

9. Click Finish.

10. Close the Add Or Remove Programs window.

Lesson Review

The following questions are intended to reinforce key information presented in this lesson. If you are unable to answer a question, review the lesson materials and try the question again. You can find answers to the questions in the "Questions and Answers" section at the end of this chapter.

1. Why would you need an Lmhosts file on a computer that is already capable of using the broadcast method for NetBIOS name resolution?

   _____

   _____

2. Which type of WINS replication partner is preferable when the two servers are connected by a slow WAN link?

   _____

   _____

3. Which Lmhosts extension enables you to access an Lmhosts file on a shared network drive?

   a. #DOM

   b. #INCLUDE

   c. #PRE

   d. \0nn

Lesson Summary

- Lmhosts files enable a computer that is not a WINS client to resolve the NetBIOS names of systems on other networks.

- In addition to name and address mappings, Lmhosts files can contain extensions that provide additional functions, such as name cache preloading and access to Lmhosts files on shared network drives.

- A WINS server can register and resolve NetBIOS names immediately after installation, but you must manually configure WINS servers to replicate their databases.

- You must create a WINS replication topology that enables every WINS server to have a database containing records for all the WINS clients on the network.

Lesson 5: Planning DNS Security

Although DNS servers perform functions that are intrinsically benign, the possibility of their compromise does pose a significant threat to your network security. Part of the design process for your name resolution strategy is keeping your DNS servers, and the information they contain, safe from intrusion by potential predators.

After this lesson, you will be able to

- List the potential threats to a DNS server
- Describe the techniques you can use to protect a DNS server from unauthorized access

Estimated lesson time: 20 minutes

Determining DNS Security Threats

As you have learned, DNS name resolution is an essential part of TCP/IP networking. Both Internet and Active Directory communications rely on the ability of DNS servers to supply clients with the IP addresses they need. There are two primary security threats associated with DNS: interruption of service and compromise of DNS data. As part of your name resolution strategy, you must evaluate the threats to your DNS servers and the possible consequences, and then take steps to protect the servers without compromising their functionality.

Some of the potential threats to your DNS servers are as follows:

- **Denial-of-Service (DoS) attacks**   Flooding a DNS server with huge numbers of recursive queries can eventually force the processor to 100 percent usage, preventing the server from processing name resolution requests from actual clients. This type of attack does not require a great deal of skill from the attacker, and can be extremely effective in shutting down a network. The inability to resolve DNS names can prevent users from accessing Internet resources, and even from logging on to Active Directory servers.

- **Footprinting**   Intruders gather information about a network's infrastructure by intercepting DNS data, usually to identify targets. By capturing DNS traffic, intruders can learn the domain names, host names, and IP addresses you are using on your network. This information frequently discloses the functions of specific computers on the network, enabling the intruder to decide which ones are worth attacking in other ways.

- **IP spoofing**   Intruders can use a legitimate IP address (often obtained through footprinting) to gain access to network services or to send damaging packets to network computers. Spoofing can enable packets to get through filters that are designed to block traffic from unauthorized IP addresses. Once granted access to computers and services using this technique, the attacker can cause a great deal of damage.

- **Redirection**   In this type of attack, an intruder causes a DNS server to forward name resolution request messages to an incorrect server that is under the attacker's control. The attacker usually accomplishes this by corrupting the DNS cache in a server that is using unsecured dynamic updates.

Securing DNS

A number of techniques can protect your DNS servers and your namespace data from attack, and it is up to you to locate the threats to your servers and to determine what steps to take to protect against them. As with most security problems, it is just as possible to err on the side of caution as it is to be negligent. As an example of negligence, not implementing security measures can leave your DNS servers open to access from the Internet and can allow them to exchange zone transfers and dynamic updates with any other computer. This leaves the servers vulnerable to any of the attacks described in the previous section.

At the opposite extreme, you can close off your network from the outside world by denying all Internet access, creating an internal root, using Active Directory domain controllers for your DNS servers, limiting administrative access to the DNS servers, and encrypting all DNS communications. These measures secure the DNS servers from most forms of attack, but they also compromise the functionality of the network by preventing users from accessing the Internet. There certainly are times when extreme measures like these are warranted, but it is up to you to decide what level of security your network requires.

Some of the security measures you can use to protect your DNS servers from outside (and even internal) intrusion are described in the following sections.

Providing Redundant DNS Services

When you use registered domain names on your network, your DNS servers must be accessible from the Internet, and they are therefore vulnerable to DoS attacks and other forms of intrusion. To prevent intruders from crippling your network by these attacks, it is a good idea to use multiple DNS servers to provide redundant services to your users. This type of protection can be as simple as configuring your DNS clients to use your ISP's DNS server when yours is unavailable or unresponsive. This way, your users can continue to access Internet services, even when someone disables your own DNS server by a DoS attack. Unless the intruder attacks both your DNS server and the ISP's server, name resolution services continue to function properly.

Planning   You can also deploy your own redundant DNS servers, to provide even more protection. Placing a second server on another subnet, or at another site, can give your users a fallback in case an attack takes place on one of the servers. In addition, running your own servers enables you to provide redundant name resolution services for Active Directory, which your ISP's DNS servers probably cannot do.

Deploying multiple DNS servers is also a way to protect your namespace from footprinting. Install one server on your perimeter network, for Internet name resolution, and another on your internal network, to host your private namespace and provide internal name resolution services. Then, configure the internal DNS server to forward all Internet name resolution requests to the external DNS server. This way, no computers on the Internet communicate directly with your internal DNS server, making it less vulnerable to all kinds of attacks.

Limiting DNS Interface Access

Another way of securing DNS servers against unauthorized access from the Internet is to limit the network interfaces over which the server can receive name resolution requests. If you have configured your DNS server computer with multiple IP addresses, you can click the Interfaces tab in the server's Properties dialog box in the DNS console and specify the IP addresses that DNS clients can use to contact the server (see Figure 4-14). For example, if a server is connected to both an internal network and to the Internet, you can prevent the server from receiving name resolution requests that originate on the Internet.

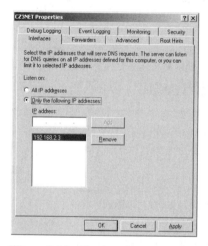

Figure 4-14   The Interfaces tab in a DNS server's Properties dialog box

Securing Zone Replication

Although it is possible to footprint a namespace by capturing name resolution traffic, a more efficient method (for the attacker) is to intercept zone replication traffic. By capturing zone transfer packets, for example, an intruder can get a complete picture of a zone and all its domains and hosts at once.

The best and simplest way to secure zone replication traffic is to deploy all your DNS servers on your domain controllers and store all your zones in Active Directory. Active Directory is then responsible for performing all zone replication. All Active Directory domain controllers perform a mutual authentication procedure before they exchange data, so a potential intruder cannot use IP spoofing to impersonate a domain controller. In addition, Active Directory encrypts all traffic, which prevents anyone capturing the packets from reading the data they contain. Finally, access to the domain controllers themselves is restricted by the policies you already have in place to protect your other Active Directory data.

Planning   If you cannot use Active Directory–integrated zones on your network, you must create standard file-based zones and use zone transfers to replicate the DNS namespace data. Although zone transfers are inherently less secure than Active Directory replication, there are still techniques you can use to prevent intruders from intercepting your DNS data.

One way to protect zone transfer data is to specify the IP addresses of the DNS servers that you allow to participate in zone transfers. If you do not do this, a potential intruder can simply install a DNS server, create a secondary zone, and request a zone transfer from your primary zone. The intruder then has a complete copy of your zone and all the information in it. To limit zone transfers on a Windows Server 2003 DNS server, you open the DNS console, display the Properties dialog box for a primary zone and then click the Zone transfers tab to display the dialog box shown in Figure 4-15. Select the Allow Zone Transfers check box and then choose either the Only To Servers Listed On The Name Servers Tab or the Only To The Following Servers option button. You can then specify the IP addresses of the DNS servers that contain your secondary zones, in either the IP Address text box or the Name Servers tab.

Exam Tip   Be sure to understand the various methods of securing zone transfer traffic and the conditions under which zone transfers are necessary. For example, Active Directory-integrated zones do not need to be replicated using zone transfers.

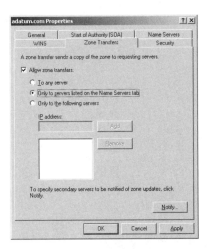

Figure 4-15   The Zone Transfers tab in a DNS zone's Properties dialog box

Although the preceding technique can prevent unauthorized DNS servers from receiving zone transfers, it does not protect the packets containing the zone transfer data themselves. An intruder with a protocol analyzer, such as Microsoft's System Monitor application, can capture the zone transfer traffic and read the data inside the packets. To prevent this, you can configure your DNS servers to encrypt their traffic using the Internet Protocol Security extensions (IPSec) or virtual private networking.

> **See Also**   For more information on securing network traffic using encryption, see Chapter 12, "Securing Network Communications Using IPSec."

Preventing Cache Corruption

Potential attackers might try to load a DNS server's name cache with incorrect information, in an effort to redirect client connections to other servers and gather information from the clients. The Windows Server 2003 DNS server includes a feature that helps to prevent cache corruption. In a DNS server's Properties dialog box, click the Advanced tab (see Figure 4-16) and then select the Secure Cache Against Pollution check box under Server Options. Activating this feature prevents the server from caching unrelated resource records included in reply messages. For example, if a DNS server sends a query to an Internet server requesting the resolution of a name in the adatum.com domain, it would normally cache all the resource records supplied by the Internet server, no matter what information they contained. If you activate the Secure Cache Against Pollution option, however, the DNS server caches only resource records for names in the adatum.com domain. The server ignores all records for names in other domains.

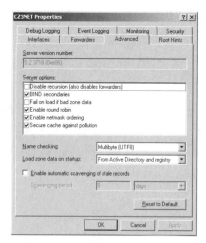

Figure 4-16   The Advanced tab in a DNS server's Properties dialog box

Using Secure Dynamic Update

As the DNS was originally designed, administrators had to create all resource records by hand, typing the host name of each computer and its IP address or other information. This eventually became a problem as the use of automatic IP addressing solutions such as the Dynamic Host Configuration Protocol (DHCP) became more prevalent. DHCP is designed to automatically supply IP addresses and other TCP/IP configuration parameters to computers, which means that it is possible for a computer's IP address to change periodically. Because it would be impractical for network administrators to keep track of these changes and modify the appropriate resource records manually, the developers of the DNS created a new standard, referred to as *dynamic update*.

> **See Also**   Dynamic updates are defined in a standard published by the IETF as RFC 2136, "Dynamic Updates in the Domain Name System (DNS Update)."

Dynamic update enables DNS clients on the network to send messages to their DNS servers during system startup. These messages contain the IP addresses the DHCP server has assigned to the clients, and this information is used by the DNS server to update its resource records with the new information.

Although dynamic update saves DNS administrators a lot of work, it also leaves the DNS servers vulnerable to serious forms of attack. An intruder could create a false dynamic update message and send it to your network's DNS server. The message could state that your company's Internet Web server has changed its IP address, forcing your DNS server to add a counterfeit address to the resource record for the Web server's host name. From now on, Internet traffic intended for your company Web server is redirected to a server under the attacker's control.

To prevent this from occurring, you should create Active Directory-integrated zones whenever possible, and configure them to accept only secure dynamic updates. The procedure is to display the zone's Properties dialog box, click the General tab, and, from the Dynamic Updates drop-down list, select Secure Only (see Figure 4-17).

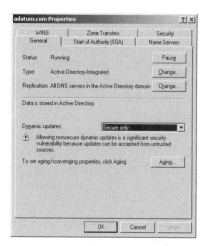

Figure 4-17 The General tab in a DNS zone's Properties dialog box

Using Standard Security Measures

In addition to these specialized DNS security measures, you can also protect your Windows Server 2003 DNS servers from attack using the same techniques you use for any computer on your network. Limiting physical access to the server and using permissions to control administrative access are basics that you should not omit in the case of a DNS server, because intruders can come from inside the organization as well as from outside. You can also use the packet filtering capabilities of your firewall to control access to the computer itself and to Transmission Control Protocol (TCP) and User Datagram Protocol (UDP) port number 53, which is the well-known port number for DNS.

Practice: Understanding DNS Security Techniques

For each of the following DNS security techniques, specify which types of attack they help to prevent: DoS, IP spoofing, redirection, footprinting. (Choose all correct answers.)

1. Using only secure dynamic updates

2. Installing redundant DNS servers on different networks

3. Encrypting zone transfer traffic

4. Using Active Directory-integrated zones

5. Preventing cache pollution

6. Restricting zone transfers to specific IP addresses

Lesson Review

The following questions are intended to reinforce key information presented in this lesson. If you are unable to answer a question, review the lesson materials and try the question again. You can find answers to the questions in the "Questions and Answers" section at the end of this chapter.

1. Which of the following forms of protection does Active Directory provide when you create Active Directory-integrated zones instead of file-based zones? (Choose all correct answers.)

   a. Cache pollution prevention

   b. Encrypted zone replication

   c. Authenticated zone replication

   d. Secure dynamic updates

2. The DNS Update standard was developed as a response to the widespread use of which of the following?

   a. Active Directory

   b. DHCP

   c. Zone transfers

   d. Protocol analyzers

3. Using your ISP's DNS servers as a redundant name resolution mechanism helps to combat which type of attack?

   _____

   _____

Lesson Summary

- DNS servers are subject to several forms of attack, including DoS, footprinting, IP spoofing, and redirection.

- Using redundant DNS servers on different networks provides protection from DoS attacks.

- Securing zone replication prevents attackers from footprinting the network. The best form of protection is to create Active Directory-integrated zones, but you can also protect zone transfers by limiting them to specific IP addresses and by encrypting network traffic.

- Securing dynamic updates and using cache pollution protection prevents intruders from loading a DNS server with false data.

- Use standard network security measures, such as physical access control and permissions, to protect DNS servers from internal attacks.

Lesson 6: Troubleshooting Name Resolution

As you learned in Chapter 3, "Planning Internet Connectivity," DNS name resolution failure is one of the common causes of Internet access problems. On a network running Windows Server 2003 servers, the inability to resolve DNS names can bring client activities to a standstill, because Active Directory relies on DNS and is responsible for controlling all client access to Windows server resources. When a client's attempts to resolve DNS names fail, there are usually two possible causes: either the client is incorrectly configured, or the DNS server itself is inaccessible or not functioning properly. These problems are discussed in the following sections.

After this lesson, you will be able to

- List the reasons that a DNS client might experience name resolution failures
- List the reasons that a DNS server might supply incorrect information
- List the reasons that a DNS server might be unable to resolve names for which it is not the authority

Estimated lesson time: 20 minutes

Troubleshooting Client Configuration Problems

When a client reports a failure to access a TCP/IP resource, such as a "Name Not Found" error message, the first order of business is to determine whether the computer has any TCP/IP connectivity at all. After you have determined that the computer is connected to the network and that it can access TCP/IP resources, the usual method for isolating a name resolution problem is to try accessing a server using its IP address instead of its DNS name. If the computer can access the server using the IP address, you know that the problem is related to the name resolution process.

The next order of business is to check the client computer's TCP/IP configuration parameters. Assuming that the client is running Windows 2000 or Windows XP, display a Command Prompt window, type **ipconfig/all** at the prompt, and press ENTER. The resulting display contains all the computer's TCP/IP settings, including the IP addresses of the DNS servers it is configured to use.

Check to see that the IP addresses listed under DNS Servers in the Ipconfig.exe display are correct for a computer on the client's network. If they are not correct, you can modify them using the Network Connections tool. If the IP addresses of the DNS servers are correct, use the Ping.exe tool at the command prompt to determine if the client computer can contact them, using the following syntax, where ipaddress is the address of the DNS server:

```
ping ipaddress
```

If the ping test fails, you know that either the DNS server is not running at all, or a network connectivity problem is preventing the client from accessing the DNS server. If you have already checked the client computer's general network connectivity, there might be a problem with the router or other connection device that provides access to the network on which the DNS server is located. If this is the case, follow the protocol established at your organization for troubleshooting a network connectivity problem. This protocol might require you to escalate the incident to another technician, or to begin the troubleshooting process yourself. In either case, if the client's computer can access the network and is configured with the correct DNS server addresses, you can be sure that the problem lies elsewhere in the network.

Troubleshooting DNS Server Problems

If a client computer is able to access the network, and you have ruled out other network connectivity problems, the cause of the name resolution failures lies in the DNS server itself. A variety of conditions can prevent DNS servers from fulfilling their functions, as described in the following sections.

Non-Functioning DNS Servers

If a client is unable to ping a DNS server, and there is no client configuration or network connectivity problem, the DNS server itself might not be functioning, or might be suffering from its own configuration or connectivity problem. Assuming the server is turned on and the operating system is running as it should, you should begin by checking the server's own TCP/IP client configuration parameters.

> ### DNS and TCP/IP Configuration
> Windows Server 2003 DNS servers should have static IP addresses. If the server is configured to obtain its IP address from DHCP, then make sure that the DHCP server is manually allocating the address so that it never changes, and that the DNS server is actually using the IP address that the DNS clients are configured to use. You can use the same **ipconfig/all** command to view the DNS server's IP address and other TCP/IP settings, whether or not they are assigned by DHCP.

If clients are able to ping the DNS server but are not receiving replies to name resolution requests, the problem could be that the DNS Server service is not running. Display the Services console and check to see that its status is Started. In nearly all cases, the Startup Type selector for the service should be set to Automatic. If the Startup Type selector is set to Manual, then it is likely that the server restarted and no one manually started the DNS Server service. If the Startup Type selector for the DNS Server service is Automatic and the service is not running, either someone stopped it deliberately or a problem caused it to stop. Check the logs in the Event Viewer console for any indication of a problem, and check with your colleagues to see if someone is working on the server and has stopped it for a reason.

If you can find no reason for the DNS Server service to have stopped, you can try to start it again. Then test it carefully to see if it is functioning properly.

> **Tip** To test the functionality of a Windows Server 2003 DNS server, display the server's Properties dialog box in the DNS console and then click the Monitoring tab. Choose whether you want to perform a simple (iterative) query or a recursive query test and then click Test Now. Windows Server 2003 also includes a tool called Nslookup.exe, which you can use to test the functionality of a specific DNS server from any location on the network.

Troubleshooting DNS Server Health

You can use the Dcdiag.exe command-line tool to analyze the state of domain controllers in a forest or enterprise and report any problems to assist in troubleshooting. Windows Server 2003 Service Pack 1 (SP1) contains an updated version of the tool that includes two significant improvements.

DCDiag /test:DNS This set of tests checks the health of DNS settings for your enterprise. There are seven new DNS-related tests that you can run individually or simultaneously. You can perform these tests on one or all domain controllers in an Active Directory forest. When the tests have completed, Dcdiag.exe presents a summary of the results, along with detailed information for each domain controller tested.

> **Note** You can run the new DNS tests only against Windows 2000 Server (SP3 or later) or Windows Server 2003 family domain controllers.

The new DNS dcdiag test in Windows Server 2003 SP1 uses the following syntax:

```
dcdiag  /test:DNS [/DnsBasic | /DnsForwarders | /DnsDelegation | /DnsDynamicUpdate |
/DnsRecordRegistration | /DnsResolveExtName [/DnsInternetName:InternetName] | /DnsAll]
[/f:LogFile] [/ferr:ErrLog] /s:DomainController [/e] [/v]
```

For example, typing **dcdiag /test:DNS /DnsRecordRegistration /s:TargetDCName /f:LogFileName** at a command prompt performs the /DnsBasic test, and also checks if the address (A), canonical name (CNAME), and well-known service (SRV) resource records are registered for the target domain controller. It also creates a detailed test results report in the log file location specified.

DCDiag /test:CheckSecurityError This new test detects security configuration errors that can cause Active Directory replication to fail, and performs initial diagnosis of the problems. You can perform the CheckSecurityError test on one or all domain controllers in an Active Directory forest. The test performs the following operations:

■ Checks for the availability of a Key Distribution Center (KDC) in both the destination and source domain controller's domains

■ Verifies that the destination domain controller can transmit and receive sufficiently large UDP-formatted packets (used by Kerberos)

■ Verifies that the system clock of the destination domain controller is no more than 5 minutes different from the system time of the KDC in the destination and source domain, and the source domain controller

■ Confirms that the root of each naming context on the source domain controller is configured with the necessary permission

■ Confirms that the source and destination domain controller computer accounts are not disabled, are trusted for delegation, and contain all required service principal names

When the test has completed, Dcdiag.exe presents a summary of the results for each domain controller tested and the diagnosis of the security errors encountered.

This test can be run from the command line using the following syntax:

```
dcdiag /test:CheckSecurityError [/DnsBasic | /DnsForwarders | /DnsDelegation
```

Optionally, you can add the switch **/ReplSource:SourceDC** to the command to identify a specific domain controller as a source in a replication attempt.

> **Important**   You can run the CheckSecurityError test against domain controllers running Windows 2000 Server with SP3 or later, Windows Server 2003 with no service pack installed, and Windows Server 2003 with SP1. However, you can only execute the test itself on a domain controller that is running Windows Server 2003 with SP1.

Troubleshooting Incorrect Name Resolutions

In some cases, client computers are able to complete the DNS name resolution process, but the DNS server supplies them with outdated or incorrect information. If the clients are attempting to resolve names for which the DNS server is the authoritative source, it is possible that the DNS server has bad information in its resource records. This could be attributable to any of the following causes:

■ **Incorrect resource records**   If your DNS servers rely on administrators to manually create and modify resource records, the possibility of typographical errors always exists. If this is the case, the only solution is to manually check and correct the resource records on the server.

- **Dynamic updates failed to occur**   If you have configured your DNS servers to use dynamic updates, and those updates have not occurred for any reason, the server's resource records could contain incorrect or outdated IP addresses. In this event, you can correct the resource records manually, or trigger a new dynamic update by traveling to the computer whose resource record is wrong and typing **ipconfig /registerdns** at a command prompt. This causes the DNS client on the computer to re-register its IP address with the DNS server. If dynamic updates still fail to occur, check to see whether the server supports them and is configured to accept them.

- **Zone transfers failed to occur**   If the DNS server is incorrectly resolving names from a secondary zone, it is possible that a zone transfer has failed to occur, leaving outdated information in the secondary zone database file. Try to manually trigger a zone transfer. If the zone transfer still does not occur, the problem might be due to incompatible DNS server implementations, such as different compression formats or unsupported resource record types. If this is the case, you might have to update the secondary zone's resource records manually, until you can update one or both servers to compatible DNS software implementations.

If the DNS server supplying incorrect information is not the authority for the names it is resolving, it is possible that the server's cache contains incorrect or outdated information. The best solution for this problem is to clear the cache, which you do in Windows Server 2003 by clicking the server's icon in the DNS console and, from the Action menu, selecting Clear Cache.

> **Caution**   DNS servers supplying incorrect information, whether from their own zones or from the cache, might be doing so because an unauthorized user has planted the incorrect information or polluted the cache. See Lesson 5 of this chapter for more information on DNS-related security hazards, and techniques for protecting your servers from them.

Troubleshooting Outside Name Resolution Failures

In some cases, you might discover that a DNS server can successfully resolve names for which it is the authority, but fails to resolve names in other domains. This problem is typically due to a recursion failure, meaning that the server is not forwarding queries for other domains to the appropriate place, or is not forwarding queries at all.

One possible cause of recursion failures is that the server is configured with incorrect root hints. The *root hints* are a DNS server's list of root name server addresses, which it uses to resolve names outside its domain. If the server cannot contact one of the root name servers, it cannot discover the IP addresses of the authoritative servers for the domain that contains the name it is trying to resolve. The DNS server in Windows Server 2003 comes preconfigured with root hints for the Internet root name servers, as shown in Figure 4-18.

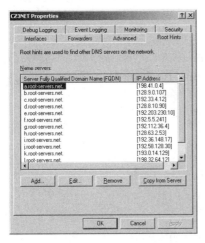

Figure 4-18   The Root Hints tab in a DNS server's Properties dialog box

Off the Record   The addresses of the Internet root name servers rarely change, and it is not likely that a Windows DNS server would be unable to contact even one of these servers, unless someone modifies the root hints. It is more common for a network connectivity problem to be affecting the server's communication with the root name servers.

Incorrect root hints are more likely to cause problems in a DNS namespace that is isolated from the Internet and contains its own internal root. If this is the case, the person who initially configured the DNS server probably forgot to add the internal root name server to the list of root hints, or typed the root name server's address incorrectly. Correcting the root hints in the DNS console should resolve the problem.

It is also possible that the server is configured not to use recursion at all. Windows Server 2003 DNS servers use recursion by default, but it is possible to prevent the server from using recursion by selecting the Disable Recursion check box under Server Options in the Advanced tab in the server's Properties dialog box. You can also prevent recursion when configuring a Windows DNS server to use forwarders. When you display a DNS server's Properties dialog box, you can select the Do Not Use Recursion For This Domain check box. This prevents the server from using any recursion, should the forwarder be unable to resolve a name. If you require the server to use recursion, be sure that these options are not selected.

Lesson Review

The following questions are intended to reinforce key information presented in this lesson. If you are unable to answer a question, review the lesson materials and try the question again. You can find answers to the questions in the "Questions and Answers" section at the end of this chapter.

1. A DNS server that can resolve names for which it is the authority, but not other names, is experiencing a failure in which of the following processes?

   a. Zone transfer

   b. Dynamic update

   c. Authentication

   d. Recursion

2. Which of the following is *not* a reason for a DNS server to supply an incorrect IP address for a name for which it is authoritative?

   a. An incorrect IP address is in the root hints list.

   b. A zone transfer failed to occur.

   c. A dynamic update failed to occur.

   d. A typographic error is in a resource record.

3. When a client can successfully ping a DNS server, but fails to receive any response to a name resolution query from that server, which of the following might be the cause of the problem?

   a. The server is not the authority for the requested name.

   b. The server's cache is polluted.

   c. The DNS Server service is not started.

   d. The server has an incorrect IP address.

Lesson Summary

- When a client computer is unable to resolve a DNS name, and the DNS server is functioning properly, the problem is usually due to a client configuration or network connectivity problem.

- Use Ipconfig.exe to display a computer's TCP/IP configuration settings, Ping.exe to test TCP/IP connectivity, and Nslookup.exe to test a DNS server's name resolution capabilities.

- If a Windows Server 2003 DNS server computer is accessible from the network but is not resolving names, the DNS Server service might not be running.

- A DNS server might supply outdated or incorrect name resolution information because of an error in a resource record, a dynamic update failure, or a zone transfer failure.

- A DNS server that can resolve names for which it is authoritative, but not other names, might have incorrect root hints, or its recursion capabilities might be disabled.

Case Scenario Exercise

You are the network infrastructure design specialist for Litware Inc., a manufacturer of specialized scientific software products, and you have already created a network design for their new office building, as described in the Case Scenario Exercise in Chapter 1. The office building is a three-story brick structure built in the late 1940s, which has since been retrofitted by various tenants with several different types of network cabling. Your network design for the building calls for the installation of four LANs, each of which is connected to a fifth, backbone network. The backbone is connected to the company's home office using a T-1 leased line, and a second T-1 connects the backbone to an ISP's network, for Internet access.

The network in the new building uses the Active Directory directory service, with four computers that run Windows Server 2003 functioning as domain controllers. Each of the four domain controllers has the Microsoft DNS Server service installed. Although the other Litware offices do not use Active Directory, corporate management is considering deploying the directory service throughout the enterprise. This installation is considered the pilot program.

The company owns the litware.com domain name, which it uses for its Internet servers. Because the company Web servers have been moved to your network, you are also responsible for hosting this domain name on the Internet. In addition, the home office wants you to design a DNS namespace that would be scalable enough to eventually include the entire enterprise.

Given this information, answer the following questions:

1. Which of the following domain naming solutions is most suitable for the company network?

    a. Use the litware.com domain for the company's Internet servers and for the enterprise network's internal Active Directory domain.

    b. Use the litware.com domain for the company's Internet servers and create an internal.litware.com domain for the enterprise network's Active Directory servers.

    c. Create an external.litware.com domain for the company's Internet servers and an internal.litware.com domain for the enterprise network's Active Directory servers.

    d. Use the litware.com domain for the company's Internet servers and register a new domain called litware-int.com for the enterprise network's Active Directory servers.

2. Which of the following zoning solutions provides the most security for the internal network and Web servers?

    a. Connect one of the Active Directory domain controllers to the same network as the Web servers and create an Active Directory-integrated primary zone for the litware.com domain.

    b. Connect one of the Active Directory domain controllers to the same network as the Web servers and create a file-based primary zone for the litware.com domain.

    c. Install the DNS Server service on one of the Web servers and create a file-based primary zone for the litware.com domain.

    d. Connect a new computer running Windows Server 2003 to the same network as the Web servers, install the DNS Server service, and create a file-based primary zone for the litware.com domain.

3. In the company's Active Directory deployment plan, each of the other Litware Inc. offices is to be responsible for maintaining its own DNS records, once they deploy their own Active Directory domain controllers. Which of the following DNS namespace designs would best facilitate this intention?

    a. Create a separate third-level domain beneath litware.com for each of the Litware Inc. offices. Create a separate file-based primary zone for each third-level domain at the home office, and a file-based secondary zone at each branch office for that office's domain only. Then give the administrators at each office permission to modify the zone on their local domain controller.

    b. Use the litware.com domain for the entire enterprise. Create a file-based primary zone containing that domain at the home office and a file-based secondary zone at each of the branch offices. Then give the administrators at each office the permissions needed to modify their local zone.

    c. Create a separate third-level domain beneath litware.com for each of the Litware Inc. offices. Create a separate Active Directory-integrated primary zone at each office for that office's domain only, and replicate it on the domain controllers at the other offices. Then give the administrators at each office permission to modify the zone for their domain only on their local domain controller.

    d. Use the litware.com domain for the entire enterprise. Create an Active Directory-integrated primary zone containing that domain at the home office and replicate it to the Active Directory domain controllers at each of the branch offices. Then give the administrators at each office permission to modify the zone on their local domain controller.

Troubleshooting Lab

Using the elements listed at the end of this lab (lettered a through h), create a trouble-shooting flowchart that proceeds logically from step 1 to step 10.

1. A client computer fails to access an intranet Web server.

2. _____

3. _____

4. _____

5. _____

6. _____

7. _____

8. _____

9. _____

10. The resource record for the intranet Web site has not been modified due to a dynamic update failure. The client can now access the Web server using its DNS name.

a. Use Ipconfig.exe to check the source of the Web server's IP address. The Web server uses DHCP to obtain its address.

b. On the Web server, type **ipconfig/registerdns** at a command prompt and then press ENTER.

c. Use Ping.exe to test the client computer's TCP/IP connection to the DNS server. The test succeeds.

d. Use Ipconfig.exe to check the Web server's DNS server addresses. The addresses are correct.

e. Use Ipconfig.exe to check the client computer's DNS server addresses. The addresses are correct.

f. Check the resource record for the Web server on the DNS server. The IP address in the resource record does not match the Web server's current IP address.

g. Check the DNS server to see if the DNS service is running. The service is running normally.

h. Try to connect to the Web server using its IP address instead of its DNS name. The connection succeeds.

Chapter Summary

- DNS is a hierarchical, distributed database of names and IP addresses that is stored on servers all over the Internet. A DNS name consists of a single host name plus a domain name that consists of two or more words, separated by periods.

- Windows versions earlier than Windows 2000 use NetBIOS names to identify network computers. Windows supports a number of NetBIOS name resolution mechanisms, including WINS.

- When creating a DNS namespace, devise naming rules for domains and hosts and stick to them.

- Creating subdomains enables you to delegate authority over parts of the namespace and balance the DNS traffic load among multiple servers.

- When combining internal and external domains, recommended practice is to use a registered domain name for the external network and to create a subdomain beneath it for the internal network.

- Lmhosts files enable a computer that is not a WINS client to resolve the NetBIOS names of systems on other networks.

- WINS servers can register and resolve NetBIOS names immediately after installation, but you must manually configure them to replicate their databases.

- Securing zone replication prevents attackers from footprinting the network. The best form of protection is to create Active Directory-integrated zones, but you can also protect zone transfers by limiting them to specific IP addresses and encrypting network traffic.

- Securing dynamic updates and using cache pollution protection prevents intruders from loading a DNS server with false data.

- When a client computer is unable to resolve a DNS name, and the DNS server is functioning properly, the problem is usually due to a client configuration or network connectivity problem.

Exam Highlights

Before taking the exam, review the key points and terms that are presented below to help you identify topics you need to review. Return to the lessons for additional practice, and review the "Further Reading" sections in Part 2 for pointers to more information about topics covering the exam objectives.

Key Points

- When designing a DNS name resolution strategy, you decide how many domains you need and what to name them. Then you populate those domains with hosts.

- NetBIOS name resolution is required only on networks with computers running Windows operating systems earlier than Windows 2000. For NetBIOS name resolution, you either deploy WINS servers on your network or use the broadcast method with an Lmhosts file for resolving names on other networks.

- To implement a DNS name resolution strategy, you create zones on your DNS servers and populate them with resource records. A zone represents a part of the DNS namespace that can consist of one or more domains.

- To implement WINS, you only have to install the WINS service. However, you must manually configure the WINS servers on your network to replicate their databases with each other.

- Name resolution problems are caused primarily by incorrect configuration of the TCP/IP client. However, the DNS server can also be at fault, due to outdated cache information or a non-functioning service.

Key Terms

Resolver   The DNS client component included in all operating systems supporting TCP/IP. The resolver queries the name server for a host name or address and then returns that information to the requesting client.

Fully-qualified domain name (FQDN)   The combination of a computer's host name and all its domain names, tracing all the way to the root of the DNS namespace.

Iterative query   A DNS name resolution request that instructs the receiving server to respond immediately with the best information in its possession, whether that information is a resolved name or a referral to another server. DNS servers typically send iterative queries to other servers.

Recursive query   A DNS name resolution request that instructs the receiving server to take full responsibility for resolving the name, including sending the query to other servers. The only acceptable replies to a recursive query are a successfully resolved name or name resolution failure. Client resolvers typically send recursive queries to their DNS servers.

Questions and Answers

Page
4-16
Lesson 1 Practice

For each of the following DNS server functions, specify whether you must have:

    a. A DNS server with a registered IP address

    b. A registered domain name

    c. A DNS server with a connection to the Internet

    d. Administrative access to the DNS server

1. Internet domain hosting

    a, b, c, and d

2. Internet client name resolution

    c

3. Web server hosting

    a, c, and d

4. Active Directory domain hosting

    d

Page
4-16
Lesson 1 Review

1. What is the technical term for a DNS client implementation?

    Resolver

2. In what domain would you find the PTR resource record for a computer with the IP address 10.11.86.4?

    a. 10.11.86.4.in-addr.arpa

    b. in-addr.arpa.4.86.11.10

    c. 4.86.11.10.in-addr.arpa

    d. in-addr.arpa.10.11.86.4

    c

3. What is the maximum length of a single DNS domain name?

    a. 255 characters

    b. 15 characters

    c. 16 characters

    d. 63 characters

    d

4. Which of the following statements are true about the broadcast transmission method of NetBIOS name resolution? (Choose all correct answers.)

   a. The broadcast method generates more network traffic than the WINS method.

   b. Broadcasts can only resolve the names of computers on local networks.

   c. To use the broadcast method, a computer must have an Lmhosts file.

   d. The broadcast method is faster than WINS.

   a and b

Lesson 2 Practice

Using the information provided in the Practice, write the fully qualified domain name for each computer in the space provided.

The following diagram contains an example of a correctly designed namespace:

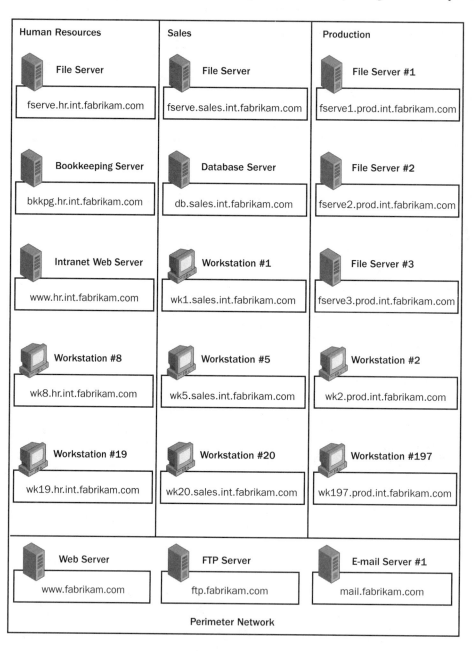

Human Resources	Sales	Production
File Server fserve.hr.int.fabrikam.com	**File Server** fserve.sales.int.fabrikam.com	**File Server #1** fserve1.prod.int.fabrikam.com
Bookkeeping Server bkkpg.hr.int.fabrikam.com	**Database Server** db.sales.int.fabrikam.com	**File Server #2** fserve2.prod.int.fabrikam.com
Intranet Web Server www.hr.int.fabrikam.com	**Workstation #1** wk1.sales.int.fabrikam.com	**File Server #3** fserve3.prod.int.fabrikam.com
Workstation #8 wk8.hr.int.fabrikam.com	**Workstation #5** wk5.sales.int.fabrikam.com	**Workstation #2** wk2.prod.int.fabrikam.com
Workstation #19 wk19.hr.int.fabrikam.com	**Workstation #20** wk20.sales.int.fabrikam.com	**Workstation #197** wk197.prod.int.fabrikam.com
Web Server www.fabrikam.com	**FTP Server** ftp.fabrikam.com	**E-mail Server #1** mail.fabrikam.com

Perimeter Network

Correct answers for this practice can vary, but they should contain the following characteristics:

- The servers in the perimeter network should have FQDNs consisting of host names in the second-level domain fabrikam.com.

- All three internal divisions should be in a third-level domain beneath fabrikam.com.

- Each of the three divisions should have a fourth-level domain name beneath the internal network's third-level domain.

- Each computer should have a unique host name that reflects its function and differentiates it from other computers performing the same function.

Page
4-26
Lesson 2 Review

1. Which of the following is the best reason to create subdomains in a DNS namespace?

    a. To speed up the name resolution process

    b. To delegate administrative authority over parts of the namespace

    c. To create identical host names in different domains

    d. To duplicate an existing Internet namespace

    b

2. Why should you never use the same domain name for your internal and external namespaces?

    Because this practice makes it possible to assign computers duplicate FQDNs that would interfere with the name resolution process.

3. Which of the following domain naming examples, for an organization with the registered domain adatum.com, conforms to the practices recommended by Microsoft?

    a. An external domain called ext-adatum.com and an internal domain called int-adatum.com

    b. An external domain called ext.adatum.com and an internal domain called adatum.com

    c. An external domain called ext.adatum.com and an internal domain called int.adatum.com

    d. An external domain called adatum.com and an internal domain called int.adatum.com

    d

Page
4-35

Lesson 3 Practice

For each of the following statements, specify whether the DNS server being described is an example of:

a. A caching-only server

b. A forwarder

c. Conditional forwarding

d. A server with a stub zone

1. A DNS server that contains only SOA, NS, and A resource records

d

2. A DNS server that receives all the unresolvable queries from another server, which has been specifically configured to send them

b

3. A DNS server with no zones that services client name resolution requests

a

4. A DNS server that sends all name resolution requests for a specific domain to another server

c ·

Page
4-40

Lesson 3 Review

1. Which of the following DNS zone types cannot be stored in the Active Directory database?

   a. Primary

   b. Secondary

   c. Stub

   d. None of the above

   b

2. Storing DNS resource records in the Active Directory database eliminates the need for which of the following? (Choose all correct answers.)

   a. Stub zones

   b. Secondary zones

   c. Zone transfers

   d. Primary zones

   b and c

3. The DNS namespace for a company consists of one second-level domain, which has three child subdomains. Each of the three child subdomains also has three subdomains, at the fourth level. What is the maximum number of domains that you can include in a zone that does not contain the second-level domain?

   a. 1

   b. 3

   c. 4

   d. 12

   c

Page
4-49

Lesson 4 Review

1. Why would you need an Lmhosts file on a computer that is already capable of using the broadcast method for NetBIOS name resolution?

   The Lmhosts file enables the computer to resolve the NetBIOS names of computers on other network segments, which broadcasts cannot do.

2. Which type of WINS replication partner is preferable when the two servers are connected by a slow WAN link?

   A pull partner is preferable.

3. Which Lmhosts extension enables you to access an Lmhosts file on a shared network drive?

   a. #DOM

   b. #INCLUDE

   c. #PRE

   d. \0nn

   b

Page
4-56

Lesson 5 Practice

For each of the following DNS security techniques, specify which types of attack they help to prevent: DoS, IP spoofing, redirection, footprinting. (Choose all correct answers.)

1. Using only secure dynamic updates

   Redirection

2. Installing redundant DNS servers on different networks

   DoS

3. Encrypting zone transfer traffic

   Footprinting

4. Using Active Directory-integrated zones

IP spoofing, footprinting

5. Preventing cache pollution

Redirection

6. Restricting zone transfers to specific IP addresses

Footprinting

Page
4-57
Lesson 5 Review

1. Which of the following forms of protection does Active Directory provide when you create Active Directory-integrated zones instead of file-based zones? (Choose all correct answers.)

    a. Cache pollution prevention

    b. Encrypted zone replication

    c. Authenticated zone replication

    d. Secure dynamic updates

b and c

2. The DNS Update standard was developed as a response to the widespread use of which of the following?

    a. Active Directory

    b. DHCP

    c. Zone transfers

    d. Protocol analyzers

b

3. Using your ISP's DNS servers as a redundant name resolution mechanism helps to combat which type of attack?

Denial-of-service (DoS)

Page
4-64
Lesson 6 Review

1. A DNS server that can resolve names for which it is the authority, but not other names, is experiencing a failure in which of the following processes?

    a. Zone transfer

    b. Dynamic update

    c. Authentication

    d. Recursion

d

2. Which of the following is *not* a reason for a DNS server to supply an incorrect IP address for a name for which it is authoritative?

   a. An incorrect IP address is in the root hints list.

   b. A zone transfer failed to occur.

   c. A dynamic update failed to occur.

   d. A typographic error is in a resource record.

   a

3. When a client can successfully ping a DNS server but fails to receive any response to a name resolution query from that server, which of the following might be the cause of the problem?

   a. The server is not the authority for the requested name.

   b. The server's cache is polluted.

   c. The DNS Server service is not started.

   d. The server has an incorrect IP address.

   c

Page 4-65

Case Scenario Exercise

Given the information provided in the Case Scenario Exercise, answer the following.

1. Which of the following domain naming solutions is most suitable for the company network?

   a. Use the litware.com domain for the company's Internet servers and for the enterprise network's internal Active Directory domain.

   b. Use the litware.com domain for the company's Internet servers and create an internal.litware.com domain for the enterprise network's Active Directory servers.

   c. Create an external.litware.com domain for the company's Internet servers and an internal.litware.com domain for the enterprise network's Active Directory servers.

   d. Use the litware.com domain for the company's Internet servers and register a new domain called litware-int.com for the enterprise network's Active Directory servers.

   b

2. Which of the following zoning solutions provides the most security for the internal network and Web servers?

    a. Connect one of the Active Directory domain controllers to the same network as the Web servers and create an Active Directory-integrated primary zone for the litware.com domain.

    b. Connect one of the Active Directory domain controllers to the same network as the Web servers and create a file-based primary zone for the litware.com domain.

    c. Install the DNS Server service on one of the Web servers and create a file-based primary zone for the litware.com domain.

    d. Connect a new computer running Windows Server 2003 to the same network as the Web servers, install the DNS Server service, and create a file-based primary zone for the litware.com domain.

d

3. In the company's Active Directory deployment plan, each of the other Litware Inc. offices is to be responsible for maintaining its own DNS records, once they deploy their own Active Directory domain controllers. Which of the following DNS namespace designs would best facilitate this intention?

    a. Create a separate third-level domain beneath litware.com for each of the Litware Inc. offices. Create a separate file-based primary zone for each third-level domain at the home office, and a file-based secondary zone at each branch office for that office's domain only. Then give the administrators at each office permission to modify the zone on their local domain controller.

    b. Use the litware.com domain for the entire enterprise. Create a file-based primary zone containing that domain at the home office and a file-based secondary zone at each of the branch offices. Then give the administrators at each office the permissions needed to modify their local zone.

    c. Create a separate third-level domain beneath litware.com for each of the Litware Inc. offices. Create a separate Active Directory-integrated primary zone at each office for that office's domain only, and replicate it on the domain controllers at the other offices. Then give the administrators at each office permission to modify the zone for their domain only on their local domain controller.

    d. Use the litware.com domain for the entire enterprise. Create an Active Directory-integrated primary zone containing that domain at the home office and replicate it to the Active Directory domain controllers at each of the branch offices. Then give the administrators at each office permission to modify the zone on their local domain controller.

c

Page
4-67**Troubleshooting Lab**

Using the elements a through h, create a troubleshooting flowchart that proceeds logically from step 1 to step 10.

1. A client computer fails to access an intranet Web server.

2.

3.

4.

5.

6.

7.

8.

9.

10. The resource record for the intranet Web site has not been modified due to a
    dynamic update failure. The client can now access the Web server using its DNS
    name.

a. Use Ipconfig.exe to check the source of the Web server's IP address. The Web
   server uses DHCP to obtain its address.

b. On the Web server, type **ipconfig/registerdns** at a command prompt and then
   press ENTER.

c. Use Ping.exe to test the client computer's TCP/IP connection to the DNS server.
   The test succeeds.

d. Use Ipconfig.exe to check the Web server's DNS server addresses. The addresses
   are correct.

e. Use Ipconfig.exe to check the client computer's DNS server addresses. The
   addresses are correct.

f. Check the resource record for the Web server on the DNS server. The IP address
   in the resource record does not match the Web server's current IP address.

g. Check the DNS server to see if the DNS service is running. The service is running
   normally.

h. Try to connect to the Web server using its IP address instead of its DNS name. The
   connection succeeds.

2. h, 3. e, 4. c, 5. g, 6. d, 7. a, 8. f, 9. b

5 Using Routing and Remote Access

Exam Objectives in this Chapter:

- Plan a routing strategy.
    - ❑ Identify routing protocols to use in a specified environment.
    - ❑ Plan routing for IP multicast traffic.
- Plan security for remote access users.
    - ❑ Plan remote access policies.
    - ❑ Analyze protocol security requirements.
    - ❑ Plan authentication methods for remote access clients.
- Troubleshoot TCP/IP routing. Tools might include the route, tracert, ping, path-ping, and netsh commands, and Network Monitor.

Why This Chapter Matters

Modern network installations frequently consist of local area networks (LANs) connected by routers. The LANs might be located at a single site or some distance apart. As a network designer or administrator, you are likely to be responsible for ensuring that the networks can communicate. Routers are complex devices that require a great deal of study, and the Routing and Remote Access (RRAS) service in the Microsoft Windows Server 2003 family includes many of the standard functions and protocols used on routed networks today. Even if you work on an installation that uses hardware routers or software routers with a different operating system from Windows Server 2003, the experience you gain by working with RRAS can benefit you on other platforms.

Lessons in this Chapter:

Before You Begin

Before you begin this chapter, you should have a basic understanding of TCP/IP communications and IP routing principles, as provided in Chapter 2, "Planning a TCP/IP Network Infrastructure." Reading Chapter 3, "Planning Internet Connectivity," is also useful, since it contains applications of some of the concepts discussed in this chapter.

Before performing the practice exercises in this chapter, you must install Windows Server 2003 on a computer, using the Setup instructions in "About This Book."

Lesson 1: Planning a Routing and Remote Access Strategy

The common need to connect networks at different locations compounds the challenges that network designers and administrators face in planning, implementing, and maintaining an internal network. As you learned in Chapter 3, "Planning Internet Connectivity," a connection between networks at remote locations requires a wide area network (WAN) connection of some type and a router at each site. The WAN is essentially a two-node network that serves only to carry traffic between the two sites, and the routers determine what traffic is permitted to enter and leave each site. Computers running Windows Server 2003 can function as the routers in this arrangement, using RRAS to provide dynamic routing, traffic management, and security features.

After this lesson, you will be able to

- Describe the characteristics of the WAN technologies most commonly used for remote network connections
- Decide whether to use static routing or dynamic routing on your network
- Select the dynamic routing protocol most suitable for your network
- List the components needed to route IP multicast traffic to an internetwork

Estimated lesson time: 15 minutes

Choosing a WAN Topology

When an enterprise consists of multiple networks at remote locations, connecting them into a single large internetwork is nearly always desirable, but not always economically practical. When deciding whether to connect the network sites, an important part of the process is considering what topologies you can use for the internetwork. Just as with LAN design, in which there are a variety of wiring topologies you can use to connect the computers, internetwork design lets you connect your sites in several different ways.

When you have only two network sites, there is obviously only one topology available. You install a router at each site and connect the routers using a WAN link, as shown in Figure 5-1. In this case, you decide which WAN technology to use based primarily on the bandwidth you need and the cost of the link.

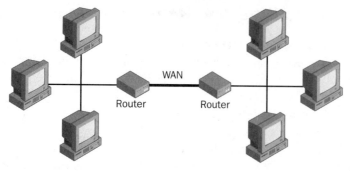

Figure 5-1   Two networks connected with a WAN link

When you have more than two sites to connect, you have more topology choices. The most efficient, and usually the most expensive, remote networking solution is to have a separate WAN link connecting each pair of sites, forming a *mesh topology*, as shown in Figure 5-2. Because each pair of sites has its own dedicated link, the arrangement is highly fault tolerant. Failure of a single link affects only the communications between the two sites connected by that link, and the other connections can compensate by relaying information to the disconnected sites.

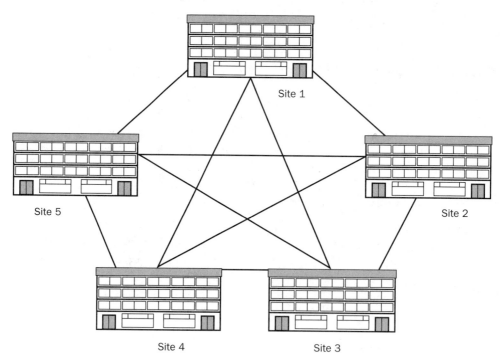

Figure 5-2   Five network sites connected by WAN links in a mesh topology

The problem with the mesh topology becomes obvious when your enterprise has more than three or four sites. Because each connection requires a router at each site and a separate WAN connection, the amount of time and money required to install and maintain them can quickly become astronomical. A network with three sites requires only three WAN connections to create the mesh, but four sites require six WAN connections. By the time you get to an enterprise with eight sites, you must install 28 separate WAN connections and 56 routers to create the mesh.

Off the Record   You can implement a large mesh topology using relatively inexpensive equipment, such as dial-up modems and telephone lines, but the performance of an internetwork using slow connections like these is usually not worth the effort.

Another method for connecting sites is to create a *ring topology*. In this topology, the network designer connects each site to its two closest neighbors, as shown in Figure 5-3. This topology requires only two routers and two WAN connections at each site, so it is much easier to install and maintain, as well as being more affordable. However, the ring topology is less efficient than the mesh, because it is not possible for the network at each site to communicate directly with every other site. Unless two sites are adjacent in the ring, traffic has to pass through one or more intermediate sites to get to its destination. This means more traffic on each WAN link, possibly requiring a faster connection than is needed with a mesh topology.

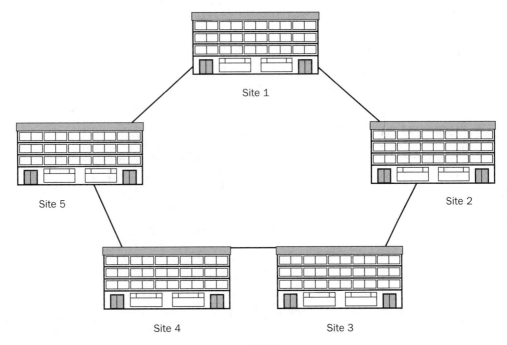

Figure 5-3   Five network sites connected by WAN links in a ring topology

Planning   You must determine whether a large number of relatively slow connections is more manageable and affordable than a smaller number of fast connections.

A ring topology is reasonably fault tolerant. Because every site connects to two other sites, the internetwork can compensate for the failure of any single router or WAN connection by sending traffic around the ring in the other direction. This increases the traffic on the other links, but data can still get through to any destination.

For an enterprise that consists of a corporate headquarters and a number of branch offices, the *star topology* can be a viable compromise between a mesh and a ring. In this topology, one site functions as the hub of the star by having a connection to each of the other sites, as shown in Figure 5-4. A star topology with a single hub site requires as many WAN connections as there are branch offices, substantially fewer than a mesh topology, but more than a ring. However, the star is more efficient than the ring topology, because traffic running between any two sites never has to pass through more than one intermediate network (the hub). The star topology is not as fault tolerant as the ring and mesh topologies. The failure of a single WAN connection affects only the branch office involved, but that office is completely isolated as a result of the failure.

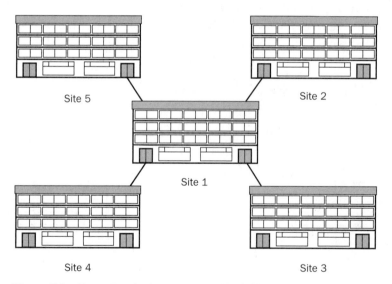

Figure 5-4   Five network sites connected by WAN links in a star topology

The selection of a WAN topology for your enterprise often depends on the type of WAN connection you elect to use. In addition to varying amounts of bandwidth, WAN technologies also provide varying connection capabilities, which can have a significant effect on the overall cost and efficiency of your internetwork connections.

Selecting a WAN Technology

In Chapter 3, "Planning Internet Connectivity," you learned about some of the WAN technologies for connecting a private network to the Internet. You can use these same technologies to connect private networks (except for cable television networks, which provide Internet connections only). Leased telephone lines, Digital Subscriber Line (DSL), Integrated Services Digital Network (ISDN), and dial-up modem connections provide varying amounts of bandwidth at various costs, but it would be a mistake to select a WAN technology for your remote network connections based solely on these two criteria. You should also consider the nature of the connections and whether their capabilities suit your needs.

Using Leased Lines

Leased telephone lines are a common type of WAN link used to connect remote networks. A T-1 connection runs at 1.544 megabits/second (Mbps), which is a good deal of bandwidth for internetwork traffic, and fractional T-1 services provide less bandwidth at lower prices. Leased lines can be expensive to install and maintain. After purchasing or leasing the necessary hardware and paying for installation (remembering that hardware and installation costs apply at both ends of the connection), you pay a monthly fee based on the distance between the two sites. DSL connections have many of the same characteristics as traditional leased lines, and are available in a range of speeds and prices.

In addition to bandwidth and cost, two characteristics of leased lines are important to consider: leased lines are persistent connections, and they are permanent. A *persistent connection* remains open at all times. With a leased line, you pay for the allotted bandwidth around the clock whether you use it or not. For organizations that do not use the connection during off hours, this can waste money. However, it is often possible to use the WAN link even when the offices are closed. You can perform automated tasks such as remote backups and database replications during off hours. A *permanent connection* is one that is fixed between two sites. After you install a leased line between two locations, moving one of the offices is a lengthy and expensive proposition.

Using Dial-on-Demand Connections

The WAN connections provided by standard asynchronous modems and ISDN are generally slower than leased lines—sometimes much slower—but they have one great advantage. Because these are dial-up services, you can disconnect them at will, and use them to connect to different destinations. The ability to disconnect means that you are paying for only the bandwidth you are using. Both standard telephone lines and ISDN connections typically have a per-minute charge in addition to a monthly fee, so disconnecting during off hours can result in substantial savings.

The ability to connect to different destinations by dialing alternative numbers can have a profound effect on your internetwork design, particularly when you use the dial-on-demand feature incorporated into Windows Server 2003 Routing and Remote Access and into many other routers. *Dial-on-demand* enables a router to connect to a remote network only when a computer sends traffic to a destination on that network.

Real World   Dial-on-Demand

You can install a Windows Server 2003 router with an ISDN line at a branch office and configure it to remain idle until someone in the office requires access to a resource at the corporate headquarters. When a user attempts to access a remote resource, the router dials the appropriate number, connects to the headquarters network, and begins routing data. After the transmissions are completed and the ISDN connection has been idle for a specified interval, the router drops the connection until someone needs it again. For WAN technologies that charge by the minute, dial-on-demand prevents you from paying for bandwidth your network is not using, without requiring manual intervention from administrators.

The other advantage of dial-on-demand is that you can use a single dial-up connection to access multiple remote sites. For an organization with ten locations, a mesh topology of WAN connections might be completely impractical using leased lines, but by using a single ISDN line with dial-on-demand at each office, any network can connect to any other network, as needed, simply by dialing the appropriate number. There are drawbacks to this arrangement; for example, each network can connect to only one other network at a time, but for situations where networks need only occasional remote access, dial-on-demand can be an effective and economical solution.

Exam Tip   Be sure to understand the ramifications of using persistent WAN connections as opposed to dial-on-demand connections.

Using Frame Relay

Frame relay is a popular WAN technology because it provides both flexibility and economy. A frame relay connection consists of a standard leased line linking the network site to the frame relay provider's nearest point of presence (POP). The provider then furnishes the connection to the frame relay cloud. When you use a frame relay provider for a private network-to-network connection, you must install a leased line at each site that connects the network to the provider's nearest POP. The provider then connects both lines to the same cloud so that the networks can establish a link.

> **See Also**   For more information on frame relay, see Lesson 1 in Chapter 3, "Planning Internet Connectivity."

A private frame relay connection provides the same benefits as a frame relay Internet connection, such as the ability to pay for only the bandwidth you use, and the ability to exceed your contracted bandwidth during heavy traffic periods. In addition, if you select the right provider, frame relay enables you to connect each of your sites to a local POP, reducing the cost of the leased lines. Another major benefit is the ability to connect to multiple sites using a single frame relay connection. You can actually create a mesh topology among all the networks in your enterprise by using a single leased line at each site to connect to a common cloud. Because connections in a frame relay cloud are ephemeral, a single network can simultaneously establish multiple links to different destinations (see Figure 5-5).

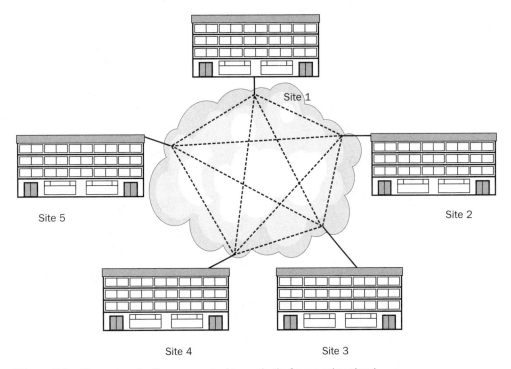

Figure 5-5   Five network sites connected to a single frame relay cloud

Using VPNs

All the WAN technologies discussed so far use private carriers to make the connections between networks. However, you can also use virtual private networks (VPNs) to connect networks at remote sites. VPNs are generally practical only for connections between distant locations, because you still must install a standard WAN connection from each network site to a local Internet service provider (ISP). The benefits of VPN connections are evident when you compare them to leased lines and other technologies that charge based on the distance between the connected sites.

> **Planning**   A company with two offices thousands of miles apart might find it cheaper to install two short-distance leased lines connecting the offices to nearby ISPs instead of one long-distance line connecting the offices directly.

Lesson Review

The following questions are intended to reinforce key information presented in this lesson. If you are unable to answer a question, review the lesson materials and try the question again. You can find answers to the questions in the "Questions and Answers" section at the end of this chapter.

1. Which of the following WAN technologies would be practical to use to create a mesh remote networking topology? (Choose all answers that apply.)

   a. ISDN

   b. Dial-up modems

   c. T-1

   d. Frame relay

   e. VPNs

2. What term do frame relay providers use to describe the network to which they connect their subscribers' leased lines?

   _____

   _____

3. In which of the following WAN topologies can a single cable break totally disconnect one site from the other sites?

   a. Mesh

   b. Ring

   c. Star

   d. None of the above

Lesson Summary

- A WAN topology is the pattern of connections among your network's various sites. When selecting a topology, be sure to consider the characteristics of the WAN technology you plan to use.

- The WAN technologies you can use to connect remote networks use either persistent connections or dial-on-demand connections.

- Persistent connections provide consistent amounts of bandwidth, usually for a flat monthly fee.

- Dial-on-demand connections enable you to pay for only the bandwidth you use.

- Dial-up services, frame relay, and VPNs all make it possible to create a mesh topology without having to install a separate WAN link for every pair of sites.

Lesson 2: Static and Dynamic Routing

In addition to WAN connections, you also need routers to connect remote networks. Because many of today's networks use switches internally, many router products are designed primarily to connect remote networks using WAN links. When you are selecting routers for this purpose, one of your first decisions is whether to use hardware or software routers. The Routing and Remote Access service in Windows Server 2003 provides the same routing services as most dedicated hardware routers.

After this lesson, you will be able to

- Describe the characteristics of the WAN technologies most commonly used for remote network connections
- Decide whether to use static or dynamic routing on your network
- Select the dynamic routing protocol most suitable for your network
- List the components needed to route IP multicast traffic to an internetwork

Estimated lesson time: 30 minutes

Selecting Routers

Compared to switches and bridges, which operate at the data-link layer of the Open Systems Interconnection (OSI) reference model, routers are relatively slow devices because they perform more extensive processing on each packet. Hardware-based router products are optimized to perform this type of processing and are therefore generally faster and more efficient than a computer running a software-based router. However, hardware routers also tend to be more expensive and less versatile than software routers. A computer running Windows Server 2003, for example, can handle routing chores as well as performing other server functions as needed.

> **Planning**   The rule of thumb is that when you have a high-speed WAN connection, such as a T-1, that carries heavy traffic, hardware routers are preferable. When the WAN connection is a relatively slow one, such as an ISDN link, or does not carry heavy traffic, a software router can function adequately, usually with far less expense.

Using Static Routing

Another important element of your routing strategy is your decision to use static or dynamic routing on your network. To forward network traffic to the proper locations, the routers on your network must have the correct entries in their routing tables. With static routing, network administrators must manually create and modify the routing table entries. Dynamic routing uses a specialized routing protocol to build and update the table entries automatically. Static and dynamic routing both provide the same level of router performance. The drawbacks of static routing are the amount of manual maintenance the process requires and the routers' inability to compensate for changes in the network configuration. Dynamic routing enables routers to compensate for a failed router or WAN link, but it can generate a considerable amount of additional network traffic.

The decision to use static or dynamic routing depends on your routing strategy for the entire enterprise, not just the routers connecting remote networks. If you are using routers to connect multiple LANs at each site, these routers' tables must have entries that direct traffic destined for other networks to the WAN routers in addition to their internal routing entries. The WAN router tables must have entries that enable them to forward traffic to the appropriate remote site.

Planning   When you consider the number of networks, routers, and sites that make up your enterprise, you can decide whether the amount of time and effort needed to maintain static routes is worth the savings in network traffic.

Real World   Modifying Routing Tables

The traditional tool for modifying routing tables on a TCP/IP computer, dating back to the earliest UNIX incarnations, is a command line program called *route*. Most operating systems include a version of this tool; in Windows Server 2003 (and all other versions of the Microsoft Windows operating system), the program is called Route.exe. Using Route.exe's four subcommands (PRINT, ADD, DELETE, and CHANGE), you can create new routing table entries and modify or delete existing ones.

The ROUTE PRINT command displays the contents of the routing table on a computer running a Windows operating system, as in the following example:

```
Network Destination  Netmask          Gateway        Interface      Metric
0.0.0.0              0.0.0.0          192.168.2.99   192.168.2.2    1
127.0.0.0            255.0.0.0        127.0.0.1      127.0.0.1      1
192.168.87.0         255.255.255.0    192.168.2.21   192.168.2.2    2
192.168.2.0          255.255.255.0    192.168.2.2    192.168.2.2    1
192.168.2.2          255.255.255.255  127.0.0.1      127.0.0.1      1
192.168.2.255        255.255.255.255  192.168.2.2    192.168.2.2    1
224.0.0.0            224.0.0.0        192.168.2.2    192.168.2.2    1
255.255.255.255      255.255.255.255  192.168.2.2    192.168.2.2    1
```

For each routing table entry, the Network Destination and Netmask columns identify a destination network (or host). The Gateway column specifies the IP address of the router the computer should use to transmit packets to the destination. The Interface column specifies which of its network interfaces the computer should use when transmitting data to the Gateway router. The Metric column indicates the relative distance to the destination. For example, the third entry in the sample routing table specifies that to send traffic to any system on the network 192.168.87.0, the computer should transmit the packets to a router with the IP address 192.168.2.21, using its 192.168.2.2 interface.

To create a new entry in the routing table, you use the ROUTE ADD command with parameters that specify the values for the various columns. For example, the command to add the third entry in the sample routing table might appear as follows:

```
route ADD 192.168.87.0 MASK 255.255.255.0 192.168.2.21 METRIC 2 IF 1
```

The address following the ADD parameter is the Network Destination column value. The subnet mask for the destination network address follows the MASK parameter. The IP address following the subnet mask is the Gateway column value. The Metric column value follows the METRIC parameter, and the number following the IF parameter identifies one of the computer's network interfaces. By substituting the DELETE or CHANGE parameter for ADD, you can create commands that remove entries from the routing table or modify existing entries.

When you use the Routing and Remote Access service to configure a computer running Windows Server 2003 as a router, you can view the system's routing table and create new static routes using a graphical interface provided by the Routing And Remote Access snap-in for Microsoft Management Console (MMC), as shown in the following illustration.

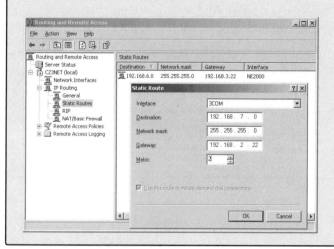

Using Dynamic Routing

Dynamic routing uses specialized protocols that enable routers to communicate with each other and share their routing table information. Routers have direct knowledge of only the networks to which they are connected. For a router to efficiently forward traffic to a distant network, it must have information in the form of routing table entries it has obtained from a router connected to that network. When you configure a router to use dynamic routing, it transmits the contents of its routing table to other routers at various intervals.

Dynamic routing eliminates the need for network administrators to manually create static routes on each router. More importantly, dynamic routing enables routers to compensate for changes in the network. For example, network designers often create redundant routes between networks, so that if a router or a connection fails, traffic can still reach any destination. For this type of failover system to work, routing table entries must be changed when a failure occurs. It is possible for administrators to make the changes, if they are on duty when the failure occurs and if they are aware of the failure. However, dynamic routing enables the routers to make these changes automatically.

When a router fails to transmit its routing table entries on schedule, the other routers detect the absence of incoming messages and remove the failed router from their routing tables. This prevents the routers from forwarding traffic to the failed router; instead, they use other paths through the network. When the failed router is back in operation, it resumes transmitting its dynamic routing messages and the other routers on the network begin to use it again by modifying their routing tables accordingly.

Off the Record   On a complex enterprise network, it would be extremely difficult for administrators to monitor all the routers on the network and keep their routing tables updated using manual programs such as Route.exe. Dynamic routing provides a more efficient, automatic solution.

Selecting a Routing Protocol

After you decide to use dynamic routing on your network, the next step is to select the routing protocol. The IP routing that occurs on even the largest private network is relatively simple when compared with the massive routing problems found on the Internet. The TCP/IP standards define many routing protocols, of which private networks only use a few.

Planning   The routing protocols most commonly used on private networks are the two supported by the Routing and Remote Access service in Windows Server 2003: Routing Information Protocol (RIP) and Open Shortest Path First (OSPF). In most cases, the designer of a routing strategy selects one of these two protocols.

The following sections compare the characteristics and capabilities of RIP and OSPF, providing the information you need to select the appropriate one for your network.

Understanding Routing Metrics

One of the most important functions of dynamic routing protocols is to evaluate the relative efficiency of routes to a specific destination. On a network with redundant routers, there might be several paths that packets can take from a particular source to a particular destination. When this is the case, a router might have multiple entries for the same destination in its routing table, and it is up to the router to forward packets using the most efficient route available. Routing table entries all include a numeric qualifier called a *metric*, which the router uses to evaluate routes to the same destination. The lower the metric value, the more efficient the route.

Although IP routers all use the metric the same way, there is no standardized definition for what the metric actually represents, if anything. On a network that uses static routing, network administrators can arbitrarily assign metrics to the routing table entries they create. As long as the routes the administrators want the traffic to take have lower metric values, the routers will choose them instead of routes with higher values. Keeping track of the relative metric values for all the routing tables on the network is another chore that falls to the network administrator who opts to use static routing on a large network.

In dynamic routing, the metric values must represent a specific attribute for routing protocols to compute them. However, different routing protocols use different algorithms to compute the metric for each routing table entry; this is one of the main characteristics that differentiates between routing protocols.

Distance Vector Routing   RIP uses one of the simplest and most obvious methods for computing routing table metrics. The metric value for each entry in a computer's routing table represents the number of hops between that computer and the destination. A *hop* is defined as a passage through a router from one network to another. Therefore, to reach a destination that is three hops away, packets must pass through three routers. This method is called *distance vector routing*.

When an enterprise network consists of nothing but LANs all running at the same speed, distance vector routing is an effective method for measuring the relative speeds of different routes through the internetwork. On a network running at one speed, the time it takes for a router to process a packet (called the router's *latency* period) is the single largest source of delay between the packet's transmission and its arrival at the destination. Therefore, a packet traveling to a destination three hops away is almost certainly going to take longer to arrive than a packet traveling two hops, no matter how long the relative cable segments are.

The distance vector routing that RIP uses is an excellent solution on a network located at a single site, with LANs running at the same speed. However, for an enterprise network that consists of LANs running at different speeds, or that includes slow WAN links to remote sites, distance vector routing is not as effective.

Real World   Distance Vector Routing

RIP makes no distinction between different types of networks. A hop is a hop, whether the packets are passing over a 1,000 Mbps Gigabit Ethernet network or a 33 Kbps dial-up modem connection. When you use a distance vector routing protocol like RIP on a mixed-speed network, it is possible for packets using a route with a metric value of 2 to take far longer to reach their destinations than those using a route with a metric value of 3. RIP metrics are therefore not reliable indicators of a route's efficiency on this kind of a network.

Exam Tip   Be sure to understand that the metrics in distance vector routing protocols represent the number of hops to the destination, regardless of the type or speed of the network connecting the routers at each hop. RIP is a distance vector routing protocol.

Link State Routing   The primary difference between RIP and OSPF is the method each protocol uses to compute the metric values for routing table entries. OSPF is called a *link state routing* protocol because it calculates metrics in a way that provides a much more realistic estimate of each route's relative efficiency. Instead of relying solely on the number of hops, OSPF uses a method called the Dijkstra algorithm, which uses multiple criteria to evaluate the efficiency of a route. In addition to counting the number of hops, these criteria include the link's transmission speed and delays caused by network traffic congestion.

Real World **Link State Routing**

Network administrators can also supply a *route cost value,* which OSPF factors into the equation. This enables administrators to skew the metric values in favor of certain links that they want the routers to use by default. For example, an organization might use a 128 Kbps fractional T-1 connection to link two office networks, while also maintaining an ISDN connection between the two offices as a fallback. The two links run at the same speed, but the administrators want the routers to use the T-1 by default, because they are paying a flat monthly fee for it, while the ISDN connection has a per minute charge. Ordinarily, OSPF would probably assign the same metric to both routes, because they run at the same speed; OSPF might even give the ISDN route a lower metric when the T-1 is experiencing traffic delays. By assigning a lower route cost value to the T-1 route, administrators can ensure that traffic uses the T-1 connection by default, only falling back to the ISDN link when the T-1 fails.

Link state routing is more processor intensive than distance vector routing, but it is also more precise and more capable of compensating for changes in the network infrastructure.

Understanding Routing Protocol Communications

Link state routing is one of the main reasons that administrators choose OSPF over RIP, but there are other considerations when choosing a routing protocol. One of the biggest criticisms leveled at RIP has always been the amount of network traffic it generates. When a RIP router starts, it generates a RIP request message and transmits it as a broadcast over all its network interfaces. The other RIP routers on the connected networks, on receiving the request, generate reply messages containing all the entries in their routing tables. On receiving the reply, the router assimilates the information about the other networks in the enterprise into its own routing table. By exchanging routing table information with all the other routers on their connected networks, RIP routers eventually develop a picture of the entire internetwork, enabling them to forward traffic to any destination.

Note When a RIP router receives routing table entries from another router, it increments the metric value for each entry before adding it to the table. This enables the routers to keep track of the number of hops needed to reach each destination.

After the initial exchange of messages, the RIP routers all transmit periodic updates at regular intervals. These updates are broadcast messages containing the entire contents of the system's routing table. An essential part of the RIP communications process, these updates enable RIP routers to determine when another router on the network has stopped functioning. When a RIP router fails to receive update messages from another router for a specified amount of time, the router recognizing the absence removes the failed router's entries from its routing table. When the failed router starts transmitting updates again, the other routers add its routing table entries back to their tables.

With every RIP router on the network broadcasting its entire routing table over and over, the amount of network traffic generated by the routers can be enormous. RIP version 2 (included with Windows Server 2003) addresses this problem by adding support for multicast transmissions. A *multicast* is a transmission addressed to a group of computers with a common attribute or trait. In this case, RIP version 2 routers can transmit their messages to a RIP multicast address so that only the other RIP routers on the network process the messages. This is an improvement over broadcast transmissions because non-routers don't have to process the RIP messages. However, RIP routers still generate a lot of traffic that can add a significant burden to a busy network.

Planning   In addition to its multicasting ability, RIP version 2 can share more routing information than version 1. A RIP version 1 message can carry only a Network Destination and Metric value for each routing table entry. The router receiving the message uses the transmitting router's IP address for the Gateway value. Most importantly, RIP version 1 messages do not include Netmask values, which is a serious shortcoming if you have subnetted your network. RIP version 2 addresses these problems by including Gateway and Netmask values for each routing table entry. In most cases, if you plan to use RIP on your network, you should make sure that all the RIP routers on your network support RIP version 2.

OSPF routers do not repeatedly broadcast their routing tables as RIP routers do, and they do not send messages to other routers unless a change in the network has taken place. This makes OSPF more suitable for large enterprise networks. Rather than repeatedly transmit routing table entries, each OSPF router compiles a map of the network called the *link state database*. The routers use the information in the database to compute the metrics for routes to specific destinations. OSPF routers synchronize their link state databases with adjacent routers, enabling each router to build a complete picture of the network's topology. Whenever a change to the network topology occurs, the OSPF routers nearest the change update their link state databases and then replicate the changes to other nearby routers. Soon the changes have propagated to all the other OSPF routers on the network.

Off the Record   To prevent the OSPF link state replication process from dominating a large network, it is possible to split the network into discrete *areas*. Each area is a group of adjacent networks, connected to a *backbone area*. The OSPF routers in each area are responsible only for maintaining a link state database for the networks in that area. Other routers, called *area border routers*, are responsible for sharing routing information between areas.

Administering Routing Protocols

OSPF's link state routing capabilities and its ability to form areas make it more efficient and scaleable than RIP, but it does have drawbacks. Deploying RIP on a network is usually simplicity itself. In Windows Server 2003, all you have to do is install the RIP protocol in the Routing and Remote Access service, and RIP immediately begins transmitting its messages. In most cases, RIP requires no additional configuration and no maintenance. OSPF is a different story, however. Deploying OSPF in a large network requires planning so that you can properly create areas and the backbone area. OSPF also requires more configuration and administration than RIP.

> **Exam Tip**   When preparing for the exam, no time spent familiarizing yourself with the RIP and OSPF configuration parameters in the Routing And Remote Access console will be wasted. Use the online help to learn the functions of the routing protocol parameters.

> **Planning**   RIP is usually the preferable routing protocol on any network that can tolerate its drawbacks. If your network can tolerate the amount of traffic RIP generates, and the network provides a suitably homogeneous environment, you can benefit from the protocol's simplicity and ease of installation. On a large network that uses WAN links to connect remote sites, or that a large amount of broadcast traffic would hamper, you are probably better off expending the time and effort to use OSPF.

Routing IP Multicast Traffic

IP multicasting is a technique that is designed to provide a more efficient method of one-to-many communications than unicast or broadcast transmissions. A unicast transmission, by definition, involves two systems only, a source and a destination. To use unicasts to send the same message to a group of computers, a system must transmit the same message many times. A broadcast message can reach multiple destinations with a single transmission, but broadcasts are indiscriminate. The message reaches every system on the network, whether or not it is an intended recipient. Broadcasts are also limited to the local network, so they can't reach recipients on other networks.

Multicast transmissions use a single destination IP address that identifies a group of systems on the network, called a *host group*. Multicasts use Class D addresses, as assigned by the Internet Assigned Numbers Authority (IANA), which can range from 224.0.1.0 to 238.255.255.255. Because one Class D address identifies an entire group of systems, the source computer requires only a single transmission to send a message to the entire group.

Members of a multicast group can be located on any LAN in an internetwork and are still accessible with a single transmission. However, for the transmission to reach the entire multicast group, the routers on the network must know which hosts are members of the group in order to forward messages to them.

Off the Record   Most of the routers on the market today, including the Routing and Remote Access service in Windows Server 2003, support IP multicasting.

Computers that will be members of a multicast host group must register themselves with the routers on the local network, using the Internet Group Management Protocol (IGMP). To support multicasting, all the members of the host group and all the routers providing access to the members of the host group must support IGMP.

Off the Record   All the Windows operating systems that include a TCP/IP client include support for IGMP.

To receive all the IP multicast traffic on the network, the network interface adapters in a router must support a special mode called *multicast promiscuous mode*. Unlike *promiscuous mode*, in which the network interface adapter processes all incoming packets, multicast promiscuous mode has the network interface adapter process all incoming packets with the multicast bit (that is, the last bit of the first byte of the destination hardware address) set to a value of 1.

Planning   Most network interface adapters on the market support multicast promiscuous mode, but make sure that the adapters in your routers have this support if you intend to use multicasting on your network.

To support multicasting on a large internetwork, the routers must be able to share their information about host group memberships. To do this, the routers use a multicast routing protocol, such as the Distance Vector Multicast Routing Protocol (DVMRP), the Multicast Open Shortest Path First (MOSPF) protocol, or the Protocol Independent Multicast (PIM) protocol. The Routing and Remote Access service in Windows Server 2003 does not include support for these, or any, multicast routing protocols other than the IGMP routing protocol component, but a Windows Server 2003 router can run a third-party implementation of such a protocol.

Practice: Installing RIP

In this practice, you configure RRAS to function as a LAN router and then install and configure the RIP routing protocol. If you are working on a network, your server will be able to exchange routing table information messages with other RIP routers on the same LAN.

Exercise 1: Configuring Routing and Remote Access as a LAN Router

In this procedure, you configure RRAS to function as a basic LAN router.

1. Log on to Server01 as Administrator.

2. Click Start, point to All Programs, point to Administrative Tools, and then click Routing And Remote Access. The Routing And Remote Access console appears and SERVER01 (local) is listed in the console tree.

3. Click SERVER01 (local) and, on the Action menu, click Configure And Enable Routing And Remote Access. The Routing And Remote Access Server Setup Wizard appears.

4. Click Next. The Configuration page appears.

5. Select the Custom Configuration. Select the Any Combination Of The Features Available In Routing And Remote Access option button and then click Next. The Custom Configuration page appears.

6. Select the LAN Routing check box and then click Next. The Completing The Routing And Remote Access Server Setup Wizard page appears.

7. Click Finish. A Routing And Remote Access message box appears, asking if you want to start the service.

8. Click Yes. The Routing and Remote Access service starts, and new entries appear in the console tree.

9. Leave the Routing And Remote Access console open for the next exercise.

Exercise 2: Installing RIP

In this procedure, you install the RIP routing protocol on your RRAS router.

1. In the Routing And Remote Access console, expand the IP Routing icon.

2. Click the General icon, and on the Action menu, click New Routing Protocol. The New Routing Protocol dialog box appears.

3. In the Routing Protocols list, select RIP Version 2 For Internet Protocol and then click OK. A RIP icon appears below the IP Routing icon.

4. Click the RIP icon and, on the Action menu, click New Interface. The New Interface For RIP Version 2 For Internet Protocol dialog box appears.

5. In the Interfaces list, select the interface that connects your computer to the LAN and then click OK. A RIP Properties dialog box for your selected interface appears.

   In the General tab, you can specify whether the RIP outgoing messages your server transmits should use the RIP version 1 or version 2 packet format, broadcasts or multicasts, or no transmissions at all. You can also specify whether the server should process incoming RIP messages that use the version 1 format, version 2, or both.

6. Click the Advanced tab and then change the Periodic Announcement Interval (Seconds) setting to 300 seconds.

   The Periodic Announcement Interval (Seconds) setting is the frequency at which the router transmits its RIP messages. In a stable network where configuration changes and communications failures are rare, you can safely increase this setting to reduce the amount of broadcast traffic RIP generates.

7. Change the Time Before Routes Expire (Seconds) setting to 1800 and the Time Before Route Is Removed (Seconds) setting to 1200.

   If you increase the Periodic Announcement Interval (Seconds) value on all the RIP servers on your network, you must increase these two settings as well so that the router does not purge the routing table too quickly of information from RIP.

8. Click OK. The interface you selected appears in the details pane, along with statistical indicators displaying the number of RIP messages the server transmits and receives.

9. Leave the Routing And Remote Access console open for the next exercise.

Exercise 3: Disabling Routing and Remote Access

In this procedure, you disable RRAS, removing the configuration you just created. This leaves RRAS in its original state, so that you can create different configurations later in this chapter.

1. Click SERVER01 (local) and, on the Action menu, click Disable Routing And Remote Access. A Routing And Remote Access message box appears, warning you that you are disabling the router.

2. Click Yes. The Routing and Remote Access service is stopped, and the subheadings beneath the SERVER01 (local) icon disappear.

3. Close the Routing And Remote Access console.

Lesson Review

The following questions are intended to reinforce key information presented in this lesson. If you are unable to answer a question, review the lesson materials and try the question again. You can find answers to the questions in the "Questions and Answers" section at the end of this chapter.

1. To support IP multicasting, which of the following components must be installed on a Windows Server 2003 router? (Choose all correct answers.)

   a. The Protocol Independent Multicast (PIM) protocol

   b. A network interface adapter that supports multicast promiscuous mode

   c. The Routing And Remote Access MMC snap-in

   d. Internet Group Management Protocol

2. Specify whether each of the following characteristics describes distance vector routing, link state routing, or both.

   a. Used by OSPF

   b. Uses the number of hops to the destination when calculating metrics

   c. Uses link speed when calculating metrics

   d. Used by RIP

   e. Unsuitable for enterprises with networks running at various speeds

Lesson Summary

- Static routing is the manual creation of routing table entries, and can require extensive maintenance. It is not practical for large networks with frequent infrastructure changes.

- Dynamic routing uses a specialized routing protocol that automatically compensates for changes in the network. Routing protocols enable routers to exchange messages containing information about their networks.

- RIP is a distance vector routing protocol that is suitable for small networks running at a single speed, but it generates a lot of broadcast traffic. OSPF is a link state routing protocol that is scaleable to support networks of almost any size, but requires more planning, configuration, and maintenance than RIP.

- To support IP multicasting, a router must support IGMP and have network interface adapters that support multicast promiscuous mode.

Lesson 3: Securing Remote Access

The Routing and Remote Access service in Windows Server 2003 provides routing capabilities that enable the computer to forward traffic between LANs, whether they are at the same or distant locations. However, RRAS can also give individual computers at remote locations access to a network, enabling users on the road or working at home to connect to network resources. While remote access can be a tremendous convenience, both to users and to network administrators, it can also be a serious security hazard. Unless you protect your network from unauthorized access, any user with a modem and a telephone line can gain access to your data.

After this lesson, you will be able to

■ Determine the security requirements of your remote access installation

■ Control remote access with user account properties

■ Create remote access policies

Estimated lesson time: 30 minutes

Determining Security Requirements

Before you implement a remote access solution, you should consider what security measures are necessary to grant users the access they need while preventing them from accessing resources for which they lack authorization. To determine what security measures you should use, you must ask questions like the following:

■ **Which users require remote access?**   In most organizations, not every user needs remote access, and you should take steps to limit that access to users who need it. You can specify users who are permitted remote access by authenticating them as they log on and by using remote access policies to dictate conditions that users must meet.

■ **Do users require different levels of remote access?**   Depending on users' standing in the organization and the resources they need, you can use permissions to assign different levels of remote access.

■ **Do users need access to the network?**   In the case of users whose needs can be met by access to the remote access server, you can prevent them from accessing the entire network.

■ **What applications must users run?**   You can limit users to specific applications by creating packet filters that permit only traffic using specific protocols and port numbers onto the network.

Controlling Access Using Dial-In Properties

The most basic method for securing remote access to your network through a Routing and Remote Access server is to use the properties of the individual accounts that clients use to connect to the network. When you display the Properties dialog box for a user account in the Active Directory Users And Computers console and click the Dial-In tab, you see the interface shown in Figure 5-6.

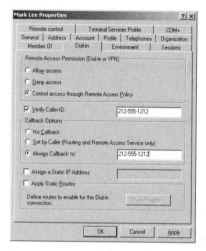

Figure 5-6 The Dial-In tab in a user account's Properties dialog box

The security-related options in this tab are as follows:

- **Remote Access Permission (Dial-in Or VPN)**   In this group box, you can specify whether the individual user is allowed or denied remote access, or you can specify that remote access be controlled by using group memberships, as specified in remote access policies.

- **Verify Caller ID**   This check box option enables you to specify the user's telephone number, which the system will verify during the connection process using caller ID. If the number the user calls from does not match the number supplied, the system denies the connection.

- **Callback Options**   This group box enables you to specify that the user cannot use callback, that the user sets the callback options, or that the user must use callback. The callback options cause the Routing and Remote Access server to break the connection after it authenticates a user and then dial the user to reconnect. You can use this mechanism to save on long distance charges by having the remote access calls originate at the server's location, but it can also function as a security mechanism if you select the Always Callback To option and then furnish a specific callback number in this option's text box. If you select the Always Callback To option, the user must be dialing in from the location you specify to connect to the server.

Planning Authentication

Authentication is the most basic form of remote access security. Without it, anyone can connect to your remote access server and gain access to the network. In addition, many of the other remote access security measures that Windows Server 2003 provides are keyed off the user's identity, which is confirmed by the authentication process.

When you display the Properties dialog box of a Routing and Remote Access server and select the Security tab, you can select the authentication protocol you want to use by clicking Authentication Methods, as shown in Figure 5-7. You should base your selection of an authentication protocol on the amount of security your network needs and the capabilities of your remote access clients, which must be able to support the same protocol.

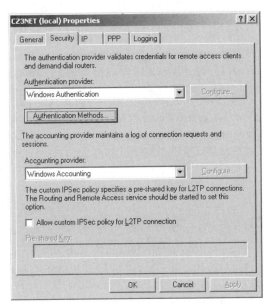

Figure 5-7   The Security tab in a Routing and Remote Access server's Properties dialog box

Real World   Authentication

Most forms of authentication are based on an exchange of user names and passwords. However, passwords are subject to compromise by a variety of methods. Intruders might capture network data packets containing passwords and other account information, and users might write their passwords down and then store them in an insecure place, share them with other users, or even disclose them to social engineers who specialize in providing convincing reasons for needing a person's private information. The Routing And Remote Access service in Windows Server 2003 includes support for several authentication protocols, which provide varying degrees of protection, primarily by controlling how the systems transmit their passwords to each other. These protocols can't prevent users from giving away their passwords, but they can stop intruders from intercepting them.

Using RADIUS

In addition to supporting multiple authentication protocols, RRAS enables you to use the Remote Authentication Dial-In User Service (RADIUS), a standard defining a service that provides authentication, authorization, and accounting for remote access installations. RADIUS proxy and server support is a new feature in Windows Server 2003. You can install and use the Microsoft Internet Authentication Service (IAS) server for both RADIUS servers and RADIUS proxies. (You install IAS using Network Services in the Add/ Remove Windows Components tool.)

Connection request processing determines how the IAS processes a RADIUS request. When you use an IAS server as a RADIUS server, the server attempts to authenticate and authorize the connection request. If it determines that the request's credentials are authentic, the RADIUS server authorizes the user's connection attempt and access, and then logs the remote access connection as an accounting event. When you use IAS as a RADIUS proxy, the proxy forwards the connection request to a member of a remote RADIUS server group for authentication and authorization.

Changing the Authentication Provider setting in the Security tab in the Routing and Remote Access server's Properties dialog box to RADIUS Authentication activates the Configure button, which enables you to specify the RADIUS server you want to use for remote access authentication.

After you have configured a Routing and Remote Access server to use RADIUS, RRAS transmits all authentication traffic to the RADIUS server for confirmation. The RADIUS server stores all the user accounts and passwords, as well as other account information. The real advantage of RADIUS is that you can run multiple remote access servers and configure them all to use a single RADIUS server for authentication. This way, remote users can access any remote access server, and you have to maintain only a single set of user accounts on the RADIUS server. Organizations that use RADIUS typically have large remote access installations, for example, ISPs.

The Authentication Methods dialog box, shown in Figure 5-8, lists the authentication protocols that Windows Server 2003 RRAS supports. The characteristics of the authentication protocols are as follows:

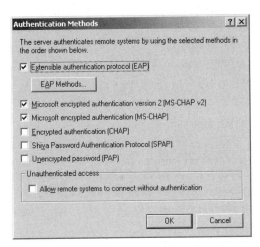

Figure 5-8   The RRAS Authentication Methods dialog box

- **Extensible Authentication Protocol (EAP)**   An open-ended system that allows RRAS to use third-party authentication protocols as well as those supplied with Windows Server 2003. To use EAP, you select the Extensible Authentication Protocol (EAP) check box in the Authentication Methods dialog box and then click EAP Methods to display the EAP Methods dialog box. This dialog box contains a list of the EAP methods currently installed on the system. EAP is the only authentication protocol supported by Windows Server 2003 RRAS that enables you to use mechanisms other than passwords (such as digital certificates stored on smart cards) to verify a user's identity. In addition to providing the infrastructure to support third-party authentication mechanisms, Windows Server 2003 RRAS supports the following EAP types:

❑ Extensible Authentication Protocol–Message Digest 5 Challenge Handshake Authentication Protocol (EAP–MD5 CHAP)—Uses the same authentication mechanism as CHAP (explained later in this list), but packages the authentication messages in EAP packets

❑ Extensible Authentication Protocol–Transport Level Security (EAP–TLS)—Required to authenticate remote access users with smart cards or other security mechanisms based on certificates

❑ Protected EAP (PEAP)—A password-based EAP type designed for wireless networks

❑ EAP–RADIUS—Not a true EAP type, but a mechanism that enables the Routing and Remote Access server to encapsulate EAP authentication messages in the RADIUS message formation and send them to a RADIUS server

- **Microsoft Encrypted Authentication Version 2 (MS-CHAP v2)**   A password-based authentication protocol that enables the client and the server to mutually authenticate each other using encrypted passwords. This makes it all but impossible for potential intruders to compromise passwords by capturing packets. Microsoft Challenge Handshake Authentication Protocol Version 2 (MS-CHAP v2) is the simplest and most secure option to use when your clients are running Microsoft Windows 98 or later.

- **Microsoft Encrypted Authentication (MS-CHAP)**   An earlier version of the Microsoft Challenge Handshake Authentication Protocol (MS-CHAP) that uses one-way authentication and a single encryption key for transmitted and received messages. The security that MS-CHAP v1 provides is inferior to that of version 2, but RRAS includes it as well to support remote access clients running Windows 95 and Windows NT 3.51, which cannot use MS-CHAP v2.

- **Encrypted Authentication (CHAP)**   A standard authentication protocol included in RRAS to support non-Microsoft remote access clients that cannot use MS-CHAP or EAP. Less secure than either version of MS-CHAP, Challenge Handshake Authentication Protocol (CHAP) requires access to users' passwords, and by default, Windows Server 2003 does not store the passwords in a form that CHAP can use. To authenticate users with CHAP, you must open the group policy governing users and enable the Store Passwords Using Reversible Encryption password policy. Then you must have every user's password reset or changed so that it is stored in the reversible form that CHAP can use.

- **Shiva Password Authentication Protocol (SPAP)**   A relatively insecure authentication protocol designed for use with Shiva remote access products.

- **Unencrypted Password (PAP)**   A password-based authentication protocol that transmits passwords in clear text, leaving them open to interception by packet captures. Some RRAS administrators use Password Authentication Protocol (PAP) as a fallback authentication mechanism for clients that support none of the more secure authentication protocols. Using PAP is better than no authentication at all, but you should be careful not to use it for accounts that have administrative access to servers or other resources, as it can compromise the passwords for these accounts.

- **Allow Remote Systems To Connect Without Authentication**   Enables remote access clients to connect to the Routing and Remote Access server with no authentication at all, enabling anyone to access the network. The use of this option is strongly discouraged.

> **Exam Tip**   You should understand the differences among these authentication protocols and how they provide their respective levels of security.

Using Remote Access Policies

After a Routing and Remote Access server successfully authenticates remote access users and verifies their identities, it attempts to authorize the users. *Authorization* is the process of determining whether the server should permit the connection to proceed. Even though the server might have successfully authenticated a user, that user must also satisfy a set of conditions before the server can grant the connection. To specify these conditions, you create remote access policies in the Routing And Remote Access console.

> **Note**   The use of remote access policies is limited to the Windows Server 2003 family or to Windows 2000 native-mode domains. Mixed-mode and Windows NT domains cannot use them.

Remote access policies are sets of conditions that users must meet before RRAS authorizes them to access the server or the network. You can create policies that limit user access based on group memberships, day and time restrictions, and many other criteria. Remote access policies can also specify what authentication protocol and what type of encryption clients must use. You can also create different policies for different types of connections, such as dial-up, VPN, and wireless.

Remote Access Policy Components

Remote access policies consist of three elements, as follows:

- **Conditions**   Specific attributes that the policy uses to grant or deny authorization to a user. A policy can have one or more conditions. If there is more than one condition, the user must meet all the conditions before the server can grant access.

Some of the conditions that RRAS remote access policies can require clients to meet are as follows:

❑ Authentication type—Specifies the authentication protocol that the client must use

❑ Day and time restrictions— Specifies the time of day and the day of the week when users must connect

❑ Framed protocol—Specifies the data-link layer protocol that the client must be using

❑ Tunnel type—Specifies the tunneling protocol that a VPN client must be using to connect to the server

❑ Windows groups—Specifies the groups to which the user must belong

- **Remote access permission**   Clients receive permission to access the remote network either by satisfying the conditions of the Routing and Remote Access server's remote policies, or by an administrator explicitly granting them the permission in the Dial-in tab in each user's Properties dialog box.

- **Remote access profile**   A set of attributes associated with a remote access policy that the Routing and Remote Access server applies to a client once it has authenticated and authorized it. The profile can consist of any of the following elements:

❑ Dial-in constraints—You can use a profile to set limitations to a dial-in connection, such as a time limit for the duration of the connection, an idle time limit before the server terminates the connection, and the hours and days when the client can connect. You can also limit client access to specific server telephone numbers or specific media types.

❑ IP—You can specify whether the clients or the server should supply the IP addresses the clients use, or you can specify a static IP address that the server should assign to the client. You can also create input and output filters that limit the types of traffic exchanged by the clients and the server, based on IP addresses, port numbers, or both.

❑ Multilink—Grants the client permission to use the Windows Multilink feature, which enables the client to combine the bandwidth of multiple modem connections into a single data pipe. You can also limit the number of connections you permit a client to use, and you can specify Bandwidth Allocation Protocol (BAP) settings.

❑ Authentication—Enables you to specify the authentication protocol the client must use to connect to the server, using the same selection of protocols as in the Authentication Methods dialog box, described earlier in this lesson.

❑ Encryption—Enables you to specify the types of encryption that clients can use when connecting to the server.

❑ Advanced—Enables you to set values for special attributes that RADIUS servers use when communicating with the Routing and Remote Access server.

Creating Remote Access Policies

To create a remote access policy, you open the Routing And Remote Access console, expand the icon for your Routing and Remote Access server, and click the Remote Access Policies subheading (see Figure 5-9). In the details pane is a list of the policies that already exist on the server. You can modify these policies or add new ones.

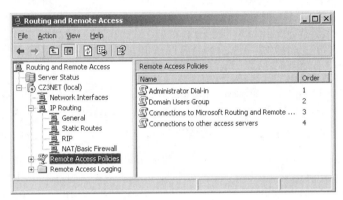

Figure 5-9   The Remote Access Policies node in the Routing And Remote Access console

Important   Before RRAS can use remote access policies to regulate access to the server by group membership, you must configure the user's account by selecting the Control Access Through Remote Access Policy option button in the Dial-in tab in the user's Properties dialog box in the Active Directory Users And Computers console.

When you select New Remote Access Policy from the console's Action menu, the New Remote Access Policy Wizard launches and walks you through the steps of creating the new policy by specifying values for the conditions described earlier. After you finish using the wizard, the console adds the new policy to the bottom of the list in the details pane.

Tip   Administrators can configure remote access policies to either grant or deny user access based on the specified conditions. In some cases, it is easier to deny access based on a smaller set of conditions than it is to grant them based on a larger set. For example, if nine groups should receive permission to access the network remotely, and one group should be denied permission, it is easier to grant all users permission by default and explicitly deny permission to that one group rather than grant permission to nine different groups.

When multiple policies are listed in the details pane, you can control the order of the list by clicking a policy and choosing Move Up or Move Down from the Action menu. The order of the policies is important, because the RRAS applies them in order to each connection attempt. The logic sequence for the connection process is as follows:

1. RRAS checks the incoming connection against the first remote access policy in the list. If there are no policies in the list, RRAS rejects the connection attempt.

2. If the incoming connection does not satisfy all the conditions in the first policy, RRAS proceeds to check the connection against the next policy in the list.

   If the incoming connection does not satisfy all the conditions in any one of the policies in the list, RRAS rejects the connection attempt.

3. When the incoming connection does satisfy all the conditions of one of the policies in the list, RRAS checks the value of the user's Ignore-User-Dialin-Properties attribute, which you set in the Advanced tab of the profile settings for a remote access policy.

4. If the Ignore-User-Dialin-Properties attribute is set to False, RRAS checks the remote access permission setting for the user account attempting to connect.

   If the Deny Access option is selected, RRAS rejects the connection attempt.

   If the Allow Access option is selected, RRAS applies the user account and profile properties to the connection. If the connection attempt does not match the settings of the user account and profile properties, RRAS rejects the connection attempt. If the connection attempt matches the settings of the user account and profile properties, RRAS accepts the connection attempt.

   If the Control Access Through Remote Access Policy option is selected, RRAS checks the remote access permission setting of the policy. If Deny Access is selected, RRAS rejects the connection attempt. If Allow Access is selected, RRAS applies the user account and profile properties, accepting the connection attempt if it matches the user account and profile properties settings, and rejecting the attempt if it does not.

5. If the Ignore-User-Dialin-Properties attribute is set to True, RRAS checks the remote access permission setting of the policy.

   If Deny Access is selected, RRAS rejects the connection attempt.

   If Allow Access is selected, RRAS applies the profile properties, accepting the connection attempt if it matches the profile properties settings, and rejecting the attempt if it does not.

Using Network Access Quarantine Control

The remote access security measures you have seen so far have all related to authenticating the incoming user. Network Access Quarantine Control, a new feature in Windows Server 2003 with Service Pack 1 (SP1), gives network administrators the ability to validate the configuration of remote client computers before granting access to the entire corporate network.

Typical remote access configurations can only validate the credentials of the remote access user and check that the user has permission to make a remote connection. Therefore, a remote computer can access internal network resources even when the remote computer's configuration does not comply with organization network policy. Therefore, the remote computer might not have:

- The correct service pack or the latest security patches installed.

- The correct antivirus software and signature files installed.

- Routing disabled. A remote access client computer with routing enabled might pose a security risk, providing an opportunity for a malicious user to access corporate network resources through the client computer, which has an authenticated connection to the private network.

- Firewall software installed and active on the Internet interface.

- A password-protected screensaver with an adequate wait time.

Despite the efforts made within organizations to ensure that computers physically attached to the network comply with network policy, those computers that remote or mobile workers use for remote access connections can present significant risk to the network.

Network Access Quarantine Control delays full access to a private network until the configuration of a connecting remote computer has been examined and validated. When a remote computer initiates a connection to a remote access server, the user is authenticated and the remote access computer is assigned an IP address. However, the computer is placed in quarantine mode with limited network access. The client component of the administrator-provided script is run on the remote access computer. When the script notifies the remote access server that it has successfully run and the remote access computer complies with current network policies, quarantine mode is removed and the remote access computer is granted normal remote access.

The quarantine restrictions placed on individual remote access connections consist of the following:

- A set of quarantine packet filters that restrict the traffic that can be sent to and from a quarantined remote access client

■ A quarantine session timer that restricts the amount of time the client can remain connected in quarantine mode before being disconnected

You can use either restriction, or both, as needed.

> **Important**   Network Access Quarantine Control is not a security solution. It is designed to help prevent computers with unsafe configurations from connecting to a private network, rather than to protect a private network from malicious users who have obtained a valid set of credentials.

The Components of Network Access Quarantine Control

The components required for this remote access quarantine solution include the following:

■ **Quarantine-compatible remote access clients**   Client computers must be configured to run the Remote Access Quarantine Client and the validation script. The supported client operating systems are Windows Server 2003, Windows XP, Windows 2000, Windows Me, and Windows 98 SE. These versions of Windows support Connection Manager (CM) profiles that are created with the Connection Manager Administration Kit (CMAK) provided in Windows Server 2003 with SP1. The CM profile contains the following:

❑ A postconnect action that runs a network policy requirements script. This is configured when the CM profile is created with CMAK.

❑ A validation script that performs validation checks to verify that the remote access client computer conforms to the minimum security guidelines required to access the corporate network. If the script does not run successfully and the connecting computer does not satisfy all of the network policy requirements, the script should direct the remote access user to a quarantine resource such as an internal Web page, which describes how to install the components that are required for network policy compliance.

❑ A notifier component that sends a message that indicates a successful execution of the script to the quarantine-compatible remote access server. You can use your own notifier component or you can use Rqc.exe, which is provided with the Windows Server 2003 Resource Kit Tools for computers running

Windows Server 2003 with no service packs installed. For computers running Windows Server 2003 with SP1, Rqc.exe is installed with the CMAK component in the Program Files\CMAK\Support folder. The CMAK component is installed through the Add/Remove Windows Components option, accessed through the Add Or Remove Programs Control Panel icon.

- **Quarantine-compatible remote access server**   The Remote Access Quarantine Service (Rqs.exe) or Listener runs on the RRAS server and listens for requests from the remote clients for removal of quarantine restrictions.

- **Quarantine-compatible RADIUS server (optional)**   If RRAS on the remote access server is configured for RADIUS authentication, a quarantine-compatible RADIUS server running Windows Server 2003 and IAS is required.

- **Quarantine resources**   These resources consist of servers that a remote access client in quarantine mode can access to perform name resolution (such as DNS servers), obtain the latest version of the CM profile (file servers with anonymous access allowed), or access instructions and components needed to make the remote access client comply with network policies (Web servers with anonymous access allowed). Anonymous access to file and Web resources are needed because, although the remote access user has the correct credentials to create the remote access connection, he or she might not be using the correct domain credentials to access protected file and Web resources.

- **Accounts database**   For Windows Server 2003 or Windows 2000–based networks, Active Directory is used as the accounts database to store user accounts and their dial-in properties.

- **Quarantine remote access policy**   Configured with the required conditions for remote access connections, and with profile settings that can specify the MS-Quarantine-IPFilter or MS-Quarantine-Session-Timeout attributes. The packet filters configured for the MS-Quarantine-IPFilter attribute provide the quarantine of the remote access client until the notifier component on the remote access client indicates that the computer is in compliance with network policies. You use the MS-Quarantine-Session-Timeout attribute to specify how long the remote access server must wait to receive the notification that the script has run successfully before terminating the connection.

Figure 5-10 shows the components of Network Access Quarantine Control with RADIUS as the authentication provider.

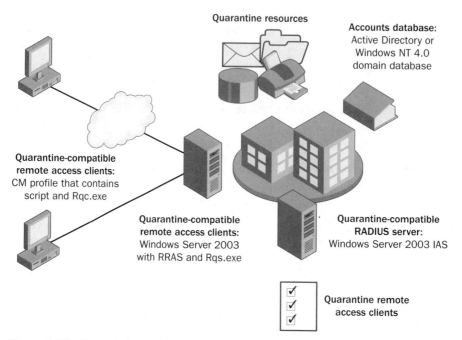

Figure 5-10   Network Access Quarantine Control components with RADIUS authentication

Practice: Installing a Routing and Remote Access Server

In this practice, you configure the Routing and Remote Access service on Server01 to function as a remote access server. For the purposes of this exercise, the Microsoft Loopback Adapter is assumed to be connected to a WAN device providing a connection to an ISP. Remote access clients can access the server using VPN connections. The other adapter (which is the actual network interface card in the computer) is connected to the local private network. After configuring RRAS, you create separate remote access policies for your domain users and administrators, with different security conditions.

Exercise 1: Configuring Routing and Remote Access as a Remote Access Server

In this procedure, you configure RRAS on Server01 to function as a remote access server, supporting both dial-in and VPN connections.

1. Log on to Server01 as Administrator.

2. Click Start, point to All Programs, point to Administrative Tools, and then click Routing And Remote Access. The Routing And Remote Access console appears and SERVER01 (local) is listed in the console tree.

3. Click SERVER01 (local) and, on the Action menu, click Configure And Enable Routing And Remote Access. The Routing And Remote Access Server Setup Wizard appears.

4. Click Next. The Configuration page appears.

5. Accept the (default) Remote Access (Dial-up Or VPN) option button and then click Next. The Remote Access page appears.

6. Select both the VPN and Dial-up check boxes and then click Next. The VPN Connection page appears.

7. Click the WAN Connection interface in the Network Interfaces box and then click Next. The IP Address Assignment page appears.

8. Accept the (default) Automatically option button and then click Next. The Managing Multiple Remote Access Servers page appears.

9. Accept the (default) No, Use Routing And Remote Access To Authenticate Connection Requests option button and then click Next. The Completing The Routing And Remote Access Server Setup Wizard page appears.

10. Click Finish. A Routing And Remote Access message box appears, warning you to configure the DHCP Relay Agent to service clients on other networks.

11. Click OK. The Routing and Remote Access service starts, and new entries appear in the console tree.

    Notice that the IP Routing icon contains four subheadings: General, Static Routes, DHCP Relay Agent, and IGMP, and that the SERVER01 (local) icon now has Remote Access Clients, Remote Access Policies, and Remote Access Logging subheadings.

12. Leave the Routing And Remote Access console open for later practices.

Exercise 2: Creating a Remote Access Policy for Domain Users

In this procedure, you create a remote access policy that is designed to grant your domain users remote access to the network using VPN connections only. You do this using one of the common scenarios scripted into the New Remote Access Policy Wizard.

1. In the Routing And Remote Access console, click the Remote Access Policies subheading in the console tree and, on the Action menu, click New Remote Access Policy. The New Remote Access Policy Wizard appears.

2. Click Next. The Policy Configuration Method page appears.

3. Accept the (default) Use The Wizard To Set Up A Typical Policy For A Common Scenario option button, and in the Policy Name text box, type **Domain Users VPN**. Click Next. The Access Method page appears.

4. Select the VPN, Use For All VPN Connections, To Create A Policy For A Specific VPN Type, Go Back To The Previous Page, And Select Set Up A Custom Policy option button and then click Next. The User Or Group Access page appears.

5. Accept the (default) Group, Individual User Permissions Override Group Permissions option button and then click Add. A Select Groups dialog box appears.

6. Type **Domain Users** in the Enter The Object Names To Select text box and then click Check Names. Domain Users now appears underlined.

7. Click OK. The Domain Users group is added to Group Name box in the User Or Group Access page. Click Next. The Authentication Methods page appears.

8. Accept the (default) Microsoft Encrypted Authentication Version 2 (MS-CHAPv2) option button and then click Next. The Policy Encryption Level page appears.

9. Accept the default options and then click Next. The Completing The New Remote Access Policy Wizard page appears.

10. Click Finish. The Domain Users VPN policy you created now appears in the console's details pane in the Remote Access Policies list.

Exercise 3: Creating a Remote Access Policy for Domain Administrators

In this procedure, you create a remote access policy that enables the domain administrators to connect to the remote access server using dial-in connections, but only with specific authentication and encryption protocols. You do this using the custom policy capabilities of the New Remote Access Policy Wizard.

1. In the Routing And Remote Access console, click the Remote Access Policies subheading in the console tree and, on the Action menu, click New Remote Access Policy. The New Remote Access Policy Wizard appears.

2. Click Next. The Policy Configuration Method page appears.

3. Click the Set Up A Custom Policy option button and then type **Administrators Dial-in** in the Policy Name text box. Click Next. The Policy Conditions page appears.

4. Click Add. The Select Attribute dialog appears.

5. Scroll down the Attribute Types list and click Windows-Groups. Click Add. The Groups dialog box appears.

6. Click Add. A Select Groups dialog box appears.

7. Type **Domain Admins** in the Enter The Object Names To Select text box and then click Check Names. Domain Admins now appears underlined.

8. Click OK. The Domain Admins group is added to the Groups list in the Groups dialog box.

9. Click OK. The Windows-Groups condition you just created is added to the Policy Conditions list. Click Next. The Permissions page appears.

10. Click the Grant Remote Access Permission option button and then click Next. The Profile page appears.

11. Click Edit Profile. The Edit Dial-In Profile dialog box appears.

12. Click the Authentication tab and clear all the check boxes except Microsoft Encrypted Authentication Version 2 (MS-CHAP v2).

13. Click the Encryption tab and clear all the check boxes except Strongest Encryption (MPPE 128 bit).

14. Click OK to return to the Profile page and then click Next. The Completing The New Remote Access Policy Wizard page appears.

15. Click Finish. The Administrators Dial-In policy you just created now appears in the console's details pane in the Remote Access Policies list.

16. Close the Routing And Remote Access console.

Lesson Review

The following questions are intended to reinforce key information presented in this lesson. If you are unable to answer a question, review the lesson materials and try the question again. You can find answers to the questions in the "Questions and Answers" section at the end of this chapter.

1. Which of the following authentication protocols do you use with smart cards?

   a. MS-CHAP v2

   b. EAP-TLS

   c. PEAP

   d. PAP

2. What is the function of a RADIUS server in a remote access installation?

   _____

   _____

3. How does the callback option in a user account's dial-in properties function as a security feature?

   _____

   _____

4. Which of the following is *not* a component of a remote access policy?

   a. Authentication protocol

   b. Conditions

   c. Remote access profile

   d. Remote access permission

Lesson Summary

■ To determine the security requirements you need for your remote access server, determine which users need remote access to the network, what type of access they need, and whether different users require different degrees of access.

■ RRAS supports several authentication protocols, including EAP, MS-CHAP (versions 1 and 2), CHAP, SPAP, and PAP.

■ Remote access policies are sets of conditions that remote clients attempting to connect to the Routing and Remote Access server must meet. You can use policies to control remote access based on group membership and other criteria.

■ RRAS matches each connection attempt against the list of remote access policies you create on the server. The server grants access only when a connection meets all the conditions in one of the policies.

■ Remote access profiles are sets of attributes that RRAS applies to connections after successfully authenticating and authorizing them. You can use profiles to control when clients can connect to the network, what types of IP traffic you permit them to use, and what authentication protocols and encryption algorithms they must use.

Lesson 4: Troubleshooting TCP/IP Routing

The Routing and Remote Access service is one of the more complex components in Windows Server 2003. Because RRAS can perform so many functions, it has a large number of configurable settings. Even a minor misconfiguration can prevent the server from routing traffic properly. The TCP/IP implementation in Windows Server 2003 includes a variety of tools that you can use to troubleshoot RRAS and its various functions.

After this lesson, you will be able to

- Use TCP/IP tools to isolate a router problem
- Check an RRAS installation for configuration problems
- Troubleshoot static and dynamic routing problems

Estimated lesson time: 20 minutes

Isolating Router Problems

In most cases, administrators discover router problems when communications fail between computers on the network. However, once the troubleshooter suspects that there might be a routing problem, the next step is to determine which router is malfunctioning. Some of the TCP/IP tools in the Windows operating system that can help you in this respect are discussed in the following sections.

Using Ping.exe

PING is the standard TCP/IP tool for testing connectivity; virtually every TCP/IP client includes a PING implementation. In the Windows operating systems, PING takes the form of a command line program called Ping.exe. By typing **ping** followed by an IP address on the command line, you can test any TCP/IP system's connectivity with any other system.

Note   PING functions by transmitting a series of Echo Request messages containing a sample of random data to the destination you specify, using the Internet Control Message Protocol (ICMP). The system that receives the Echo Request messages is required to generate an Echo Reply message for each request that contains the same data sample and return the messages to the sender.

Compared to other tools, PING has limited utility when you are trying to locate a malfunctioning router. You might be able to ping a router's IP address successfully even when it is not routing traffic properly. However, as part of your initial troubleshooting efforts, you can use PING to test a routed network connection in the following manner:

1. Ping the computer's loopback address (127.0.0.1) to confirm that the TCP/IP client is installed and functioning.

   If this test fails, there is a problem with the TCP/IP installation on the computer, with the network interface adapter, or with the network adapter driver. The problem is not caused by network cables or other external hardware, because messages addressed to the loopback address never leave the system.

2. Ping the computer's own IP address to confirm that the routing table contains the appropriate entries.

   A properly configured routing table contains an entry with the computer's own IP address as the network destination and the loopback address as the gateway the system should use to reach that destination. If this test fails (after you have successfully pinged the loopback address), this entry in the routing table is missing or incorrect. You should check the routing table carefully at this point, because other important entries might also be missing or incorrect.

3. Ping the IP address of another computer on the same LAN.

   This test confirms that the computer is not being prevented from accessing the network by problems with TCP/IP configuration or network hardware. If this test fails, you should check that the computer has a correct IP address and subnet mask, and that the computer's physical connection to the network is intact.

4. Ping the DNS name of another computer on the same LAN.

   If this test fails, and you are able to successfully ping the IP address of the same computer, there is a name resolution problem. Check the computer's DNS server address and that the DNS server is functioning properly.

5. Ping the computer's designated default gateway address.

   Successfully pinging the default gateway does not confirm that the gateway is routing packets as it should, but it does verify that gateway system is up and running, and that its TCP/IP client is properly configured. If this test fails (after you have successfully completed all the previous tests), you should examine the router functioning as the default gateway for TCP/IP configuration or network hardware problems.

6. Ping several computers on another network that are accessible through the default gateway.

   If this test fails (and the previous test succeeded), then you know that although the default gateway is up and running, it might not be routing packets properly. A failure to ping a single computer on another network could indicate that the destination system is not running, but if you cannot ping several systems on another network, it is likely that there is a routing problem.

> **Tip**   For best results, you should try to ping systems on a network to which the default gateway is directly connected. This way, you know that if the test fails, the default gateway is the problem. If the packets are passing through two or more routers to get to their destinations, any one of the routers could be at fault, and you must use another tool (such as Tracert.exe or Pathping.exe) to determine which router is malfunctioning.

Using Tracert.exe

Tracert.exe is the Windows operating system's implementation of the UNIX traceroute program. TRACERT enables you to view the path that packets take from a computer to a specific destination. When you type **tracert** and an IP address at the Windows command prompt, the program displays a list of the hops to the destination, including the IP address and DNS name (where available) of each router along the way, as follows:

```
Tracing route to www.adatum.co.uk [10.146.1.1]
over a maximum of 30 hops:
    1     <10 ms       1 ms    <10 ms    192.168.2.99
    2     105 ms      92 ms      98 ms   qrvl-67terminal01.epoch.net [172.24.67.3]
    3     101 ms     110 ms      98 ms   qrvl.epoch.net [172.24.67.1]
    4     123 ms     109 ms     118 ms   svcr03-7b.epoch.net [172.24.103.125]
    5     123 ms     112 ms     114 ms   clsm02-2.epoch.net [172.24.88.26]
    6     136 ms     130 ms     133 ms   sl-0-T3.sprintlink.net [10.228.116.5]
    7     143 ms     126 ms     138 ms   sl-3.sprintlink.net [192.168.5.117]
    8     146 ms     129 ms     133 ms   sl-12-0.sprintlink.net [192.168.5.1]
    9     131 ms     128 ms     139 ms   sl-13-0.sprintlink.net [192.168.18.38]
   10     130 ms     134 ms     134 ms   sl-8-0.sprintlink.net [192.168.7.94]
   11     147 ms     149 ms     152 ms   sl-0.sprintlink.net [192.168.173.10]
   12     154 ms     146 ms     145 ms   ny2-ge021.router.demon.net [172.21.173.121]
   13     230 ms     225 ms     226 ms   tele-ge023.router.demon.net [172.21.173.12]
   14     233 ms     220 ms     226 ms   tele-fxp1.router.demon.net [10.159.252.56]
   15     223 ms     224 ms     224 ms   tele-14.router.demon.net [10.159.254.245]
   16     236 ms     221 ms     226 ms   tele-165.router.demon.net [10.159.36.149]
   17     220 ms     224 ms     210 ms   www.adatum.co.uk [10.146.1.1]
Trace complete.
```

Tracert.exe is an excellent tool for locating a malfunctioning router, because it is able to inform you how far packets have gotten on the way to their destination. When one of the routers on the path is not forwarding packets properly, the TRACERT output stops at the last functioning router. You know then that the next router on the path is the one experiencing the problem.

How Tracert.exe Works

Tracert.exe works by sending ICMP Echo Request messages to the destination, much as PING does, but with a special difference. For the first group of three Echo Request messages, TRACERT assigns a value of 1 to the IP header's Time to Live (TTL) field. The TTL field is a safety measure designed to prevent packets from circulating endlessly around an internetwork. Normally, computers running Windows operating systems assign a value of 128 to the TTL field. When a router processes a packet, it reduces the TTL value by 1; if the TTL value reaches 0, the router discards the packet and returns an error message to the system that transmitted it.

Because the first three TRACERT packets have a TTL value of 1, when they reach the first router on their path, the router reduces their TTL values to 0 and discards them, sending error messages back to the sender. Then, for each successive group of three Echo Request messages, TRACERT increments the initial TTL value by 1, causing each group of packets to travel one more hop on the way to the destination before the router discards them. The TRACERT program uses the error messages generated by the routers (which contain the routers' IP addresses) to create the output display.

Tip   It is important to understand that routes through a large internetwork can change frequently, for a variety of reasons, and packets can take different paths to the same destination. Therefore, when you use TRACERT, it is possible (although not probable) for the path through the internetwork taken by successive sets of Echo Request messages to be different. When you are using TRACERT to locate a malfunctioning router, you should run the program at least twice, using the same destination, to ensure that you are seeing an accurate path through the network.

Using Pathping.exe

Pathping.exe is another tool available from the Windows command prompt that is similar to Tracert.exe in that it traces a path through the network to a particular destination and displays the names and addresses of the routers along the path. PATHPING is different, however, because it reports packet loss rates at each of the routers on the path. TRACERT is the preferred tool for locating a router failure that completely interrupts communications, while PATHPING is more useful when you can connect to a destination, but you are experiencing data loss or transmission delays.

After displaying the path to the destination, PATHPING sends 100 packets (by default) to each of the routers on the path and computes the packet loss rate in the form of a percentage. A typical PATHPING output display appears as follows:

```
Computing statistics for 125 seconds...
                  Source to Here    This Node/Link
    Hop    RTT    Lost/Sent=Pct     Lost/Sent    =    Pct    Address
     0                                                        172.16.87.35
                                     0/ 100      =    0%      |
     1    41ms   0/ 100 =   0%       0/ 100      =    0%      172.16.87.218
                                    13/ 100      =    13%     |
     2    22ms   16/ 100 = 16%       3/ 100      =    3%      192.68.52.1
                                     0/ 100      =    0%      |
     3    24ms   13/ 100 = 13%       0/ 100      =    0%      192.68.80.1
                                     0/ 100      =    0%      |
     4    21ms   14/ 100 = 14%       1/ 100      =    1%      192.168.247.14
                                     0/ 100      =    0%      |
     5    24ms   13/ 100 = 13%       0/ 100      =    0%       192.168.54.76
Trace complete.
```

Troubleshooting the Routing and Remote Access Configuration

The most common symptom of trouble for an RRAS router is simply that the server is not routing traffic. However, although the symptom might be simple, the cause might not be. To begin troubleshooting, it is best to start with the most obvious possible causes, such as the following:

- **Verify that the Routing and Remote Access service is running**   Display the Services tool on the Administrative Tools menu to verify that the status of the Routing and Remote Access service is Started. In most cases, you should set the Startup Type selector to Automatic. If the service had been running and has now stopped for no apparent reason, check the Event Viewer console for error messages related to the stoppage.

- **Verify that routing is enabled**   In the Routing And Remote Access console, display the Properties dialog box for your server and, in the General tab, make sure that the Router check box and the appropriate routing option for your network (Local Area Network (LAN) Routing Only or LAN And Demand-Dial Routing) are selected. If your router is also functioning as a remote access server, you should select that check box as well. If RRAS is not configured with the correct options, you should check the other configuration parameters or disable the Routing and Remote Access service completely and reconfigure it from scratch.

- **Check the TCP/IP configuration settings**   Just like any other TCP/IP computer, a router must have the proper TCP/IP configuration settings in order to function properly. Make sure that you've configured all the router's interfaces with the correct IP addresses, subnet masks, and other settings.

- **Check the IP addresses of the router interfaces**   When you use the Routing And Remote Access Server Setup Wizard to configure RRAS to function as a router, the wizard creates interfaces in the router configuration using the computer's current interface settings. If you change the interface settings, such as the IP address or subnet mask, you must change the corresponding setting in the RRAS interface as well. In the Routing And Remote Services console, display the Properties dialog boxes for the interfaces listed in the IP Routing's General subheading and check to see that their IP addresses and subnet masks match the actual interface addresses, and that the interfaces show Operational status.

Troubleshooting the Routing Table

If you have configured RRAS correctly, and you are still experiencing routing problems, another cause could be that the routing table does not contain the information needed to route network traffic properly. The cause of this problem depends largely on whether you use static routing or dynamic routing. If you use static routing, someone might have deleted, omitted, or mistyped important routing table entries. If you use dynamic routing, your routing protocol might not be functioning properly.

Troubleshooting Static Routing

Because static routing requires human beings to create all the specialized entries in a routing table, the only possible source of problems in the routing table (excluding hardware failures) is human error. If you have created your static routes in the Routing And Remote Access console, you can view and modify them there by selecting the IP Routing's Static Routes subheading in the console tree (see Figure 5-11). Note, however, that doing this displays only the static routes you have created in the Routing And Remote Access console.

> **Important**   If someone has created static routes using the Route.exe command line utility, these routes do not appear in the Routing And Remote Access console's Static Routes display, nor do the default entries in the routing table appear. The only way to modify or delete routing table entries created with Route.exe is to use Route.exe.

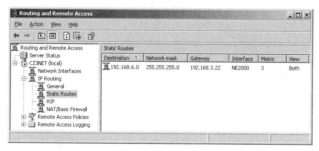

Figure 5-11   The Static Routes display in the Routing And Remote Access console

To display the entire routing table for the computer using the Routing And Remote Access console, click the Static Routes subheading and, on the Action menu, click

Show IP Routing Table to produce a display like the one in Figure 5-12. You cannot modify the routing table in this display, however, just view it.

Destination	Network mask	Gateway	Interface
0.0.0.0	0.0.0.0	192.168.2.99	3COM
127.0.0.0	255.0.0.0	127.0.0.1	Loopback
127.0.0.1	255.255.255.255	127.0.0.1	Loopback
192.168.2.0	255.255.255.0	192.168.2.3	3COM
192.168.2.0	255.255.255.0	192.168.2.3	3COM
192.168.2.3	255.255.255.255	127.0.0.1	Loopback
192.168.2.255	255.255.255.255	192.168.2.3	3COM
192.168.3.0	255.255.255.0	192.168.3.3	NE2000
192.168.3.0	255.255.255.0	192.168.3.3	NE2000
192.168.3.3	255.255.255.255	127.0.0.1	Loopback
192.168.3.255	255.255.255.255	192.168.3.3	NE2000
192.168.5.0	255.255.255.0	192.168.3.21	NE2000
192.168.6.0	255.255.255.0	192.168.3.22	NE2000
224.0.0.0	240.0.0.0	192.168.3.3	NE2000
224.0.0.0	240.0.0.0	192.168.2.3	3COM
255.255.255.255	255.255.255.255	192.168.3.3	NE2000
255.255.255.255	255.255.255.255	192.168.2.3	3COM

Figure 5-12   The RRAS IP Routing Table window

The Route.exe command-line utility enables you to view, add, modify, or delete any entries in the computer's routing table, regardless of how you created them.

> **Tip**   Although it might take you a bit of time to get used to its command line syntax, Route.exe is a much better tool for creating static routes than the Routing And Remote Access console. For example, if you try to create a routing table entry with a gateway address that does not exist on one of the router's connected networks, Route.exe refuses to create the entry and displays an error message. The Static Route dialog box in the Routing And Remote Access console allows you to create this incorrect table entry without complaining.

Troubleshooting Routing Protocols

If you use dynamic routing, the lack of the proper entries in a router's routing table is the result of the routing protocol failing to put them there. Assuming that no network communications problem is preventing the routers from exchanging messages, it is likely that the routing protocol on one or more of the routers is not configured properly. To verify the functionality of the routing protocol, use the following procedures:

1. Verify that the routing protocol is installed on all the participating routers.

   On an RRAS router, you must install the routing protocol manually after you configure the Routing and Remote Access service. Other operating systems and standalone routers might have their own procedures for installing or enabling the routing protocol. Make sure that all the routers on the network are configured to use the same routing protocol, and that the protocol implementations are compatible.

2. Verify that the routing protocol is configured to use the correct interfaces.

   After you install RIP or OSPF on an RRAS router, you must specify the interfaces over which you want the protocol to transmit its messages. To do this, you click the routing protocol icon in the console tree and, on the Action menu, click New Interface. In the New Interface dialog box, you select the interface in the computer that provides access to the network where the other routers are located. If other routers are located on both networks to which the Routing and Remote Access server is connected, you should perform this procedure twice, to install both interfaces.

After you have ascertained that RRAS has the routing protocol installed and the interfaces selected, you can begin checking elements specific to the individual routing protocol, as described in the following sections.

Troubleshooting RIP

To determine whether RIP is functioning properly, you can select the RIP subheading in the console tree, as shown in Figure 5-13.

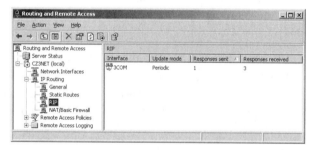

Figure 5-13   The RIP display in the Routing And Remote Access console

The details pane shows the number of RIP packets transmitted and received by the router. If RRAS is not sending or receiving RIP messages (or both), you should check the RIP configuration settings, as described in the following procedures:

1. Verify that all the RIP routers are using the same message types.

   The RIP implementation in Windows Server 2003 supports version 2 of the protocol, but you can configure RIP on each interface to transmit its messages as either version 1 or version 2 broadcasts, or version 2 multicasts. By default, RRAS uses RIP version 2, but you may have to modify these settings so that the router functions with other RIP implementations on your network. Be sure to check every RIP router on your network to see which version of the protocol it uses, and then modify your RRAS configuration accordingly.

> **Tip**   When configuring the RIP version properties, remember that you must configure ingoing traffic, outgoing traffic, and each interface separately.

2. Check RIP security properties.

In the Security tab in each RIP interface's Properties dialog box, you can specify the address ranges of routes that you want RIP to accept from other routers. By default, RRAS RIP accepts all incoming routes, but if new entries are not appearing in the computer's routing table, check to make sure that no one has changed the security settings inappropriately.

3. Check the RIP timing interval settings.

By default, the RRAS RIP implementation transmits update messages every 30 seconds, and RRAS removes RIP entries from the routing table if they are not refreshed at least every 20 minutes (1200 seconds). If you decide to modify these defaults (as a bandwidth conservation measure), make sure that the Periodic Announcement Interval value is lower than the Time Before Route Is Removed setting. Otherwise, RRAS will remove entries from the table before they have a chance to be refreshed.

> **Tip**   If you change the RIP timing interval settings on one router, you should change them on all the other RIP routers in the same way.

Troubleshooting OSPF

As with RIP, when you click the OSPF subheading in the Routing And Remote Access console tree, the details pane shows the number of OSPF packets the router has sent and received, so you can tell if the protocol is functioning. If the router is not sending or receiving OSPF packets, the first thing to check is whether OSPF is enabled on each of the interfaces you installed. Display the Properties dialog box for each interface and check to see that the Enable OSPF For This Address option button is selected.

If OSPF is enabled on the interfaces and your routers are still not communicating, it is time to check whether each router is configured in accordance with your OSPF deployment plan. Unlike RIP, which requires little or no configuration, an OSPF deployment requires you to make decisions such as how many areas you want to create, and which routers will handle the communication between areas by functioning as area border routers. Make sure that you have configured each OSPF router on the network to perform its designated roles.

Lesson Review

The following questions are intended to reinforce key information presented in this lesson. If you are unable to answer a question, review the lesson materials and try the question again. You can find answers to the questions in the "Questions and Answers" section at the end of this chapter.

1. Which of the following TCP/IP tools is best suited to troubleshooting a situation in which a router is dropping packets?

   a. Ping.exe

   b. Tracert.exe

   c. Pathping.exe

   d. Route.exe

2. What would happen if a router on your network supported only RIP version 1, and all your other routers were Routing and Remote Access servers using RIP with its default configuration?

   _____

   _____

3. If you use static routing on your network, and several administrators are responsible for creating the routing table entries on your routers, what should you do if you open the Routing And Remote Access console on one of your routers, click the Static Routes subheading, and see no entries?

   _____

   _____

Lesson Summary

- Tracert.exe is a command line tool that can help you locate a non-functioning router on the network. TRACERT uses ICMP Echo Request messages with incrementing TTL values to test the connection to each router on the path to a given destination.

- Pathping.exe is a command line tool that sends large numbers of test messages to each router on the path to a particular destination and compiles statistics regarding dropped packets. Pathping.exe is best suited to locating a router that is malfunctioning but still operational.

- When a routing table lacks the proper entries, the cause depends on whether you use static or dynamic routing on the network.

■ For an RRAS router to use either RIP or OSPF, you must install the routing protocol and then select the interfaces over which the protocol will transmit messages.

■ Incorrect routing protocol configurations can prevent the routers on the network from sharing their routing table entries, which in turn prevents the routers from forwarding traffic properly.

Case Scenario Exercise

You are the network infrastructure design specialist for Litware Inc., a manufacturer of specialized scientific software products, and you have already created a network design for their new office building, as described in the Case Scenario Exercise in Chapter 1. The office building is a three-story brick structure built in the late 1940s, which has since been retrofitted with several types of network cabling by various tenants. Your network design for the building calls for the installation of four LANs, each of which is connected to a fifth, backbone network. The backbone is connected to the company's home office using a T-1 leased line, and a second T-1 connects the backbone to an ISP's network, for Internet access.

To connect the building's internetwork to the company's home office and to the ISP, you must install two routers, and you have decided to use computers running Windows Server 2003 and the Routing and Remote Access service. The first computer running Windows Server 2003 is called Router01 and two network interface adapters are installed in it. In the Network Connections tool, the adapter connecting the computer to the local network is called LAN Connection and the adapter connected to the T-1 providing access to the home office network is called WAN Connection. The second computer, Router02, also has two network interface adapters, named LAN Connection and ISP Connection, respectively.

The Litware home office network and all the company's other branch offices use RIP, and you have already configured the routers connecting the building's LANs to use RIP.

Based on this information, answer the following questions:

1. When you are running the Routing And Remote Access Server Setup Wizard on Router2, which option should you select in the Configuration page?

   a. Network Address Translation (NAT)

   b. Remote Access (Dial-Up Or VPN)

   c. Secure Connection Between Two Private Networks

   d. Virtual Private Network (VPN) Access And NAT

2. When configuring RIP on Router01, which interfaces should you install?

   a. None

   b. LAN Connection only

   c. WAN Connection only

   d. Both LAN Connection and WAN Connection

3. On which of the two routers must you install RIP? Explain why.

   _____

   _____

4. Which of the following methods can you use to reduce the amount of RIP traffic passing over the T-1 link to the home office?

   a. Set the Outgoing Packet Protocol setting to RIP Version 1 Broadcast

   b. Increase the Periodic Announcement Interval setting

   c. Set the Incoming Packet Protocol setting to RIP Version 1 Only

   d. Decrease the time Before Route Is Removed setting

5. On which of the RRAS configurations should you enable demand-dial routing?

   a. Neither

   b. Router01 only

   c. Router02 Only

   d. Both

Troubleshooting Lab

For each of the following scenarios, specify which of the following tools you would use to troubleshoot the problem: Ping.exe, Tracert.exe, Route.exe, or Pathping.exe.

1. A router on a private internetwork is forwarding traffic to some destination networks properly, but is failing to forward traffic to others. Which tool do you use to repair the problem?

   _____

   _____

2. On a large corporate internetwork, packets originating on one LAN are not reaching destination systems on another LAN, and both the source and destination computers are functioning properly on their local networks. How do you determine which router on the network is not forwarding packets properly?

_____

_____

3. Traffic levels on your company network have risen precipitously, and you have determined that this is due to a dramatic increase in packet retransmissions. You suspect that one of the routers on the network is dropping packets. How do you determine which one?

_____

_____

Chapter Summary

- A WAN topology is the pattern of connections among your network's sites. When selecting a topology, be sure to consider the characteristics of the WAN technology you plan to use.

- Dial-up services, frame relay, and VPNs all make it possible to create a mesh topology without having to install a separate WAN link for every pair of sites.

- Static routing is the manual creation of routing table entries, and can require extensive maintenance. It is not practical for large networks with frequent infrastructure changes.

- Dynamic routing uses a specialized routing protocol, such as RIP or OSPF, that enables the routers to exchange messages containing information about their networks.

- RIP is a distance vector routing protocol that is suitable for smaller networks running at a single speed, but it generates a lot of broadcast traffic. OSPF is a link state routing protocol that is scaleable to support networks of almost any size, but requires more planning, configuration, and maintenance than RIP.

- To support IP multicasting, a router must support IGMP and have network interface adapters that support multicast promiscuous mode.

- RRAS supports multiple authentication protocols, including EAP, MS-CHAP (versions 1 and 2), CHAP, SPAP, and PAP. You should configure RRAS to use the strongest protocol that your clients and servers have in common.

- Remote access policies are sets of conditions that remote clients attempting to connect to the Routing and Remote Access server must meet. You can use policies to control remote access based on group membership and other criteria.

- Tracert.exe is a command line tool that can help you locate a non-functioning router. TRACERT uses ICMP Echo Request messages with incrementing TTL values to test the connection to each router on the path to a given destination.

- Pathping.exe is a command line tool that sends large numbers of test messages to each router on the path to a particular destination and compiles statistics regarding dropped packets. Pathping.exe is best suited for locating a router that is malfunctioning but still operational.

Exam Highlights

Before taking the exam, review the key points and terms that are presented below to help you identify topics you need to review. Return to the lessons for additional practice, and review the "Further Reading" sections in Part 2 for pointers to more information about topics covering the exam objectives.

Key Points

- A distance vector routing protocol like RIP is the preferred routing protocol for an internetwork with LANs that all run at the same speed, because the number of hops is a viable measure of a route's efficiency.

- Link state routing protocols like OSPF are preferable on internetworks with links running at different speeds, such as remote offices connects by WAN links, because their metrics use a more realistic measurement of a route's efficiency.

- To route IP multicast traffic, you must install IGMP on your routers, so that client computers on the networks can register their memberships in a host group.

- Windows Server 2003 includes a variety of security measures to protect remote access servers against unauthorized access, including multiple authentication protocols and encryption algorithms.

- Tracert.exe is the best tool for locating a non-functioning router, while Pathping.exe is better for locating a router that is dropping some packets.

Key Terms

Distance vector routing   A dynamic routing method that rates the relative efficiency of specific routes through the network by counting the number of hops between the source and the destination

Link state routing   A dynamic routing method that rates the relative efficiency of specific routes through the network using link speed, network congestion delays, and a route cost value assigned by an administrator, in addition to the number of hops

Authentication   The process of confirming the identity of a connecting user

Authorization   The process of determining whether the server should permit the connection to proceed

Questions and Answers

Page
5-10 **Lesson 1 Review**

1. Which of the following WAN technologies would be practical to use to create a mesh remote networking topology? (Choose all answers that apply.)

    a. ISDN

    b. Dial-up modems

    c. T-1

    d. Frame relay

    e. VPNs

    a, d, and e

2. What term do frame relay providers use to describe the network to which they connect their subscribers' leased lines?

    A cloud

3. In which of the following WAN topologies can a single cable break totally disconnect one site from the other sites?

    a. Mesh

    b. Ring

    c. Star

    d. None of the above

    c

Page
5-24 **Lesson 2 Review**

1. To support IP multicasting, which of the following components must be installed on a Windows Server 2003 router? (Choose all correct answers.)

    a. The Protocol Independent Multicast (PIM) protocol

    b. A network interface adapter that supports multicast promiscuous mode

    c. The Routing And Remote Access MMC snap-in

    d. Internet Group Management Protocol

    b, c, and d

2. Specify whether each of the following characteristics describes distance vector routing, link state routing, or both.

   a. Used by OSPF

Link state routing

   b. Uses the number of hops to the destination when calculating metrics

Both

   c. Uses link speed when calculating metrics

Link state routing

   d. Used by RIP

Distance vector routing

   e. Unsuitable for enterprises with networks running at various speeds

Distance vector routing

Page 5-41

Lesson 3 Review

1. Which of the following authentication protocols do you use with smart cards?

   a. MS-CHAP v2

   b. EAP-TLS

   c. PEAP

   d. PAP

b

2. What is the function of a RADIUS server in a remote access installation?

   RADIUS is a service that can provide authentication, authorization, and accounting services for multiple remote access servers.

3. How does the callback option in a user account's dial-in properties function as a security feature?

   The callback feature can provide additional security when an administrator specifies the telephone number that the Routing and Remote Access server will use to call the user back during the connection process.

4. Which of the following is *not* a component of a remote access policy?

   a. Authentication protocol

   b. Conditions

   c. Remote access profile

   d. Remote access permission

a

Page
5-52

Lesson 4 Review

1. Which of the following TCP/IP tools is best suited to troubleshooting a situation in which a router is dropping packets?

    a. Ping.exe

    b. Tracert.exe

    c. Pathping.exe

    d. Route.exe

    c

2. What would happen if a router on your network supported only RIP version 1, and all your other routers were Routing and Remote Access servers using RIP with its default configuration?

    The RIP version 1 router would not be able to process the incoming packets from the RRAS routers, because they use RIP version 2 messages by default.

3. If you use static routing on your network, and several administrators are responsible for creating the routing table entries on your routers, what should you do if you open the Routing And Remote Access console on one of your routers, click the Static Routes subheading, and see no entries?

    You should use Route.exe to view the computer's routing table, because static routes not created in the Routing And Remote Access console do not appear in the Static Routes display.

Page
5-53

Case Scenario Exercise

Based on the information provided in the Case Scenario Exercise, answer the following questions:

1. When you are running the Routing And Remote Access Server Setup Wizard on Router2, which option should you select in the Configuration page?

    a. Network Address Translation (NAT)

    b. Remote Access (Dial-Up Or VPN)

    c. Secure Connection Between Two Private Networks

    d. Virtual Private Network (VPN) Access And NAT

    a

2. When configuring RIP on Router01, which interfaces should you install?

   a. None

   b. LAN Connection only

   c. WAN Connection only

   d. Both LAN Connection and WAN Connection

d

3. On which of the two routers must you install RIP? Explain why.

You only have to install RIP on Router01 because this is the router connecting the building network to the home office. Router02 does not need RIP because it only routes traffic to the Internet.

4. Which of the following methods can you use to reduce the amount of RIP traffic passing over the T-1 link to the home office?

   a. Set the Outgoing Packet Protocol setting to RIP Version 1 Broadcast

   b. Increase the Periodic Announcement Interval setting

   c. Set the Incoming Packet Protocol setting to RIP Version 1 Only

   d. Decrease the time Before Route Is Removed setting

b

5. On which of the RRAS configurations should you enable demand-dial routing?

   a. Neither

   b. Router01 only

   c. Router02 Only

   d. Both

a

Page
5-54

Troubleshooting Lab

For each of the following scenarios, specify which of the following tools you would use to troubleshoot the problem: Ping.exe, Tracert.exe, Route.exe, or Pathping.exe.

1. A router on a private internetwork is forwarding traffic to some destination networks properly, but is failing to forward traffic to others. Which tool do you use to repair the problem?

Route.exe

2. On a large corporate internetwork, packets originating on one LAN are not reaching destination systems on another LAN, and both the source and destination computers are functioning properly on their local networks. How do you determine which router on the network is not forwarding packets properly?

Tracert.exe

3. Traffic levels on your company network have risen precipitously, and you have determined that this is due to a dramatic increase in packet retransmissions. You suspect that one of the routers on the network is dropping packets. How do you determine which one?

Pathping.exe

6 Maintaining Server Availability

Exam Objectives in this Chapter:

- Plan network traffic monitoring. Tools might include Network Monitor and System Monitor.
- Identify system bottlenecks, including memory, processor, disk, and network related bottlenecks.
  - ❏ Identify system bottlenecks by using System Monitor.
- Plan a backup and recovery strategy.
  - ❏ Identify appropriate backup types. Methods include full, incremental, and differential.
  - ❏ Plan a backup strategy that uses volume shadow copy.
  - ❏ Plan system recovery that uses Automated System Recovery (ASR).

Why This Chapter Matters

The tools discussed in this chapter should be part of every network administrator's basic tool kit. Keeping your servers running smoothly and protecting their data are top priorities that you should observe before any signs of trouble occur. In the real world, you can use the Performance console to monitor virtually every aspect of the performance of a computer running the Microsoft Windows Server 2003 family, and to alert you when conditions signal any kind of trouble. Network Monitor enables you to examine any kind of traffic on your network, and is also a valuable aid for learning about network protocols.

Lessons in this Chapter:

Before You Begin

To perform the practice exercises in this chapter, you must have installed and configured Windows Server 2003 using the procedure described in "About This Book."

Lesson 1: Monitoring Network Traffic

An important part of a network administrator's job is to keep track of network traffic patterns and to notice developing trends before they become major problems. Windows Server 2003 includes several tools that you can use to view network traffic statistics in real time, maintain logs of network conditions, and capture packets as they travel over the network.

After this lesson, you will be able to

- Use System Monitor to view computer performance statistics in real time
- Use Performance Logs And Alerts to capture counter information to log files
- Use Network Monitor to capture and analyze network traffic

Estimated lesson time: 30 minutes

Using the Performance Console

The Windows Server 2003 Performance console consists of two Microsoft Management Console (MMC) snap-ins: System Monitor and Performance Logs And Alerts. System Monitor enables you to display real-time statistics for a wide variety of system and network performance parameters, in graphical, histogram, or report form. Performance Logs And Alerts enables you to capture performance data from computers anywhere on the network and to create alarms to notify you when specific events or conditions occur.

The System Monitor and Performance Logs And Alerts snap-ins provide detailed data about the resources used by specific components of the operating system and by server programs that have been designed to collect performance data. The graphs provide a display for performance-monitoring data; logs provide recording capabilities for the data; and alerts send notifications to users by means of the Messenger service when a counter value reaches, rises above, or falls below a defined threshold.

Viewing Statistics with System Monitor

With the System Monitor snap-in, you can select from among hundreds of statistics, called *performance counters*, to display the information you need about the computer on which System Monitor is running, or any other computer on the network. Windows Server 2003 includes hundreds of counters, providing information about virtually any component installed in the computer.

Note   The variety of counters that you can choose in System Monitor depends on the software that is running on the computer. When you install additional Windows Server 2003 services, many of them add new performance objects and counters to System Monitor. Some third-party software developers also take advantage of the System Monitor engine and include their own counters with their products.

System Monitor counters are grouped in categories called *performance objects*. A performance object represents a specific hardware or software element in the computer. For example, on a default Windows Server 2003 installation, there are performance objects corresponding to hardware elements, such as the system's processor, memory, and network interface, and to software elements, such as the protocols and services running on the system. When you select a performance object from the Performance Object drop-down list, you see a list of the counters for that object in the Select Counters From List box, and also a list of instances for each counter in the Select Instances From List box. *Instances* enable you to monitor statistics for components individually, when there are two or more in the computer. For instance, on a server with two network interface adapters, you can select a particular network interface counter, such as Bytes Received/Sec, and then select the instance that specifies the particular adapter you want to monitor.

Using System Monitor   When you launch the Performance console from the Administrative Tools program group, you see the graph display of the System Monitor snap-in by default, as shown in Figure 6-1. The graph contains a line for each counter you select for display. By clicking the View Histogram (Ctrl+B) or View Report (Ctrl+R) button on the toolbar, you can display the same information in different formats. The snap-in also provides controls that enable you to change the appearance of the graph in many ways, such as specifying colors for the counter lines and scale increments for the axis.

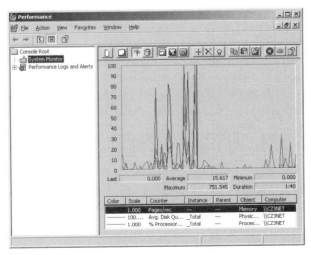

Figure 6-1   The Windows Server 2003 Performance console

To add counters to the System Monitor display, you click the Add (+) button on the toolbar, press Ctrl+I, or right-click anywhere on the graph and select Add Counters from the shortcut menu. (There is no standard menu equivalent for this function.) In the Add Counters dialog box (see Figure 6-2), you specify the name of the computer that you want to monitor, select a performance object, counter, and instance, and then click Add.

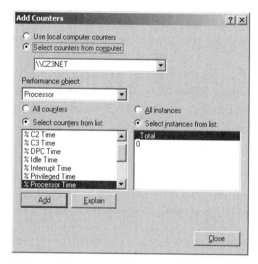

Figure 6-2   The Performance console's Add Counters dialog box

You can add as many counters as you need, after which you click Close. The counters you selected now appear as lines in the graph and as entries in the legend at the bottom of the window.

Although you can add a large number of counters to the System Monitor display, this generally produces a crowded and incoherent graph. Consider the following tips when selecting counters and configuring the display options:

- **Limit the number of counters**   Too many counters make the graph more difficult to understand. To display a large number of statistics, you can display multiple windows in the console and select different counters in each window, or use the Report view to display the counters in the more compact numeric form.

- **Modify the counter display properties**   Depending on the size and capabilities of your monitor, the default colors and line widths that System Monitor uses in its graph might make it difficult to distinguish counters from each other. In the Data tab in the System Monitor Properties dialog box for each counter, you can modify the color, style, and width of that counter's line in the graph, to make it easier to distinguish. (You display the Properties dialog box for each counter by clicking the Properties button on the toolbar or by pressing Ctrl+Q.)

Tip   On a complex System Monitor graph with multiple counters, you can highlight the display of a particular counter by selecting it in the legend and clicking the Highlight button on the toolbar (or pressing Ctrl+H). The line in the graph representing that counter changes to white and becomes thicker, making it easier to see among the other lines.

■ **Choose counters with comparable values**   System Monitor imposes no limitations on the combinations of counters you can select for a single graph, but some statistics are not practical to display together, because of their disparate values. When a graph contains a counter with a value under twenty and a counter with a value in the hundreds, it is difficult to arrange the display so that both counters are easy to read. Choose counters with values that are reasonably comparable, so that you can display them legibly. Here again, if you must display counters with different value ranges, you might use Report view instead of Graph view.

■ **Adjust the vertical scale**   The vertical axis of the System Monitor graph specifies the range of counter values the graph can display. When all the counter lines are compressed to the bottom of the graph, it is difficult to distinguish them and read their values. Reducing the maximum value of the scale can make the graph easier to read. In the Graph tab in the System Monitor Properties dialog box, you can modify the vertical scale by specifying new minimum and maximum values. You can also add horizontal or vertical grid lines, or both, to the display.

Once you create and configure a System Monitor graph, you can save it as an MMC console file (with the .msc filename extension) by selecting Save As from the File menu. Opening the console file later restores your configuration just as you left it, complete with your counter selection and display settings.

Network Traffic Monitoring with System Monitor   In addition to providing information about hardware components in the computer, such as the processor and memory, System Monitor also includes counters for many network statistics. You can use these counters to monitor the network traffic the computer is sending and receiving in a variety of ways. Some of the performance objects that provide network traffic monitoring capabilities are as follows:

■ **Network Interface**   Contains counters providing overall traffic statistics for one of the network interfaces in the computer. In addition to measuring the number of packets and bytes sent and received, in both unicast and broadcast transmissions, you can monitor the network interface for errors and discarded packets.

■ **IPv4**   Contains counters that monitor the number of Internet Protocol (IP) datagrams the computer has sent and received, plus the number of datagrams discarded because they were undeliverable for various reasons. You can also monitor the IP fragmentation process, which is especially useful on a router that connects two different types of networks.

- **ICMP**   Tracks total number of messages using the Internet Control Message Protocol (ICMP). TCP/IP computers use ICMP for diagnostic purposes and to send error messages. Using this performance object, you can track the total number of ICMP messages that the computer has transmitted and received, as well as the statistics for specific ICMP message types. This is a particularly useful device for monitoring network traffic, as it enables you to detect increases in error messages that might be caused by changes in the condition of the network.

- **TCPv4**   Tracks the number of successful and failed Transmission Control Protocol (TCP) connections. You can monitor both the number of TCP segments the computer has sent and received, and their success rate. TCP is the transport layer protocol that most applications use to transmit data over the network, so monitoring the number of TCP segments over time is a good way of evaluating the overall network traffic load.

- **UDPv4**   Monitors the number of User Datagram Protocol (UDP) packets the computer transmits and receives. Service applications, such as the Domain Name System (DNS) and the Dynamic Host Configuration Protocol (DHCP), typically use UDP for client–server communications.

Tip   The System Monitor snap-in in Windows Server 2003 includes performance objects for both version 4 and version 6 of the IP protocol. IPv6 expands the IP address space from 32 to 128 bits and uses a different packet format than version 4. As a result, the monitoring of ICMP, TCP, and UDP messages (which are carried inside IP datagrams) is also different, so there are separate performance objects for version 6 of these protocols as well. Virtually all networks today still use version 4 of these protocols, but the version 6 standards are currently in the process of ratification and deployment. Unless you know that you are using version 6 on your network, you should use the version 4 performance objects.

In addition to monitoring protocol traffic, System Monitor also includes counters for many of the network services you can run on a computer running Windows Server 2003. Installing services such as DNS and Windows Internet Name Service (WINS) adds new performance objects to System Monitor, containing dozens of counters that enable you to monitor the activities of these services in great detail.

See Also   For more information on monitoring network services, see Lesson 2 of this chapter.

Using Performance Logs And Alerts

Few network administrators have the time or inclination to sit around watching the System Monitor display, looking for signs of trouble on the network. The Performance Logs And Alerts snap-in eliminates the need to do this: it uses the same performance counters as System Monitor to capture information to log files over a period of time. When you select the Performance Logs And Alerts snap-in in the Performance console, you see three subheadings, as follows:

- **Counter logs**   Enables the Performance console to capture statistics for specific counters to a log file at regular intervals over a specified time

- **Trace logs**   Enables the Performance console to record information about system applications when certain events occur, such as disk I/O operations or page faults

- **Alerts**   Enables the Performance console to monitor the values of a specific counter at regular intervals and perform an action when the counter reaches a specified value

One of the main benefits of Performance Logs And Alerts is the ability to capture performance counter information for later study. The snap-in supports a variety of file formats that enable you to import the captured information into spreadsheet and database programs. You can use counter logs to establish a baseline for network performance, then periodically check the logs for deviation from that baseline. You can also create alerts to warn you when specific network conditions deviate too far from the norm.

> **Note**   Performance Logs And Alerts runs as a service, which means that it loads during system startup and continues to operate even if no user is logged on to the system.

Analyzing Network Traffic with Network Monitor

While the Performance console is an excellent tool for monitoring a wide range of network performance parameters over time, you can also examine network traffic in much greater detail by using the Network Monitor application included with Windows Server 2003. Network Monitor is a protocol analyzer that captures the packets the computer sends and receives, and then displays their contents for examination. Network Monitor includes parsers for all the major protocols that Windows Server 2003 uses, enabling the program to interpret the protocol header fields and display them in a comprehensible format.

> **Caution**   Because Network Monitor can intercept and read the contents of packets transmitted over the network, it is a potentially serious security hazard. Passwords or other sensitive data transmitted in unencrypted form can easily be read from packets captured with Network Monitor. Therefore, you should take steps to prevent unauthorized users from having access to the application.

Network Monitor Versions

The Network Monitor application included with Windows Server 2003 is a subset of the full version of the program included with the Microsoft Systems Management Server (SMS) product. The Windows Server 2003 Network Monitor is limited to capturing the traffic transmitted and received by the computer on which the program is running. The SMS version can switch the computer's network interface adapters into *promiscuous mode*, enabling the program to capture all traffic passing over the network, even packets not transmitted or received by the computer running Network Monitor. The SMS version also enables you to install a Network Monitor Agent on other computers, so that you can use them to capture packets on other networks and send them to the computer running Network Monitor for display.

In addition to these features, the SMS version of Network Monitor can also perform the following actions:

- Determine the top user of network bandwidth
- Determine which protocol consumes the most bandwidth
- Locate routers on the network
- Resolve a device name into a Media Access Control (MAC) address
- Edit and retransmit network traffic

Using Network Monitor

When you first launch Network Monitor, you see a Capture window for the computer's network interface adapter. When you select Start from the Capture menu, the program copies the packets processed by the network interface adapter to a buffer file on the hard drive, and displays a variety of statistics about the network traffic (see Figure 6-3).

Note   Windows Server 2003 does not include Network Monitor in its default Setup configuration. You must install the program yourself, using the Add Or Remove Programs tool.

Tip   If your computer has more than one network interface, Network Monitor prompts you to select one of the interfaces the first time you launch the program. Afterwards, you can switch interfaces at any time by selecting Networks from the Capture menu.

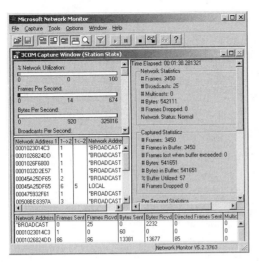

Figure 6-3   The Network Monitor Capture window

When you have captured enough data to the buffer, you select Stop And View from the Capture menu to display a Capture Summary window containing a list of the packets in the buffer (see Figure 6-4). Each entry in the list contains the following information:

■ **Frame**   The frame number, beginning with 1, in the order in which the packets are captured

■ **Time**   The number of seconds since the beginning of the captured traffic sample

■ **Src MAC Addr**   The hardware address of the computer that transmitted the packet

■ **Dst MAC Addr**   The hardware address of the computer that received the packet

■ **Protocol**   The protocol that defines the primary function of the packet

■ **Description**   The function of the protocol, often including values of important header fields

■ **Src Other Addr**   The IP address or the Internetwork Packet Exchange (IPX) address of the computer that transmitted the packet

■ **Dst Other Addr**   The IP address or the IPX address of the computer that received the packet

■ **Type Other Addr**   The network layer protocol responsible for carrying the packet across the network

Tip   By default, the size of the capture buffer in Network Monitor is 1 megabyte. You can modify the buffer size by selecting Buffer Settings from the Capture menu.

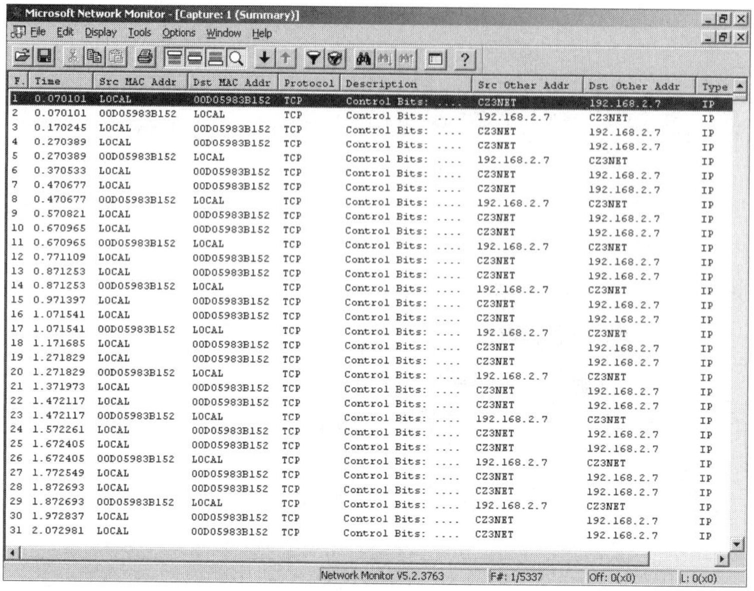

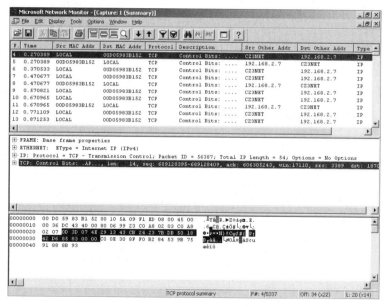

Figure 6-4   The Network Monitor Capture Summary window

Figure 6-5   The Capture Summary window's Summary, Detail, and Hexadecimal panes

Double-clicking one of the entries in the Capture Summary window splits the screen into three panes (see Figure 6-5), which contain the following information:

■ **Summary**   The same list of frames as the ones appearing in the full-size Capture Summary window

■ **Detail**   The decoded contents of the selected packet in the form of an expandable tree

■ **Hexadecimal**   The raw contents of the selected packet, in hexadecimal notation

The Detail pane is the most useful one in this display, as you can expand any of the protocols in the packet to display the values of specific header fields, as shown in Figure 6-6.

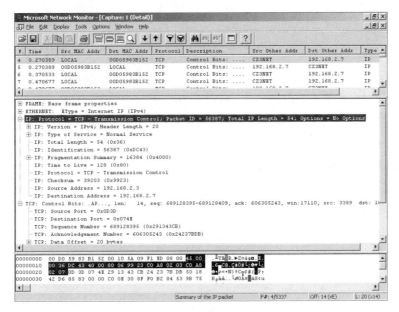

Figure 6-6   Network Monitor's expandable protocol display

Using Capture and Display Filters

One of the things you learn quickly when using Network Monitor is that the tool can often provide an embarrassment of riches. Even a brief network traffic sample can contain hundreds of packets performing many different functions, and it can be difficult to home in on the information you need. However, Network Monitor provides the ability to filter the traffic you capture and display, so that you can concentrate on specific computers or protocols.

Network Monitor includes both capture and display filters. Capture filters enable you to specify which packets the program should copy to its buffer, and display filters enable you to control which packets already stored in the buffer the program displays in the Capture Summary window.

You use capture filters when you want to capture specific traffic to the buffer over a long period of time. For example, if you want to examine the traffic that a server exchanges with a particular computer over the course of an entire day, you can use a capture filter to save only the packets containing the addresses of those two computers. Without the capture filter, an enormous amount of data would be captured during an entire day. Display filters are best when you want to capture a relatively short traffic sample and examine in it in different ways. For example, you might capture five minutes of traffic in the buffer and then create a series of display filters to examine the traffic generated by various protocols.

To create a capture filter, you display the Capture Filter dialog box by selecting Filter from the Capture menu in the Capture window. To create a display filter, you display the Display Filter dialog box (see Figure 6-7), by selecting Filter from the Display menu in the Capture Summary window. In this dialog box, you can use Boolean logic to select the combination of protocols and addresses you want to display. When you click OK, the program modifies the display to hide all the packets that don't meet the conditions specified by the filter.

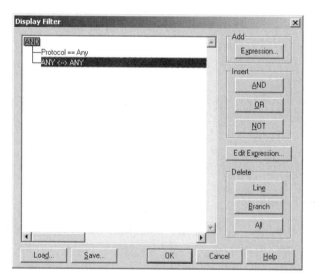

Figure 6-7 The Display Filter dialog box

Exam Tip Be sure to understand the differences between System Monitor and Network Monitor. System Monitor displays performance data for specific hardware and software components in a computer, while Network Monitor captures, analyzes, and displays traffic as it is transmitted over the network.

Practice: Using Network Monitor

For the purposes of this practice, assume that you are a network administrator planning to use Network Monitor to capture a representative traffic sample on your network. Once you have the sample, you want to check the ICMP traffic for error messages the computer might have sent or received. First, you install Network Monitor on your Server01 computer and use it to capture traffic on your network. Then, you create a display filter that causes Network Monitor to display only the ICMP packets in the traffic sample.

Exercise 1: Installing Network Monitor

In this procedure, you install the Network Monitor application.

1. Click Start, point to Control Panel, and then click Add Or Remove Programs.

2. Click Add/Remove Windows Components to launch the Windows Components Wizard.

3. Scroll down in the Components list, select Management And Monitoring Tools, and then click Details.

4. Select Network Monitor Tools, and then click OK.

5. Click Next to perform the installation. You might be prompted to insert your Windows Server 2003 distribution CD in the CD-ROM drive.

6. Click Finish to close the wizard and complete the installation.

7. Close the Add Or Remove Programs tool.

Exercise 2: Capturing Frames

In this procedure, you use Network Monitor to capture a sample of the traffic on your network.

1. Click Start, point to All Programs, point to Administrative Tools, and then click Network Monitor.

   The Microsoft Network Monitor window opens and a Microsoft Network Monitor message box appears, prompting you to specify the network on which you want to capture data.

2. Click OK. A Select A Network dialog box appears.

3. Expand the Local Computer heading, select the Local Area Connection subheading, and then click OK. The Local Area Connection Capture Window window appears.

4. From the Capture menu, choose Start. Network Monitor begins capturing frames.

5. In Microsoft Windows Explorer, copy a series of files from a drive on the computer running Network Monitor to a shared folder on another computer on the network running a Windows operating system.

6. Display a Command Prompt window and use the Ping.exe utility to test the connection to one of the other computers on the network.

   To use Ping.exe, type **ping *ipaddress*** at the command prompt, where *ipaddress* is the address of another computer on the network.

7. Back in Network Monitor, from the Capture menu, choose Stop And View. The Capture Summary window appears, containing a list of the frames in the traffic sample.

8. Close the Command Prompt window.

9. Leave Network Monitor open for the next exercise.

Exercise 3: Creating a Display Filter

In this procedure, you create a display filter to restrict the display to ICMP packets.

1. From the Display menu, select Filter. The Display Filter dialog box appears.

2. Double-click Protocol == Any. The Expression dialog box appears.

3. In the Protocol tab, click Disable All. All the protocols in the Enabled Protocols list move to the Disabled Protocols list.

4. Scroll down the Disabled Protocols list, select ICMP, and then click Enable. The ICMP protocol entry moves to the Enabled Protocols list.

5. Click OK to close the Expression dialog box.

6. Click OK to close the Display Filter dialog box.

7. Notice that the Capture Summary window now contains only the ICMP Echo and Echo Reply packets created when you pinged the other computer in Exercise 2. The Frame numbers and Time stamp retain their original values.

8. Close the Network Monitor window. A Microsoft Network Monitor message box appears.

9. Click No when asked if you want to save the capture.

Lesson Review

The following questions are intended to reinforce key information presented in this lesson. If you are unable to answer a question, review the lesson materials and try the question again. You can find answers to the questions in the "Questions and Answers" section at the end of this chapter.

1. Why do System Monitor performance counters sometime have multiple instances?

_____

_____

2. In System Monitor, which performance object would you select to monitor the number of TCP/IP error messages transmitted and received by a computer?

   a. Network Interface

   b. TCPv4

   c. ICMP

   d. UDPv4

3. When using Network Monitor, under what conditions is it preferable to use a capture filter instead of a display filter?

_____

_____

Lesson Summary

- System Monitor is an MMC snap-in that monitors specific computer resources in real time, displaying the information in Graph, Histogram, or Report view.

- You can use System Monitor to monitor network traffic by selecting performance counters corresponding to network interfaces, protocols, or applications.

- Performance Logs And Alerts is an MMC snap-in that uses System Monitor's performance counters to capture information to log files over a long period of time.

- You can use Performance Logs And Alerts to establish a network performance baseline, and then compare the baseline to current performance levels.

- Network Monitor is a protocol analyzer that can capture packets from the network and analyze their contents in detail.

Lesson 2: Monitoring Network Servers

Servers are the mainstay of most networks, and keeping them running efficiently is a major part of the network administrator's job. You can use the Performance console and other Windows Server 2003 tools to monitor the activities of your servers and the applications running on them.

After this lesson, you will be able to

- Monitor the network services included with Windows Server 2003
- Locate bottlenecks in the four primary server subsystems

Estimated lesson time: 30 minutes

Monitoring Network Server Services

Network services are applications that always run in the background, listening for and processing client requests. In many cases, it is easy to forget that they are even there—until something goes wrong. However, it is the job of the network administrator to try to anticipate problems before they become disasters, and this means regularly keeping a watchful eye on these services. Most of the network services included with Windows Server 2003 provide several ways to monitor their activities, including status screens, logs, and performance counters. The procedures for monitoring the major Windows Server 2003 network services are covered in the following sections.

Keeping Services Running

Obviously, the most important consideration for network services is for them to be running when clients need them. It is common for a network administrator to find that DNS name resolution or DHCP address assignment is failing simply because the service is not running. There are several reasons that this might be the case, including the following:

- The service might not have started when an administrator restarted the server last.
- Another administrator might have manually stopped the service for some reason, and failed to restart it.
- Conditions on the server might have caused the service to stop.

To check the current status of the services running on a computer running Windows Server 2003, display the Services console (see Figure 6-8) from the Administrative Tools program group. For every service that you expect to be running, Started should appear in the Status column.

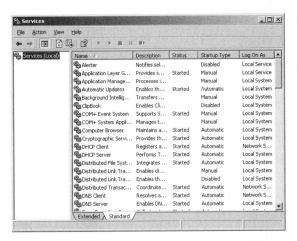

Figure 6-8   The Services console

In most cases, system administrators configure the services that always need to be running with a startup type of Automatic, so that the services load when the operating system starts. If a service does not start, and you have configured it for automatic startup, you should determine why it is not running. If the service failed to start when the system started or if it has stopped, there must be a problem, such as insufficient system memory or some other fault. In most cases, the System log in the Event Viewer console should contain an entry explaining why the service stopped or failed to load. If there is no such entry, it is possible that someone manually stopped the service, and you should find out why before you start it again.

Monitoring DHCP

DHCP is a vital service for the networks designed to rely on it, but a failure of the DHCP service might not be readily apparent in some cases. By default, DHCP servers lease IP addresses to clients for eight days at a time. If all the computers on your network successfully obtain an address from a DHCP server, and the DHCP server then fails, the computers can still use their addresses until the leases expire in eight days. You might not even know that the DHCP service is not running unless a new client attempts to obtain an address and cannot do so.

Tip   Along with monitoring the DHCP service for faults or errors, it is also important to be aware of the number of addresses available in the DHCP scopes. If all the addresses in a scope are in use, new clients requiring address assignments cannot obtain them from that server. If you have the addresses for a particular subnet split between two scopes on different servers, you can modify the scope configurations to add some addresses to the scope that is depleted.

Viewing DHCP Server Statistics   The DHCP console includes a Server Statistics dialog box that you can display by clicking the Server icon and then, from the Action menu, choosing Display Statistics (see Figure 6-9). This dialog box contains the following information.

Figure 6-9   The DHCP Server Statistics window

- **Start Time**   The date and time that the DHCP service was last started

- **Up Time**   The amount of time that the DHCP service has been running since it was last started

- **Discovers**   The number of DHCPDISCOVER messages that the server has received from clients, requesting IP address assignments

- **Offers**   The number of DHCPOFFER messages that the server has transmitted to clients, offering them IP address assignments

- **Requests**   The number of DHCPREQUEST messages that the server has received from clients, accepting offered IP addresses and renewing address leases

- **Acks**   The number of DHCPACK messages that the server has transmitted to clients, confirming IP address assignments

- **Nacks**   The number of DHCPNAK messages that the server has transmitted to clients, denying IP address assignments

- **Declines**   The number of DHCPDECLINE messages that the server has received from clients, declining offered IP addresses

- **Releases**   The number of DHCPRELEASE messages that the server has received from clients, releasing IP addresses

- **Total Scopes**   The number of operational scopes (IP address pools) on the DHCP server

- **Total Addresses**   The total number of IP addresses available in all the server's scopes

- **In Use**   The number of IP addresses that are currently assigned by the DHCP server, in both numerical and percentage forms

- **Available**   The number of IP addresses that are currently available for allocation by the DHCP server, in both numeric and percentage form

Important   The Available value specifies the number of IP addresses available for allocation by all the scopes on the server combined. This means that one or more of the scopes could still be depleted even though this value is positive.

DHCP Logging   Although a failure of the DHCP service to start or an incident causing the service to shut down will usually show up as an entry in the Event Viewer console's System log, DHCP does not log its everyday activities there. Instead, the DHCP service maintains its own log files in the *%Systemroot%*\System32\Dhcp folder on the system drive. Every entry in the DHCP log contains the following information:

- **ID**   A numerical code that identifies the reason for the log entry

See Also   Windows Server 2003 DHCP Server uses a list of codes that represent common DHCP activities (such as the starting and stopping of the DHCP service) and common error conditions. The code values are accessible from the DHCP console's online help system.

- **Date**   The date on which the log entry was created

- **Time**   The time at which the log entry was created

- **Description**   Describes the event that triggered the log entry

- **IP Address**   The IP address of the DHCP client (if any) involved in the event that triggered the log entry

- **Host Name**   The host name of the DHCP client (if any) involved in the event that triggered the log entry

- **MAC Address**   The hardware address of the network interface adapter in the DHCP client (if any) involved in the event that triggered the log entry

Using DHCP Performance Counters   Installing the DHCP Server service on a computer running Windows Server 2003 also adds the following performance counters, which you can use to track DHCP performance in the System Monitor and Performance Logs And Alerts snap-ins:

- **Acks/Sec**   Specifies the number of DHCPACK messages being transmitted by the DHCP server each second

- **Active Queue Length**   Specifies the number of incoming packets waiting to be processed by the DHCP server

- **Conflict Check Queue Length**   Specifies the number of outgoing conflict detection (ping) packets waiting to be transmitted by the DHCP server

- **Declines/Sec**   Specifies the number of DHCPDECLINE messages being received by the DHCP server each second

- **Discovers/Sec**   Specifies the number of DHCPDISCOVER messages being received by the DHCP server each second

- **Duplicates Dropped/Sec**   Specifies the number of duplicate packets being received by the DHCP server each second

- **Informs/Sec**   Specifies the number of DHCPINFORM messages being received by the DHCP server each second

- **Milliseconds Per Packet (Avg)**   Specifies the amount of time (in milliseconds) that the server is taking to respond to an incoming message

- **Nacks/Sec**   Specifies the number of DHCPNAK messages being transmitted by the DHCP server each second

- **Offers/Sec**   Specifies the number of DHCPOFFER messages being transmitted by the DHCP server each second

- **Packets Expired/Sec**   Specifies the number of packets in the DHCP server's message queue that are expiring each second

- **Packets Received/Sec**   Specifies the number of packets received by the DHCP server each second

- **Releases/Sec**   Specifies the number of DHCPRELEASE messages being received by the DHCP server each second

- **Requests/Sec**   Specifies the number of DHCPREQUEST messages being received by the DHCP server each second

Monitoring these counters is one way of determining how much network traffic the DHCP clients and servers are generating. If the two queue length counters frequently contain high values, you should check the server for a bottleneck that is slowing down DHCP operations.

Monitoring DNS

A malfunctioning DNS server can have much a more drastic and immediate effect on a network than a DHCP server failure. Depending on the functions that the DNS server performs, a failure could have any or all of the following effects:

- Internet clients cannot access Internet servers.

- Internet users cannot access your company's World Wide Web servers.

- Internet e-mail directed to your domain bounces.

- Active Directory directory service clients cannot locate a domain controller and therefore cannot log on.

Because your DNS servers might be accessible from the Internet, they are also more susceptible than internal services such as DHCP to attacks that can prevent them from functioning. It is therefore important that you monitor your DNS servers regularly.

DNS Logging   Unlike most of the network services in Windows Server 2003, DNS has its own log in the Event Viewer console (see Figure 6-10). This log can contain informational entries about the service's activities, as well as errors and warnings concerning dangerous conditions.

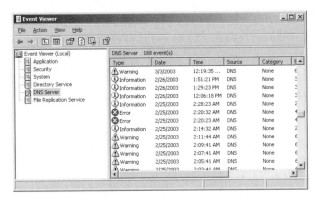

Figure 6-10   The DNS Server log in the Event Viewer console

Tip   You can specify what information the DNS service saves to the Event Log by displaying the DNS server icon's Properties dialog box in the DNS console, clicking the Event Logging tab, and selecting from the following options: No Events, Errors Only, Errors And Warnings, or All Events.

In addition to the Event Viewer log, the Windows Server 2003 DNS Server service has debug logging capabilities, which you configure in the Debug Logging tab in the DNS server icon's Properties dialog box, as shown in Figure 6-11. In this dialog box, you can specify the types of messages and the amount of detail you want to log. You can also create filters to log only the messages to or from specific IP addresses.

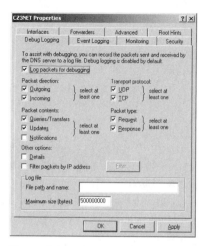

Figure 6-11   The Debug Logging tab in a DNS server's Properties dialog box

By default, the DNS service saves the debugging log as a standard text file in the *%Systemroot%*\System32\Dns folder on the computer's local drive. In the Debug Logging tab, you can also specify an alternative file name and a maximum size for the log.

> **Important**   The DNS service's debug logging feature can log a great deal of detailed information. The log file can therefore take up a lot of disk space and consume a substantial number of processor cycles, if you let it. You should not leave this feature on all the time. Use it only when you are troubleshooting a problem with the DNS service or when you are performing regular maintenance.

Using DNS Performance Counters   A computer running Windows Server 2003 with the DNS Server service installed also has a DNS performance object that contains over 60 performance counters to monitor virtually every DNS server activity, using the Performance console. The DNS performance counters include virtually every type of DNS message, incoming and outgoing. Monitoring these counters is particularly useful when the DNS server is accessible from the Internet. For example, using Performance Logs And Alerts to track the number of incoming name resolution requests can help you detect a denial-of-service (DoS) attack before it completely overwhelms your server.

Monitoring WINS

Because it is not an Internet service and because it is largely self-sufficient, WINS doesn't require a lot of monitoring. The most important element to consider in a large WINS deployment is the database replication process. If replication events don't occur as planned, some of the WINS servers on the network might not be able to resolve NetBIOS names.

The WINS Server Statistics dialog box (see Figure 6-12), which you access by clicking the Server icon in the WINS console and selecting Display Server Statistics from the Action menu, specifies the number of name registrations and resolutions the server has performed, as well as information about the most recent replication processes.

Figure 6-12   The WINS Server Statistics dialog box

The Performance console also includes WINS performance counters that roughly correspond to the statistics in the WINS Server Statistics dialog box, which enable you to monitor the same statistics over time. You can also set alarms to notify you of certain conditions, such as the number of name resolution failures reaching a critically high amount, possible signaling a failure in the replication process.

Monitoring Routing And Remote Access

As you have learned throughout this book, the Routing And Remote Access service (RRAS) in Windows Server 2003 can perform a wide variety of tasks; as a result, there are many different status screens scattered throughout the Routing And Remote Access console.

Monitoring Remote Access Activities   When you click the Server Status icon at the top of the console tree, the details pane contains a list of all the Routing And Remote Access servers you've added to the console, specifying each server's current operational state, the number of ports it has, and the number of ports that are currently in use (see Figure 6-13). If you have multiple RRAS servers on your network, configured to provide remote access to clients, this is a good way to track your current port usage at any time.

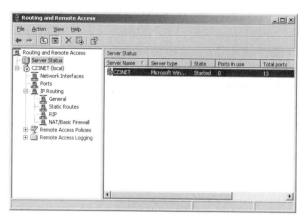

Figure 6-13   The Routing And Remote Access console's Server Status display

When you click the Ports icon in the console tree, you see a list of the server's ports in the details pane. Double-clicking one of the ports displays a Port Status dialog box (see Figure 6-14) specifying the number of bytes the port has transmitted and received, the number of errors that have occurred, and the IP address of the client connected to the port.

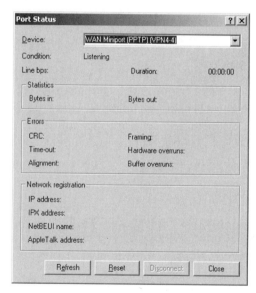

Figure 6-14   A Routing And Remote Access console Port Status dialog box

To monitor remote access port activities over time, you can use the Remote Access Service (RAS) counters in the Performance console. The System Monitor and Performance Logs And Alerts snap-ins have two performance objects, called RAS Port and RAS Total. The RAS Port performance object enables you to select a particular port to monitor, and RAS Total monitors the combined activity on all ports. Individual counters in each of these performance objects enable you to track the same statistics as in the Port Status dialog box. Here again, you can set alerts to notify you when errors reach a certain level, or when other possible signs of trouble arise.

Monitoring Router Activities   When you have configured RRAS to function as a router, you can view some basic routing statistics in the TCP/IP Information window for your server (see Figure 6-15) by clicking the IP Routing's General subheading in the console tree and, from the Action menu, choosing Show TCP/IP Information. This window specifies the number of entries in the routing table and the number of IP datagrams the router has forwarded, as well as statistics for the IP, ICMP, TCP, and UDP protocols.

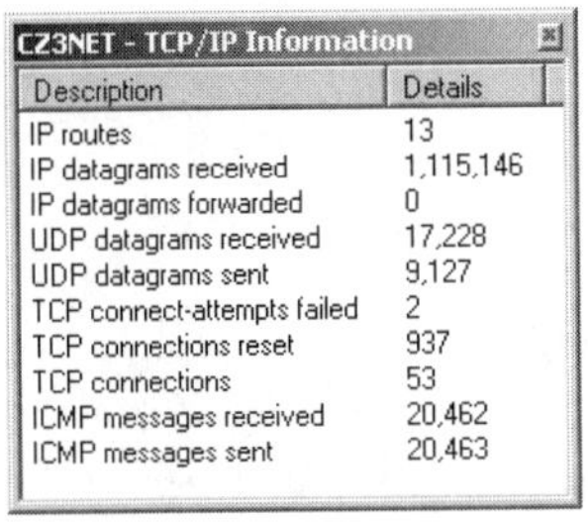

CZ3NET – TCP/IP Information	
Description	Details
IP routes	13
IP datagrams received	1,115,146
IP datagrams forwarded	0
UDP datagrams received	17,228
UDP datagrams sent	9,127
TCP connect-attempts failed	2
TCP connections reset	937
TCP connections	53
ICMP messages received	20,462
ICMP messages sent	20,463

Figure 6-15   The Routing And Remote Access console's TCP/IP Information window

If you have installed a dynamic routing protocol on your RRAS server, such as Routing Information Protocol (RIP) or Open Shortest Path First (OSPF), you can monitor it using any of the following procedures:

■ Select RIP, and then choose Show Neighbors from the Action menu—Displays a list of the other RIP routers exchanging messages with RRAS, along with the number of bad packets and bad routes attributable to each one

■ Select OSPF, and then choose Show Areas from the Action menu—Displays a list of the OSPF areas configured on the server, whether they are operational or not, and how many link state calculations have been performed on the interface

■ Select OSPF, and then choose Show Link-State Database from the Action menu— Displays the entire OSPF link state database

■ Select OSPF, and then choose Show Neighbors from the Action menu—Displays a list of the other OSPF routers exchanging messages with RRAS, along with information about them

■ Select OSPF, and then choose Show Virtual Interfaces from the Action menu— Displays a list of the OSPF virtual interfaces you have configured in RRAS

Locating System Bottlenecks

It is not uncommon for network administrators to be faced with performance problems that are not attributable to an obvious cause, such as a service failure. Users might complain that their network performance is slow at certain times of the day, or that performance has been declining gradually over the course of weeks or months. When this occurs, one of the most common causes is a bottleneck somewhere in the path between the client and the data on the network that the client needs.

> **Note**   A *bottleneck* is a component that is not providing the same level of performance as the other components in the system. For example, users might complain that their file server performance is slow, and you might spend a great deal of time and money upgrading your network from 10Base-T to 100Base-TX, expecting to see a dramatic improvement. However, if your server is an old computer using a first generation Pentium processor, the improvement is likely to be minimal, because the server's processor, not the LAN technology, is the bottleneck. All the other components are running well, but the processor cannot keep up with the data flow provided by the new, faster network.

Locating the bottleneck that is hindering performance can be a complicated task, but Windows Server 2003 provides most of the tools you need. To find a bottleneck, you usually examine the four main subsystems of a computer, which are covered in the following sections. The Performance console in Windows Server 2003 is usually the best tool for detecting bottlenecks, because it includes performance counters that enable you to monitor each of these subsystems in detail.

> **Tip**   To monitor these four subsystems, it is always a good idea to establish a performance baseline first, under normal operating conditions, so that you can compare the baseline to future statistics and discern trends that might eventually affect performance.

Monitoring Processor Performance

An inadequate or improperly configured processor array can cause a server to queue incoming client requests, preventing the server from fulfilling them promptly. For processor monitoring, the % Processor Time counter is the primary indicator of processor activity. If this counter frequently reaches 100 percent, the processor is likely to be the bottleneck. To remedy the problem, you could use faster processors, more processors (in a multiprocessor server), or processors with larger Level 2 caches.

Monitoring Memory Performance

An inadequate amount of memory in a server can prevent the computer from caching frequently used data aggressively enough, causing processes to rely on disk reads more than memory reads, and slowing down the entire system. To monitor memory performance, you can use counters in the Memory performance object, such as Pages/ Sec and Available MBytes. If the server gets to a point where the amount of available memory is dwindling, you can probably improve the performance of the entire system by installing more.

Monitoring Storage Subsystem Performance

A storage subsystem that is overburdened with Read and Write commands can slow down the rate of processing client requests. The server's hard disk drives carry a greater physical burden than the other three subsystems, because in satisfying the I/O requests of many clients, the drive heads must continually move to different locations on the drive platters. The drive head mechanism can move only so fast, however, and once the drive reaches its maximum read/write speed, additional requests can begin to pile up in the queue, waiting to be processed. For this reason, the storage subsystem is a prime location for a bottleneck.

To monitor the storage subsystem in the Performance console, you can use the counters in the PhysicalDisk performance object, such as % Disk Time. When trying to remedy a storage bottleneck, adding more hard drives as separate entities generally does not do any good, unless you split your data among the drives so that the I/O requests are divided equally among them. Instead, you should consider adding drives and combining them in a RAID (redundant array of independent disks) installation. With RAID, the more disks in the array, the faster the I/O performance. If you find that the disk time percentage is frequently at a higher level, you can remedy the situation by adding more drives to the RAID array.

Monitoring Network Performance

The bandwidth of the network connections limits the amount of traffic reaching the server through its network interfaces. If counters in the Network Interface performance object, such as Output Queue Length, indicate that the network itself is the bottleneck, there are two remedies, and neither one is a simple fix:

- **Increase the speed of the network** This means replacing the network interfaces in all the computers, hubs, routers, and other devices on the network, and possibly replacing the cabling as well.

- **Install additional network adapters in the server and redistribute the network** If traffic frequently saturates the network interfaces already in the server, the only way to increase the network throughput without increasing the network's speed is to install more network interfaces. However, connecting more interfaces to the same network will not permit any more traffic to reach the server. Instead, you must create additional subnets on the network and redistribute the computers among them, so that there is less traffic on each subnet.

Exam Tip   Be sure to familiarize yourself with the performance counters commonly used to locate system bottlenecks in a computer running Windows Server 2003.

Practice: Establishing a Performance Baseline

In this practice, you configure the Performance Logs And Alerts snap-in to create a counter log containing baseline performance information for your server, and then view the results. In the future, if your server's performance degrades, you can repeat the procedure and compare the results to this baseline.

Exercise 1: Creating a Counter Log

In this procedure, you configure the Performance Logs And Alerts snap-in to create a log file containing information about the computer's four primary subsystems.

1. Click Start, point to All Programs, point to Administrative Tools, and then click Performance. The Performance console appears.

2. Expand the Performance Logs And Alerts heading in the console tree and select the Counter Logs subheading.

3. From the Action menu, select New Log Settings. The New Log Settings dialog box appears.

4. In the Name text box, type **Baseline,** and then click OK. A Baseline dialog box appears.

5. Click Add Counters. An Add Counters dialog box appears.

6. Click Add to select the default % Processor Time counter.

7. In the Performance Object field, select Memory.

8. Click Add to select the default Pages/Sec counter.

9. In the Performance Object field, select PhysicalDisk.

10. Click Add to select the default % Disk Time counter.

11. In the Performance Object field, select Network Interface.

12. Click Add to select the default Bytes Total/Sec counter.

13. In the Select Counters From List box, select Output Queue Length, and then click Add.

14. Click Close to return to the Baseline dialog box. The counters you selected appear in the Counters list.

15. Click the Schedule tab.

16. In the Start Log group box, click the Manually (Using The Shortcut Menu) option button.

17. In the Stop Log group box, click the After option button, and then set the time interval to one hour.

18. Click OK. If this is the first time you are creating a log file, a Baseline message box appears asking if you'd like to create the default C:\PerfLogs log folder.

19. Click Yes. An entry for the Baseline log you created appears in the Counter Logs details pane.

20. Select the Baseline entry in the details pane and, from the Action menu, click Start. The icon for the log changes from red to green, indicating that the service is capturing data.

21. Leave the Performance console open for the next exercise.

Exercise 2: Viewing Counter Log Data

In this procedure, you view the data that the Performance Logs And Alerts service has collected in the counter log using System Monitor.

1. In the Performance console, click the System Monitor heading in the console tree.

2. Click the View Log Data button on the toolbar. The System Monitor Properties dialog box appears.

3. Click the Log Files option button, and then click Add. A Select Log File dialog box appears.

4. Browse to the folder containing the counter logs, select the Baseline_000001.blg file, and then click Open. The counter log you selected appears in the Log Files list in the System Monitor Properties dialog box.

> **Tip**   By default, Performance Logs And Alerts creates counter logs in the PerfLogs folder on the system drive.

5. Click Time Range to display the starting and ending times for the range of information in the counter log file.

6. Use the slider bars in the Time Range indicator to display the entire range of information in the log. Click OK.

7. Click the Add button on the System Monitor toolbar. The Add Counters dialog box appears.

   The performance objects and counters available in the Add Counters dialog box are now limited to those you captured in the log.

8. Select each Performance Object value in turn and add all five counters to the System Monitor graph. A System Monitor Control message box may appear to inform you that a selected counter is already present. If this message box appears, click OK.

9. Click Close. The counter log information now appears on the System Monitor graph.

10. Close the Performance console.

Lesson Review

The following questions are intended to reinforce key information presented in this lesson. If you are unable to answer a question, review the lesson materials and try the question again. You can find answers to the questions in the "Questions and Answers" section at the end of this chapter.

1. Why is the Available value in the DHCP console's Server Statistics dialog box usually not an adequate means of determining whether a DHCP scope's IP address pool is depleted?

   _____

   _____

2. Which of the following are correct reasons that it is more critical to monitor DNS performance than DHCP or WINS performance? (Choose all answers that are correct.)

   a. DNS servers might be accessible from the Internet, and DHCP and WINS servers are not.

   b. DNS servers are more likely to malfunction than DHCP or WINS servers.

   c. DNS server failures can have an immediate effect on network client performance.

   d. DNS servers have less effective monitoring tools.

3. What is the best remedy for a disk subsystem that is the bottleneck in a server's performance?

   _____

   _____

Lesson Summary

- Use the Services console to ensure that vital network services are running, and that they are configured with the correct startup type. Check the Event Viewer console to determine why a service might have stopped.

- Network services such as DHCP, DNS, WINS, and RRAS, have various mechanisms you can use to track their statistics and ongoing activities, including log files, status screens, and performance counters.

- Server performance degradations are frequently caused by a bottleneck, that is, a slowdown of a key component that prevents the system from performing up to its potential.

- When looking for the bottleneck on a server, check its four primary subsystems: processor, memory, storage, and network.

Lesson 3: Planning a Backup Strategy

Performing regular backups is one of the most basic functions of the network administrator. Unlike most of the key components in a computer, hard drives have parts that move at high speeds, working at very close tolerances. As a result, hard drive failures are relatively common, and you must prepare for them by regularly saving your data on another storage medium.

Off the Record   The most common analogy used to describe the relationship between a hard drive's platters (where the data is stored) and its heads (which read and write data to the platters) is that of a 747 airliner flying at 500 miles an hour, five feet above the ground. When you consider this, it is amazing that hard drives work as well and as long as they do.

After this lesson, you will be able to

- Describe the elements of a backup strategy and their functions
- Understand the difference between full, incremental, and differential backup jobs
- List the steps involved in creating a backup plan

Estimated lesson time: 30 minutes

Understanding Network Backups

A network backup solution consists of three elements: one or more backup drives, a backup software product, and a backup plan that details the use of the other two items.

Backup Hardware

The storage medium that most administrators choose for backing up their networks is magnetic tape. Magnetic tape drives have high capacities, low media costs, and are a reliable means of long-term data storage. High capacity is a major requirement for a backup medium, because administrators usually like to create unattended backup solutions that can run at night, or while the business is closed. The higher the capacity of the storage device, the fewer times an administrator has to change the medium to complete the backup.

Off the Record   Many removable storage devices that would otherwise be acceptable backup media, such as Compact Disk-Recordable drives (CD-Rs) and Zip cartridges, are almost never used for backups, because an administrator would have to hang around the office all night swapping new disks or cartridges into the drive.

Many magnetic tape formats are suitable for backups. Table 6-1 lists some of these formats. The general rule of magnetic tape drives is that you trade speed and capacity for cost. The best drives on the market can hold up to 200 gigabytes on a single tape, and write data at speeds of nearly 60 megabytes per second. For a drive like this, however, you can easily pay $5,000 or more. Slower drives with lower media capacities can be much less expensive.

Table 6-1 Magnetic Tape Drive Types

Type	Tape Width	Cartridge Size	Capacity (uncompressed)	Speed
Quarter-inch cartridge (QIC), Travan	.25 inch	4 × 6 × 0.625 inches (data cartridge); 3.25 × 2.5 × 0.6 inches (minicartridge)	50 GB	600 MB/min
Digital audio tape (DAT)	4 mm	2.875 × 2.0625 × 0.375 inches	20 GB	360 MB/min
8 mm	8 mm	3.7 × 2.44 × 0.59 inches	100 GB	1,400 MB/min
Digital linear tape (DLT), Super DLT	.50 inch	4.16 × 4.15 × 1 inches	160 GB	960 MB/min
Linear Tape-Open (LTO), Ultrium	.50 inch	4.0 × 4.16 × 0.87 inches	200 GB	3,600 MB/min

Real World Magnetic Tape Compression

Virtually all magnetic tape drives support hardware compression, which means that a drive compresses all data before writing it to the tape. This is why most tape drive manufacturers are careful to mention the compressed and uncompressed capacities of their products. Drive manufacturers all use the traditional ratio of 2:1 when describing the compressed capacities of their drives. However, the actual compression ratio you achieve depends on the type of data you are backing up. Executables and other application files do generally compress at approximately a 2:1 ratio. However, some file types, such as uncompressed bitmap graphics, compress at a much higher rate, such as 8:1, meaning that you can fit even more on a tape. On the other hand, when you are backing up files that are already compressed, such as .jpg images, .mpg audio files, and .zip archives, the drive cannot compress them any more, so the ratio for these files is 1:1.

For organizations with an enormous amount of data to back up, there are also devices on the market called *autochangers* or *tape libraries*. An autochanger combines one or more magnetic tape drives with a robotic mechanism that inserts tapes into drives and removes them. Autochangers range from small desktop devices with one drive that hold a handful of tapes, to huge units the size of a refrigerator, with several drives and holding hundreds of tapes. The advantage of an autochanger is that you can create a single unattended backup job that spans multiple tapes. When the first tape is full, the autochanger removes it from the drive and inserts a new one, repeating the sequence until the job finishes. With a large autochanger, network administrators can sometimes go for weeks or months without having to swap tapes in and out of the device, while their backups proceed automatically every night.

Off the Record   As with high-end tape drives, the prices of autochangers can be shockingly high. A ten-drive LTO unit holding 100 tapes can easily cost $75,000 or more.

Real World   Media Costs

When evaluating backup hardware, cost is always important. However, in addition to the cost of the drive itself, you must also consider the media costs. You might be able to purchase a drive at what seems to be a bargain price, only to discover that the cost of the media makes the solution more expensive than a higher-priced drive. The traditional method of evaluating storage media costs is to divide the price of one storage device (such as a tape) by the number of megabytes it holds, which tells you the medium's cost per megabyte. However, with storage capacities constantly increasing and media costs decreasing, it is now often more practical to compute the cost per gigabyte.

Backup Software

A backup software product is an application that enables you to select the files you want to back up and sends them to the backup drive. Most backup software also includes features that enable you to create repeating backup jobs and schedule them to occur regularly. The usual objective of a network administrator is to create a backup solution that requires as little intervention as possible. With a properly configured hardware and software combination, daily backups should occur with the administrator doing nothing but swapping tapes in and out of the drive.

The backup software must also provide a way to restore data from the backup tapes. When the software backs up data, it creates a catalog of the files it processes, so that you can locate specific data for restoration. You can usually choose individual files for restoration, or restore entire drives, in the case of a disaster.

Off the Record   The difference between various backup software products is usually in the extra features that the application includes. Most tape drives come with a rudimentary backup program that gets the job done, but offers few of the extra features needed by most network backup administrators.

Network backup software typically differs in several important ways from a software product designed for a standalone computer. Some of these differences are as follows:

- **Backup scheduling**   Some rudimentary backup software products only enable you to perform a backup in real time. Network backup software enables you to schedule backup jobs to occur at any time, and to repeat at regular intervals.

- **Remote backup agents**   Virtually all backup software products can back up a shared network drive mapped to a drive letter on the server, but a remote agent enables the server to back up the entire remote computer, including system state information, such as the registry and Active Directory databases.

- **Backup file database**   Some higher-end network backup software products store the catalogs of the backed up data in a database on the server, providing various ways for administrators to search for files to be restored and to create reports about the data stored on the backup media. Lower-end products store the catalogs on the individual tapes, which can make it difficult to locate the tape containing the specific files you need to restore.

- **Media rotation schemes**   An efficient backup strategy uses a specified number of tapes to back up the network, and rotates them so that the drive overwrites them at regular intervals. However, it is vital that you reuse only tapes that are outdated, and that you don't overwrite data that you might someday need to restore. Network backup software products typically include a media rotation scheme that helps you schedule your backup jobs and tells you which tape to insert each day.

- **Open file backup**   A backup software product usually cannot back up a file that a running process has locked open. For example, if a user leaves a document open in an application before leaving for the day, the backup software will usually fail to copy that file, because the application has it open. Many network backup products include an open file option that enables the software to back up certain types of files while they are in use.

- **Disaster recovery**   When a computer's primary hard drive fails completely, you cannot restore the data from your backup right away, because the computer must be able to run the backup program or agent. This means that you must reinstall the operating system and the backup software before the restoration can proceed, which can be a time-consuming process. Disaster recovery software circumvents this problem by creating a backup in combination with a boot disk that you can use on the target computer. The boot disk contains only the operating system software needed for the restoration to occur. After booting from the disk, you can perform the restore, and the computer is back to its original condition much more quickly than if you had to install the operating system manually.

Tip   The Backup program included in Windows Server 2003 contains a disaster recovery feature called ASR. The Automated System Recovery Preparation Wizard backs up the System State data, system services, and all disks associated with the operating system components. It also writes to a floppy disk information about the backup, the disk configurations (including basic and dynamic volumes), and how to accomplish a restore. If you have a system failure, make sure you have your previously created Automated System Recovery (ASR) floppy disk, your previously created backups, and the original operating system installation CD. If you have a mass storage controller and the manufacturer has supplied a separate driver file for it (different from the driver files available on the Setup CD), obtain the file on a floppy disk. To begin the recovery procedure, insert the original operating system installation CD into your CD drive. Restart your computer. If you are prompted to press a key to start the computer from CD, press the appropriate key. If you have a separate driver file for a mass storage controller, use the driver as a part of Setup by pressing F6 when prompted. Press F2 when prompted at the beginning of the text-only section of Setup. You will be prompted to insert your ASR floppy disk. Follow the directions onscreen. If you have a separate driver file, press F6 a second time when prompted after the system reboots.

- **Database backup**   Database software products have always been a problem when it comes to backups, because users perpetually leave the databases themselves open. Many network backup software products provide agents that make it possible to back up specific types of databases while they are operational. The agent typically works by intercepting all database access requests and redirecting them to a temporary file called a delta file. While this is occurring, the agent can close the database files themselves and back them up. Once the backup is completed, the agent reopens the database files, and applies any changes that are queued up in the delta file.

Note   The features listed here are often called by different names by software manufacturers, and in some cases, they are not included with the standard network backup software product. Some manufacturers adopt a modular approach, which requires you to purchase add-on products to back up special types of data, such as databases or e-mail servers.

Exam Tip   Most network installations use a third-party software product to perform backups, but you should familiarize yourself with the functions of the Windows Server 2003 Backup program, even if you do not intend to use it.

Creating a Backup Plan

Once the hardware and software components for your backup solution are in place, the next step is to create a plan that contains elements such as the following:

- What data will be backed up
- When backups will occur
- Which tapes to use and when

Selecting Backup Targets

The easiest way to perform backups of your network is to simply back up all the data on all your computers every day. However, in most cases, this is not a practical approach for reasons such as the following:

- **There is too much data to back up.**   The hard drives that are typically included in today's computers hold more than ever, and on a large network, total storage capacity can easily add up to thousands of gigabytes. Unless you want to spend an enormous amount of money on tape drive and autochanger hardware, it would not be possible to back up all the data in every computer every day.

- **There is not enough time to perform the backups.**   Most network administrators schedule network backup jobs to occur at night, or whenever the organization is closed. Backing up during off hours makes it less likely for the backup to skip files because they are locked open, and minimizes the impact of the network traffic generated by remote backup processes. For some organizations, the amount of time available to perform backups (called the *backup window*) would be insufficient to back up the entire network, unless multiple high-speed drives were used.

- **There is too much redundant data.**   Much of the data stored on a typical computer's hard drive is static; it does not change every day. Application and operating system files never change, and some document files can go for long periods without users changing them. Backing up files like these every day means saving the same data to tape over and over, which is a waste of time and media.

For these and other reasons, backup software products enable you to be selective about the files you back up. As a rule, you should back up every day only the files that change every day, such as frequently used data files. Files that change less frequently are best served by a weekly, or even a monthly, backup. Some operating system and application files need never be backed up because, in the event of a disaster, you would have to reinstall the operating system and applications from your original distribution disks anyway.

> **Tip**   Ease of backup is one of the primary reasons that many network administrators insist that users store their data files on servers, rather than on their local hard drives. By giving each user a home directory on a server, it is possible to back up everyone's data files with a single server backup, rather than having to configure the backup software to connect to each individual workstation every day.

Most backup software products enable you to select backup targets in two ways, by checking files and folders in a directory tree display (see Figure 6-16) or by using filters. Filters enable you to select the files you want included or excluded from a backup by specifying a combination of factors, including file names, extensions, dates, sizes, and attributes. For example, you can select an entire folder containing your Microsoft Word files for backup, and then exclude all the backup copies that Word automatically creates by applying a filter with the file mask *Backup*.**.

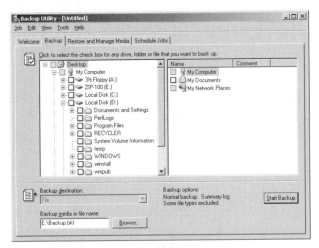

Figure 6-16   The Windows Server 2003 Backup Utility window

Understanding Backup Job Types

To simplify the process of backing up only the necessary files, backup software products enable you to select different types of backup jobs. The three most common types are as follows:

- **Full backup**   Copies all the selected files to the backup medium and resets the archive bits for all the copied files

- **Incremental backup**   Copies only the selected files that have archive bits, and then resets those archive bits

- **Differential backup**   Copies only the selected files that have archive bits without resetting those archive bits

The archive bit is a one-bit flag (called an attribute) on every file, which backup software products use to determine whether that file has changed recently. When you perform a full backup, the software resets all the archive bits for the files it has copied to the backup medium by changing the bit values to 0. Later, whenever an application modifies one of these files, it sets the archive bit for that file by changing its value to 1. The next time you perform an incremental or differential backup, the software checks the archive bits of the files targeted for backup and copies only those with archive bit values of 1. The result is that the incremental or differential job has backed up only the files that have changed. You can still restore all the other files from the last full backup, because they have not changed since then.

The difference between an incremental backup and a differential backup is the way that the software treats the archive bits of the files it has just copied. Incremental jobs reset the archive bits and differential jobs don't. This means that an incremental job consists of only the files that have changed since the last full or incremental backup. A differential job consists of all the files that have changed since the last full backup. The advantage of using incremental jobs is that they occupy the least amount of storage space and take the least amount of time, because the software only writes each changed file to the backup medium once. Differential jobs take up more storage space and take longer to run because the software backs up all the files that have changed repeatedly during each successive differential job until the next full backup.

The advantage of using differential jobs is that the restoration process is simpler and faster. To restore an entire drive that has been lost, you must first restore the last full backup, and then the incremental or differential backups. With incremental backups, you must perform a separate restore for each incremental backup you performed since the last full backup, to ensure that you are getting the latest version of every changed file. With differentials, you only have to restore the most recent differential backup since the last full backup, because the differential contains all the files that have changed since the full backup in their latest versions.

> **Exam Tip**   Be sure to understand the differences between a full backup, an incremental backup, and a differential backup. Incremental and differential backups are identical except that incremental backups do reset archive bits and differential backups do not.

Scheduling Backup Jobs

Most organizations perform incremental or differential backups daily and a full backup once a week. This arrangement provides a good compromise between protection and the amount of time and media devoted to backups. The ideal situation for a backup administrator is having each daily incremental or differential job fit on a single tape. This enables the administrator to schedule the job to run unattended in the middle of the night or during other off hours, without the need to have someone change media. Once you have created your backup schedule, you can simply insert the correct tape into the drive each day. Full backups might require more than one tape, so someone might have to be there to change media.

Tip   The ability to create an unattended backup schedule like this is one of the primary factors to consider when evaluating backup hardware products. Before selecting a drive, you should estimate the amount of data you will have to back up each day (allowing some leeway for growth) and look at drives that can store at least that much data on a single tape. While you can certainly shop for a drive that can store an entire full backup on a single tape, this practice is generally not economically sound, because you are paying for tape capacity you are usually not.

Creating a media rotation scheme is also part of backup scheduling. The media rotation scheme enables you to use a specified number of tapes for your entire backup strategy, and tells you which tape to insert in the drive each day. As mentioned earlier, some network backup products have preconfigured media rotation schemes that work everything out for you, but the best schemes are those that you can modify to meet your own needs.

Using the Grandfather-Father-Son Method

One of the most common media rotation schemes is called the Grandfather-Father-Son method. In this method, the terms grandfather, father, and son refer to monthly, weekly, and daily tapes, respectively. For daily backups, you have one set of "son" tapes that you reuse every week. For the weekly full backup, you have "father" tapes that you reuse every month. Then, every month, you perform an additional full backup to tapes in your "grandfather" set, which you reuse every year. This method enables you to perform a complete restore at any time, and maintains a year's history of your files.

Performing Restores

Obviously, exercising all this care when planning and performing your backups is pointless if you cannot restore the data you have backed up. A good backup software product gives you a lot of flexibility in restoring. The software should provide the following basic options:

- **File selection**   You should be able to select any combination of files, folders, or drives on any tape. Some software products enable you to switch between a media view, which displays the contents of each tape in the library, and a disk view, which displays your backup targets and a list of the multiple versions of each file available on your tapes.

- **Restore location**   You should be able to restore your selected files to their original locations automatically, or specify an alternative location; you should also be able to recreate the original directory tree or dump all the files into a single folder.

- **Overwrite options**   When restoring files to their original locations, you should be able to specify the criteria for overwriting existing files with the same names—based on their dates or using other criteria.

Performing Test Restores

If there is one piece of advice that every backup administrator should follow, it would be to perform frequent test restores. Even though your backup software might say that your jobs have completed successfully, even though your backup logs don't show any errors, and even though your tape drive seems to be functioning properly, there is no way to be absolutely positive that your backups have completed properly other than to perform a test restore. There are all kinds of horror stories in the backup industry about administrators who diligently perform backups every day, carefully label the tapes, and store them under stringently controlled conditions, only to discover when a disaster occurs that all their carefully labeled tapes are, in fact, blank.

Using Volume Shadow Copy

Volume shadow copy is a Windows Server 2003 feature that maintains a library containing multiple versions of selected files. Although not a replacement for system backups, volume shadow copy enables users to access saved versions of files they have accidentally damaged or deleted. This eliminates one of the most onerous chores of the backup administrator: performing single file restores for users who have inadvertently deleted their own files.

To enable volume shadow copy for a volume on your server, you display the Properties dialog box for the volume and click the Shadow Copies tab (see Figure 6-17). When you select a volume on the list and click Enable, Windows Server 2003 makes a copy of all the files in shared folders on that volume and stamps the copies with the current date and time. As long as shadow copying is enabled for that volume, Windows Server 2003 continues to make two copies a day of these files and saves them until the amount of space designated for volume shadow copies is full. You can modify both the frequency at which the Windows operating system makes copies and the size of the space used to store the copies.

Only computers running Windows Server 2003, Windows XP, and Windows 2000 (with Service Pack 3 or higher) can access the shadow copies of files on your designated volumes. On Windows XP and Windows 2000 workstations, you must first install the client software that makes this possible. Then, a user can access shadow copies by displaying the Properties dialog box for a file in a shadow volume and clicking the Previous Versions tab (see Figure 6-18).

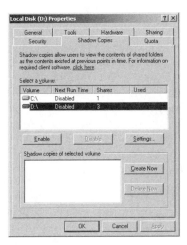

Figure 6-17   The Shadow Copies tab in a volume's Properties dialog box

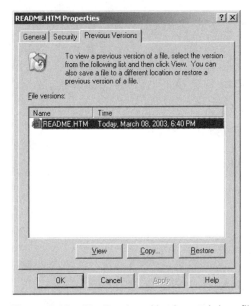

Figure 6-18   The Previous Versions tab in a file's Properties dialog box

Tip   Windows Server 2003 includes the client software for volume shadow copy in its *%Systemroot%*\System32\Clients\Twclient folder. You can deploy the software by installing it manually on the clients or by using an automated method, such as group policies. This client is also available as a free download from Microsoft's Web site at *http://www.microsoft.com /technet/downloads/winsrvr/shadowcopyclient.mspx.*

Practice: Using Windows Server 2003 Backup

In this practice, you use the Windows Server 2003 Backup program to create a backup of your server, and then restore selected files from the backup.

Exercise 1: Creating a Backup Job

In this procedure, you create a normal job to back up the Windist folder on your server.

1. Click Start, point to All Programs, point to Accessories, point to System Tools, and then click Backup. The Backup Or Restore Wizard appears.

2. Clear the Always Start In Wizard Mode check box, and then click the Advanced Mode hyperlink. The Backup Utility window appears.

3. Click the Backup tab. In the directory tree, expand the C drive, and then select the check box for the \Windist folder.

4. In the Backup Media Or File Name text box, clear any text that appears, type **C:\Normal.bkf** and then click Start Backup. The Backup Job Information dialog box appears.

5. Click Start Backup. The backup job begins, displaying a Backup Progress window.

6. When the job completes, click the Close button.

7. Leave the Backup Utility window open for the next exercise.

Exercise 2: Creating a Differential Backup Job

In this procedure, you modify a file in the Windist folder and then perform a differential backup.

1. Start Windows Explorer and browse to the \Windist folder on the C drive.

2. Double-click the Eula.txt file in the \Windist folder to open it in Notepad.exe.

3. Type your name in the Eula.txt file and close Notepad, saving the file as you do so.

4. In the Backup Utility window, expand the C drive in the directory tree and select the check box for the \Windist folder.

5. In the Backup Media Or File Name text box, type **C:\Diff.bkf** and then click Start Backup. The Backup Job Information dialog box appears.

6. Click Advanced. The Advanced Backup Options dialog box appears.

7. In the Backup Type selector, choose Differential, and then click OK.

8. Click Start Backup. The backup job begins, displaying a Backup Progress window. Notice that the Backup program backs up only one file.

9. When the job completes, click the Close button.

10. Leave the Backup Utility and Windows Explorer windows open for the next exercise.

Exercise 3: Restoring a File

In this procedure, you restore the file you modified and backed up in Exercise 2.

1. In the Backup Utility window, click the Restore And Manage Media tab.

2. Expand the File tree in the left pane, and then open the Diff.bkf file icon and expand the C drive icon.

3. Click the \Windist folder in the left pane and, in the right pane, select the check box for the Eula.txt file.

4. In the Restore Files To selector, choose Alternate Location. An Alternate Location text box appears.

5. In the Alternate Location text box, type **C:** and then click Start Restore. A Confirm Restore message box appears.

6. Click OK. The Restore Progress dialog box appears.

7. When the restore job finishes, click Close.

8. In Windows Explorer, verify that the Backup program restored the Eula.txt file to the root of the C drive. Open the file with Notepad and verify that it is the copy you modified by adding your name.

9. Close the Windows Explorer and Backup windows.

Lesson Review

The following questions are intended to reinforce key information presented in this lesson. If you are unable to answer a question, review the lesson materials and try the question again. You can find answers to the questions in the "Questions and Answers" section at the end of this chapter.

1. Why is it best to perform backups when the organization is closed?

   _____

   _____

2. Which of the following backup job types does not reset the archive bits on the files that it copies to the backup medium?

   a. Full

   b. Incremental

   c. Differential

   d. None of the above

3. Which of the following tape drive devices has the greatest capacity?

   a. LTO

   b. QIC

   c. DAT

   d. DLT

Lesson Summary

- A network backup solution consists of backup drives, backup software, and a backup plan.

- When evaluating backup hardware, higher speed and greater capacity nearly always means higher price.

- The function of the backup software is to enable the administrator to select the targets for backup and then send them to the tape drive or other device.

- Incremental and differential backup jobs save tape by backing up only the files that have changed since the last backup, based on the status of each file's archive bit.

- Performing regular test restores is a crucial part of backup administration.

- Volume shadow copy is a Window Server 2003 feature that enables users to access multiple copies of files they have accidentally deleted or damaged.

Case Scenario Exercise

You are the network infrastructure design specialist for Litware Inc., a manufacturer of specialized scientific software products, and you have already created a network design for their new office building, as described in the Case Scenario Exercise in Chapter 1. The office building is a three-story brick structure built in the late 1940s, which has since been retrofitted by various tenants with several different types of network cabling. Your network design for the building calls for the installation of four LANs, each of which is connected to a fifth, backbone network.

You are designing a backup solution for the building's entire internetwork. To make it easier to back up valuable company data, you have supplied each of the network's 125 users with a home folder on a shared server drive, and have instructed the users to store all their data files in their home folders. You have also created disk quotas granting each user a maximum of 1 gigabyte of storage space.

Because of this arrangement, you will be backing up only the network servers, not user workstations. In addition to the file servers hosting the users' home folders, there are also six Web servers, each with a 40 GB drive, a database server with an 80 GB drive hosting approximately 10 GB of database files, and an e-mail server with 25 GB of mail archives.

Based on this information, answer the following questions:

1. What is the approximate total amount of volatile data that you might have to back up each day?

   a. 60 GB

   b. 160 GB

   c. 360 GB

   d. 480 GB

2. Assuming that you decide to perform a weekly full backup and daily incremental backups, approximately how much data from the six Web servers can you expect to find on each incremental backup tape? Explain your answer.

   _____

   _____

3. Using the information in Table 6-1, which type of magnetic tape drive would best be suited for this network, assuming that you want to use only a single tape for your daily incremental backups?

   a. DLT

   b. 8 mm

   c. QIC

   d. DAT

Troubleshooting Lab

While working at a corporate help desk, you suddenly start to receive calls from users all over the network, complaining that response times when trying to access Internet Web sites are extremely slow. Other users are also having difficulty logging on to

Active Directory. You also notice several e-mails from Internet users who are unable to access the company Web site. You begin to suspect that the network's DNS server is the target of a DoS attack from the Internet. Based on this information, answer the following questions:

1. What makes you suspect that the DNS server might be the source of the problem?

   _____

   _____

2. Which of the following System Monitor performance counters can you use to determine whether the DNS server is the target of a DoS attack? (Choose all answers that are correct.)

   a. Segments Retransmitted/Sec in the TCPv4 performance object

   b. Zone Transfer Failure in the DNS performance object

   c. Datagrams Received/Sec in the UDPv4 performance object

   d. Total Query Received/Sec in the DNS performance object

   e. Messages/Sec in the ICMP performance object

Chapter Summary

- System Monitor is an MMC snap-in that monitors specific computer resources in real time, displaying the information in Graph, Histogram, or Report view.

- Performance Logs And Alerts is an MMC snap-in that uses System Monitor's performance counters to capture information to log files over a long period of time.

- Network Monitor is a protocol analyzer that can capture packets from the network and analyze their contents in detail.

- Network services such as DHCP, DNS, WINS, and RRAS all have various mechanisms you can use to track their statistics and ongoing activities, including log files, status screens, and performance counters.

- Server performance degradations are frequently caused by a bottleneck, that is, a slowdown of a key component that prevents the system from performing up to its potential.

- When looking for the bottleneck on a server, check its four primary subsystems: processor, memory, storage, and network.

- A network backup solution consists of backup drives, backup software, and a backup plan.

- Incremental and differential backup jobs save tape by backing up only the files that have changed since the last backup, based on the status of each file's archive bit.

- Performing regular test restores is a crucial part of backup administration.

- Volume shadow copy is a Window Server 2003 feature that enables users to access multiple copies of files they have accidentally deleted or damaged.

Exam Highlights

Before taking the exam, review the key points and terms that are presented below to help you identify topics you need to review. Return to the lessons for additional practice, and review the "Further Reading" sections in Part 2 for pointers to more information about topics covering the exam objectives.

Key Points

- The Performance console can monitor specific computer resources in real time, displaying the information in Graph, Histogram, or Report view. You can use System Monitor to monitor network traffic by selecting performance counters corresponding to network interfaces, protocols, or applications.

- Network Monitor is a protocol analyzer that can capture packets from the network and analyze their contents by displaying the values of the individual header fields in each protocol.

- The MMC consoles for the various Windows Server 2003 network services have a variety of screens that enable you to monitor the operational status of the services. Most of the services can also maintain logs and include performance counters that you can use in System Monitor.

- Server performance degradations are frequently caused by a bottleneck, that is, a slowdown of a key component that prevents the system from performing up to its potential. When looking for the bottleneck on a server, check its four primary subsystems: processor, memory, storage, and network, using the performance counters provided in System Monitor.

- Planning a network backup solution consists of selecting backup drives and backup software, and devising a backup plan. Incremental and differential backup jobs save tape by backing up only the files that have changed since the last backup, based on the status of each file's archive bit.

- Automated System Recovery is a disaster recovery feature included in Windows Server 2003 that enables you to restore an entire computer without reinstalling the operating system. Volume shadow copy is another feature that enables users to access multiple copies of files they have accidentally deleted or damaged.

Key Terms

Promiscuous mode   An operational mode that enables a network interface adapter to receive and process all the packets transmitted on the network, not just those transmitted to or by the computer containing the adapter

Bottleneck   A condition in which a single component in a computer or on a network is preventing the rest of the system from operating up to its full potential

Incremental backup   A type of backup job that copies only the files that have changed since the last backup of any kind, and then resets the files' archive bits

Differential backup   A type of backup job that copies only the files that have changed since the last full backup, and does not reset the files' archive bits

Questions and Answers

Page
6-15
Lesson 1 Review

1. Why do System Monitor performance counters sometime have multiple instances?

   If the computer contains more than one of the same type of component, such as two network interface adapters, instances enable you to monitor each one independently.

2. In System Monitor, which performance object would you select to monitor the number of TCP/IP error messages transmitted and received by a computer?

   a. Network Interface

   b. TCPv4

   c. ICMP

   d. UDPv4

   c

3. When using Network Monitor, under what conditions is it preferable to use a capture filter instead of a display filter?

   Capture filters, which prevent the buffer from filling too quickly, are preferable when you want to capture a traffic sample over a long period of time.

Page
6-30
Lesson 2 Review

1. Why is the Available value in the DHCP console's Server Statistics dialog box usually not an adequate means of determining whether a DHCP scope's IP address pool is depleted?

   Because the Available value specifies the total number of available addresses on all the scopes on the server. One of the scopes could still be depleted, even though the Available value is positive.

2. Which of the following are correct reasons that it is more critical to monitor DNS performance than DHCP or WINS performance? (Choose all answers that are correct.)

   a. DNS servers might be accessible from the Internet, and DHCP and WINS servers are not.

   b. DNS servers are more likely to malfunction than DHCP or WINS servers.

   c. DNS server failures can have an immediate effect on network client performance.

   d. DNS servers have less effective monitoring tools.

   a and c

3. What is the best remedy for a disk subsystem that is the bottleneck in a server's performance?

Install additional drives in the form of a RAID array.

Page
6-43

Lesson 3 Review

1. Why is it best to perform backups when the organization is closed?

Because files are less likely to be locked open and the network is not affected by the amount of traffic that backups generate.

2. Which of the following backup job types does not reset the archive bits on the files that it copies to the backup medium?

  a. Full

  b. Incremental

  c. Differential

  d. None of the above

c

3. Which of the following tape drive devices has the greatest capacity?

  a. LTO

  b. QIC

  c. DAT

  d. DLT

a

Page
6-44

Case Scenario Exercise

Based on the information provided in the Case Scenario Exercise, answer the following questions:

1. What is the approximate total amount of volatile data that you might have to back up each day?

  a. 60 GB

  b. 160 GB

  c. 360 GB

  d. 480 GB

b

2. Assuming that you decide to perform a weekly full backup and daily incremental backups, approximately how much data from the six Web servers can you expect to find on each incremental backup tape? Explain your answer.

   Almost none, because the data used to host Internet sites on Web servers typically does not change.

3. Using the information in Table 6-1, which type of magnetic tape drive would best be suited for this network, assuming that you want to use only a single tape for your daily incremental backups?

   a. DLT

   b. 8 mm

   c. QIC

   d. DAT

   a

Page 6-45 **Troubleshooting Lab**

Based on the information provided in the Troubleshooting Lab, answer the following questions:

1. What makes you suspect that the DNS server might be the source of the problem?

   The DNS server is related to all the processes that are causing problems. A DNS server can contain Active Directory records, provide name resolution services to internal network clients, and host the company's domain on the Internet. If the DNS server is not available, all three of these services might be interrupted.

2. Which of the following System Monitor performance counters can you use to determine whether the DNS server is the target of a DoS attack? (Choose all answers that are correct.)

   a. Segments Retransmitted/Sec in the TCPv4 performance object

   b. Zone Transfer Failure in the DNS performance object

   c. Datagrams Received/Sec in the UDPv4 performance object

   d. Total Query Received/Sec in the DNS performance object

   e. Messages/Sec in the ICMP performance object

   c and d

7 Clustering Servers

Exam Objectives in this Chapter:

- Plan services for high availability.
    - ❑ Plan a high availability solution that uses clustering services.
    - ❑ Plan a high availability solution that uses Network Load Balancing.
- Implement a cluster server.
    - ❑ Recover from cluster node failure.
- Manage Network Load Balancing. Tools might include the Network Load Balancing Monitor Microsoft Management Console (MMC) snap-in and the WLBS cluster control utility.

Why This Chapter Matters

As organizations become increasingly dependent on their computer networks, clustering is becoming an increasingly important element of those networks. Many businesses now rely on the World Wide Web for all their contact with customers, including order taking and other revenue-producing tasks. If the Web servers go down, business stops. Understanding how clustering works, and how Microsoft Windows Server 2003 supports clustering, is becoming an important element of the network administrator's job.

Lessons in this Chapter:

Before You Begin

This chapter assumes a basic understanding of Transmission Control Protocol/Internet Protocol (TCP/IP) communications, as described in Chapter 2, "Planning a TCP/IP Network Infrastructure," and of Microsoft Windows network services, such as DNS and DHCP.

To perform the practice exercises in this chapter, you must have installed and configured Windows Server 2003 using the procedure described in "About This Book."

Lesson 1: Understanding Clustering

A cluster is a group of two or more servers dedicated to running a specific application (or applications) and connected to provide fault tolerance and load balancing. Clustering is intended for organizations running applications that must be available, making any server downtime unacceptable. In a server cluster, each computer is running the same critical applications, so that if one server fails, the others detect the failure and take over at a moment's notice. This is called *failover*. When the failed node returns to service, the other nodes take notice and the cluster begins to use the recovered node again. This is called *failback*. Clustering capabilities are installed automatically in the Windows Server 2003 operating system. In Microsoft Windows 2000 Server, you had to install Microsoft Clustering Service as a separate module.

After this lesson, you will be able to

- List the types of server clusters
- Estimate your organization's availability requirements
- Determine which type of cluster to use for your applications
- Describe the clustering capabilities of the Windows Server 2003 operating systems

Estimated lesson time: 30 minutes

Clustering Types

Windows Server 2003 supports two different types of clustering: *server clusters* and *Network Load Balancing (NLB)*. The difference between the two types of clustering is based on the types of applications the servers must run and the nature of the data they use.

Important   Server clustering is intended to provide high availability for applications, not data. Do not mistake server clustering for an alternative to data availability technologies, such as RAID (redundant array of independent disks) and regular system backups.

Server Clusters

Server clusters are designed for applications that have long-running in-memory states or large, frequently changing data sets. These are called *stateful applications*, and include database servers such as Microsoft SQL Server, e-mail and messaging servers such as Microsoft Exchange, and file and print services. In a server cluster, all the computers (called *nodes*) are connected to a common data set, such as a shared SCSI bus or a storage area network. Because all the nodes have access to the same application data, any one of them can process a request from a client at any time. You configure each node in a server cluster to be either active or passive. An active node receives and processes requests from clients, while a passive node remains idle and functions as a fallback, should an active node fail.

For example, a simple server cluster might consist of two computers running both Windows Server 2003 and Microsoft SQL Server, connected to the same Network-Attached Storage (NAS) device, which contains the database files (see Figure 7-1). One of the computers is an active node and one is a passive node. Most of the time, the active node is functioning normally, running the database server application, receiving requests from database clients, and accessing the database files on the NAS device. However, if the active node should suddenly fail, for whatever reason, the passive node detects the failure, immediately goes active, and begins processing the client requests, using the same database files on the NAS device.

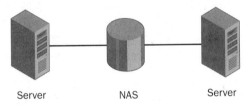

Server   NAS   Server

Figure 7-1   A simple two-node server cluster

> **See Also**   The obvious disadvantage of this two-node, active/passive design is that one of the servers is being wasted most of the time, doing nothing but functioning as a passive standby. Depending on the capabilities of the application, you can also design a server cluster with multiple active nodes that share the processing tasks among themselves. You learn more about designing a server cluster later in this lesson.

A server cluster has its own name and Internet Protocol (IP) address, separate from those of the individual computers in the cluster. Therefore, when a server failure occurs, there is no apparent change in functionality to the clients, which continue to send their requests to the same destination. The passive node takes over the active role almost instantaneously, so there is no appreciable delay in performance. The server cluster ensures that the application is both highly available and highly reliable, because, despite a failure of one of the servers in the cluster, clients experience few, if any, unscheduled application outages.

Windows Server 2003, Enterprise Edition, and Windows Server 2003, Datacenter Edition, both support server clusters consisting of up to eight nodes. This is an increase over the Microsoft Windows 2000 operating system, which supports only two nodes in the Advanced Server product and four nodes in the Datacenter Server product. Neither Windows Server 2003, Standard Edition, nor Windows 2000 Server supports server clusters at all.

> **Planning**   Although Windows Server 2003, Enterprise Edition, and Windows Server 2003, Datacenter Edition, both support server clustering, you cannot create a cluster with computers running both versions of the operating system. All your cluster nodes must be running either Enterprise Edition or Datacenter Edition. You can, however, run Windows 2000 Server in a Windows Server 2003, Enterprise Edition, or Windows Server 2003, Datacenter Edition, cluster.

Network Load Balancing

Network Load Balancing (NLB) is another type of clustering that provides high availability and high reliability, with the addition of high scalability as well. NLB is intended for applications with relatively small data sets that rarely change (or may even be read-only), and that do not have long-running in-memory states. These are called *stateless applications*, and typically include Web, File Transfer Protocol (FTP), and virtual private network (VPN) servers. Every client request to a stateless application is a separate transaction, so it is possible to distribute the requests among multiple servers to balance the processing load.

Instead of being connected to a single data source, as in a server cluster, the servers in an NLB cluster all have identical cloned data sets and are all active nodes (see Figure 7-2). The clustering software distributes incoming client requests among the nodes, each of which processes its requests independently, using its own local data. If one or more of the nodes should fail, the others take up the slack by processing some of the requests to the failed server.

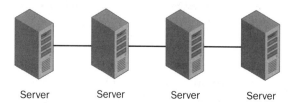

Server   Server   Server   Server

Figure 7-2   A Network Load Balancing cluster

Network Load Balancing and Replication

Network Load Balancing is clearly not suitable for stateful applications such as database and e-mail servers, because the cluster nodes do not share the same data. If one server in an NLB cluster were to receive a new record to add to the database, the other servers would not have access to that record until the next database replication. It is possible to replicate data between the servers in an NLB cluster, for example, to prevent administrators from having to copy modified Web pages to each server individually. However, this replication is an occasional event, not an ongoing occurrence.

Network Load Balancing provides scalability in addition to availability and reliability, because all you have to do when traffic increases is add more servers to the cluster. Each server then has to process a smaller number of incoming requests. Windows Server 2003, Standard Edition, Windows Server 2003, Enterprise Edition, and Windows Server 2003, Datacenter Edition, all support NLB clusters of up to 32 computers.

Off the Record   There is also a third type of clustering, called component load balancing (CLB), designed for middle-tier applications based on Component Object Model (COM+) programming components. Balancing COM+ components among multiple nodes provides many of the same availability and scalability benefits as Network Load Balancing. The Windows Server 2003 operating systems do not include support for CLB clustering, but it is included in the Microsoft Windows 2000 Application Center product.

Exam Tip   Be sure you understand the differences between a server cluster and a Network Load Balancing cluster, including the hardware requirements, the difference between stateful and stateless applications, and the types of clusters supported by the various versions of Windows Server 2003.

Designing a Clustering Solution

The first thing to decide when you are considering a clustering solution for your network is just what you expect to realize from the cluster—in other words, just how much availability, reliability, or scalability you need. For some organizations, high availability means that any downtime at all is unacceptable, and clustering can provide a solution that protects against three different types of failures:

- **Software failures**   Many types of software failure can prevent a critical application from running properly. The application itself could malfunction, another piece of software on the computer could interfere with the application, or the operating system could have problems, causing all the running applications to falter. Software failures can result from applying upgrades, from conflicts with newly installed programs, or from the introduction of viruses or other types of malicious code. As long as system administrators observe basic precautions (such as not installing software updates on all the servers in a cluster simultaneously), a cluster can keep an application available to users despite software failures.

- **Hardware failures**   Hard drives, cooling fans, power supplies, and other hardware components all have limited life spans, and a cluster enables critical applications to continue running despite the occurrence of a hardware failure in one of the servers. Clustering also makes it possible for administrators to perform hardware maintenance tasks on a server without having to bring down a vital application.

- **Site failures**   In a geographically dispersed cluster, the servers are in different buildings or different cities. Apart from making vital applications locally available to users at various locations, a multisite cluster enables the applications to continue running even if a fire or natural disaster shuts down an entire site.

Estimating Availability Requirements

The degree of availability you require depends on a variety of factors, including the nature of the applications you are running, the size, location, and distribution of your user base, and the role of the applications in your organization. In some cases, having applications available at all times is a convenience; in others, it is a necessity. The amount of availability an organization requires for its applications can affect its clustering configuration in several ways, including the type of clustering you use, the number of servers in the cluster, the distribution of applications across the servers in the cluster, and the locations of the servers.

> **Real World**   **High Availability Requirements**
>
> The technical support department of a software company might need the company's customer database available to be fully productive, but can conceivably function without it for a time. For a company that sells its products exclusively through an e-commerce Web site, however, Web server downtime means no incoming orders, and therefore no income. For a hospital or police department, non-functioning servers can literally be a matter of life and death. Each of these organizations might be running similar applications and servicing a similar number of clients, but their availability requirements are quite different, and so should their clustering solutions be.

Availability is sometimes quantified in the form of a percentage reflecting the amount of time that an application is up and running. For example, 99% availability means that an application can be unavailable for up to 87.6 hours during a year. An application that is 99.9% available can be down for no more than 8.76 hours a year.

Achieving a specific level of availability often involves more than just implementing a clustering solution. You might also have to install fault tolerant hardware, create an extensive hardware and software evaluation and testing plan, and establish operational policies for the entire IT department. As availability requirements get higher, the amount of time, money, and effort needed to achieve them grows exponentially. You might find that achieving 95% to 99% reliability is relatively easy, but pushing reliability to 99.9% becomes very expensive indeed.

Scaling Clusters

Both server clusters and Network Load Balancing are scalable clustering solutions, meaning that you can improve the performance of the cluster as the needs of your organization grow. There are two basic methods of increasing cluster performance, which are as follows:

- **Scaling up**   Improving individual server performance by modifying the computer's hardware configuration. Adding random access memory (RAM) or level 2 (L2) cache memory, upgrading to faster processors, and installing additional processors are all ways to scale up a computer. Improving server performance in this way is independent of the clustering solution you use. However, you do have to consider the individual performance capabilities of each server in the cluster. For example, scaling up only the active nodes in a server cluster might establish a level of performance that the passive nodes cannot meet when they are called on to replace the active nodes. It might be necessary to scale up all the servers in the cluster to the same degree, to provide optimum performance levels under all circumstances.

- **Scaling out**   Adding servers to an existing cluster. When you distribute the processing load for an application among multiple servers, adding more servers reduces the burden on each individual computer. Both server clusters and NLB clusters can be scaled out, but it is easier to add servers to an NLB cluster.

  In Network Load Balancing, each server has its own independent data store containing the applications and the data they supply to clients. Scaling out the cluster is simply a matter of connecting a new server to the network and cloning the applications and data. Once you have added the new server to the cluster, NLB assigns it an equal share of the processing load.

  Scaling out a server cluster is more complicated because the servers in the cluster must all have access to a common data store. Depending on the hardware configuration you use, scaling out might be extremely expensive or even impossible. If you anticipate the need for scaling out your server cluster sometime in the future, be sure to consider this when designing its hardware configuration.

Real World Scalability in the Real World

Be sure to remember that the scalability of your cluster is also limited by the capabilities of the operating system you are using. When scaling out a cluster, the maximum numbers of nodes supported by the Windows operating systems are as follows:

Operating System	Network Load Balancing	Server Clusters
Windows Server 2003, Standard Edition	32	Not Supported
Windows Server 2003, Enterprise Edition	32	8
Windows Server 2003, Datacenter Edition	32	8
Windows 2000 Advanced Server	32	2
Windows 2000 Datacenter Server	32	4

When scaling up a cluster, the operating system limitations are as follows:

Operating System	Maximum Number of Processors	Maximum RAM
Windows Server 2003, Standard Edition	2	4 GB
Windows Server 2003, Enterprise Edition	8	32 GB
Windows Server 2003, Datacenter Edition	32	64 GB
Windows 2000 Advanced Server	8	8 GB
Windows 2000 Datacenter Server	32	64 GB

How Many Clusters?

If you want to deploy more than one application with high availability, you must decide how many clusters you want to use. The servers in a cluster can run multiple applications, of course, so you can combine multiple applications in a single cluster deployment, or you can create a separate cluster for each application. In some cases, you can even combine the two approaches.

For example, if you have two stateful applications that you want to deploy using server clusters, the simplest method would be to create a single cluster and install both applications on every computer in the cluster, as shown in Figure 7-3. In this arrangement, a single server failure affects both applications, and the remaining servers must be capable of providing adequate performance for both applications by themselves.

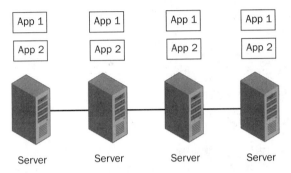

Figure 7-3   A cluster with two applications running on each server

Another method is to create a separate cluster for each application, as shown in Figure 7-4. In this model, each cluster operates independently, and a failure of one server only affects one of the applications. In addition, the remaining servers in the affected cluster only have to take on the burden of one application. Creating separate clusters provides higher availability for the applications, but it can also be an expensive solution, because it requires more servers than the first method.

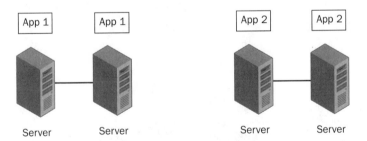

Figure 7-4   Two separate clusters running two different applications

It is also possible to compromise between these two approaches by creating a single cluster, installing each of the applications on a separate active node, and using one passive node as the backup for both applications, as shown in Figure 7-5. In this arrangement, a single server failure causes the passive node to take on the burden of running only one of the applications. Only if both active nodes fail would the passive node have to take on the full responsibility of running both applications. It is up to you to evaluate the odds of such an occurrence and to decide whether your organization's availability requirements call for a passive node server with the capability of running both applications at full performance levels, or whether a passive node scaled to run only one of the applications is sufficient.

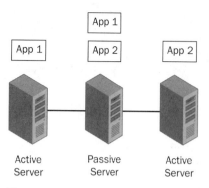

Figure 7-5 Two active nodes sharing a single passive node

Combining Clustering Technologies

The decision to use server clustering or Network Load Balancing on your clusters is usually determined by the applications you intend to run. However, in some cases it might be best to deploy clusters of different types together to create a comprehensive high availability solution.

The most common example of this approach is an e-commerce Web site that enables Internet users to place orders for products. This type of site requires Web servers (which are stateless applications) to run the actual site, and (stateful) database servers to store customer, product, and order entry information. In this case, you can build an NLB cluster to host the Web servers and a server cluster for the database servers, as shown in Figure 7-6. The two clusters interface just as though the applications were running on individual servers.

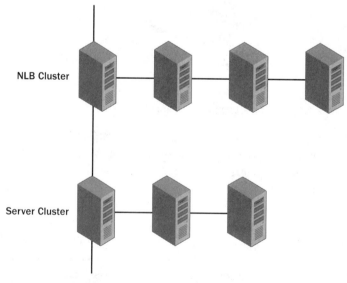

Figure 7-6 An NLB cluster interacting with a server cluster

Dispersing Clusters

Deploying geographically dispersed clusters enables applications to remain available in the event of a catastrophe that destroys a building or even a city. Having cluster servers at different sites can also enable users to access applications locally, rather than having to communicate with a distant server over a relatively slow wide area network (WAN) connection.

Geographically dispersed server clusters can be extremely complex affairs: in addition to the regular network, you have to construct a long-distance storage area network (SAN) that gives the cluster servers access to the shared application data. This usually means that you have to combine privately owned hardware and software products with WAN links for the SAN supplied by a third-party service provider.

Geographically dispersing Network Load Balancing clusters is much easier, because there is no shared data store. However, in most cases, an NLB cluster that is dispersed among multiple sites is not actually a single cluster at all. Instead of installing multiple servers at various locations and connecting them all into a single cluster, you can create a separate cluster at each location and use another technique to distribute the application load among the clusters. This is possible with stateless applications. In the case of a geographically dispersed cluster of Web or other Internet servers, the most common solution is to create a separate NLB cluster at each site, and then use the DNS round robin technique to distribute client requests evenly among the clusters.

Dispersing Network Load Balancing Clusters

Normally, DNS servers contain resource records that associate a single host name with a single IP address. For example, when clients try to connect to an Internet Web server called www.contoso.com, the clients' DNS servers always supply the same IP address for that name. When the www.contoso.com Web site is actually a Network Load Balancing cluster, there is still only one name and one IP address, and it is up to the clustering software to distribute the incoming requests among the servers in the cluster. In a typical geographically dispersed NLB cluster, each site has an independent cluster with its own separate IP address. The DNS server for the contoso.com domain associates all the cluster addresses with the single www.contoso.com host name and supplies the addresses to incoming client requests in a round robin fashion. The DNS server thus distributes the requests among the clusters, and the clustering software distributes the requests for the cluster among the servers in that cluster.

Lesson Review

The following questions are intended to reinforce key information presented in this lesson. If you are unable to answer a question, review the lesson materials and try the question again. You can find answers to the questions in the "Questions and Answers" section at the end of this chapter.

Specify whether each of the following is a characteristic of server clusters, CLB clusters, or NLB clusters.

1. Used for database server clusters

   _____

   _____

2. Supports clusters of up to 8 nodes in Windows Server 2003, Datacenter Edition

   _____

   _____

3. Supported by Windows Server 2003, Standard Edition

   _____

   _____

4. Makes stateless applications highly available

   _____

   _____

5. Used for applications with frequently changing data

   _____

   _____

6. Used for Web server clusters

   _____

   _____

7. Not supported by Windows Server 2003, Enterprise Edition

   _____

   _____

8. Requires a shared data store

   _____

   _____

9. Makes stateful applications highly available

_____

_____

10. Used for read-only applications

_____

_____

11. Used for COM+ applications

_____

_____

12. Supports clusters of up to 32 nodes in Windows Server 2003

_____

_____

Lesson Summary

- A cluster is a group of servers that appears to users as a single resource, and which provides high availability, reliability, and scalability for specific applications.

- A server cluster is a group of servers running a stateful application, such as a database server, and sharing a common data store. Servers in this type of cluster can be configured as active or passive nodes.

- A Network Load Balancing cluster is a group of servers running a stateless application, such as a Web server, each of which has an identical, independent data store.

- Scaling out is the process of adding more servers to an existing cluster, while scaling up is the process of upgrading the hardware of servers already in a cluster.

- Geographically dispersed clusters have servers in different locations. If the cluster is a server cluster, it requires a long-distance storage area network to provide the common data store. NLB typically uses separate clusters at each location, with a technique like DNS round robin to distribute client requests among the clusters.

Lesson 2: Using Network Load Balancing

Of the two types of clusters supported by Windows Server 2003, Network Load Balancing is the easier one to install, configure, and maintain. You can use the existing hardware and applications in your computers, and there is no additional software to install. You use the Network Load Balancing Manager application in Windows Server 2003 to create, manage, and monitor NLB clusters.

After this lesson, you will be able to

- Describe how Network Load Balancing works
- Understand the differences among the four NLB operational modes
- List the steps involved in deploying an NLB cluster
- Monitor NLB using Windows Server 2003 tools

Estimated lesson time: 30 minutes

Understanding Network Load Balancing

A Network Load Balancing cluster consists of up to 32 servers, referred to as hosts, each of which is running a duplicate copy of the application you want the cluster to provide to clients. Network Load Balancing works by creating on each host a *virtual network adapter* that represents the cluster as a single entity. The virtual adapter has its own IP and media access control (MAC) addresses, independent of the addresses assigned to the physical network interface adapters in the computers. Clients address their application requests to the cluster IP address, instead of an individual server's IP address.

Off the Record   In an Ethernet or Token Ring network interface adapter, the MAC address, also known as the adapter's hardware address, is a unique six-byte hexadecimal value hardcoded into the adapter by the manufacturer. Three bytes of the address contain a code identifying the manufacturer, and three bytes identify the adapter itself.

NLB Clustering and DNS

Directing clients to the IP address of the cluster is a task left to the name resolution mechanism that provides clients with IP addresses. For example, if you are currently running an individual Web server on the Internet, the DNS server hosting your domain has a record associating your Web server's name with the Web server computer's IP address. If you change from the single Web server to a Network Load Balancing cluster to host your Web site, you must modify the DNS resource record for the Web site's name so that it supplies clients with the cluster IP address, not your original Web server's IP address.

When an incoming client request addressed to the cluster IP address arrives, all the hosts in the cluster receive and process the message. On each host in an NLB cluster, a Network Load Balancing service functions as a filter between the cluster adapter and the computer's TCP/IP stacks. This filter enables NLB to calculate which host in the cluster should be responsible for resolving the request. No communication between the hosts is required for this purpose. Each host performs the same calculations independently and decides whether it should process that request or not. The algorithm the hosts use to perform these calculations changes only when hosts are added to or removed from the cluster.

Planning a Network Load Balancing Deployment

Before you deploy a Network Load Balancing cluster, you must create a plan for the network infrastructure that will support your cluster servers. The high availability provided by NLB will do you no good if your users can't access the servers due to a failure in a router, switch, or Internet connection. In addition, because many NLB installations provide Web and other services to Internet users, you must consider the security of your cluster servers and the rest of your internal network.

Real World   NLB Network Design

For a high-traffic Web site with high availability requirements, a typical network infrastructure design would consist of a Web server farm located on a perimeter network, as shown in the following figure. The perimeter network has redundant connections to the Internet, preferably with different Internet service providers (ISPs) or with one ISP that has connections to multiple Internet backbones. A firewall at each Internet access router protects the perimeter network from Internet intruders, and another firewall isolates the perimeter network from the internal network.

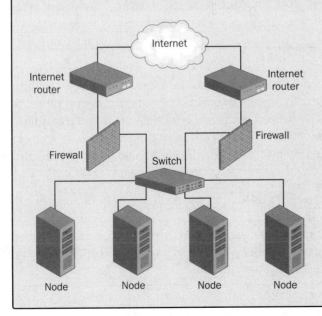

> **Important**   Deploying a Network Load Balancing cluster is not a task to undertake casually or haphazardly. As with any major network service, the NLB deployment process must be planned carefully, tested thoroughly on a lab network, and then implemented in a pilot program before proceeding with the full production deployment.

NLB Operational Modes

The servers that are going to be the hosts in your NLB cluster do not require any special hardware. There is no shared data store as in a server cluster, for example, so you do not have to build a storage area network. However, NLB imposes certain limitations on a server with a single network interface adapter in a standard configuration, and in some cases, you can benefit from installing a second network interface adapter in each of your servers.

Windows Server 2003 Network Load Balancing has two operational modes: *unicast mode* and *multicast mode*. In unicast mode, Network Load Balancing replaces the MAC address of the physical network interface adapter in each server with the MAC address of the virtual adapter representing the cluster. The server does not use the computer's original MAC address at all, effectively transforming the computer's physical network interface adapter into a virtual cluster adapter. The Address Resolution Protocol (ARP) resolves both of the server's IP addresses (the IP address originally assigned to the network interface adapter and the cluster IP address) to the single MAC address for the cluster.

> **Off the Record**   NLB does not actually modify the MAC address in the network interface adapter itself; the address assigned to the adapter by the manufacturer is permanent and cannot be changed. NLB only replaces the MAC address in the computer's memory, substituting a virtual cluster address for the physical address the system reads from the network adapter card.

NLB and ARP

ARP is a TCP/IP protocol that resolves IP addresses into MAC or hardware addresses. To transmit to a particular IP address, a TCP/IP computer must first discover the MAC address associated with that IP address, so that it can build a data-link layer protocol frame. ARP functions by transmitting a broadcast message containing an IP address to the local network. The computer using that IP address is responsible for replying with a message containing its MAC address.

In the case of an NLB cluster in unicast mode, each server in the cluster replies to ARP requests that contain either its original IP address or the cluster IP address by sending a response containing the cluster MAC address. Therefore, no computer on the network can transmit to the MAC address assigned for NLB server's physical network interface adapter.

Because the network interface adapters of all the servers in the cluster have the same MAC address, the cluster servers cannot communicate among themselves in the normal way, using their individual MAC addresses. The servers can, however, communicate with other computers on the same subnet, and with computers on other subnets, as long as the IP datagrams don't contain the cluster MAC address.

Note   When you configure the servers in an NLB cluster to use unicast mode with a single network interface adapter, you cannot use the Network Load Balancing Manager application on one of the servers to manage the other servers in the cluster.

In some cases, this is not a problem. Dedicated Web servers hosting the same site, for example, don't often need to communicate with each other under normal conditions. However, if you determine that it is necessary for the servers in your NLB cluster to communicate with each other, there are two possible solutions:

■ Configure the cluster servers to operate in NLB multicast mode—In multicast mode, NLB assigns a cluster MAC address to the physical network interface adapter, but also retains the adapter's original MAC address. The cluster IP address resolves to the cluster MAC address and the server's original IP address resolves to the original MAC address. For this configuration to function properly, the routers on the network must support the use of multicast MAC addresses.

■ Install a second network interface adapter in each server—One of the adapters becomes the cluster adapter, with its original MAC address replaced by the cluster MAC address. Both the cluster IP address and the adapter's original IP address resolve to the cluster MAC address. The system does not use this adapter's original MAC address. Like a single adapter in unicast mode, the cluster adapter cannot communicate with the other servers in the cluster. The second adapter retains its original MAC address and assigned IP address and handles all noncluster network communications.

Tip   In a Windows Server 2003 Network Load Balancing cluster, you must configure all the servers to operate in either unicast or multicast mode. You cannot mix unicast and multicast servers in the same cluster. However, you can mix network interface adapter configurations, installing two network interface adapters in some of a cluster's servers, while leaving a single adapter in others. In the case of a unicast cluster, only the servers with multiple adapters are able to communicate with the other servers.

In summary, a server in an NLB cluster can have either one network interface adapter or multiple adapters, and it can run in either unicast or multicast mode. By combining these options, you can use four possible NLB configurations, each of which has advantages and disadvantages, as shown in Table 7-1.

Table 7-1   NLB Configuration Advantages and Disadvantages

NLB Configuration	Advantages	Disadvantages
Single network interface adapter in unicast mode	■ Requires no special hardware ■ No router incompatibility problems	■ Ordinary communications with other servers in the cluster are not possible ■ Network performance might degrade when one network interface adapter is handling both ordinary traffic and cluster traffic
Single network interface adapter in multicast mode	■ Requires no special hardware ■ Permits ordinary communications among cluster servers	■ Some routers cannot support multicast MAC addresses ■ Network performance might degrade when one network interface adapter is handling both ordinary traffic and cluster traffic
Multiple network interface adapters in unicast mode	■ No router incompatibility problems ■ Permits ordinary communications among cluster servers ■ Network performance enhanced, because cluster traffic and ordinary network traffic use different network interface adapters	■ Requires installation of second network interface adapter
Multiple network interface adapters in multicast mode	■ Permits ordinary communications among cluster servers ■ Network performance enhanced, because cluster traffic and ordinary network traffic use different network interface adapters	■ Requires installation of second network interface adapter ■ Some routers cannot support multicast MAC addresses

The most popular configuration for large NLB installations is to install two network interface adapters in each server and run them in unicast mode. This enables the servers to function as normal participants on the network, in addition to performing their

NLB server duties. There are also no problems with routers handling multicast MAC addresses and no bottlenecks caused by cluster traffic and ordinary network traffic sharing a single network interface adapter.

NLB Networking

Although the servers in a Network Load Balancing cluster do not share a single data store, as in a server cluster, and perform their own independent calculations to determine which server will service an incoming request, the servers do communicate with each other. The cluster servers must exchange information to know many servers are in the cluster, and to determine when a server has been added or removed from the cluster. This communication enables the cluster to compensate for a failed server and to take advantage of new servers in the cluster by redistributing the traffic load.

Important   A single computer running Windows Server 2003 cannot be a member of a Network Load Balancing cluster and a server cluster at the same time, because these two clustering solutions use network interface adapters in different ways. If you want to deploy both an NLB cluster and a server cluster on your network, you must use separate servers for each cluster.

The cluster traffic between NLB servers takes the form of a *heartbeat* message that each server transmits once per second to the other servers in the cluster. If one cluster server fails, it stops transmitting its heartbeat messages, and the other servers detect the absence of the heartbeats. Once the other servers in the cluster miss five consecutive heartbeat messages from a server, they begin a process called *convergence*, in which they recalculate their traffic distribution algorithm to compensate for the missing server. In the same way, adding a new server to an NLB cluster introduces a new heartbeat to the network, which triggers a convergence in the other servers, enabling them to redistribute the traffic so that the new server receives an equal share of the load.

Note   Because all the servers in the cluster are using the same cluster MAC address, transmitting the heartbeats is simply a matter of directing the packets to that address. The servers don't need to broadcast the heartbeat messages, reducing the impact of the cluster traffic on the network.

When you deploy NLB cluster servers with a single network interface adapter in each computer, obviously all the cluster-related traffic must travel over the same network as your ordinary traffic. This is usually not a major burden, because the heartbeat packets are small, less than 1,500 bytes, so they fit into a single Ethernet packet. If you decide to install multiple network interface adapters in each cluster server, you can connect both adapters to the same local area network (LAN) or construct a separate network for the cluster traffic.

> **Planning**   If your NLB cluster consists of servers that are already isolated on a perimeter network, there is probably no need to create a separate LAN for cluster traffic. However, if you are deploying an NLB cluster on a heavily trafficked internal network, you might benefit from installing a dedicated cluster LAN.

Deploying a Network Load Balancing Cluster

Once you have planned the network infrastructure for your NLB cluster and decided on the operational mode, you can plan the actual deployment process. The basic steps in deploying NLB for a cluster of Web servers on a perimeter network are as follows:

1. Construct the perimeter network on which the Network Load Balancing servers will be located.

   Create a separate LAN on your internetwork and isolate it from the internal network and from the Internet using firewalls. Install the hardware needed to give the Web servers Internet access.

2. Install additional network interface adapter cards in the NLB servers if necessary.

   If you intend to use a separate network interface adapter for cluster-related communications, you must first install the second adapter card in the computer. During the Windows Server 2003 installation, you configure the network interface adapter driver for the second card just as you normally would.

3. Install Windows Server 2003 on the NLB servers.

4. Configure the TCP/IP configuration parameters for the network interface adapters on the NLB servers.

   When using two network interface adapters, you must configure them both in the normal manner, using the Internet Protocol (TCP/IP) Properties dialog box, and assigning them standard IP addresses and subnet masks, just as you would configure any other computer on the network.

> **Important**   If you are using a second network interface adapter for cluster traffic, at this point do not configure that adapter with the IP address you want to use to represent the cluster. Use a standard IP address for the subnet to which you have connected the adapter. Later, when you create the cluster, you specify the cluster IP address and NLB reconfigures the adapter's TCP/IP configuration parameters.

5. Join the NLB servers to an Active Directory domain created specifically for managing servers on the perimeter network.

6. Install the additional applications required by the NLB servers.

   For Web servers, you must install Internet Information Services (IIS), using the Add Or Remove Programs tool. At this point, you should also install any other applications that the servers need, such as the Microsoft DNS Server service.

7. Create and configure the cluster on the first host server.

   You use the Network Load Balancing Manager (see Figure 7-7) to create the new cluster and configure its parameters.

8. Add additional hosts to the cluster.

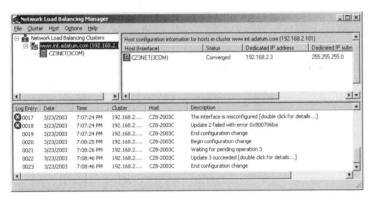

Figure 7-7   Network Load Balancing Manager

Monitoring Network Load Balancing

Once you have created and configured your Network Load Balancing cluster, several tools included in Windows Server 2003 can be used to monitor the cluster's ongoing processes.

Using Network Load Balancing Manager

When you display the Network Load Balancing Manager application, the bottom pane of the window displays the most recent log entries generated by activities in the NLB Manager (see Figure 7-8). These entries detail any configuration changes and contain any error messages generated by improper configuration parameters on any host in the cluster.

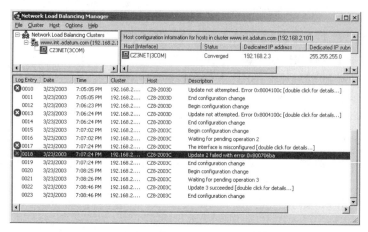

Figure 7-8   The Network Load Balancing Manager's log pane

By default, the log entries that Network Load Balancing Manager displays are not saved. To save a continuing log, you must enable logging by selecting Log Settings from the NLB Manager's Options menu. In the Log Settings dialog box, select the Enable Logging check box, and then, in the Log Filename text box, specify the name you want to use for the log file. The NLB Manager creates the file in the Documents And Settings folder's subfolder named for the account used to log on to the server.

Using Event Viewer

The Network Load Balancing Manager's log pane and log file contain information only about the NLB Manager's activities. To display log information about the Network Load Balancing service, you must look at the System log in the Event Viewer console, as shown in Figure 7-9. Entries concerning the Network Load Balancing service are labeled WLBS. (This stands for Windows Load Balancing Service, a holdover from the Windows NT name for the service.)

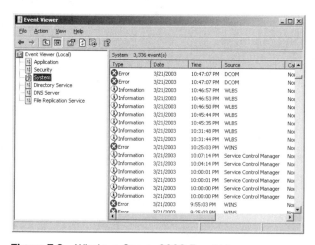

Figure 7-9   Windows Server 2003 Event Viewer

Using Nlb.exe

You can control many of an NLB cluster's functions from the Windows Server 2003 command line using a utility called Nlb.exe. Some of the program's most useful parameters are as follows:

> **Tip**   Nlb.exe is the Windows Server 2003 equivalent of the Wlbs.exe program included with earlier versions of the Windows operating system. If you are accustomed to using wlbs on your command lines, or more importantly, if you have existing scripts that use wlbs, you can continue to use them, because Windows Server 2003 includes the Wlbs.exe program as well.

■ **display**   Displays the configuration parameters stored in the registry for a specific cluster, plus the most recent cluster-related System log entries, the computer's IP configuration, and the cluster's current status.

■ **drain** *port*   Prevents a specified cluster from handling any new traffic conforming to the rule containing the port specified by the *port* variable.

■ **drainstop**   Disables all cluster traffic handling after completing the transactions currently in process.

■ **params**   Displays all the current configuration parameters for a specified cluster on the local host, as follows:

```
WLBS Cluster Control Utility V2.4 (c) 1997-2003 Microsoft Corporation.
Cluster 192.168.2.101
Retrieving parameters
Current time            = 3/19/2003 1:55:24 AM
HostName                = cz3net.int.adatum.com
ParametersVersion       = 4
CurrentVersion          = 00000204
EffectiveVersion        = 00000201
InstallDate             = 3E779B7C
HostPriority            = 3
ClusterIPAddress        = 192.168.2.101
ClusterNetworkMask      = 255.255.255.0
DedicatedIPAddress      = 192.168.2.3
DedicatedNetworkMask    = 255.255.255.0
McastIPAddress          = 0.0.0.0
ClusterName             = www.int.adatum.com
ClusterNetworkAddress   = 03-bf-c0-a8-02-65
IPToMACEnable           = ENABLED
MulticastSupportEnable   = ENABLED
IGMPSupport             = DISABLED
MulticastARPEnable      = ENABLED
MaskSourceMAC           = ENABLED
AliveMsgPeriod          = 1000
AliveMsgTolerance       = 5
NumActions              = 100
NumPackets              = 200
```

```
NumAliveMsgs                = 66
DescriptorsPerAlloc         = 512
MaxDescriptorAllocs         = 512
TCPConnectionTimeout        = 60
IPSecConnectionTimeout      = 86400
FilterICMP                  = DISABLED
ClusterModeOnStart          = STARTED
HostState                   = STARTED
PersistedStates             = NONE
ScaleSingleClient           = DISABLED
NBTSupportEnable            = ENABLED
NetmonAliveMsgs             = DISABLED
IPChangeDelay               = 60000
ConnectionCleanupDelay      = 300000
RemoteControlEnabled        = ENABLED
RemoteControlUDPPort        = 2504
RemoteControlCode           = 00000000
RemoteMaintenanceEnabled    = 00000000
BDATeaming                  = NO
TeamID                      =
Master                      = NO
ReverseHash                 = NO
IdentityHeartbeatPeriod     = 10000
IdentityHeartbeatEnabled    = ENABLED


PortRules (1):
        VIP         Start  End  Prot   Mode    Pri Load Affinity
---------------     -----  ---- ----   -------- --- ---- --------
All                  80     80  TCP   Multiple      Eql  None


Statistics:
Number of active connections  =   0
Number of descriptors allocated=  0
```

- **query**   Displays the current state of all hosts in a specified cluster, as follows:

```
WLBS Cluster Control Utility V2.4 (c) 1997-2003 Microsoft Corporation.
Cluster 192.168.2.101
Host 3 has entered a converging state 3 time(s) since joining the cluster
  and the last convergence completed at approximately: 3/19/2003 12:06:20 AM
Host 3 converged with the following host(s) as part of the cluster:
1, 3
```

- **queryport** *port*   Displays the current status of the rule containing the port specified by the *port* variable, as follows:

```
WLBS Cluster Control Utility V2.4 (c) 1997-2003 Microsoft Corporation.
Cluster 192.168.2.101
Retrieving state for port rule 80
Rule is enabled
Packets: Accepted=0, Dropped=17
```

Practice: Creating a Network Load Balancing Cluster

In this practice, you configure your Server01 computer to function as an IIS Web server, and then create a Network Load Balancing cluster, enabling clients to access the Web server using a cluster name and IP address. For the purposes of this practice, you are going to create a cluster consisting of a single server.

Exercise 1: Installing IIS

In this exercise, you install Internet Information Services on your Server01 computer, and create a simple home page so that your computer can function as a Web server.

1. Click Start, point to Control Panel, click Add Or Remove Programs. The Add Or Remove Programs window appears.

2. Click Add/Remove Windows Components. The Windows Components Wizard appears.

3. In the Components list, click the Application Server entry (but do not select its check box), and then click Details. The Application Server dialog box appears.

4. Select the Internet Information Services (IIS) check box, and then click OK.

5. Click Next. The Configuring Components page appears as the wizard installs the new software. Insert your Windows Server 2003, Enterprise Edition distribution disk, if the wizard prompts you to do so.

6. When the Completing the Windows Components Wizard page appears, click Finish.

7. Close the Add Or Remove Programs window.

8. Click Start, point to All Programs, point to Accessories, and then click Notepad. An Untitled – Notepad window opens.

9. In the Untitled – Notepad window, type the following:

```
<html>
<title>Hello, world.</title>
<body>
<h1>Hello, world.</h1>
</body>
</html>
```

This simple Hypertext Markup Language (HTML) script will function as the contents of your newly installed Web server.

10. From the File menu, select Save As. The Save As dialog box appears.

11. Using the Save In drop-down list, browse to the C:\Inetpub\Wwwroot folder and save the file using the name **default.htm**.

12. From the File menu, select Open. The Open dialog box appears.

13. Using the Look In drop-down list, browse to the C:\Windows\System32\Drivers\Etc folder and open the file called Hosts. (To open the Hosts file, you might need to select All Files from the Files Of Type drop-down list.)

14. At the end of the Hosts file, add a line like the following:

    ```
    10.0.0.100      www.contoso.com
    ```

    The IP address in this Hosts file entry is the address that you will later use to represent the cluster on the network.

15. From the File menu, select Save.

16. Close Notepad.

Exercise 2: Creating a Network Load Balancing Cluster

In this exercise, you create a new cluster and configure it to balance incoming Web server traffic.

1. Click Start, point to All Programs, point to Administrative Tools, and then click Network Load Balancing Manager. The Network Load Balancing Manager window appears.

2. Click the Network Load Balancing Clusters icon in the left pane and, from the Cluster menu, select New. The Cluster Parameters dialog box appears.

3. In the IP Address text box, type **10.0.0.100**.

    This IP address will represent the entire cluster on the network. Web clients use this address to connect to the Web server cluster.

4. In the Subnet Mask text box, type **255.0.0.0**.

5. In the Full Internet Name text box, type **www.contoso.com**.

    This fully qualified domain name (FQDN) will represent the cluster on the network. Web users type this name in their browsers to access the Web server cluster.

Important   Specifying a name for the cluster in this dialog box does not in itself make the cluster available to clients by that name. You must register the name you specify here in a name resolution mechanism. For an Internet Web server cluster, you must create a resource record on the DNS server hosting your domain, associating the name you specified with the cluster IP address you specified. For the purposes of this practice, you added the cluster name and IP address to the Hosts file on the computer in Exercise 1.

6. In the Cluster Operation Mode group box, click the Multicast option button. Then click Next. The Cluster IP Addresses dialog box appears.

   Selecting the Multicast option button on a computer with a single network interface adapter enables the computer to communicate normally with other hosts in the cluster.

7. Click Next. The Port Rules dialog box appears.

8. Click Edit. The Add/Edit Port Rule dialog box appears.

   A cluster's port rules specify which ports and which protocols the NLB service should monitor for traffic that is to be balanced among the servers in the cluster.

9. In the Port Range box, change the values of both the From and To selectors to 80.

   Port 80 is the well-known port for the Hypertext Transfer Protocol (HTTP), the application layer protocol that Web servers and clients use to communicate. By changing the Port Range values, you configure the NLB service to balance only Web traffic.

10. In the Protocols group box, click the TCP option button. Then click OK.

    When defining a port rule, you can specify whether one server or multiple servers should process the traffic for that rule. You can also configure the rule's *affinity*, which specifies whether multiple requests from the same client should be processed by a single server or distributed among multiple servers.

11. In the Port Rules dialog box, click Next. The Connect dialog box appears.

12. In the Host text box, type Server01, and then click Connect.

    The Host text box specifies the name of the server that you want to add to the cluster. You can use the Network Load Balancing Manager to create a cluster from any computer on the network running Windows Server 2003.

13. The Connection Status group box reads Connected, and the computer's network interfaces appear in the Interfaces Available For Configuring A New Cluster list.

14. Click Local Area Connection in the Interfaces Available For Configuring A New Cluster list, and then click Next. The Host Parameters dialog box appears.

15. Click Finish. The new cluster appears in the left pane in the Network Load Balancing Clusters list.

16. Close the Network Load Balancing Manager window.

Tip   If your computer is connected to a network that contains other computers running Windows Server 2003, you can create additional hosts in your cluster by selecting Add Host from the Cluster menu.

Exercise 3: Testing the Cluster

In this exercise, you connect to the Web server using the NLB cluster IP address, to prove that the NLB service is functioning.

1. Open Internet Explorer, and in the Address drop-down list, type **http:// 10.0.0.100**, and then press ENTER. The "Hello, world" page you created earlier appears in the browser.

   This test is successful because the NLB service has created the 10.0.0.100 address you specified for the cluster.

2. Next, type **http://10.0.0.1** in the Address drop-down list, and then press ENTER. The "Hello, world" page appears again.

   This test is successful because you have configured the NLB service to operate in multicast mode. Because of this, the network interface adapter's original IP address, 10.0.0.1, remains active.

3. Now, type **http://www.contoso.com** in the Address drop-down list, and then press ENTER. The "Hello, world" page appears yet again.

   This test is successful because you added the name www.contoso.com to the computer's Hosts file earlier, and associated it with the cluster IP address.

4. Close the Internet Explorer window.

Lesson Review

The following questions are intended to reinforce key information presented in this lesson. If you are unable to answer a question, review the lesson materials and try the question again. You can find answers to the questions in the "Questions and Answers" section at the end of this chapter.

1. You are the administrator of a Network Load Balancing cluster consisting of six Web servers running in unicast mode, with a single network interface adapter in each server. You are using the Network Load Balancing Manager application on one of the cluster servers to try to shut down the NLB service on one of the other servers so that you can upgrade its hardware. Why is the Manager not letting you do this?

_____

_____

2. Which of the following Nlb.exe commands do you use to shut down NLB operations on a cluster server without interrupting transactions currently in progress?

   a. Nlb drain

   b. Nlb params

   c. Nlb drainstop

   d. Nlb queryport

3. How long does it take a Network Load Balancing cluster to begin the convergence process after one of the servers in the cluster fails?

   _____

   _____

Lesson Summary

- Network Load Balancing works by creating a virtual network adapter with IP and MAC addresses that represent the cluster as a single unit.

- When NLB is running in unicast mode, the service replaces the network interface adapter's MAC address with the cluster MAC address, making ordinary communications between cluster servers impossible.

- When NLB is running in multicast mode, the service uses both the network interface adapter's MAC address and the cluster MAC address, enabling cluster servers to communicate normally.

- Although NLB can function with a single network interface adapter installed in each server, using multiple adapters in each server can prevent network performance degradation.

- NLB cluster servers transmit a heartbeat message once every second. If a server fails to transmit five successive heartbeats, the other servers in the cluster begin the convergence process, redistributing the incoming traffic among the remaining servers.

Lesson 3: Designing a Server Cluster

Server clusters are, by definition, more complicated than Network Load Balancing clusters, both in the way they handle applications and in the way they handle the application data. When designing a server cluster implementation, you still must evaluate your organization's high availability needs, but you must do so in light of a server cluster's greater deployment cost and greater capabilities.

After this lesson, you will be able to

- List the shared storage hardware configurations supported by Windows Server 2003
- Understand how to partition applications
- Describe the quorum models you can use in a server cluster
- List the steps involved in creating a server cluster
- Describe the different types of failover policies you can use with server clusters

Estimated lesson time: 40 minutes

Designing a Server Cluster Deployment

As you learned in Lesson 1 of this chapter, server clusters are intended to provide advanced failover capabilities for stateful applications, particularly database and e-mail servers. Because the data files maintained by these applications change frequently, it is not practical for individual servers in a cluster to maintain their own individual copies of the data files. If this were the case, the servers would have to immediately propagate changes that clients make to their data files to the other servers, so that the server could present a unified data set to all clients at all times.

As a result, server clusters are based on a shared data storage solution. The cluster stores the files containing the databases or e-mail stores on a drive array (typically using RAID or some other data availability technique) that is connected to all the servers in the cluster. Therefore, all the application's clients, no matter which server in the cluster they connect to, are working with the same data files, as shown in Figure 7-10.

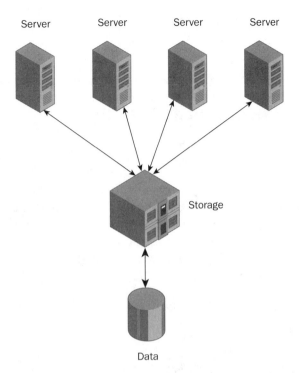

Figure 7-10   Server cluster nodes share application data

The shared data store adds significantly to the cost of building a server cluster, especially if you plan to create a geographically dispersed cluster. Unlike geographically dispersed NLB clusters, which are usually separate clusters unified by an external technology, such as round robin DNS, the hosts in server clusters must be connected to the central data store, even when the servers are in different cities. This means that you must construct a SAN connecting the various sites, as well as a standard WAN. When considering a deployment of this type, you must decide whether the impact of having your applications offline justifies the expense of building the required hardware infrastructure.

Planning a Server Cluster Hardware Configuration

The computers running Windows Server 2003 that you use to build a server cluster must all use the same processor architecture, meaning that you cannot mix 32-bit and 64-bit systems in the same cluster. Each server in the cluster must have at least one standard network connection giving it access to the other cluster servers and to the client computers that use the cluster's services. For maximum availability, having two network interface adapters in each computer is preferable, one providing the connection to the client network, and one connecting to a network dedicated to communications between the servers in the cluster.

In addition to standard network connections, each server must have a separate connection to the shared storage device. Windows Server 2003 supports three types of storage connections: Small Computer System Interface (SCSI) and two types of Fibre Channel, as discussed in the following sections.

> **Planning**   Microsoft strongly recommends that all the hardware components you use in your cluster servers for Windows Server 2003, and particularly those that make up the shared storage solution, be properly tested and listed in the Windows Server Catalog.

Using SCSI

SCSI is a bus architecture used to connect storage devices and other peripherals to personal computers. SCSI implementations typically take the form of a host adapter in the computer, and a number of internal or external devices that you connect to the card, using appropriate SCSI cables. In a shared SCSI configuration, however, you use multiple host adapters, one for each server in the cluster, and connect the adapters and the storage devices to a single bus, as shown in Figure 7-11.

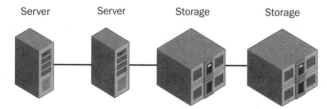

Figure 7-11   A cluster using a SCSI bus

Understanding SCSI

The SCSI host adapter is the component responsible for receiving device access requests from the computer and feeding them to the appropriate devices on the SCSI bus. Although you can use SCSI devices on any personal computer by installing a host adapter card, SCSI is usually associated with servers, because it can handle requests for multiple devices more efficiently than other interfaces.

When the Integrated Drive Electronics (IDE) devices used in most PC workstations receive an access request from the computer's host adapter, the device processes the request and sends a response to the adapter. The adapter remains idle until it receives the response from that device. Only when that response arrives can the adapter send the next request. SCSI host adapters, by contrast, can send requests to many different devices in succession, without having to wait for the results of each one. Therefore, SCSI is better for servers that must handle large numbers of disk access requests.

Many personal computers marketed as servers have an integrated SCSI host adapter. If the computers you use for your cluster servers do not already have SCSI adapters, you must purchase and install a SCSI host adapter card for each one.

Because of the limitations of the SCSI architecture, Windows Server 2003 only supports two-node clusters using SCSI, and only with the 32-bit version of Windows Server 2003, Enterprise Edition. SCSI hubs are also not supported. In addition, you cannot use SCSI for a geographically dispersed cluster, as the maximum length for a SCSI bus is 25 meters.

Real World   SCSI Clustering

SCSI is designed to support multiple devices and multiple device types on a single bus. The original SCSI standard supported up to eight devices (including the SCSI host adapter), while some newer versions of the standard can support up to 16. For the SCSI adapter to communicate with each device individually, you must configure each device on the bus with a unique SCSI ID. SCSI IDs range from 0 to 7 on the standard bus, and SCSI host adapters traditionally use ID 7. When you create a shared SCSI bus for your server cluster, you must modify the SCSI ID of one of the host adapters on the bus, so that both are not using the same ID.

The other requirement for all SCSI buses is that both ends of the bus be terminated so that the signals generated by the SCSI devices do not reflect back in the other direction and interfere with new signals. A terminator uses resistors to remove the electrical signals from the cable. You must have appropriate terminators installed at the ends of your shared SCSI bus, and Microsoft recommends physical terminating devices, rather than the termination circuits built into many SCSI devices.

Using Fibre Channel

Fibre Channel is a high-speed serial networking technology that was originally conceived as a general purpose networking solution, but which has instead been adopted primarily for connections between computers and storage devices. Unlike SCSI, which is a parallel signaling technology, Fibre Channel uses serial signaling, which enables it to transmit over much longer distances. Fibre Channel devices can transmit data at speeds up to 100 megabytes per second using *full duplex communications*, which means that the devices can transmit at full speed in both directions simultaneously.

Off the Record   The nonstandard spelling of the word "fibre" in Fibre Channel is deliberate. The designers of the technology want to avoid confusion with the term "fiber optic," because Fibre Channel connections can use copper-based as well as fiber-optic cable as a network medium.

The most common method for implementing a Fibre Channel storage solution on a server cluster is to install a Fibre Channel host adapter in each cluster server and then use them to connect the computers to one or more external storage devices. The storage devices are typically self-contained drive arrays or NAS devices, using RAID to provide high data availability.

Windows Server 2003 supports two types of Fibre Channel topologies for connecting cluster servers to storage devices: Fibre Channel arbitrated loop (FC-AL) and Fibre Channel switched fabric (FC-SW).

Fibre Channel Arbitrated Loop   In the context of Windows Server 2003 server clusters, a Fibre Channel arbitrated loop is a ring topology that connects cluster servers with a collection of storage devices, as shown in Figure 7-12. The total number of devices in an arbitrated loop is limited to 126, but Windows Server 2003 limits the number of servers in an arbitrated loop cluster to two.

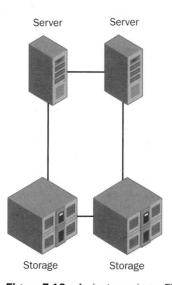

Server   Server

Storage   Storage

Figure 7-12   A cluster using a Fibre Channel arbitrated loop network

A Fibre Channel arbitrated loop is a shared network medium, which is one reason for the two-server limit. Data packets transmitted by one device on the loop might have to pass through other devices to reach their destinations, which lowers the overall bandwidth available to the individual devices. Compared to switched fabric, arbitrated loop is a relatively inexpensive clustering hardware technology that enables administrators to easily expand their storage capacity (although not the number of cluster nodes).

Fibre Channel Switched Fabric   The only shared storage solution supported by Windows Server 2003 that is suitable for server clusters of more than two nodes is the Fibre Channel switched fabric network. FC-SW is similar in configuration to a switched Ethernet network, in which each device is connected to a switch, as shown in Figure 7-13. Switching enables any device on the network to establish a direct, dedicated connection to any other device. There is no shared network medium, as in FC-AL; the full bandwidth of the network is available to all communications.

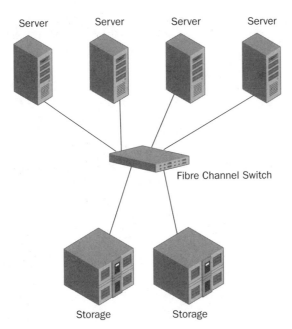

Figure 7-13   A cluster using a Fibre Channel switched fabric network

An FC-SW network that is wholly dedicated to giving servers access to data storage devices is a type of SAN. Building a SAN to service your server cluster provides the greatest possible amount of flexibility and scalability. You can add nodes to the cluster by installing additional servers and connecting them to the SAN, or expand the cluster's shared storage capacity by installing additional drives or drive arrays. You can also build a geographically dispersed server cluster by extending the SAN to locations in other cities.

Creating an Application Deployment Plan

The stateful applications that server clusters host usually have greater capabilities than the stateless applications used on Network Load Balancing clusters. This means that you have more flexibility in how you deploy the applications on the cluster. Windows Server 2003 can host the following two basic types of applications in a server cluster:

- **Single-instance applications**   Applications that can run on no more than one server at a time, using a given configuration. The classic example of a single-instance application is the DHCP service. You can run a DHCP server with a particular scope configuration on only one server at a time, or you risk the possibility of having duplicate IP addresses on your network. To run an application of this type in a cluster, the application can be running on only one node, while other nodes function as standbys. If the active node malfunctions, the application fails over to one of the other nodes in the cluster.

■ **Multiple-instance applications** Applications in which duplicated (or *cloned*) code can run on multiple nodes in a cluster (as in an NLB cluster) or in which the code can be *partitioned,* or split into several instances, to provide complementary services on different cluster nodes. With some database applications, you can create partitions that respond to queries of a particular type, or that furnish information from a designated subset of the database.

Deploying Single-Instance Applications

Deploying one single-instance application on a cluster is simply a matter of installing the same application on multiple nodes and configuring one node to be active, while the others remain passive until they are needed. This type of deployment is most common in two-node clusters, unless the application is so vital that you feel you must plan for the possibility of multiple server failures.

When you plan to run more than one single-instance application on a cluster, you have several deployment alternatives. You can create a separate two-node cluster for each application, with one active and one passive node in each, but this requires having two servers standing idle. You can create a three-node cluster, with two active nodes, each running one of the applications, and one passive node functioning as the standby for both applications. If you choose this configuration, the passive node must be capable of running both applications at once, in the event that both active nodes fail. A third configuration would be to have a two-node cluster with one application running on each, and each server active as a standby for the other. In this instance, both servers must be capable of running both applications.

Capacity Planning

This talk of running multiple applications on a server cluster introduces one of the most important elements of cluster application deployment: capacity planning. The servers in your cluster must have sufficient memory and enough processing capabilities to function adequately in your worst-case scenario.

For example, if your organization is running five critical applications, you can create a six-node cluster with five active nodes running the five applications and a single passive node functioning as the standby for all five. If your worst-case scenario is that all five active nodes fail, the single passive node had better be capable of running all five applications at one time with adequate performance for the entire client load.

In this example, the possibility of all five active nodes failing is remote, but you must decide on your own worst-case scenario, based on the importance of the applications to your organization.

Deploying Multiple-Instance Applications

In a multiple-instance application, more than one node in the cluster can be running the same application at the same time. When deploying multiple-instance applications, you either clone them or partition them. Cloned applications are rare on server clusters. Most applications that require this type of deployment are stateless and are better suited to a Network Load Balancing cluster than to a server cluster.

Partitioning an application means that you split the application's functionality into separate instances and deploy each one on a separate cluster node. For example, you can configure a database application on a four-node server cluster so that each node handles requests for information from one fourth of the database, as shown in Figure 7-14. When an application provides a number of different services, you might be able to configure each cluster node to handle one particular service.

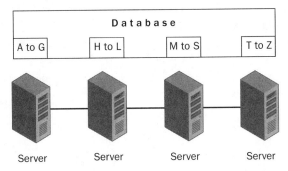

Figure 7-14   A partitioned database application

Note   With a partitioned application, some mechanism must distribute the requests to the appropriate nodes and assemble the replies from multiple nodes into a single response for the client. This mechanism, like the partitioning capability itself, is something that developers must build into the application; these functions are not provided by the clustering capability in Windows Server 2003 by itself.

Partitioning by itself can provide increased application efficiency, but it does not provide high availability. Failure of a node hosting one partition renders part of the database or certain services unavailable. In addition to partitioning the application, you must configure its failover capabilities. For example, in the four-node, partitioned database application mentioned earlier, you can configure each partition to fail over to one of the other nodes in the cluster. You can also add one or more passive nodes to function as standbys for the active nodes. Adding a single passive node to the four-node cluster would enable the application to continue running at full capacity in the event of a single node failure. It would be necessary for servers to run multiple partitions at once only if multiple server failures occurred.

Planning Here again, you must decide what is the worst-case scenario for the cluster and plan your server capacity accordingly. If you want the four-node cluster to be able to compensate for the failure of three out of four nodes, you must be sure that each server is capable of running all four of the application's partitions at once.

If you plan to deploy more than one multiple-instance application on your cluster, the problem of configuring partitions, failover behavior, and server capacity becomes even more complex. You must plan for all possible failures and make sure that all the partitions of each application have a place to run in the event of each type of failure.

Selecting a Quorum Model

Every node in a server cluster maintains a copy of the cluster database in its registry. The cluster database contains the properties of all the cluster's elements, including physical components such as servers, network adapters, and shared storage devices; and cluster objects such as applications and other logical resources. When a cluster node goes offline for any reason, its cluster database is no longer updated as the cluster's status changes. When the mode comes back online, it must have a current copy of the database to rejoin the cluster, and it obtains that copy from the cluster's *quorum resource*.

A cluster's quorum contains all the configuration data needed for the recovery of the cluster, and the quorum resource is the drive where the quorum is stored. To create a cluster, the first node must be able to take control of the quorum resource, so that it can save the quorum data there. Only one system can have control of the quorum resource at any one time. Additional nodes must be able to access the quorum resource so that they can create the cluster database in their registries.

Selecting the location for the quorum is a crucial part of creating a cluster. Server clusters running Windows Server 2003 support the following three types of quorum models:

- **Single-node cluster**   A cluster that consists of only one server. Because there is no need for a shared storage solution, the application data store and the quorum resource are located on the computer's local drive. The primary reason for creating single-node clusters is for testing and development.

- **Single-quorum device cluster**   The cluster uses a single quorum resource, which is one of the shared storage devices accessible by all the nodes in the cluster. This is the quorum model that most server cluster installations use.

- **Majority node set cluster**   A separate copy of the quorum is stored in each cluster node, with the quorum resource responsible for keeping all copies of the quorum consistent. Majority node set clusters are particularly well suited to geographically dispersed server clusters and clusters that do not have shared data storage devices.

Exam Tip   Be sure to understand the differences between the various quorum models supported by Windows Server 2003.

Creating a Server Cluster

Before you actually create the cluster, you must select, evaluate, and install a shared storage resource and install the critical applications on the computers running Windows Server 2003. All the computers that are to become cluster nodes must have access to the shared storage solution you have selected; you should know your applications' capabilities with regard to partitioning; and you should have decided how to deploy them. Once you have completed these tasks, you will use the Cluster Administrator tool to create and manage server clusters (see Figure 7-15).

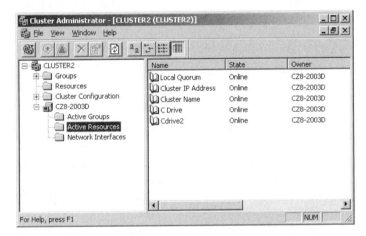

Figure 7-15   Cluster Administrator

To create a new cluster, you must have the following information available:

- The name of the domain in which the cluster will be located
- The host name to assign to the cluster
- The static IP address to assign to the cluster
- The name and password for a cluster service account

With this information in hand, you can proceed to deploy the cluster, taking the following basic steps:

1. Start up the computer running Windows Server 2003 that will be the first node in the cluster.

   At this time, the other servers that you will later add to the cluster should not be running.

2. Use the Cluster Administrator application on the first server to create a new cluster.

   During this process, the New Server Cluster Wizard detects the storage devices and network interfaces on the computer, and determines whether they are suitable for use by the cluster. You also supply the name and IP address for the cluster and the name and password for the cluster service account.

3. Verify that the cluster is operational and that you can access the cluster disks.

   At this point, you have created a single-node cluster.

4. Start up the computers running Windows Server 2003 that will become the other nodes in the cluster.

5. Use the Add Nodes Wizard in Cluster Administrator to make the other servers part of the cluster.

6. Test the cluster by using Cluster Administrator to stop the cluster service on each node in turn, verifying that the cluster disks are still available after each stoppage.

Once you have added all the nodes to the cluster, you can view information about the nodes in Cluster Administrator as well as manage the nodes and their resources from a central location. In addition, there are many clustering features you can use to configure how the cluster behaves under various conditions.

Understanding Cluster Resources

When managing a cluster, you frequently work with cluster resources. A cluster resource is any physical or logical element that the cluster service can manage by bringing it online or offline and moving it to a different node. By default, the cluster resources supported by server clusters running Windows Server 2003 include storage devices, configuration parameters, scripts, and applications. When you deploy a third-party application on a server cluster, the application developer typically includes resource types that are specific to that application.

Some of the configuration tasks you can perform in Cluster Administrator are as follows:

- **Create resource groups**   A resource group is a collection of cluster resources that functions as a single failover unit. When one resource in the group malfunctions, the cluster service fails the entire group over to another node. You use the New Group Wizard to create resource groups, after which you can create new resources or move existing resources into the group.

- **Define resource dependencies**   You can configure a specific cluster resource to be dependent on other resources in the same resource group. The cluster service uses these dependencies to determine the order in which it starts and stops the resources on a node in the event of a failover. For example, when an application is dependent on a particular shared disk where the application is stored, the cluster service always brings down the application on a node before bringing down the disk. Conversely, when launching the application on a new node, the service will always start the disk before the application, so that the disk is available to the application when it starts.

- **Configure the cluster network role** For each network to which a cluster is connected, you can specify whether the cluster should use that network for client access only, for internal cluster communications only, or for both.

- **Configure failover relationships** For each resource that the cluster manages, you can specify a list of nodes that are permitted to run that resource. With this capability, you can configure a wide variety of failover policies for your applications.

Exam Tip It is a good idea to spend some time exploring the Network Load Balancing Manager and Cluster Administrator applications. Learn the function of each parameter or setting in these two programs, using the online help for assistance.

Configuring Failover Policies

By configuring the failover relationships of your cluster applications and other resources, you can implement a number of different failover policies that control which cluster nodes an application uses and when. With small server clusters, failover is usually a simple affair because you don't have that many nodes to choose from. As server clusters grow larger, however, their failover capabilities become more flexible. Some of the failover policies you might consider using are as follows:

- **Failover pairs** In a large server cluster running several applications, each application is running on one node and has one designated standby node. This makes server capacity planning simple, as the servers are never running more than one application. However, half of the cluster's processing capacity is not in use, and, in the event of multiple node failures, some applications could go offline unless an administrator intervenes.

- **Hot-standby server** A single node functions as the designated standby server for two or more applications. This option uses the cluster's processing capacity more efficiently (fewer servers are idle), but might not handle multiple node failures well. For capacity planning, the standby server only has to be able to support the most resource-intensive application it might run, unless you want to plan for multiple node failures, in which case the standby must be capable of running multiple applications at once.

- **N+I** An expanded form of the hot-standby server policy, in which you configure a number of active nodes running different applications (N) to fail over to any one of a number of idle servers (I). As an example, you can create a six-node server cluster with four applications running on four separate nodes, plus two standby nodes that are idle. When one of the active nodes malfunctions, its application fails over to one of the standby servers. This policy is better at handling multiple server failures than failover pairs or hot-standby servers.

- **Failover ring** Each node in a server cluster runs an application, and you configure each application to fail over to the next node. This policy is suitable for relatively small applications, because in the event of a failure, a server might have to run two or more applications at once. In the event of multiple node failures, the application load could be unbalanced across the active nodes. For example, in a four-node cluster, if Server 1 fails, Server 2 must run its own application and that of Server 1. If Server 2 then fails, Server 3 must take on the Server 2 and Server 1 applications in addition to its own, while Server 4 continues to run only one application. This makes server capacity planning difficult.

- **Random** In some cases, the best policy is for the administrator not to define any specific failover relationships at all, and let the cluster service be responsible for failing over resources to other nodes in the cluster. This policy is usually preferable for smaller applications, so that a single node can conceivably run multiple applications if necessary. Random failovers also place less of a burden on the cluster administrator.

Practice: Creating a Single Node Cluster

In this practice, you create a server cluster on your Server01 computer. Because you are not likely to have access to shared storage hardware that would enable you to create a multinode cluster, this will be a cluster with only one server. However, the process of creating a single node cluster is the same as the first step of creating a cluster with multiple nodes.

Exercise 1: Creating a Server Cluster

In this exercise, you use the Cluster Administrator to create a new server cluster on your Server01 computer.

> **Important** If you have previously created a Network Load Balancing cluster on your server, as described in the Lesson 2 practice in this chapter, you must disable it before you perform this practice. To do this, open Network Load Balancing Manager, select the cluster you created, and, from the Cluster menu, click Delete.

1. Click Start, point to All Programs, point to Administrative Tools, and then click Cluster Administrator. The Cluster Administrator window appears and the Open Connections To Cluster dialog box appears.

2. In the Action selector, choose Create New Cluster, and then click OK. The New Server Cluster Wizard appears.

3. Click Next. The Cluster Name And Domain page appears. Verify that the correct domain name is chosen in the Domain selector. Type **cluster** in the Cluster Name text box, and then click Next. The Select Computer page appears.

   The name of your computer appears in the Computer Name text box.

4. Click Next. The Analyzing Configuration page appears.

   The wizard proceeds to analyze the system resources and configuration to determine whether it can create a cluster. When the process is complete, notice that the Finding Common Resources On Nodes and Checking Cluster Feasibility entries are flagged with a yellow triangle containing an exclamation point. When you expand these entries, you see that the flags indicate that the wizard failed to locate a shared quorum resource and that it found only one network interface adapter in the computer. Neither of these conditions prevents you from creating the single-node cluster.

5. Click Next. The IP Address page appears.

6. Type **10.0.0.110** in the IP Address text box, and then click Next. The Cluster Service Account page appears.

7. Type **Administrator** in the User Name text box and the password for the Administrator account in the Password text box. Then click Next. The Proposed Cluster Configuration page appears.

   When creating an actual production cluster, you should create a new account with administrative privileges to the servers that will become your cluster nodes and use that as the cluster service account. For the purposes of this practice, you need not bother.

8. Review the configuration analysis displayed on the page, and then click Next. The Creating The Cluster page appears.

9. The wizard proceeds to create the cluster and start the cluster service.

10. When the wizard completes the process and activates the Next button, click it. The Completing The New Server Cluster Wizard page appears.

11. Click Finish.

12. Leave the Cluster Administrator window open for the next exercise.

Exercise 2: Creating a Cluster Resource

In this exercise, you create a File Share resource on your new cluster, which you will later access using the cluster name you assigned in Exercise 1.

1. From the Cluster Administrator's File menu, point to New, and then click Resource. The New Resource Wizard appears.

2. In the Name text box, type **Cdrive**.

3. In the Resource Type selector, choose File Share, and then click Next. The Possible Owners page appears.

4. In the Possible Owners page, your computer appears in the Possible Owners list. Click Next. The Dependencies page appears.

5. Click Next. The File Share Parameters page appears.

6. In the Share Name text box, type **Cdrive**.

7. In the Path text box, type **C:**.

8. Click Finish. A Cluster Administrator message box appears, stating that the resource was created successfully. Click OK.

9. In Cluster Administrator's scope pane, click the Resources folder.

   The newly created Cdrive resource appears in the details pane, displaying its state as Offline.

10. Click the Cdrive icon in the details pane and, from the File menu, select Bring Online.

    The state of the Cdrive resource changes to Online.

11. Close the Cluster Administrator window.

Exercise 3: Access the Server Cluster

In this exercise, you access your newly created cluster using its name and IP address.

1. Click Start, point to All Programs, point to Accessories, and then click Command Prompt. A Command Prompt window appears.

2. In the Command Prompt window, type **ping 10.0.0.110**, and then press ENTER.

   The Ping.exe program successfully tests the connection to the cluster IP address you specified in Exercise 1.

3. Click Start, and then select Run. The Run dialog box appears.

4. In the Open text box, type **cluster**, and then click OK.

   A \\Cluster window appears, containing icons for Scheduled Tasks and for the File Share resource you created in Exercise 2.

5. Double-click the Cdrive icon. You can now access the contents of the computer's C drive using a share you created as a cluster resource.

   At this point, if your server was connected to a network with other computers running Windows Server 2003 and had the appropriate shared storage hardware, you could add other nodes to the cluster to provide failover capabilities.

6. Close the Command Prompt window.

Lesson Review

The following questions are intended to reinforce key information presented in this lesson. If you are unable to answer a question, review the lesson materials and try the question again. You can find answers to the questions in the "Questions and Answers" section at the end of this chapter.

1. Explain why planning server capacity is an important element of deploying a server cluster.

   _____

   _____

2. Which shared storage hardware configuration is the only possible solution for a server cluster with more than two nodes?

   _____

   _____

3. Which of the following failover policies provides the best compensation for multiple node failures?

   a. Failover pairs

   b. Hot-standby servers

   c. N+I

   d. Failover ring

Lesson Summary

- A server cluster requires a storage resource shared by the nodes in the cluster. Windows Server 2003 supports shared SCSI and Fibre Channel arbitrated loop for 2-node clusters, and Fibre Channel switched fabric for server clusters with more than two nodes.

- Some of the stateful applications you can deploy in a server cluster support partitioning, which enables you to split the functionality of the application among the servers in the cluster.

- A quorum is a storage resource that contains cluster configuration data, which nodes use to create their configuration databases as they join the cluster. Server clusters running Windows Server 2003 support three quorum models: single-node cluster, single-quorum device cluster, and majority node set cluster.

- To create and manage server clusters, you use the Cluster Administrator application. This tool enables you to create new clusters, add nodes and resources to a cluster, and control all aspects of cluster performance from a central location.

- You can configure a cluster to use various failover policies by specifying which nodes are permitted to run various cluster resources. Some of the policies include failover pairs, hot-standby servers, N+I, and failover rings.

Case Scenario Exercise

You are the network administrator for Litware Inc., a manufacturer of specialized scientific software products, and you have already created a network design for their new office building, as described in the Case Scenario Exercise in Chapter 1. The office building is a three-story brick structure built in the late 1940s, which has since been retrofitted by various tenants with several different types of network cabling. Your network design for the building calls for the installation of five LANs, each of which is connected to a sixth, backbone network.

The corporation's six Web servers running Windows Server 2003 are housed in the basement of the building, on a dedicated perimeter network. The company also has a computer running both Windows Server 2003 and Microsoft SQL Server on the second floor, which is hosting the customer database used by the Sales staff. This server is currently running at near peak capacity almost all the time.

You have been directed by the home office to see to it that the company Web servers are accessible by Internet users at all times. You are also ordered to make sure that the customer database is always available to the sales staff. After informing your superiors of the database server's operational state, they have authorized you to purchase three new database servers and the additional hardware needed to connect them to the network.

You have decided to use the clustering capabilities in Windows Server 2003 to achieve both of these goals. For the Web servers, you are going to create a Network Load Balancing cluster, and to host the customer database, you are going to create a four-node server cluster. Based on this information, answer the following questions:

1. Each of the six Web servers on the perimeter network has a single network interface adapter installed. What additional hardware is absolutely required to implement the NLB cluster on the Web servers?

   _____

   _____

2. You want to be able to use Network Load Balancing Manager, running on one of the Web servers, to configure all the servers in the NLB cluster. Other than this, very little noncluster communication between the Web servers is required. Which of the following communication models should you use to make this possible with the greatest economy? Explain your answer.

   a. Single network interface adapter in unicast mode

   b. Single network interface adapter in multicast mode

   c. Multiple network interface adapters in unicast mode

   d. Multiple network interface adapters in multicast mode

3. Which of the following storage hardware configurations should you use for the 4-node database server cluster? Explain your answer.

   a. Install a SCSI host adapter in each server and connect them all to a single SCSI bus

   b. Install a SCSI host adapter in each server and connect them all to a SCSI hub

   c. Install a Fibre Channel adapter in each server and connect them in an arbitrated loop

   d. Install a Fibre Channel adapter in each server and connect them all to a Fibre Channel switch

4. You have decided to partition your database server application to spread the load among the servers in the cluster. Which of the following failover policies will ensure that the entire database is constantly available without any server running multiple partitions, even if two servers fail? Explain your answer.

   a. Failover pairs. Split the database into two partitions and assign each one to an active server. Then, configure each of the active servers to fail over to one of the two remaining servers.

   b. Hot-standby server. Split the database into three partitions and assign each one to an active server. Then, configure each of the active servers to fail over to the one remaining server.

   c. N+I. Split the database into two partitions and assign each one to an active server. Then, configure each of the active servers to fail over to either one of the two remaining servers.

   d. Failover ring. Split the database into four partitions and assign each one to an active server. Then, configure each of the four servers to failover to the next server.

5. If you need to expand the server cluster, how many more servers can you add?

Troubleshooting Lab

You are a network administrator who has recently installed a four-node Network Load Balancing cluster on the company internetwork. The cluster provides fault tolerance for the company's Internet Web servers. The cluster servers are located on a dedicated LAN in the building's basement data center, with routers connecting the LAN to the Internet and to the rest of the company network. When you installed the cluster, you used multicast mode on the servers so that they could communicate with each other. However, you now discover that when you try to use the Network Load Balancing Manager application on your office workstation on the third floor, you cannot connect to any of the cluster servers. For each of the following procedures, state whether it might resolve the problem and explain your answer.

1. Reconfigure the Network Load Balancing cluster servers to use unicast mode rather than multicast mode.

   _____

   _____

2. Install a second network interface adapter in each Network Load Balancing cluster server.

   _____

   _____

3. Replace the router connecting the Web server LAN to the company network with a computer running Windows Server 2003 that you have configured to function as a router.

   _____

   _____

Chapter Summary

- A cluster is a group of servers that appears to users as a single resource and which provides high availability, reliability, and scalability for specific applications.

- A server cluster is a group of servers running a stateful application, such as a database server, and sharing a common data store. Servers in this type of cluster can be configured as active or passive nodes.

- A Network Load Balancing cluster is a group of servers running a stateless application, such as a Web server, each of which has an identical, independent data store.

- Network Load Balancing works by creating a virtual network adapter with IP and MAC addresses that represent the cluster as a single unit.

- When NLB is running in unicast mode, ordinary communication between cluster servers is impossible. In multicast mode, the cluster servers can communicate normally.

- Although NLB and server clusters can both function with a single network interface adapter installed in each server, using multiple adapters in each server can prevent network performance degradation.

- A server cluster requires a storage resource shared by the nodes in the cluster. Windows Server 2003 supports shared SCSI and Fibre Channel arbitrated loop for two-node clusters, and Fibre Channel switched fabric for server clusters with more than two nodes.

- In a server cluster, the quorum is a storage resource that contains cluster configuration data, which nodes use to create their configuration databases as they join the cluster.

- You can configure a cluster to use various failover policies by specifying which nodes are permitted to run various cluster resources. Some of the policies include failover pairs, hot-standby servers, N+I, and failover rings.

- To create and manage server clusters, you use the Cluster Administrator application. To manage Network Load balancing clusters, you use Network Load Balancing Manager.

Exam Highlights

Before taking the exam, review the key points and terms that are presented below to help you identify topics you need to review. Return to the lessons for additional practice, and review the "Further Reading" sections in Part 2 for pointers to more information about topics covering the exam objectives.

Key Points

- Server clusters are for stateful applications, such as database servers, that have frequently changing data. NLB clusters are for stateless applications, such as Web servers, in which the data seldom changes.

- While both types of clusters can benefit from multiple network interface adapters, only server clusters require additional hardware, in the form of a shared storage solution that enables all the servers in the cluster to access the same application data.

- All Windows Server 2003 versions support NLB clusters, but only Enterprise Edition and Datacenter Edition support server clusters.

- To monitor Network Load Balancing, you can use the Network Load Balancing Manager itself, the Event Viewer console, and the Nlb.exe command line utility.

- Cluster servers continually exchange heartbeat messages, which they use to determine when a node has failed. To recover from a node failure, the remaining servers begin a process called convergence, which enables them to compensate for the loss.

Key Terms

Failover and failback   Failover is the process of shifting specific application tasks to another node in the cluster when one or more servers malfunction. Failback is the process of shifting application tasks back to their original nodes after a failed server comes back online.

Stateful and stateless applications   A stateful application is one in which the application data frequently changes or that has long-running in-memory states, such as a database server. A stateless application is one in which data changes infrequently, or that does not have long-running in-memory states.

Convergence   The process by which a cluster compensates for the failure of one or more servers. In an NLB cluster, convergence consists of redistributing the incoming client traffic among the remaining servers. In a server cluster, convergence consists of failing over the application tasks performed by the malfunctioning node to another server in the cluster.

Quorum resource   A storage device containing continually updated configuration data about a server cluster, which the cluster uses to rejoin nodes that have been offline.

Questions and Answers

Lesson 1 Review

Specify whether each of the following is a characteristic of server clusters, CLB clusters, or NLB clusters.

1. Used for database server clusters

   Server clusters

2. Supports clusters of up to 8 nodes in Windows Server 2003, Datacenter Edition

   Server clusters

3. Supported by Windows Server 2003, Standard Edition

   NLB clusters

4. Makes stateless applications highly available

   NLB clusters

5. Used for applications with frequently changing data

   Server clusters

6. Used for Web server clusters

   NLB clusters

7. Not supported by Windows Server 2003, Enterprise Edition

   CLB clusters

8. Requires a shared data store

   Server clusters

9. Makes stateful applications highly available

   Server clusters

10. Used for read-only applications

    NLB clusters

11. Used for COM+ applications

    CLB clusters

12. Supports clusters of up to 32 nodes in Windows Server 2003

    NLB clusters

Page
7-28

Lesson 2 Review

1. You are the administrator of a Network Load Balancing cluster consisting of six Web servers running in unicast mode, with a single network interface adapter in each server. You are using the Network Load Balancing Manager application on one of the cluster servers to try to shut down the NLB service on one of the other servers, so that you can upgrade its hardware. Why is the Manager not letting you do this?

   Because when cluster servers with one network interface adapter are running in unicast mode, the adapters on all the host servers are using the same cluster MAC address, making ordinary communications between the cluster servers impossible.

2. Which of the following Nlb.exe commands do you use to shut down NLB operations on a cluster server without interrupting transactions currently in progress?

   a. Nlb drain

   b. Nlb params

   c. Nlb drainstop

   d. Nlb queryport

   c

3. How long does it take a Network Load Balancing cluster to begin the convergence process after one of the servers in the cluster fails?

   Five seconds

Page
7-45

Lesson 3 Review

1. Explain why planning server capacity is an important element of deploying a server cluster.

   Server capacity planning is the process of estimating the resources needed by each node in a cluster during a worst-case scenario. When one or more nodes in a cluster malfunction, their applications fail over to other nodes, and those nodes must be capable of running them efficiently for the applications to remain available. Depending on the failover policies you configure for the cluster, you might have to use servers that are capable of running several applications at once in the event of a node failure, and the servers must have sufficient memory, processing power, and disk space to do so.

2. Which shared storage hardware configuration is the only possible solution for a server cluster with more than two nodes?

   Fibre Channel switched fabric

3. Which of the following failover policies provides the best compensation for multiple node failures?

    a. Failover pairs

    b. Hot-standby servers

    c. N+I

    d. Failover ring

c

Page
7-46

Case Scenario Exercise

Given the information provided in the Case Scenario Exercise, answer the following questions:

1. Each of the six Web servers on the perimeter network has a single network interface adapter installed. What additional hardware is absolutely required to implement the NLB cluster on the Web servers?

No additional hardware is required.

2. You want to be able to use Network Load Balancing Manager, running on one of the Web servers, to configure all the servers in the NLB cluster. Other than this, very little noncluster communication between the Web servers is required. Which of the following communication models should you use to make this possible with the greatest economy? Explain your answer.

    a. Single network interface adapter in unicast mode

    b. Single network interface adapter in multicast mode

    c. Multiple network interface adapters in unicast mode

    d. Multiple network interface adapters in multicast mode

b. Running the cluster in multicast mode enables the servers to communicate with each other without having to install a second network interface adapter in each server.

3. Which of the following storage hardware configurations should you use for the 4-node database server cluster? Explain your answer.

    a. Install a SCSI host adapter in each server and connect them all to a single SCSI bus

    b. Install a SCSI host adapter in each server and connect them all to a SCSI hub

    c. Install a Fibre Channel adapter in each server and connect them in an arbitrated loop

    d. Install a Fibre Channel adapter in each server and connect them all to a Fibre Channel switch

d. The Fibre Channel switched fabric solution is the only one that Windows Server 2003 supports for a 4-node server cluster.

4. You have decided to partition your database server application to spread the load among the servers in the cluster. Which of the following failover policies will ensure that the entire database is constantly available without any server running multiple partitions, even if two servers fail? Explain your answer.

   a. Failover pairs. Split the database into two partitions and assign each one to an active server. Then, configure each of the active servers to fail over to one of the two remaining servers.

   b. Hot-standby server. Split the database into three partitions and assign each one to an active server. Then, configure each of the active servers to fail over to the one remaining server.

   c. N+I. Split the database into two partitions and assign each one to an active server. Then, configure each of the active servers to fail over to either one of the two remaining servers.

   d. Failover ring. Split the database into four partitions and assign each one to an active server. Then, configure each of the four servers to failover to the next server.

   c. To guarantee that no server ever has to run more than one partition, you must have two standby servers, so answers b and d are incorrect. Answer a is incorrect because the failure of an active server and its designated standby would cause one of the partitions to go offline.

5. If you need to expand the server cluster, how many more servers can you add?

   4

Page 7-48

Troubleshooting Lab

Given the information provided in the Troubleshooting Lab, answer the following questions:

1. Reconfigure the Network Load Balancing cluster servers to use unicast mode rather than multicast mode.

   The cause of the problem might be that the router connecting the Web server LAN to the rest of the company network does not support the use of multicast MAC addresses. This inability would prevent the Network Load Balancing Manager on a different LAN from communicating with the Web servers. Changing the cluster servers to unicast mode would eliminate the multicast addresses, enabling the communication to take place.

2. Install a second network interface adapter in each Network Load Balancing cluster server.

   If the router connecting the Web server LAN to the company network does not support multicast MAC addresses, adding a second network interface adapter would not by itself resolve the problem, because the servers would still use the same multicast address.

3. Replace the router connecting the Web server LAN to the company network with a computer running Windows Server 2003 that you have configured to function as a router.

   If the router currently connecting the Web server LAN to the company network does not support multicast MAC addresses, replacing the router with a Windows Server 2003 router would resolve the problem.

8 Planning a Secure Baseline Installation

Exam Objectives in this Chapter:

- Plan a secure baseline installation.
  - ❑ Identify client operating system default security settings.
  - ❑ Identify all server operating system default security settings.
- Plan a framework for planning and implementing security.
  - ❑ Plan for security monitoring.
  - ❑ Plan a change and configuration management framework for security.
- Evaluate and select the operating system to install on computers in an enterprise.
  - ❑ Identify the minimum configuration to satisfy security requirements.

Why This Chapter Matters

When you install an operating system on a computer, the Setup program creates a default configuration that, from a security perspective, might or might not be suitable for your network environment. When designing a new network, you should keep security in mind from the start, and select your hardware and software with support and security capabilities as criteria. When designing a deployment plan for your computers, you should create a baseline installation that provides a secure starting point for the final configuration. For the majority of your systems, the baseline configuration should be adequate. For computers with extraordinary security requirements, you can build on the baseline installation by modifying the default configuration settings or by installing additional security hardware and software.

Designing a baseline operating system installation is crucial to creating a secure network and smooth-running technical support. As a network administrator, you must understand the security capabilities of the operating systems on your network and be familiar with the default security settings that the installation program creates. You configure many of the security settings discussed in this chapter with tools that network administrators use every day, so the more familiarity you have with these tools, the better.

Lessons in this Chapter:

Before You Begin

This chapter requires only a basic understanding of the Microsoft Windows Server 2003 family's interface and of the operating system's security features. To perform the practice exercises in this chapter, you must have installed and configured Windows Server 2003 using the procedure documented in "About This Book."

Lesson 1: Selecting Computers and Operating Systems

Selecting the appropriate operating systems for your network's servers and worksta-tions is essential to deploying an effective network installation. A well-governed net-work has policies that control which operating systems are permitted for the types of computers your organization uses and the roles that the computers play. Before you evaluate computers for purchase, you should have prepared a list of hardware require-ments for each role your computers have to fill, based on the hardware products sup-ported by the operating systems you plan to use. You should also have policies in place regarding how long you expect the organization to be using the computers and how frequently you will be upgrading the operating systems and applications.

After this lesson, you will be able to

■ List the roles of servers, desktop workstations, and portable workstations on a network

■ Describe the elements of server and workstation hardware specifications

■ List the criteria for selecting operating systems for network servers and workstations

Estimated lesson time: 15 minutes

Understanding Computer Roles

A network is a group of computers connected to each other, but in a typical organiza-tion, the computers have different capabilities and are used for a variety of tasks. Before you select the computers for your network, you should completely understand what tasks they will perform and what components they need. At the highest level, you can usually categorize the computers on a network using three basic roles: server, desktop workstation, and portable workstation.

Understanding the Server's Role

Servers perform a variety of roles and sometimes need specialized equipment to per-form them. Servers typically have faster processors, more memory, and more disk space than workstations, but the differences are not strictly quantitative. The types of components in a server are often just as important as their speed, quantity, or capacity.

Off the Record   For example, servers not only tend to have more disk space than worksta-tions, they also tend to have Small Computer System Interface (SCSI) disks rather than Inte-grated Drive Electronics (IDE) disks, because SCSI is better suited to handling read/write requests from multiple users at once.

The applications it runs define a server's role, and the applications dictate which components are most important. Some of the most common server roles are as follows:

- **Backup server** Runs a network backup software program that enables the server to execute backup jobs at scheduled times. Backup servers must have access to at least one backup device, such as a tape drive, and must have the network bandwidth, memory, and processing power needed to stream data at high speeds from locations all over the network to the backup device.

- **Database server** Runs a database server application that hosts large amounts of information and processes client requests for that information. Database servers usually require superior disk capacity and performance to handle large amounts of data, and enough processing power to manipulate the data as clients request.

- **Domain controller** Hosts a copy of the Active Directory directory service database and provides services such as authentication for Active Directory clients on the network. Domain controllers require enough processing power to handle client traffic and to perform security-related tasks, such as encryption and decryption.

- **E-mail server** Provides a number of mail-related services for network clients by storing their mail and running specialized mail protocols, such as Simple Mail Transfer Protocol (SMTP), Post Office Protocol 3 (POP3), and Internet Message Access Protocol (IMAP). E-mail servers typically require superior disk capacity and performance to store large amounts of e-mail data, process client requests, and receive incoming mail from the Internet.

- **File and print server** Stores data files for network users and queues print jobs generated by network clients. File and print servers typically require large amounts of storage space and disk equipment that can handle large numbers of simultaneous client requests.

- **Infrastructure server** Runs network services such as a DNS server, a DHCP server, or a Windows Internet Name Service (WINS) server. Infrastructure servers typically require superior network performance to handle large numbers of client requests.

- **Web server** Hosts a copy of a World Wide Web site and might run Web-based programs for clients. Web servers typically require superior network performance to handle large numbers of client requests, and might also need additional processing power for executing scripts and applications.

Understanding the Desktop Workstation's Role

Servers are expected to require better hardware, because, by definition, they provide services to multiple clients at once. Desktop workstations, on the other hand, can have a wide range of functionality, from simple systems designed to run one or two small applications to high-powered computers performing complex graphics, video, and computer-aided design (CAD) functions.

At the low end, workstations require little more than the basic components needed to run the operating system. If you want the users to be limited to a specific workstation configuration, you might even want to omit the CD-ROM and floppy disk drives, so they cannot install their own applications or boot the computer with another operating system. Workstations that have to perform resource-intensive tasks can start to look a lot like servers in terms of processor speed, amount of memory, and disk capacity, but they don't typically have the same availability requirements as a server.

The basic function of a desktop workstation on a network is to access server applications or files stored on servers so that the user can work with the data. Here again, the capabilities of the workstation are defined by the applications it runs. In some cases, the applications your workstations use are dictated by the applications you selected for your servers. For example, you might have to run a specific client program to connect to a server application.

Understanding the Portable Workstation's Role

Portable workstations can also perform a number of different roles, depending on the needs of the users. In most cases, a portable workstation refers to a notebook computer, but personal digital assistants (PDAs) and other handhelds are becoming viable options for the traveling user. In some cases, portable computers must be capable of supporting all the functions of a desktop workstation, while other users prefer to sacrifice functionality for a smaller size and less weight.

Creating Hardware Specifications

Creating hardware specifications before you begin evaluating computers for your network enables you to decide which components a computer needs to fulfill a particular role. Administering a large fleet of computers is easiest when you define your computers' roles and standardize the hardware and software needed for each role. This way, support personnel know what to expect when they troubleshoot a problem.

Server Hardware Specifications

When you create the hardware specification for a server, you must consider the requirements and capabilities of the applications that the server will run. Computers that are marketed as servers typically have more robust power supplies than normal PCs. A server might also have integrated components not usually found in a workstation, such as network interface adapters, SCSI host adapters, and drive arrays.

Planning   For all computers, but especially for servers, be sure that the hardware components you select are on the operating system manufacturer's list of tested and approved products. For the Microsoft Windows operating systems, check the Hardware Compatibility List for Windows 2000 and earlier operating systems and the Windows Server Catalog for Microsoft Windows XP and later operating systems for system compatibility.

The amount of random access memory (RAM) and the speed and number of processors should always be part of a hardware specification for a server. Furthermore, in addition to the components that you want in the server when you purchase it, you should also specify the server's maximum capacity for these components, to account for future upgrades. For example, if you intend to purchase a server with one gigabyte of RAM, make sure that the computer can support at least two gigabytes (or more) so that you can install additional memory later, if necessary.

You might also purchase a server that supports multiple processors, even if you are only going to use one right now. This way, you can always scale up the server's performance by installing additional processors. In the same way, you should plan for future as well as current server disk capacity. For example, select disk arrays with slots for additional disks, or computer cases with enough internal bays for expansion.

In addition to the performance levels your organization and your applications require, you should also consider your requirements for fault tolerance and availability because these elements might affect your hardware specifications. Disk arrays that use hot plugging and redundant array of independent disks (RAID), redundant power supplies, shared storage solutions, tape backup drives, and server clusters all can be substantial additions to your server configurations.

See Also   For more information on using clustering for fault tolerance and high availability, see Chapter 7, "Clustering Servers."

Desktop Hardware Specifications

Unlike the hardware specifications for servers, which tend to be more specialized, depending on their role, desktop workstations are more general-purpose computers. Your objective in creating desktop hardware specifications is to design systems suitable for a wide variety of tasks. The ideal situation would be a single desktop computer design that is suitable for all the users on your network. From a purchasing standpoint, this would enable you to order a larger number of identical computers and get the best price. From a support standpoint, your technicians would have to familiarize themselves with only one hardware configuration.

Most organizations have a variety of user requirements, however. For example, you might have a large group of order entry clerks who only have to run a single database client program and a small graphic design department that needs better equipped computers for manipulating large images. It would not be practical to create a hardware specification for a high-end computer that fulfills the graphic designers' needs and use the same expensive computers in the order entry department just for the sake of uniformity. In this case, you would create two hardware specifications, one to suit each class of users.

> **Real World   Desktop Hardware Specifications**
>
> In the real world, your organization is likely to have more than two classes of users, but you should refrain from creating a hardware specification for each class of users. This would defeat the purpose of standardizing in the first place. Instead, try to consolidate your users' needs into three or four desktop hardware specifications, at most.

In some cases, your organization's security requirements might affect your desktop hardware specifications. If you want to limit users' access to the computer by preventing them from installing outside applications, you might decide to use desktop systems without CD-ROM drives. For high-security applications, you might want to equip the desktop computers with card readers, so that users can use smart cards to authenticate themselves when they log on.

Portable Hardware Specifications

When creating hardware specifications for portable computers, two configurations are usually enough because portable computers fall into two categories that reflect the needs and tastes of their users: small and light or large and heavy. Large, heavy notebook computers typically include all the features and capabilities of a desktop computer, including audio speakers, CD-ROM or DVD-ROM drives, high-capacity hard drives, and large screens. These computers are capable of being a user's primary workstation and not just a traveling alternative. Salespeople and others who spend a lot of time on the road are usually best served by this type of computer, which they can use in the office as is, or connected to a docking station. Smaller and lighter portables are better suited for people with limited computing needs who don't want to carry a seven-pound machine. However, you often pay a premium for light weight, and these smaller portables are not necessarily a step down from the larger models.

Selecting Operating Systems

Selecting operating systems for your network computers must be coordinated with developing your hardware specifications. The reasons for this include the need to purchase compatible hardware, or from the opposite starting point, to meet the hardware requirements of the operating systems. However, several other factors are important, such as the following:

- **Application compatibility**   Obviously, the operating systems you choose must be capable of running the applications you need. In some cases, people select an operating system to run a particular application. In other cases, you can find comparable applications for each operating system you are considering.

- **Support issues**   If you already have technical support personnel who are accustomed to working with a particular operating system, you must consider the costs involved in retraining them if you change to a different one.

- **Security features**   The operating system you select must have the security features your organization requires. In many instances, this is the main criterion for selecting a particular operating system.

- **Cost**   Cost is always a factor when selecting an operating system. Sometimes free operating systems can provide capabilities equal or superior to those of commercial products.

> **Exam Tip**   Although MCSE exams like 70-293 are developed and administered by Microsoft, you should also consider the operating systems produced by other companies when preparing for the exam.

Choosing Workstation Operating Systems

The vast majority of workstation computers on networks today run some version of the Windows operating system, but there are still a number of alternatives. The releases of Windows operating systems for workstations have run in two parallel tracks over the years, one track based on DOS and the other based on Microsoft Windows NT (see Figure 8-1).

Microsoft has discontinued the track based on DOS, which started with Windows 3.1, ran through Windows 95 and Windows 98, and culminated in Windows Me. Some of these operating systems are still in use on many networks and work well. However, for a network, the Windows operating systems based on DOS are severely deficient in their security capabilities. As security becomes important to network administrators, these older operating systems become less viable.

The Windows NT track started with Windows NT Workstation and proceeded through Microsoft Windows 2000 Professional. Microsoft Windows XP Professional is the version currently shipping. Microsoft built all these operating systems with networking in mind, and they far exceed their DOS-based counterparts in their security capabilities.

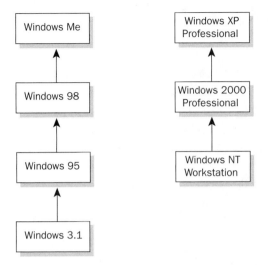

Figure 8-1   The DOS and Windows NT workstation operating system tracks

Planning   Windows XP, Home Edition, as the name implies, is targeted at the home user and is not suitable for most networks. The operating system lacks an Active Directory client, which means that you cannot join it to a domain, and many security mechanisms built into the Windows XP model are disabled to provide greater ease of use.

Although PC manufacturers install one of the current Windows operating systems on most of the PCs sold today, you can opt for one of the many UNIX or Linux alternatives. UNIX is still primarily a programmer's and power user's operating system, but a number of graphical shells make it friendly enough for the average user. However, although you might save money by purchasing a UNIX operating system for your workstations, the after-purchase costs of installing, configuring, and supporting the computers might outweigh those savings.

Choosing Server Operating Systems

As in the case of hardware specifications, servers' specific requirements often compel you to make individual choices based on each computer's role. While it is a good idea to choose a single operating system for all your workstations if possible, you can more easily select different operating systems for your servers.

The Windows server operating systems have always been available in multiple versions, to support different hardware and software configurations (see Figure 8-2). For Windows Server 2003, the primary differences among the operating systems are listed in Table 8-1.

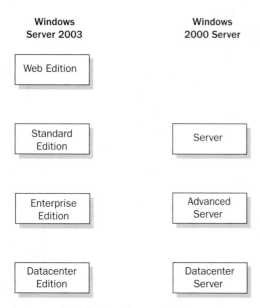

Figure 8-2   Windows Server 2003 and Windows 2000 Server versions

Table 8-1   Windows Server 2003 Versions

	Windows Server 2003, Web Edition	Windows Server 2003, Standard Edition	Windows Server 2003, Enterprise Edition	Windows Server 2003, Datacenter Edition
Minimum Processor Speed	133 MHz	133 MHz	133 MHz	400 MHz
Multiprocessor Support	Up to 2	Up to 4	Up to 8	From 8 to 64
Minimum RAM	128 MB	128 MB	128 MB	512 MB
Maximum RAM	2 GB	4 GB	32 GB	64 GB
Active Directory Support	Member server only	Domain controller or member server	Domain controller or member server	Domain controller or member server

There are more viable alternatives to Windows operating systems for servers than for workstations. Novell NetWare, now in version 6.0, is a server operating system that is comparable to Windows Server 2003 in many ways, including support for TCP/IP protocols and services and an enterprise directory service called Novell eDirectory. There are also dozens of UNIX and Linux versions that provide many of the same services as Windows operating systems and the NetWare operating system, including several that are available for free on the Internet.

It is not unusual for servers on a network in different roles to run different operating systems. You might use Windows Server 2003 for your file and print servers, but use UNIX servers running the Apache Web server product for your organization's Internet site. For some server applications, you have no choice. For example, if you plan to use Active Directory on your network, you obviously have to use servers running the Windows operating system for your domain controllers. However, TCP/IP services, such as Web, File Transfer Protocol (FTP), and DNS, can run on virtually any operating system platform.

Lesson Review

The following questions are intended to reinforce key information presented in this lesson. If you are unable to answer a question, review the lesson materials and try the question again. You can find answers to the questions in the "Questions and Answers" section at the end of this chapter.

1. What is the primary reason for using workstation operating systems based on Windows NT on a network, rather than operating systems based on DOS?

_____

_____

2. Which of the following Windows Server 2003 versions cannot function as a domain controller?

    a. Standard Edition

    b. Enterprise Edition

    c. Web Edition

    d. Datacenter Edition

3. Which of the following server roles require superior network performance? (Choose all correct answers.)

    a. Domain controllers

    b. Infrastructure servers

    c. Web servers

    d. Database servers

Lesson Summary

- Servers can perform a variety of roles in the enterprise, acting as domain controllers, Web servers, database servers, e-mail servers, infrastructure servers, file and print servers, and backup servers.

- While servers are often constructed and configured for specialized applications, workstations are usually set up for more general purposes.

- When creating server hardware specifications, plan for future upgrades when selecting the number and type of processors, the amount of memory, and storage solutions.

- The Windows workstation operating systems have followed two tracks: one based on DOS and one based on Windows NT; the latter is preferable for networks.

- When selecting operating systems for servers, you can choose the platform best suited to the server's role. When selecting workstation operating systems, standardization takes precedence over specialization.

Lesson 2: Planning a Security Framework

In recent years, security has become an increasingly important part of the network designer's and administrator's jobs. Security is no longer an afterthought; you must include security considerations in all your network planning from the outset, and at every level. Nearly all the remaining lessons in this book are concerned with security issues, but before you deploy the security features in Windows Server 2003, your organization should have a framework for designing and implementing security policies.

After this lesson, you will be able to

- Understand the process of designing, implementing, and managing a security strategy
- Create a security design team
- Map a security life cycle

Estimated lesson time: 15 minutes

High-Level Security Planning

Windows Server 2003 includes a great many security features, tools, and capabilities. Much of this book is devoted to the processes involved in planning, implementing, and maintaining these features. However, before you deploy specific security features, someone must decide which features are appropriate for your organization. A security framework is a logical, structured process by which your organization performs tasks like the following:

- Estimating security risks
- Specifying security requirements
- Selecting security features
- Implementing security policies
- Designing security deployments
- Specifying security management policies

This lesson, therefore, is concerned not so much with developing a security solution for your organization, but with the process your organization uses to develop a security solution.

Creating a Security Design Team

Security is not strictly an IT issue anymore, so the first step in creating a security framework is to determine which people in your organization are going to be responsible for designing, implementing, and maintaining the security policies. Technical people, such as network administrators, might be familiar with the capabilities of specific security mechanisms and how to implement them, but they are not necessarily the best people to identify the resources that are most at risk or the forces that threaten them. Management might be more familiar with the resources that need to be protected and the potential ramifications of their being compromised, but is probably not familiar with the tools that can be used to protect those resources. There are also economic issues to consider, and the effect of new security policies on employee productivity and morale.

All these arguments lead to the conclusion that most organizations need to assemble a team or committee responsible for providing a balanced picture of the organization's security status and capable of deciding how to implement security policies. The number of people on the team and their positions in the company depend on the organization's size and political structure. A well-balanced team should consist of people who can answer questions such as the following:

- What are your organization's most valuable resources?
- What are the potential threats to your organization's resources?
- Which resources are most at risk?
- What are the consequences if specific resources are compromised?
- What security features are available?
- Which security features are best for protecting specific resources?
- How secure is secure enough?
- What is involved in implementing specific security features?
- How do particular security features affect users, administrators, and managers?

Mapping Out a Security Life Cycle

Creating a security framework is not a one-time project that ends when you have finished designing the initial security plan for your network. Security is an ongoing concern, and the responsibilities of the security design team are ongoing as well. A security life cycle typically consists of three basic phases:

- Designing a security infrastructure
- Implementing security features
- Ongoing security management

These phases are discussed in the following sections.

Designing a Security Infrastructure

The initial design phase of a security infrastructure should run concurrently with the network design. Security issues can have a major effect on many elements of your network design, including the hardware components you purchase, the locations you select for the hardware, and how you configure individual devices. The design phase begins with identifying the resources that need protection and evaluating the threats to those resources.

Even the smallest organization has information it should protect, such as financial data and customer lists. Other valuable commodities might include order entry data, research and development information, and confidential correspondence. In more extreme cases, your organization might possess secret government or military information. The threats to your data can range from the casual to the felonious. In many cases, a modicum of security can protect your confidential data from curious employees and casual Internet predators. However, targeted threats, such as those mounted by business competitors and even rival governments, require more serious security measures.

Tip   In addition to deliberate attempts to penetrate security, your confidential data is in danger from accidents, thefts of equipment, and natural disasters. When planning the protection of your data, don't forget to include fault tolerance solutions that can prevent data loss due to drive failures, fires, and other accidents.

After your team has identified the resources that need protection and has determined how severe the threats are, you can plan how to secure them. This is where the technically oriented members of the team come into play, because they are familiar with the security measures that are available and what is involved in deploying them. Depending on the requirements of the organization, the security plan might consist of merely taking advantage of the features already included in the network's operating systems and other hardware and software components or you might have to purchase additional security products, such as firewalls, smart card readers, or biometric devices.

A typical security plan for a network includes implementations of the following security principles:

- **Access control**   The granting of specific levels of access based on a user's identity. Access control capabilities are built into most network operating systems and applications.

- **Auditing**   A process by which administrators monitor system and network activities over extended periods. Most network operating systems and applications include some form of auditing that administrators can configure to their needs.

- **Authentication**   The verification of a user's identity before providing access to secured resources. Authentication mechanisms can use encrypted passwords, certificates, and hardware devices such as smart cards and biometric sensors, depending on the degree of security required.

- **Encryption**   The process of protecting data through the application of a cryptographic algorithm that uses keys to encrypt and decrypt data. The strength of an encryption mechanism is based on the capabilities of the algorithm itself, the number and types of keys the system uses, and the method of distributing the keys.

- **Firewalls**   A system designed to prevent unauthorized access to a private network from outside. Firewalls can use a variety of mechanisms to secure a network, including packet filtering, network address translation, application gateways, and proxy servers.

> **Note**   Windows Server 2003 with Service Pack 1 (SP1) includes the Windows Firewall, a remotely manageable host-based firewall that provides basic packet filtering and intrusion prevention services similar to those in Windows XP Service Pack 2.

The security plan is not just a matter of technology. Your security team is also responsible for creating security policies for the organization. For example, you might agree to use encrypted passwords for user authentication, but you must also decide who is going to supply the passwords, how long the passwords should be, how often they should change, and so forth.

Implementing Security Features

After deciding what security mechanisms you are going to use and designing your security policies, the next step is to devise an implementation plan for these mechanisms and policies. In some cases, the implementation plan might consist of a procedure and timetable for the process of evaluating, purchasing, installing, and configuring security hardware and software products. For security mechanisms included with operating systems and applications, the implementation plan might consist of modifications to an existing installation or configuration routine.

Implementing security policies can be more problematic than implementing security technologies, because you must devise a way to disseminate the policies to everyone who needs them and to ensure compliance. In some cases, your software will contain mechanisms that enable you to enforce your policies; in other cases, you might have to compel your users to comply using other methods (such as gentle reason and logic or, failing that, bribes and threats).

Enforcing Security Policies

For a simple example, your team might decide that the network users must use passwords at least eight characters long, containing numeric characters and symbols as well as letters, and that users must change their passwords once a month. You can advise the users of these new requirements by sending a general e-mail, but the most important part of the implementation plan would be using a tool like Windows Server 2003 group policies to enforce your requirements. In this case, Windows Server 2003 has preconfigured password policies that enable you to require the use of eight-character, complex passwords, modified every 30 days. In other cases, however, enforcing compliance might be more complicated, for example, asking them not to store their password information in their unlocked desks.

Ongoing Security Management

With your security mechanisms and policies in place, you might be tempted to think that the work of your team is finished, but this is definitely not the case. Security is an ongoing concern that requires the continued attention of the entire team.

For the technical staff, security management means regular checking of audit logs and other resources as well as monitoring individual systems and network traffic for signs of intrusion. Administrators must also update the security software products as needed. Beyond these regular tasks, however, the entire team must be aware that the organization's security situation changes constantly. Every day can bring new resources to protect or new threats to existing resources. Security is often an arms race between the intruders and the protectors, and whichever side allows itself to become lax or complacent ends up losing the race.

Lesson Review

The following questions are intended to reinforce key information presented in this lesson. If you are unable to answer a question, review the lesson materials and try the question again. You can find answers to the questions in the "Questions and Answers" section at the end of this chapter.

1. List the three phases of a security life cycle.

_____

_____

2. Which of the following Windows Server 2003 features can you use to ensure that users supply passwords of a specified length?

   a. Audit policies

   b. Group policies

   c. Authentication protocols

   d. Access control lists

3. List three of the tasks that a security design team typically performs.

   _____

   _____

Lesson Summary

- Security is a concern through the entire process of network design and implementation.

- For most organizations, the best strategy is to create a security design team responsible for all aspects of the organization's security strategy.

- The typical functions of a security design team are to determine what resources need protection, to identify the threats to those resources, and to specify what mechanisms the organization will use to protect the resources.

- Security mechanisms can include authentication, access control, encryption, firewalls, and auditing. The team should also create security policies for the organization and a way to enforce them.

- After the design and implementation of the security strategy is completed, the team is still responsible for the ongoing management of the security mechanisms, as well as for constantly reevaluating the threats to the organization's resources.

Lesson 3: Identifying Client and Server Default Security Settings

When you install an operating system, the Setup program includes default configuration settings for security features; these settings might or might not be suitable for your needs. When you create a secure baseline installation for your computers, you have to be familiar with the operating system's default security settings, understand the effects of those settings on your overall security strategy, and determine whether you want to change them on your computers.

After this lesson, you will be able to

■ List the default security settings for the Windows Server 2003 and Windows XP Professional operating systems

Estimated lesson time: 25 minutes

Evaluating Security Settings

Windows Server 2003 and Windows XP Professional are the current operating systems that Microsoft has designated for use on network servers and clients. Security was a major concern to their designers, and the systems contain many configurable security features. The following sections examine some of these features and their default settings and discuss how to manipulate these settings to modify the security of your baseline installation.

File System Permissions

File system permissions constitute one of the basic security tools in any network operating system; one that network administrators are likely to use every day. Access permissions are a feature of the Windows NTFS file system that enables you to specify which users and groups are given access to a specific folder or drive and what degree of access they have. To modify the permissions for a drive or folder, you display its Properties dialog box, and then click the Security tab (see Figure 8-3). When you install Windows Server 2003 or Windows XP Professional on a network that uses Active Directory and format the system drive using NTFS, the Setup program automatically assigns the file system permissions shown in Table 8-2.

Caution   File system permissions are available only when you format your computer's drives using NTFS. If you format your drives using the FAT file system, there are no permissions and all users have full access to the drive.

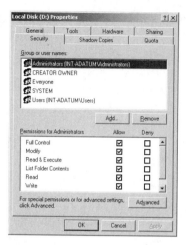

Figure 8-3 The Security tab in a folder's Properties dialog box

Table 8-2 Default Windows File System Permissions for System Drive

	System Drive (Root)	Documents And Settings Folder	Program Files Folder	Windows Folder
Administrators	Full Control	Full Control	Full Control	Full Control
Users Group	Read & Execute List Folder Contents Read Create Folders / Append Data Create Files / Write Data (in subfolders only)	Read & Execute List Folder Contents Read	N/A	N/A
Everyone Group	Read & Execute (in root only, not subfolders)	Read & Execute List Folder Contents Read	N/A	N/A
Authenticated Users Group	N/A	N/A	Read & Execute List Folder Contents Read	Read & Execute List Folder Contents Read
Server Operators Group	N/A	N/A	Modify Read & Execute List Folder Contents Read Write	Modify Read & Execute List Folder Contents Read Write

As you can see in the table, the Windows operating system assigns almost all file system permissions to groups, not to users, which makes the task of managing permissions much easier. Not surprisingly, the Windows operating system assigns the Administrators group the Full Control permission over the entire drive, enabling members of this group to perform any action on existing files and folders as well as create new ones. The Windows operating system grants the members of the Users group permission to read and execute files anywhere on the drive, but Users members cannot modify or delete existing files or folders anywhere except in their home folders. Users can create folders and write to files in those home folders, which makes it possible for them to install applications. The Everyone group receives only the ability to execute, list, and read files.

Note   In addition to the permissions in the table, the Windows operating system grants each user the Full Control permission for the subfolder named after that user in the Documents And Settings folder. This is the location of the user's profile and home folder.

Off the Record   Technically speaking, groups like Authenticated Users and Everyone are not really groups at all, in the accepted sense of the word; instead, they are called *special identities*. Although you can choose a special identity group when you are assigning permissions, you cannot manage the group in the usual manner. The Windows operating system creates the special identity groups automatically, and you cannot delete them or modify their member lists. The Windows operating system also creates a number of Built-in groups, such as Administrators and Users, but these are actual groups that you can modify or delete.

The Server Operators group is intended for system support personnel who need more access to the file system than normal users, but who are not yet trusted with the Full Control permission. Server operators have full access to the key Program Files and Windows folders. Their only limitation is that without the Full Control permission, they cannot grant their permissions to other users.

Warning   If you have NTFS drives other than the system drive on the computer running a Windows operating system, the Setup program does not create any special permissions there. The program grants the Everyone group Full Control over the entire drive, so that anyone can perform any action, including modifying or deleting existing files. It is up to the administrators to implement a system of permissions on these drives once users have populated them with files and folders.

Share Permissions

Share permissions constitute an access control mechanism that enables you to specify which users and groups are permitted to access a shared resource over the network, and what degree of access they should have. By default, when the Windows Server 2003 operating system is installed, the Windows Setup program creates only administrative shares. Each drive on the computer has a hidden administrative share, named with the drive letter followed by a dollar sign ($). These are special shares that you cannot delete, and you cannot modify their permissions.

> **Tip**   When creating a file system share, appending a dollar sign to the share name causes the Windows operating system to keep the share hidden. You cannot see hidden shares when you browse the network using My Network Places, but you can still access them by typing the share name in the Run dialog box. For example, to access the administrative share on drive C on a computer called Server01, you would type **\\Server01\C$** in the Open text box in the Run dialog box.

When you create a new file system share on a computer running Windows Server 2003, by default the Everyone group receives only the Read permission. You must modify the defaults to give users greater access to the share. The Permissions dialog box you use to modify the share permissions is shown in Figure 8-4. This default is new to Windows Server 2003. On computers running the Windows XP and Windows 2000 operating systems, the Everyone group receives the Full Control permission on all newly created shares. You must modify or remove this permission to control access to the shares.

Real World   File System and Share Permissions

Share permissions are completely separate from file system permissions. File system permissions affect all users, whether they are accessing the drive over the network or sitting at the computer console. Share permissions affect only users who are accessing the resource over the network. A network user must therefore have both the appropriate file system permissions and the appropriate share permissions to access a shared drive or folder on a remote computer.

Many network administrators use either file system permissions or share permissions to secure their drives, but not both, to avoid confusion. Keep in mind, however, that securing a share does not prevent users from accessing the share's files from the computer's console. For this reason, it is common practice among many administrators to rely entirely on file system permissions and not to use share permissions for access control.

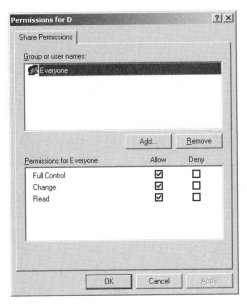

Figure 8-4   The Permissions dialog box for a file share

Registry Permissions

The registry of the Windows operating system contains a great deal of configuration data for many applications and many elements of the operating system. Installing applications and configuring operating system settings modifies registry elements. It is also possible to modify the registry manually, but this is a dangerous practice because even the slightest incorrect setting can cause a catastrophic malfunction. To protect the registry, the Windows operating system includes a separate system of permissions that enable you to specify who has access to the registry and to what degree. You modify registry permissions using the Registry Editor (Regedit.exe) program, using a Permissions dialog box like the one shown in Figure 8-5.

By default, members of the Administrators group have the Full Control permission for all the keys in the registry. The Everyone group has the Read permission only for the HKEY_LOCAL_MACHINE and HKEY_USERS keys, and the Server Operators group members have permissions that enable them to read, add, and modify certain registry keys without giving them full control. In most cases, there is no need to modify registry permissions manually, but if you want to create a class of administrative users that has limited access, you might want to modify the permissions of the Server Operators group.

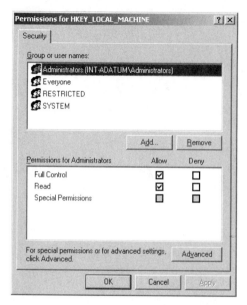

Figure 8-5   A Permissions dialog box for a registry key

Active Directory Permissions

Windows Server 2003 has yet another system of permissions, which you can use to specify who can access and manage objects in the Active Directory database. On a large network, working with Active Directory objects is a common administrative task. Administrators frequently have to create or delete user objects or modify the properties of existing objects. To delegate these tasks to other people, you might want to modify the default permissions for all or part of the Active Directory database.

When you create a new Active Directory domain by assigning a computer running Windows Server 2003 the role of domain controller, the system creates default permissions for the following groups:

- **Enterprise Admins**   Enterprise Admins is the only group that receives the Full Control permission over the entire domain.

- **Domain Admins and Administrators**   The Domain Admins and Administrators groups both get a selection of permissions that enable them to perform most Active Directory object maintenance tasks. They can create objects and modify their properties, for example, but they cannot delete objects.

- **Authenticated Users**   The Authenticated Users group receives the Read permission for the entire domain, plus a small selection of very specific Modify permissions. For example, members of this group receive the Unexpire Password permission, which enables them to change their own passwords after an expiration period specified by an administrative policy.

There are two ways to modify the default permissions that the Windows operating system assigns to Active Directory objects. You can use the Delegation Of Control Wizard in the Active Directory maintenance snap-ins for the Microsoft Management Console (MMC), or you can modify the permissions directly. The Delegation Of Control Wizard simplifies the process of delegating responsibility for a part of the Active Directory database to a user or group (see Figure 8-6).

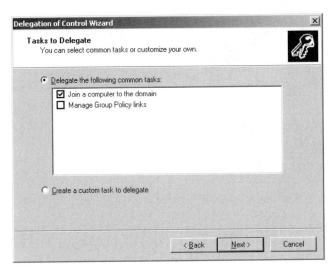

Figure 8-6   The Delegation Of Control Wizard

The drawback of using the Delegation Of Control Wizard is that you cannot view the permissions you have set after you have assigned them. To do this, you must work with the permissions directly. By default, Windows directory service tools such as Active Directory Users And Computers do not provide direct access to the permissions. To modify this default, you select the Advanced Features option from the console's View menu. Once you do this, the Properties dialog box for each Active Directory object displays a standard Security tab, as shown in Figure 8-7.

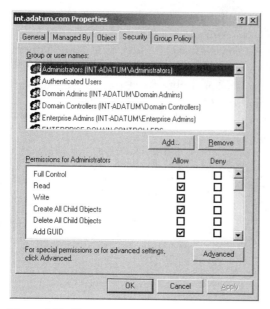

Figure 8-7   The Security tab in a domain's Properties dialog box

Account Policy Settings

Group policies are among the most powerful security features included with Windows Server 2003. You can create *Group Policy Objects (GPOs)* that do everything from distributing new software to configuring system security settings to remapping directories. You then associate the Group Policy Object with an Active Directory container object, such as a domain, a site, or an organizational unit, and the Windows operating system applies the policy to all the objects in that container.

One of the security modifications that Microsoft has made in Windows Server 2003 is to enable some of the most commonly used policies by default. These are the account policies, which you can find in the Computer Configuration\Windows Settings\Security Settings heading in the Group Policy Object Editor console (see Figure 8-8).

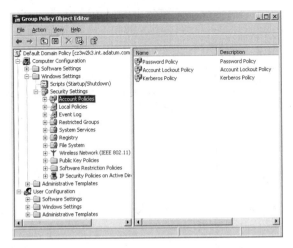

Figure 8-8   Account policies in the Group Policy Object Editor console

In previous versions of the Windows operating system, these policies are undefined by default. However, Windows Server 2003 enables the following account policies by default and applies them to each domain:

- **Enforce Password History**   Specifies the number of unique passwords that users have to supply before the Windows operating system permits them to reuse an old password. The default value is 24.

- **Maximum Password Age**   Specifies how long a single password can be used before the Windows operating system forces the user to change it. The default value is 42 days.

- **Minimum Password Age**   Specifies how long a single password must be used before the Windows operating system permits the user to change it. The default value is 1 day.

- **Minimum Password Length**   Specifies the minimum number of characters the Windows operating system permits in user-supplied passwords. The default value is 7.

- **Password Must Meet Complexity Requirements**   Specifies criteria for passwords, such as length of at least six characters; no duplication of all or part of the user's account name; and inclusion of characters from at least three of the following four categories: uppercase letters, lowercase letters, numbers, and symbols. By default, the Windows operating system enables this policy.

- **Store Passwords Using Reversible Encryption**   Specifies whether the Windows operating system should store user passwords in an encrypted form that specific applications or protocols can decrypt as needed. This policy weakens the security of the authentication system; you should not enable it unless you are forced to use an application or protocol that requires it. By default, this policy is disabled.

- **Account Lockout Threshold**   Specifies the number of failed logon attempts that causes the Windows operating system to lock out users from future attempts until an administrator resets the account. The default value is zero, which means that users are allowed unlimited failed logon attempts.

- **Enforce User Logon Restrictions**   Specifies whether the Kerberos Key Distribution Center (KDC) should validate every request for a session ticket against the user rights policy of the requesting user's account. By default, this policy is enabled.

- **Maximum Lifetime For Service Ticket**   Specifies the amount of time that clients can use a Kerberos session ticket to access a particular service. The default value is 600 minutes.

- **Maximum Lifetime For User Ticket**   Specifies the maximum amount of time that users can utilize a Kerberos ticket-granting ticket (TGT) before requesting a new one. The default value is 10 hours.

- **Maximum Lifetime For User Ticket Renewal**   Specifies the amount of time during which users can renew a Kerberos TGT. The default value is 7 days.

- **Maximum Tolerance For Computer Clock Synchronization**   Specifies the maximum time difference that Kerberos allows between the client computer and the authentication server. The default value is 5 minutes.

> **Tip**   Windows account policies have three possible states: enabled, disabled, and undefined. The difference between disabled and undefined comes into play when multiple Group Policy Objects apply to the same objects and the Windows operating system must resolve policy conflicts. An enabled policy always overrides an undefined instance of the same policy, but a policy that is explicitly disabled might override an enabled instance of the same policy.

This default configuration forces users to change their passwords every 6 weeks, and compels them to use passwords that are not easy to guess. Policies like Minimum Password Age and Enforce Password History prevent the users from working around the password requirements by reusing the same few passwords and repeatedly changing passwords over a short time. If you want to increase the password security on your network, you can modify these defaults by requiring longer passwords and more frequent changes. You can also relax security by disabling some or all of these policies.

> **Exam Tip**   Be sure to understand the functions of the security configuration parameters in a Group Policy Object.

Audit Policies

Group Policy Objects can contain audit policies specifying the activities that the system should record in a log. You find the audit policies in the Computer Configuration/ Windows Settings/Security Settings/Local Policies header in the Group Policy Object Editor console (see Figure 8-9). By default, domain objects do not have any audit policies defined, but the GPO for the Domain Controllers organizational unit in each domain does have audit policies.

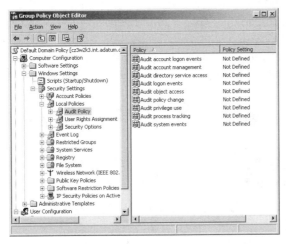

Figure 8-9   Audit policies in the Group Policy Object Editor console

By default, Windows Server 2003 enables the following audit policies for the Domain Controllers organizational unit:

- Audit Account Logon Events

- Audit Account Management

- Audit Directory Service Access

- Audit Logon Events

- Audit Policy Change

- Audit System Events

For each of these policies the default setting is to record only successful events in the log. For example, with these settings, the system logs all successful logons, but not the logon failures. If you are concerned about people trying to penetrate account passwords using the brute force method (trial and error), you might want to audit unsuccessful logon attempts as well.

Tip   To prevent brute force attacks, in addition to auditing unsuccessful logons, you should consider modifying the default value of the Account Lockout Threshold policy. This policy limits the number of unsuccessful logon attempts by locking the account for a specified period or until an administrator releases it.

Security Configuration Wizard

Windows Server 2003 with SP1 includes a new feature in the form of the Security Configuration Wizard (SCW). You can use the SCW to implement security policies on servers that run Windows Server 2003 with SP1. Two examples of security policies that you can implement with the SCW are modifying the security on critical system files and implementing an audit policy.

See Also   For more information on the SCW, see Chapter 9, "Hardening Servers."

Practice: Modifying Default Security Settings

In this practice, you modify some of the default settings on the computer running Windows Server 2003, to increase the overall security of the system.

Exercise 1: Modifying File System Permissions

In this exercise, you modify the file system permissions on the C drive of the server running Windows Server 2003, so that members of the Users group have access to a common folder called Xfer.

1. Log on as Administrator.

2. Click Start, point to All Programs, point to Accessories, and then click Windows Explorer. The Windows Explorer window appears.

3. On the computer's C drive, create a new folder called Xfer.

    The Xfer directory is intended to be a place where network users can store copies of files that they want to share freely with other users.

4. Click the Xfer folder you created and, from the File menu, select Properties. The Xfer Properties dialog box appears.

5. Click the Security tab, and then, in the Group Or User Names list, click the Users object.

    The Users group currently has the Read & Execute, List Folder Contents, and Read permissions, plus the Create Files/Write Data and Create Folders/Append Data special permissions. The group has inherited these permissions from the root of the drive.

6. Click the Modify and Write check boxes in the Allow column.

   Adding these permissions enables the members of the Users group to freely modify and delete files in the Xfer folder.

7. Click Add. The Select Users, Computers, Or Groups dialog box appears.

8. In the Enter The Object Names To Select text box, type **Everyone**, and then click OK. The Everyone group appears in the Group Or User Names list.

   The Everyone group receives the Read & Execute, List Folder Contents, and Read permissions automatically.

9. Click OK. Leave Windows Explorer running for the next exercise.

Exercise 2: Creating Share Permissions

In this exercise, you create a new share from the Xfer directory and assign share permissions to it.

1. In Windows Explorer, click the Xfer directory you created and then, from the File menu, select Properties. The Properties dialog box appears.

2. Click the Sharing tab.

3. Click the Share This Folder option button and leave Xfer as the default Share Name value.

4. Click Permissions. The Permissions For Xfer dialog box appears.

5. In the Group Or User Names list, select the Everyone group, and then click the Full Control check box under the Allow column. Click OK.

   Because you are using file system permissions to control access to the Xfer folder, you can safely grant the Full Control share permission to the Everyone group.

6. Click OK, and then close Windows Explorer.

Exercise 3: Modifying Account Policies

In this exercise, you modify the default account policy settings for your domain to increase the security of your authentication system.

1. Click Start, point to Administrative Tools, and then click Active Directory Users And Computers. The Active Directory Users And Computers console appears.

2. Click the contoso.com domain in the scope pane and then, from the Action menu, select Properties. The Contoso.com Properties dialog box appears.

3. Click the Group Policy tab, and then click Edit. The Group Policy Object Editor console appears.

4. In the scope pane, under Computer Configuration, expand the Windows Settings folder, the Security Settings icon, and the Account Policies icon. Then click the Password Policy icon.

5. In the details pane, double-click the Maximum Password Age policy. The Maximum Password Age Properties dialog box appears.

6. Change the Password Will Expire In selector value to 7 days, and then click OK.

   Reducing the Maximum Password Age policy value forces users to change their passwords more frequently, reducing the damage that can be caused by a compromised password.

7. Double-click the Minimum Password Length policy. The Minimum Password Length Properties dialog box appears.

8. Change the Password Must Be At Least selector value to 10, and then click OK.

   Increasing the length of users' passwords makes it more difficult to compromise them.

9. In the scope pane, click the Account Lockout Policy icon.

10. Double-click the Account Lockout Threshold policy. The Account Lockout Threshold Properties dialog box appears.

11. Change the Account Will Not Lock Out selector value to 3, and then click OK.

    Changing this value causes the Windows operating system to lock the user out from future logon attempts after three consecutive logon failures. This prevents potential intruders from trying to access an account using different passwords.

12. A Suggested Value Changes message box might appear. It informs you that because the Account Lockout Threshold value has changed, the Windows operating system will change two other policy settings to their suggested values. The Account Lockout Duration and the Reset Account Lockout Counter After values will change from Not Defined to 30 minutes. Click OK.

13. Double-click the Account Lockout Duration policy. The Account Lockout Duration Properties dialog box appears.

14. Select the Define This Policy Setting check box. Change the selector value to 0, and then click OK.

    Assigning a value of 0 to the Account Lockout Duration policy causes the Windows operating system to lock accounts indefinitely after three failed logon attempts. An administrator must manually reenable the account before the user can attempt to log on again.

15. Close the Group Policy Object Editor console.

16. Click OK to close the Contoso.com Properties dialog box.

17. Close the Active Directory Users And Computers console.

Lesson Review

The following questions are intended to reinforce key information presented in this lesson. If you are unable to answer a question, review the lesson materials and try the question again. You can find answers to the questions in the "Questions and Answers" section at the end of this chapter.

1. In which of the following folders on a Windows Server 2003 NTFS system drive with default permissions can a member of the Users group create a new file? (Choose all correct answers.)

   a. The root folder

   b. Documents And Settings

   c. The user's home folder

   d. Windows

2. How do the default share permissions on a computer running Windows Server 2003 differ from those on a computer running Windows XP?

   _____

   _____

3. For which of the following account policies should you modify the default setting to prevent brute force attempts at password penetration?

   a. Minimum Password Age

   b. Store Passwords Using Reversible Encryption

   c. Account Lockout Threshold

   d. Enforce User Logon Restrictions

Lesson Summary

- When you install Windows Server 2003 or Windows XP Professional, the operating system Setup program configures a number of security settings with default values that you can either keep or choose to modify for your baseline installation.

- When you use the NTFS file system for your system drive, Windows Server 2003 gives the Administrators group the Full Control permission. The Users group receives permissions that enable members to read and execute files and to create folders and files, but they cannot modify or delete files created by members of any other group.

- Shares have a separate system of permissions, independent of the file system permissions. For network users to access a share, they must have both share and file system permissions.

- Account policies enable you to control password requirements and authentication parameters, among other things. Unlike earlier versions of the Windows operating system, Windows Server 2003 implements a number of password policies by default.

- Windows Server 2003 enables a number of audit policies for the Domain Controllers organizational unit, which causes the system to create log entries when specific activities occur.

Case Scenario Exercise

You are the network administrator for Litware Inc., a manufacturer of specialized scientific software products, and you have already created a network design for their new office building, as described in the Case Scenario in Chapter 1. The office building is a three-story brick structure built in the late 1940s, which various tenants have since retrofitted with several different types of network cabling. Your network design for the building calls for the installation of five LANs, each of which is connected to a sixth, backbone network.

To protect the computers on the network, you have devised a series of account policy values that impose password requirements on users and control the response to failed logon attempts. After configuring these policies in a Group Policy Object, you associated the GPO with the Active Directory domain that encompasses the entire network. The policies you have configured and their values are shown in the following table:

Policy	Status	Value
Enforce Password History	Enabled	2 passwords
Maximum Password Age	Enabled	28 days
Minimum Password Age	Undefined	N/A
Minimum Password Length	Enabled	8 characters
Password Must Meet Complexity Requirements	Undefined	N/A
Store Passwords Using Reversible Encryption	Undefined	N/A
Account Lockout Duration	Enabled	60 minutes
Account Lockout Threshold	Enabled	6 attempts
Reset Account Logon Counter After	Enabled	10 minutes

Based on this information, answer the following questions:

1. Which of the following policy modifications could you make to ensure that user passwords cannot be intercepted by analyzing captured packets?

   a. Change the Enforce Password History value to 10.

   b. Enable the Password Must Meet Complexity Requirements policy.

   c. Change the Account Lockout Threshold value to 3.

   d. Disable the Store Passwords Using Reversible Encryption policy.

2. Which of the following policy modifications would make it harder for intruders to penetrate user passwords by trial and error? (Choose all correct answers.)

   a. Change the Reset Account Logon Counter After value to 60 minutes.

   b. Enable the Password Must Meet Complexity Requirements policy.

   c. Change the Account Lockout Threshold value to 10.

   d. Enable the Minimum Password Age policy and set its value to 3.

3. You have discovered that some users are bypassing your security requirements by changing their passwords as required, and then immediately changing them back again. Which of the following policy changes would prevent this practice? (Choose all correct answers.)

   a. Change the Account Lockout Duration value to 600.

   b. Enable the Minimum Password Age policy and set its value to 28.

   c. Change the Enforce Password History value to 10.

   d. Change the Reset Account Logon Counter After value to 60.

Chapter Summary

- Servers can perform a variety of roles in the enterprise, acting as domain controllers, Web servers, database servers, e-mail servers, infrastructure servers, file and print servers, and backup servers.

- While servers are often constructed and configured for specialized applications, workstations are usually set up for more general purposes.

- When creating server hardware specifications, plan for future upgrades when selecting the number and type of processors, the amount of memory, and storage solutions.

- When selecting operating systems for servers, you can choose the platform best suited to the server's role. When selecting workstation operating systems, standardization takes precedence over specialization.

- For most organizations, the best way to integrate security into the network design and implementation process is to create a security design team responsible for all aspects of the organization's security strategy.

- The typical functions of a security design team are to determine what resources need protection, to identify the threats to those resources, and to specify what mechanisms the organization will use to protect the resources.

- After the design and implementation of the security strategy is completed, the team is still responsible for the ongoing management of the security mechanisms, as well as for constantly reevaluating the threats to the organization's resources.

- When you install Windows Server 2003 or Windows XP Professional, the operating system Setup program configures a number of security settings with default values that you can either keep or choose to modify for your baseline installation.

- The default security settings for the Windows operating systems include file system permissions, share permissions, Active Directory account policies, and audit policies.

Exam Highlights

Before taking the exam, review the key points and terms that are presented below to help you identify topics you need to review. Return to the lessons for additional practice, and review the "Further Reading" sections in Part 2 of this book for pointers to more information about topics covering the exam objectives.

Key Points

- When selecting operating systems for your network, the objective for workstations should be to choose an operating system that is suitable for as many of your users as possible. For servers, you have more freedom in selecting operating systems with capabilities appropriate to the applications each computer will run.

- A baseline installation is an operating system configuration that provides the minimum level of security required by your organization. For computers with special security requirements, you can alter the baseline installation by modifying or configuring settings or installing additional security software or hardware.

- When designing a network, you should create a security team, composed of members from various parts of the organization, that is responsible for specifying the resources that need protection, identifying the threats to those resources, deciding how to protect the resources, and monitoring their ongoing security status.

- Operating systems have default security settings that might or might not be appropriate to your organization. You should be familiar with the defaults for the operating systems you select and should decide in advance whether you want to change the security settings for your baseline installation.

Key Terms

Special identities   Entities built into Windows Server 2003 and other Windows operating systems, such as Everyone and Authenticated Users, that function like groups, but which you cannot modify by adding or deleting members.

Group Policy Object   A collection of configuration settings and other features that you associate with specific Active Directory container objects, such as domains, sites, and organizational units. All the objects in the container receive the settings specified in the GPO.

Account policies   Specific elements of a Group Policy Object that you use to implement features such as password restrictions and account lockout behavior.

Page
8-11
Lesson 1 Review

1. What is the primary reason for using workstation operating systems based on Windows NT on a network, rather than operating systems based on DOS?

   The operating systems based on Windows NT have more and better security features than the operating systems based on DOS.

2. Which of the following Windows Server 2003 versions cannot function as a domain controller?

   a. Standard Edition

   b. Enterprise Edition

   c. Web Edition

   d. Datacenter Edition

   c

3. Which of the following server roles require superior network performance? (Choose all correct answers.)

   a. Domain controllers

   b. Infrastructure servers

   c. Web servers

   d. Database servers

   b and c

Page
8-17
Lesson 2 Review

1. List the three phases of a security life cycle.

   Design, implementation, and management

2. Which of the following Windows Server 2003 features can you use to ensure that users supply passwords of a specified length?

   a. Audit policies

   b. Group policies

   c. Authentication protocols

   d. Access control lists

   b

3. List three of the tasks that a security design team typically performs.

Determine the resources to protect, identify threats to those resources, and specify how to protect the resources.

Page
8-33

Lesson 3 Review

1. In which of the following folders on a Windows Server 2003 NTFS system drive with default permissions can a member of the Users group create a new file? (Choose all correct answers.)

    a. The root folder

    b. Documents And Settings

    c. The user's home folder

    d. Windows

b, c, and d

2. How do the default share permissions on a computer running Windows Server 2003 differ from those on a computer running Windows XP?

On a Windows Server 2003 share, the Everyone group receives only the Read permission. On a computer running Windows XP, the Everyone group receives the Full Control permission.

3. For which of the following account policies should you modify the default setting to prevent brute force attempts at password penetration?

    a. Minimum Password Age

    b. Store Passwords Using Reversible Encryption

    c. Account Lockout Threshold

    d. Enforce User Logon Restrictions

c

Page
8-34

Case Scenario Exercise

Given the information provided in the Case Scenario Exercise, answer the following questions:

1. Which of the following policy modifications could you make to ensure that user passwords cannot be intercepted by analyzing captured packets?

    a. Change the Enforce Password History value to 10.

    b. Enable the Password Must Meet Complexity Requirements policy.

    c. Change the Account Lockout Threshold value to 3.

    d. Disable the Store Passwords Using Reversible Encryption policy.

d

2. Which of the following policy modifications would make it harder for intruders to penetrate user passwords by trial and error? (Choose all correct answers.)

   a. Change the Reset Account Logon Counter After value to 60 minutes.

   b. Enable the Password Must Meet Complexity Requirements policy.

   c. Change the Account Lockout Threshold value to 10.

   d. Enable the Minimum Password Age policy and set its value to 3.

   a and b

3. You have discovered that some users are bypassing your security requirements by changing their passwords as required, and then immediately changing them back again. Which of the following policy changes would prevent this practice? (Choose all correct answers.)

   a. Change the Account Lockout Duration value to 600.

   b. Enable the Minimum Password Age policy and set its value to 28.

   c. Change the Enforce Password History value to 10.

   d. Change the Reset Account Logon Counter After value to 60.

   b and c

9 Hardening Servers

Exam Objectives in this Chapter:

- Plan a secure baseline installation.
  - ❑ Plan a strategy to enforce system default security settings on new systems.
- Configure security for servers that are assigned specific roles.
- Plan security for servers that are assigned specific roles. Roles might include domain controllers, Web servers, database servers, and mail servers.

Why This Chapter Matters

In Chapter 8, "Planning a Secure Baseline Installation," you learned about the preliminary phases of creating a secure baseline installation. This chapter discusses the mechanics of creating a baseline installation and hardening servers that perform specific roles using Group Policy Objects (GPOs). GPOs constitute one of the most powerful tools included in the Microsoft Windows Server 2003 family, and understanding how to use them effectively can help you deploy large numbers of computers on a network without having to configure each one manually. Windows Server 2003 with Service Pack 1 (SP1) includes the Security Configuration Wizard (SCW). The SCW is a powerful tool that you can use to harden servers running Windows Server 2003 SP1.

Lessons in this Chapter:

Before You Begin

This chapter requires a basic understanding of Active Directory and the Active Directory administration tools included with Windows Server 2003. The chapter continues the discussion of security issues and baseline installation begun in Chapter 8, "Planning a Secure Baseline Installation." You should complete that chapter before beginning this one. The practices for each lesson in this chapter require you to have installed Windows Server 2003 using the procedure described in "About This Book." The three practices build on each other and should be performed in the order in which they appear.

Lesson 1: Creating a Baseline for Member Servers

The Windows Server 2003 default configuration is far more secure than those of previous versions of the Microsoft Windows operating system, but there are still security settings that you should consider modifying from their defaults. The security requirements for the various servers on your network might differ, but a good place to start is creating a security configuration for a standard member server. This gives you a baseline security configuration for member servers and a starting point for modifications needed by servers performing specific roles.

> **After this lesson, you will be able to**
>
> - Use a GPO to create a secure baseline installation for a member server
> - Configure audit and Event Log policies using GPOs
> - Configure service startup types using GPOs
> - Configure security options using GPOs
>
> **Estimated lesson time: 30 minutes**

Creating a Baseline Policy

Many of the Windows Server 2003 security parameters used to create a baseline installation can be configured using a *Group Policy Object (GPO)*. A GPO can contain settings for a myriad of different configuration parameters associated with the operating system and the applications running on it. To use a GPO, you associate it with a particular Active Directory directory service object, such as a domain, a site, or an organizational unit. When you associate a GPO with an object, that object's contents receive all the configuration settings in the GPO. For example, when you associate a GPO with a domain, all the objects in that domain inherit the GPO settings.

> **Note**   Member servers are computers running Windows Server 2003 that are joined to a domain, but are not domain controllers.

By default, Windows Server 2003 places all the member servers joined to a domain in a container object, beneath the domain, called Computers (see Figure 9-1). The Computers object is not a domain, site, or organizational unit object, however, so you cannot associate a GPO with it. Furthermore, this container also contains the computer objects for all your workstations, so you would not want to apply a member server baseline to it.

Exam Tip   You should have a basic familiarity with all of the security settings found in Group Policy Objects.

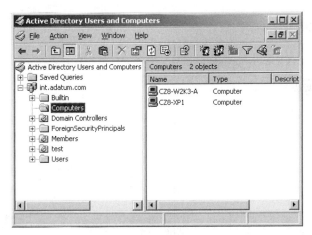

Figure 9-1   The Computers container in the Active Directory Users And Computers console

Understanding Container Objects

The Computers container object is a special Active Directory object called a *container*, which Windows Server 2003 creates by default when you create the first domain controller for a new domain. The system also creates other container objects called Users, Builtin, and ForeignSecurityPrincipals. The term container can be misleading in the case of these four container objects, because many directory services, including Active Directory, refer to any object that can have other objects beneath it as a container. Objects that cannot contain other objects are called *leaves*.

The Computers, Users, Builtin, and ForeignSecurityPrincipals container objects are different, however, because their object type is literally called a container. These container objects do not have the same properties as Active Directory objects, such as domains, sites, and organizational units, which function as generic containers. You cannot delete the Computers, Users, Builtin, and ForeignSecurityPrincipals container objects, nor can you create new objects using the container object type. You also cannot associate GPOs with these objects. You can, however, create new generic containers, such as organizational units, and associate GPOs with them.

To create a baseline installation for your member servers only, the best practice is to create a new organizational unit in your domain, then move the computer objects representing the member servers into it, as shown with the Members object in Figure 9-2. This way, you can associate a GPO containing your security baseline with the member servers' organizational unit and all the objects in that container will inherit the baseline security settings.

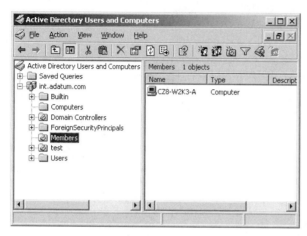

Figure 9-2   A container object for member servers in the Active Directory Users And Computers console

Tip   Do not put the computer objects for other types of systems, such as domain controllers or workstations, in your member servers organizational unit unless you want them to have the same baseline configuration as your member servers. Workstations do not need most of the configuration settings discussed in this lesson, and domain controllers have their own requirements. As a rule, you should place each type of computer that requires a different configuration in its own organizational unit.

Setting Audit Policies

Auditing is an important part of a secure baseline installation because it enables you to gather information about the computer's activities as they happen. If a security incident occurs, you want to have as much information about the event as possible, and auditing specific system elements makes the information available. The problem with auditing is that it can easily give you an embarrassment of riches. You can't have too much information when a security breach occurs, but most of the time your servers will be operating normally. If you configure the system to audit too many events, you can end up with enormous log files consuming large amounts of disk space and making it difficult to find the information you need. The object of an audit configuration is to achieve a balance between enough auditing information and too much.

When you configure Windows Server 2003 to audit events, the system creates entries in the Security log that you can see in the Event Viewer console (see Figure 9-3). Each audit entry contains the action that triggered the event, the user and computer objects involved, and the event's date and time.

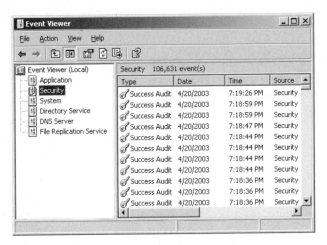

Figure 9-3   The Event Viewer console

A GPO's audit policies are located in the Group Policy Object Editor console in the Computer Configuration\Windows Settings\Security Settings\Local Policies\Audit Policy container, as shown in Figure 9-4. Each policy creates an audit entry in response to the following events:

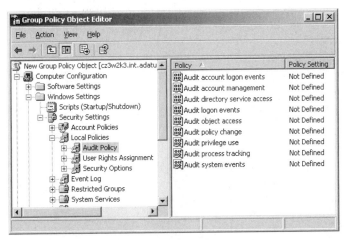

Figure 9-4   The Audit Policy container in the Group Policy Object Editor console

- **Audit Account Logon Events** A user logging on to or off another computer. The policy uses this computer to authenticate the account. This policy is intended primarily for domain controllers, which authenticate users as they log on to other computers. There is typically no need to activate this policy on a member server.

- **Audit Account Management** Each account management event that occurs on the computer, such as creating, modifying, or deleting a user object, or changing a password. On a member server, this policy only applies to local account management events. If your network relies on Active Directory for its accounts, administrators seldom have to work with local accounts. However, activating this policy can detect unauthorized users who are trying to gain access to the local computer.

- **Audit Directory Service Access** A user accessing an Active Directory object that has its own system access control list (SACL). This policy only applies to domain controllers, so there is no need for you to enable it on your member servers.

- **Audit Logon Events** Users logging on to or off the local computer when the local computer or a domain controller authenticates them. You use this policy to track user logons and logoffs, enabling you to determine which user was accessing the computer when a specific event occurred.

- **Audit Object Access** A user accesses an operating system element such as a file, folder, or registry key. To audit elements like these, you must enable this policy and you must enable auditing on the resource that you want to monitor. For example, to audit user accesses of a particular file or folder, you display its Properties dialog box with the Security tab active, navigate to the Auditing tab in the Advanced Security Settings dialog box for that file or folder (see Figure 9-5), and then add the users or groups whose access to that file or folder you want to audit.

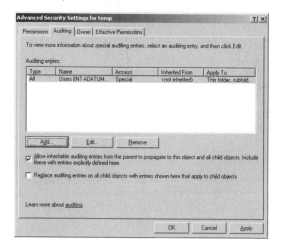

Figure 9-5 The Advanced Security Settings dialog box

- **Audit Policy Change** Someone changes one of the computer's audit policies, user rights assignments, or trust policies. This policy is a useful tool for tracking changes administrators make to the computer's security configuration. For example, an administrator might disable a policy temporarily to perform a specific task and then forget to reenable it. Auditing enables you to track the administrator's activities and notice the oversight.

- **Audit Privilege Use** A user exercises a user right. By default, Windows Server 2003 excludes the following user rights from auditing because they tend to generate large numbers of log entries: Bypass Traverse Checking, Debug Programs, Create A Token Object, Replace Process Level Token, Generate Security Audits, Backup Files And Directories, and Restore Files And Directories.

Tip It is possible to enable auditing of the user rights listed here by adding the following key to the registry in the Windows operating system: HKEY_LOCAL_MACHINE\SYSTEM\Current-ControlSet\Control\Lsa\FullPrivilegeAuditing=3,1. However, if you do this, you should be prepared to deal with the large number of log entries that auditing these user rights generates by increasing the maximum size of the logs and having a policy for frequent evaluation and clearance of the logs.

- **Audit Process Tracking** The computer experiences an event such as a program activation or a process exit. While this policy gathers information that is valuable when analyzing a security incident, it also generates a large number of log entries.

- **Audit System Events** Someone shuts down or restarts the computer or an event affecting system security or the security log occurs.

When you enable one of these audit policies, you can select three possible values, which determine the conditions for creating an audit entry, as follows:

- **Success only (select the Success check box)** Only when the specified action completes successfully

- **Failure only (select the Failure check box)** Only when the specified action fails

- **Success and Failure (select both the Success and Failure check boxes)** Whether the specified action succeeds or fails

- **No auditing (clear both the Success and Failure check boxes)** No audit entries for the specified actions under any circumstances

Real World **GPO Application**

Although it might appear that the no auditing option is the same as leaving the policy disabled, this is not necessarily the case. You can associate multiple GPOs with a single Active Directory object and control the order in which the system applies the GPO settings. If you have a GPO that enables a particular policy, you can override the value for that policy by creating another GPO with a different value for the same policy and configuring it to override the first GPO's settings. For example, if one GPO enables the Success and Failure options for the Audit Logon Events policy, you can override this setting with another GPO that has the same policy enabled, but the Success and Failure check boxes are cleared.

For security purposes, auditing failures can often be more valuable than auditing successes. For example, the default Audit Account Logon Events policy value for domain controllers is to audit successful logons only. This enables you to determine who was logged on to the network at any time. However, if an unauthorized user attempts to penetrate an administrative account by guessing passwords, the audit log would not contain any evidence of these attempts. Selecting the Failure check box for the Audit Account Logon Events policy gives you information about the failed logon attempts as well as the successful ones.

Setting Event Log Policies

The Event Log is an essential tool for Windows Server 2003 administrators, and the Event Log policies control various aspects of the log's performance, including the maximum size of the logs, who has access to them, and how the logs behave when they reach their maximum size. The Event Log policies in a GPO are located in the Computer Configuration\Windows Settings\Security Settings\Event Log container, as shown in Figure 9-6.

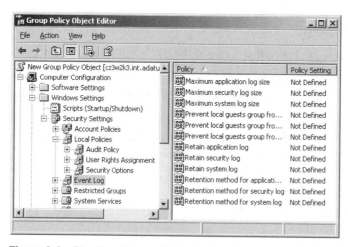

Figure 9-6 The Event Log container in the Group Policy Object Editor console

For each of the following, there are three policies, one for each of the logs: application, security, and system.

- **Maximum log size**   Specifies the maximum size the system permits, in kilobytes. Values must be in 64 KB increments, and the maximum value is 4,194,240 (4 gigabytes).

- **Prevent local Guests group from accessing log**   Specifies whether members of the local Guests group on the computer are permitted to view the log file.

- **Retain log**   Specifies the number of days for which the log should retain information.

- **Retention method for log**   Specifies the behavior of the log when it reaches its maximum size, using the following options:

  - Overwrite Events By Days—The log retains the number of days of entries specified by the retain log policy. Once the log grows to the specified number of days, the system erases the oldest day's entries each day.

  - Overwrite Events As Needed—The log erases the oldest individual entries as needed once the log file has reached the size specified in the maximum log size policy.

  - Do Not Overwrite Events (Clear Log Manually)—The system stops creating new entries when the log reaches the size specified in the maximum log size policy.

Creating an event logging configuration for a member server usually requires some experimentation. The best way to proceed is to configure the events and resources that you want to audit, and then let the logs accrue for several days. Calculate the average number of entries for each log per day and then decide how many days of history you want to retain. This enables you to determine a suitable maximum size for your logs.

Before setting the retain log and retention method for log policies, you should decide how often someone is going to review the logs and clear or archive them when necessary. If it is essential to retain all log information, you can specify a maximum size for the log and then enable the Security Options policy, Audit: Shut Down System Immediately If Unable To Log Security Audits, which forces you to manage the logs regularly.

Configuring Services

Windows Server 2003 installs a great many services with the operating system, and configures quite a few with the Automatic startup type, so that these services load automatically when the system starts. Many of these services are not needed in a typical member server configuration, and it is a good idea to disable the ones that the computer doesn't need. Services are programs that run continuously in the background, waiting for another application to call on them. For this reason, services are also potential points of attack, which intruders might be able to exploit.

Instead of controlling the services manually, using the Services console, you can configure service parameters as part of a GPO. Applying the GPO to a container object causes the services on all the computers in that container to be reconfigured. To configure service parameters in the Group Policy Object Editor console, you browse to the Computer Configuration\Windows Settings\Security Settings\System Services container and select the policies corresponding to the services you want to control (see Figure 9-7).

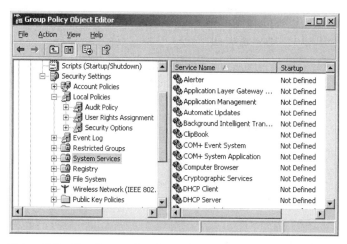

Figure 9-7   The System Services container in the Group Policy Object Editor console

Tip   When a service policy is left undefined, the service retains the default status that the Windows Server 2003 Setup program assigned it during the operating system installation. For example, even if you do not configure a particular service with the Automatic startup type, Windows Server 2003 itself might configure that service to load automatically. If you want to be certain that a service is disabled, you must activate the System Services policy and choose the Disabled option.

Table 9-1 contains the services that Windows Server 2003 typically installs on a member server. The Automatic column contains the services that Windows Server 2003 requires for basic system management and communications. The Manual column contains services that do not have to be running all the time, but which must be available so that other processes can activate them. The Disabled column contains services that the typical member server does not need, and which you can permanently deactivate, unless the computer has a specific need for them.

Table 9-1 Typical Member Server Service Assignments

Automatic	Manual	Disabled
Automatic Updates	Background Intelligent Transfer Service	Alerter
Computer Browser	COM+ Event System	Application Management
DHCP Client	Logical Disk Manager Administrative Service	ClipBook
Distributed Link Tracking Client	Network Connections	Distributed File System
DNS Client	NT LM Security Support Provider	Distributed Transaction Coordinator
Event Log	Performance Logs And Alerts	Fax Service (only present when a modem is installed)
IPSEC Services	Terminal Services	Indexing Service
Logical Disk Manager	Windows Installer	Internet Connection Firewall (ICF)/Internet Connection Sharing (ICS)
Net Logon	Windows Management Instrumentation Driver Extensions	License Logging
Plug And Play		Messenger
Protected Storage		NetMeeting Remote Desktop Sharing
Remote Procedure Call (RPC)		Network (DDE)
Remote Registry		Network DDE DSDM
Security Accounts Manager		Print Spooler
Server		Remote Access Auto Connection Manager
System Event Notification		Remote Access Connection Manager
TCP/IP NetBIOS Helper		Removable Storage
Windows Management Instrumentation		Routing And Remote Access
Windows Time		Secondary Logon
Workstation		Smart Card
		Task Scheduler
		Telephony
		Telnet
		Uninterruptible Power Supply

In a default Windows Server 2003 member server installation, the Setup program has already configured many of the services listed in Table 9-1 with the startup type values listed there. However, controlling service configurations with a GPO enables you to be sure that only the services you need are running.

> **Caution** Member servers might need other services to perform certain functions. You can create and apply additional GPOs to configure the services that servers performing particular roles need. Before deploying a server in a live environment, be sure to test the configuration thoroughly, to ensure that the modifications to the default setup do not interfere with the server's operation.

Configuring Security Options

The Security Options container in the Group Policy Object Editor console contains a long list of policies that you can use to secure specific server elements. Almost all these policies are undefined in a default member server installation, but you can activate them and use them to secure your servers against a wide variety of accidents and threats. To configure these policies, browse to the Computer Configuration\Windows Settings\Security Settings\Local Policies\Security Options container in the Group Policy Object Editor console, as shown in Figure 9-8. Because these policies are widely divergent in their functions, the Properties dialog box for each one has different configuration options.

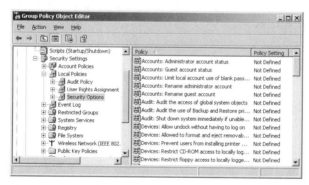

Figure 9-8   The Security Options container in the Group Policy Object Editor console

Some of the most useful Security Options policies are as follows:

- **Accounts: Administrator Account Status**   Enables or disables the computer's local Administrator account.

- **Accounts: Guest Account Status**   Enables or disables the computer's local Guest account.

- **Accounts: Rename Administrator Account**   Specifies an alternative name for the security identifier (SID) associated with the local Administrator account.

- **Accounts: Rename Guest Account**   Specifies an alternative name for the SID associated with the local Guest account.

- **Audit: Audit The Use Of Backup And Restore Privilege**   Causes the computer to audit all user privileges when the Audit Privilege Use policy is enabled, including all file system backups and restores.

- **Audit: Shut Down System Immediately If Unable To Log Security Audits**   Causes the computer to shut down if the system is unable to add auditing entries to the security log because the log has reached its maximum size.

- **Devices: Allowed To Format And Eject Removable Media**   Specifies which local groups are permitted to format and eject removable NTFS file system media.

- **Devices: Restrict CD-ROM Access To Locally Logged-on User Only**   Prevents network users from accessing the computer's CD-ROM drives.

- **Devices: Restrict Floppy Access To Locally Logged-on User Only**   Prevents network users from accessing the computer's floppy disk drive.

- **Domain Member: Maximum Machine Account Password Age**   Specifies how often the system changes its computer account password.

- **Interactive Logon: Do Not Require CTRL+ALT+DEL**   Select the Disable option to protect users against Trojan attacks that attempt to intercept users' passwords.

- **Interactive Logon: Require Domain Controller Authentication To Unlock Workstation**   Prevents unlocking the computer using cached credentials. The computer must be able to use a domain controller to authenticate the user attempting to unlock the system for the process to succeed.

- **Microsoft Network Client: Digitally Sign Communications (Always)**   The computer requires packet signatures for all Server Message Block (SMB) client communications.

- **Microsoft Network Server: Digitally Sign Communications (Always)**   The computer requires packet signatures for all Server Message Block (SMB) server communications.

- **Network Access: Do Not Allow Anonymous Enumeration Of SAM Accounts And Shares**   Prevents anonymous users from determining the names of local user accounts and shares. This prevents potential intruders from gathering information about the computer without being authenticated.

- **Network Access: Remotely Accessible Registry Paths And Sub-Paths**   Specifies which registry paths and subpaths qualified users can access over the network.

- **Network Access: Shares That Can Be Accessed Anonymously** Specifies which shares anonymous users are permitted to access.

- **Network Security: Force Logoff When Logon Hours Expire** Causes the computer to terminate existing local user connections when they reach the end of their specified logon time.

- **Shutdown: Allow System To Be Shut Down Without Having To Log On** Activates the Shut Down button in the Log On To Windows dialog box.

Practice: Creating a Group Policy Object

In this practice, you create a secure baseline installation for the member servers on your network. For the purposes of this exercise, you don't actually have any member servers, but you will create an Active Directory container for them, create a GPO, and then associate the GPO with the container object.

> **Note** This practice assumes that you have installed a computer running Windows Server 2003 according to the procedure documented in "About This Book."

Exercise 1: Creating an Active Directory Container

In this procedure, you create a new container in the Active Directory tree on your Server01 computer, to hold the (imaginary) member servers on your network.

1. Log on to your Server01 computer as Administrator.

2. Click Start, point to All Programs, point to Administrative Tools, and then click Active Directory Users And Computers. The Active Directory Users And Computers console appears.

3. Select the contoso.com domain object, point to New on the Action menu, and then click Organizational Unit. The New Object—Organizational Unit dialog box appears.

4. Type **Member Servers** in the Name text box and click OK. A new organizational unit object appears in the directory service tree in the contoso.com domain.

   If there were member servers in the contoso.com domain on your network, they would be located in the Computers container object by default. You would then move them to the new Member Servers organization unit you just created.

5. Leave the Active Directory Users And Computers console open for the next exercise.

Exercise 2: Creating a Group Policy Object

In this procedure, you create a new GPO for the Member Servers organizational unit object you just created and use it to create a secure baseline configuration for your (imaginary) member servers.

▶ **To create a new GPO**

1. In the Active Directory Users And Computers console, select the Member Servers organizational unit you created in Procedure 1 and, on the Action menu, click Properties. The Member Servers Properties dialog box appears.

2. Click the Group Policy tab and then click New. A New Group Policy Object entry appears in the Group Policy Object Links list, with the name of the entry highlighted for renaming.

3. Type **Member Server Baseline** and then press ENTER.

4. Click Edit. The Group Policy Object Editor console appears, with the Member Server Baseline GPO at the root of the console tree.

5. In the Computer Configuration container, expand the Windows Settings, Security Settings, and Local Policies containers.

6. Click the Audit Policy container. A list of audit policies appears in the console's details pane.

7. Double-click the Audit Account Logon Events policy. The Audit Account Logon Events Properties dialog box appears.

8. Select the Define These Policy Settings check box. The two Audit These Attempts check boxes are activated, with the Success check box selected by default.

9. Select the Failure check box and click OK.

10. Configure the remaining audit policies using the following settings:

    ❑ Audit Account Management—Success and Failure

    ❑ Audit Directory Service Access—Success and Failure

    ❑ Audit Logon Events—Success and Failure

    ❑ Audit Object Access—Success and Failure

    ❑ Audit Policy Change—Success and Failure

    ❑ Audit Privilege Use—Failure only

    ❑ Audit Process Tracking—No auditing

    ❑ Audit System Events—Success and Failure

You are configuring the Audit Process Tracking policy to audit neither successes nor failures because of the large number of log entries this policy creates. However, you should still select the Define These Policy Settings check box in the Audit Process Tracking Properties dialog box, leaving the Success and Failure check boxes cleared, to ensure that the configuration you want overrides any existing settings for that policy.

11. In the console's scope pane, click the Event Log container. A list of Event Log policies appears in the details pane.

12. Configure the Event Log policies using the following settings:

   ❑ Maximum Application Log Size—10240 KB

   ❑ Maximum Security Log Size—184320 KB

   ❑ Maximum System Log Size—10240 KB

   ❑ Prevent Local Guests Group From Accessing Application Log—Enabled

   ❑ Prevent Local Guests Group From Accessing Security Log—Enabled

   ❑ Prevent Local Guests Group From Accessing System Log—Enabled

   ❑ Retention Method For Application Log—Overwrite Events As Needed

   ❑ Retention Method For Security Log—Overwrite Events As Needed

   ❑ Retention Method For System Log—Overwrite Events As Needed

13. Click the System Services container in the scope pane. A list of services appears in the details pane.

14. Double-click the Alerter service entry. The Alerter Properties dialog box appears.

15. Select the Define This Policy Setting check box. The Disabled service startup mode is selected by default.

16. Leave the default service startup mode unchanged, and then click OK.

17. Activate each of the other service policies listed in Table 9-1 and configure their service startup modes using the table's values.

18. On the File menu, click Exit to close the Group Policy Object Editor console.

19. Click Close to close the Member Servers Properties dialog box.

20. Close the Active Directory Users And Computers console.

Lesson Review

The following questions are intended to reinforce key information presented in this lesson. If you are unable to answer a question, review the lesson materials and try the question again. You can find answers to the questions in the "Questions and Answers" section at the end of this chapter.

1. Which of the following audit policies enables you to tell what applications were running when a security event occurred?

   a. Audit Object Access

   b. Audit Privilege Use

   c. Audit Process Tracking

   d. Audit System Events

2. After installing several member servers running Windows Server 2003 on your Active Directory network, you want to deploy a baseline security configuration that you have designed for the member servers only, using group policies. Which of the following tasks must you perform to accomplish this objective? (Choose all correct answers.)

   a. Create a new domain

   b. Create a new organizational unit

   c. Move the computer objects representing the member servers

   d. Create a new GPO

   e. Modify the domain GPO

   f. Apply a GPO to the Computers container

   g. Apply a GPO to an organizational unit

3. With which of the following Active Directory object types can you associate a GPO? (Choose all correct answers.)

   a. Domain

   b. Computer

   c. Site

   d. Organizational unit

   e. Container

   f. Group

Lesson Summary

- A Group Policy Object (GPO) is a collection of configuration parameters that you can use to create a secure baseline installation for a computer running Windows Server 2003.

- To deploy a GPO, you associate it with an Active Directory container, and all the objects in the container inherit the GPO configuration settings.

■ Audit and Event Log policies enable you to specify what information a computer logs, how much information the computer retains in logs, and how the computer behaves when logs are full.

■ Windows Server 2003 loads many services by default that a member server usually doesn't need. You can use a GPO to specify the startup type for each service on a computer.

■ GPOs include a great many security options that you can use to configure specific behaviors of a computer running Windows Server 2003.

Lesson 2: Creating Role-Specific Server Configurations

Once a baseline security configuration for your servers is in place, you can consider the special needs of the servers performing particular roles in your enterprise. Domain controllers, infrastructure servers, file and print servers, and application servers all are vulnerable to unique threats, and their security requirements can be quite different. By combining the policy settings in a role-specific GPO with those in your baseline configuration, you can create a secure environment for each server role without much duplication of effort.

See Also   For servers running Windows Server 2003 with SP1, you can use the SCW to create role-specific server configurations. Lesson 4 in this chapter contains more information about the SCW.

After this lesson, you will be able to
- Configure security for the domain controller role
- Configure security for the infrastructure server role
- Configure security for the file and print server role

Estimated lesson time: 30 minutes

Securing Domain Controllers

On a Windows Server 2003 network that uses Active Directory, no servers are more vital than the domain controllers. Because domain controllers provide authentication services for most network operations and store and distribute group policies, their failure or compromise can be a catastrophe for network productivity. The domain controller role requires special security considerations that go beyond those of the baseline configuration discussed in Lesson 1 of this chapter.

Exam Tip   Be sure to understand the operational differences between the various server roles, including domain controllers, infrastructure servers, application servers, and file and print servers.

Isolating Domain Controllers

Because of the importance of domain controllers, your security measures should minimize the threats to the computers in every possible way. Physically, domain controllers should always be in a secured location, such as a server closet or a data center, which is accessible only to administrative personnel who have reason to be there.

Secure the console with a complex password, so that even people who are in the room for other reasons are not able to access the server.

In addition to limiting physical access to your domain controller, you should limit the access provided by the network connection. This means reducing the number of open ports on the computer by minimizing the number of applications and services it runs. Many domain controllers running Windows Server 2003 also run the DNS Server service, because DNS is intimately associated with Active Directory, but you should avoid running services and applications that are unnecessary to the domain controller role.

Setting Audit and Event Log Policies

When you install Active Directory on a computer running Windows Server 2003 and create a new domain, the system puts the domain controller's computer object in an organizational unit called Domain Controllers and creates a GPO that is linked to that organizational unit. The Domain Controllers container's GPO provides some additional security settings beyond the default settings in the domain's GPO, but you might want to augment or modify them.

For example, the Domain Controllers container's GPO enables the following audit policies, but configures them to audit only successes:

- Audit Account Logon Events
- Audit Account Management
- Audit Directory Service Access
- Audit Logon Events
- Audit Policy Change
- Audit System Events

Depending on the policy settings you use in your baseline security configuration, you might want to modify these settings to audit failures as well as successes, or to define additional policies such as Audit Object Access and Audit Process Tracking. If you decide to implement additional audit policies, be sure to consider the Event Log policies as well, because you might have to specify a larger maximum size for the security log to hold all the entries that these policies create.

See Also   If you decide to apply the GPO for the baseline security configuration discussed in Lesson 1 to your domain controllers, be sure to consider the effect of using multiple GPOs on the same container. You must be familiar with all the policy settings in both GPOs and know the order in which the system applies the GPOs to the container. For more information on combining GPOs, see Lesson 3 of this chapter.

Assigning User Rights

The default domain GPO created by Windows Server 2003 contains no user rights assignments, but the default Domain Controllers container's GPO does. Most of the user rights that the GPO assigns using these policies are intended to give administrators the access they need to manage the domain controller, while granting users only the minimum rights they need to use the domain controller's services. For the most part, the settings for the User Rights Assignment policy in the default Domain Controllers container's GPO are acceptable, and you should use them on your domain controllers. However, there are a few changes that you might want to make.

Debug Programs   The Debug Programs user right enables you to use a debugging tool to access any process running on the computer or even the operating system kernel itself. Software developers use these tools to debug applications that they are in the process of creating. This user right provides access to sensitive areas of the operating system that a potential intruder might be able to abuse. By default, the GPO linked to the Domain Controllers organizational unit grants this right to the Administrators group (see Figure 9-9). However, if no one in your organization is developing or debugging software, you can revoke the Debug Programs user right from the Administrators group and close what could be a serious security breach.

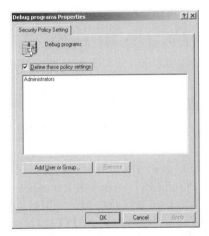

Figure 9-9   The Debug Programs Properties dialog box

Add Workstations To Domain   By default, all authenticated users have the right to add up to ten computer accounts to an Active Directory domain. Adding an account creates a new computer object in the Computers container. Computer accounts are full security principals in Windows Server 2003, able to authenticate and access domain resources. This right can allow any authenticated user to create unauthorized domain workstations that an intruder could use when the computer account is idle.

Many large network installations rely on IT support personnel to install new workstations and manually create new computer objects. In this case, you can revoke the Authenticated Users group's Add Workstations To Domain right without causing problems.

Allow Log On Locally   The Allow Log On Locally user right enables specified users and groups to log on to the computer interactively from the console. Obviously, users with this right have access to many important operating system elements, and could cause a great deal of damage, either accidentally or deliberately. It is therefore important to grant this right only to users and groups that absolutely need it.

> **Tip**   Users who connect to a domain controller using Terminal Services also require the Allow Log On Locally user right. Be sure to account for these users when modifying the default user rights assignments.

The default Domain Controllers container's GPO grants the Allow Log On Locally user right to the following built-in groups:

- Account Operators
- Administrators
- Backup Operators
- Print Operators
- Server Operators

How (or whether) you use the built-in groups is your decision, but, based on their intended use, the Account Operators and Print Operators groups typically do not need to perform their tasks from a domain controller console, so you can usually revoke these two groups' Allow Log On Locally right.

Shut Down The System   You should control the ability to shut down a domain controller very carefully, because shutting down a domain controller can affect systems all over the network. The default Domain Controllers container's GPO grants this user right to the following groups:

- Administrators
- Backup Operators
- Print Operators
- Server Operators

In most environments, members of the Backup Operators and Print Operators groups should not need to shut down a domain controller, so you can revoke their right to do this.

> **Important**   For the restrictions imposed by your assignments of Shut Down The System user right to be meaningful, you must also revoke the Security Options policy, Shutdown: Allow System To Be Shut Down Without Having To Log On. If you enable this option, any user can shut down the computer without authentication, which means that they are not subject to user rights restrictions.

Configuring Services

In addition to the services required by member servers, as listed earlier in Table 9-1, domain controllers require the following additional services, which you should enable in the System Services container of your Domain Controllers container's GPO, using the Automatic startup type:

- Distributed File System
- File Replication Service
- Intersite Messaging
- Kerberos Key Distribution Center
- Remote Procedure Call (RPC) Locator

Securing Infrastructure Servers

Infrastructure servers are computers that run network support services such as DNS, DHCP, and Windows Internet Name Service (WINS). An infrastructure server can run any or all of these services and might also fill other roles, such as an application or file and print server.

For an infrastructure server that provides all these services, you should modify the System Services policies in your infrastructure servers' GPO to include the following services, using the Automatic startup type:

- DHCP Server
- DNS Server
- NT LM Security Support Provider
- Windows Internet Name Service (WINS)

Configuring DNS Security

It is common for administrators to run the DNS Server service on Windows Server 2003 domain controllers, particularly when they use Active Directory-integrated zones. One benefit of storing the zone database in Active Directory is that the directory service takes over securing and replicating the DNS data. However, even if you do use Active Directory-integrated zones, there are additional security measures you might consider.

> **See Also**   The Microsoft DNS Server service has its own security features, such as secured dynamic update and authorized zone transfers. For more information on implementing these features, see Lesson 5 in Chapter 4, "Planning a Name Resolution Strategy."

Protecting Active Directory-Integrated DNS   When you create Active Directory-integrated zones on your DNS server, the zone database is stored as part of the Active Directory database, which protects it from direct access by unauthorized users. However, you should still take steps to ensure that the MicrosoftDNS container object in Active Directory (shown in Figure 9-10) is secure.

Figure 9-10   The MicrosoftDNS container in the Active Directory Users And Computers console

> **Tip**   To access the MicrosoftDNS container object in the Active Directory Users And Computers console, you must first select the Advanced Features option from the console's View menu. The console then displays additional containers, including the System container, which contains MicrosoftDNS.

By default, the DnsAdmins, Domain Admins, and Enterprise Admins groups all have the Full Control permission for the MicrosoftDNS container. The local Administrators group lacks the Full Control permission, but it does have the permissions needed to create new objects and modify existing ones. You might modify these defaults to limit the number of users with permission to modify this container.

Protecting DNS Database Files   For DNS zones that are not integrated into Active Directory, the zone databases are simple text files stored in the C:\Windows\System32\Dns folder by default. Windows Server 2003 creates DNS debug logs in the same folder. The permissions for this folder grant the Administrators group Full Control, while the Server Operators group receives all permissions except Full Control. The Authenticated Users group receives the permissions needed to read and execute files in this folder (see Figure 9-11).

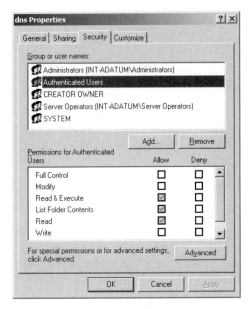

Figure 9-11   The DNS Properties dialog box

You don't need file system permissions to maintain the DNS zone databases using the DNS console or to access DNS server information using a client. Therefore, there is no reason for the Authenticated Users group to have file system permissions. By enabling users to view the DNS data files, you give them an opportunity to gather information about your domain that they could use to stage an attack against the network. You can safely revoke the Authenticated Users group's permissions for this folder, and even limit the Server Operators group to read-only access, if desired.

Configuring DHCP Security

The interruption of a DHCP server's functions might not have an immediate effect on your network, but eventually your DHCP clients' leases will expire and they will be unable to obtain new ones. Apart from enabling the DHCP Server service itself, there

is little you can do to configure DHCP using a GPO. However, there are security measures that can help to ensure uninterrupted performance.

Denial of service attacks (DoS) constitute one of the biggest threats to DHCP servers.
DoS attacks can result in system shutdowns or service disruptions. One relatively simple way for an unscrupulous individual to commit a DoS attack is to create a script that
sends repeated requests for IP address assignments to the server until all the addresses
in the scope are depleted. Legitimate clients are then unable to obtain addresses until
the bogus leases expire. Several techniques can defend against denial of service
attacks, including the following:

■ Use of 802.1x-enabled hardware; 802.1x can authenticate clients prior to obtaining
  a DHCP lease. If the attacker cannot be authenticated, he will not be able to obtain
  any leases.

■ Ensure that unauthorized persons do not have access to the physical or wireless
  network.

■ Use the 80/20 address allocation method. Use two DHCP servers to provide
  addresses for each subnet, with 80 percent of the available addresses in one
  server's scope and 20 percent in the other. This ensures that there are addresses
  available to clients, even if one of the servers fails.

■ Create a DHCP server cluster. Clustering enables you to use multiple servers to
  create a single network entity. If one server fails, the other servers in the cluster
  take up the slack.

> **See Also**   See Chapter 7, "Clustering Servers," for more information on clustering.

■ Monitor DHCP activity. You can monitor the activity of a DHCP server by using
  tools such as the Performance console and Network Monitor or by enabling audit
  logging on the DHCP server.

DHCP audit logging is not integrated into the main Windows Server 2003 auditing facility. You can enable DHCP audit logging using group policies but you cannot access the
logs using the Event Viewer console. To enable DHCP audit logging, you must open
the DHCP console, display the Properties dialog box for the DHCP server, and then
select the Enable DHCP Audit Logging check box in the General tab. The server stores
the log files in the C:\Windows\System32\Dhcp folder, by default.

Securing File and Print Servers

Security for a file and print server requires policy settings similar to those of the baseline installation you created in Lesson 1 of this chapter. The two main changes you must make for the file and print server role are as follows:

- **Enable the Print Spooler service**   Use the appropriate policy in the System Services container of your GPO to enable the Print Spooler service with the Automatic startup type. The server needs this service to receive print jobs from other computers on the network.

- **Disable the Microsoft Network Server: Digitally Sign Communications (Always) security policy**   When this security option is enabled, users are unable to view the print queue on the server, even though they are able to submit print jobs. Defining this policy with a value of Disabled in the Security Options container of your GPO ensures that your clients can access the print queue on the server.

> **Note**   To view print queues on file and print servers, client computers must have the Security Options policy, Microsoft Network Client: Digitally Sign Communications (Always) (or its equivalent) disabled as well.

Configuring Permissions Using a GPO

One of the most important security measures for a file and print server is protection for the user data stored on the server drives. You create this protection by using the NTFS file system on your drives and by using NTFS permissions to control access to the server drives. You can specify the permissions for your NTFS drives in a GPO by browsing to the File System container in the Group Policy Object Editor console and, from the Action menu, selecting Add File. In the series of dialog boxes that appear, you perform the following tasks:

1. Specify the files or folders for which you want to configure file system permissions.

2. Specify the permissions you want to assign to the selected files or folders.

3. Specify whether you want the permissions to be inherited by subfolders.

By default, all the NTFS drives on a computer running Windows Server 2003, except the system drive, have Full Control permission assigned to the Everyone group. Therefore, it is up to you to design a directory structure and a system of permissions for your drives that gives users only the access they need to the files stored there.

> **Tip**   In addition to file system permissions, you can also use a GPO to configure registry permissions on a computer running Windows Server 2003. Browse to the Registry container and, from the Action menu, choose Add Key. The process resembles configuring file system permissions, except that you select a registry key instead of a file or folder.

Securing Application Servers

It is difficult, if not impossible, to create a generic security configuration for application servers, because the requirements of the individual applications are usually unique. Windows Server 2003 includes some software that enables the computer to function as an application server, most notably Internet Information Services (IIS), which provides World Wide Web, File Transfer Protocol (FTP), and other Internet server services, but in most cases, application servers run external software products, such as database or e-mail servers. To secure these applications, you must compare the security requirements of your network and your users with the security features provided by the application itself.

Practice: Modifying the GPO for the Domain Controllers Container's GPO

In this practice, you increase the security of your domain controllers by modifying the GPO for the Domain Controllers container that Windows Server 2003 creates by default.

Exercise: Modify the Domain Controllers Container's GPO

1. Log on to your Server01 computer as Administrator.

2. Click Start, point to All Programs, point to Administrative Tools, and then click Active Directory Users And Computers. The Active Directory Users And Computers console appears.

3. Highlight the Domain Controllers organizational unit and, on the Action menu, click Properties. The Domain Controllers Properties dialog box appears.

4. Click the Group Policy tab, and then click Edit. The Group Policy Object Editor console appears, with the Default Domain Controllers Policy object at the root of the scope pane.

5. Expand the Windows Settings, Security Settings, and Local Policies containers, and then select the Audit Policy container. The list of audit policies appears in the details pane.

6. Double-click the Audit Account Logon Events policy. The Audit Account Logon Events Properties dialog box appears.

7. Windows Server 2003 defines this policy for domain controllers by default, with only the Success option selected.

8. Select the Failure check box, and then click OK.

9. Modify the following audit policies in the same way, by selecting the Failure check box.

   ❑ Audit Account Management

   ❑ Audit Directory Service Access

   ❑ Audit Logon Events

   ❑ Audit Policy Change

   ❑ Audit System Events

10. In the scope pane, select the User Rights Assignment container. The list of user rights appears in the details pane.

11. Double-click the Debug Programs user right. The Debug Programs Properties dialog box appears.

12. Select the Administrators group, and then click Remove. Click OK.

13. Double-click the Add Workstations To Domain user right. The Add Workstations To Domain Properties dialog box appears.

14. Select the Authenticated Users group, and then click Remove. Click OK.

15. Double-click the Allow Log On Locally user right. The Allow Log On Locally Properties dialog box appears.

16. Select the Account Operators and Print Operators groups, and then click Remove. Click OK.

17. Select the System Services container. The list of services appears in the details pane.

18. Double-click the Distributed File System service policy. The Distributed File System Properties dialog box appears.

19. Select the Define This Policy Setting check box, and then click the Automatic option button. Click OK.

20. Modify the following System Services policies in the same way, assigning them the Automatic startup type.

    ❑ File Replication Service

    ❑ Intersite Messaging

    ❑ Kerberos Key Distribution Center

    ❑ Remote Procedure Call (RPC) Locator

❑ Close the Group Policy Object Editor console.

❑ Click OK in the Domain Controllers Properties dialog box.

21. Close the Active Directory Users And Computers console.

Lesson Review

The following questions are intended to reinforce key information presented in this lesson. If you are unable to answer a question, review the lesson materials and try the question again. You can find answers to the questions in the "Questions and Answers" section at the end of this chapter.

1. Under what conditions can you not revoke the Debug Programs user right from all users and groups?

_____

_____

2. Which of the following tasks can users not perform when you enable the Security Options policy, Microsoft Network Server: Digitally Sign Communications (Always) on a computer running Windows Server 2003?

   a. Submit jobs to a print queue on the server

   b. View the print queues on the server

   c. Install printer drivers stored on the server

   d. Create printer shares on the server

3. Enabling which of the following audit policies is likely to require changing the Maximum Security Log Size value as well?

   a. Audit Process Tracking

   b. Audit Policy Change

   c. Audit Account Logon Events

   d. Audit Directory Service Access

Lesson Summary

■ The domain controller role is only assigned its own default GPO by Windows Server 2003. To create your own policy settings for domain controllers, you can modify the existing GPO or create a new one.

- Domain controllers require more security than any other server role. You should secure the server physically, and then use group policies to specify auditing and Event Log settings, user rights assignments, and the services the computer should run.

- Infrastructure servers run network support services such as DNS, DHCP, and WINS.

- DNS servers using Active Directory-integrated zones use the directory service to secure their data, but for servers that use file-based zones, you must take steps to secure the DNS database and log files.

- For NTFS drives other than the system drive on computers running Windows Server 2003 the Full Control permission is assigned to the Everyone group by default. You can use a GPO to protect the files on your server drives by assigning your own file systems permissions.

Lesson 3: Deploying Role-Specific GPOs

The function of the secure baseline configuration for member servers discussed in Lesson 1 is to implement a general form of security for all your network servers. Most, if not all, of the configuration settings in your baseline should apply to all your servers. However, you undoubtedly also have servers that perform specific roles and that have different security requirements. The best way to accommodate these servers is to create Group Policy Objects that build on the baseline configuration you have already created.

> **See Also** For servers running Windows Server 2003 with SP1, you can use the SCW to create role-specific server configurations. Lesson 4 in this chapter contains more information about the SCW.

After this lesson, you will be able to
- Assign multiple GPOs to one object
- Understand group policy inheritance rules

Estimated lesson time: 20 minutes

Combining GPO Policies

To modify the security configuration for a group of servers performing a particular role without altering your baseline configuration, you can create a separate GPO for a server role and, after these computers receive the GPO containing the baseline configuration, you can apply the role-specific GPO to them. The settings in the role-specific GPO override those in the baseline. You can use the role-specific GPO to do any of the following:

- Modify settings you configured in the baseline
- Configure settings that are not defined in the baseline
- Leave the baseline settings for specific parameters unchanged

Because a GPO assigned to an Active Directory container affects all the objects in that container, you must create separate organizational units for the servers running the Windows operating system on your network that are performing different roles. You can deploy your server GPOs in two ways: by creating role-specific organizational units anywhere in the Active Directory tree and assigning multiple GPOs to each organizational unit, or by creating a hierarchy of organizational units and letting group policy inheritance do some of the work for you.

Applying Multiple GPOs

When you create a GPO, you must associate it with a specific Active Directory domain, site, or organizational unit object. However, once you have created the GPO, you can link it to as many other objects as you want. Therefore, if servers running Windows Server 2003 on your network are performing different roles, you can create separate organizational units for them at the same level, as shown in Figure 9-12.

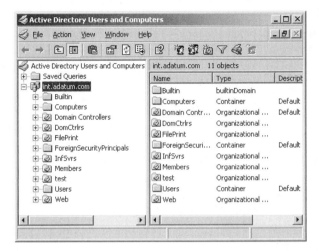

Figure 9-12   Organizational units for server roles

In the figure, you see the Domain Controllers organizational unit that the Windows Server 2003 creates by default when you create the domain, as well as new organizational units for member servers (named Members), infrastructure servers (named InfSvrs), file and print servers (named FilePrint), and application servers (named Web). To create a separate security configuration for each server role, you would use a procedure like the following:

1. Create a new GPO for the Members container and use it to create your baseline security configuration.

2. Create a new GPO in each of the role-specific containers and use it to create a role-specific security configuration.

3. Link the Members GPO to each of the role-specific containers and move it to the bottom of the Group Policy Object Links list in the Group Policy tab in the Domain Controllers Properties dialog box.

> **Important**   When you link a GPO to multiple container objects, you are only creating links between the object pairs; you are not creating copies of the GPO. Therefore, when you modify the policy settings for the GPO from one of the linked containers, the changes you make affect all the containers to which you have linked the GPO.

The order in which the GPOs appear in the Group Policy Object Links list is critical. GPOs that are higher in the list have higher priority, so that a setting in the first policy listed will overwrite a setting in the second. If you list the GPOs in the wrong order, a different set of policy values than you had planned might be in effect.

> **Tip**   Although Active Directory objects inherit group policy settings from their parent objects by default, it is possible to block the inheritance. Display the Properties dialog box for an object, click the Group Policy tab, and then select the Block Policy Inheritance check box to prevent that object from inheriting group policy settings from its parent objects.

Creating a Container Hierarchy

Instead of manually linking your GPOs to the various organizational unit objects in your Active Directory tree, you can also create a hierarchy of organizational unit objects, as shown in Figure 9-13. In this figure, you see the Members organizational unit, with the role-specific organizational units beneath it.

Figure 9-13   An organizational unit hierarchy

As with most tree hierarchies in Windows operating systems, the properties of a parent object are passed down to the child objects beneath it. Therefore, when you create a GPO and link it to the Members container, not only the computer objects in Members receive the policy settings from the GPO; all the computers in the role-specific organizational units receive these settings.

> **Note**   The one exception to the rule of group policy inheritance is that subdomains do not inherit group policy settings from their parent domains.

> **Tip**   If you plan to create a hierarchy of organizational units that includes domain controllers in one of the role-specific containers, you will not be able to move the Domain Controllers organizational unit object that Windows Server 2003 creates automatically at domain creation to another location in the tree. However, you can create a new organizational unit object in the hierarchy and move the computer objects there from the Domain Controllers container.

To create security configurations for the servers in the role-specific organizational units, you create a new GPO for each container. When you do this, the policy settings in the GPOs linked to the role-specific containers take precedence over the settings for the same policies in the parent container's GPO. The rules governing the combination of inherited and direct policy settings are as follows:

- If the parent container's GPO contains a policy setting, and the same policy is undefined in the child container's GPO, the objects in the child container use the setting from the parent GPO.

- If the child container's GPO contains a policy setting, and the same policy is undefined in the parent container's GPO, the objects in the child container use the setting from the child GPO.

- If the parent container's GPO contains a policy setting, and the same policy has a different setting in the child container's GPO, the objects in the child container use the setting from the child GPO.

> **Real World   GPO Combination**
>
> When you apply multiple GPOs to a container, whether with multiple links or with a hierarchical GPO arrangement, it is important to understand the difference between an undefined policy and an explicit policy setting. An undefined policy is not necessarily the same as a Disabled setting. When you leave a policy undefined in the GPO, the computers to which that GPO applies use the operating system's default setting, which might be Enabled, Disabled, or something else, depending on the policy. If you define a policy with an Enabled value in the parent container's GPO, you must explicitly define the same policy in the child container's GPO to assign it a different value, even if that value is the same as the Windows Server 2003 default setting.

Practice: Deploying Multiple GPOs

In this practice, you use two different methods to combine the policies in the GPOs you created for the Member Servers and Domain Controllers organizational units in the practices for Lessons 1 and 2 of this chapter. First, you link both GPOs to a single container and modify the order in which the system applies them. Then, you create a hierarchy of organizational units and use group policy inheritance to combine policy settings.

Exercise 1: Creating GPO Links

The GPO you created for the Domain Controllers container in the practice for Lesson 2 is not intended to stand alone. It builds on the Member Servers container's GPO you created in the practice for Lesson 1. In this practice, you link the Member Servers container's GPO to the Domain Controllers organizational unit.

1. Log on to your Server01 computer as Administrator.

2. Click Start, point to All Programs, point to Administrative Tools, and then click Active Directory Users And Computers. The Active Directory Users And Computers console appears.

3. Select the Domain Controllers organizational unit object you modified in the practice for Lesson 2 and, on the Action menu, click Properties. The Domain Controllers Properties dialog box appears.

4. Click the Group Policy tab and then click Add. The Add A Group Policy Object Link dialog box appears.

5. In the Look In drop-down list, select contoso.com.

6. In the Domains, OUs, And Linked Group Policy Objects list, double-click the Member Servers.contoso.com entry.

7. Select the Member Server Baseline GPO, and then click OK. A link to the Member Server Baseline GPO appears in the Group Policy Object Links list.

8. Select the Member Server Baseline entry in the Group Policy Object Links list, and then click Up. The Member Server Baseline entry moves to the top of the list.

9. Click OK.

10. Leave the Active Directory Users And Computers console open for the next exercise.

Exercise 2: Creating an Organizational Unit Hierarchy

In this procedure, you create a new hierarchy of organizational units and link your existing GPOs to them.

1. In the Active Directory Users And Computers console, select the contoso.com object in the scope pane. Then, on the Action menu, point to New and click Organizational Unit. The New Object — Organizational Unit dialog box appears.

2. In the Name text box, type **Members** and then click OK. A new Members organizational unit appears in the scope pane.

3. With the Members container highlighted, click Properties on the Action menu. The Members Properties dialog box appears.

4. Click the Group Policy tab and then click Add. The Add A Group Policy Object Link dialog box appears.

5. In the Look In drop-down list, select contoso.com.

6. In the Domains, OUs, And Linked Group Policy Objects list, double-click the Member Servers.contoso.com entry.

7. Select the Member Server Baseline GPO, and then click OK. A link to the Member Server Baseline GPO appears in the Group Policy Object Links list.

8. Click OK.

9. In the console scope pane, highlight the Members organizational unit and, on the Action menu, point to New, and then click Organizational Unit. The New Object — Organizational Unit dialog box appears.

10. Type **DomCtrlrs** in the Name text box, and then click OK. A new DomCtrlrs organizational unit appears in the scope pane beneath the Members object.

11. With the Members container highlighted, click Properties on the Action menu. The Members Properties dialog box appears.

12. Click the Group Policy tab, and then click Add. The Add A Group Policy Object Link dialog box appears.

13. In the Look In drop-down list, select contoso.com.

14. In the Domains, OUs, And Linked Group Policy Objects list, double-click the Domain Controllers.contoso.com entry.

15. Select the Default Domain Controllers Policy GPO, and then click OK. A link to the Default Domain Controllers Policy GPO appears in the Group Policy Object Links list.

16. Click OK.

17. Close the Active Directory Users And Computers console.

Lesson Review

The following questions are intended to reinforce key information presented in this lesson. If you are unable to answer a question, review the lesson materials and try the question again. You can find answers to the questions in the "Questions and Answers" section at the end of this chapter.

1. In the GPO for your adatum.com domain, you define the Audit Account Logon Events policy by specifying that both successes and failures be audited. In the GPO for the sales.adatum.com domain, you leave the Audit Account Logon Events policy undefined. What will be the effective value for this policy for a computer in the sales.adatum.com domain?

_____

_____

2. Although Windows Server 2003 creates a GPO for the Domain Controllers container with default role-specific policy settings in it, you have other policy settings that you want to apply to your domain controllers. Which of the following methods can you use to apply these settings? (Choose all correct answers.)

   a. Modify the policy settings in the Domain Controllers container's existing GPO.

   b. Create a new organizational unit object and create a GPO for it containing the desired policy settings. Then, move the Domain Controllers container to make it a child of the new object.

   c. Create a second GPO for the Domain Controllers container.

   d. Create a new child organizational unit object beneath the Domain Controllers container object, and then create a GPO for the new object containing the desired policy settings.

3. When creating a GPO for an organizational unit called Servers, you define a particular audit policy and configure it to audit successes only. When creating a GPO for an organizational unit called Infrastructure, which is a child of the Servers organizational unit, you configure the same policy to audit failures only. What is the effective value of that policy for a computer object in the Infrastructure container?

   a. Undefined

   b. Success only

   c. Failure only

   d. Success and Failure

Lesson Summary

- When creating security configurations for servers that perform specific roles, you can build on your secure baseline configuration.

- An Active Directory object can receive policy settings from multiple GPOs and apply them in a particular order.

- Active Directory objects do not contain GPOs; they are only linked to them. You can link a single GPO to multiple objects and make global changes by modifying that single GPO.

- Organizational unit objects inherit policy settings from the GPOs applied to their parent objects.

- Policy settings from a GPO linked directly to an object take precedence over settings inherited from a parent object's GPO.

Lesson 4: Using the SCW to Harden Servers

The SCW can be used to harden computers running Windows Server 2003 with SP1. The SCW determines the minimum functionality required for a server's role or roles, and disables functionality that is not required. The SCW can be used in addition to the role-specific GPOs discussed in the previous lessons.

After this lesson, you will be able to

- Deploy the SCW
- Create and deploy SCW policies
- Convert SCW policies to GPOs

Estimated lesson time: 20 minutes

Deploying the SCW

You can install the SCW only on computers running Windows Server 2003 with SP1, which includes the SCW as an optional Windows component. The SCW is not installed by default. To install SCW, in Control Panel, open Add Or Remove Programs, and then select Add/Remove Windows Components to open the Windows Components Wizard shown in Figure 9-14. To install the SCW, you need to be a member of the Administrators group on the server.

Tip   The SCW can be deployed using an unattended installation. Consult the SCW Help file for information about unattended installation of the SCW.

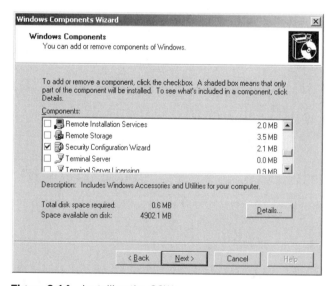

Figure 9-14   Installing the SCW

SCW Components

There are three main components to the SCW: the SCW itself (the user interface), a command-line tool, and the Security Configuration Database.

SCW User Interface (UI)   You will find the SCW UI in Administrative Tools in All Programs, which you can find in the Start menu. When run, the SCW UI displays the initial wizard page shown in Figure 9-15. You can target the SCW UI on the local server or any server on the network that is running Windows Server 2003 with SP1 and perform the following tasks:

- Create a new security policy.
- Edit an existing SCW-generated security policy.
- Apply an existing SCW-generated security policy.
- Roll back the last applied SCW policy.

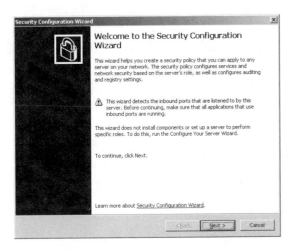

Figure 9-15   Running the SCW

Tip   Each page of the SCW contains a link to online help that is specific to that wizard page. You can view the online help file in its entirety from the command line by typing **hh scwhelp.chm**.

Warning   You must not use the SCW on servers running Microsoft Windows Small Business Server 2003. Instead of the SCW, Windows Small Business Server 2003 uses the default settings in Setup and in the Configure E-Mail and Internet Connection Wizard to help secure your server.

SCW Command-Line Tool   The SCW includes the Scwcmd.exe command-line tool. You can use scwcmd for the following tasks:

- Configure one or many servers with an SCW-generated policy.

- Analyze one or many servers with an SCW-generated policy.

- View analysis results in HTML format.

- Roll back SCW policies.

- Transform an SCW-generated policy into native files that are supported by Group Policy.

- Register a Security Configuration Database extension with the SCW.

> **Note** When you use scwcmd to configure, analyze, or roll back a policy on a remote server, the SCW must be installed on the remote server.

Security Configuration Database   The Security Configuration Database consists of a set of Extensible Markup Language (XML) documents that define server roles, as shown in Figure 9-16. In addition to server roles, these XML documents define the security settings for client features, administration options, services, ports, and other settings that are used in the server roles. If necessary, you can use the SCW to modify these security settings for a nonstandard server role.

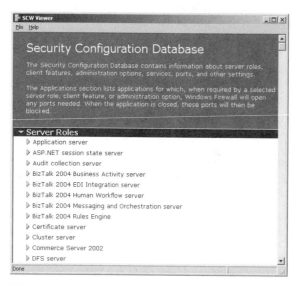

Figure 9-16   Security Configuration Database

SCW Security Policies

The SCW allows you to create security policies and apply the policies to multiple servers running Windows Server 2003 with SP1. The SCW establishes the minimum functionality required for a server's role or roles, and disables functionality that is not required. Specifically, the SCW assists in creating a security policy that:

- Disables unneeded services.

- Prohibits unnecessary IIS Web extensions, if applicable.

- Reduces protocol exposure to SMB, LAN Manager, and Lightweight Directory Access Protocol (LDAP).

- Defines a high signal-to-noise audit policy.

- Blocks unused ports and implements additional address or security restrictions for open ports.

> **See Also**   This chapter does not include details on using the SCW to block or configure security restrictions on ports. For more information on blocking and securing ports, see Chapter 12, "Securing Network Communications Using IPSec."

Creating SCW Security Policies   Use the SCW UI to create security policies on prototype servers of the same type as the servers that will receive the policy. When creating the policy, ensure that the server roles shown on the Select Server Roles page (see Figure 9-17) are correct for the prototype server. The SCW bases all subsequent security settings on the server roles detected.

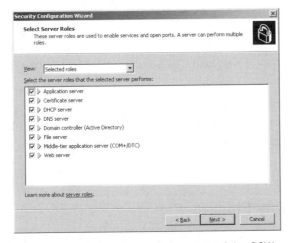

Figure 9-17   Select Server Roles page of the SCW

> **Note** SCW security policy files are created as XML files that are saved by default in %systemdir%\Security\Msscw\Policies.

Deploying SCW Security Policies SCW Security Policies can be deployed by using the SCW UI as shown in Figure 9-18 or by using the Scwcmd.exe command-line tool included with the SCW.

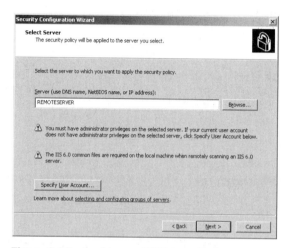

Figure 9-18 Applying an SCW Security Policy

Converting SCW Security Policy Files into GPOs

The SCW saves its security policies as XML files, and the Scwcmd.exe command-line utility allows you to convert these and save them as GPOs by using the scwcmd transform command. The SCW UI itself does not support GPOs.

After the GPO is created, you must manually link the GPO to the target organizational unit (OU) by using Active Directory Users and Computers, or by using the Group Policy Management Console (GPMC).

> **Security Alert** Any IIS settings that are defined in the SCW policy will be lost during the scwcmd transform operation because Group Policy does not support configuration of IIS settings.

Practice: Deploying SCW Security Policies

In this practice, you install the SCW and create a security policy. You then convert the SCW security policy into a GPO.

Important   Before starting this practice, ensure the computer is running Windows Server 2003 with SP1.

Exercise 1: Installing the SCW

A default installation of Windows Server 2003 with SP1 does not include the SCW. Therefore, in this exercise, you install the SCW by completing the following steps:

1. In Control Panel, double-click Add Or Remove Programs.

2. Click Add/Remove Windows Components, select the Security Configuration Wizard check box, and then click Next.

3. When the installation has completed, close Add/Remove Windows Components.

4. Close Control Panel.

Exercise 2: Creating an SCW Security Policy

In this exercise, you create an SCW Security Policy and exclude any network security settings. To create an SCW Security Policy, complete the following steps:

1. Click Start, click Administrative Tools, and then click Security Configuration Wizard.

2. Read the Welcome page and click Next.

3. Select Create A New Security Policy and then click Next.

4. Leave the default name for the prototype server and then click Next.

5. When processing is complete, click Next.

6. On the Role-Based Service Configuration page, click Next.

7. On the Select Server Roles page, click Next.

8. On the Select Client Features page, click Next.

9. On the Select Administration And Other Options page, click Next.

10. On the Select Additional Services page, click Next.

11. On the Handling Unspecified Services page, select Do Not Change The Startup Mode Of The Service and click Next.

12. On the Confirm Service Changes page, click Next.

13. On the Network Security page, select the Skip This Section check box and click Next.

14. On the Registry Settings page, click Next.

15. On the Require SMB Security Signatures page, click Next.

16. On the Require LDAP Signing page, click Next.

17. On the Outbound Authentication Methods page, click Next.

18. On the Outbound Authentication Methods Using Domain Accounts page, click Next.

19. On the Registry Settings Summary page, click Next.

20. On the Audit Policy page, click Next.

21. On the System Audit Policy page, click Next.

22. On the Audit Policy Summary page, click Next.

23. On the Internet Information Services page, click Next.

24. On the Select Web Service Extensions For Dynamic Content page, click Next.

25. On the Select The Virtual Directories To Retain page, click Next.

26. On the Prevent Anonymous Users From Accessing Content Files page, click Next.

27. On the IIS Settings Summary page, click Next.

28. On the Save Security Policy page, click Next.

29. On the Security Policy File Name page, type **70-293.XML** for the prototype policy, and then click Next.

30. On the Apply Security Policy page, click Next.

31. On the Completing The Security Configuration Wizard page, click Finish.

Exercise 3: Converting an SCW Security Policy into a GPO

In this exercise, you convert the SCW Security Policy you created in Exercise 2 into a GPO and link it to an OU you created in the practice for Lesson 3. To convert the SCW Security Policy, complete the following steps:

1. At the command prompt, type **cd %systemroot%\security\msscw\Policies**.

2. Next, type **scwcmd transform /p:70-293.XML /g:SCW-GPO**.

   After a short delay you will see the message "Command completed successfully."

3. Click Start, point to All Programs, point to Administrative Tools, and then click Active Directory Users And Computers. The Active Directory Users And Computers console appears.

4. Select the DomCtrls OU you created in the practice for Lesson 3 and, on the Action menu, click Properties. The DomCtrls Properties dialog box appears.

5. Click the Group Policy tab and then click Add. The Add A Group Policy Object Link dialog box appears.

6. Click the All tab, select the SCW-GPO, and then click OK. A link to the SCW-GPO appears in the Group Policy Object Links list.

7. Click OK to close the DomCtrls Properties dialog box.

8. Close the Active Directory Users And Computers console.

Lesson Review

The following questions are intended to reinforce key information presented in this lesson. If you are unable to answer a question, review the lesson materials and try the question again. You can find answers to the questions in the "Questions and Answers" section at the end of this chapter.

1. List the operating systems supported by the SCW.

   _____

   _____

2. Which of the following tasks can you not do using the SCW UI?

   a. Create an SCW policy.

   b. Apply an SCW policy to a computer.

3. What is the command line required to convert an SCW policy named C:\SCW\SQLPOLICY.XML into a GPO named SQL-SERVERS?

   _____

   _____

Lesson Summary

- The SCW is a powerful tool for securing servers running Windows Server 2003 with SP1.

- Use the SCW UI on prototype servers to create a standard policy that you will apply to servers with the same roles.

- Apply the SCW policy to the target servers using the SCW UI or command line.

- SCW policies can be converted (transformed) to GPOs using the SCW command line.

Case Scenario Exercise

You are the network infrastructure design specialist for Litware, Inc., a manufacturer of specialized scientific software products, and you have already created a basic network design for their new office building, as described in the Case Scenario Exercise in Chapter 1. You are currently designing a security infrastructure for the company's computers running Windows Server 2003. The servers running Windows Server 2003 on the network are as follows:

- Three Active Directory domain controllers also running the DNS Server service with Active Directory-integrated zones

- Four file and print servers

- Six Web servers running IIS

Your first task is to create a GPO for a baseline installation. This baseline GPO leaves the audit and Event Log policies undefined but uses the System Services policies to disable the following services:

Alerter	Network DDE DSDM
Application Management	Print Spooler
ClipBook	Remote Access Auto Connection Manager
Distributed File System	Remote Access Connection Manager
Distributed Transaction Coordinator	Removable Storage
Fax Service	Routing And Remote Access
Indexing Service	Secondary Logon
Internet Connection Firewall (ICF)/ Internet Connection Sharing (ICS)	Smart Card
License Logging	Task Scheduler
Messenger	Telephony
NetMeeting Remote Desktop Sharing	Telnet
Network DDE	Uninterruptible Power Supply

The baseline GPO also enables the following Security Options policies:

- Devices: Restrict CD-ROM Access To Locally Logged-on User Only

- Devices: Restrict Floppy Access To Locally Logged-on User Only

- Interactive Logon: Require Domain Controller Authentication To Unlock Workstation

- Microsoft Network Client: Digitally Sign Communications (Always)

- Microsoft Network Server: Digitally Sign Communications (Always)

To deploy the baseline GPO, you create a new organizational unit called Servers in your Active Directory domain. You then create four organizational units beneath Servers, called DomCtrlrs, DHCP, FilePrint, and WebSvrs. Your plan is to create a GPO with role-specific settings for each of these four containers.

Based on this information, answer the following questions:

1. For the domain controllers, you want to capture as much auditing information as possible, and you have decided to configure all the audit policies in the Domain Controllers container's GPO to audit both successes and failures. Which of the following policies should you also configure to accomplish this goal? (Choose all correct answers.)

   a. Increase the default value of the Event Log policy, Maximum System Log Size

   b. Enable the Security Options policy, Audit: Audit The Use Of Backup And Restore Privilege

   c. Increase the default value of the Event Log policy, Maximum Security Log Size

   d. Disable the Security Options policy, Microsoft Network Client: Digitally Sign Communications (Always)

2. Which of the following system service policies should you set in the Domain Controllers container's GPO with a startup type of Automatic? (Choose all correct answers.)

   a. File Replication Service

   b. Routing And Remote Access

   c. Intersite Messaging

   d. Kerberos Key Distribution Center

   e. Remote Procedure Call (RPC) Locator

   f. Remote Access Auto Connection Manager

   g. License Logging

3. Each file and print server has one printer and two hard drives for user data storage in addition to the system drive. You want users to be able to access the data drives on all the servers using a single directory structure and you want all users on the network to be able to send jobs to the printer on every server. Which of the following policy settings should you include in the FilePrint container's GPO? (Choose all correct answers.)

   a. Add the shares on the file and print server drives to the Network Access: Shares That Can Be Accessed Anonymously security option

   b. Enable the Print Spooler service

   c. Disable the Microsoft Network Server: Digitally Sign Communications (Always) security option

   d. Enable the Distributed File System service

4. Which of the following policy changes can you configure in the GPO for the WebSvrs container to add protection from Internet intruders? (Choose all correct answers.)

   a. Enable the Network Access: Do Not Allow Anonymous Enumeration Of SAM Accounts And Shares security option

   b. Enable the Accounts: Rename Administrator Account security option

   c. Revoke the Administrators group's Debug Programs user right

   d. Disable the Interactive Logon: Do Not Require CTRL+ALT+DEL security option

Troubleshooting Lab

1. A user calls your company's network help desk to report that she has just sent a large print job to her departmental print server by mistake and wants to delete it from the print queue. However, when she tries to access the queue, she receives the error message "Unable to connect. Access denied." You log on from your workstation with the user's account and are able to access the print queue in the normal manner. Which of the following could be the problem?

   a. The Microsoft Network Server: Digitally Sign Communications (Always) security option is enabled on the print server.

   b. The Microsoft Network Server: Digitally Sign Communications (Always) security option is enabled on the user's workstation.

   c. The Microsoft Network Client: Digitally Sign Communications (Always) security option is enabled on the print server.

   d. The Microsoft Network Client: Digitally Sign Communications (Always) security option is enabled on the user's workstation.

2. In an effort to cooperate with your company's new emphasis on security, you have used GPOs to enable all the available audit policies on the computers that are running Windows Server 2003. A few days after making these changes, you unlock the data center to find that your domain controller has shut down during the night. Which of the following modifications might prevent this from happening again? (Choose all correct answers.)

   a. Revoke the Administrators group's Debug Programs user right.

   b. Increase the default value specified in the Maximum Security Log Size policy.

   c. Disable the Shutdown: Allow System To Be Shut Down Without Having To Log On security option.

   d. Disable the Audit: Shut Down System Immediately If Unable To Log Security Audits security option.

Chapter Summary

■ A Group Policy Object (GPO) is a collection of configuration parameters that you can use to secure a Windows Server 2003 installation. To deploy a GPO, you associate it with an Active Directory container, and all the objects in the container inherit the GPO configuration settings.

■ Audit and Event Log policies enable you to specify what types of information a computer logs, how much information the computer retains in the logs, and how the computer behaves when the logs are full.

■ Windows Server 2003 loads many services by default that a member server usually doesn't need. You can use a GPO to specify the startup types for the services on a computer.

■ The domain controller role is the only one that has its own default GPO assigned by Windows Server 2003. To create your own policy settings for domain controllers, you can modify the existing GPO or create a new one.

■ Infrastructure servers run network support services such as DNS, DHCP, and WINS.

■ DNS servers using Active Directory-integrated zones use the directory service to secure their data, but for servers that use file-based zones, you must take steps to secure the DNS database and log files.

■ On NTFS drives other than the system drive on computers running Windows Server 2003, the operating system assigns the Full Control permission to the Everyone group by default. You can use a GPO to protect the files on your server drives by assigning your own file systems permissions.

■ An Active Directory object can receive policy settings from multiple GPOs and apply them in a particular order.

■ Active Directory objects do not contain GPOs; they are only linked to them. You can link a single GPO to multiple objects and make global changes by modifying that single GPO.

■ Organizational unit objects inherit policy settings from the GPOs applied to their parent objects. Policy settings from a GPO linked directly to an object take precedence over settings inherited from a parent object's GPO.

■ The SCW is a powerful security tool in Windows Server 2003 with SP1. SCW creates XML-based security policies that can be applied directly to a server or converted to a GPO.

Exam Highlights

Before taking the exam, review the key points and terms that are presented below to help you identify topics you need to review. Return to the lessons for additional practice, and review the "Further Reading" sections in Part 2 for pointers to more information about topics covering the exam objectives.

Key Points

■ To create a secure baseline installation for computers that are running Windows Server 2003, you can use Group Policy Objects (GPOs) to deploy a wide variety of configuration settings.

■ Servers on a network usually perform specific roles that have their own security requirements. You can accommodate these roles by creating GPOs that build on your secure baseline.

■ Different server roles can require modifications to the baseline policy settings, new policy settings, or protection provided by other security features in the operating system or application.

■ You can apply multiple GPOs to a single Active Directory object, with the policy settings that the system applies last taking precedence.

■ Group policies flow downward through the Active Directory tree, much like file system permissions. A parent container with a GPO linked to it passes the policy settings down to its child containers.

■ Using Windows Server 2003 with SP1, you can create an SCW XML security template and apply it directly to a server, so you do not have to use a GPO.

Key Terms

Group Policy Object (GPO)   An Active Directory object that contains a hierarchy of policies that represent configuration parameters for users and computers. When you link a GPO to an Active Directory container object, Active Directory applies the policies in the GPO to all the objects in that container.

Infrastructure server   A server that provides network support services, such as DNS, DHCP, and WINS.

Organizational unit   A type of Active Directory object you can use to create a directory service hierarchy. Creating organizational units enables you to delegate administrative responsibility for parts of the Active Directory database and use inheritance to disseminate properties downward through the Active Directory tree.

Questions and Answers

Page
9-16

Lesson 1 Review

1. Which of the following audit policies enables you to tell what applications were running when a security event occurred?

    a. Audit Object Access

    b. Audit Privilege Use

    c. Audit Process Tracking

    d. Audit System Events

    c

2. After installing several member servers running Windows Server 2003 on your Active Directory network, you want to deploy a baseline security configuration that you have designed for the member servers only, using group policies. Which of the following tasks must you perform to accomplish this objective? (Choose all correct answers.)

    a. Create a new domain

    b. Create a new organizational unit

    c. Move the computer objects representing the member servers

    d. Create a new GPO

    e. Modify the domain GPO

    f. Apply a GPO to the Computers container

    g. Apply a GPO to an organizational unit

    b, c, d, and g

3. With which of the following Active Directory object types can you associate a GPO? (Choose all correct answers.)

    a. Domain

    b. Computer

    c. Site

    d. Organizational unit

    e. Container

    f. Group

    a, c, and d

Lesson 2 Review

1. Under what conditions can you not revoke the Debug Programs user right from all users and groups?

   When software developers are working with debugging tools on your network.

2. Which of the following tasks can users not perform when you enable the Security Options policy, Microsoft Network Server: Digitally Sign Communications (Always) on a computer running Windows Server 2003?

   a. Submit jobs to a print queue on the server

   b. View the print queues on the server

   c. Install printer drivers stored on the server

   d. Create printer shares on the server

   b

3. Enabling which of the following audit policies is likely to require changing the Maximum Security Log Size value as well?

   a. Audit Process Tracking

   b. Audit Policy Change

   c. Audit Account Logon Events

   d. Audit Directory Service Access

   a

Lesson 3 Review

1. In the GPO for your adatum.com domain, you define the Audit Account Logon Events policy by specifying that both successes and failures be audited. In the GPO for the sales.adatum.com domain, you leave the Audit Account Logon Events policy undefined. What will be the effective value for this policy for a computer in the sales.adatum.com domain?

   The policy will be undefined for computers in the sales.adatum.com domain.

2. Although Windows Server 2003 creates a GPO for the Domain Controllers container with default role-specific policy settings in it, you have other policy settings that you want to apply to your domain controllers. Which of the following methods can you use to apply these settings? (Choose all correct answers.)

   a. Modify the policy settings in the Domain Controllers container's existing GPO.

b. Create a new organizational unit object and create a GPO for it containing the desired policy settings. Then, move the Domain Controllers container to make it a child of the new object.

c. Create a second GPO for the Domain Controllers container.

d. Create a new child organizational unit object beneath the Domain Controllers container object, and then create a GPO for the new object containing the desired policy settings.

a and c

3. When creating a GPO for an organizational unit called Servers, you define a particular audit policy and configure it to audit successes only. When creating a GPO for an organizational unit called Infrastructure, which is a child of the Servers organizational unit, you configure the same policy to audit failures only. What is the effective value of that policy for a computer object in the Infrastructure container?

    a. Undefined

    b. Success only

    c. Failure only

    d. Success and Failure

    c

Page
9-47

Lesson 4 Review

1. List the operating systems supported by the SCW.

    Windows Server 2003 with SP1 and later

2. Which of the following tasks can you not do using the SCW UI?

    a. Create an SCW policy.

    b. Apply an SCW policy to a computer.

    c. Convert (transform) an SCW policy to a GPO.

    c

3. What is the command line required to convert an SCW policy named C:\SCW\SQLPOLICY.XML into a GPO named SQLSRVS?

    scwcmd transform /p:C:\SCW\SQLPOLICY.XML /g:SQLSRVS

Page
9-47
Case Scenario Exercise

Based on the information provided in the Case Scenario Exercise, answer the following questions:

1. For the domain controllers, you want to capture as much auditing information as possible, and you have decided to configure all the audit policies in the Domain Controllers container's GPO to audit both successes and failures. Which of the following policies should you also configure to accomplish this goal? (Choose all correct answers.)

    a. Increase the default value of the Event Log policy, Maximum System Log Size

    b. Enable the Security Options policy, Audit: Audit The Use Of Backup And Restore Privilege

    c. Increase the default value of the Event Log policy, Maximum Security Log Size

    d. Disable the Security Options policy, Microsoft Network Client: Digitally Sign Communications (Always)

    b and c

2. Which of the following system service policies should you set in the Domain Controllers container's GPO with a startup type of Automatic? (Choose all correct answers.)

    a. File Replication Service

    b. Routing And Remote Access

    c. Intersite Messaging

    d. Kerberos Key Distribution Center

    e. Remote Procedure Call (RPC) Locator

    f. Remote Access Auto Connection Manager

    g. License Logging

    a, c, d, and e

3. Each file and print server has one printer and two hard drives for user data storage in addition to the system drive. You want users to be able to access the data drives on all the servers using a single directory structure and you want all users on the network to be able to send jobs to the printer on every server. Which of the following policy settings should you include in the FilePrint container's GPO? (Choose all correct answers.)

    a. Add the shares on the file and print server drives to the Network Access: Shares That Can Be Accessed Anonymously security option

b. Enable the Print Spooler service

c. Disable the Microsoft Network Server: Digitally Sign Communications (Always) security option

d. Enable the Distributed File System service

b and d

4. Which of the following policy changes can you configure in the GPO for the Web-Svrs container to add protection from Internet intruders? (Choose all correct answers.)

a. Enable the Network Access: Do Not Allow Anonymous Enumeration Of SAM Accounts And Shares security option

b. Enable the Accounts: Rename Administrator Account security option

c. Revoke the Administrators group's Debug Programs user right

d. Disable the Interactive Logon: Do Not Require CTRL+ALT+DEL security option

a and b

Page
9-50
Troubleshooting Lab

1. A user calls your company's network help desk to report that she has just sent a large print job to her departmental print server by mistake and wants to delete it from the print queue. However, when she tries to access the queue, she receives the error message "Unable to connect. Access denied." You log on from your workstation with the user's account and are able to access the print queue in the normal manner. Which of the following could be the problem?

a. The Microsoft Network Server: Digitally Sign Communications (Always) security option is enabled on the print server.

b. The Microsoft Network Server: Digitally Sign Communications (Always) security option is enabled on the user's workstation.

c. The Microsoft Network Client: Digitally Sign Communications (Always) security option is enabled on the print server.

d. The Microsoft Network Client: Digitally Sign Communications (Always) security option is enabled on the user's workstation.

d

2. In an effort to cooperate with your company's new emphasis on security, you have used GPOs to enable all the available audit policies on the computers that are running Windows Server 2003. A few days after making these changes, you unlock the data center to find that your domain controller has shut down during the night. Which of the following modifications might prevent this from happening again? (Choose all correct answers.)

   a. Revoke the Administrators group's Debug Programs user right.

   b. Increase the default value specified in the Maximum Security Log Size policy.

   c. Disable the Shutdown: Allow System To Be Shut Down Without Having To Log On security option.

   d. Disable the Audit: Shut Down System Immediately If Unable To Log Security Audits security option.

   b and d

10 Deploying Security Configurations

Exam Objectives in this Chapter:

- Plan a strategy to enforce system default security settings on new systems.
- Deploy the security configuration for servers that are assigned specific roles.
- Create custom security templates based on server roles.

Why This Chapter Matters

In Chapter 9, "Hardening Servers," you learned how to configure security parameters for a computer running the Microsoft Windows Server 2003 family using Group Policy Objects (GPOs) and, for servers running Windows Server 2003 with Service Pack 1 (SP1), the Security Configuration Wizard (SCW). However, for a large network installation, the process of developing and deploying security policies consists of a good deal more than merely creating GPOs. To administer a large network, configuration techniques adequate to single computers or small installations are often impractical. Once you decide the security settings your network requires, you must test them carefully to determine whether they provide the security you need and to make sure that they do not interfere with your standard network operations. When you are ready to deploy your security configurations, you can use security templates to simplify the process.

Lessons in this Chapter:

Before You Begin

This chapter requires an understanding of the security parameters provided by Windows Server 2003 and the process of configuring them using Group Policy Objects. To perform the practice exercises in this chapter, you must install and configure Windows Server 2003 on your computer using the Setup procedure in "About This Book."

Lesson 1: Creating a Testing and Deployment Plan

Before you actually implement security policies on your production network, you must be sure that the settings you choose are suitable for your computer, that they function properly, and that they satisfy your organization's security requirements. To verify the functionality of your security configuration, the best practice is to first test it in a lab environment, and then to create a limited pilot deployment on your live network. Then, if the configuration exhibits no major problems, you can proceed to deploy it throughout your network.

After this lesson, you will be able to

- Create a plan for testing security configuration settings in a lab environment
- Plan a pilot deployment of new configuration settings on a live network

Estimated lesson time: 20 minutes

Creating a Testing Environment

For the initial testing phase of deploying a configuration, you want to implement your security parameter settings in a lab environment. The lab network environment should closely resemble the actual environment in which you will deploy your configurations, but should be isolated from your live production environment. The testing process consists of the following five basic steps:

- Creating a test plan
- Creating test cases
- Building a lab
- Conducting the tests
- Evaluating the results

These steps are discussed in the following sections.

Creating a Test Plan

For the first phase of the testing process, you should create a test plan that specifies what you want to accomplish and how the testing process will proceed. The specific goals for your test plan will vary depending on the nature of your organization and how it uses the network, but some of the most typical testing objectives are as follows:

- Hardware compatibility testing
- Application and operating system compatibility testing

- Hardware and software product evaluation

- Performance baseline determination

- Security testing

- Documentation of installation and configuration procedures

- Documentation of administrative procedures

Tip   While the focus of this lesson, and of the related 70-293 exam objectives, is on the configuration and deployment of security parameters, your test plan can and should encompass all aspects of network compatibility and performance.

In addition to general testing objectives such as these, you will probably also have goals that are specific to your organization and its security requirements. To achieve your testing objectives, your plan should specify elements such as the following:

- The structure of the test lab

- A list of all hardware, software, and personnel required for the testing process

- What tools and techniques the testers will use

- The methodology and duration for each phase of the testing

- How the testers will document the testing process and the results

Creating Test Cases

To test specific elements of your network installation, you create test cases. A *test case* is a procedure that fully tests a particular feature or setting. For example, if you have decided to use a particular set of account policy values to control your users' passwords, the test case for those policies might consist of implementing them on the lab network and then having people log on and off those computers, deliberately duplicating common user logon errors and attempting to guess passwords using the brute force method. The results for that test case might lead you to use the account policy parameters as is or it might lead you to modify them to enhance or reduce the security they provide.

As documented in the test plan, each test case should include the following information:

- The purpose of the test case

- The hardware and software required to perform the test

- The installation and configuration procedures required before the test can proceed

- The procedure for performing the test

Creating detailed and complete test cases is one of the most critical elements of the test plan. For the example given, it might be tempting to create a brief test case that specifies what account policy settings to use and, in general terms, how the testing should proceed. However, this practice introduces an element of chance that can jeopardize the validity of the test. If you create detailed, step-by-step testing procedures for your test cases, not only can you repeat the test using the exact same methodology, it is also possible for different people to perform the same test in the same way.

Building a Lab

The nature of the testing lab itself depends on a variety of factors, including the size and nature of the organization, the amount of testing to be done, the complexity of the network, and the duration of the testing process. Security configuration testing is not the only part of designing and constructing a network in which a lab environment is useful. You can use a lab for any or all of the following purposes:

- Developing the overall design of the network
- Evaluating hardware and software products
- Planning performance and capacity
- Determining bandwidth requirements
- Establishing administrative policies
- Training users and support staff
- Documenting deployment and administration procedures

For a large organization, a permanent lab installation can be a worthwhile investment that enables network administrators to continually evaluate upgrades and new technologies, in preparation for their deployment on the live network. For organizations that are not quite so large, or that have limited budgets, the lab can be an ad hoc arrangement that consists of computers and other equipment that administrators will later deploy in a production environment.

The object of creating a lab is to duplicate the organization's live computing environment as closely as possible, within practical limits. For some organizations, a simple isolated local area network (LAN), consisting of a handful of computers connected to a hub, is sufficient. For larger organizations, a more elaborate lab setup might be necessary. For example, if your network consists of offices at remote locations connected by wide area network (WAN) links, you might want to integrate the WAN links into your lab environment as well.

Real World   WAN Testing

While it would be impractical for most organizations to install expensive WAN connections solely for testing purposes, there are other ways to incorporate WAN links into your lab network. For a new network rollout, you might be able to use the WAN connections for the production network during a preliminary testing phase, and then use the same connections for the live deployment when you have completed the testing. You can also substitute lower-cost WAN technologies in the lab for the real ones on the production network.

For example, if your network design calls for T-1 leased lines to connect your offices, you can create a reasonable facsimile of the live network in the lab using modems and dial-up connections. Obviously, this type of arrangement does not enable you to test technology-dependent elements such as WAN bandwidth utilization, but it can provide a more accurate representation of your live production network than you could achieve with LAN technology alone.

Creating a WAN testing environment using actual WAN links obviously requires that you disperse the testing facilities among your network locations. Depending on the needs of your organization, you might want to build a lab network at each site so that the staff at each location can use its own lab network for its own testing and training operations, or you can create a satellite installation at each site, accessible through remote control and intended only to provide a terminus for the WAN connection.

Conducting the Tests

The ease or difficulty of the actual testing process depends largely on the amount of detail in your test plan. If you create highly specific test cases with step-by-step instructions for the testing procedure, virtually anyone can do the testing, as many times as needed. If your test cases are more general, you might have to count on the insight of the particular individuals who perform the tests to determine the results.

The first step of the testing process is to configure the computers and other components required for the test according to the specifications in your test case. Once you have created the environment you need, you can begin the actual testing.

Tip   In many cases, you can use this configuration process as an opportunity to test your deployment plans for hardware, software, or configuration settings. This is just one way you can integrate testing your security configuration into a comprehensive program of testing network administration and rollout.

When testing security configurations, your two main objectives are to determine whether the parameter settings you have chosen provide the security you need and whether the settings interfere with normal operation of the network. Your test cases should include procedures that duplicate all the network's standard functions with the security parameters in place. For example, you should have testers run all the applications and access all the network shares your users need, to ensure that the security parameters don't inhibit access to these resources. Then, the testers should attempt to bypass the security measures you have implemented, to see if they are secure enough, and duplicate typical user errors, such as incorrect logon passwords, to document the system's reaction.

Evaluating the Results

One of the most important elements of the testing process is careful documentation of every action and its results. Once the testing process is finished, you should have a complete record of everything that occurred, to be used in evaluation. With detailed test cases and well-documented test results, it is even possible for individuals not involved in making the decisions to do the testing, leaving the evaluation to the organization's policy makers.

As a result of the testing, you might decide that your security configuration parameters are acceptable as is, or you might have to modify them, in which case you should repeat the tests using the new settings. It is when you have to repeat the tests that you realize the benefits of creating detailed test cases. When you document the testing procedures completely, you can repeat them exactly and compare the results with the original tests.

Creating a Pilot Deployment

The one element that is extremely difficult to duplicate adequately in a lab environment, no matter what your budget, is network activity. While there are ways to generate traffic on a lab network, it is hard to duplicate actual working conditions. For this reason, it is a good idea to follow up your lab testing with a pilot deployment. A *pilot deployment* is an implementation of your actual configuration on the production network in a limited and controlled fashion.

The object of a pilot deployment is to select a small sampling of network users, deploy your tested hardware and software configurations on their computers, and have them work under normal operating conditions. A limited deployment like this enables you to monitor the performance of the network more closely and react quickly to any problems that arise. In addition, the pilot program enables you to refine and practice the deployment process you will use on the entire network; it is also an opportunity to train the help desk and other support personnel who will troubleshoot problems when the configuration goes live.

> **Important**   It is extremely important that your pilot deployment not include technologies or configuration settings that you haven't previously tested in a lab setting. Modifying the deployment between the lab phase and the pilot phase contaminates the results of the pilot project. If problems occur, you might not be able to determine whether they result from a fault in your original configuration or from the changes you made after testing.

Creating a Pilot Deployment Plan

As with the testing phase, planning and preparation are crucial to a successful pilot deployment. The users in the pilot program are not as rigidly controlled in their activities as the lab testers are, so there is no need to create specific user procedures. After all, the object of the pilot deployment is to have users work as they normally do. What does require careful planning, however, is the selection of the pilot users and creating a support system for them.

Selecting Users for a Pilot Deployment

There are three factors to consider when selecting the users who will participate in your pilot deployment: the nature of the configuration parameters you are rolling out, the users' roles in the organization, and the users' own capabilities. Depending on what parameters you are testing, you might want to select a single workgroup or department for the pilot plan, or you might want to select a cross-section of users throughout the organization. A single group or department is easier to monitor and troubleshoot, but a cross-section provides a better picture of the new configuration's effect on the entire network.

The users participating in a pilot plan should not be performing critical roles. The users must be able to tolerate some down time, should problems occur, without unduly affecting the company's business or reputation. In addition, the users you select should have temperaments that enable them to deal with problems without panic or hysterics.

Training Users and Support Staff

Your pilot plan should specify the training your selected users need to work with the new configuration. For a pilot deployment of new security parameters, the user training might consist of nothing more than a new logon procedure, but if you are deploying new applications or operating systems, more extensive training might be necessary. You can treat the user training as a dry run for the enterprise-wide deployment that is to follow, so the pilot program should include a complete training plan, including a curriculum, and identifying who will be performing the training and when.

Providing Technical Support

Because problems are likely to occur during a pilot deployment, your plan should also specify what technical support the users will receive and who will provide it. Depending on the nature of the deployment, you might want to have your regular help desk staff handle the pilot users' problems, or you might want to assemble a support staff specifically for the pilot project. If you choose the latter, you must create an entirely separate support network and inform the users how to report problems and to whom. As with the users, you might have to provide additional training for your support personnel if you are introducing new technologies in the pilot deployment.

The support staff for the pilot deployment must have protocols in place for rapidly escalating problems, particularly those that point to problems with the new technologies you are deploying. If serious problems occur, it might become necessary to abort the pilot deployment and return the network to its original configuration.

Creating a Rollback Procedure

Because of the limited scope of the pilot deployment, any problems that occur as a result of undiscovered incompatibilities or misconfigurations will not be widespread and should not have a serious effect on network productivity. However, you should always have a rollback procedure as part of your pilot deployment plan, so that you can return to your original network configuration if serious problems arise that demand further development and testing. Your plan should include detailed procedures for the rollback, plus specific conditions under which the rollback should occur.

> **See Also**   One of the best ways to implement a rollback strategy is to create a rollback security template using the Secedit.exe utility. For more information on using this tool, see Lesson 3 of this chapter.

Lesson Review

The following questions are intended to reinforce key information presented in this lesson. If you are unable to answer a question, review the lesson materials and try the question again. You can find answers to the questions in the "Questions and Answers" section at the end of this chapter.

1. What are the two main reasons for creating test cases with specific step-by-step testing procedures?

   _____

   _____

2. How does a pilot deployment differ from a lab testing program?

_____

_____

3. What is the function of a rollback procedure in a pilot deployment?

_____

_____

Lesson Summary

- Testing is an essential part of any security configuration deployment. A proper testing program consists of two main phases: lab testing and a pilot deployment.

- A testing lab is defined as a network that is isolated from the organization's production network and used to test specific network elements.

- A testing plan consists of individual test cases. A test case is a detailed procedure that fully tests a particular feature or setting.

- A pilot deployment is the introduction of technologies or configuration parameters that have already been tested in a lab onto a live production network on a limited basis.

- A pilot deployment plan specifies which users will participate in the deployment, how the users will be supported, and should include a rollback plan in the event that serious problems occur.

Lesson 2: Introducing Security Templates

Windows Server 2003 includes another mechanism for deploying security configuration settings called security templates. A *security template* is a collection of configuration settings stored as a text file with the .inf extension. A security template contains many of the same security parameters you learned to configure using Group Policy Objects and the SCW in Chapter 9, "Hardening Servers." Similar to the SCW, the security template presents settings in a unified interface and enables you to save your configurations as files and deploy them when and where they are needed.

After this lesson, you will be able to

- List the parameters you can modify using a security template
- Use the Security Templates snap-in for Microsoft Management Console (MMC)
- Describe the functions of the Windows Server 2003 pre-defined security templates

Estimated lesson time: 20 minutes

Understanding Security Templates

Security templates consist of policies and settings that you can use to control a computer's security configuration using local policies or group policies. You can use security templates to configure any of the following types of policies and parameters:

- **Account Policies**   Enables you to specify password restrictions, account lockout policies, and Kerberos policies

- **Local Policies**   Enables you to configure audit policies, user rights assignments, and security options policies

- **Event Log policies**   Enables you to configure maximum Event Log sizes and rollover policies

- **Restricted Groups**   Enables you to specify the users who are permitted to be members of specific groups

- **System Services**   Enables you to specify the startup types and permissions for system services

- **Registry permissions**   Enables you to set access control permissions for specific registry keys

- **File System permissions**   Enables you to specify access control permissions for NTFS files and folders

You can deploy security templates in a variety of ways, using Active Directory directory service Group Policy Objects, the Windows Server 2003 Security Configuration And

Analysis snap-in, the Secedit.exe command-line utility, or for servers running Windows Server 2003 with SP1, the SCW. When you associate a security template with an Active Directory object, the settings in the template become part of the GPO associated with the object. You can also apply a security template directly to a computer, in which case the settings in the template become part of the computer's local policies.

There are several advantages to storing your security configuration parameters in security templates. Because the templates are plain text files, you can work with them manually as with any text file, cutting and pasting sections as needed. Second, templates make it easy to store security configurations of various types, so that you can easily apply different levels of security to computers performing different roles.

Tip   Storing your security settings in templates also provides an adequate backup of a computer's security configuration that you can use to quickly and easily restore the system to its original configuration. For example, when working with GPOs, it is easy to forget what changes you have made, and manually restoring the GPO to its original configuration can be difficult. If you have a security template containing your original settings, you can simply apply it to the GPO to return to your default settings.

Using the Security Templates Console

To work with security templates, you use the Security Templates snap-in for Microsoft Management Console. By default, the Windows Server 2003 Administrative Tools menu does not include an MMC console containing the Security Templates snap-in, so you have to create one yourself using the MMC Add/Remove Snap-in function. When you do this, the console provides an interface like the one shown in Figure 10-1.

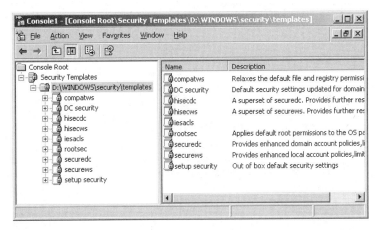

Figure 10-1   The Security Templates snap-in

The scope pane of the Security Templates snap-in contains a list of all the template files the program finds in the Windows\Security\Template folder on the system drive. The snap-in interprets any file in this folder that has an .inf extension as a security template, even though the extensions do not appear in the console.

Tip You can add security templates in other folders to the console by selecting New Template Search Path from the Action menu and then browsing to the folder containing your templates. Please note, however, that not all the files with .inf extensions on a computer running Windows Server 2003 are security templates. The operating system uses files with .inf extensions for other purposes as well.

When you expand one of the templates in the scope pane, you see a hierarchical display of the policies in the template (see Figure 10-2) as well as their current settings. You can modify the policies in each template just as you would using the Group Policy Object Editor console.

Exam Tip It is important to gain a familiarity with the functions and the interface of the Security Templates snap-in.

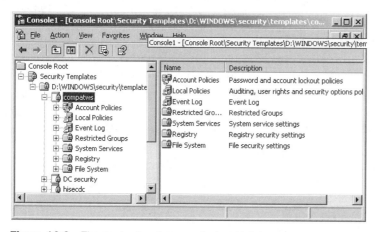

Figure 10-2 The contents of a security template

See Also For more information about configuring security policies, see Lessons 1 and 2 in Chapter 9, "Hardening Servers."

Using the Supplied Security Templates

Windows Server 2003 includes a selection of predefined security templates that you can use as is or modify to your needs. These templates provide different levels of security for servers performing specific roles. The predefined templates are as follows:

Setup Security.inf   Contains the default security settings created by the Windows Server 2003 Setup program. The settings in the template depend on the nature of the installation, such as whether it was an upgrade or a clean install. You can use this template to restore the original security configuration to a computer that you have modified.

Important   When you use a security template to restore a computer's default settings, remember that the template might overwrite existing permissions modified by the installation of other applications. After you restore the default settings, you might have to reinstall your applications or modify certain file system or registry permissions manually.

DC Security.inf   A computer running Windows Server 2003 creates this template only when you promote the computer to a domain controller. The template contains the default file system and registry permissions for domain controllers, as well as system service modifications.

Caution   The "Setup Security.inf" and "DC Security.inf" templates contain a large number of settings, and in particular a long list of file system permission assignments. For this reason, you should not apply these templates to a computer using group policies. Computers running Microsoft Windows operating systems periodically refresh group policy settings by accessing the GPOs on the network's domain controllers, and a template of this size can generate a great deal of Active Directory traffic on the network. Instead of using group policies, you should apply the template using the Security Configuration And Analysis snap-in or the Secedit.exe utility.

Compatws.inf   By default, the members of the local Users group on a computer running a Windows operating system can only run applications that meet requirements of the Designed for Windows Logo Program for Software. To run applications that are not compliant with the program, a user must be a member of the Power Users group. Some administrators want to grant users the ability to run these applications without giving them all the privileges of the Power Users group. The Compatws.inf template modifies the default file system and registry permissions for the Users group, enabling the members to run most applications, and also removes all members from the Power Users group.

> **Caution**   The Compatws.inf template is not intended for domain controllers, so you should not apply it to the default domain GPO or the Domain Controllers container's GPO.

Securedc.inf   This template contains policy settings that increase the security on a domain controller to a level that remains compatible with most functions and applications. The template includes more stringent account policies, enhanced auditing policies and security options, and increased restrictions for anonymous users and LanManager systems.

Securews.inf   This template contains policy settings that increase the security on a workstation or member server to a level that remains compatible with most functions and applications. The template includes many of the same account and local policy settings as Securedc.inf, and implements digitally signed communications and greater anonymous user restrictions.

Hisecdc.inf   This template contains policy settings that provide an even greater degree of security for domain controllers than the Securedc.inf template. Applying this template causes the computer to require digitally-signed communications and encrypted secure channel communications, instead of just requesting it, as Securedc.inf does.

Hisecws.inf   This template contains policy settings that provide higher security than Securews.inf on a workstation or member server. In addition to many of the same settings as Hisecdc.inf, the template remove all members from the Power Users group and makes the Domain Admins group and the local Administrator account the only members of the local Administrators group.

> **Tip**   The Securedc.inf, Securews.inf, Hisecdc.inf, and Hisecws.inf templates are all designed to build on the default Windows security settings, and do not themselves contain those default settings. If you have modified the security configuration of a computer substantially, you should first apply the "Setup Security.inf" template (and the "DC Security.inf" template as well, for domain controllers) before applying one of the secure or highly secure templates.

Rootsec.inf   This template contains only the default file system permissions for the system drive on a computer running Windows Server 2003. You can use this template to restore the default permissions to a system drive that you have changed, or to apply the system drive permissions to the computer's other drives.

> **Tip**   If you want to make changes to any of the policies in the pre-defined templates, it is a good idea to make a backup copy of the template file first, to preserve its original configuration. You can copy a template by simply copying and pasting the file in the normal manner using Microsoft Windows Explorer, or you can use the Security Templates snap-in by selecting a template and, from the Action menu, choosing Save As and supplying a new file name.

Exam Tip   Be sure to familiarize yourself with the security templates supplied with Windows Server 2003 and what settings they use to provide different levels of security.

Practice: Using the Security Templates Snap-in

In this practice, you use the Security Templates snap-in to create a new security template from one of the existing ones and modify it to provide a customized security level.

Exercise 1: Creating a Security Templates Console

Windows Server 2003 includes the Security Templates snap-in, but the operating system does not include a shortcut to a console containing the snap-in. In this procedure, you use Microsoft Management Console to create a Security Templates console.

1. Log on to Windows Server 2003 as Administrator.

2. Click Start and then click Run. The Run dialog box appears.

3. In the Open text box, type **mmc** and then click OK. The Console1 window appears.

4. From the File menu, select Add/Remove Snap-in. The Add/Remove Snap-in dialog box appears with the Standalone tab selected.

5. Click Add. The Add Standalone Snap-in dialog box appears.

6. Scroll down in the Available Standalone Snap-ins list and select Security Templates.

7. Click Add and then click Close. Security Templates appears in the Add/Remove Snap-in dialog box.

8. Click OK. A Security Templates entry appears in the Console Root window.

9. From the File menu, select Save As. The Save As dialog box appears.

10. In the File Name text box, type **Security Templates.msc** and then click Save. The name of the console shown in the title bar changes to Security Templates.

11. Leave the Security Templates console open for the next procedure.

Exercise 2: Modifying an Existing Template

In this procedure, you create a copy of one of the pre-defined Windows Server 2003 security templates and modify its policies to create a more secure environment.

1. In the Security Templates console, expand the Security Templates heading and the C:\Windows\Security\Templates subheading.

2. Click the Securews template in the scope pane and, from the Action menu, select Save As. The Save As dialog box appears.

3. In the File Name text box, type **Custom.inf** and then click Save. The Custom template appears in the scope pane of the console.

4. Expand the Custom template and Account Policies container. Click the Password Policy subheading.

5. In the details pane, double-click the Maximum Password Age policy. The Maximum Password Age Properties dialog box appears.

6. Change the Password Will Expire In selector value to 7 days and then click OK.

7. Click the Account Lockout Policy subheading and change the selector values of the account lockout policies to the following settings:

   ❑ Account Lockout Duration—0 Minutes

   ❑ Account Lockout Threshold—3 Invalid Logon Attempts

   ❑ Reset Account Lockout Counter After—180 Minutes

8. Expand the Local Policies container and then click the Security Options subheading.

9. Modify the values of the following security options as shown:

   ❑ Devices: Restrict CD-ROM Access To Locally Logged-on User Only—Enabled

   ❑ Interactive Logon: Prompt User To Change Password Before Expiration—1 Day

   ❑ Shutdown: Allow System To Be Shut Down Without Having To Log On—Disabled

10. Click the File System subheading and, from the Action menu, click Add File. The Add A File Or Folder dialog box appears.

11. In the Folder text box, type **D:** and then click OK. The Database Security For D:\ dialog box appears.

12. Click the Users group and, in the Permissions For Users box, select the Modify and Write check boxes in the Allow column. Then click OK. The Add Object dialog box appears.

13. Accept the default option button by clicking OK. The D:\ drive appears in the File System list.

14. Close the Security Templates console. A Microsoft Management Console dialog box appears asking whether you want to save the console settings to Security Templates.msc. Click Yes.

15. A Save Security Templates dialog box appears, prompting you to save the changes you made. Click Yes.

Lesson Review

The following questions are intended to reinforce key information presented in this lesson. If you are unable to answer a question, review the lesson materials and try the question again. You can find answers to the questions in the "Questions and Answers" section at the end of this chapter.

1. You are the new administrator for an Active Directory network, and while it is clear that someone has changed the security configuration of the network's domain controllers, your predecessor left no records of the exact changes he made. Which of the following security templates should you apply to the domain controllers to restore their default security settings, and then implement the highest possible level of security?

    a. Compatws.inf and then Securedc.inf

    b. Securedc.inf and then Hisecdc.inf

    c. Hisecdc.inf and then Setup Security.inf

    d. DC Security.inf and then Hisecdc.inf

    e. Setup Security.inf and then Securedc.inf

2. Why should you not use group policies to apply the "Setup Security.inf" template to a computer?

_____

_____

3. What are the four ways to apply a security template to a computer running Windows Server 2003 with SP1?

_____

_____

Lesson Summary

- A security template is a collection of configuration settings stored as a text file with an .inf extension.

- Security templates contain basically the same security parameters as Group Policy Objects, including account, local, and event log policies, file system and registry permissions, system service parameters, and restricted groups.

■ To create and modify security templates, you use the Security Templates snap-in for Microsoft Management Console.

■ To apply a security template to a computer, you can use group policies, the Security Configuration And Analysis snap-in, the Secedit.exe utility and, for servers running Windows Server 2003 with SP1, the SCW.

■ Windows Server 2003 includes a number of pre-defined templates that enable you to restore the default security parameters created by the Windows Setup program and to implement secure and highly secure configurations for workstations, member servers, and domain controllers.

Lesson 3: Deploying Security Templates

Once you have created or modified your security templates, it is time to deploy them on your computers running Windows operating systems. There are several methods you can use to apply security templates, which provide different capabilities, including mass deployments to groups of computers, scripted deployments, and analysis of a computer's existing security configuration.

After this lesson, you will be able to

- Use group policies to deploy security templates
- Use the Security Configuration And Analysis snap-in to compare a computer's security settings with a security template and apply a template to the computer
- Understand the functions of the Secedit.exe command line program
- Include a security template in an SCW security policy (XML file)

Estimated lesson time: 30 minutes

Using Group Policies

To configure a large group of computers in a single operation, you can import a security template into the Group Policy Object for a domain, site, or organizational unit object in Active Directory. However, there are a few cautions that you must observe when using group policies to deploy security templates.

Group Policy Deployment Cautions

As with other security settings, the configuration parameters you import into the Group Policy Object for a specific container are inherited by all the objects in that container, including other containers. Most networks use different levels of security for computers performing various roles, so it is relatively rare for administrators to apply a security template to a domain or site object, because then all the computers in that domain or site receive the same settings. At the very least, your domain controllers should have a higher level of security than the other computers on your network.

> **Tip**   When creating security templates for importation into group policies, the best practice is to place your computers into organizational units according to their roles and create individual templates for each organizational unit. This way you can customize the security configuration for each role, and modify the template for each role as needed, without affecting the others.

Another consideration when importing security templates into Group Policy Objects is the amount of data in the template itself. Every computer running a Windows operating system in an Active Directory container refreshes its group policy settings every 90 minutes, except for domain controllers, which refresh their settings every 5 minutes. It is possible for a security template to contain a large number of settings, and the continual refreshing of large templates to a large fleet of computers can generate a great deal of Active Directory traffic and place a heavy burden on the network's domain controllers.

> **Note** When you look at the sizes of the pre-defined security templates included with Windows Server 2003, it is easy to see which ones you should not deploy using group policies. Most of the templates are less than ten kilobytes, with the notable exceptions of the "DC Security.inf" and "Setup Security.inf" templates, which are 127 and 784 kilobytes respectively.

Deploying Security Templates Using Group Policies

To deploy a security template using group policies, you select an Active Directory object that has a GPO and import the template into the GPO. The template's settings then become part of the GPO, overwriting any existing values. The importation process proceeds as follows:

1. Open the Active Directory Users And Computers console.

2. Select the domain or organizational unit object to which you want to apply the template and, from the Action menu, choose Properties. The Properties dialog box for that object appears.

3. Click the Group Policy tab, select a Group Policy Object from the Group Policy Object Links list, and then click Edit. The Group Policy Object Editor console appears.

> **Tip** Instead of using an existing Group Policy Object, you can also create a new one by clicking New and then supplying a name for the GPO.

4. Under Computer Configuration, expand the Windows Settings subheading, and then click Security Settings.

5. From the Action menu, select Import Policy. The Import Policy From dialog box appears (see Figure 10-3).

6. Select the security template file you want to import, and then click Open. The settings in the template are imported into the Group Policy Object.

7. Close the Group Policy Object Editor console, and then click OK in the Properties dialog box for the object you selected.

8. Close the Active Directory Users And Computers console.

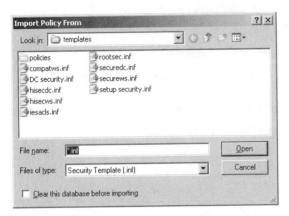

Figure 10-3   The Import Policy From dialog box

Using the Security Configuration And Analysis Tool

Security Configuration And Analysis is an MMC snap-in that you can use to apply a security template to the local computer interactively. However, in addition to configuring the security settings for the computer, the snap-in also provides the ability to analyze the current system security configuration and compare it to a baseline saved as a security template. This enables you to quickly determine whether someone has changed a computer's security settings and whether the system conforms to your organization's security policies.

As with the Security Templates snap-in, Windows Server 2003 does not include a shortcut to a Security Configuration And Analysis console, so you must add the snap-in to a console yourself. When you do this for the first time, the console contains nothing but the Security Configuration And Analysis heading, as shown in Figure 10-4.

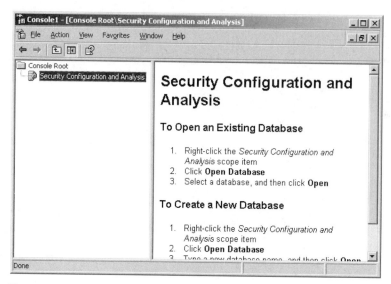

Figure 10-4   The Security Configuration And Analysis snap-in

Analyzing a System

To use the Security Configuration And Analysis snap-in, you must first create a database that will contain a collection of security settings. The database is the interface between the actual security settings on the computer and the settings stored in your security templates. After you create a database (or open an existing one), you then import a security template of your choice. Once you have imported a template you can proceed to apply the settings in that template to the computer or analyze the computer's current settings.

When you begin the analysis by selecting Analyze Computer Now from the Action menu, the system prompts you for the location of its error log file, and then proceeds to compare the settings in the template to the computer's current settings. Once the analysis is complete, the console produces a display similar to that of the Security Templates snap-in (see Figure 10-5), containing all the standard security settings found in a template.

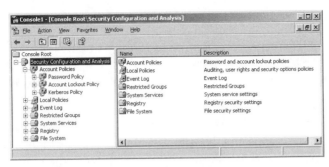

Figure 10-5   The contents of a security database

The big difference between the Security Templates console and this display, however, is that the policies listed in the details pane have columns containing the database settings and the computer settings. The Database Settings column contains the values imported from the template you selected, while the Computer Settings column contains the system's current settings. The comparison of the two values for each policy is reflected in the flag on each policy name, as shown in Figure 10-6. The meanings of the flags are as follows;

- **X in a red circle**   Indicates that the policy is defined in both the database and on the computer, but that the configured values do not match

- **Green check mark in a white circle**   Indicates that the policy is defined in both the database and on the computer, and that the configured values do match

- **Question mark in a white circle**   Indicates that the policy is not defined in the database and therefore was not analyzed, or that the user running the analysis did not have the permissions needed to access the policy on the computer

- **Exclamation point in a white circle**   Indicates that the policy is defined in the database, but does not exist on the computer

- **No flag**   Indicates that the policy is not defined in the database or on the computer

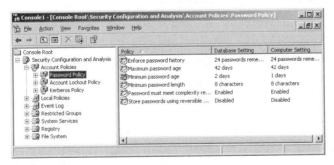

Figure 10-6   Results of a security analysis

Changing Security Settings

As you examine the elements of the database and compare the template values with those of the computer, you might find discrepancies and want to make changes to the computer's configuration. There are several ways in which you can do this, such as the following:

Apply the database settings to the computer   If you want to use the exact settings from the template that you imported into the database, you can simply select Configure Computer Now from the Action menu to apply them to the computer.

Modify the database settings   You can double-click any policy in the console tree to display its Properties dialog box and modify its value in the database.

> **Caution**   Modifying a policy value in the Security Configuration And Analysis snap-in changes the database value only, not the actual computer setting. For the changes you make to take effect on the computer, you must either apply the database settings to the computer using the Configure Computer Now command or export the database to a new template and apply it to the computer using any of the standard methods.

Create a new template   You can select Export Template from the Action menu to create an entirely new template from the settings currently in the database, and then apply the template to the computer using any of the standard methods.

> **Important**   The Export Template feature creates a new template from the current database settings at the time you execute the command, not from the computer's current settings.

Modify the computer's settings manually   You can always modify the computer's security settings directly by using a member server's Local Security Settings console (open the console by selecting Local Security Policy from the Administrative Tools menu), by modifying the appropriate Group Policy Object, or by manually manipulating file system or registry permissions.

Using Secedit.exe

Secedit.exe is a command prompt utility that can perform the same functions as the Security Configuration And Analysis snap-in. The advantage of Secedit.exe is that you can call it from scripts and batch files, enabling you to automate your security template deployments. Another big advantage of Secedit.exe is that you can use it to apply only part of a security template to a computer, something that you cannot do with the Security Configuration And Analysis snap-in or with Group Policy Objects. For example, if you want to apply the file system's permissions from a template, but leave all the other settings alone, Secedit.exe is the only way to do it.

To use Secedit.exe, you run the program from the command prompt with one of the following six main parameters, plus additional parameters for each function:

- **Configure** Applies all or part of a security database to the local computer. You can also configure the program to import a security template into the specified database before applying the database settings to the computer.

- **Analyze** Compares the computer's current security settings with those in a security database. You can configure the program to import a security template into the database before performing the analysis. The program stores the results of the analysis in the database itself, which you can view later using the Security Configuration And Analysis snap-in.

- **Import** Imports all or part of a security template into a specific security database.

- **Export** Exports all or part of the settings from a security database to a new security template.

- **Validate** Verifies that a security template is using the correct internal syntax.

- **Generaterollback** Creates a security template that you can use to restore a system to its original configuration after applying another template.

Using the Security Configuration Wizard

The SCW security policy settings overlap with those set using security templates (.inf files). On the SCW Security Policy File Name page (see Figure 10-7) you can include a security template if you want to add settings that cannot be configured directly from the SCW. If you attach a security template, and it contains settings that conflict with settings configured in the SCW, the SCW-configured settings have precedence.

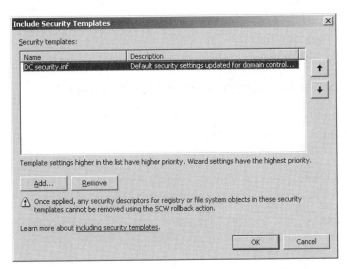

Figure 10-7 Including a security template in an SCW policy

In an environment utilizing Group Policy, the SCW, and multiple security templates, use the following guidelines to anticipate the precedence of security settings:

- Security policy applied through Active Directory–based GPOs has higher precedence than security policy applied through the SCW policy files (.xml files).

- Precedence among GPOs is unaffected by whether each GPO was created by Scwcmd.exe or not; only the standard Active Directory inheritance rules (in which local, site, domain, and organization unit GPOs are applied in succession) and link order determine precedence for GPOs.

- Security policy set in the SCW UI has higher precedence than conflicting policy set in .inf security templates that are attached to the .xml policy file.

- If multiple security templates are attached to the .xml security template, a template that is listed higher in the Include Security Templates dialog box has precedence over a template that appears lower in the list.

Important   Always test security policy in a lab before deploying it to your live production servers.

See Also   See Lesson 4 in Chapter 9, "Hardening Servers," for more information on the SCW UI and command line Scwcmd.exe.

Practice: Using the Security Configuration And Analysis Snap-in

In this practice, you add the Security Configuration And Analysis snap-in to the Security Templates console you created in the practice for Lesson 2 of this chapter, and then use the snap-in to analyze the computer in relation to one of the pre-defined security templates included with Windows Server 2003.

Exercise 1: Adding the Security Configuration And Analysis Snap-in

In this procedure, you create a comprehensive security template management tool by adding the Security Configuration And Analysis snap-in to the Security Templates console.

1. Log on to your computer running Microsoft Windows Server 2003 as Administrator.

2. Click Start, point to All Programs, point to Administrative Tools, and then click Security Templates.msc. The Security Templates console you created in the practice for Lesson 2 of this chapter appears.

3. From the File menu, select Add/Remove Snap-in. The Add/Remove Snap-in dialog box appears.

4. Click Add. The Add Standalone Snap-in dialog box appears.

5. Scroll down in the Available Standalone Snap-ins list and select Security Configuration And Analysis.

6. Click Add and then click Close. Security Configuration And Analysis appears in the Add/Remove Snap-in dialog box, along with the Security Templates snap-in that you added in the Lesson 2 practice.

7. Click OK. A Security Configuration And Analysis entry appears in the Console Root window.

8. From the File menus, select Save. Leave the console open for the next exercise.

Exercise 2: Analyzing a Computer

In this procedure, you use the Security Configuration And Analysis snap-in to compare the computer's current configuration with that of a security template.

1. In the Security Templates console you created, click the Security Configuration And Analysis heading in the scope pane.

2. From the Action menu, select Open Database. The Open Database dialog box appears.

3. In the File Name text box, type **Windb.sdb** and then click Open. The Import Template dialog box appears.

4. Click the Hisecdc.inf template, and then click Open.

5. From the Action menu, select Analyze Computer Now. The Perform Analysis dialog box appears.

6. Click OK to accept the default log file name. An Analyzing System Security message box appears to show a progress indicator as the snap-in performs the analysis.

7. When the analysis is complete, expand the Security Configuration And Analysis heading and the Account Policies heading in the console's scope pane.

8. Click the Password Policy subheading in the scope pane.

   Notice that the console has flagged three of the six password policies with a red X, indicating that the database settings for those policies do not match the template settings.

9. Double-click the Minimum Password Age policy in the details pane. The Minimum Password Age Properties dialog box appears.

10. Modify the Password Can Be Changed After selector value from 2 to 1, and then click OK.

    Notice that the red X next to the Minimum Password Age policy has changed to a green check mark. This is because you have changed the setting in the database to match that of the computer.

11. Click the Security Configuration And Analysis header in the scope pane.

12. From the Action menu, select Configure Computer Now. The Configure System dialog box appears.

13. Click OK to accept the default log file path. A Configuring Computer Security message box displays to show a progress indicator as the snap-in configures the computer using the settings in the database.

14. From the Action menu, select Analyze Computer Now a second time. The Perform Analysis dialog box appears.

15. Click OK to accept the default log file path. An Analyzing System Security message box appears to show a progress indicator as the snap-in performs the analysis.

16. When the analysis is complete, expand the Security Configuration And Analysis heading and the Account Policies heading in the console's scope pane.

17. Click the Password Policy subheading in the scope pane.

    Notice that all the password policies are now flagged with green check marks, indicating that the computer settings match the database settings. This is because you have just applied the database settings to the computer. Notice also that the Minimum Password Age value is 1 day instead of the 2 days specified in the His-ecdc.inf template. This is because you changed the value of this policy in the database prior to applying the database to the computer.

18. Close the Security Templates console. A Microsoft Management Console dialog box appears asking whether you want to save the console settings to Security Templates.msc. Click Yes.

Lesson Review

The following questions are intended to reinforce key information presented in this lesson. If you are unable to answer a question, review the lesson materials and try the question again. You can find answers to the questions in the "Questions and Answers" section at the end of this chapter.

1. Why is it not common practice to apply security templates to Active Directory domain objects?

    _____

    _____

2. Name two security template deployment tasks that the Secedit.exe utility can perform, which group policies and the Security Configuration And Analysis snap-in cannot.

_____

_____

3. When you use the Security Configuration And Analysis snap-in to export a template, where do the settings in the new template come from?

   a. From the computer's current security settings

   b. From the snap-in's currently loaded database

   c. From the security template you imported into the database

   d. From a Group Policy Object you specify

Lesson Summary

- You can use group policies to deploy security templates on multiple computers, but you must be aware that the GPO applies the template settings to all the computers in the container to which the GPO is linked.

- You should not use group policies to deploy large security templates, because of the burden they create on the network and on the domain controllers.

- You can use the Security Configuration And Analysis snap-in to deploy security templates on the local computer.

- The Security Configuration And Analysis snap-in can also analyze the computer's security configuration by comparing its current security settings to those of a security template and flagging the discrepancies.

- Secedit.exe is a command line tool that performs the same functions as the Security Configuration And Analysis snap-in, and can also apply specific parts of templates to the computer. You can use Secedit.exe in scripts and batch files to automate security template deployments.

- In the SCW, you can include a security template if you want to add settings that cannot be configured directly from SCW. If you attach a security template, and it contains settings that conflict with settings configured in the SCW, the SCW-configured settings have precedence.

Case Scenario Exercise

You are the network infrastructure design specialist for Litware Inc., a manufacturer of specialized scientific software products, and you have already created a basic network design for their new office building, as described in the Case Scenario Exercise in Chapter 1. You are currently in the process of designing a security infrastructure for the company's computers that run Windows Server 2003.

Unbeknownst to you, the IT directory at the home office has engaged a consulting firm to create a security configuration for all the company's Windows Server 2003 networks. Based on the requirements supplied by the home office, the consultants have supplied you with a series of security templates to implement their configurations for the various server roles. Based on this information, answer the following questions.

1. After receiving the security templates from the consultant, you examine one of them by creating a new database in the Security Configuration And Analysis snap-in on one of your Web servers, importing the new security template into the database, and performing an analysis. While examining the results of the analysis, you notice that there are quite a few discrepancies between the security settings you have configured on the computer and the settings in the template. You decide that you want to use a combination of the settings in the template and the settings you have already configured on the computer. Which of the following procedures should you use to create a composite security configuration and implement it on all your Web servers?

   a. In the new database you created, modify the values of the policies corresponding to the template settings you want to use. Then export the database to a new template and apply it to the Web servers' organizational unit object.

   b. In the new database you created, modify the values of the policies corresponding to the current computer settings you want to use. Then export the database to a new template and apply it to the Web servers' organizational unit object.

   c. Export the database to a new template without making any changes and apply it to the Web servers' organizational unit object.

   d. Use the Secedit.exe program to apply only the individual policy settings from the template you want to use on the Web servers.

2. Which of the following tools can you use to compare the templates supplied by the consultant with the security configurations you have already created on your servers? (Choose all correct answers.)

   a. The Security Templates snap-in

   b. Secedit.exe

   c. The Security Configuration And Analysis snap-in

   d. The Group Policy Object Editor console

3. To deploy the security templates, you begin by creating an organizational unit object for each server role in your Active Directory tree. Which of the following procedures can you use to apply the security templates to the organizational units?

   a. Use the Security Templates snap-in to create Group Policy Objects for each organizational unit using the supplied templates.

   b. Apply the templates to the correct organizational units using the Security Configuration And Analysis snap-in.

   c. Use Secedit.exe to apply the security templates to the appropriate Group Policy Objects.

   d. Create a Group Policy Object for each organizational unit and apply the appropriate template to it using the Group Policy Object Editor console.

Troubleshooting Lab

The director of IT for a growing company plans to install three new Windows Server 2003 domain controllers on the network, so she assigns each of the three new network administrators who have recently joined the firm the task of installing one of the new servers. She gives each of the administrators a worksheet containing the information they need to perform the installation, including the proper domain names and IP addresses. She also informs them that all the domain controllers on the company network must use the Hisecdc.inf security template included with Windows Server 2003, but with several key changes to certain security policies, which she supplies to them as a printed list of policies and their new values.

The three administrators, Tom, Dick, and Harry, each go off to perform their tasks separately. They proceed as follows:

■ Tom opens the Security Configuration And Analysis snap-in on his domain controller, creates a new database, and imports the Hisecdc.inf security template into it. After performing an analysis using the snap-in, Tom opens each policy on the list of changes the director has given him and modifies it to the value on the list.

■ Dick uses the Security Templates snap-in to create a new template containing the settings on the list of changes the director has given him. Then he creates two Group Policy Objects, links them both to the Domain Controllers organizational unit in Active Directory, and applies the templates to the Group Policy Objects, Hisecdc.inf to the first one and the new template he created to the second.

■ Harry uses the Security Templates snap-in to modify the Hisecdc.inf template by changing the policies on the list of changes to the values specified on the list. Then he uses the Secedit.exe utility to apply the modified template to the domain controller.

1. Based on this information, which of the following statements is true?

    a. None of the three administrators has correctly configured the new domain controllers with the appropriate security settings.

    b. One of the three domain controllers is correctly configured with the appropriate security settings; the other two are not.

    c. Two of the three domain controllers are correctly configured with the appropriate security settings; the other one is not.

    d. All three of the new domain controllers are correctly configured with the appropriate security settings.

Chapter Summary

- A proper testing program for a security configuration consists of two main phases: lab testing and a pilot deployment.

- A testing lab is defined as a network that is isolated from the organization's production network and is used to test specific network elements.

- A testing plan consists of individual test cases. A test case is a detailed procedure that fully tests a particular feature or setting.

- A pilot deployment is the introduction of technologies or configuration parameters that have already been tested in a lab onto a live production network on a limited basis.

- A security template is a collection of configuration settings stored as a text file with an .inf extension.

- Security templates contain basically the same security parameters as Group Policy Objects, including account, local, and event log policies, file system and registry permissions, system service parameters, and restricted groups. To apply a security template to a computer, you can use group policies, the Security Configuration And Analysis snap-in, or the Secedit.exe utility.

- Windows Server 2003 includes a number of pre-defined templates that enable you to restore the default security parameters created by the Windows installation program and to implement secure and highly secure configurations for workstations, member servers, and domain controllers.

- You should not use group policies to deploy large security templates, because of the burden they create on the network and on the domain controllers.

- You can use the Security Configuration And Analysis snap-in to deploy security templates on the local computer. The Security Configuration And Analysis snap-in can also analyze the computer's security configuration by comparing its current security settings to those of a security template and flagging the discrepancies.

■ Secedit.exe is a command line tool that performs the same functions as the Security Configuration And Analysis snap-in, and can also apply specific parts of templates to the computer. You can use Secedit.exe in scripts and batch files to automate security template deployments.

Exam Highlights

Before taking the exam, review the key points and terms that are presented below to help you identify topics you need to review. Return to the lessons for additional practice, and review the "Further Reading" sections in Part 2 for pointers to more information about topics covering the exam objectives.

Key Points

■ Security templates are text files containing security parameters that enable you to deploy configuration settings on your computers in a variety of ways, including group policies, the Security Configuration And Analysis snap-in, and the Secedit.exe utility.

■ You can create different security templates for the computers on your network performing specific roles, and deploy them for each role using a Group Policy Object linked to an Active Directory organizational unit object.

■ Using the Security Configuration And Analysis snap-in and a security template, you can analyze a computer to determine whether any of its security settings have been changed, and then, if necessary, apply the template to the computer to restore the modified parameters to their correct settings.

■ Secedit.exe enables you to apply all or part of a template to a computer from the command line. You can therefore integrate Secedit commands into scripts, to perform unattended system configurations.

Key Terms

Pilot deployment   The implementation of a tested configuration on a representative portion of a live production network. A pilot deployment enables you to test a configuration under real-world conditions with actual users, before you perform a general deployment on the entire network.

Rollback procedure   In the event that severe problems occur during a pilot deployment, you should always be prepared to roll your systems back to their original configuration. Before you begin the deployment, you should have a rollback procedure in place to make this possible.

Security template   A security template is a collection of configuration settings stored as a text file with an .inf extension. You can deploy templates in a variety of ways on multiple computers.

Questions and Answers

Page
10-8

Lesson 1 Review

1. What are the two main reasons for creating test cases with specific step-by-step testing procedures?

   To make it possible to repeat the tests exactly the same way

   To enable any user to perform the tests

2. How does a pilot deployment differ from a lab testing program?

   A pilot deployment is conducted on a live network using actual users performing their daily tasks in the usual manner.

3. What is the function of a rollback procedure in a pilot deployment?

   A rollback procedure enables you to abort the pilot deployment and return the network to its original configuration.

Page
10-17

Lesson 2 Review

1. You are the new administrator for an Active Directory network, and while it is clear that someone has changed the security configuration of the network's domain controllers, your predecessor left no records of the exact changes he made. Which of the following security templates should you apply to the domain controllers to restore their default security settings, and then implement the highest possible level of security?

   a. Compatws.inf and then Securedc.inf

   b. Securedc.inf and then Hisecdc.inf

   c. Hisecdc.inf and then Setup Security.inf

   d. DC Security.inf and then Hisecdc.inf

   e. Setup Security.inf and then Securedc.inf

   d

2. Why should you not use group policies to apply the "Setup Security.inf" template to a computer?

   Because the template contains a large number of file system and registry permissions, and the repeated refreshing of the group policy would generate a large amount of Active Directory traffic.

3. What are the four ways to apply a security template to a computer running Windows Server 2003 with SP1?

   Group policies, the Security Configuration And Analysis snap-in, the Secedit.exe command-line utility, and the SCW.

Page
10-28

Lesson 3 Review

1. Why is it not common practice to apply security templates to Active Directory domain objects?

   Because a security template applied to a domain object confers its settings on all the computers in the domain, and it is rare for computers performing different roles to use exactly the same security settings.

2. Name two security template deployment tasks that the Secedit.exe utility can perform, which group policies and the Security Configuration And Analysis snap-in cannot.

   Apply just a part of a security template to a computer and perform unattended template deployments using scripts or batch files.

3. When you use the Security Configuration And Analysis snap-in to export a template, where do the settings in the new template come from?

   a. From the computer's current security settings

   b. From the snap-in's currently loaded database

   c. From the security template you imported into the database

   d. From a Group Policy Object you specify

   b

Page
10-29

Case Scenario Exercise

Based on the information provided in the Case Scenario Exercise, answer the following:

1. After receiving the security templates from the consultant, you examine one of them by creating a new database in the Security Configuration And Analysis snap-in on one of your Web servers, importing the new security template into the database, and performing an analysis. While examining the results of the analysis, you notice that there are quite a few discrepancies between the security settings you have configured on the computer and the settings in the template. You decide that you want to use a combination of the settings in the template and the settings you have already configured on the computer. Which of the following procedures should you use to create a composite security configuration and implement it on all your Web servers?

   a. In the new database you created, modify the values of the policies corresponding to the template settings you want to use. Then export the database to a new template and apply it to the Web servers' organizational unit object.

   b. In the new database you created, modify the values of the policies corresponding to the current computer settings you want to use. Then export the database to a new template and apply it to the Web servers' organizational unit object.

   c. Export the database to a new template without making any changes and apply it to the Web servers' organizational unit object.

   d. Use the Secedit.exe program to apply only the individual policy settings from the template you want to use on the Web servers.

   b

2. Which of the following tools can you use to compare the templates supplied by the consultant with the security configurations you have already created on your servers? (Choose all correct answers.)

   a. The Security Templates snap-in

   b. Secedit.exe

   c. The Security Configuration And Analysis snap-in

   d. The Group Policy Object Editor console

   b and c

3. To deploy the security templates, you begin by creating an organizational unit object for each server role in your Active Directory tree. Which of the following procedures can you use to apply the security templates to the organizational units?

   a. Use the Security Templates snap-in to create Group Policy Objects for each organizational unit using the supplied templates.

   b. Apply the templates to the correct organizational units using the Security Configuration And Analysis snap-in.

   c. Use Secedit.exe to apply the security templates to the appropriate Group Policy Objects.

   d. Create a Group Policy Object for each organizational unit and apply the appropriate template to it using the Group Policy Object Editor console.

   d

<table>
<tr><td>Page
10-31</td><td>

Troubleshooting Lab

</td></tr>
</table>

The director of IT for a growing company plans to install three new Windows Server 2003 domain controllers on the network, so she assigns each of the three new network administrators who have recently joined the firm the task of installing one of the new servers. She gives each of the administrators a worksheet containing the information they need to perform the installation, including the proper domain names and IP addresses. She also informs them that all the domain controllers on the company network must use the Hisecdc.inf security template included with Windows Server 2003, but with several key changes to certain security policies, which she supplies to them as a printed list of policies and their new values.

The three administrators, Tom, Dick, and Harry, each go off to perform their tasks separately. They proceed as follows:

■ Tom opens the Security Configuration And Analysis snap-in on his domain controller, creates a new database, and imports the Hisecdc.inf security template into it. After performing an analysis using the snap-in, Tom opens each policy on the list of changes the director has given him and modifies it to the value on the list.

■ Dick uses the Security Templates snap-in to create a new template containing the settings on the list of changes the director has given him. Then he creates two Group Policy Objects, links them both to the Domain Controllers organizational unit in Active Directory, and applies the templates to the Group Policy Objects, Hisecdc.inf to the first one and the new template he created to the second.

■ Harry uses the Security Templates snap-in to modify the Hisecdc.inf template by changing the policies on the list of changes to the values specified on the list. Then he uses the Secedit.exe utility to apply the modified template to the domain controller.

1. Based on this information, which of the following statements is true?

   a. None of the three administrators has correctly configured the new domain controllers with the appropriate security settings.

   b. One of the three domain controllers is correctly configured with the appropriate security settings; the other two are not.

   c. Two of the three domain controllers are correctly configured with the appropriate security settings; the other one is not.

   d. All three of the new domain controllers are correctly configured with the appropriate security settings.

   c

11 Creating and Managing Digital Certificates

Exam Objectives in this Chapter:

- Configure Active Directory directory service for certificate publication.
- Plan a public key infrastructure (PKI) that uses Certificate Services.
    - Identify the appropriate type of certificate authority to support certificate issuance requirements.
    - Plan the enrollment and distribution of certificates.
    - Plan for the use of smart cards for authentication.

Why This Chapter Matters

The public key infrastructure (PKI) is an important element of the security philosophy of the Microsoft Windows Server 2003 family, and digital certificates provide the cornerstone of the PKI. With certificates, you can protect network data and secure communications using a variety of cryptographic algorithms and key lengths that enable you to implement as much security as you need for your organization. Before you actually use certificates on your network, you must understand the architecture of the PKI and create a plan that is suitable for your network.

Lessons in this Chapter:

Before You Begin

This chapter requires a basic understanding of Windows Server 2003 security, Active Directory directory service, and group policies. You should complete Chapter 8, "Planning a Secure Baseline Installation," and Chapter 9, "Hardening Servers," before beginning this chapter.

To perform the practice exercises in this chapter, you must have installed and configured Windows Server 2003 according to the procedure in "About This Book," and you must have installed Internet Information Services (IIS) on the computer, as described in the practice exercises for Chapter 7, "Clustering Servers."

Lesson 1: Introducing Certificates

As an increasing number of important business transactions are performed digitally, the issue of security for network communications has become vitally important. Digital transactions both within an organization and between organizations require protection from a variety of threats, including message interception, identity spoofing, and message repudiation. To provide this protection, Windows Server 2003 includes the components needed to create a PKI.

After this lesson, you will be able to

- List the capabilities of secret key encryption
- Describe the contents of a certificate
- Describe the function of a certification authority

Estimated lesson time: 20 minutes

Introducing the Public Key Infrastructure

A *public key infrastructure* is a collection of software components and operational policies that govern the distribution and use of public and private keys, using digital certificates. To protect data transmitted over a network, computers use various types of encryption to encode messages and create digital signatures that verify their authenticity. For one computer to encrypt a message and another computer to decrypt it, both must possess a key.

Understanding Secret Key Encryption

Encryption is essentially a system in which one character is substituted for another. If you create a key specifying that the letter A should be replaced by Q, the letter B by O, the letter C by T, and so forth, any message you encode using that key can be decoded by anyone else who has that key. This is called *secret key encryption*, because you must protect the key from compromise. For computer transactions, this simple type of encryption is all but useless, because there is usually no practical way to distribute the secret key to all recipients. After all, if the object is to send an encrypted message to a recipient over the network, it would hardly be appropriate to first send the secret encryption key in an unsecured message.

For encryption on a data network to be both possible and practical, computers typically use a form of public key encryption. In *public key encryption*, every user has two keys, a public key and a private key. As the names imply, the public key is freely available to anyone, while the private key is carefully secured and never transmitted over the network. The way the system works is that data encrypted with the public key can only be decrypted with the private key, and conversely, data encrypted with the private key can only be decrypted using the public key. It is the protection of the private key that guarantees the security of messages encrypted using this system.

Encrypting Data   If someone wants to send you a message making sure that no one but you can read it, that person must obtain your public key and use it to encrypt the message. The person can then transmit the message to you over the network, secure in the knowledge that only you possess the private key needed to decrypt it. Even if an intruder were to intercept the message during transmission, it would still be in its encrypted form, and therefore impenetrable. Once you receive the message and decrypt it using your private key, you could reply to it by using the other party's own public key to encrypt your response, which only that person can decrypt, using the private key.

Digitally Signing Data   If you want to send someone a message and have them be absolutely sure that it came from you, you can digitally sign it by using your private key to encrypt all or part of the data. Anyone receiving the message can then decrypt the encoded data using your public key. The fact that your public key successfully decrypted the message proves that you sent it, because only your private key could have encrypted it. This not only prevents other users from impersonating you by sending messages in your name, it also provides the recipient with proof that you sent the message, so that you cannot repudiate it later.

> **Note**   It is usually not practical to encrypt an entire message for the purpose of digitally signing it. Instead, most PKI systems create a hash from the message and then encrypt the hash using the private key. A *hash* is a digital summary of the message created by removing redundant bits according to a specialized hashing algorithm.

Verifying Data   When you want to be certain that the message you are sending to a recipient is not modified en route, you can use a hashing algorithm to create a hash from the message, and then encrypt both the message and the hash using your private key. When the message arrives at its destination, the recipient's computer decrypts the message using your public key, and then uses the same hashing algorithm to create a hash from the incoming message. If the hash included with the message matches the hash calculated by the receiving system, the message is verified as being unchanged since its transmission.

Using Certificates

For public key encryption to be a reliable form of communication, there has to be a verifiable mechanism for the distribution of public keys. Otherwise, an imposter could distribute a public key using another person's name, and receive encrypted messages intended for that person, which the imposter could decrypt using the corresponding private key. To distribute public keys, Windows Server 2003 and most other systems supporting a PKI use digital certificates. A *digital certificate* is a document that verifiably associates a public key with a particular person or organization.

Understanding Certificate Contents

A digital certificate contains the public key for a particular entity, such as a user or an organization, plus information about the entity and about the certification authority (CA) that issued the certificate. The Telecommunication Standardization Sector of the International Telecommunication Union (ITU-T) has published a standard called X.509 (03/00), "The Directory: Public-key and Attribute Certificate Frameworks," which defines the format of the certificates used by most PKI systems, including Windows Server 2003. In addition to the public key, every digital certificate contains these attributes:

- **Version**   Identifies the version of the X.509 standard used to format the certificate

- **Serial number**   A value assigned by the CA that uniquely identifies the certificate

- **Signature algorithm identifier**   Specifies the algorithm that the CA used to calculate the certificate's digital signature

- **Issuer name**   Specifies the name of the entity that issued the certificate

- **Validity period**   Specifies the period during which the certificate is valid

- **Subject name**   Specifies the name of the entity for which the certificate is issued

Most certificates also contain other attributes, which are specific to the certificates' intended functions.

To use public key encryption, you must obtain a certificate from an administrative entity called a *certification authority (CA)*. A CA can be a third-party company that is trusted to verify the identities of all parties involved in a digital transaction, or it can be a piece of software on a computer running Windows Server 2003 or another operating system. The type of CA you use for your organization depends on who is involved in the secure transactions.

Obtaining a certificate from a CA can be manual, with the user explicitly requesting that a CA issue a certificate, or automatic, with an application requesting and obtaining a certificate in the background as part of its normal function. No matter how the process occurs, the CA issues a public key and a private key as a matched pair. The private key is stored on the user's computer in encrypted form, and the public key is issued as part of a certificate. The certificate is essentially a carrier for the public key and related information, and facilitates the distribution of the key to the people that need it.

Using Internal and External CAs

For a certificate to be useful in securing a digital transaction, it must be issued by an authority that both parties to the transaction trust to verify each other's identities. When you are designing your own PKI for your network, you can deploy your own certificate authorities, or use a third-party CA, or both. Your choice typically depends on whether the parties involved in the transaction work for the same company or different ones.

If you want to ensure that internal communications in your organization are secure, you would be best served by installing your own CAs. Windows Server 2003 includes Certificate Services, a service that functions as a CA. All the users in your organization can usually trust a CA run by the company to verify other users' identities. However, if your organization engages in digital transactions with other companies, an internal CA is typically not useful, because the other companies are not going to trust your own CA to verify your identity.

For securing external transactions, the best practice is to obtain certificates from a neutral third-party organization that functions as a commercial certification authority. Companies such as Thawte and VeriSign, Inc., are examples of commercial CAs that are trusted throughout the IT industry.

Real World   Using Certificates

For a Windows operating system user, one of the most common occasions for encountering certificates occurs when you download software from the Internet and Microsoft Internet Explorer displays a dialog box, like the one in the following illustration, that prompts you to confirm that you want to install the software. This dialog box specifies the manufacturer of the software and indicates whether the download includes a certificate that verifies the source of the download.

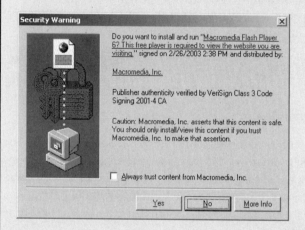

If a certificate is included, it contains the software manufacturer's public key, which your computer uses to decrypt the download's digital signature. If decryption is successful, you know that the software you downloaded was digitally signed using the private key corresponding to the public key in the certificate. As long as you trust the authority that issued the certificate to verify the software manufacturer's identity, you know that the download came from the manufacturer and was not tampered with en route.

Understanding PKI Functions

With a Windows Server 2003 PKI in place, network administrators can perform the following tasks:

- **Publish certificates**   Certificate Services can create certificates and publish them on a Web site or in Active Directory, where clients, such as users, computers, and applications, can retrieve them.

- **Enroll clients**   Enrollment is the term used to describe the process by which a client requests and receives a certificate from a certification authority. When a client requests a certificate, the CA (or the CA administrator) verifies the client's identity, and then issues a certificate in the client's name.

- **Use certificates**   Once a client requests and receives a certificate, the client can use it to secure its communications in various ways, depending on the capabilities of the certificate and the functions for which it was issued.

- **Renew certificates**   Certificates are typically valid for a finite period. At the end of that period, the client must either renew the certificate with the CA or stop using it.

- **Revoke certificates**   When a CA administrator explicitly revokes a certificate, the CA adds it to a certificate revocation list (CRL). The CA publishes this list at regular intervals, to inform the other systems on the network of certificates that they should no longer honor.

Practice: Viewing a Certificate

In this practice, you install the Macromedia Shockwave Player software on a computer running Windows Server 2003. During the installation procedure, you can display the certificate that verifies the identity of the software's publisher.

1. Log on to Windows Server 2003 as Administrator.

2. Click Start, point to All Programs, and then click Internet Explorer. A Microsoft Internet Explorer window appears.

3. From the Tools menu, select Internet Options, and then click the Security tab.

4. Move the Security Level For This Zone slider to Medium, and then click OK.

   Changing the Security Level prevents the Internet Explorer Enhanced Security Configuration feature from blocking access to the Certificate Services Web page.

5. In the Address text box, type **http://sdc.shockwave.com/shockwave/download** and then press Enter. The Macromedia Shockwave & Macromedia Flash Player Download Center page appears.

6. Click the Install Now button. The Security Warning dialog box appears.

   This dialog box specifies that you are about to install the Shockwave Player software and states that the computer has confirmed the authenticity of the publisher.

7. Click the Macromedia, Inc., hyperlink. The Certificate dialog box appears with the General tab active.

   Notice that the software uses a certificate supplied by VeriSign, which provides assurance that the software comes from the specified publisher and has not been modified.

8. Click the Details tab.

   This tab displays a list of all the certificate's attributes.

9. Click OK to close the Certificate dialog box, and then click Yes in the Security Warning dialog box. The software installation proceeds.

10. Close Internet Explorer after the installation completes.

Lesson Review

The following questions are intended to reinforce key information presented in this lesson. If you are unable to answer a question, review the lesson materials and try the question again. You can find answers to the questions in the "Questions and Answers" section at the end of this chapter.

1. Which of the following pieces of information is not included as part of a digital certificate?

   a. Validity period

   b. Private key

   c. Signature algorithm identifier

   d. Public key

2. For each of the following messaging scenarios, specify which key you should use to encrypt the message: the sender's public key, the sender's private key, the recipient's public key, or the recipient's private key.

   a. To send a message that can't be read by anyone but the recipient

   b. To assure the recipient that the message you are sending actually came from you

Lesson Summary

- Public key encryption uses two keys, a public key and a private key.

- Data encrypted with the public key can only be decrypted using the private key, and data encrypted using the private key can only be decrypted with the public key.

- A PKI is a collection of software components and operational policies that govern the distribution and use of public and private keys.

- Private keys must never be transmitted over a network. Public keys are distributed in digital certificates.

- Certificates are issued by a certification authority (CA). You can run your own CA using Windows Server 2003, or you can obtain your certificates from a third-party commercial CA.

Lesson 2: Designing a Public Key Infrastructure

As with most elements of a network, implementing a public key infrastructure requires careful planning before you begin deployment. Planning a PKI typically consists of the following basic steps:

- Defining certificate requirements

- Creating a certification authority infrastructure

- Configuring certificates

***

After this lesson, you will be able to

- List the types of certificates a Windows Server 2003 CA can issue
- Describe the structure of a CA hierarchy
- List the differences between enterprise and stand-alone CAs
- Configure certificate parameters

Estimated lesson time: 30 minutes

***

Defining Certificate Requirements

As in most phases of designing a network, the first step of the planning phase is to determine the requirements of the users. In the case of a PKI design, you must determine what your client's security needs are, how certificates can help provide that security, which users, computers, services, and applications will use certificates, and what kinds of certificates your clients need. In many cases, you will have already answered some or all of these questions as you developed an overall security strategy.

A PKI using computers running Windows Server 2003 can create certificates that support any or all of the following applications:

- **Digital signatures**   Used to confirm that the person sending a message, file, or other data is actually who he or she purports to be. Digital signatures do not protect the data itself from compromise; they only verify the identity of the sender.

- **Encrypting File System user and recovery certificates**   The Windows Server 2003 Encrypting File System (EFS) enables users to store data on disk in encrypted form, to prevent other users from accessing it. To prevent loss of data resulting from users leaving the organization or losing their encryption keys, EFS allows designated recovery agents to create public keys that can decode the encrypted information. As with IPSec, EFS does not have to use the PKI for its encryption keys, but the use of a PKI simplifies managing EFS.

- **Internet authentication** You can use the PKI to authenticate clients and servers as they establish connections over the Internet, so that servers can identify the clients connecting to them and clients can confirm that they are connecting to the correct servers.

- **IP Security** The IP Security extensions (IPSec) enable you to encrypt and digitally sign communications, to prevent them from being compromised as they are transmitted over a network. The Windows Server 2003 IPSec implementation does not have to use a PKI to obtain its encryption keys, but you can use the PKI for this purpose.

- **Secure e-mail** Internet e-mail protocols transmit mail messages in plain text, making it relatively easy to intercept them and read their contents. With the PKI, you can secure e-mail communications by encrypting the actual message text using the recipient's public key, and you can digitally sign the messages using your private key.

- **Smart card logon** A smart card is a credit card-size device that contains memory and possibly an integrated circuit. Windows Server 2003 can use a smart card as an authentication device that verifies the identity of a user during logon. The smart card contains the user's certificate and private key, enabling the user to log on to any workstation in the enterprise with full security.

- **Software code signing** Microsoft's Authenticode technology uses certificates to confirm that the software users download and install actually comes from the publisher and has not been modified.

- **Wireless network authentication** The increasing popularity of wireless local area networking (LAN) technologies, such as those based on the 802.11 standard, raises an important security issue. When you install a wireless LAN, you must make sure that only authorized users can connect to the network and that no one can eavesdrop on the wireless communications. You can use the Windows Server 2003 PKI to protect a wireless network by identifying and authenticating users before they are granted access to the network.

Once you have decided what applications you want to secure with certificates, you can create a plan indicating the level of security for each user. For example, you might decide that you want everyone on your network to use secured e-mail, while only the Research and Development and Accounting departments need IPSec for all their network communications. Users' locations can also be significant. You might want to use software code signing and Internet authentication for clients who connect to your network over the Internet, but omit these requirements for internal users.

When defining the certificate security requirements for your network, the best practice is to create a small set of security definitions and apply them to your users and computers as needed. For example, Table 11-1 shows a certificate plan for an organization that includes four levels of security: basic, medium, high, and external. The basic security level, applied to most of the users in the organization, uses certificates to provide encrypted e-mail and EFS services. Medium-level security, which is used for general users in more sensitive departments, adds IPSec to secure their LAN communications. Top-level executives and people working with highly sensitive information use high security and must use a smart card to log on to the network. Because the organization runs a Web site where registered customers can download software products, a special classification for external users calls for certificates that provide software code signing and Internet authentication.

Table 11-1   Sample Certificate Plan

Basic Security	Medium Security	High Security	External Security
Secure e-mail	Secure e-mail	Secure e-mail	Software code signing
EFS	EFS	EFS	Internet authentication
	IPSec	IPSec	
		Smart card logon	

Creating a CA Infrastructure

Once you have decided what you are going to use certificates for and who is going to need them, you can plan the infrastructure of certificate authorities that will provide the certificates you need. Certificate authorities function using a hierarchy in which each CA is validated by a CA at a higher level until you reach the root CA, the ultimate authority for the organization. CAs issue certificates not only to applications and users, but also to other CAs. If you trust a particular root CA, you should also trust any lower-level CAs that are authenticated and validated by that root CA. Trusts between CAs flow downward through the hierarchy, just as file system permissions do (see Figure 11-1).

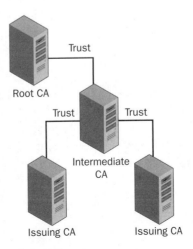

Figure 11-1   Certification authority trusts flow downward

When creating a CA infrastructure for your organization, you must decide how many CAs you need, who is going to provide them, where to locate them, and what the trust relationships between them should be.

Using Internal or External CAs

You can use either internal CAs running on your own computers or external CAs provided by a commercial service for all your certificate needs. Some applications (such as software code signing) clearly call for one or the other, but in many cases, the choice depends on the needs and capabilities of your organization. The advantages and disadvantages of using internal and external CAs are summarized in Table 11-2.

Table 11-2   Advantages and Disadvantages of Internal and External CAs

Advantages of an Internal CA	Disadvantages of an Internal CA	Advantages of an External CA	Disadvantages of an External CA
Direct control over certificates	Increased certificate management overhead	Instills customers with greater confidence in the organization	High cost per certificate
No per-certificate fees	Longer, more complex deployment	Provider liable for PKI failures	No autoenrollment possible
Can be integrated into Active Directory	Organization must accept liability for PKI failures	Expertise in the technical and legal ramifications of certificate use	Less flexibility in configuring and managing certificates
Allows configuring and expanding PKI for minimal cost	Limited trust by external customers	Reduced management overhead	Limited integration with the organization's infrastructure

In many cases, organizations use a combination of internal and external CAs. They use their own CAs to secure their internal communications and use external CAs when they must secure communications with outside parties, such as customers.

How Many CAs?

If you decide to use internal CAs for your network, the next step is to determine how many CAs you need and where to locate them. A single CA running on Windows Server 2003 can support as many as 35 million certificates, issuing two million or more a day. As a result, most organizations use multiple CAs due to logistical factors other than the number of certificates required.

A variety of factors affect the performance of a CA, and can influence your decision as to how many CAs you need. Some of these factors are as follows:

- **Number and speed of processors** The CPU performance of a server is the single most influential factor in that server's performance as a CA. A server with multiple processors or faster processors will perform better as a CA, particularly when issuing certificates with long encryption keys.

- **Key length** The length of the encryption keys in your certificates is a major factor in the impact of CA service on the computer's CPU. Longer keys require more processing time and can slow down the certificate enrollment process.

- **Disk performance** A high-performance disk subsystem in a CA can influence the certificate enrollment rate; however, the degree of influence depends on other factors, such as the CPU performance and key length. If the CA issues certificates with unusually long keys, processing time for each certificate increases, slowing down the enrollment rate and lessening the impact on the disk subsystem. With shorter keys, disk performance is more critical, because the disk subsystem can more easily become the bottleneck slowing down the enrollment rate.

Based on these criteria, many organizations would be adequately served by a single CA, but there are several reasons implementing multiple CAs anyway. One reason is fault tolerance. Having two or more CAs enables the PKI to service clients even if one of the servers fails. Another reason is load distribution when servicing an organization spread out over multiple locations. A corporation with several offices might want a CA in each office to reduce wide area network (WAN) traffic and to keep the certificate enrollment process local. It might also be necessary to deploy multiple CAs so that different servers can issue certificates for different purposes.

Creating a CA Hierarchy

When you deploy multiple CAs in a single organization, the relationships between them are hierarchical, based on a network of parent/child relationships. Every CA in a PKI is either a *root CA* or a *subordinate CA*. A root CA is the parent that issues certificates to the subordinate CAs beneath it. If a client trusts the root CA, it must also trust all the subordinate CAs that have been issued certificates by the root CA.

> **Note**   Root CAs are the only CAs that do not have a certificate issued by a higher authority. A root CA issues its own *self-signed certificate,* which functions as the top of the certificate chain for all the certificates issued by all the CAs subordinate to the root.

Subordinate CAs can also issue certificates to other subordinate CAs. In this case, the CA in the middle is called an *intermediate CA.* An intermediate CA is subordinate to the root CA but higher than the other subordinate CAs to which it issues certificates.

Every certificate issued by every CA in the hierarchy can trace its trust relationships back to a root CA. The CA that issues your certificate might possess a certificate issued by another CA, which in turn might possess a certificate issued by a root CA. This hierarchy of relationships is called a *certificate chain*. In Windows Server 2003, you can display the certificate chain for any certificate by clicking the Certification Path tab in the Certificate dialog box, as shown in Figure 11-2.

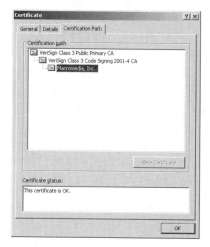

Figure 11-2 The Certification Path tab in the Certificate dialog box

In a large PKI implementation, a three-layer CA hierarchy like the one in Figure 11-1 is typical. The root CA exists only to issue certificates to the intermediate CAs, thereby functioning as the ultimate authority for the PKI. Beneath the CA are one or more intermediate CAs, which issue certificates to the subordinate CAs at the next level. Generally speaking, you create multiple intermediate CAs to separate different classes of certificates, for example, one intermediate CA for internal user certificates and one for external certificates. At the bottom layer of the hierarchy are the subordinate CAs, also known as *issuing CAs* because these servers actually enroll client users and applications. Intermediate and root CAs usually do not issue certificates directly to clients, only to subordinate CAs.

Tip The security of the higher-level CAs in a PKI hierarchy is critical, because if an intruder penetrates the security of one high-level CA, all its subordinates are compromised as well. For this reason, it is common practice to leave root and intermediate CAs offline after they issue certificates to their subordinates. You can take a CA offline by shutting down Certificate Services, by disconnecting the Windows Server 2003 CA server from the network, or by shutting the server down completely.

Understanding Windows Server 2003 CA Types

When you configure a server running Windows Server 2003 to function as a CA, you can configure it to be either a root CA or a subordinate CA. In addition, you select one of the following two types for the CA:

- **Enterprise**   *Enterprise CAs* are integrated into the Active Directory directory service. They use certificate templates, publish their certificates and CRLs to Active Directory, and use the information in the Active Directory database to approve or deny certificate enrollment requests automatically. Because the clients of an enterprise CA must have access to Active Directory to receive certificates, enterprise CAs are not suitable for issuing certificates to clients outside the enterprise.

- **Stand-alone**   *Stand-alone CAs* do not use certificate templates or Active Directory; they store their information locally. In addition, by default, stand-alone CAs do not automatically respond to certificate enrollment requests, as enterprise CAs do. Requests wait in a queue for an administrator to manually approve or deny them. Stand-alone CAs are intended for situations in which users outside the enterprise submit requests for certificates.

Whether you choose to create an enterprise CA or a stand-alone CA, you can also specify that the CA be a root or a subordinate. An enterprise root CA is the top of the hierarchy. There can only be one enterprise root in any CA hierarchy. All the other CAs in the hierarchy must be enterprise subordinate CAs.

Stand-alone CAs can function in the same type of hierarchy as enterprise CAs; you can create a stand-alone root CA with stand-alone subordinate CAs beneath it. If you want to create only one stand-alone CA for your PKI, it must be a root CA, because every CA hierarchy must be traceable back to a root.

Tip   If you plan to use smart cards to authenticate users on your network, you must create enterprise CAs, because smart card certificates must be associated with Active Directory user accounts to be functional.

Exam Tip   Be sure to understand the differences between enterprise root CAs, enterprise subordinate CAs, stand-alone root CAs, and stand-alone subordinate CAs.

Configuring Certificates

With your security requirements and your CA hierarchy design in place, you can decide on a configuration for the certificates that the CA will issue to your clients. Some of the criteria to consider when planning certificate configurations are as follows:

- **Certificate type**   Specifies the function of the certificate. Windows Server 2003 includes a collection of certificate templates that enable you to easily configure a CA to issue specific types of certificates.

- **Encryption key length and algorithm**   The length of the encryption keys included in your certificates and the encryption algorithm the certificates use dictate how difficult certificates are to penetrate and how secure the information they protect is. Longer keys provide greater security, but also require more processor time when creating and processing certificates. Different algorithms provide various degrees of security, also at the expense of processor time.

- **Certificate lifetime**   The lifetime of a certificate specifies how long the client can use it before it must be renewed. Longer lifetimes increase the chances that a certificate can be compromised. For certificates with longer encryption keys and stronger algorithms, however, longer lifetimes are often justified. Shorter lifetimes increase the number of certificates your CAs must issue, affecting network traffic and the server processing load. The default certificate lifetime for enterprise and stand-alone root CAs is two years.

- **Renewal policies**   You can configure a CA to issue new public and private keys when renewing a certificate or to re-use the existing keys. Issuing new keys increases the security the certificate provides, but also increases the processing load on the CA.

Practice: Installing a Windows Server 2003 Certification Authority

In this practice, you install Certificate Services on a computer running Windows Server 2003 and configure it to function as a stand-alone root CA.

> **Important**   Make sure that you have Internet Information Services (IIS) installed on the computer before you install Certificate Services.

1. Log on to Windows Server 2003 as Administrator.

2. Click Start, point to Control Panel, and then click Add Or Remove Programs. The Add Or Remove Programs dialog box appears.

3. Click Add/Remove Windows Components. The Windows Components Wizard appears.

4. Click Certificate Services (without selecting the check box), and then click Details. The Certificate Services dialog box appears.

5. Select the Certificate Services CA and the Certificate Services Web Enrollment Support check boxes, and then click OK.

   A Microsoft Certificate Services message box appears, warning you that once you install Certificate Services, you cannot change the computer's machine name or domain membership without affecting the function of the CA. Click Yes to continue.

6. Click OK in the Certificate Services dialog box.

7. In the Windows Components Wizard, click Next. The CA Type page appears.

8. Click the Stand-alone Root CA option button, and then click Next. The CA Identifying Information page appears.

9. In the Common Name For This CA text box, type **Issuing** and then click Next. The Certificate Database Settings page appears.

10. Click Next to accept the default database settings.

11. A Microsoft Certificate Services message box appears, stating that the system must temporarily stop the IIS service to complete the installation. Click Yes to proceed. The Configuring Components page appears, displaying a progress indicator as the wizard installs Certificate Services.

12. Another Microsoft Certificate Services message box appears, stating that the system must activate Active Server Pages (ASP) in IIS. Click Yes to proceed. The Configuring Components page finishes showing the progress of the installation.

13. When the Completing the Windows Components Wizard page appears, click Finish.

14. Close the Add Or Remove Programs dialog box.

Lesson Review

The following questions are intended to reinforce key information presented in this lesson. If you are unable to answer a question, review the lesson materials and try the question again. You can find answers to the questions in the "Questions and Answers" section at the end of this chapter.

1. Which of the following types of certificates can be issued only by an enterprise certification authority?

   a. IPSec

   b. Smart card logon

   c. Software code signing

   d. Wireless network authentication

2. Which of the following modifications to a certificate configuration does not increase the burden on the CA's processor?

   a. Increasing the key length

   b. Increasing the certificate's lifetime

   c. Issuing new keys with each certificate renewal

   d. Changing the certificate type

3. Where does a root CA obtain its own certificate?

   a. From a third-party certification authority

   b. From a subordinate CA

   c. From another root CA

   d. From itself

Lesson Summary

■ The first step in planning a PKI is to study what the security enhancements certificates can provide and determine which of your organization's security requirements you can satisfy with certificates.

■ Certificates are issued by certification authorities, which you can run on your own computers or obtain from third-party providers.

■ When running multiple CAs in an enterprise, you configure them in a hierarchy, with a root CA at the top, intermediate CAs at the second level, and subordinate (or issuing) CAs at the bottom.

■ Every certificate has a chain of trust relationships running from the CA that issued it all the way up to a root CA.

■ The configuration parameters of certificates themselves include the certificate type, the encryption algorithm and key length the certificates use, the certificate's lifetime, and the renewal policies that dictate how the CA behaves when processing certificate renewal requests.

Lesson 3: Managing Certificates

Once you have completed your PKI design and installed your CAs, the next step in deploying PKI to consider is the ongoing management of your CAs and their certificates. This includes administering certificate enrollment, managing the certificates themselves, and publishing certificate revocation lists.

After this lesson, you will be able to

- Control auto-enrollment in enterprise CAs
- Submit certificate requests to a CA using the Certificates console or the pages created by the Certificate Services Web Enrollment Support interface
- Publish certificate revocation lists

Estimated lesson time: 30 minutes

Understanding Certificate Enrollment and Renewal

The actual process by which CAs issue certificates to clients varies, depending on the types of CAs you have installed. If you have installed enterprise CAs, you can use *auto-enrollment*, in which the CA receives certificate requests from clients, evaluates them, and automatically determines whether to issue the certificate or deny the request. If you have installed stand-alone CAs, you cannot use auto-enrollment, so you must arrange for an administrator to monitor the CA (using the Certification Authority console) for incoming requests and to make decisions about whether to issue or deny the requests.

 Exam Tip   Be sure to understand the circumstances in which clients use auto-enrollment and manual enrollment, and to be familiar with the Microsoft Management Console (MMC) snap-ins used to manage certificates and certification authorities.

Using Auto-Enrollment

Auto-enrollment enables clients to automatically request and receive certificates from a CA with no manual intervention from administrators. To use auto-enrollment, you must have domain controllers running Windows Server 2003, an enterprise CA running on Windows Server 2003, and clients running Microsoft Windows XP Professional. You control the auto-enrollment process using a combination of group policy settings and certificate templates.

By default, Group Policy Objects (GPOs) contain settings that enable auto-enrollment for all user and computer objects in a domain. You configure these settings by opening the Autoenrollment Settings policy, located in the Windows Settings\Security Settings\Public Key Policies folder in both the Computer Configuration and User Configuration nodes in the Group Policy Object Editor. In the Autoenrollment Settings Properties dialog box (see Figure 11-3), you can disable auto-enrollment entirely for the objects receiving these GPO settings. You can also enable the objects to renew and update their certificates automatically.

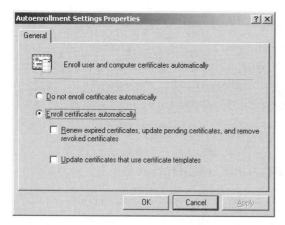

Figure 11-3   The Autoenrollment Settings Properties dialog box

The other mechanism you can use to control auto-enrollment is built into the certificate templates that define the properties of specific certificate types. To manage certificate templates, you use the Certificate Templates snap-in, as shown in Figure 11-4. Using this tool, you can specify the validity and renewal periods of specific certificate types and choose cryptographic service providers for them. Using the Security tab for a particular template, you can also specify which users and groups are allowed to request certificates using that template.

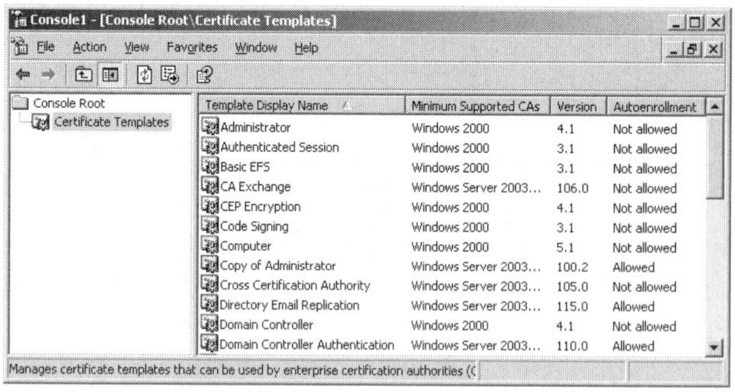

Figure 11-4   The Certificate Templates snap-in

When a client requests a particular type of certificate, the CA checks the properties of the client's Active Directory object to determine if the client has the permissions needed to receive the certificate. If the client has the appropriate permissions, the CA issues the certificate automatically.

Using Manual Enrollment

Stand-alone CAs cannot use auto-enrollment, so when a stand-alone CA receives a certificate request from a client, it stores the request in a queue until an administrator decides whether to issue the certificate. To monitor and process incoming requests, administrators use the Certification Authority console, as shown in Figure 11-5.

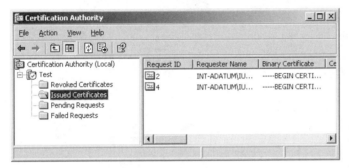

Figure 11-5   The Certification Authority console

In the Certification Authority console, incoming certificate enrollment requests appear in the Pending Requests folder. After evaluating the information in each request, an administrator can choose to issue or deny each request. Administrators can also view the properties of issued certificates and revoke certificates as needed.

Manually Requesting Certificates

In some cases, the process of requesting a certificate and receiving it from a CA is invisible to both the client and the administrator. Certain applications might request certificates and receive them in the background, then proceed to function in the normal manner. In other cases, however, users must explicitly request certificates, using one of the tools that Windows Server 2003 provides.

Using the Certificates Snap-in

The Certificates snap-in (see Figure 11-6) is a tool that you can use to view and manage the certificates of a specific user or computer. The snap-in's main display consists of folders that contain categories for all the certificates accessible to the designated user or computer. If your organization uses enterprise CAs, the Certificates snap-in also enables you to request and renew certificates using the Certificate Request Wizard and Certificate Renewal Wizard.

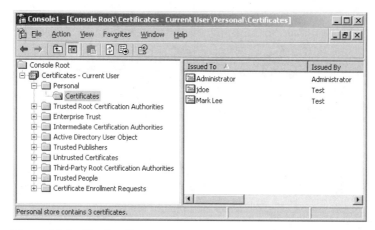

Figure 11-6   The Certificates snap-in

Off the Record   The Certificates snap-in is limited to use with enterprise CAs because the snap-in reads certificate information for the user or computer from Active Directory, and clients of stand-alone CAs are not expected to have access to Active Directory resources.

Using Web Enrollment

When you install Certificate Services on a computer running Windows Server 2003, you have the option of installing the Certificate Services Web Enrollment Support module as well. To function properly, this module requires you to have IIS installed on the computer first, along with support for ASP. Selecting this module during the Certificate Services installation creates a series of Web pages on the computer running the CA (see Figure 11-7); these pages enable users to submit requests for particular types of certificates.

Tip   You can also install the Certificate Services Web Enrollment Support module on a server running Windows Server 2003 that is not a CA, enabling you to integrate this module into existing Web servers.

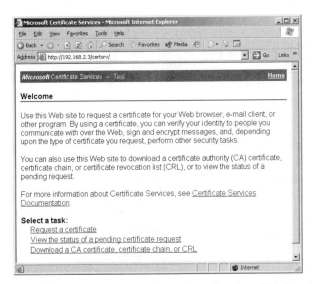

Figure 11-7   The Microsoft Certificate Services Web Enrollment Support interface

The Web Enrollment Support interface is intended to give internal or external network users access to stand-alone CAs. Because stand-alone servers do not use certificate templates, the requests submitted by clients must include all the necessary information about the certificates being requested and about the users of the certificates. When clients request certificates using the Web Enrollment Support interface, they can select from a list of predefined certificate types or create an advanced certificate request in which they specify all the required information in a Web-based form (see Figure 11-8).

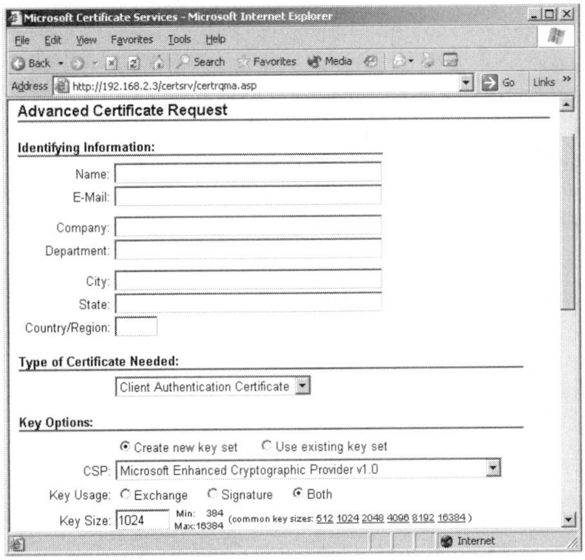

Figure 11-8   The Web Enrollment Support interface's Advanced Certificate Request page

Off the Record The Web Enrollment Support interface can generate requests for most certificate types, but not for certificates that are exclusive to enterprise CAs, such as smart card logon certificates.

Revoking Certificates

Several conditions can prompt an administrator to revoke a certificate. If a private key is compromised, or an unauthorized user has gained access to the CA, or even if you want to issue a certificate using different parameters, such as longer keys, you must revoke the certificates that are no longer usable. A CA maintains a CRL, which it publishes to clients on a regular basis. Enterprise CAs publish their CRLs in the Active Directory database, so clients can access them using the standard Active Directory communication protocol, called Lightweight Directory Access Protocol (LDAP). A stand-alone CA stores its CRL as a file on the server's local drive, so clients must access it using an Internet communications protocol, such as Hypertext Transfer Protocol (HTTP) or File Transfer Protocol (FTP).

Every certificate contains the path to the CA's distribution point for CRLs. You can modify this path in the Certification Authority console by displaying the Properties dialog box for the CA, and then clicking the Extensions tab (see Figure 11-9). However, if you plan to modify a CA's CRL distribution point, you must do so before it issues certificates. When an application authenticates a client using a certificate, it checks the CRL distribution point specified in the certificate, to make sure that the certificate has not been revoked. If the CRL is not at its specified distribution point, the application rejects the certificate.

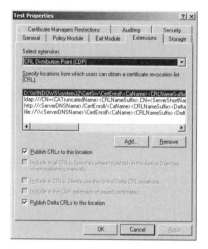

Figure 11-9 The Extensions tab in a CA's Properties dialog box

By selecting the Revoked Certificates folder in the Certification Authority console and then displaying its Properties dialog box (see Figure 11-10), you can specify how often the CA should publish a new CRL, and also configure the CA to publish delta CRLs. A *delta CRL* is a list of all certificates revoked since the last CRL publication. In organizations with large numbers of certificates, using delta CRLs instead of base CRLs can save a great deal of network bandwidth. For example, rather than publishing a base CRL every week, you can choose to publish delta CRLs weekly, and publish the base CRLs monthly.

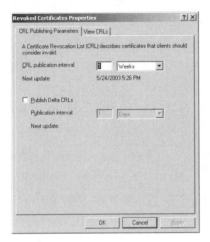

Figure 11-10   The Revoked Certificates Properties dialog box

Practice: Requesting a Certificate

In this practice, you use the Web Enrollment Support interface to request a certificate from the CA you installed in the Lesson 2 practice. Then, you instruct the CA to issue the certificate and use the Web Enrollment Support interface to retrieve it. Finally, you view the contents of the certificate using the Certificates snap-in.

Important   These practice exercises require you to have installed Certificate Services, as described in the Lesson 2 practice. In addition, you must have installed IIS on the computer before you installed Certificate Services, and have adjusted the security setting in Microsoft Internet Explorer as described in the Lesson 1 practice.

Exercise 1: Requesting a Certificate

In this exercise, you access the CA using the Web Enrollment Support interface and request a certificate from the CA.

1. Log on to Windows Server 2003 as Administrator.

2. Click Start, and then click Internet Explorer. A Microsoft Internet Explorer window appears.

3. In the Address text box, type **http://10.0.0.1/certsrv** and press Enter. The Microsoft Certificate Services Web page appears.

4. Click Request A Certificate. The Request A Certificate page appears.

5. Click Advanced Certificate Request. The Advanced Certificate Request page appears.

6. Click Create And Submit A Request To This CA. The Advanced Certificate Request form appears.

7. In the Name text box, type **Mark Lee**.

8. In the Type Of Certificate Needed drop-down list, select IPSec Certificate.

9. In the CSP drop-down list, select Microsoft Strong Cryptographic Provider.

10. In the Key Size text box, type **2048**, and then click Submit at the bottom of the form.

11. A Potential Scripting Violation message box appears, prompting you to confirm your request. Click Yes.

12. An Internet Explorer message box might appear to inform you that others might intercept information sent over the Internet. Click Yes to continue.

13. The Certificate Pending page appears, informing you that your request has been submitted to the CA.

14. Leave Internet Explorer running.

Exercise 2: Issuing a Certificate

In this exercise, you use the Certification Authority console to issue the certificate you requested in the first exercise.

1. Click Start, point to Administrative Tools, and then click Certification Authority. The Certification Authority console appears.

2. Expand the Issuing icon in the scope pane, and then click the Pending Requests folder.

3. The request you generated in the first exercise appears in the details pane.

4. Right-click the request and, from the shortcut menu, point to All Tasks, and then select Issue. The request disappears from the folder.

5. Click the Issued Certificates folder. Notice that the request you just approved now appears in the Issued Certificates list.

6. Close the Certification Authority console.

Exercise 3: Retrieving a Certificate

In this exercise, you use the Web Enrollment Support interface to retrieve the certificate you just issued.

1. Return to the Internet Explorer window.

2. In the Address text box, type **http://10.0.0.1/certsrv** and then press Enter. The Microsoft Certificate Services Web page appears.

3. Click View The Status Of A Pending Certificate Request. The View The Status Of A Pending Certificate Request page appears.

4. Click IPSec Certificate. The Certificate Issued page appears, stating that the certificate you requested was issued to you.

5. Click Install This Certificate. A Potential Scripting Violation message box appears, prompting you to confirm the installation of the certificate.

6. Click Yes. The Certificate Installed page appears.

7. Close Internet Explorer.

Exercise 4: Viewing a Certificate

In this exercise, you use the Certificates snap-in to view the certificate you just installed.

1. Click Start, and then click Run. The Run dialog box appears.

2. In the Open text box, type **mmc** and then click OK. The Console1 window appears.

3. From the File menu, select Add/Remove Snap-in. The Add/Remove Snap-in dialog box appears.

4. Click Add. The Add Standalone Snap-in dialog box appears.

5. In the Available Standalone Snap-ins list, select Certificates.

6. Click Add. The Certificates Snap-in dialog box appears.

7. Click Finish to accept the default My User Account option button, and then click Close. The Certificates—Current User snap-in appears in the Add/Remove Snap-in dialog box.

8. Click OK. A Certificates—Current User entry appears in the Console Root window.

9. Expand the Certificate—Current User icon, expand the Personal folder, and then click the Certificates subfolder. The certificate issued to Mark Lee appears in the details pane.

10. Double-click the Mark Lee certificate. A Certificate dialog box appears.

11. Click the Details tab.

    Notice that the Public Key entry detail shows the 2048-bit key length you specified in your request and the Enhanced Key Usage detail indicates that the certificate is to be used for IP Security.

12. Click OK to close the Certificate dialog box.

13. Close the Console1 window.

14. If a Microsoft Management Console message box appears, click No to save the console settings.

Lesson Review

The following questions are intended to reinforce key information presented in this lesson. If you are unable to answer a question, review the lesson materials and try the question again. You can find answers to the questions in the "Questions and Answers" section at the end of this chapter.

1. Which of the following tools does an administrator use to manually issue certificates to clients of a stand-alone CA?

   a. The Certificates snap-in

   b. The Certification Authority console

   c. The Web Enrollment Support interface

   d. The Certificate Templates snap-in

2. What is the advantage of using delta CRLs instead of base CRLs?

   _____

   _____

3. Which of the following must a user have to receive certificates from an enterprise CA using auto-enrollment? (Choose all correct answers.)

   a. Permission to use certificate templates

   b. Membership in an organizational unit to which administrators have applied a Group Policy Object

   c. Access to Active Directory

   d. Access to the Certificates snap-in

Lesson Summary

- Only enterprise CAs can use auto-enrollment, in which clients send certificate requests to a CA and the CA automatically issues or denies the certificate.

- For a client to receive certificates using auto-enrollment, it must have permission to use the certificate template for the type of certificate it is requesting.

- Stand-alone CAs do not use certificates or auto-enrollment. Certificate requests are stored in a queue on the CA until an administrator approves or denies them.

- Clients can request certificates using the Certificates console (for enterprise CAs only) or Web Enrollment Support pages (for stand-alone CAs).

- CAs publish certificate revocation lists (CRLs) at regular intervals, to inform authenticating computers of certificates that they should no longer honor.

Case Scenario Exercise

You are the network infrastructure design specialist for Litware Inc., a manufacturer of specialized scientific software products, and you have already created a network design for their new office building, as described in the Case Scenario in Chapter 1. You are designing a PKI solution for the entire corporate network, which will enable all network users to encrypt and digitally sign their e-mail. In addition, you want the employees of the R&D department, who work with highly sensitive data, to be authenticated using smart card logons, to store their data files using EFS, and to transmit their files in encrypted form using IPSec. You also want to enable registered users of the company's products to be able to download software updates from your company's Web servers without fear of viruses or other forms of tampering.

To achieve these goals, you have designed a hierarchy of certificate authorities using three levels. The design calls for a single enterprise root CA at the company's headquarters and one or more enterprise subordinate CAs at each of the company's branch offices. Depending on the number of users, an office might have a single issuing CA or an intermediate CA and two subordinate issuing CAs.

1. After the initial deployment of the PKI, which of the CAs can safely be taken offline? (Choose all correct answers.)

    a. The root CA

    b. The intermediate CAs

    c. One of the issuing CAs at each office with an intermediate CA

    d. All the issuing CAs

   2. Does the PKI design described here satisfy all the specified goals?

   a. Yes, the design satisfies all the specified goals.

   b. No, the design satisfies the goals for the network's internal users, but not for the external users.

   c. No, the design satisfies all the stated goals except for the goal of smart card logons.

   d. No, the design does not satisfy any of the stated goals.

   3. Which of the following procedures can you use to ensure that only the employees in the R&D department receive certificates for smart card logons, EFS, and IPSec?

   a. Grant the R&D users the permissions they need to access the Certificates console, which they can use to request the appropriate certificates.

   b. Using Group Policy Objects, turn off auto-enrollment for the domain and enable auto-enrollment for an organizational unit containing the R&D users.

   c. Grant the R&D users permission to use the Smartcard Logon, Basic EFS, and IPSec certificate templates.

   d. Install the Certificate Services Web Enrollment Support module and restrict access to the certificate enrollment Web pages to the R&D users.

Troubleshooting Lab

You are a user on a large corporate network, trying to secure your network communications using IPSec. After capturing a traffic sample, you discover that your transmissions are not being encrypted. The network uses certificates to provide IPSec encryption keys, issued by a hierarchy of stand-alone CAs that service the entire enterprise. You think that your transmissions are not being encrypted because you don't possess the correct certificate, so you open Microsoft Management Console, load the Certificates snap-in, and attempt to request an IPSec certificate. However, the snap-in displays an error message stating that the Certificate Request Wizard cannot start because no trusted CAs are available.

   1. Which of the following procedures would enable you to request the certificate you need?

   a. Log on to the workstation as Administrator and try requesting the certificate again.

   b. Use the Web Enrollment Support pages for your CA instead of the Certificates snap-in.

c. Call the network help desk and have someone give you the permissions you need to request the certificate.

d. Activate the Secure Server (Require Security) policy in your workstation's Local Security Settings console.

Chapter Summary

- Public key encryption uses two keys, a public key and a private key. Data encrypted with the public key can only be decrypted using the private key, and data encrypted using the private key can only be decrypted with the public key.

- A public key infrastructure is a collection of software components and operational policies that govern the distribution and use of public and private keys.

- Certificates are issued by a certification authority (CA). You can run your own CA using Windows Server 2003, or you can obtain your certificates from a third-party commercial CA.

- The first step in planning a PKI is to study what the security enhancements certificates can provide and determine which of your organization's security requirements you can satisfy with certificates.

- When running multiple CAs in an enterprise, you configure them in a hierarchy, with a root CA at the top, intermediate CAs at the second level, and subordinate (or issuing) CAs at the bottom.

- The configuration parameters of certificates themselves include the certificate type, the encryption algorithm and key length the certificates use, the certificate's lifetime, and the renewal policies that dictate how the CA behaves when processing certificate renewal requests.

- Only enterprise CAs can use auto-enrollment, in which clients send certificate requests to a CA and the CA automatically issues or denies the certificate.

- For a client to receive certificates using auto-enrollment, it must have permission to use the certificate template for the type of certificate it is requesting.

- Stand-alone CAs do not use certificates or autoenrollment. Certificate requests are stored in a queue on the CA until an administrator approves or denies them.

- CAs publish certificate revocation lists (CRLs) at regular intervals, to inform authenticating computers of certificates that they should no longer honor.

Exam Highlights

Before taking the exam, review the key points and terms that are presented next to help you identify topics you need to review. Return to the lessons for additional practice, and review the "Further Reading" sections in Part 2 for pointers to more information about topics covering the exam objectives.

Key Points

- In an Active Directory environment, you should create enterprise (as opposed to stand-alone) CAs. Enterprise CAs support auto-enrollment and use certificate templates and Active Directory object information to automatically issue certificates to clients.

- Certificate Services is a Windows Server 2003 service that enables administrators to configure, issue, and revoke digital certificates for specific security functions, such as secure e-mail, EFS, IPSec, Internet server authentication, and smart card logons.

- Windows Server 2003 Certificate Services supports two basic types of certification authorities: enterprise and stand-alone. Enterprise CAs are intended for internal clients and store their information in Active Directory. Stand-alone CAs are intended for external clients, and store their information in a database file.

- Clients can obtain certificates in three ways: through autoenrollment, by using the Certificates snap-in, and by using the Web Enrollment Support interface.

- A smart card is a portable device that contains a user's certificate and private key, enabling the user to log on to the network from any workstation equipped with the appropriate hardware. Support for smart card logons is provided only by enterprise CAs, in conjunction with Active Directory.

Key Terms

Public key encryption   A security system in which each user has two encryption keys, a public key and a private key. Data encrypted using the public key can only be decrypted by the private key and data encrypted using the private key can only be decrypted using the public key.

Hash   A digital summary of a message created by removing redundant bits according to a specialized hashing algorithm. Hashes are used to digitally sign messages and to confirm that messages have not been tampered with in transmission.

Delta CRL   A list containing only the certificates that have been revoked since the last certificate revocation list was published. Using delta CRLs instead of base CRLs (which contain the entire list of all revoked certificates) can save network bandwidth.

Questions and Answers

Page
11-8

Lesson 1 Review

1. Which of the following pieces of information is not included as part of a digital certificate?

    a. Validity period

    b. Private key

    c. Signature algorithm identifier

    d. Public key

    b

2. For each of the following messaging scenarios, specify which key you should use to encrypt the message: the sender's public key, the sender's private key, the recipient's public key, or the recipient's private key.

    a. To send a message that can't be read by anyone but the recipient

    The recipient's public key

    b. To assure the recipient that the message you are sending actually came from you

    The sender's private key

Page
11-17

Lesson 2 Review

1. Which of the following types of certificates can be issued only by an enterprise certification authority?

    a. IPSec

    b. Smart card logon

    c. Software code signing

    d. Wireless network authentication

    b

2. Which of the following modifications to a certificate configuration does not increase the burden on the CA's processor?

    a. Increasing the key length

    b. Increasing the certificate's lifetime

    c. Issuing new keys with each certificate renewal

    d. Changing the certificate type

    d

3. Where does a root CA obtain its own certificate?

   a. From a third-party certification authority

   b. From a subordinate CA

   c. From another root CA

   d. From itself

   d

Page
11-28

Lesson 3 Review

1. Which of the following tools does an administrator use to manually issue certificates to clients of a stand-alone CA?

   a. The Certificates snap-in

   b. The Certification Authority console

   c. The Web Enrollment Support interface

   d. The Certificate Templates snap-in

   b

2. What is the advantage of using delta CRLs instead of base CRLs?

   Delta CRLs only contain a list of the certificates revoked since the last CRL publication. They therefore save network bandwidth by reducing the size of the published list.

3. Which of the following must a user have to receive certificates from an enterprise CA using auto-enrollment? (Choose all correct answers.)

   a. Permission to use certificate templates

   b. Membership in an organizational unit to which administrators have applied a Group Policy Object

   c. Access to Active Directory

   d. Access to the Certificates snap-in

   a and c

Page
11-29

Case Scenario Exercise

Based on the information provided in the Case Scenario Exercise, answer the following questions:

1. After the initial deployment of the PKI, which of the CAs can safely be taken offline? (Choose all correct answers.)

   a. The root CA

   b. The intermediate CAs

   c. One of the issuing CAs at each office with an intermediate CA

   d. All the issuing CAs

   a and b

2. Does the PKI design described here satisfy all the specified goals?

   a. Yes, the design satisfies all the specified goals.

   b. No, the design satisfies the goals for the network's internal users, but not for the external users.

   c. No, the design satisfies all the stated goals except for the goal of smart card logons.

   d. No, the design does not satisfy any of the stated goals.

   b

3. Which of the following procedures can you use to ensure that only the employees in the R&D department receive certificates for smart card logons, EFS, and IPSec?

   a. Grant the R&D users the permissions they need to access the Certificates console, which they can use to request the appropriate certificates.

   b. Using Group Policy Objects, turn off auto-enrollment for the domain and enable auto-enrollment for an organizational unit containing the R&D users.

   c. Grant the R&D users permission to use the Smartcard Logon, Basic EFS, and IPSec certificate templates.

   d. Install the Certificate Services Web Enrollment Support module and restrict access to the certificate enrollment Web pages to the R&D users.

   c

Troubleshooting Lab

Based on the information provided in the Troubleshooting Lab, answer the following questions:

1. Which of the following procedures would enable you to request the certificate you need?

   a. Log on to the workstation as Administrator and try requesting the certificate again.

   b. Use the Web Enrollment Support pages for your CA instead of the Certificates snap-in.

   c. Call the network help desk and have someone give you the permissions you need to request the certificate.

   d. Activate the Secure Server (Require Security) policy in your workstation's Local Security Settings console.

   b

12 Securing Network Communications Using IPSec

Exam Objectives in this Chapter:

- Implement secure access between private networks.
    - Create and implement an IPSec policy.
- Configure network protocol security.
    - Configure protocol security in a heterogeneous client computer environment.
    - Configure protocol security by using IPSec policies.
- Configure security for data transmission.
    - Configure IPSec policy settings.
- Plan for network protocol security.
    - Specify the required ports and protocols for specified services.
    - Plan an IPSec policy for secure network communications.
- Plan security for data transmission.
    - Secure data transmission between client computers to meet security requirements.
    - Secure data transmission by using IPSec.
- Troubleshoot security for data transmission. Tools might include the IP Security Monitor MMC snap-in and the Resultant Set of Policy (RSoP) MMC snap-in.

Why This Chapter Matters

The Microsoft Windows Server 2003 family of operating systems includes a variety of security mechanisms, some of which you have studied in previous chapters. Until now, however, you have not learned how to protect data as it is transmitted across a network. In Windows Server 2003, IPSec is the primary mechanism for securing network transmissions, by both digitally signing and encrypting them. Although IPSec is easy to deploy in its default configuration, it is important for a network administrator to understand what is going on behind the scenes in IPSec communications, so you can implement a level of security appropriate to your needs and troubleshoot problems as they arise.

Lessons in this Chapter:

Before You Begin

This chapter assumes a basic understanding of TCP/IP communications, as described in Chapter 2, "Planning a TCP/IP Network Infrastructure." To perform the practice exercises in this chapter, you must have installed and configured Windows Server 2003 using the procedure described in "About This Book."

Lesson 1: Securing Internetwork Communications

Computers running Windows Server 2003 are designed to receive traffic from other computers over the network. The primary function of a server is to receive and process requests sent by clients. However, a computer that is left open to transmissions from other computers is also a security hazard, particularly if the server is accessible from the Internet. Unauthorized users might attempt to access the server for destructive purposes, such as to access confidential data files, introduce outside software, or simply to prevent others from using the server. One of the most common techniques firewalls use to prevent these kinds of intrusions is called *packet filtering*.

After this lesson, you will be able to

- Describe the function and usefulness of packet filtering
- List the well-known port numbers used by common applications and services
- List the criteria you can use to filter network traffic
- Describe the packet filtering functionality included in Windows Server 2003

Estimated lesson time: 30 minutes

Introducing Packet Filtering

Packet filtering is a method for regulating the TCP/IP traffic that is permitted to reach a computer or a network, based on criteria such as IP addresses, protocols, and port numbers. The system implementing the filter examines each packet as it arrives and determines whether it meets the criteria for admission. Packets that do meet the admission criteria are processed by the system in the normal manner; those that do not are silently discarded. For example, Internet e-mail servers typically use the Simple Mail Transfer Protocol (SMTP) and the Post Office Protocol 3 (POP3). These protocols use the port numbers 25 and 110, respectively. You can create a packet filter that permits only packets addressed to port numbers 25 and 110 to reach the server.

Understanding Ports and Protocols

In the packet header of each TCP/IP protocol at each layer of the Open Systems Interconnection (OSI) reference model, identifiers specify which protocol at the next layer should receive the packet. For example, a data-link layer protocol, such as Ethernet, has an Ethertype value in its header that specifies which network-layer protocol should process the packet. In the same way, at the network layer, the Internet Protocol (IP) has a Protocol field that specifies the transport-layer protocol that should receive the packet, and each transport-layer protocol has a Port field that specifies the application that should be the final recipient of the data in the packet.

The values for the TCP/IP port and protocol fields are assigned by an administrative body called the Internet Assigned Numbers Authority (IANA). Commonly used server applications have permanent port number assignments; these are called *well-known ports*. Clients often connect to a server using a port number chosen at random and used only for the duration of the transaction; this is called an *ephemeral port*. Some of the most commonly used well-known ports are listed in Table 12-1. (For the complete, updated list, refer to the IANA Port Numbers online database at *http://www.iana.org/assignments/port-numbers.*)

Table 12-1   Well-Known Port Numbers

Application	Abbreviation	Protocol	Port Number
File Transfer Protocol (Default Data)	ftp-default data	TCP	20
File Transfer Protocol (Control)	ftp-control	TCP	21
Telnet	telnet	TCP	23
Simple Mail Transfer Protocol	smtp	TCP	25
Domain Name Service	domain	TCP/UDP	53
Dynamic Host Configuration Protocol (Server) Bootstrap Protocol Server (nondynamic)	dhcps bootps	UDP	67
Dynamic Host Configuration Protocol (Client) Bootstrap Protocol Client (nondynamic)	dhcpc bootpc	UDP	68
World Wide Web HTTP	http	TCP	80
Post Office Protocol version 3	pop3	TCP	110
Simple Network Management Protocol	snmp	UDP	161
Simple Network Management Protocol Trap	snmptrap	UDP	162

Exam Tip   Be sure to familiarize yourself with the well-known port numbers assigned to the most commonly used services in Windows Server 2003, as listed in Table 12-1.

Packet filtering is used primarily by routers and firewalls that connect a private network to the Internet. However, you can use packet filtering inside a private network as well, to isolate one part of the network from the others. For example, you might have a separate local area network (LAN) dedicated to your organization's accounting department. You want to prevent unauthorized users on the rest of the network from trying to access information on the accounting servers, but the users on the accounting LAN still need to access resources elsewhere on the network. By installing a firewall between the accounting LAN and the rest of the network, you can regulate the traffic that is permitted onto the accounting LAN.

Most routers have packet filtering capabilities built into them, enabling you to implement filters at the boundaries between networks. The problem with integrating packet filters into a router is that the filters can introduce a large amount of overhead, slowing down the router's performance. The router must compare each incoming packet against all the filters, and then decide whether to admit the packet to the network. If you have a large, complex system of filters, the amount of time needed for the router to process each packet can become a major network performance bottleneck.

Separate firewall products are also likely to have packet filtering capabilities. Using firewall-based filters can be advantageous in two ways. First, by separating the routing and filtering functions on different systems, you are less likely to experience degraded network performance. Second, firewalls are likely to have more advanced packet filtering capabilities, such as preset filter configurations designed to protect against specific types of attacks.

> **See Also**   The capabilities of most packet filtering implementations are the same; what differs is the interface and the configurability of the filters. Two products might have the same basic filtering capabilities, but one with preset configurations and detailed documentation will be far easier to use than one that requires you to understand the ramifications of the filters you are creating.

Packet filtering is not a perfect security solution. It is still possible for intruders to attack a server using the ports and protocols that the firewall lets through, or to find a clever new way to bypass the filters you have in place. In some cases, packet filtering can be an ongoing battle of wits between the protector and a determined attacker. Every time the attacker finds a way to penetrate the filters, the system administrator modifies them to close the opening that is being exploited. Advanced packet filtering requires a detailed understanding of the TCP/IP protocols and the applications that use them.

Packet Filtering Criteria

Creating packet filters is a matter of selecting the specific criteria you want the system to examine and specifying the values that you want to allow or deny passage. Packet filters can be inclusive or exclusive. This means that you can start with a network connection that is completely blocked and use filters to specify what traffic can pass through, or you can start with a completely open connection and specify the types of traffic you want to block. The former is inherently more secure but can be more difficult to debug, because you must make sure that all the traffic that needs to pass through the filters is getting through.

> **Note**   Packet filtering can also work in either direction. You can use filters to prevent users on the Internet from accessing your private network, or you can use them to limit the Internet access granted to your internal users.

The criteria most commonly used in packet filtering are as follows:

■ **Port numbers**   Filtering by port numbers, also know as *service-dependent filtering*, is the most common type of packet filtering, and the most flexible. Because port numbers represent specific applications, you can use them to prevent traffic generated by other applications from reaching a network. For example, to protect a perimeter network containing your company's Web servers, you can create filters that allow only traffic using port 80 to enter from the Internet. Port 80 is the well-known port assigned to World Wide Web HTTP, the main application layer protocol used by Web servers.

■ **Protocol identifiers**   The Protocol field in every packet's IP header contains a code that identifies the protocol that should receive the packet next. In most cases, the code represents a transport layer protocol, such as Transmission Control Protocol (TCP) or User Datagram Protocol (UDP). However, IP datagrams frequently carry Internet Control Message Protocol (ICMP) messages as well. ICMP is another network layer protocol, but IP frequently uses it to transmit error messages and diagnostic packets, such as the Echo Request messages used by the Ping utility. Filtering using protocol identifiers is not very precise, because it blocks or allows all the traffic that uses a particular protocol. However, for certain applications, blocking an entire protocol is warranted, and is easier than anticipating the specific applications an attacker might use. For example, you might use protocol filters on a network that contains only Internet Web and FTP servers to limit incoming traffic to TCP packets. Because these servers rely on TCP for their primary functions, you can usually block all UDP and ICMP traffic, preventing attackers from using any application that relies on these protocols to attack your servers.

■ **IP addresses**   IP address filtering enables you to limit network access to specific computers. For example, if you have an Internet Web server on a LAN with other computers, and you want Internet clients to be able to access only the Web server, you can create a filter permitting only packets addressed to the Web server to enter the network from the Internet. IP address filtering is also useful for protecting part of a private network from users on the other parts. You can create filters that give only certain computers access to the protected LAN, while preventing all others from accessing it.

Security Alert   Filtering using IP addresses is not particularly secure if potential attackers have any way to discover the IP addresses of the computers on your network. Once an attacker finds out the IP addresses for which the filter allows access to the network, it is simple to impersonate another computer by using its IP address (which is called *spoofing*).

- **Hardware addresses**   Hardware addresses (also called media access control or MAC addresses) are coded into network interface adapters at the factory. Filtering based on hardware addresses provides the same basic functionality as IP address filtering. However, it is much more difficult to spoof a hardware address than an IP address, so using hardware addresses is inherently more secure than using IP addresses. Hardware address filtering is rarely used on Internet routers or firewalls, primarily because computers outside the private network have no way to discover the hardware addresses of the computers on the inside. For internal filtering, however, hardware addresses are a useful means of restricting access to specific resources.

The four criteria listed here correspond to the transport, network, data-link, and physical layers of the OSI reference model, as shown in Figure 12-1. Filters get more specific as you move up the OSI model. Filtering by port numbers enables you to specify which applications you want to permit through the filter, while filtering by IP addresses and hardware addresses enables you to block access by entire computers.

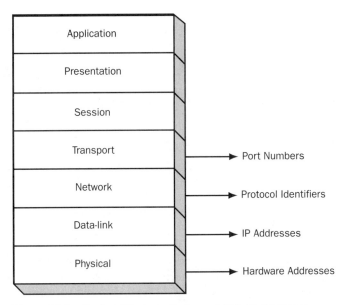

Figure 12-1   Packet filtering criteria and OSI model layers

The real strength of packet filtering as a security mechanism comes when you combine different types of filters to create a composite solution. For example, you might want to open up the Telnet port (port 23) so that administrators can remotely manage the company Web servers from home, using the Internet. However, leaving this port open is an invitation for unauthorized Internet users to access your servers for their own illicit reasons. By adding a filter that limits port 23 access to only your administrators' IP addresses, you add a measure of protection to the network.

Windows Server 2003 Packet Filtering

Windows Server 2003 contains three packet filtering implementations: the first is integrated into the TCP/IP client itself, the second is included in Windows Firewall (Windows Server 2003 Service Pack 1), and the third is included in the Routing and Remote Access service (RRAS). You can use these implementations to filter specific types of traffic entering the computer.

> **Caution**   You cannot use both Windows Firewall and RRAS. You must disable Windows Firewall /Internet Connection Sharing service before you can configure and enable RRAS.

Using TCP/IP Packet Filtering

The TCP/IP client in all the current versions of the Microsoft Windows operating system (including Windows Server 2003, Microsoft Windows XP, and Microsoft Windows 2000) includes a rudimentary packet filtering capability that you can use to specify what types of traffic are permitted to reach the TCP/IP protocol stack on the computer. This packet filtering implementation is relatively limited. You cannot filter out ICMP traffic and you cannot create exclusive filters. Exclusive filters enable you to specify the ports and protocols that you want to prevent from entering the system. TCP/IP client packet filtering is only inclusive: it can only specify the ports and protocols you want to allow in.

To configure the packet filtering capabilities of the TCP/IP client, use the following procedure:

1. From Control Panel, display the Network Connections window.

2. Select one of the connections in the window, and display its Properties dialog box.

   Each network interface has its own independent packet filtering implementation. You can create separate filters for each interface, providing different degrees of access to each network connection.

3. Display the Internet Protocol (TCP/IP) Properties dialog box for the connection.

4. Click Advanced, click the Options tab, and then click Properties. The TCP/IP Filtering dialog box appears, as shown in Figure 12-2.

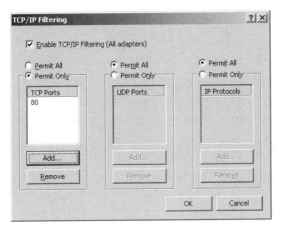

Figure 12-2   The TCP/IP Filtering dialog box

In this dialog box, you can specify the TCP ports, UDP ports, and IP protocols that packets must use if they are to access the TCP/IP stack. In each case, you must use the standard code numbers to reference the ports and protocols. The port numbers are listed in Table 12-1, earlier in this lesson, and the protocol codes are listed in Table 12-2. (For the complete, updated list, refer to the IANA Protocol Numbers online database at *http://www.iana.org/assignments/protocol-numbers.*)

Table 12-2   Protocol Codes

Protocol	Protocol Code
Internet Protocol (IP)	0
Internet Control Message Protocol (ICMP)	1
Transmission Control Protocol (TCP)	6
User Datagram Protocol (UDP)	17

Note   Although the codes for the IP and ICMP protocols are listed in Table 12-2, and you can specify them in the TCP/IP Filtering dialog box, they are both useless under normal conditions. The TCP/IP client cannot filter ICMP traffic, so specifying code 1 in the dialog box has no effect. Specifying code 0 indicates that you are permitting IP datagrams to contain other IP datagrams, which under normal conditions is not possible.

Using Windows Firewall Packet Filtering

Windows XP Service Pack 2 and Windows Server 2003 Service Pack 1 include the Windows Firewall, which provides a packet filtering mechanism that is more flexible than the TCP/IP client is for controlling inbound traffic. Windows Firewall implements exclusive inbound packet filtering and drops all inbound packets unless there is an enabled exception.

Windows Firewall supports two types of exceptions: ports and programs (applications or services).

- **Port exceptions**   Adding a port exception allows any program running on Windows Server 2003 to receive inbound traffic on the specified port number. For example, adding a port exception for port 80 will allow inbound World Wide Web (WWW) access.

- **Program exceptions**   Adding a program exception allows the specified program to receive inbound traffic on any port on which the program listens. For example, adding a program exception for an FTP server allows the FTP server to listen on the well-known ports 20 and 21 and allows it to open a dynamic port for each connecting client.

Security Alert   In most cases, it is more secure to add a program exception rather than a port exception.

Another benefit of Windows Firewall over the TCP/IP client packet filtering is the ability to configure the scope of an exception. By default, the scope of a Windows Firewall exception is Any Computer, which potentially includes computers on the Internet. By changing the scope of the exception, you can limit inbound access to other computers on the same network (subnet) or to a range of IP addresses.

See Also   The best resources to help you fully understand how Windows Firewall works are Windows Firewall Information and Help topics and the "Windows Firewall Operations Guide" available on the Microsoft TechNet Web site at *http://technet2.microsoft.com/WindowsServer /en/Library/c52a765e-5a62-4c28-9e3f-d5ed334cadf61033.mspx*.

Using Routing and Remote Access Service Packet Filtering

Windows Server 2003 RRAS includes a packet filtering mechanism that is more capable than that of the TCP/IP client, but you can only use it when you have configured Windows Server 2003 to function as a router. As with the TCP/IP client packet filtering mechanism, you can create different filters for each network interface on the computer. However, in RRAS packet filtering, there are a number of capabilities that TCP/IP client filtering does not have, such as the following:

- Creating filters based on the IP addresses, protocols, and port numbers of a packet's source or destination
- Creating inclusive or exclusive filters
- Creating filters for ICMP messages, specified by the message type and code values
- Creating multiple filters of the same type

Practice: Creating Packet Filters in Routing and Remote Access Service

In this practice, you use the Windows Server 2003 Routing And Remote Access console to examine the default packet filters created by RRAS and to create new packet filters of your own. This practice assumes that you've installed Windows Server 2003 on your computer according to the Setup procedure in "About This Book," and that the RRAS configuration has not changed since the Lesson 3 practice in Chapter 5, "Using Routing and Remote Access," in which you configured RRAS to function as a remote access server.

Exercise 1: Examining the Default Routing and Remote Access Service Packet Filters

In this exercise, you examine the packet filters that RRAS creates by default when you configure it to function as a remote access server using virtual private networks (VPNs).

1. Log on to Windows Server 2003 as Administrator.

2. Click Start, point to All Programs, point to Administrative Tools, and then select Routing And Remote Access. The Routing And Remote Access console appears.

3. Expand the SERVER01 (local) header, expand the IP Routing subheader, and then click the General icon. A list of network interfaces appears in the details pane.

4. In the details pane, click the WAN Connection interface and, from the Action menu, select Properties. The WAN Connection Properties dialog box appears.

5. In the General tab, click Inbound Filters. The Inbound Filters dialog box appears.

    Notice that there are six packet filters listed in the Filters list, and that the Drop All Packets Except Those That Meet The Criteria Below option button is selected.

6. Select the third entry in the Filters list, and then click Edit. The Edit IP Filter dialog box appears.

    Notice that this filter is designed to admit only packets in which the destination IP address is that of the RRAS server; the Protocol field selector value is the code for TCP; and the destination port number is 1723, which is the well-known port number for Point-to-Point Tunneling Protocol (PPTP). PPTP is a protocol used to establish VPN connections across the Internet. The other five filters in the Filters list enable traffic carrying messages generated by other applications, such as the Layer 2 Tunneling Protocol (L2TP) and Internet Key Exchange (IKE), to reach the system.

7. Click OK three times to close the Edit IP Filter, Inbound Filters, and WAN Connection Properties dialog boxes.

8. Leave the Routing And Remote Access console open for the next exercise.

Exercise 2: Creating New Packet Filters

In this exercise, you create a new packet filter using the Routing And Remote Access console.

1. In the details pane of the Routing And Remote Access console, select the Local Area Connection interface and, from the Action menu, select Properties. The Local Area Connection Properties dialog box appears.

2. In the General tab, click Inbound Filters. The Inbound Filters dialog box appears.

   Notice that there are no default packet filters created by RRAS for the Local Area Connection interface.

3. Click New. The Add IP Filter dialog box appears.

4. Select the Destination Network check box.

5. In the IP Address text box (under the Destination Network check box), type **10.0.0.1**.

6. In the accompanying Subnet Mask text box, type **255.255.255.255**.

   This filter will apply only to incoming packets that have the RRAS server's IP address as their destination.

7. In the Protocol selector, click ICMP. Two new text boxes, ICMP Type and ICMP Code, appear in the dialog box.

   Of the incoming packets addressed to the RRAS server, this filter will apply only to those in which the Protocol field of the IP header has a value of 1, signifying that the packets carry ICMP messages.

8. In the ICMP Type text box, type **8**.

9. In the ICMP Code text box, type **0** and then click OK. The new filter appears in the Inbound Filters dialog box.

   The function of an ICMP message is specified by the values of its ICMP Type and ICMP Code fields. This filter will block only the incoming ICMP messages addressed to the RRAS server that have a Type value of 8 and a Code value of 0, indicating that the packets contain ICMP Echo Request messages. Echo Requests are the messages used by the Ping utility to determine whether a system on the network with a specific IP address is functioning. Sometimes people use ICMP Echo Request messages to stage a denial-of-service attack against another computer. The computer that is the target of the attack is so busy processing Echo Request messages that it cannot perform its regular functions. This type of filter can prevent such an attack from succeeding.

10. Click OK twice to close the Inbound Filters and Local Area Connection Properties dialog boxes.

11. Close the Routing And Remote Access console.

Lesson Review

The following questions are intended to reinforce key information presented in this lesson. If you are unable to answer a question, review the lesson materials and try the question again. You can find answers to the questions in the "Questions and Answers" section at the end of this chapter.

1. Specify the well-known port numbers for each of the following applications.

   a. World Wide Web HTTP

   _____

   _____

   b. Dynamic Host Configuration Protocol (Server)

   _____

   _____

   c. Simple Mail Transfer Protocol

   _____

   _____

   d. Domain Name Service

   _____

   _____

   e. Telnet

   _____

   _____

2. Which of the following packet filtering criteria enable you to prevent a denial-of-service attack using ICMP messages?

    a. Port numbers

    b. Hardware addresses

    c. Protocol identifiers

    d. IP addresses

3. For each of the following packet filtering capabilities, identify whether the feature is supported in Windows Server 2003 with SP1 by TCP/IP client packet filtering, Windows Firewall, RRAS packet filtering, two of these, or all three of these.

    a. Creating filters that admit all port numbers except for the ones you specify

    TCP/IP client packet filtering: YES/NO

    Windows Firewall: YES/NO

    RRAS packet filtering: YES/NO

    b. Creating filters that block all ICMP messages

    TCP/IP client packet filtering: YES/NO

    Windows Firewall: YES/NO

    RRAS packet filtering: YES/NO

    c. Creating filters that block all protocols except for the ones you specify

    TCP/IP client packet filtering: YES/NO

    Windows Firewall: YES/NO

    RRAS packet filtering: YES/NO

    d. Creating filters that admit only packets using specific IP protocol code numbers

    TCP/IP client packet filtering: YES/NO

    Windows Firewall: YES/NO

    RRAS packet filtering: YES/NO

Lesson Summary

■ Packet filtering is a method for regulating the TCP/IP traffic that is permitted to reach a computer or a network, based on criteria such as IP and hardware addresses, protocols, and port numbers.

■ Packet filtering is a technique used primarily by routers and firewalls that connect a private network to the Internet, to protect the private network from Internet intrusion.

■ Windows Server 2003 with SP1 includes three packet filtering implementations: one in the TCP/IP client, one in Windows Firewall, and one in RRAS.

■ Service-dependent filtering using port numbers enables you to restrict traffic based on the application that generated the traffic or is destined to receive it.

■ The IANA assigns well-known port numbers to applications and services.

Lesson 2: Planning an IPSec Implementation

Many of the Windows Server 2003 security mechanisms you have studied so far in this book are designed to protect valuable data, but few of them are capable of protecting data while it is in transit over the network. You can store your files in encrypted form using the Encrypting File System (EFS), for example, or an individual application might be able to protect files with a password, but when you access the file over the network or send it to someone else, your computer always decrypts it first. The *IP Security extensions (IPSec)* are a means of securing the actual network communications themselves, so that intruders cannot compromise your data by intercepting it as it travels over the network.

After this lesson, you will be able to

- List the major threats to network communications
- Describe the functions of IPSec
- Understand the functions and architecture of the IPSec protocols

Estimated lesson time: 30 minutes

Evaluating Threats

When you log on to an FTP server on your network, you have to supply a user name and a password to be granted access. The FTP client program you use probably does not display the password on the screen as you type it, but of course the password must be included in the data packets the client sends over the network to the FTP server. Figure 12-3 shows a screen capture from Microsoft Network Monitor, which is displaying the contents of an FTP packet that the program captured from the network.

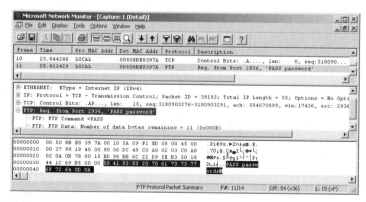

Figure 12-3   Network Monitor, displaying an FTP password

In this packet, you can clearly see the password (which is "password") associated with the user account that the client is supplying to the server. If you are a network administrator, and you use the Administrator account to access the FTP server, someone capturing the packets in this way could learn the Administrator password and possibly wreak havoc on the network.

Not all applications transmit passwords in clear text this way, however. When you log on to Active Directory, for example, the computer transmits your password in encrypted form. This is just an example of how easy it is for unauthorized people to capture and access your data as it is being transmitted. A user running a protocol analyzer such as Network Monitor can capture the packets containing your data files, your e-mail messages, or other confidential communications, and reconstruct the data for their own use.

There are many ways that unauthorized personnel can use this captured data against you, including the following:

- **Compromising keys**   In the same way that captured packets can contain passwords, they can also contain encryption keys. An intruder capturing a key can then decrypt any data using that key. The Public Key Infrastructure (PKI) used on networks running Microsoft Windows is not threatened by this practice, because it uses separate public and private keys for encryption and decryption, and the private keys are never transmitted over the network. However, other encryption systems use a single key to encrypt and decrypt data, and if an intruder captures that key, the entire security system is compromised.

- **Spoofing**   Spoofing is digitally masquerading as another person by using captured IP addresses and other information. By capturing network packets, an intruder can discover an actual user's IP address, packet sequence numbers, and the other personal information needed to create new packets that originated from the actual user's computer. Using this method, the intruder can send messages in the victim's name, receive data that was meant for the victim, and even engage in financial or other transactions using the victim's accounts. Sometimes an attacker will simultaneously initiate a denial-of-service attack on the victim's computer to prevent the victim from sending any further messages while the attacker assumes the victim's identity.

Security Alert   Even when you use applications that encrypt your passwords for transmission, it is still sometimes possible for intruders to use those passwords by simply pasting the encrypted string into a spoofed message. Even though the intruder doesn't actually know what the password is, the authenticating system could decrypt it and accept it as genuine.

- **Modifying data**   When intruders capture data packets from the network, they can not only read the information inside, they can also modify it, then send the packets to the recipient. The packets arriving at the destination therefore might contain information that the true sender did not create, even though the packets appear to be genuine.

- **Attacking applications**   In addition to modifying the data in captured packets, intruders might add their own software to the packets and use the packets to introduce the software into the destination computer. Viruses, worms, and Trojan horses are just some of the dangerous types of code that can infiltrate your network in this way.

Introducing IPSec

IPSec is designed to protect data by digitally signing and encrypting it before transmission. IPSec encrypts the information in IP datagrams by encapsulating it so that even if the packets are captured, none of the data inside can be read. Using IPSec protects your network against all the threats listed in the previous section.

Because IPSec operates at the network layer as an extension to the IP protocol, it provides end-to-end encryption, meaning that the source computer encrypts the data, and it is not decrypted until it reaches its final destination. Intermediate systems, such as routers, treat the encrypted part of the packets purely as payload, so they do not have to perform any decryption; they just forward the encrypted payload as is. The routers do not have to possess the keys needed to decrypt the packets, nor do they have to support the IPSec extensions in any way.

> **Off the Record**   By contrast, encrypting network traffic at the data-link layer would require that each router that forwards packets must decrypt the incoming data, then re-encrypt it again before transmitting it. This would add a tremendous amount of processing overhead to each router and slow down the entire network.

There are other protocols besides IPSec that provide network traffic encryption, such as Secure Sockets Layer (SSL), but these are application layer protocols that can encrypt only specific types of traffic. For example, SSL only encrypts communications between Web clients and servers. IPSec can encrypt any traffic that takes the form of IP datagrams, no matter what kind of information is inside them.

IPSec Functions

In addition to encrypting IP datagrams, the IPSec implementation in Windows Server 2003 provides a variety of security functions, including the following:

- **Key generation**   For two computers to communicate over the network using encrypted IP datagrams, both must have access to a shared encryption key. This key enables each computer to encrypt its data and the other computer to decrypt it. However, the key cannot be transmitted over the network without compromising the security of the system. Therefore, computers preparing to communicate with each other using IPSec both use a technique called the Diffie–Hellman algorithm to compute identical encryption keys. The computers publicly exchange information about the calculations that enable them to arrive at the same result, but they do not exchange the keys themselves or information that would enable a third party to calculate the key.

■ **Cryptographic checksums**   In addition to encrypting the data transmitted over the network, IPSec uses its cryptographic keys to calculate a checksum for the data in each packet, called a *hash message authentication code (HMAC),* then transmits it with the data. If anyone modifies the packet while it is in transit, the HMAC calculated by the receiving computer will be different from the one in the packet. This prevents attackers from modifying the information in a packet or adding information to it (such as a virus). IPSec supports two hash functions: HMAC in combination with Message Digest 5 (MD5) and HMAC in combination with Secure Hash Algorithm-1 (SHA1). HMAC-SHA1 is the more secure function, partly due to SHA1's longer key length (SHA1 uses a 160-bit key as opposed to the 128-bit key used by MD5). HMAC-MD5 is strong enough for a normal security environment, but HMAC-SHA1 is the better choice for a high-level security environment, and it meets the U.S. government's security requirements for high-level security.

■ **Mutual authentication**   Before two computers can communicate using IPSec, they must authenticate each other to establish a trust relationship. Windows Server 2003 IPSec can use Kerberos, digital certificates, or a preshared key for authentication. Once the computers have authenticated each other, the cryptographic checksum in each packet functions as a digital signature, preventing anyone from spoofing or impersonating one of the computers.

■ **Replay prevention**   In some cases, it is possible for attackers to use data from captured packets against you, even when the data in the packets is encrypted. Using traffic analysis, it is possible to determine the function of some encrypted packets. For example, the first few packets that two computers exchange during a secured transaction are likely to be authentication messages. Sometimes, by retransmitting these same packets, still in their encrypted form, attackers can use them to gain access to secured resources. IPSec prevents packet replays from being effective by assigning a sequence number to each packet. An IPSec system will not accept a packet that has an incorrect sequence number.

■ **IP packet filtering**   IPSec includes its own independent packet filtering mechanism that enables you to prevent denial-of-service attacks by blocking specific types of traffic using IP addresses, protocols, ports, or any combination of the three.

IPSec Protocols

The IPSec standards define two protocols that provide different types of security for network communications: IP Authentication Header (AH) and IP Encapsulating Security Payload (ESP). These protocols are discussed in the following sections.

IP Authentication Header

The IP Authentication Header protocol does not encrypt the data in IP packets, but it does provide authentication, anti-replay, and integrity services. You can use AH by itself or in combination with ESP. Using AH alone provides basic security services, with relatively low overhead. AH by itself does not prevent unauthorized users from reading the contents of captured data packets. However, using AH does guarantee that no one has modified the packets en route, and that the packets did actually originate at the system identified by the packet's source IP address.

> **See Also**   IPSec is capable of operating in two modes: transport mode and tunnel mode. These descriptions of the AH and ESP protocols refer to transport mode operations. For more information on tunnel mode, see "Transport Mode and Tunnel Mode" later in this lesson.

When a computer uses AH to protect its transmissions, the system inserts an AH header into the IP datagram, immediately after the IP header and before the datagram's payload, as shown in Figure 12-4.

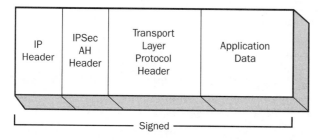

Figure 12-4   The AH header location

The contents of the AH header are shown in Figure 12-5, and the functions of the header fields are as follows:

- **Next Header**   Contains a code specifying the protocol that generated the header immediately following the AH header, using the protocol codes specified by the IANA. If IPSec is using AH alone, this field contains the code for the protocol that generated the datagram's payload, which is usually TCP, UDP, or ICMP.

> **Note**   The IP header has a Protocol field that contains a code identifying the protocol that generated the datagram's payload. Normally, this code has a value of 6 for the TCP protocol, 17 for UDP, or 1 for ICMP. However, in a packet using AH, the Protocol field has a value of 51, because the AH header immediately follows the IP header. The Next Header field in the AH header contains the code representing the TCP, UDP, or ICMP protocol that generated the payload.

- **Payload Length**   Specifies the length of the AH header.
- **Reserved**   Unused.
- **Security Parameters Index**   Contains a value that, in combination with the packet's destination IP address and its security protocol (AH), defines the datagram's *security association*. A security association is a list of the security measures, negotiated by the communicating computers, that the systems will use to protect the transmitted data.
- **Sequence Number**   Contains a value that starts at 1 in the first packet using a particular security association, and is incremented by 1 in every subsequent packet using the same security association. This field provides IPSec's anti-replay service. If an IPSec system receives packets with the same sequence numbers and the same security association, it discards the duplicates.
- **Authentication Data**   Contains an *integrity check value (ICV)* that the sending computer calculates, based on selected IP header fields, the AH header, and the datagram's IP payload. The receiving system performs the same calculation and compares its results to this value.

> **Note**   The ICV is the message authentication code. Its main purpose is to authenticate a message and verify its integrity.

Next Header	Payload Length	Reserved
Security Parameters Index		
Sequence Number		
Authentication Data		

Figure 12-5   The AH header format

IP Encapsulating Security Payload

The IP Encapsulating Security Payload (ESP) protocol is the one that actually encrypts the data in an IP datagram, preventing intruders from reading the information in packets they capture from the network. ESP also provides authentication, integrity, and anti-replay services. Unlike AH, which inserts only a header into the IP datagram, ESP inserts a header and a trailer, which surround the datagram's payload, as shown in Figure 12-6. The protocol encrypts all the data following the ESP header, up to and including the ESP trailer. Therefore, someone who captures a packet encrypted using ESP could read the contents of the IP header, but could not read any part of the datagram's payload, including the TCP, UDP, or ICMP header.

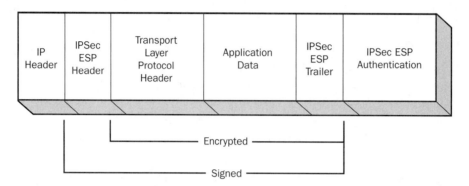

Figure 12-6   The ESP header and trailer locations

An IPSec packet can use ESP by itself or in combination with AH. When a packet uses both protocols, the ESP header follows the AH header, as shown in Figure 12-7. Although AH and ESP perform some of the same functions, using both protocols provides the maximum possible security for a data transmission. When ESP computes its ICV, it calculates the value only on the information between the ESP header and trailer; no IP header fields are included in an ESP ICV. Therefore, it is possible for an attacker to modify the contents of the IP header in an ESP-only packet, and have those changes go undetected by the recipient. AH includes most of the IP header in its ICV calculation, so combining AH with ESP provides more protection than ESP alone.

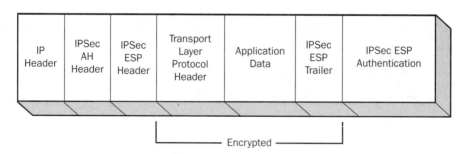

Figure 12-7   An IP datagram using AH and ESP

The contents of the ESP header are shown in Figure 12-8, and the functions of the header fields are as follows:

- **Security Parameters Index**   Contains a value that, in combination with the packet's destination IP address and its security protocol (AH or ESP), defines the datagram's *security association*.

- **Sequence Number**   Contains a value that starts at 1 in the first packet using a particular security association, and is incremented by 1 in every subsequent packet using the same security association. This field provides IPSec's anti-replay service. If an IPSec system receives packets with the same sequence numbers and the same security association, it discards the duplicates.

- **Payload Data**   Contains the TCP, UDP, or ICMP information carried inside the original IP datagram.

- **Pad Length**   Specifies the number of bytes of padding the system added to the Payload Data field to fill out a 32-bit word.

- **Next Header**   Contains a code specifying the protocol that generated the header immediately following the ESP header, using the protocol codes specified by the IANA. In virtually all cases, this field contains the code for the protocol that generated the datagram's payload, which is usually TCP, UDP, or ICMP.

> **Note**   When an IPSec system is using AH and ESP together, the Protocol field in the IP header contains the value 51, because the AH header immediately follows the IP header. The Next Header field in the AH header has the value 50, because the ESP header immediately follows the AH header. Finally, the Next header field in the ESP header contains the code for the protocol that generated the payload, which is usually TCP, UDP, or ICMP.

- **Authentication Data**   Contains an ICV based on the information after the ESP header, up to and including the ESP trailer. The receiving system uses the ICV to verify the packet's integrity by performing the same calculation and comparing the results with this value.

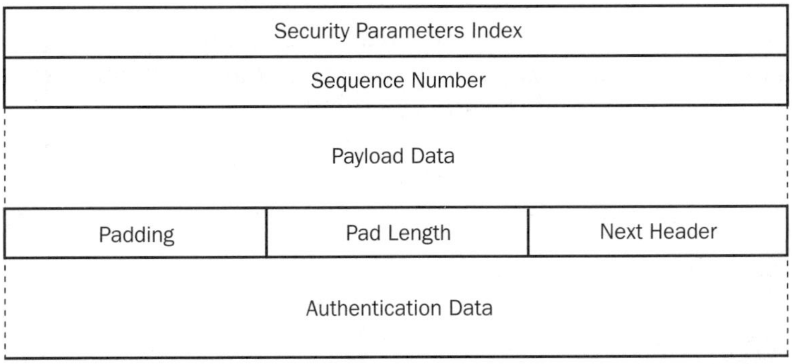

Security Parameters Index		
Sequence Number		
Payload Data		
Padding	Pad Length	Next Header
Authentication Data		

Figure 12-8   The ESP message format

Transport Mode and Tunnel Mode

IPSec can operate in two modes: *transport mode* and *tunnel mode*. To protect communications between computers on a network, you use transport mode, in which the two end systems must support IPSec, but intermediate systems (such as routers) need not. All the discussion of the AH and ESP protocols so far in this lesson applies to transport mode.

Tunnel mode is designed to provide security for wide area network (WAN) connections, and particularly virtual private network (VPN) connections, which use the Internet as a communications medium. In a tunnel mode connection, the end systems do not support and implement the IPSec protocols; the routers at both ends of the WAN connection do this.

The tunnel mode communications process proceeds as follows:

1. Computers on one of the private networks transmit their data using standard, unprotected IP datagrams.

2. The packets reach the router that provides access to the WAN, which encapsulates them using IPSec, encrypting and hashing data as needed.

3. The router transmits the protected packets to a second router at the other end of the WAN connection.

4. The second router verifies the packets by calculating and comparing ICVs, and decrypts them if necessary.

5. The second router repackages the information in the packets into standard, unprotected IP datagrams and transmits them to their destinations on the private network.

IPSec also uses a different packet structure in tunnel mode. Unlike transport mode, in which IPSec modifies the existing IP datagram by adding its own headers, tunnel mode implementations create an entirely new datagram and use it to encapsulate the existing datagram, as shown in Figure 12-9. The original datagram, inside the new datagram, remains unchanged. The IPSec headers are part of the outer datagram, which exists only to get the inner datagram from one router to the other.

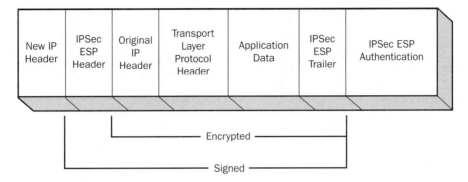

Figure 12-9   An IPSec tunnel mode packet

Lesson Review

The following questions are intended to reinforce key information presented in this lesson. If you are unable to answer a question, review the lesson materials and try the question again. You can find answers to the questions in the "Questions and Answers" section at the end of this chapter.

1. Which of the following ESP header fields provides the protocol's anti-replay capability?

   a. Sequence Number

   b. Security Parameters Index

   c. Pad Length

   d. Next Header

2. Specify the proper order for the following components in an IPSec transport mode packet using both AH and ESP and containing TCP data.

   a. ESP trailer

   b. IP header

   c. ESP header

   d. TCP header

   e. AH header

   f. TCP data

3. Which of the following IPSec characteristics is different when a connection is operating in tunnel mode instead of transport mode? (Choose all that apply.)

   a. The order of the fields in the ESP header

   b. The location of the ESP header in the datagram

    c. The location of the ESP trailer in the datagram

    d. The value of the Next Header field in the ESP header

Lesson Summary

■ IPSec is a set of extensions to the IP protocol that provide protection for data as it is transmitted over the network. IPSec includes two protocols, IP Authentication Header and IP Encapsulating Security Payload, which can be used separately or together.

■ IPSec features include Diffie–Hellman key generation, cryptographic checksums, mutual authentication, replay prevention, and IP packet filtering.

■ The IP Authentication Header protocol provides authentication, anti-replay, and data integrity services, but it does not encrypt data.

■ The IP Encapsulating Security Payload protocol encrypts the information in IP datagrams, and provides authentication, anti-replay, and data integrity services.

■ IPSec can operate in transport mode or tunnel mode. Transport mode is for securing communications between end users on a network, and tunnel mode is for securing WAN communications between routers.

Lesson 3: Deploying IPSec

All versions of Microsoft Windows beginning with Windows 2000 include support for IPSec, as do other operating systems. IPSec is based on standards published by the Internet Engineering Task Force (IETF), so all IPSec implementations conforming to those standards should be compatible. In Windows operating systems, the administration of IPSec is based on *IPSec policies*, which specify when and how IPSec should be used to secure network communications.

After this lesson, you will be able to

- List the components of a Windows Server 2003 IPSec implementation
- List the default IPSec policies included with Windows Server 2003 and their applications
- Understand the functions of an IPSec policy's components
- Use the IP Security Policies snap-in to manage IPSec policies

Estimated lesson time: 20 minutes

IPSec Components

The IPSec implementation in Windows Server 2003 consists of the following components:

- **IPSec Policy Agent**   A service (appearing as IPSEC Services on every computer running Windows Server 2003) that accesses IPSec policy information stored in the Active Directory database or the Windows registry.

- **Internet Key Exchange (IKE)**   IKE is the protocol that IPSec computers use to exchange information about generating Diffie–Hellman keys and to create a security association (SA). The IKE communication process proceeds in two stages. The first stage, called the Phase 1 SA, includes the negotiation of which encryption algorithm, hashing algorithm, and authentication method the systems will use. The second stage consists of the establishment of two Phase 2 SAs, one in each direction. This stage includes the negotiation of which IPSec protocols, hashing algorithm, and encryption algorithm the systems will use, as well as the exchange of information about authentication and key generation.

- **IPSec Driver**   Performs the actual preparations that enable secure network communication to take place, including the generation of checksums, the construction of IPSec packets, and the encryption of the data to be transmitted. The driver receives a filter list from the IPSec policy the system is using and compares each outgoing packet to that list. When a packet meets the criteria of the filter list, the IPSec driver initiates the IKE communications process with the destination system, adds the AH and ESP headers to the outgoing packet, and encrypts the data inside, if necessary. For incoming packets, the IPSec driver calculates hashes and check-sums as needed and compares them to those in the packet that just arrived.

Planning an IPSec Deployment

Configuring computers running Windows Server 2003 to use IPSec is relatively simple. However, before the actual deployment, you must consider just what network traffic you need to protect and how much protection you want to provide. IPSec is resource intensive in two different ways. First, the addition of AH and ESP headers to each packet increases the amount of traffic on your network. Second, calculating hashes and encrypting data both require large amounts of processor time. Unless you have planned your network design to account for the resources that IPSec needs, using IPSec for all your network traffic simply because you can is usually not a good idea.

A new installation of a slipstream version of Windows Server 2003 with Service Pack 1 (or later) has Windows Firewall enabled by default. Before implementing IPSec, you must disable Windows Firewall by running the Post-Setup Security Updates (PSSU).

Windows Server 2003 IPSec enables you to specify exactly what traffic to protect using IPSec, and what degree of protection to apply. IPSec does this using packet filters much like those described in Lesson 1 of this chapter. You can specify IP addresses, protocols, and ports when creating a filter, and the system secures all traffic that meets the filter criteria using IPSec.

Another factor to consider when planning an IPSec deployment is support for the protocols on your network's various computers. Systems running versions of the Windows operating system earlier than Windows 2000 cannot use IPSec. In the case of operating systems other than the Windows operating system, you must determine whether they support IPSec and do your own testing to be sure that the implementations are compatible.

Working with IPSec Policies

The IP Security Policies snap-in for Microsoft Management Console (MMC) is the tool you use to view and manage IPSec policies on a computer running Windows Server 2003. By default, the snap-in is incorporated into the Group Policy Object Editor console and, on member servers, into the Local Security Policy console. You can also add the snap-in to a new MMC console and configure it to manage the policies on any individual computer or Active Directory domain.

You deploy IPSec policies in much the same way as other types of Windows Server 2003 policy settings; you can apply them to individual computers, but for network installations it is more common to deploy IPSec policies by assigning them to Active Directory objects. IPSec policies flow down through the Active Directory hierarchy just like other group policy settings. When you apply an IPSec policy to a domain, for example, all the computers in the domain inherit that policy.

Once you have created IPSec policies in the appropriate places, you must then activate them by selecting Assign from the Action menu in the IP Security Policies snap-in. You can view the policy that is currently in effect for any computer on the network, as well as detailed information about IPSec activities, using the IP Security Monitor snap-in.

Using the Default IPSec Policies

When you open the IP Security Policies snap-in (see Figure 12-10), you see the three policies that Windows Server 2003 always creates by default. These three policies are as follows:

■ **Client (Respond Only)**   Configures the computer to use IPSec only when another computer requests IPSec. The computer using this policy never initiates an IPSec negotiation; it only responds to requests from other computers for secured communications.

■ **Secure Server (Require Security)**   Configures the computer to require IPSec security for all communications. If the computer attempts to communicate with a computer that does not support IPSec, the initiating computer terminates the connection.

■ **Server (Request Security)**   Configures the computer to request the use of IPSec when communicating with another computer. If the other computer supports IPSec, the IPSec negotiation begins. If the other computer does not support IPSec, the systems establish a standard, unsecured IP connection.

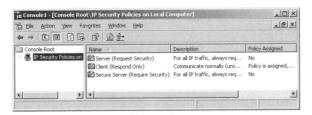

Figure 12-10   The IP Security Policies snap-in

These default policies are intended for computers performing different roles. The Client (Respond Only) policy is intended for computers that connect sometimes to secured servers, and sometimes to systems that do not require the security of IPSec. Using the Client (Respond Only) policy, the system incurs the additional overhead generated by IPSec only when necessary. The Secure Server (Require Security) policy is intended for computers working with sensitive data that must be secured at all times. Before implementing this policy, you must make sure that all the computers that need to access the secured server support IPSec. The Server (Request Security) policy is intended for computers that do not require the highest levels of security and might communicate with systems not supporting IPSec.

Modifying IPSec Policies

In addition to using the default IPSec policies as they are, you can modify them, or create new policies of your own. IPSec policies consist of three elements, which are as follows:

> **Tip**   Although you can modify the properties of the default IPSec policies, the best practice is to leave them intact and create new policies of your own instead, using the default policies as models.

- **Rules**   A rule is a combination of an IP filter list and a filter action that specifies when and how the computer should use IPSec. An IPSec policy can consist of multiple rules, as shown in Figure 12-11.

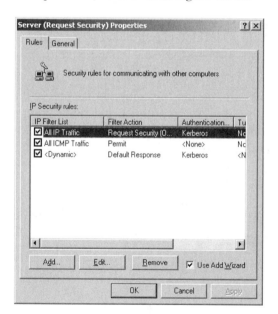

Figure 12-11   The IP Security Rules list

- **IP filter lists**   A collection of filters that specify what traffic the system should secure with IPSec, based on IP addresses, protocols, or port numbers. You can also create filters using a combination of these criteria, as shown in Figure 12-12.

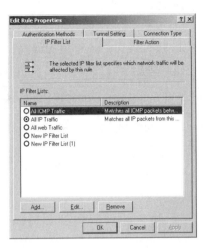

Figure 12-12   The IP Filter Lists list

■ **Filter actions**   Configuration parameters that specify exactly how IPSec should secure the filtered packets. Filter actions specify whether IPSec should use AH, ESP, or both, as well as what data integrity and encryption algorithms the system should use (see Figure 12-13).

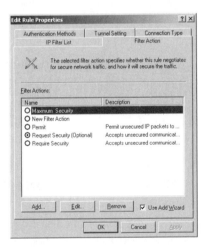

Figure 12-13   The Filter Actions list

To help create a new policy, the IP Security Policies snap-in provides wizards for creating rules, filter lists, and filter actions. However, you can elect not to use the wizards and create the policy elements using standard dialog boxes.

Exam Tip   Be sure you are familiar with the components of an IPSec policy and with the functions of each component.

Practice: Creating an IPSec Policy

In this practice, you use the IP Security Policies snap-in to view the properties of the default IPSec policies and create a new policy of your own.

Exercise 1: Creating an MMC Console and Viewing the Default Policies

In this exercise, you create an MMC console containing the IP Security Policies snap-in and use it to view the default IPSec policies on your server.

1. Log on to Windows Server 2003 as Administrator.

2. Click Start, and then click Run. The Run dialog box appears.

3. In the Open text box, type **mmc** and then click OK. The Console1 window appears.

4. From the File menu, select Add/Remove Snap-in. The Add/Remove Snap-in dialog box appears.

5. Click Add. The Add Standalone Snap-in dialog box appears.

6. Scroll down the Available Standalone Snap-ins list, select IP Security Policy Management, and then click Add. The Select Computer Or Domain dialog box appears.

7. With the default Local Computer option button selected, click Finish.

8. Click Close to close the Add Standalone Snap-in dialog box. The IP Security Policies On Local Computer snap-in now appears in the Add/Remove Snap-in dialog box.

9. Click OK to close the Add/Remove Snap-in dialog box. The snap-in you selected now appears in the scope pane of the MMC console.

10. Click the IP Security Policies on Local Computer heading in the scope pane. The three default IPSec policies described earlier in this lesson appear in the details pane.

11. Select the Secure Server (Require Security) policy in the details pane and, from the Action menu, select Properties. The Secure Server (Require Security) Properties dialog box appears.

    Notice that the Rules tab in the Secure Server (Require Security) Properties dialog box contains three rules, one applying to all IP traffic, one for all ICMP traffic, and one dynamic.

12. Select All IP Traffic from the IP Security Rules list, and then click Edit. The Edit Rule Properties dialog box appears.

    Notice that the All IP Traffic option button is selected in the IP Filter List tab.

13. Click the Filter Action tab.

   Notice that the Require Security option button is selected in the Filter Actions list.

14. Click the Authentication Methods tab.

   Notice that the policy is configured to use Kerberos for authentication.

15. Click OK to close the Edit Rule Properties dialog box.

16. Click OK to close the Secure Server (Require Security) Properties dialog box.

Exercise 2: Creating a New IPSec Policy

In this exercise, you use the IP Security Policies snap-in to create a new IPSec policy on the computer.

1. In the console you created in Exercise 1, select the IP Security Policies On Local Computer heading in the scope pane and, from the Action menu, select Create IP Security Policy. The IP Security Policy Wizard appears.

2. Click Next. The IP Security Policy Name page appears.

3. In the Name text box, type **Web Server Security** and then click Next. The Requests for Secure Communication page appears.

4. Click Next to accept the default Activate The Default Response Rule setting. The Default Response Rule Authentication Method page appears.

   The default authentication method for Active Directory systems is Kerberos V5 protocol, but on this page, you could elect to use a digital certificate or a pre-shared key in the form of a character string that you supply to all the computers involved in secured communications.

5. Click Next to accept the default Active Directory Default (Kerberos V5 Protocol) option button. The Completing The IP Security Policy Wizard page appears.

6. Make sure the Edit Properties check box is selected, and then click Finish. The Web Server Security Properties dialog box appears.

7. In the Rules tab, make sure that the Use Add Wizard check box is selected, and then click Add. The Security Rule Wizard appears.

8. Click Next. The Tunnel Endpoint page appears.

   On this page, you specify whether you want IPSec to run in transport mode or tunnel mode. To use tunnel mode, you must specify the IP address of the system functioning as the tunnel endpoint. This is usually a router that provides a WAN connection to a remote site.

9. Click Next to accept the default This Rule Does Not Specify A Tunnel option button. The Network Type page appears.

This page enables you to specify whether you want the rule to apply to local area network (LAN) traffic only, remote access traffic only, or both.

10. Click Next to accept the default All Network Connections option button. The IP Filter List page appears.

11. Click Add. The IP Filter List dialog box appears.

12. In the Name text box, type **All Web Traffic** and then click Add. The IP Filter Wizard appears.

13. Click Next. The IP Filter Description And Mirrored Property page appears.

14. Click Next to accept the default Mirrored, Match Packets With The Exact Opposite Source And Destination Addresses check box. The IP Traffic Source page appears.

15. In the Source Address selector , click Any IP Address, and then click Next. The IP Traffic Destination page appears.

16. In the Destination Address selector, click My IP Address, and then click Next. The IP Protocol Type page appears.

17. In the Select A Protocol Type selector, click TCP, and then click Next. The IP Protocol Port page appears.

18. Click the To This Port option button, type **80** in the text box provided, and then click Next. The Completing The IP Filter Wizard page appears.

19. Click Finish. The new IP filter you created appears in the IP Filters list. Click OK to close the IP Filter List dialog box.

20. In the IP Filter List page of the Security Rule Wizard, select the All Web Traffic filter list you just created, and then click Next. The Filter Action page appears.

21. Make sure the Use Add Wizard check box is selected, and then click Add. The Filter Action Wizard appears.

22. Click Next. The Filter Action Name page appears.

23. In the Name text box, type **Maximum Security** and then click Next. The Filter Action General Options page appears.

24. Click the Negotiate Security option button, and then click Next. The Communicating With Computers That Do Not Support IPSec page appears.

25. Click Next to accept the default Do Not Communicate With Computers That Do Not Support IPSec option button. The IP Traffic Security page appears.

26. Click the Custom option button, and then click Settings. The Custom Security Method Settings dialog box appears.

27. Select the Data And Address Integrity Without Encryption (AH) check box to activate the IP Authentication Header protocol, and then click OK to return to the IP Traffic Security page.

28. Click Next. The Completing The IP Security Filter Action Wizard page appears.

29. Click Finish to return to the Filter Action page in the Security Rule Wizard.

30. Select the Maximum Security filter action you just created, and then click Next. The Authentication Method page appears.

31. Click Next to accept the default Active Directory Default (Kerberos V5 Protocol) option button. The Completing The Security Rule Wizard page appears.

32. Clear the Edit Properties check box, and then click Finish.

33. Click OK to close the Web Server Security Properties dialog box.

34. The new Web Server Security policy you created now appears in the IP Security Policies On Local Computer snap-in.

35. Click the Web Server Security policy in the details pane and, from the Action menu, select Assign.

36. Close the IP Securities Policies On Local Computer snap-in.

Lesson Review

The following questions are intended to reinforce key information presented in this lesson. If you are unable to answer a question, review the lesson materials and try the question again. You can find answers to the questions in the "Questions and Answers" section at the end of this chapter.

1. Which IPSec policy can you use to encrypt all traffic to and from a particular database application on a server running Windows Server 2003?

   a. Client (Respond Only)

   b. Secure Server (Require Security)

   c. Server (Request Security)

   d. You must create a new custom policy

2. Which of the following pieces of information must you supply when creating a policy that configures IPSec to use tunnel mode?

   a. The IP address of the router's WAN interface

   b. The port number associated with the WAN technology used for the tunnel

   c. The IP address of the router at the far end of the tunnel

   d. The network layer protocol used for the WAN connection

3. Which IPSec component is responsible for actually encrypting the information in IP datagrams?

   a. Internet Key Exchange

   b. IPSEC Services

   c. IPSec driver

   d. The IP Security Policies snap-in

Lesson Summary

- The IPSec implementation in Windows Server 2003 consists of IPSEC Services, Internet Key Exchange (IKE), and the IPSec driver.

- When planning an IPSec deployment, you must consider the impact of using IPSec on your computers and on your network. IPSec hashing and encryption calculations can be extremely processor intensive, and the added overhead of the AH and ESP headers can increase the level of network traffic. You must also consider whether all the computers on your network support IPSec.

- The Windows Server 2003 IPSec implementation is based on IPSec policies. You can manage IPSec policies using the IP Security Policies snap-in for Microsoft Management Console.

- Windows Server 2003 IPSec has three default policies: Client (Respond Only), Secure Server (Require Security), and Server (Request Security). You can use these policies or create your own.

- IPSec policies consist of rules, IP filter lists, and filter actions. A rule is a combination of an IP filter list and a filter action. IP filter lists specify what traffic IPSec should protect, and filter actions specify what type of protection IPSec should apply.

Lesson 4: Troubleshooting Data Transmission Security

When network communications fail to occur because of IPSec problems, the most common cause of the difficulty is improper configuration of the IPSec components on one or both of the systems trying to communicate. You can take steps to check the configuration settings on the computers to see if they are compatible. Windows Server 2003 also includes tools that you can use to monitor and troubleshoot IPSec and other policy-based security mechanisms, including the IPSec Security Monitor snap-in and the Resultant Set of Policy (RSoP) snap-ins for Microsoft Management Console.

After this lesson, you will be able to

- List possible causes of policy mismatches
- Describe the functions of the IP Security Monitor and Resultant Set of Policy snap-ins

Estimated lesson time: 10 minutes

Troubleshooting Policy Mismatches

One common cause of IPSec communications problems is incompatible IPSec policies or policy settings. This is particularly true when you create your own IPSec policies. For example, one of your computers might require IPSec for a particular port, while the other computer is not configured to use IPSec for that port. It is also possible for two computers to be configured to use IPSec for a particular type of traffic but have incompatible filter action settings, such as different authentication methods or encryption algorithms. This prevents the computers from negotiating a common IPSec configuration, and communications fail.

To determine if a policy mismatch is the cause of a communications problem, you should examine the Security logs in the Event Viewer console. The Security log should contain a warning message if the system attempted to perform an IKE negotiation that failed.

Tip   In addition to IKE-related messages, the logs in the Event Viewer console can contain other valuable information related to IPSec processes. However, logging some IPSec events requires that you use the appropriate audit policy settings. To include IPSec events in the logs, make sure the Audit Logon Events and Audit Policy Change policies are enabled. To configure the IPSec driver to log dropped inbound and outbound packets, type the following command at a command prompt, and then reboot the computer: **netsh ipsec dynamic set config ipsecdiagnostics 7**.

To troubleshoot policy mismatches, you have to examine the policy settings for each computer involved. You can examine the policies using the IP Security Policies snap-in, but this tool does not tell you which policy is active on a particular computer. To view the policy settings currently in use, you must run one of the tools discussed in the next sections.

Using the IP Security Monitor Snap-in

IP Security Monitor is an MMC snap-in that you can use to view the currently active policy on any network computer, plus other detailed information, including IPSec statistics, filter details, security associations, and more. To use IPSec Security monitor, you must manually add the snap-in to an MMC console, as shown in Figure 12-14.

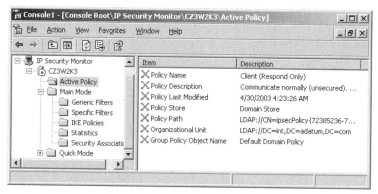

Figure 12-14   The IP Security Monitor snap-in

When you open IP Security Monitor, the Active Policy folder specifies the policy that is currently in effect on the computer, where the policy is stored, and what Group Policy Object (GPO) applied it. In some cases, you might discover that a policy mismatch is caused by a computer that is running a different policy than you thought. If you have IPSec policies deployed by Group Policy Objects at different levels of the Active Directory tree, the IPSec policy that is closest to the computer object is the one that takes effect. For example, if you assign the Client (Respond Only) policy to your domain object and the Secure Server (Require Security) policy to an organizational unit, Secure Server (Require Security) will be the effective policy for the computers in that organizational unit.

If you have recently made changes to IPSec policies that you deploy using Group Policy Objects, your computers might not yet have received the new policy settings from a domain controller. You can use IP Security Monitor to examine the details of a computer's current policy, such as the details of the IP filter lists shown in Figure 12-15. If you determine that the policy settings that the computer is using are outdated, you can wait for the system to refresh its group policy settings or reboot the computer to force an update from the domain controller.

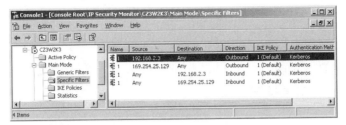

Figure 12-15   IP Filter Lists details

Using the Resultant Set of Policy Snap-in

The Resultant Set of Policy snap-in is a more comprehensive tool than IP Security Monitor. You can use RSoP to view all the effective group policy settings for a computer or user, including the IPSec policies. To use RSoP, you must first load the snap-in into an MMC console, and then perform a query on a specific computer (select Generate RSoP Data from the Action menu), specifying the information you want to gather. The result is a display of the group policy settings that the selected computer is using, similar to the display of the Group Policy Object Editor console (see Figure 12-16).

> **Important**   If Windows Firewall is installed on Windows Server 2003 with Service Pack 1, remote access to RSoP data no longer works from that target computer. If you need to access RSoP data remotely, refer to the RSoP documentation on the Microsoft TechNet Web site at *http://technet2.microsoft.com/WindowsServer/en/Library/c52a765e-5a62-4c28-9e3f-d5ed334cadf61033.mspx*.

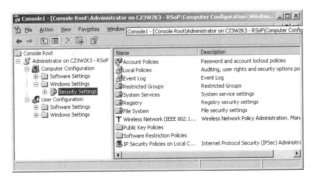

Figure 12-16   The Resultant Set of Policy snap-in

When you expand the Windows Settings\Security Settings header in RSoP and then click the IP Security Policies On Local Computer subheading, the details pane contains a list of the computer's assigned policies (see Figure 12-17). The display specifies the Group Policy Object from which the computer received the policy (something the IP

Security Monitor snap-in cannot do) and enables you to display a read-only Properties dialog box for the IPSec policy, so you can review its settings.

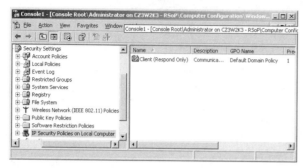

Figure 12-17   The RSoP snap-in, displaying the computer's effective policy

Exam Tip   Be sure you understand the differences between the IP Security Monitor snap-in and the Resultant Set of Policy snap-in, and know when it is preferable to use each one.

Examining IPSec Traffic

Another valuable tool for IPSec troubleshooting is the Network Monitor application included with Windows Server 2003. You can use Network Monitor to capture traffic from your network and examine the structure of the various protocol headers. Windows Server 2003 Network Monitor includes parsers for IKE, AH, and ESP traffic. However, you cannot use Network Monitor to examine packet information that has been encrypted using ESP.

To examine the IPSec packet structure when ESP is in use, you can temporarily configure the operative filter action to use null encryption from the IP Security Policies snap-in by selecting None for the Encryption Algorithm setting in the Custom Security Method Settings dialog box, as shown in Figure 12-18. This enables IPSec to create packets that include the ESP components without actually encrypting the contents. (To arrive at this dialog box, double-click the security policy in the IP Security Policies snap-in that you want to modify, click Edit for the desired rule, click the Filter Action tab, click Edit for the filter action you want to modify, click Edit for the desired security method, click Settings, and then specify your settings for the custom security method in the Custom Security Method Settings dialog box.)

Figure 12-18   The Custom Security Method Settings dialog box

 Note   If you use null encryption, be sure to activate the encryption algorithm of your choice after you are finished testing or troubleshooting, so that your data is protected.

Practice: Using Resultant Set of Policy

In this practice, you use the Resultant Set of Policy snap-in to view the policy settings on your computer.

Exercise 1: Creating a Resultant Set of Policy Console

In this exercise, you install the Resultant Set of Policy snap-in into Microsoft Management Console (MMC).

1. Log on to Windows Server 2003 as Administrator.

2. Click Start, and then click Run. The Run dialog box appears.

3. In the Open text box, type **mmc** and then click OK. The Console1 window appears.

4. From the File menu, select Add/ Remove Snap-in. The Add/Remove Snap-in dialog box appears.

5. Click Add. The Add Standalone Snap-in dialog box appears.

6. Scroll down the Available Standalone Snap-ins list, select Resultant Set of Policy, and then click Add.

7. Click Close to close the Add Standalone Snap-in dialog box. The Resultant Set of Policy snap-in now appears in the Add/Remove Snap-in dialog box.

8. Click OK to close the Add/Remove Snap-in dialog box. The snap-in you selected now appears in the scope pane of the MMC console.

9. Leave the MMC console window open for the next exercise.

Exercise 2: Performing an RSoP Scan

In this exercise, you use the Resultant Set of Policy snap-in to scan the computer and display the active policy settings.

1. Click the Resultant Set of Policy heading in the MMC console's scope pane. An Action Required message appears in the details pane.

2. From the Action menu, select Generate RSoP Data. The Resultant Set of Policy Wizard appears.

3. Click Next. The Mode Selection page appears.

4. Click Next to accept the default Logging Mode option button. The Computer Selection page appears.

5. Click Next to accept the default This Computer option button. The User Selection page appears.

6. Click Next to accept the default Current User option button. The Summary of Selections page appears.

7. Click Next to begin the scanning process. When the scanning completes, the Completing The Resultant Set of Policy Wizard page appears.

8. Click Finish. An Administrator On SERVER01 — RSoP heading appears on the scope pane.

9. Expand the Administrator On SERVER01 — RSoP, Computer Configuration, Windows Settings, and Security Settings headings. Then click the IP Security Policies On Local Computer heading.

   Notice that no entries appear in the details pane, even though you assigned the Web Server Security policy to the computer in the Lesson 3 practice. This is because the Resultant Set of Policy snap-in only lists IP security policies assigned through Group Policy Objects.

10. Leave the MMC Console1 window open for the next exercise.

Exercise 3: Creating a Domain IPSec Policy

In this exercise, you recreate the Web Server Security IPSec policy from the Lesson 3 practice in Active Directory and repeat the RSoP scan.

1. From the MMC console's File menu, select Add/Remove Snap-in. The Add/ Remove Snap-in dialog box appears.

2. Click Add. The Add Standalone Snap-in dialog box appears.

3. Scroll down the Available Standalone Snap-ins list, select IP Security Policy Management, and then click Add. The Select Computer Or Domain dialog box appears.

4. Select The Active Directory Domain Of Which This Computer Is A Member option button and then click Finish.

5. In the Add Standalone Snap-in dialog box, select Group Policy Object Editor and then click Add. The Select Group Policy Object page appears.

6. Click Browse. The Browse For A Group Policy Object dialog box appears.

7. In the Domains, OUs And Linked Group Policy Objects list, select the Default Domain Policy icon and then click OK.

8. Click Finish to close the Select Group Policy Object page.

9. Click Close to close the Add Standalone Snap-in dialog box.

10. The IP Security Policies On Active Directory and the Default Domain Policy (server01.contoso.com) Policy snap-ins now appear in the Add/Remove Snap-in dialog box.

11. Click OK to close the Add/Remove Snap-in dialog box. The snap-ins you selected now appear in the scope pane of the MMC console.

12. Click the IP Security Policies On Active Directory heading in the scope pane. The three default IPSec policies appear in the details pane.

13. Ensure that you've selected the IP Security Policies On Active Directory heading and then repeat steps 1 through 34 from Exercise 2 in Lesson 3 of this chapter to create the Web Server Security policy in the Default Domain Policy Group Policy Object.

14. Expand the Default Domain Policy (server01.contoso.com) Policy heading in the scope pane. Then expand the Computer Configuration, Windows Settings, and Security Settings headings and click IP Security Policies On Active Directory (contoso.com).

15. In the details pane, click Web Server Security and, from the Action menu, select Assign.

16. Restart the computer and repeat Exercises 1 and 2 above to perform another Resultant Set of Policy scan.

    Notice that the IP Security Policies On Local Computer heading in the RSoP display now lists the Web Server Security policy and specifies that it comes from the Default Domain Policy GPO.

17. Close the MMC Console1 window.

Lesson Review

The following questions are intended to reinforce key information presented in this lesson. If you are unable to answer a question, review the lesson materials and try the question again. You can find answers to the questions in the "Questions and Answers" section at the end of this chapter.

1. Which of the following Windows Server 2003 tools enables you to tell which Group Policy Object assigned the effective IPSec policy to a particular computer?

    a. Resultant Set of Policy

    b. IP Security Monitor

    c. Network Monitor

    d. IP Security Policies

2. You have just finished making changes to the IPSec policy assigned to a particular Active Directory Group Policy Object, but the changes have not yet taken effect on the network's computers. Which of the following procedures will enable the computers to receive the new policy settings?

    a. In the IP Security Policies snap-in, remove the assignment of the IPSec policy, and then assign it again.

    b. Restart each network computer.

    c. Use the Resultant Set of Policy snap-in to refresh the policy assignment.

    d. Delete the computer objects from Active Directory and recreate them.

Lesson Summary

■ Incompatible configuration settings are a common cause of IPSec communication problems.

■ Enabling the Audit Logon Events and Audit Policy Change audit policies causes Windows Server 2003 to record IPSec-related events in the Event Viewer console's logs.

- The IP Security Monitor snap-in displays information about the IPSec policy currently in effect on a particular computer, as well as IPSec statistics.

- The Resultant Set of Policy snap-in displays all the effective group policy settings for a particular computer, including the IPSec policy and its source.

- Windows Server 2003 Network Monitor includes parsers for IKE, AH, and ESP traffic, but you cannot view IPSec packet contents that are encrypted.

Case Scenario Exercise

You are the network infrastructure design specialist for Litware Inc., a manufacturer of specialized scientific software products, and you have already created a network design for their new office building, as described in the Case Scenario Exercise in Chapter 1. You are in the process of designing an IPSec deployment for the network to protect the network transmissions of certain network users.

The primary goal of this project is to protect the network transmissions of users in the R&D department, who regularly work on government contracts using confidential company information and secret documents. The confidential material is stored on several database servers in the building's data center. Because these database servers perform no other company functions, you want to require the use of IPSec to encrypt all traffic accessing them. However, the users in the R&D department also have to access other company services that do not need such high security, such as e-mail and the company's customer database.

In addition to the R&D users in the building, the information in the R&D databases must also be available to specific people in the company's headquarters in another city. The building is connected to the headquarters by a T-1 WAN link, but you must secure this access with IPSec as well.

Based on this information, answer the following questions.

1. Which of the following IPSec policies should you assign to the organizational unit object containing the R&D users' workstations?

    a. The default Secure Server (Require Security) policy

    b. The default Client (Respond Only) policy

    c. A policy that secures all TCP traffic, using both the AH and ESP protocols

    d. A policy that secures all traffic to the port number of the database application, using the AH protocol

2. Which of the following procedures should you use to secure the WAN traffic between the users in the company headquarters and the R&D database servers? (Choose all that apply.)

   a. Configure the routers at both ends of the WAN connection to use IPSec in tunnel mode

   b. Configure the database servers with the Secure Server (Require Security) policy

   c. Configure the workstations of the users at headquarters with the Client (Respond Only) policy

   d. Configure the database servers and the workstations at headquarters to use IPSec in tunnel mode

Troubleshooting Lab

You are a network administrator for a company whose president has recently become extremely security-conscious as the result of an incident in which confidential documents found their way into the hands of a competing company. You have been ordered to encrypt all sensitive network communications, and you just finished deploying IPSec on all the network's computers. To ensure the security of the network, you assigned the Secure Server (Require Security) policy to the Group Policy Object for your Active Directory domain. Now, the day after the deployment, you are getting numerous complaints from users about slow performance from their computers.

1. Which of the following procedures might lessen the impact of IPSec on network performance, while keeping the network sufficiently secure? (Choose all that apply.)

   a. Switch the IPSec policy assigned to the domain from Secure Server (Require Security) policy to Server (Request Security)

   b. Using organizational unit objects instead of the domain, assign the Secure Server (Require Security) policy to the company servers and the Client (Respond Only) policy to the workstations

   c. Modify the Secure Server (Require Security) policy to use only the AH protocol

   d. Create a new IPSec policy that encrypts only the traffic to and from the computers containing confidential documents

   e. Install addition memory in all the network computers

   f. Upgrade the network from 10Base-T to 100Base-TX

Chapter Summary

- Packet filtering is a method for regulating the TCP/IP traffic that is permitted to reach a computer or a network based on criteria such as IP and hardware addresses, protocols, and port numbers.

- Service-dependent filtering using port numbers enables you to restrict traffic based on the application that generated it or is destined to receive it.

- IPSec is a set of extensions to the IP protocol that provide protection for data as it is transmitted over the network. IPSec includes two protocols, IP Authentication Header and IP Encapsulating Security Payload, which can be used separately or together.

- IPSec can operate in transport mode or tunnel mode. Transport mode secures communications between end users on a network, and tunnel mode secures WAN communications between routers.

- The IPSec implementation in Windows Server 2003 consists of IPSEC Services, Internet Key Exchange (IKE), and the IPSec driver.

- Windows Server 2003 IPSec has three default policies: Client (Respond Only), Secure Server (Require Security), and Server (Request Security). You can use these policies or create your own.

- IPSec policies consist of rules, IP filter lists, and filter actions. A rule is a combination of an IP filter list and a filter action. IP filter lists specify what traffic IPSec should protect, and filter actions specify what type of protection IPSec should apply.

- Incompatible configuration settings are a common cause of IPSec communication problems.

- The IP Security Monitor snap-in displays information about the IPSec policy currently in effect on a particular computer, as well as IPSec statistics.

- The Resultant Set of Policy snap-in displays all the effective group policy settings for a particular computer, including the IPSec policy and its source.

Exam Highlights

Before taking the exam, review the key points and terms that are presented below to help you identify topics you need to review. Return to the lessons for additional practice, and review the "Further Reading" sections in Part 2 for pointers to more information about topics covering the exam objectives.

Key Points

- Routers use packet filtering to protect network computers by specifying the types of traffic they are permitted to receive. You can filter traffic based on addresses, protocols, or port numbers, using code values standardized by the IANA.

- In Windows Server 2003, IPSec policies control when and how IPSec is used to protect network traffic from compromise.

- IPSec policies consist of rules, IP filter lists, and filter actions. A rule is a combination of IP filter actions and filter lists. IP filter lists are combinations of IP addresses, protocols, and ports that specify what traffic IPSec should protect. Filter actions specify which IPSec features the system should use to protect the traffic conforming to the IP filter list settings.

- To deploy IPSec on a network, you assign an IPSec policy to a Group Policy Object or to a particular computer.

- IP Security Monitor and Resultant Set of Policy are tools that you can use to examine IPSec and other group policy settings on specific computers.

Key Terms

Service-dependent filtering   The regulation of network traffic based on the port number values found in packet headers

Ephemeral port   A port number chosen by a client computer for a single transaction when communicating with a server

Spoofing   The impersonation of another user or computer, usually for illicit purposes

Questions and Answers

Page
12-13

Lesson 1 Review

1. Specify the well-known port numbers for each of the following applications.

    a. World Wide Web HTTP

    80

    b. Dynamic Host Configuration Protocol (Server)

    67

    c. Simple Mail Transfer Protocol

    25

    d. Domain Name Service

    53

    e. Telnet

    23

2. Which of the following packet filtering criteria enable you to prevent a denial-of-service attack using ICMP messages?

    a. Port numbers

    b. Hardware addresses

    c. Protocol identifiers

    d. IP addresses

    c

3. For each of the following packet filtering capabilities, identify whether the feature is supported in Windows Server 2003 with SP1 by TCP/IP client packet filtering, Windows Firewall, or RRAS packet filtering, two of these, or all three of these.

    a. Creating filters that admit all port numbers except for the ones you specify

    TCP/IP client packet filtering: NO

    Windows Firewall: NO

    RRAS packet filtering: YES

    b. Creating filters that block all ICMP messages

    TCP/IP client packet filtering: NO

    Windows Firewall: NO

    RRAS packet filtering: YES

c. Creating filters that block all protocols except for the ones you specify

TCP/IP client packet filtering: YES

Windows Firewall: YES (inbound only)

RRAS packet filtering: YES

d. Creating filters that admit only packets using specific IP protocol code numbers

TCP/IP client packet filtering: YES

Windows Firewall: NO

RRAS packet filtering: NO

Lesson 2 Review

1. Which of the following ESP header fields provides the protocol's anti-replay capability?

    a. Sequence Number

    b. Security Parameters Index

    c. Pad Length

    d. Next Header

    a

2. Specify the proper order for the following components in an IPSec transport mode packet using both AH and ESP and containing TCP data.

    a. ESP trailer

    b. IP header

    c. ESP header

    d. TCP header

    e. AH header

    f. TCP data

    b, e, c, d, f, a

3. Which of the following IPSec characteristics is different when a connection is operating in tunnel mode instead of transport mode? (Choose all that apply.)

    a. The order of the fields in the ESP header

    b. The location of the ESP header in the datagram

    c. The location of the ESP trailer in the datagram

    d. The value of the Next Header field in the ESP header

    b and d

Page
12-35

Lesson 3 Review

1. Which IPSec policy can you use to encrypt all traffic to and from a particular database application on a server running Windows Server 2003?

   a. Client (Respond Only).

   b. Secure Server (Require Security).

   c. Server (Request Security).

   d. You must create a new custom policy.

   d

2. Which of the following pieces of information must you supply when creating a policy that configures IPSec to use tunnel mode?

   a. The IP address of the router's WAN interface

   b. The port number associated with the WAN technology used for the tunnel

   c. The IP address of the router at the far end of the tunnel

   d. The network layer protocol used for the WAN connection

   a

3. Which IPSec component is responsible for actually encrypting the information in IP datagrams?

   a. Internet Key Exchange

   b. IPSEC Services

   c. IPSec driver

   d. The IP Security Policies snap-in

   c

Page
12-44

Lesson 4 Review

1. Which of the following Windows Server 2003 tools enables you to tell which Group Policy Object assigned the effective IPSec policy to a particular computer?

   a. Resultant Set of Policy

   b. IP Security Monitor

   c. Network Monitor

   d. IP Security Policies

   a

2. You have just finished making changes to the IPSec policy assigned to a particular Active Directory Group Policy Object, but the changes have not yet taken effect on the network's computers. Which of the following procedures will enable the computers to receive the new policy settings?

 a. In the IP Security Policies snap-in, remove the assignment of the IPSec policy, and then assign it again.

 b. Restart each network computer.

 c. Use the Resultant Set of Policy snap-in to refresh the policy assignment.

 d. Delete the computer objects from Active Directory and recreate them.

 b

Page
12-45
Case Scenario Exercise

Based on the information provided in the Case Scenario Exercise, answer the following questions:

1. Which of the following IPSec policies should you assign to the organizational unit object containing the R&D users' workstations?

 a. The default Secure Server (Require Security) policy

 b. The default Client (Respond Only) policy

 c. A policy that secures all TCP traffic, using both the AH and ESP protocols

 d. A policy that secures all traffic to the port number of the database application, using the AH protocol

 b

2. Which of the following procedures should you use to secure the WAN traffic between the users in the company headquarters and the R&D database servers? (Choose all that apply.)

 a. Configure the routers at both ends of the WAN connection to use IPSec in tunnel mode

 b. Configure the database servers with the Secure Server (Require Security) policy

 c. Configure the workstations of the users at headquarters with the Client (Respond Only) policy

 d. Configure the database servers and the workstations at headquarters to use IPSec in tunnel mode

 b and c

Page
12-46

Troubleshooting Lab

You are a network administrator for a company whose president has recently become extremely security-conscious as the result of an incident in which confidential documents found their way into the hands of a competing company. You have been ordered to encrypt all sensitive network communications, and you just finished deploying IPSec on all the network's computers. To ensure the security of the network, you assigned the Secure Server (Require Security) policy to the Group Policy Object for your Active Directory domain. Now, the day after the deployment, you are getting numerous complaints from users about slow performance from their computers.

1. Which of the following procedures might lessen the impact of IPSec on network performance, while keeping the network sufficiently secure? (Choose all that apply.)

   a. Switch the IPSec policy assigned to the domain from Secure Server (Require Security) policy to Server (Request Security)

   b. Using organizational unit objects instead of the domain, assign the Secure Server (Require Security) policy to the company servers and the Client (Respond Only) policy to the workstations

   c. Modify the Secure Server (Require Security) policy to use only the AH protocol

   d. Create a new IPSec policy that encrypts only the traffic to and from the computers containing confidential documents

   e. Install addition memory in all the network computers

   f. Upgrade the network from 10Base-T to 100Base-TX

   d and f

13 Designing a Security Infrastructure

Exam Objectives in this Chapter:

- Plan a security update infrastructure. Tools might include Microsoft Baseline Security Analyzer and Microsoft Software Update Services.

- Plan security for wireless networks.

- Plan secure network administration methods.

    - Create a plan to offer Remote Assistance to client computers.

    - Plan for remote administration by using Terminal Services.

Why This Chapter Matters

In addition to the basic security issues treated thus far in this book, many special situations require attention to security. Because security is an ongoing concern, the problem of keeping systems updated with the latest security patches is one that all network administrators must face, and the larger the network, the more complex the update process. Whenever you deploy new technologies on your network, such as wireless local area network (WLAN) equipment or remote administration software, you must consider the security ramifications and take steps to ensure that you do not introduce new security hazards into your environment.

Lessons in this Chapter:

Before You Begin

This chapter assumes a basic understanding of security implementation in the Microsoft Windows Server 2003 family and of how to use group policies to apply settings to large numbers of computers, as covered throughout this book. To perform the practice exercises in this chapter, you must have installed and configured Windows Server 2003 using the procedure described in "About This Book."

Lesson 1: Planning a Security Update Infrastructure

Securing a network is not simply a matter of designing a protected environment and implementing it. You must also maintain that environment, because the threats to your network are constantly changing and you must continually compensate for those threats. Microsoft regularly releases updates and patches for its operating systems, but obtaining and deploying these releases on a large network installation is more complicated than updating a single computer. To keep your network protected, you must create a plan for obtaining the latest security update releases on a timely basis and deploying them on your network in a controlled manner.

After this lesson, you will be able to

- List the types of software updates that Microsoft releases
- Describe the problems inherent in keeping the software on a large network installation updated
- Use Microsoft Baseline Security Analyzer (MBSA)
- Use Microsoft Software Update Services (SUS)
- Describe the enhancements in Microsoft Windows Server Update Services (WSUS)

Estimated lesson time: 20 minutes

Understanding Software Update Practices

Virtually all software products have to be updated, some more frequently than others. Operating systems are usually updated on a regular basis, and Microsoft releases its primary updates in the form of service packs. A *service pack* is a collection of patches and updates that have been tested as a single unit. Service packs are a distinct improvement over the previous system, in which operating system updates were released as a series of individual patches, each addressing a separate issue. For support personnel, the large number of patches available and the uncertainty surrounding which patches had been installed on a particular computer made the task of troubleshooting software problems extremely difficult. Service packs install all the available patches at one time, enabling the support staff to know which updates are present on the computer.

See Also   Microsoft uses service packs to update all its major applications, as well as its operating systems. Other software manufacturers also use the same basic method for updating their products, although their releases often have different names.

Service packs are not the only updates that Microsoft releases, however. Because service packs require a great deal of testing, Microsoft releases them relatively infrequently. In between service pack releases, Microsoft releases individual patches called hotfixes. A *hotfix* is a small patch designed to address a specific issue. While Microsoft recommends that all users install the service pack releases, hotfixes are often intended only for computers experiencing a particular problem.

Update releases might include bug fixes, new features, or drivers, but for network administrators, security updates are often the most important releases. In many cases, Microsoft releases hotfixes to address specific security issues that cannot wait until the next service pack release. Security updates are relatively frequent, and in some cases must be installed as quickly as possible to eliminate a potential hazard.

Using Windows Update

Windows Update is a World Wide Web site that Microsoft maintains, which enables a computer to locate and download the latest updates to the Windows operating system and some hardware driver updates. Windows Update is fully supported on Windows 2000 with Service Pack 4, Windows XP with Service Pack 2, and Windows Server 2003 with Service Pack 1 (SP1).

See Also   For the latest details on the operating systems that Windows Update supports, visit the Windows Update Web site at *http://update.microsoft.com/windowsupdate/v6 /about.aspx?ln=en-us#SupportVL*

When a computer connects to the Windows Update site, shown in Figure 13-1, the user can select an Express update to download and install all updates identified by Microsoft as high priority. Alternatively, the user can select a Custom update and select from a list of critical and optional updates. By using the Custom update, the user can also install any available hardware driver updates.

Tip   Windows Update only provides a limited number of hardware driver updates. You should always check with the vendor of your computer or peripherals for the latest hardware driver updates.

See Also   In Windows Server 2003 SP1, Microsoft Update is a service that provides all the features and benefits of Windows Update plus downloads for other Microsoft applications including Office. For more information on Microsoft Update, see *http://update.microsoft.com /microsoftupdate/v6/muoptdefault.aspx.*

Figure 13-1   The Windows Update Web site interface

For a single computer, a network of home computers, or a small business with a peer-to-peer LAN, Windows Update is a great way to keep a computer current, but it is generally not suitable for use on larger networks, for the following reasons:

- **Bandwidth**   Each time a computer receives an update release using Windows Update, it downloads the software from a Microsoft server on the Internet. On a large network, this would mean that hundreds or thousands of computers are downloading the same files. For small updates, this might not be a problem, but Windows service packs are usually more than 100 megabytes (MB), and downloading the same file for every computer could monopolize an enormous amount of the network's Internet bandwidth.

- **Testing**   Although Microsoft tests its updates carefully before releasing them, the company cannot possibly test every combination of configuration settings and software products. Therefore, it is possible for a particular update to cause problems with some or all of the computers on your network. Here again, for a single computer, this might not be a major issue, but if an update causes a problem on all a network's computers, the loss of productivity and the added burden on technical support personnel could be catastrophic.

Updating a Network

In a network environment, deciding which updates to install and when to install them should not be left up to the individual user. Administrators must be responsible for obtaining updates when they are released and deploying them on the network in a timely manner. However, network administrators should not immediately install every update that appears. It is important to test the update releases first. This is one of the reasons that a network installation should have a security update infrastructure.

A network *security update infrastructure* is a series of policies that are designed to help the network administrator perform the following tasks:

- Determine which computers need to be updated—In some cases, a new security update might apply only to computers performing a specific function or using a specific application or feature. Network administrators must understand each release's specific function and determine which computers require the update.

- Test update releases on multiple system configurations—A security update that causes a malfunction might be just an annoyance on a single computer, but on a large network, it could be a catastrophe. Network administrators must perform their own tests of all security updates before deploying them on the entire network.

- Determine when updates are released—Microsoft frequently releases security updates that might or might not be applicable to the systems on your network. Network administrators must be aware of new releases when they occur and must understand the specific issues each release addresses.

- Deploy update releases on large fleets—Manually installing security updates on hundreds or thousands of computers requires enormous amounts of time, effort, and expense. To deploy updates on a large network efficiently, the process must be automated.

Microsoft has made tools available that help the administrator accomplish these tasks, such as those discussed in the following sections.

Using Microsoft Baseline Security Analyzer

Microsoft Baseline Security Analyzer (MBSA) is a graphical tool (see Figure 13-2) that can check for common security lapses on a single computer or multiple computers running various versions of the Windows operating system. These lapses are typically due to incorrect or incomplete configuration of security features and failure to install security updates. The security faults that MBSA can detect are as follows:

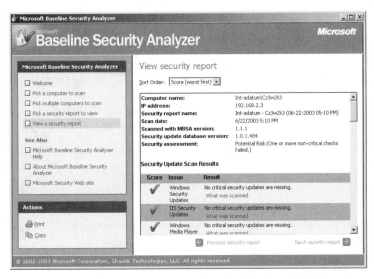

Figure 13-2   The Microsoft Baseline Security Analyzer 1.2.1 interface

- **Missing security updates**   Using a list of current update releases obtained from a Microsoft Internet server, a Microsoft SUS server (MBSA 1.2.1), or a Microsoft WSUS server (MBSA 2.0), MBSA determines whether all the required service packs and security updates have been installed on the computer, and if not, compiles a list of the updates that need to be installed.

> **Tip**   MBSA replaces an earlier Microsoft update checking utility called Hfnetchk.exe, which operates from the command line and only checks computers for missing updates. MBSA includes all the functionality of Hfnetchk.exe, including the command line interface, which you can activate by running Mbsacli.exe with the /hf parameter.

- **Account vulnerabilities**   MBSA checks to see if the Guest account is activated on the computer; whether there are more than two accounts with Administrator privileges; whether anonymous users have too much access to the computer; and whether the computer is configured to use the Autologon feature.

- **Improper passwords**   MBSA checks the passwords on all the computer's accounts, to see if they are configured to expire, are blank, or are too simple.

- **File system vulnerabilities**   MBSA checks to see whether all the disk drives on the computer are using the NTFS file system.

- **IIS and SQL vulnerabilities**   If the computer is running Microsoft Internet Information Services (IIS) or Microsoft SQL Server, MBSA examines these applications for a variety of security weaknesses.

In addition, MBSA displays other information about security on the computer, such as a list of shares, the Windows operating system version number, and whether auditing is enabled.

Microsoft Baseline Security Analyzer (MBSA) 2.0

MBSA 2.0 offers an intuitive user interface and more informative dialog boxes compared to previous versions. Using the new Windows Update Agent and Microsoft Update catalog, MBSA 2.0 has automatically expanding product support.

Other new features in MBSA 2.0 are as follows:

- Severity ratings

- Local and remote scans for Microsoft Office XP security updates

- Additional guidance for locating updates and taking appropriate action

- CVE-IDs for supported updates

- Improved help content

- Compatibility with WSUS

- Automatic Microsoft Update registration and agent update

- Detection of updates on Windows XP Embedded and on 64-bit versions of Microsoft Windows

See Also   MBSA 2.0 is not included with Windows Server 2003, but it is available without charge from the Microsoft Web site at *http://www.microsoft.com/downloads /details.aspx?FamilyID=4b4aba06-b5f9-4dad-be9d-7b51ec2e5ac9.*

MBSA 2.0 is an informational tool that can display security information about a computer, but it cannot do anything to remedy the vulnerabilities that it finds. You can use MBSA 2.0 to determine which security updates to install on specific computers, but to develop an effective security update infrastructure, you must implement a system to keep track of which security updates have been installed on every computer in the enterprise.

Testing Security Updates

Before you deploy security updates on a network, you must test them to make sure they are compatible with all your system configurations. The amount and type of testing depends on the nature of the updates and the complexity of your network. For a major update like a service pack, testing should be extensive. You might want to test the release in a lab environment first, and then do a pilot deployment on a part of your network before proceeding with the general deployment. For smaller, minor updates, a pilot deployment might be sufficient, followed by a general deployment if no problems occur.

Using Microsoft Software Update Services

Deploying any software on a large network is a complicated task, and security updates are no exception. What might be a simple task on a single computer turns into a major project when you have hundreds or thousands of computers. Microsoft SUS is a free product that notifies administrators when new security updates are available, downloads the updates, and then deploys them to the computers on the network (see Figure 13-3).

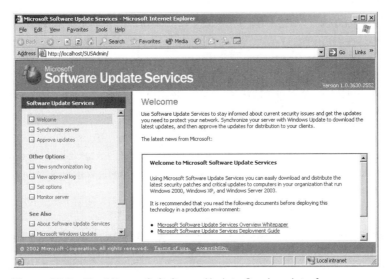

Figure 13-3   The Microsoft Software Update Services interface

See Also   For more information on SUS, see the Microsoft Web site at *http: //www.microsoft..com/windowsserversystem/updateservices/evaluation/previous /default.mspx*.

SUS is essentially an intranet version of the Windows Update Web site that eliminates the need for each computer to download software updates from the Internet and eliminates the need to deploy the updates to multiple computers manually. Administrators can control which updates are applied to the network computers and when, automating the process so that users do not need to know or do anything.

SUS consists of the following components:

■ **Synchronization server**   One computer, running SUS, functions as a synchronization server, downloading all software updates from the Windows Update Web site as they are released. The administrator can allow the downloads to occur as needed; schedule them to occur at specific times (such as off-peak traffic hours); or trigger them manually. Once SUS downloads the updates, it stores them on the server. This eliminates the need for the administrator to continually check the Windows Update Web site for new releases.

- **Intranet Windows Update server** Once the SUS server has downloaded the updates, the administrator must decide whether the server deploys them immediately to the network or saves them for testing and later deployment. When updates are ready for deployment, SUS functions as the Windows Update server for the computers on the network, except that this server is on the intranet and does not require the clients to access the Internet.

- **Automatic Updates** Automatic Updates is a Windows operating system feature that enables computers to download and install software updates with no user intervention. You can configure this feature on your client computers so that they get the updates from an SUS server on the local network rather than from the Windows Update Web site, restricting the updates to those approved by the network administrator.

Important The SUS server runs only on Windows Server 2003 and Microsoft Windows 2000 Server with Service Pack 2 or later. SUS clients must be running Windows Server 2003, Windows 2000, or Microsoft Windows XP.

To configure the computers on a network to retrieve and install updates from an SUS server, you can use group policies to avoid having to configure each system individually. The Computer Configuration\Administrative Templates\Windows Components\Windows Update container (see Figure 13-4) contains a number of policies that enable you to configure the Automatic Update behavior for all your network computers.

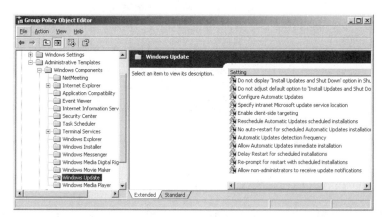

Figure 13-4 Windows Update group policies

Tip   Be sure to understand the differences between the functions of Microsoft Baseline Security Analyzer and Microsoft Software Update Services.

Windows Server Update Services

WSUS is an updated and enhanced version of SUS and is essentially an intranet version of the Microsoft Update Web site. Like SUS, WSUS eliminates the need for each computer to download software updates from the Internet, removes the need to deploy the updates onto multiple computers manually, and eliminates the requirement for user interaction.

Microsoft recommends that customers deploy (or upgrade to) WSUS.

Note   Microsoft will continue to support Software Update Services (SUS) until December 6, 2006. Microsoft will no longer support SUS after this date.

WSUS builds on the features of SUS by providing the following:

- More updates for Microsoft products, in more categories
- Ability to automatically download updates from Microsoft Update by product and type
- More language support for customers worldwide
- Maximized bandwidth efficiency through Background Intelligent Transfer Service (BITS) 2.0
- Ability to target updates to specific computers and computer groups
- Ability to verify that updates are suitable for each computer before installation, a feature that runs automatically for critical and security updates
- Flexible deployment options
- Reporting capabilities
- Flexible database options
- Data migration and import/export capabilities
- Extensibility through the WSUS application programming interface (API)

See Also   For more details on WSUS, see "Now Available: Windows Server Update Services" on the Microsoft Web site, at *http://www.microsoft.com/windowsserversystem/updateservices /default.mspx*.

> **Exam Tip**   For the exam, focus on Microsoft Baseline Security Analyzer and Microsoft Software Update Services.

Practice: Using Microsoft Baseline Security Analyzer

In this practice, you download and install Microsoft Baseline Security Analyzer on a computer running Windows Server 2003 and use it to analyze the security environment on the computer.

Exercise 1: Downloading and Installing MBSA

In this exercise, you download MBSA and install it on your computer. To complete this exercise, you must have access to the Internet.

1. Log on to the computer as Administrator.

2. Open Microsoft Internet Explorer and, in the Address box, type **http://www.microsoft.com/downloads/details.aspx?FamilyID=4b4aba06-b5f9-4dad-be9d-7b51ec2e5ac9** and press ENTER.

3. Click Continue, follow any Windows Validation steps, click MBSASetup-EN.MSI, and select Run.

4. When the download completes, in the Security Warning dialog box, click Run.

5. The Microsoft Baseline Security Analyzer Setup page appears. Click Next to continue.

6. The License Agreement page appears. Select I Accept The License Agreement and click Next.

7. The Destination Folder page appears. Click Next to accept the default destination folder.

8. The Start Installation page appears. Click Install to start the installation.

9. When the installation is completed, a message indicating that the Microsoft Baseline Security Analyzer Setup has completed successfully appears. Click OK.

10. Close Internet Explorer.

Exercise 2: Performing a Security Analysis

In this exercise, you use MBSA to analyze your computer's security configuration.

1. Click Start, point to All Programs, and then click Microsoft Baseline Security Analyzer 2.0. The Microsoft Baseline Security Analyzer window appears.

2. Click Pick A Computer To Scan. The Pick A Computer To Scan page appears in the right pane.

   By default, MBSA is configured to scan only the local computer.

3. Click Start Scan at the bottom of the page. MBSA downloads data from Microsoft, scans the computer, and then displays the View Security Report page.

4. Scroll down the list and note the potential security vulnerabilities of your computer.

5. Close the Microsoft Baseline Security Analyzer window.

Lesson Review

The following questions are intended to reinforce key information presented in this lesson. If you are unable to answer a question, review the lesson materials and try the question again. You can find answers to the questions in the "Questions and Answers" section at the end of this chapter.

1. Which of the following tools can tell you when a computer is missing an important security update? (Choose all that apply.)

   a. Security Configuration and Analysis

   b. Hfnetchk.exe

   c. Microsoft Software Update Services (SUS)

   d. Microsoft Baseline Security Analyzer (MBSA)

2. You have just implemented a Microsoft Software Update Services (SUS) server on your network, and you want workstations running Windows 2000 and Windows XP operating systems to automatically download all the software updates from the SUS server and install them. Which of the following procedures can you use to configure all the workstations at once?

   a. Configure the SUS server to push the updates to specified computers.

   b. Use group policies to configure Automatic Updates on the workstations.

   c. Use Microsoft Baseline Security Analyzer to configure Automatic Updates on the workstations.

   d. Create a login script for the workstations that downloads the update files and installs them.

3. Which of the following are valid reasons for using Microsoft Software Update Services (SUS) instead of Windows Update to update your network workstations? (Choose all that apply.)

   a. To automate the update deployment process

   b. To conserve Internet bandwidth

   c. To enable administrators to test updates before deploying them

   d. To determine which updates must be deployed on each workstation

Lesson Summary

- Microsoft regularly releases software updates for its operating systems and applications. Major updates are called service packs and include all the updates since the current version of the product was released. Between service packs, Microsoft releases individual updates called hotfixes, which address only a single issue.

- To keep a network secure, you must update the software on all the computers on a regular basis. Deploying updates on a large network is a much more complex task than updating an individual computer.

- Microsoft Baseline Security Analyzer is a tool that scans computers on a network and examines them for security vulnerabilities, such as missing security updates, improper passwords, and account vulnerabilities.

- Network administrators should test all software updates before deploying them on the network. The testing process can consist of a lab testing phase and a pilot deployment before the full deployment on the entire network.

- Microsoft Software Update Services (SUS) is a tool that informs administrators when software updates are released and functions as an intranet Windows Update server for clients on the network, so that they can automatically install new updates.

- Microsoft Windows Server Update Services (WSUS) supercedes SUS and provides a greater range of features than SUS does.

Lesson 2: Securing a Wireless Network

Wireless networking has existed for many years, but it is only recently, with the publication of the 802.11 series of standards by the Institute of Electrical and Electronics Engineers (IEEE), that *wireless local area networking (WLAN)* technologies have become mainstream products. WLANs enable home and business users to set up computer networks between places that were previously inaccessible, and enable portable computer users to roam freely while connected to the network. However, wireless networking creates unique security challenges that administrators must address.

After this lesson, you will be able to

- List the standards that define common WLAN technologies
- Describe the security problems inherent in wireless networking
- List the mechanisms that WLANs running IEEE 802.11 based on the Windows operating system can use to authenticate clients and encrypt transmitted data

Estimated lesson time: 30 minutes

Understanding Wireless Networking Standards

Until recently, wireless networking was based on standards defining physical layer technologies that, while reasonably effective, were much slower than the average network and not altogether reliable. These technologies were also expensive and difficult to implement. However, in 1999, the *Institute of Electrical and Electronics Engineers (IEEE)* released the first standard in the 802.11 working group, called "Wireless LAN Medium Access Control (MAC) and Physical Layer (PHY) Specifications," defining a new series of technologies for the WLAN physical layer. For the wireless networking industry, the key document in this series of standards was *IEEE 802.11b*, "Wireless LAN Medium Access Control (MAC) and Physical Layer (PHY) specifications—Amendment 2: higher-speed Physical Layer (PHY) extension in the 2.4 GHz band."

The 802.11b standard defines a physical layer specification that enables WLANs to run at speeds up to 11 megabits per second (Mbps), slightly faster than a standard Ethernet network. When products conforming to this standard arrived on the market, they quickly became a popular solution, both for home and business use. Prices dropped accordingly and, for the first time, wireless networking became a major force in the industry.

Development continues on standards that are designed to provide even higher WLAN transmission speeds. The 802.11a standard, "Wireless LAN Medium Access Control (MAC) and Physical Layer (PHY) specifications: Amendment 1: High-speed Physical Layer in the 5 GHz band" defines a medium with speeds running up to 54 Mbps, while 802.11g, "Wireless LAN Medium Access Control (MAC) and Physical

Layer (PHY) specifications—Amendment 4: Further Higher Data Rate Extension in the 2.4 GHz Band," calls for higher transmission speeds using the same 2.4 GHz frequencies as 802.11b.

See Also For more information on IEEE standards, and to obtain the standards themselves, see the IEEE Web site at *http://www.ieee.org*.

Wireless Networking Topologies

In computer networking, the term *topology* typically refers to the pattern of the cables used to connect the computers. Wireless networks do not use cables, but they still have a topology, which defines how the wireless devices interact at the physical layer. At the physical layer, IEEE 802.11b WLANs use direct sequence spread spectrum communications at a frequency of 2.4 GHz, and the devices can communicate with each other using two basic topologies: ad hoc and infrastructure.

Off the Record Cabled networks are sometimes referred to as *bounded* media, because their signals are confined to a given space, that is, the interior of the cable. Wireless networks are therefore called *unbounded* media, because their signals are not physically restricted in this way.

An *ad hoc network* consists of two or more wireless devices communicating directly with each other. The signals generated by WLAN network interface adapters are omnidirectional out to a range that is governed by environmental factors, as well as the nature of the equipment involved. This range is called a *basic service area (BSA)*. When two wireless devices come within range of each other, as shown in Figure 13-5, they are able to connect and communicate, immediately forming a two-node network. Wireless devices within the same basic service area are called a *basic service set (BSS)*.

Other wireless devices coming within the transmission range of the first two can also participate in the network. Ad hoc networking is not transitive, however. A wireless device that comes within range of another device, but still lies outside the range of a third, can only communicate with the device in its range.

An *infrastructure network* uses a wireless device called an access point as a bridge between wireless devices and a standard cabled network. An *access point* is a small unit that connects to an Ethernet network (or other cabled network) by cable, but that also contains an 802.11b-compliant wireless transceiver. Other wireless devices coming within range of the access point are able to communicate with the cabled network just as though they were connected by a cable themselves (see Figure 13-6). The access point functions as a transparent bridge, effectively extending the cabled local area network (LAN) to include the wireless devices.

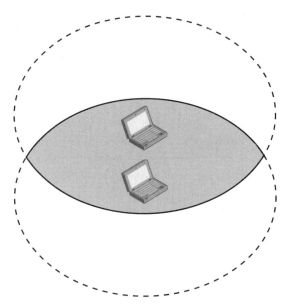

Figure 13-5   An ad hoc network

 Note   The ad hoc topology is most often used on home networks, or for very small business that have no cabled network components at all.

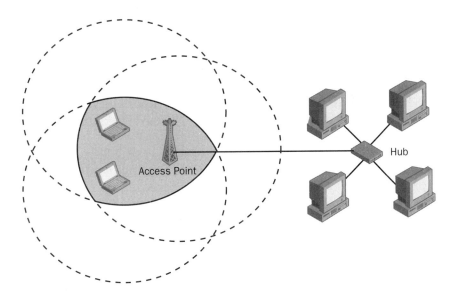

Figure 13-6   An infrastructure network

> **Note**   On an infrastructure network, wireless devices communicate only with the access point; they do not communicate with each other directly. Therefore, even if two wireless computers are within range of each other, they must still use the access point to communicate.

Most business networks use the infrastructure topology because it provides complete connectivity between wireless devices and the cabled network.

Understanding Wireless Network Security

Unlike bounded media, in which every device on the network must be physically connected to a cable for communication to occur, wireless networks transmit signals in all directions, and any compatible device coming within transmission range may be able to connect to the network. Depending on how many access points you have and where they are located, the boundary of your equipment's effective range can easily fall outside a controllable area. For example, placing an access point near a building's outer wall can enable an unauthorized user with a wireless-equipped laptop to access your network from a car parked outside the building.

For this reason, security should be a major concern for all wireless network installations. The two primary threats when it comes to wireless networking are as follows:

- **Unauthorized access**   An unauthorized user with a wireless workstation connects to the network and accesses network resources. This is the functional equivalent of a user connecting to a cabled network by plugging into an available jack or splicing into the cable, but on a wireless network the process of making the network connection is much easier. On an infrastructure network, this type of attack compromises the entire network because the user may be able to access bounded as well as unbounded resources. To prevent unauthorized users from connecting to a wireless network, you must implement a system that authenticates and authorizes users before they receive significant access.

- **Data interception**   A user running a protocol analyzer with a wireless network interface adapter may be able to capture all the packets transmitted between the other wireless devices and the access point. In this case, the device can be as simple as a laptop running Microsoft Network Monitor with a network interface adapter that supports promiscuous mode operation. This type of attack endangers only the data transmitted over the air, but it also leaves no traces, so it is virtually undetectable. The only way to protect against this type of attack is to encrypt all packets transmitted over wireless connections. This does not prevent intruders from capturing the packets, but it does prevent them from reading the data inside.

Controlling Wireless Access Using Group Policies

Windows Server 2003 provides security capabilities for wireless networking in the form of group policies that you can use to restrict users' wireless access to the network. In the Group Policy Object Editor console, you can create a policy in the Computer Configuration\Windows Settings\Security Settings\Wireless Network (IEEE 802.11) Policies subheading that enables you to specify whether wireless-equipped computers can connect to ad hoc networks only, infrastructure networks only, or both (see Figure 13-7).

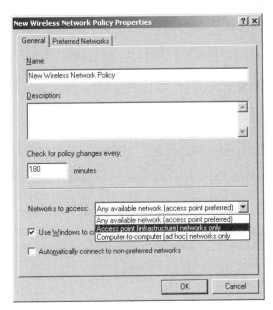

Figure 13-7   The New Wireless Network Policy Properties dialog box

In the Preferred Networks tab, you can specify the networks to which users can connect and set properties for the IEEE 802.1X security protocol, such as which authentication protocol to use (see Figure 13-8). Using these group policy settings, you can configure the wireless networking properties for all the computers on your WLAN.

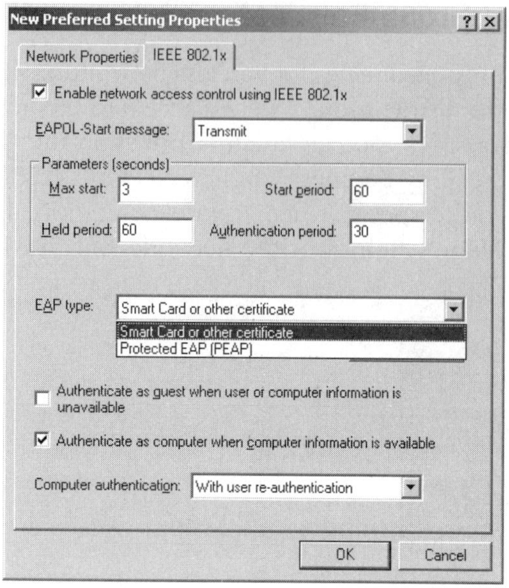

Figure 13-8   The New Preferred Setting Properties dialog box

Authenticating Users

You can use several methods to authenticate users attempting to connect to your WLAN and to prevent unauthorized access by outsiders. The IEEE 802.11 standard itself defines two methods: Open System authentication and Shared Key authentication, and Windows Server 2003 supports a third method, based on another standard called IEEE 802.1X.

Open System Authentication

Open System authentication is the default authentication method used by IEEE 802.11 devices, and it actually provides no authentication at all. Open System authentication is simply an exchange of messages in which one system identifies itself to another and the other system replies. There is no exchange of passwords, keys, or any other type of credential, and there is no way for a device configured to use Open System authentication to refuse authentication to another.

Shared Key Authentication

Shared Key authentication is a system by which wireless devices authenticate each other using a secret key that both possess. The key is assumed to have been shared before authentication using a secure channel independent of 802.11 communications to prevent it from being compromised during transmission. Shared Key authentication is not a particularly secure method because all the computers in the same BSS must possess the same key. Compromising the key on one system nullifies the authentication security for the entire BSS.

Important   Shared Key authentication requires the use of the Wired Equivalent Privacy (WEP) algorithm. If WEP is not implemented, Shared Key authentication is not available.

During a Shared Key authentication, messages are exchanged between the requester and the responder as follows:

1. The system requesting authentication asserts its identity to the other system, using a message that contains a value that identifies the shared key (not the shared key itself) that the system is using.

2. The system receiving the authentication request responds with a message containing the authentication result. If the authentication is successful, the response message includes a 128-byte block of challenge text generated by the WEP pseudo-random number generator.

3. The requester copies the challenge text from the response message to a new message and encrypts it with WEP, using the shared key as an encryption key.

4. The responder decrypts the message and compares the decrypted challenge text with the text the system transmitted in step 2. If the values match, the responder grants the authentication.

IEEE 802.1X Authentication

The *IEEE 802.1X* standard, "Port Based Network Access Control," defines a method of authenticating and authorizing users connecting to an IEEE 802 LAN, and blocking those users' access to the LAN should the authentication fail. IEEE 802.1X can authenticate users connecting to any type of LAN, such as Ethernet or Token Ring, but in this case, it is particularly valuable in the case of IEEE 802.11 wireless LANs.

Most IEEE 802.1X implementations function as clients of a server running a *Remote Authentication Dial-In User Service (RADIUS)*, such as the Internet Authentication Service (IAS) included with Windows Server 2003. The RADIUS server provides centralized authentication and authorization services for the entire network; for WLAN authentication, RADIUS typically uses one of the following two authentication protocols:

- *Extensible Authentication Protocol-Transport Level Security (EAP-TLS)*—EAP is an authentication protocol that is designed to be adaptable, so that it can carry a variety of *authentication mechanisms* within a given packet framework. TLS is an authentication mechanism that transports its messages within EAP packets and provides mutual authentication, integrity-protected negotiation of cryptographic service providers, and secret key exchange between two systems that use public key cryptography. The networks that use EAP-TLS typically have a public key infrastructure (PKI) in place and use certificates for authentication that are stored on the computer or on smart cards.

- *Protected EAP-Microsoft Challenge Handshake Authentication Protocol, version 2 (PEAP-MS-CHAP v2)*—PEAP is a variation on EAP that is designed for use on wireless networks that do not have a PKI in place. With PEAP, you can use a password-based authentication method, such as MS-CHAP, to securely authenticate wireless connections. PEAP creates an encrypted channel before the password-based authentication occurs. Therefore, password-based authentication exchanges such as those that occur in MS-CHAP v2 are not subject to offline dictionary attacks. (Put simply, an offline dictionary attack uses a brute force dictionary attack to make repeated attempts to decrypt captured packets that use an encryption key derived from a user's password. This process is made easier for the intruder when the encryption key is derived from a weak password.)

> **Important**   To use PEAP-MS-CHAP v2 for wireless network authentication, the wireless client must be running either Windows Server 2003 or Windows XP with SP1 installed.

With this system in place, an access point receiving a connection request from a wireless client forwards the request to the RADIUS server, which uses information in a data store, such as the Active Directory database, to determine whether the client should be granted access to the network.

Encrypting Wireless Traffic

To prevent data transmitted over a wireless network from being compromised through unauthorized packet captures, the IEEE 802.11 standard defines an encryption mechanism called *Wired Equivalent Privacy (WEP)*. WEP is an encryption system that uses the RC4 cryptographic algorithm developed by RSA Security Inc. WEP depends on encryption keys that are generated by a mechanism external to WEP itself. In cases where WEP is used with IEEE 802.1X to create a comprehensive wireless security solution for the Windows operating system, WEP uses the keys generated by the EAP-TLS or PEAP-MS-CHAP v2 authentication protocol to encrypt the data in the packets.

> **Off the Record**   Microsoft recommends using the WEP and IEEE 802.1X combination as a suitable security configuration for wireless clients running the Windows operating system.

The degree of protection that WEP provides is governed by configurable parameters that control the length of the keys used to encrypt the data and the frequency with which the systems generate new keys. Longer and more frequently changed keys produce better security.

Exam Tip   Be sure you are familiar with the security hazards inherent in wireless networking, and with the mechanisms that Windows operating systems can use to authenticate wireless clients and encrypt their traffic.

Wireless Provisioning Services (WPS)

Wireless Provisioning Services (WPS) are enhancements that are included in Microsoft Windows XP SP2 and Windows Server 2003 with SP1. WPS extends the wireless client software included with Windows XP and the Internet Authentication Service (IAS) included with Windows Server 2003 to allow for a consistent and automated configuration process when connecting to the following:

- Public wireless hotspots that provide access to the Internet

- Private organization wireless networks that provide guest access to the Internet

See Also   For more information on WPS, see "Wireless Provisioning Services Overview" on the Microsoft TechNet Web site at *http://www.microsoft.com/technet/community/columns /cableguy/cg1203.mspx.*

Lesson Review

The following questions are intended to reinforce key information presented in this lesson. If you are unable to answer a question, review the lesson materials and try the question again. You can find answers to the questions in the "Questions and Answers" section at the end of this chapter.

1. Which of the following authentication mechanisms enables clients to connect to a wireless network using smart cards?

    a. Open System authentication

    b. Shared Key authentication

    c. IEEE 802.1X authentication using EAP-TLS

    d. IEEE 802.1X authentication using PEAP-MS-CHAP v2

2. You are installing an IEEE 802.11b wireless network in a private home using computers running Windows XP, and you decide that data encryption is not necessary, but you want to use Shared Key authentication. However, when you try to configure the network interface adapter on the clients to use Shared Key authentication,

the option is not available. Which of the following explanations could be the cause of the problem?

   a. WEP is not enabled.

   b. Windows XP SP1 is not installed on the computers.

   c. Windows XP does not support Shared Key authentication.

   d. A PKI is required for Shared Key authentications.

3. Which of the following terms describe a wireless network that consists of two laptop computers with wireless network interface adapters communicating directly with each other? (Choose all that apply.)

   a. Basic service set

   b. Infrastructure network

   c. Ad hoc network

   d. Access point

Lesson Summary

- Most wireless LANs today are based on the 802.11 standards published by the IEEE.

- WLANs have two primary security hazards: unauthorized access to the network and eavesdropping on transmitted packets.

- To secure a wireless network, you must authenticate the clients before they are granted network access and encrypt all packets transmitted over the wireless link.

- To authenticate IEEE 802.11 wireless network clients, you can use Open System authentication, Shared Key authentication, or IEEE 802.1X.

- To encrypt transmitted packets, the IEEE 802.11 standard defines the Wired Equivalent Privacy (WEP) mechanism.

Lesson 3: Providing Secure Network Administration

For administrators of large networks, one of the main objectives is to minimize the amount of travel from site to site to work on individual computers. Many of the administration tools included with Windows Server 2003 are capable of managing services on remote computers as well as on the local system. For example, most Microsoft Management Console (MMC) snap-ins have this capability, enabling administrators to work on systems throughout the enterprise without traveling. These are specialized tools used primarily for server administration, however, that can perform only a limited number of tasks. For comprehensive administrative access to a remote computer, Windows Server 2003 includes two tools that are extremely useful to the network administrator, called Remote Assistance and Remote Desktop.

After this lesson, you will be able to

- Configure Windows Server 2003 Remote Assistance
- List the security features protecting computers that use Remote Assistance
- Configure Windows Server 2003 Remote Desktop

Estimated lesson time: 30 minutes

Using Remote Assistance

Remote Assistance is a feature of Windows XP and Windows Server 2003 that enables a user (an administrator, trainer, or technical support representative) at one location to connect to a distant user's computer, chat with the user, and either view all the user's activities or take complete control of the system. Remote Assistance can eliminate the need for administrative personnel to travel to a user's location for any of the following reasons:

See Also   In Microsoft interfaces and documentation, the person connecting to a client using Remote Assistance is referred to as an expert or a helper.

- **Technical support**   A system administrator or help desk operator can use Remote Assistance to connect to a remote computer to modify configuration parameters, install new software, or troubleshoot user problems.

- **Troubleshooting**   By connecting in read-only mode, an expert can observe a remote user's activities and determine whether improper procedures are the source of problems the user is experiencing. The expert can also connect in interactive mode to try to recreate the problem or to modify system settings to resolve it. This is far more efficient than trying to give instructions to inexperienced users over the telephone.

■ **Training**   Trainers and help desk personnel can demonstrate procedures to users right on their systems, without having to travel to their locations.

To receive remote assistance, the computer running Windows Server 2003 or Windows XP must be configured to use the Remote Assistance feature in one of the following ways:

■ **User Control Panel**   Display the System Properties dialog box from the Control Panel and click the Remote tab. Then select the Turn On Remote Assistance And Allow Invitations To Be Sent From This Computer check box (see Figure 13-9).

> **Tip**   By clicking the Advanced button in the Remote tab in the System Properties dialog box, the user can specify whether to let the expert take control of the computer or simply view activities on the computer. The user can also specify the amount of time that the invitation for remote assistance remains valid.

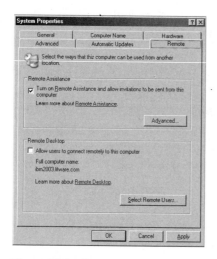

Figure 13-9   The Remote tab in the System Properties dialog box

■ **Using Group Policies**   Use the Group Policy Object Editor console to open a GPO for an Active Directory domain or organizational unit object containing the client computer. Browse to the Computer Configuration\Administrative Templates\System\Remote Assistance container and enable the Solicited Remote Assistance policy (see Figure 13-10).

> **Tip**   The Solicited Remote Assistance policy also enables you to specify the degree of control the expert receives over the client computer, the duration of the invitation, and the method for sending e-mail invitations. The Offer Remote Assistance policy enables you to specify the names of users or groups who can function as experts, and whether those experts can perform tasks or just observe.

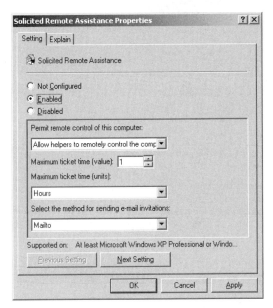

Figure 13-10   The Solicited Remote Assistance Properties dialog box

Creating an Invitation

To receive remote assistance, a client must issue an invitation and send it to a particular expert. The client can send the invitation using e-mail, Microsoft Windows Messenger, or can save it as a file to be sent to the expert in some other manner, using the interface shown in Figure 13-11.

> **Tip**   When users create invitations, they can specify a password that the expert has to supply to connect to their computers. You should urge your users to always require passwords for Remote Assistance connections, and instruct them to supply the expert with the correct password using a different medium from the one they are using to send the invitation.

Once the expert receives the invitation, invoking it launches the Remote Assistance application, which enables the expert to connect to the remote computer, as shown in Figure 13-12. Using this interface, the user and the expert can talk or type messages to each other and, by default, the expert can see everything that the user is doing on the computer. If the client computer is configured to allow remote control, the expert can also click the Take Control button and operate the client computer interactively.

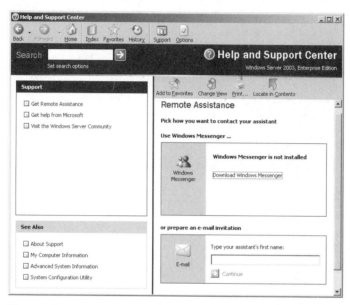

Figure 13-11   The Remote Assistance page of the Help And Support Center tool

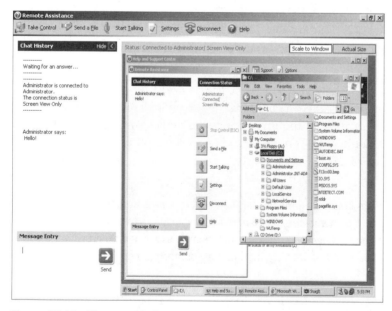

Figure 13-12   The expert's Remote Assistance interface

Securing Remote Assistance

Because an expert offering remote assistance to another user can perform virtually any activity on the remote computer that the local user can, this feature can be a significant security hazard. An unauthorized user who takes control of a computer using Remote Assistance can cause almost unlimited damage. However, Remote Assistance is designed to minimize the dangers. Some of the protective features of Remote Assistance are as follows:

- **Invitations**   No person can connect to another computer using Remote Assistance unless that person has received an invitation from the client. Clients can configure the effective lifespan of their invitations in minutes, hours, or days, to prevent experts from attempting to connect to the computer later.

- **Interactive connectivity**   When an expert accepts an invitation from a client and attempts to connect to the computer, a user must be present at the client console to grant the expert access. You cannot use Remote Assistance to connect to an unattended computer.

- **Client-side control**   The client always has ultimate control over a Remote Assistance connection. The client can terminate the connection at any time by pressing the Esc key or clicking Stop Control (ESC) in the client-side Remote Assistance page.

- **Remote control configuration**   Using the System Properties dialog box or Remote Assistance group policies, users and administrators can specify whether experts are permitted to take control of client computers. An expert who has read-only access cannot modify the computer's configuration in any way using Remote Access. The group policies also enable administrators to grant specific users expert status, so that no one else can use Remote Access to connect to a client computer, even with the client's permission.

- **Firewalls**   Remote Assistance uses Transmission Control Protocol (TCP) port number 3389 for all its network communications. For networks that use Remote Assistance internally and are also connected to the Internet, it is recommended that network administrators block this port in their firewalls, to prevent users outside the network from taking control of computers that request remote assistance. However, it is also possible to provide remote assistance to clients over the Internet, which would require leaving port 3389 open.

Using Remote Desktop

While Remote Assistance is intended to enable users to obtain interactive help from other users, Remote Desktop is an administrative feature that enables users to access computers from remote locations, with no interaction required at the remote site.

Remote Desktop is essentially a remote control program for computers running Windows Server 2003 and Windows XP; there are no invitations and no read-only capabilities. When you connect to a computer using Remote Desktop, you can operate the remote computer as though you were sitting at the console and perform most configuration and application tasks.

Off the Record   One of the most useful applications of Remote Desktop is to connect to servers, such as those in a locked closet or data center, that are not otherwise easily accessible. In fact, some administrators run their servers without monitors or input devices once the initial installation and configuration of the computer is complete, relying solely on Remote Desktop access for everyday monitoring and maintenance.

Exam Tip   Be sure that you understand the differences between Remote Assistance and Remote Desktop, and that you understand the applications for which each is used.

Remote Desktop For Administration is essentially an application of the Terminal Services service supplied with Windows Server 2003. A desktop version called Remote Desktop is included with Windows XP Professional. When you use Terminal Services to host a large number of clients, you must purchase licenses for them. However, Windows Server 2003 allows up to two simultaneous Remote Desktop connections without the need for a separate license.

When you connect to a computer using Remote Desktop, the system creates a separate session for you, independent of the console session. This means that even someone working at the console cannot see what you are doing. You must log on when connecting using Remote Desktop, just as you would if you were sitting at the console, meaning that you must have a user account and the appropriate permissions to access the host system. After you log on, the system displays the desktop configuration associated with your user account, and you can then proceed to work as you normally would.

Activating Remote Desktop

By default, Remote Desktop is disabled on computers running Windows Server 2003 and Windows XP. Before you can connect to a computer using Remote Desktop, you must enable it using the System Properties dialog box, accessed from the Control Panel. Click the Remote tab and select the Allow Users To Connect Remotely To This Computer check box, as shown earlier in Figure 13-9, and then click OK.

> **Note** Because Remote Desktop requires a standard logon, it is inherently more secure than Remote Assistance and needs no special security measures, such as invitations and session passwords. However, you can also click Select Remote Users in the Remote tab to display a Remote Desktop Users dialog box, in which you can specify the names of the only users or groups that are permitted to access the computer using Remote Desktop. All users with Administrator privileges are granted access by default.

Using the Remote Desktop Client

Both Windows Server 2003 and Windows XP include the client program needed to connect to a host computer using Remote Desktop (see Figure 13-13). In addition, both operating systems include a version of the client program that you can install on earlier Windows operating systems.

Figure 13-13 The Remote Desktop Connection client

> **Tip** Windows Server 2003 also includes a Remote Desktops console (accessible from the Administrative Tools program group) that you can use to connect to multiple Remote Desktop hosts and switch between them as needed.

Practice: Configuring Remote Assistance

In this practice, you configure a computer running Windows Server 2003 to receive remote assistance from another computer.

Exercise 1: Activating Remote Assistance Using Control Panel

In this exercise, you use the Control Panel's System Properties dialog box to activate Remote Assistance on the computer.

1. Log on to the computer as Administrator.

2. Click Start, point to Control Panel, and then click System. The System Properties dialog box appears.

3. Click the Remote tab.

4. In the Remote Assistance group box, select the Turn On Remote Assistance And Allow Invitations To Be Sent From This Computer check box.

5. Click Advanced. The Remote Assistance Settings dialog box appears.

6. Make sure that the Allow This Computer To Be Controlled Remotely check box is selected.

7. In the Invitations group box, change the Set The Maximum Amount Of Time Invitations Can Remain Open selector value to 1 hour, and then click OK.

8. Click OK to close the System Properties dialog box.

Exercise 2: Activating Remote Assistance Using Group Policies

In this exercise, you use group policies to activate remote assistance for all the computers in the domain.

> **Note**   This exercise is an alternative to the individual computer configuration you performed in Exercise 1. It is not necessary to do both.

1. Log on to the computer as Administrator.

2. Click Start, point to Administrative Tools, and then click Active Directory Users And Computers. The Active Directory Users And Computers console appears.

3. Click the icon for the contoso.com domain in the scope pane, and from the Action menu, select Properties. The Contoso.com Properties dialog box appears.

4. Click the Group Policy tab, and then click Edit. The Group Policy Object Editor console appears.

5. Expand the Computer Configuration, Administrative Templates, and System containers, and then select the Remote Assistance container.

6. In the details pane, double-click the Solicited Remote Assistance policy. The Solicited Remote Assistance Properties dialog box appears.

7. Click the Enabled option button, and then click OK to accept the default settings.

8. Close the Group Policy Object Editor console.

9. Click OK to close the Contoso.com Properties dialog box.

10. Close the Active Directory Users And Computers console.

Exercise 3: Creating an Invitation

In this exercise, you create an invitation for an expert to give you remote assistance. For the purposes of this exercise, you will save the invitation to a file, but on an actual network, you might e-mail it to the appropriate person or send it using Windows Messenger.

1. Click Start and then click Help And Support. The Help And Support Center page appears.

2. Under Support, click the Remote Assistance hyperlink. The Remote Assistance page appears.

3. Click Invite Someone To Help You. The Pick How You Want To Contact Your Assistant page appears.

4. Click Save Invitation As A File (Advanced). The Remote Assistance — Save Invitation page appears.

5. Under Set The Invitation To Expire, set the duration of the invitation to 10 minutes, and then click Continue.

6. Type a password of your choice in the Type Password text box, and again in the Confirm Password text box, and then click Save Invitation. The Save As dialog box appears.

7. Save the invitation file to the root of your computer's C drive.

> **Tip**   If you are connected to a network, and another computer running Windows Server 2003 or Windows XP is available, you can use that computer to initiate a Remote Assistance session with your server by double-clicking the invitation file.

8. Close the Help And Support Center window.

Lesson Review

The following questions are intended to reinforce key information presented in this lesson. If you are unable to answer a question, review the lesson materials and try the question again. You can find answers to the questions in the "Questions and Answers" section at the end of this chapter.

1. Your company is installing a computer running Windows Server 2003 in a utility closet that is only accessible to building maintenance personnel. Therefore, you will have to depend on Remote Desktop for maintenance access to the server. You do not have Administrator privileges to the server and your workstation is running Windows 2000 Professional. Which of the following tasks must you perform before you can connect to the server from your workstation using Remote Desktop? (Choose all that apply.)

   a. Install the Remote Desktop Connection client on the workstation.

   b. Activate Remote Desktop on the server using the System Control Panel.

   c. Enable the Solicited Remote Assistance group policy for the domain.

   d. Add your account name to the Remote Desktop users list.

2. You have just created a Remote Access invitation that you intended to send to a person at the network help desk, but you sent it to someone else instead. Which of the following measures would prevent the unintended recipient from connecting to your computer?

   a. Display the Remote Assistance Settings dialog box and reduce the duration of the invitations created by your computer.

   b. Press Esc.

   c. Refuse the incoming connection when it arrives.

   d. Change your user account password.

3. Which of the following operating systems includes the Remote Desktop Connection client program? (Choose all that apply.)

   a. Windows 2000 Server

   b. Windows XP

   c. Windows Server 2003

   d. Windows 98

Lesson Summary

- Many of the administrative tools included with Windows Server 2003 can manage services on computers all over the network.

- Remote Assistance is a Windows Server 2003 and Windows XP feature that enables users to request assistance from an expert at another location.

- Experts connecting to a computer using Remote Assistance can chat with the user, view the user's actions on the computer, and take control of the computer to provide help.

■ Remote Assistance cannot easily be abused because users must request help before experts can connect to their computers, and the users are always in control of the Remote Assistance connection.

■ Remote Desktop enables administrators to connect to distant computers that are unattended and work with them as though they are seated at the system console. A Remote Desktop client must log on to the host computer using a standard user account and receives only the permissions and rights granted to the account.

Case Scenario Exercise

You are the network infrastructure design specialist for Litware Inc., a manufacturer of specialized scientific software products, and you have already created a network design for their new office building, as described in the Case Scenario Exercise in Chapter 1. You are deploying a wireless LAN as part of your Active Directory network, which will enable users with laptop computers running Windows XP to roam anywhere in the building and remain connected to the network.

The wireless equipment you have selected conforms to the IEEE 802.11b standard and consists of network interface cards for all the laptops and an access point for each floor of the building. Because the laptop users might be working with sensitive data, you want to make sure that the wireless network is secure. You have been considering a number of security strategies for the WLAN, but have not made a final decision. Based on the information provided, answer the following questions.

1. Which of the following tasks would wireless users not be able to do if you decided to use Shared Key authentication?

   a. Use WEP encryption for all wireless transmissions

   b. Roam from one access point to another

   c. Access resources on other wireless computers

   d. Participate in an infrastructure network

2. Which of the following tasks would you need to perform to use IEEE 802.1X and WEP to secure the WLAN? (Choose all that apply.)

   a. Install IAS on a computer running Windows Server 2003.

   b. Deploy a public key infrastructure on the network by installing Certificate Services.

   c. Install smart card readers in all the laptop computers.

   d. Install SP1 on all the laptops running Windows XP.

3. If you elect to use Open System authentication with WEP encryption, to which of the following vulnerabilities would the WLAN be subject?

    a. Unauthorized users connecting to the network

    b. Compromised passwords from unencrypted WLAN authentication messages

    c. Interception of transmitted data by someone using a wireless protocol analyzer

    d. Inability of wireless computers to access resources on the cabled network

Troubleshooting Lab

You have just installed Microsoft Baseline Security Analyzer on a member server running Windows Server 2003 and have scanned the system for security vulnerabilities. The results of the scan displayed the vulnerabilities listed below. For each vulnerability in the list, state how you would correct the problem.

1. Critical Windows operating system security updates are missing.

    _____

    _____

2. Some user accounts have non-expiring passwords.

    _____

    _____

3. The computer's C drive is using the FAT file system.

    _____

    _____

4. The system is configured to use the Autologon feature, with the password stored as plain text.

    _____

    _____

5. The Guest account is enabled on the computer.

    _____

    _____

Chapter Summary

- Microsoft Baseline Security Analyzer is a tool that scans computers on a network and examines them for security vulnerabilities, such as missing security updates, improper passwords, and account vulnerabilities.

- Microsoft Software Update Services is a tool that informs administrators when software updates are released and functions as an intranet Windows Update server for clients on the network, so that they can automatically install new updates.

- Most wireless LANs in use today are based on the 802.11 standards published by the IEEE.

- To secure a wireless network, you must authenticate clients before they are granted network access and also encrypt all packets transmitted over the wireless link.

- To authenticate IEEE 802.11 wireless network clients, you can use Open System authentication, Shared Key authentication, or IEEE 802.1X.

- To encrypt transmitted packets, the IEEE 802.11 standard defines the Wired Equivalent Privacy (WEP) mechanism.

- Remote Assistance is a Windows Server 2003 and Windows XP feature that enables users to request assistance from an expert at another location.

- Remote Assistance cannot easily be abused because users must request help before experts can connect to their computers, and the users are always in control of the Remote Assistance connection.

- Remote Desktop enables administrators to connect to distant computers that are unattended and work with them as though seated at the system console. A Remote Desktop client must log on to the host computer using a standard user account, and receives only the permissions and rights granted to the account.

Exam Highlights

Before taking the exam, review the key points and terms that are presented below to help you identify topics you need to review. Return to the lessons for additional practice, and review the "Further Reading" sections in Part 2 for pointers to more information about topics covering the exam objectives.

Key Points

- Microsoft Baseline Security Analyzer is a tool that can scan multiple computers on a network and examine them for security vulnerabilities, such as missing security updates, improper passwords, and account vulnerabilities. However, MBSA cannot modify the systems or download security updates.

■ Microsoft Software Update Services is a tool that informs administrators when software updates are released and functions as an intranet Windows Update server for clients on the network, so that they can automatically install new updates.

■ Because wireless network transmissions are omnidirectional, signals may be accessed by unauthorized users. The two primary dangers are that unauthorized computers can connect to the WLAN and that they can intercept transmitted packets and read the data inside. To prevent these occurrences, you must authenticate users when they connect to the WLAN and encrypt all traffic transmitted over the WLAN.

■ To authenticate IEEE 802.11 wireless network clients, you can use Open System authentication, Shared Key authentication, or IEEE 802.1X. To encrypt transmitted packets, the IEEE 802.11 standard defines the Wired Equivalent Privacy (WEP) mechanism. Microsoft recommends the use of IEEE 802.1X authentication, in combination with WEP encryption.

■ Remote Assistance is a Windows Server 2003 and Windows XP feature that enables users to request assistance from an expert at another location. Because the user requesting help must be present and is always in control of the connection, Remote Assistance is relatively secure.

■ Remote Desktop enables administrators to connect to distant computers that are unattended and work with them as though seated at the system console. A Remote Desktop client must log on to the host computer using a standard user account, and receives only the permissions and rights granted to the account.

Key Terms

Ad hoc network   A network in which wireless computers communicate directly with each other.

Infrastructure network   A network in which wireless computers communicate with an access point that is connected to a cabled network, providing access to both bounded and unbounded network resources.

Basic service area (BSA)   The effective transmission range in which wireless devices can communicate. A new wireless device cannot connect to an existing wireless network until it enters its BSA.

Basic service set (BSS)   A group of wireless devices communicating with a basic service area.

Questions and Answers

Page
13-13
Lesson 1 Review

1. Which of the following tools can tell you when a computer is missing an important security update? (Choose all that apply.)

   a. Security Configuration and Analysis

   b. Hfnetchk.exe

   c. Microsoft Software Update Services

   d. Microsoft Baseline Security Analyzer

   b and d

2. You have just implemented a Microsoft Software Update Services server on your network, and you want workstations running Windows 2000 and Windows XP operating systems to automatically download all the software updates from the SUS server and install them. Which of the following procedures can you use to configure all the workstations at once?

   a. Configure the SUS server to push the updates to specified computers.

   b. Use group policies to configure Automatic Updates on the workstations.

   c. Use Microsoft Baseline Security Analyzer to configure Automatic Updates on the workstations.

   d. Create a login script for the workstations that downloads the update files and installs them.

   b

3. Which of the following are valid reasons for using Microsoft Software Update Services instead of Windows Update to update your network workstations? (Choose all that apply.)

   a. To automate the update deployment process

   b. To conserve Internet bandwidth

   c. To enable administrators to test updates before deploying them

   d. To determine which updates must be deployed on each workstation

   b and c

Page
13-23
Lesson 2 Review

1. Which of the following authentication mechanisms enables clients to connect to a wireless network using smart cards?

    a. Open System authentication

    b. Shared Key authentication

    c. IEEE 802.1X authentication using EAP-TLS

    d. IEEE 802.1X authentication using PEAP-MS-CHAP v2

  c

2. You are installing an IEEE 802.11b wireless network in a private home using computers running Windows XP, and you decide that data encryption is not necessary, but you want to use Shared Key authentication. However, when you try to configure the network interface adapter on the clients to use Shared Key authentication, the option is not available. Which of the following explanations could be the cause of the problem?

    a. WEP is not enabled.

    b. Windows XP SP1 is not installed on the computers.

    c. Windows XP does not support Shared Key authentication.

    d. A PKI is required for Shared Key authentications.

  a

3. Which of the following terms describe a wireless network that consists of two laptop computers with wireless network interface adapters communicating directly with each other? (Choose all that apply.)

    a. Basic service set

    b. Infrastructure network

    c. Ad hoc network

    d. Access point

  a and c

Page
13-33
Lesson 3 Review

1. Your company is installing a computer running Windows Server 2003 in a utility closet that is only accessible to building maintenance personnel. Therefore, you will have to depend on Remote Desktop for maintenance access to the server. You do not have Administrator privileges to the server and your workstation is running Windows 2000 Professional. Which of the following tasks must you perform before you can connect to the server from your workstation using Remote Desktop? (Choose all that apply.)

    a. Install the Remote Desktop Connection client on the workstation.

    b. Activate Remote Desktop on the server using the System Control Panel.

   c. Enable the Solicited Remote Assistance group policy for the domain.

   d. Add your account name to the Remote Desktop users list.

a, b, and d

2. You have just created a Remote Access invitation that you intended to send to a person at the network help desk, but you sent it to someone else instead. Which of the following measures would prevent the unintended recipient from connecting to your computer?

   a. Display the Remote Assistance Settings dialog box and reduce the duration of the invitations created by your computer.

   b. Press Esc.

   c. Refuse the incoming connection when it arrives.

   d. Change your user account password.

c

3. Which of the following operating systems includes the Remote Desktop Connection client program? (Choose all that apply.)

   a. Windows 2000 Server

   b. Windows XP

   c. Windows Server 2003

   d. Windows 98

b and c

Page
13-35

Case Scenario Exercise

Based on the information provided in the Case Scenario Exercise, answer the following questions:

1. Which of the following tasks would wireless users not be able to do if you decided to use Shared Key authentication?

   a. Use WEP encryption for all wireless transmissions

   b. Roam from one access point to another

   c. Access resources on other wireless computers

   d. Participate in an infrastructure network

b

2. Which of the following tasks would you need to perform to use IEEE 802.1X and WEP to secure the WLAN? (Choose all that apply.)

   a. Install IAS on a computer running Windows Server 2003.

   b. Deploy a public key infrastructure on the network by installing Certificate Services.

   c. Install smart card readers in all the laptop computers.

   d. Install SP1 on all the laptops running Windows XP.

   a and d

3. If you elect to use Open System authentication with WEP encryption, to which of the following vulnerabilities would the WLAN be subject?

   a. Unauthorized users connecting to the network

   b. Compromised passwords from unencrypted WLAN authentication messages

   c. Interception of transmitted data by someone using a wireless protocol analyzer

   d. Inability of wireless computers to access resources on the cabled network

   a

Page 13-36 **Troubleshooting Lab**

Based on the information provided in the Troubleshooting Lab, answer the following questions:

1. Critical Windows operating system security updates are missing.

   Access the Windows Update Web site to download the required security updates.

2. Some user accounts have non-expiring passwords.

   In the Computer Management console, access the Local Users And Groups snap-in and, in the Properties dialog box for each user account, deselect the Password Never Expires check box.

3. The computer's C drive is using the FAT file system.

   Use the Convert.exe command line utility to convert the C drive from FAT to NTFS.

4. The system is configured to use the Autologon feature, with the password stored as plain text.

   Using the Windows Registry Editor (Regedit.exe), set the value of the HKEY_LOCAL_MACHINE \SOFTWARE\Microsoft\Windows NT\CurrentVersion\Winlogon\AutoAdminLog on key to 0 and delete the DefaultUserName and DefaultPassword keys.

5. The Guest account is enabled on the computer.

   In the Computer Management console, access the Local Users And Groups snap-in and, in the Properties dialog box for the Guest account, select the Account Is Disabled check box.

Part 2
Prepare for the Exam

14 Planning and Implementing Server Roles and Server Security (1.0)

Servers are the lifeblood of a data network, and they require more protection than workstations. Servers performing different tasks also require different levels and types of security. Part of designing a network infrastructure is creating security configurations that are appropriate for each server role used on the network. The process of creating these configurations includes examining the security features provided by the operating systems that you intend to use and determining the organization's security requirements.

Tested Skills and Suggested Practices

The skills that you need to successfully master the Planning and Implementing Server Roles and Server Security objective domain on the 70-293 exam include:

- Configure security for servers that are assigned specific roles.

  - Practice 1: Compare the methods you can use to configure security parameters on a computer running the Microsoft Windows Server 2003 operating system, including Group Policy Objects (GPOs) and security templates, and devise scenarios for which each configuration method would be appropriate. For servers running Windows Server 2003 with Service Pack 1 (SP1), you can also use the Security Configuration Wizard (SCW) to create role-specific server configurations.

  - Practice 2: Examine the settings in the security templates included with Windows Server 2003 using the Security Templates snap-in. Then use the Security Configuration And Analysis snap-in to compare the secure (Securedc.inf) and highly secure (Hisecdc.inf) templates to your server and study the differences between them.

- Plan a secure baseline installation.

  - Practice 1: Examine the default security settings on a workstation running Microsoft Windows XP Professional and a server running Windows Server 2003 and evaluate the level of security they provide. Create a list of configuration changes you could make to support a maximum security environment.

  - Practice 2: Create a Group Policy Object (GPO) to apply to an Active Directory directory service domain that contains a set of baseline security settings suitable for all the computers on a maximum security network. If you are using Windows Server 2003 with SP1, create an SCW Security Policy and convert this policy into a GPO.

■ Plan security for servers that are assigned specific roles. Roles might include domain controllers, Web servers, database servers, and mail servers.

❏ Practice 1: Using the Group Policy Object Editor console, examine the default security configuration settings for the Domain Controllers organizational unit in an Active Directory tree, and compare them to the settings in the default policy for the domain object. Notice how the domain controllers have a higher level of security than other types of servers.

❏ Practice 2: Create a list of Windows Server 2003 security parameters and consider what settings would be appropriate for each of the four server roles listed in this objective.

■ Evaluate and select the operating system to install on computers in an enterprise.

❏ Practice 1: Study the product literature for various operating systems provided on manufacturers' Web sites to determine what security features each operating system provides.

❏ Practice 2: Examine the security configuration parameters of the computer you are currently using, and list the changes you could make to increase the security of the system.

Further Reading

This section lists supplemental readings by objective. We recommend that you study these sources thoroughly before taking exam 70-293.

Objective 1.1   Review Lessons 1, 2, and 3 in Chapter 10, "Deploying Security Configurations."

Microsoft Corporation. *Windows Server 2003 Security Guide.* Review Chapter 2, "Windows Server 2003 Hardening Mechanisms." This guide has been updated to include information specific to Windows Server 2003 with SP1. Available on Microsoft's Web site at *http://www.microsoft.com/technet/security/prodtech /windowsserver2003/w2003hg/sgch00.mspx.*

Microsoft Corporation. *Microsoft Solution for Securing Windows 2000 Server.* Review Chapter 7, "Hardening Specific Server Roles." Although written for Microsoft Windows 2000 Server, the concepts in this chapter are also applicable to Windows Server 2003. Available on Microsoft's Web site at *http://www.microsoft.com/technet /security/prodtech/windows2000/secwin2k/default.mspx.*

Objective 1.2   Review Lessons 1, 2, and 3 in Chapter 8, "Planning a Secure Baseline Installation," and Lessons 1 and 4 in Chapter 9, "Hardening Servers."

Microsoft Corporation. *Windows Server 2003 Security Guide.* Review Chapter 3, "The Domain Policy"; Chapter 4, "The Member Server Baseline Policy"; and Chapter 5, "The Domain Controller Baseline Policy." This guide has been updated to include information specific to Windows Server 2003 with SP1. Available on Microsoft's Web site at *http://www.microsoft.com/technet/security/prodtech/windowsserver2003 /w2003hg/sgch00.mspx.*

Microsoft Corporation. *Microsoft Solution for Securing Windows 2000 Server.* Review Chapter 6, "Hardening the Base Windows 2000 Server." Although written for Windows 2000 Server, the concepts in this chapter are also applicable to Windows Server 2003. Available on Microsoft's Web site at *http://www.microsoft.com /technet/security/prodtech/windows2000/secwin2k/default.mspx.*

Objective 1.3   Review Lessons 2, 3, and 4 in Chapter 9, "Hardening Servers," and Lessons 1, 2, and 3 in Chapter 10, "Deploying Security Configurations."

Microsoft Corporation. *Windows Server 2003 Security Guide.* Review Chapter 2, "Windows Server 2003 Hardening Mechanisms." This guide has been updated to include information specific to Windows Server 2003 with SP1. Available on Microsoft's Web site at *http://www.microsoft.com/technet/security/prodtech /windowsserver2003/w2003hg/sgch00.mspx.*

Microsoft Corporation. *Microsoft Solution for Securing Windows 2000 Server.* Review Chapter 7, "Hardening Specific Server Roles." Although written for Microsoft Windows 2000 Server, the concepts in this chapter are also applicable to Windows Server 2003. Available on Microsoft's Web site at *http://www .microsoft.com/technet/security/prodtech/windows2000/secwin2k/default.mspx.*

Objective 1.4   Review Lessons 1 and 3 in Chapter 8, "Planning a Secure Baseline Installation."

Microsoft Corporation. "How to Maintain Windows Security." This Web page enables you to compare the security capabilities of the various Microsoft Windows operating systems. Available on Microsoft's Web site at *http:// www.microsoft.com /windows/security/default.mspx.*

Configure Security for Servers That Are Assigned Specific Roles

Servers that perform different roles have different security requirements, so it is common practice to create a security configuration for each server role and deploy it at once to all the servers performing that role. This practice minimizes the number of security configurations you have to create and saves you from having to configure each server individually.

The most common method of configuring security for servers that are assigned specific roles is to use group policies. A **group policy** is an Active Directory object that consists of specific settings for a collection of configuration parameters. When you associate a **Group Policy Object (GPO)** with an Active Directory container object, all the computers in that container receive the group policy settings. To create and modify group policies, you use the Group Policy Object Editor snap-in for Microsoft Management Console (MMC). To associate Group Policy Objects with Active Directory containers, you use the Active Directory Users And Computers console or the Active Directory Sites And Services console.

To use group policies to configure servers performing different roles, you must create different Active Directory container objects for them. You can link a Group Policy Object to a domain, site, or organizational unit object. Domain and site objects typically contain many computers performing different roles, so the best practice is to create a separate **organizational unit** for each role and apply a Group Policy Object that is specific to each role to each unit.

In many cases, you might find it necessary to apply more than one Group Policy Object to a particular organization unit. Multiple assignments can be necessary because a server is performing more than one role, or because you have already created a Group Policy Object to implement a baseline configuration and want to augment it with a GPO that is specific to a role. To apply multiple policies to an organizational unit, either you can link the organizational unit object to two or more GPOs, or you can create a hierarchy of organizational units and allow group policy inheritance to combine the policy settings.

When you link a Group Policy Object to an organizational unit, every object in the organizational unit, including every subordinate organizational unit, inherits the group policy settings. Therefore, you can apply a GPO to one organizational unit and then create role-specific organizational units, with their own linked GPOs, beneath it. The settings in the role-specific GPOs will combine with those of the parent GPO to create a composite configuration on each computer.

1. As the network administrator of your company's new branch office, you are in the process of installing three new Web servers running Windows Server 2003 on your network. The branch office network, which is part of a single corporate domain, already has two servers functioning as domain controllers and three file and print servers. Corporate headquarters has given you a list of security configuration settings that must be used on all the company's Web servers. To deploy these configuration settings, you must use the Active Directory Users And Computers console. Which of the following procedures should you use to configure the settings on the new Web servers only?

   A. Access the Group Policy Object (GPO) called Default Domain Policy and then configure the settings there.

   B. Create a new GPO containing the Web server settings and then apply it to the Computers container.

   C. Create a new organizational unit called WebSvrs and then link a new GPO containing the Web server settings to it.

   D. Create a new GPO containing the Web server settings and then apply it to the site object representing the branch office.

2. Which of the following tools do you use to change the value of a specific security configuration setting for an Active Directory domain object?

   A. Active Directory Users And Computers

   B. Active Directory Sites And Services

   C. Active Directory Domains And Trusts

   D. Group Policy Object Editor

3. Which of the following Active Directory objects can you link to a Group Policy Object? (Choose all that apply.)

   A. Domain

   B. Group

   C. Organizational unit

   D. Site

Objective 1.1 Answers

1.   **Correct Answers: C**

A. **Incorrect:** If you configure the Web server settings in the Default Domain Policy GPO, every computer in the domain will receive those settings, not only the Web servers.

B. **Incorrect:** The Computers container is not an organizational unit, site, or domain object, and therefore you cannot apply a GPO to it.

C. **Correct:** By creating a new organizational unit object for the Web servers, you separate them from the rest of the Active Directory tree, enabling you to create a new GPO and apply it only to those servers by linking it to the organizational unit.

D. **Incorrect:** You cannot manage GPOs for a site object using the Active Directory Users And Computers console; you must use the Active Directory Sites And Services console instead. In addition, applying a GPO to a site object would cause all the computers in the site to inherit the GPO's settings.

2.   **Correct Answers: D**

A. **Incorrect:** You can access a domain object using the Active Directory Users And Computers console, but you cannot modify the configuration settings of a GPO associated with the domain object using that console.

B. **Incorrect:** You cannot access a domain object using the Active Directory Sites And Services console.

C. **Incorrect:** You cannot access a domain object using the Active Directory Domains And Trusts console.

D. **Correct:** The Group Policy Object Editor console enables you to modify any of the configuration settings in the Group Policy Objects associated with a domain (or any other) object.

3.   **Correct Answers: A, C, and D**

A. **Correct:** By linking a GPO to a domain object, you can configure security settings that affect all the objects in the domain.

B. **Incorrect:** Group objects can have user and group objects as members, but they are not considered container objects and you cannot link GPOs to them.

C. **Correct:** An organizational unit is a container object that can have other organizational units, computers, users, and groups as its contents. Linking a GPO to an organizational unit deploys the security settings in the GPO to all objects in the organizational unit, including subordinate containers.

D. **Correct:** A site object represents a group of Active Directory objects that are connected by network connections running at approximately the same speed. Linking a GPO to a site object deploys the GPO's settings to every object at the site.

Plan a Secure Baseline Installation

Installing an operating system on a computer gives you a default security configuration that might or might not be suitable for your network. In most cases, some modification of the security settings is necessary, and to create a consistent operating environment, the best way to make those modifications is to develop a secure baseline installation. A **secure baseline installation** is a collection of settings for the operating system's security parameters that provides a standardized starting point for the servers and workstations on your network. In many cases, servers and workstations have security needs that are different enough to warrant separate baselines. After creating a secure baseline for all the computers, you can consider the special needs of computers performing specific roles.

Before you create a secure baseline installation, you must ascertain what the operating system's default security settings are so that you can determine what modifications you need to make. To do this, you should examine the default file system, registry, and Active Directory permissions, as well as the local policy and group policy settings that are in effect on the computer.

To create a baseline, you typically use Group Policy Objects to specify values for any or all of the following types of security policy parameters:

- **Account Policies** Specify password restrictions, such as length, complexity, and age requirements, and account lockout policies

- **Audit Policies** Specify what types of system events the computer should audit and whether it should audit successes, failures, or both

- **User Rights Assignments** Specify the users and groups that are permitted to perform specific tasks on the computer

- **Security Options** Enable or disable specific operating system security parameters, such as digital signatures and secure channel encryption

- **Event Log policies** Specify the maximum sizes for the event logs and how long the system should retain information in the logs

- **System Services** Specify which services the operating system should load when it starts

- **Restricted Groups** Specify the members of particular security groups

- **Registry permissions** Specify the users and groups that are permitted to access certain registry keys

- **File System permissions** Specify the users and groups that are permitted to access certain NTFS files and folders

Objective 1.2 Questions

1. As part of the secure baseline installation for your network, you have implemented the Maximum Password Age policy with a value of seven days on all your computers. This policy forces users to change their passwords every week, which lessens the chance of passwords being compromised. However, you discover that some users have taken to changing their passwords as required, and then immediately changing them back to the original password. Which of the following account policies can you use to prevent this behavior? (Choose all that apply.)

    A. Store Passwords Using Reversible Encryption

    B. Minimum Password Age

    C. Maximum Password Age

    D. Enforce Password History

2. You are a network administrator who has been given the task of outfitting several new employees with workstations running Windows XP Professional. Two of the new employees are responsible for evaluating new software products for their departments, and must therefore be able to install new applications on their workstations. Assuming that the workstations have the default file system permissions in place, which of the following group memberships would enable the users to install new software?

    A. Everyone

    B. Users

    C. Authenticated Users

    D. Server Operators

    E. Administrators

3. Which of the following tasks can you perform using the Registry subheading in the Group Policy Object Editor console?

    A. Create new registry keys

    B. Specify values for existing registry keys

    C. Specify permissions for newly created registry keys

    D. Specify permissions for existing registry keys

4.   You are a network administrator installing a new file and print server running Windows Server 2003. To give the network users a place to store their files, you create a new file system share called Documents. Which of the following share permissions does the new share have by default?

   A. The Administrators group has the Full Control permission.

   B. The Everyone group has the Full Control permission.

   C. The Everyone group has the Read permission.

   D. The Authenticated Users group has the Read permission.

Objective 1.2 Answers

1.   Correct Answers: B and D

   A. Incorrect: The Store Passwords Using Reversible Encryption policy only affects the algorithm that Windows Server 2003 uses when encrypting user passwords. The policy has no effect on the users' ability to modify the passwords.

   B. Correct: The Minimum Password Age policy prevents users from modifying their passwords more than once in a specified period of time. Specifying a sufficiently large value for this policy would prevent your users from changing their passwords and then changing them back again.

   C. Incorrect: No possible value of the Maximum Password Age policy can prevent users from changing their passwords, so you cannot use this policy to achieve the desired end.

   D. Correct: The Enforce Password History policy prevents users from re-using the same passwords. During each successive password change users perform, they must supply a new password until the number of passwords in the history reaches the number specified by the policy. This prevents users from changing their passwords to a new value and then changing them immediately back again.

2.   Correct Answers: E

   A. Incorrect: In the default Windows XP Professional configuration, the Everyone group receives no permissions for the Program Files folder, which is where the Windows XP Professional operating system stores application files.

   B. Incorrect: The Users group receives no permissions for the Program Files folder, which makes it impossible for members of that group to install applications there.

   C. Incorrect: By default, the Authenticated Users group receives the Read & Execute, List Folder Contents, and Read permissions for the Program Files folder. These permissions enable members of the group to access the files in the folder and run the programs installed there, but they cannot install new applications themselves.

   D. Incorrect: Server Operators is a built-in group on Windows Server 2003 Domain Controllers and is designed to be used for administering domain controllers only. The Server Operators group does not exist on Windows XP Professional.

   E. Correct: The Administrators group receives the Full Control permission for the entire system drive, including the Program Files folder, which enables its members to install new applications.

3.   Correct Answers: D

    A. Incorrect: The Registry subheading enables you to work with existing registry keys, but you cannot create new keys using the Group Policy Object Editor console.

    B. Incorrect: The Group Policy Object Editor console cannot modify the values of registry keys, only the permissions that enable users to access the keys.

    C. Incorrect: Although the Group Policy Object Editor can specify permissions for registry keys, it cannot create new keys, so you cannot specify permissions for newly created keys.

    D. Correct: Using the Registry subheading in the Group Policy Object Editor console, you can select a registry key and specify the permissions that users and groups receive for that key.

4.   Correct Answers: C

    A. Incorrect: The Administrators group does not receive any share permissions to newly created file system shares.

    B. Incorrect: The Everyone group receives only the Read share permission in Windows Server 2003. In Windows 2000 Server, the Everyone group receives the Full Control permission for new shares.

    C. Correct: By default, Windows Server 2003 has a higher level of security than earlier versions of the Windows operating system. One of the changes to the default configuration implemented in Windows Server 2003 is the assignment of only the Read share permission to the Everyone group for new file system shares.

    D. Incorrect: The Authenticated Users group does not receive any share permissions for newly created file system shares.

Plan Security for Servers That Are Assigned Specific Roles

Servers performing different roles have different security requirements. In many cases, you can create role-specific configurations by modifying the same parameters you set in your baseline configuration and saving them in Group Policy Objects, security templates or, if using Windows Server 2003 with SP1, SCW security policies. When planning security for specific roles, you must consider the additional security requirements of each role, both in terms of its technical vulnerabilities and of its importance to the organization.

Some of the roles for which you might have to plan security are as follows:

- **Domain controllers** On an Active Directory network, domain controllers provide essential authentication services whenever a user accesses a network resource, and therefore they must be available at all times. Securing a domain controller might call for increased physical security, such as a locked server closet, and fault-tolerant hardware, such as disk arrays and redundant power supplies, in addition to modifications to the security configuration parameters. A typical security configuration for the domain controller role might include more comprehensive auditing, larger Event Logs, more restrictive assignments of user rights, and a more limited selection of services on the computer.

- **Infrastructure servers** An infrastructure server runs network support services, such as DNS, DHCP, and WINS servers. These services provide important functions to users and should remain available at all times. A security configuration for this role should protect the servers from unauthorized access, allow the required services to run, and take steps to secure them from the potential exploits that running the services opens on the computers. In addition to the security parameters found in Group Policy Objects, the services running on infrastructure servers often have their own security features, such as secure dynamic updates for DNS servers.

- **File and print servers** File and print servers are among the most common server roles, and are frequently combined with other roles, such as the application or infrastructure roles, on the same computers. In addition to enabling required system services, such as the Print Spooler service, security for the file and print server role typically consists of file system permissions that allow specific users and groups the appropriate amount of access to the NTFS drives on the computer.

■ **Application servers** Application servers, including Web, database, and e-mail servers, typically have their own security features, which you can implement as part of your security configuration for that role. Internet Information Services (IIS), which provides Web, File Transfer Protocol (FTP), and other Internet services, is integrated into Windows Server 2003, but most server applications are separate products with built-in security features. As a result, you might not be able to implement these features using standard Windows Server 2003 mechanisms, such as Group Policy Objects, but other ways of automating the deployment of these security mechanisms might be available.

Security templates provide a mechanism for saving, manipulating, and deploying security configurations on computers running Windows Server 2003. A security template is a plain text file, with an .inf extension, that contains values for the configuration parameters found in Group Policy Objects. Storing configurations as security templates enables you to restore a computer to its previous configuration quickly and easily; compare a computer's current configuration settings to those in a template; and integrate the deployment of security configurations into scripts or batch files.

You can deploy security templates in four ways: by importing them into Group Policy Objects, by using the **Security Configuration And Analysis** snap-in to apply them to individual computers, by using the **SECEDIT.EXE** command-line utility, or for servers running Windows Server 2003 with SP1, by using the SCW.

Objective 1.3 Questions

1. You are a network administrator who has been given a security template. Your supervisor wants you to check that all the Windows Server 2003 domain controllers are using the account policies, audit policies, event log settings, and security options stored in the template. In the case of any domain controller that is not using the same settings, you are to apply only the missing elements from the template to that computer. Which of the following procedures would enable you to perform both these tasks most efficiently?

A. Import the security template into the Security Configuration And Analysis snap-in on each domain controller, then use the snap-in to analyze the computer's current configuration and apply the required settings to the domain controllers that need them.

B. Use the Active Directory Users And Computers console to apply the template to the Group Policy Object for the Domain Controllers organizational unit.

C. Import the security template into the Security Configuration And Analysis snap-in on each domain controller, and then use the snap-in to analyze the computer's current configuration. Then, you must manually configure the computer settings that need to be changed.

D. Import the security template into the Security Configuration And Analysis snap-in on each domain controller, and then use the snap-in to analyze the computer's current configuration. Then, use the SECEDIT.EXE command-line utility to apply only the required settings to the domain controllers that need them.

2. Revoking the Add Workstations To Domain user right from the Authenticated Users group prevents the members of that group from performing which of the following tasks?

A. Joining groups

B. Creating computer objects

C. Modifying file system permissions

D. Accessing their own user objects

3. You are the network administrator responsible for equipping ten new employees of the Sales department for all their computing needs. After installing their workstations, you use the Active Directory Users And Computers console to create user accounts for the new employees in the Active Directory database. You also create computer objects for their workstations in the Sales organizational unit, which contains all the Sales department's computer objects. All ten users must also be members of a group called Salespeople, which gives them access to the server resources they need. Rather than manually add each new user object to the Salespeople group, you decide to automate the process by opening the default Group Policy Object for the Sales organizational unit and adding Salespeople to the Restricted Groups folder. Then you specify the ten new user objects as members of the Salespeople group.

Sometime later, the network help desk gets calls from dozens of other users in the Sales department, complaining that they cannot access their applications. Which of the following procedures must you perform to remedy the problem? (Choose all that apply.)

A. Add the new users to the Salespeople group using the Active Directory Users And Computers console.

B. Add the old users to the Salespeople group using the Active Directory Users And Computers console.

C. Use the Group Policy Object Editor console to remove the Salespeople group from the Restricted Groups folder.

D. Use the Group Policy Object Editor console to remove the new users from the Salespeople group in the Restricted Groups folder.

4. After using the Security Configuration And Analysis snap-in to compare a file and print server's configuration to the Hisecws.inf security template, you decide that you need to modify some of the computer's settings to match those of the template. Which of the following procedures can you use to do this?

A. Modify the parameters you want to change in the Security Configuration And Analysis snap-in's database and apply the database to the computer.

B. Open the Security Templates snap-in, create a new template, and configure the parameters you want to change with their new settings. Then apply the template to the server using the SECEDIT.EXE utility.

C. Open the Hisecws.inf template in the Security Templates snap-in and use it to apply the settings for the parameters you want to change.

D. Modify the parameters you want to change in the Security Configuration And Analysis snap-in's database and then use the SECEDIT.EXE utility to apply the database file to the computer.

Objective 1.3 Answers

1. **Correct Answers: D**

   A. **Incorrect:** Although you can use the Security Configuration And Analysis snap-in to compare each domain controller's current settings to those in the template, you cannot use the snap-in to apply only part of a template to a computer.

   B. **Incorrect:** Applying the template to the Domain Controllers GPO would deploy all the configuration settings in the template to all the domain controllers on the network. This procedure does not compare the settings in the template to those on the domain controllers, nor can it apply only part of the template.

   C. **Incorrect:** Using the Security Configuration And Analysis tool to analyze the computer's settings is the proper way to determine which settings need to be modified, but manually changing them is not the most efficient way to accomplish this goal. Instead, you should use the SECEDIT.EXE utility to apply only the Domain Controller Security Policy part of the template to the computers.

   D. **Correct:** The Security Configuration And Analysis snap-in can tell you whether each domain controller is currently configured with the same account policy and security options settings as the ones in the template, but it cannot apply only part of a template to the computer. To apply specific elements of a template, you must use the SECEDIT.EXE utility.

2. **Correct Answers: B**

   A. **Incorrect:** Users cannot join groups of their own volition unless they have the permissions needed to modify the group object in Active Directory. The Add Workstations To Domain user right has no effect on this ability.

   B. **Correct:** By default, members of the Authenticated Users group can add up to ten computer objects to the Computers container in the Active Directory domain. When you revoke the Add Workstations To Domain user right from the group, members are no longer able to create their own computer objects; an administrator must do it for them.

   C. **Incorrect:** The Add Workstations To Domain user right has no effect on a user's ability to modify file system permissions. To modify permissions, users must possess the appropriate permissions enabling them to do so.

   D. **Incorrect:** The ability to add workstations to the domain does not affect the users' ability to modify their own user objects. It is Active Directory permissions that make it possible for users to modify objects.

3.   Correct Answers: A, B, and C

A. Correct: Because the procedure you used to add the new users to the Salespeople group was incorrect, you must reverse the process and add them to the group manually, using the Active Directory Users And Computers console.

B. Correct: Creating a Salespeople group in the Restricted Groups folder and then adding the new users to it effectively removed all the other users from the Salespeople group. Therefore, you must add them to the group again manually.

C. Correct: The Restricted Groups folder in a Group Policy Object specifies all the users who are permitted to be members of a specific group. By adding only the new users to the Salespeople restricted group, you have removed all the existing users in the Sales department from that group, which prevents them from accessing the applications they need. You must remove the Salespeople group from the Restricted Groups folder, or all the users will be removed from the group the next time the server refreshes its group policies.

D. Incorrect: Removing the new users from the Salespeople restricted group would leave you with no members in the group at all, and would not resolve the problem.

4.   Correct Answers: B

A. Incorrect: The database in the Security Configuration And Analysis snap-in contains settings imported from a security template, not the computer's own settings. Modifying the database would only change the template settings, which do not need to be changed.

B. Correct: You can analyze the settings in a computer by using the Security Configuration And Analysis snap-in, but you can't modify the settings using that snap-in. The Security Templates snap-in enables you to create a new template containing only the security parameters you need to change. You can then apply the new template to the computer using the SECEDIT.EXE utility.

C. Incorrect: The Security Templates snap-in can only create and manage the templates themselves. You cannot use it to apply templates to a computer.

D. Incorrect: You cannot use the SECEDIT.EXE utility to apply a Security Configuration and Analysis database to a computer.

Evaluate and Select the Operating System to Install on Computers in an Enterprise

An important part of network design is selecting the appropriate operating systems for your servers and workstations. Your evaluation and selection of operating systems should be based on criteria such as the following:

- **Application compatibility** The operating systems you select must be able to run the applications your users need. In the case of client/server applications, you must be sure that the client and server applications are compatible if the servers are running different operating systems from the clients. In some cases, network designers select an operating system in order to run a particular application. In other cases, you can find comparable applications for each operating system you are considering.

- **Hardware compatibility** When designing a network, you must select hardware and software products that can operate together. After determining your network's hardware requirements, make sure that the operating systems you select have been tested and certified to work with the hardware you have chosen.

- **Support issues** If you have a staff of network support people who only have experience working with Microsoft Windows operating systems, choosing Linux for your network computers creates an additional support problem that might require retraining or replacing personnel.

- **Security features** The operating systems you select must have security features that can satisfy your organization's security requirements. In addition, you might want to select operating systems that have a more secure default configuration, saving you from having to reconfigure them after installation.

- **Cost** Cost is always a factor when selecting operating systems. You must consider not only the initial cost of the software, but also the cost and availability of future upgrades, documentation, and technical support. Sometimes, free operating systems provide capabilities equal or superior to those of commercial products, but they are often upgraded sporadically and do not include documentation or support.

For a large network installation, the best practice is to standardize the operating systems used for particular roles, so that technical support personnel only have to work with a limited number of system configurations.

Objective 1.4 Questions

1.   You are in the process of selecting the operating systems for your network's servers. The network will have six Web servers in a Network Load Balancing (NLB) cluster, two Active Directory domain controllers, and four file and print servers, plus approximately 150 workstations. You have decided to use Windows Server 2003 for all your servers. After checking prices with several vendors, you decide to use Windows Server 2003, Web Edition, for all your servers. Specify whether this selection is appropriate for each server role you will use on your network.

    A.   Windows Server 2003, Web Edition, is suitable for the Web servers and the file and print servers, but not for the domain controllers.

    B.   Windows Server 2003, Web Edition, is suitable for the Web servers, but not for the file and print servers or the domain controllers.

    C.   Windows Server 2003, Web Edition, is suitable for the Web servers and the domain controllers, but not for the file and print servers.

    D.   Windows Server 2003, Web Edition, is suitable for the Web servers, the file and print servers, and for the domain controllers.

2.   You are in the process of designing a network based on the Microsoft Windows operating system. For your workstations, you want an operating system that supports Active Directory as a client and that has superior security capabilities. For security reasons, you have decided to eliminate operating systems based on the DOS kernel. Which of the following Microsoft workstation operating systems support all these requirements? (Choose all that apply.)

    A.   Windows XP Home Edition

    B.   Microsoft Windows 95

    C.   Windows XP Professional

    D.   Windows NT Workstation

    E.   Microsoft Windows Me

    F.   Microsoft Windows 2000 Professional

3.   The IT director of your company has just received a new computer that will host a large Windows Server 2003 database server application and has instructed you to install the operating system on the computer. The system has four processors, a disk array using redundant array of independent disks (RAID) to provide 480 gigabytes of storage, and 8 gigabytes of random access memory (RAM). Which version of Microsoft Windows Server 2003 could you install on the computer?

A. Windows Server 2003, Web Edition

B. Windows Server 2003, Standard Edition

C. Windows Server 2003, Enterprise Edition

D. Windows Server 2003, Datacenter Edition

Objective 1.4 Answers

1. **Correct Answers: A**

   A. Correct: Windows Server 2003, Web Edition, can function as a Web server and provide file and print services, but it does not contain Active Directory server capabilities and cannot function as a domain controller.

   B. Incorrect: Windows Server 2003, Web Edition, cannot function as a domain controller, but it is capable of providing file and print services.

   C. Incorrect: Windows Server 2003, Web Edition, does not include Active Directory server capabilities, and cannot function as a domain controller.

   D. Incorrect: Windows Server 2003, Web Edition, is suitable for a Web server or a file and print server, but cannot function as a domain controller.

2. **Correct Answers: C and F**

   A. Incorrect: Windows XP Home Edition is not based on the DOS kernel, but it does not include Active Directory client capabilities.

   B. Incorrect: Windows 95 is based on the DOS kernel and does not include Active Directory client support.

   C. Correct: Windows XP Professional is based on the Microsoft Windows NT kernel and can function as an Active Directory client.

   D. Incorrect: Windows NT Workstation is not based on the DOS kernel, but it cannot function as an Active Directory client.

   E. Incorrect: Windows Me is the final Windows operating system version to be based on the DOS kernel.

   F. Correct: Windows 2000 Professional is based on the NT kernel and can function as an Active Directory client.

3. **Correct Answers: C**

   A. Incorrect: Windows Server 2003, Web Edition, only supports computers with up to two processors and two gigabytes of RAM.

   B. Incorrect: Windows Server 2003, Standard Edition, supports computers with four processors, but only supports up to four gigabytes of RAM.

   C. Correct: Windows Server 2003, Enterprise Edition, supports computers with up to 8 processors, and as much as 32 gigabytes of RAM.

   D. Incorrect: To use Windows Server 2003, Datacenter Edition, your computer must have at least 8 processors, and no more than 64.

15 Planning, Implementing, and Maintaining a Network Infrastructure (2.0)

The planning phase of deploying a network infrastructure is by far the most important part of the process. When building a large network, it is crucial that you have the entire infrastructure planned before you purchase hardware or construct the network. The plan should specify elements such as the protocols the network will use and the physical topology of the network.

The Transmission Control Protocol/Internet Protocol (TCP/IP) suite is the industry standard for network communications, and creating an effective TCP/IP infrastructure is a primary element of designing and planning a network. A TCP/IP network infrastructure plan specifies how you are going to subnet your network, what Internet Protocol (IP) addresses and subnet masks you will use, what names to assign to your computers, and how the computers will resolve these names into IP addresses.

Once you have finished deploying the network and have it up and running, the focus of the administrator's job changes to maintenance and troubleshooting. Problems with TCP/IP configuration and name resolution are common, and you must be familiar with the tools and techniques that can help determine the causes of the problems and correct them.

Tested Skills and Suggested Practices

The skills that you need to successfully master the Planning, Implementing, and Maintaining a Network Infrastructure objective domain on the 70-293 exam include:

- Plan a TCP/IP network infrastructure strategy.
  - ❏ Practice 1: Practice converting 8-bit binary numbers into decimals without using a calculator or other electronic aid.
  - ❏ Practice 2: Create a series of IP addressing scenarios in which you must subnet a network address by creating a specified number of subnets, each containing a specified number of hosts. Then, using paper and pencil only, calculate the IP addresses and the subnet mask for each subnet.

■ Plan and modify a network topology.

❑ Practice 1: Using Web sites, catalogs, or manufacturers' literature, examine the specifications for the various types of Ethernet network interface adapters, hubs, and other devices currently on the market, focusing on the compatibility of the devices for being on the same network.

❑ Practice 2: Design an imaginary network for the home or office in which you work, using the products you have evaluated. Select suitable locations for computers, printers, and hubs, and create a list of all the hardware components you would need to construct the network.

■ Plan an Internet connectivity strategy.

❑ Practice 1: Using Web sites, catalogs, or manufacturers' literature, examine the specifications for the various types of Internet access routers on the market and compare their features and capabilities.

❑ Practice 2: Contact the local cable television and telephone providers and find out which Integrated Services Digital Network (ISDN), Digital Subscriber Line (DSL), and cable television (CATV) Internet access solutions are available in your area. Find out the bandwidths that each service provides and the prices they charge and calculate the cost of each megabit per second (Mbps) of bandwidth.

■ Plan network traffic monitoring. Tools might include Network Monitor and System Monitor.

❑ Practice 1: Configure the System Monitor snap-in on a computer running Microsoft Windows Server 2003 to display a graph of the number of Transmission Control Protocol (TCP) and User Datagram Protocol (UDP) packets sent and received each second. As you perform normal activities on the computer, compare the amount of TCP traffic with the amount of UDP traffic.

❑ Practice 2: Use Network Monitor to capture the packets sent to and received by a computer running Windows Server 2003 during normal activities. Use display filters to isolate specific transactions, such as Domain Name System (DNS) name resolutions, Dynamic Host Configuration Protocol (DHCP) message exchanges, and TCP connections, and analyze the messages until you understand the function of each field in the protocol header.

■ Troubleshoot connectivity to the Internet.

❑ Practice 1: Using a modem and a standard dial-up account to connect to the Internet, and a network interface adapter to connect to a local network, configure the Windows Server 2003 Routing and Remote Access service (RRAS) to function as a NAT router.

❏ Practice 2: One at a time, modify the Preferred DNS Server and Default Gateway parameters on a computer running Windows Server 2003 to incorrect values and observe how the changes affect the computer's functionality.

■ Troubleshoot TCP/IP addressing.

❏ Practice 1: Configure a workstation computer running Windows to function as a DHCP client on a network with no DHCP server, restart the system, and observe the resulting TCP/IP configuration parameters using the IPCONFIG.EXE utility.

❏ Practice 2: Configure the DHCP Server service on a computer running Windows Server 2003 with scopes that support five subnets. Then configure DHCP options to give clients on all five scopes DNS server, default gateway, and Windows Internet Name Service (WINS) addresses, using server options wherever possible, and scope options only when necessary.

■ Plan a host name resolution strategy.

❏ Practice 1: Study the online help screen for the Windows NSLOOKUP.EXE command-line utility and learn how to send a name resolution request to a particular DNS server. (You display the online help screen for NSLOOKUP.EXE by opening the Command Prompt window, typing **nslookup** at the first command prompt, and then typing **help** at the following command prompt. You exit NSLOOKUP.EXE by typing **exit**.)

❏ Practice 2: Install the DNS Server service on a computer running Windows Server 2003, create a zone for an imaginary domain, and populate it with a series of Host (A) resource records. Then create a reverse lookup zone for the same domain and populate it with Pointer (PTR) resource records corresponding to the Host (A) resource records you created earlier. Test your configuration by resolving all the host names into IP addresses and all the IP addresses into their host names.

■ Plan a NetBIOS name resolution strategy.

❏ Practice 1: Create an LMHOSTS file on a computer running Windows Server 2003 and use the #PRE tag to preload several entries into the Network Basic Input/Output System (NetBIOS) name cache. Restart the computer, and then use the NBTSTAT.EXE command-line program to view the contents of the cache. Make sure that the entries you preloaded appear.

❏ Practice 2: Use Network Monitor to capture network traffic to and from a computer running Windows Server 2003 as you attempt to connect to another computer on the network. Then, activate the WINS client on the computer by specifying the address of a WINS server, and again perform the same connection procedure. Compare the broadcast messages generated by the first attempt with the unicast messages generated by the second attempt.

■ Troubleshoot host name resolution.

❑ Practice 1: Configure a computer running Windows Server 2003 with an incorrect Preferred DNS Server address and note the errors that result as you attempt to access network resources.

❑ Practice 2: Open the DNS console and use the Monitoring tab in the DNS server's Properties dialog box to test the server with both simple and recursive queries.

Further Reading

This section lists supplemental readings by objective. We recommend that you study these sources thoroughly before taking exam 70-293.

Objective 2.1   Review Lessons 1, 2, and 3 in Chapter 2, "Planning a TCP/IP Network Infrastructure."

Microsoft Corporation. *Microsoft Encyclopedia of Networking.* 2d ed. Redmond, Washington: Microsoft Press, 2002. See entries for "Routers," "Routing," "Subnet Mask," and "Subnetting."

Microsoft Corporation. *Microsoft Windows Server 2003 Deployment Kit.* Volume: *Deploying Network Services.* Redmond, Washington: Microsoft Press, 2003. Review Chapter 1, "Designing a TCP/IP Network." This volume can also be found on Microsoft's Web site at *http://www.microsoft.com/windowsserver2003 /techinfo/reskit/deploykit.mspx.*

Objective 2.2   Review Lessons 2, 3, and 4 in Chapter 1, "Planning a Network Topology."

Microsoft Corporation. *Microsoft Encyclopedia of Networking,* 2d ed. Redmond, Washington: Microsoft Press, 2002. See entries for "Ethernet," "topology," "unshielded twisted-pair (UTP) cabling," and "fiber optic cabling."

Objective 2.3   Review Lessons 1 and 2 in Chapter 3, "Planning Internet Connectivity."

Microsoft Corporation. *Microsoft Encyclopedia of Networking,* 2d ed. Redmond, Washington: Microsoft Press, 2002. See entries for "Integrated Services Digital Network (ISDN)," "Digital Subscriber Line (DSL)," "T1," "frame relay," "network address translation (NAT)," and "proxy server."

Objective 2.4   Review Lesson 1 in Chapter 6, "Maintaining Server Availability."

Microsoft Corporation. Windows Server 2003 Online Help. Review the "Network Monitor Overview" and "How Network Monitor Works" pages.

Microsoft Corporation. Windows Server 2003 Online Help. Review the "Performance Logs and Alerts Overview" page.

Microsoft Corporation. Windows Server 2003 Online Help. Review the "System Monitor Overview" page.

Objective 2.5 Review Lesson 3 in Chapter 3, "Planning Internet Connectivity."

Microsoft Corporation. Windows Server 2003 Online Help. Review the "Troubleshooting Network Address Translation" page.

Microsoft Corporation. *Microsoft Encyclopedia of Networking,* 2d ed. Redmond, Washington: Microsoft Press, 2002. See entry for "Transmission Control Protocol/ Internet Protocol (TCP/IP)."

Objective 2.6 Review Lesson 5 in Chapter 2, "Planning a TCP/IP Network Infrastructure."

Microsoft Corporation. *Microsoft Encyclopedia of Networking,* 2d ed. Redmond, Washington: Microsoft Press, 2002. See entry for "Transmission Control Protocol/ Internet Protocol (TCP/IP)."

Microsoft Corporation. *Microsoft Windows Server 2003 Deployment Kit.* Volume: *Deploying Network Services.* Redmond, Washington: Microsoft Press, 2003. Review Chapter 1, "Designing a TCP/IP Network." This volume can also be found on Microsoft's Web site at *http://www.microsoft.com/windowsserver2003 /techinfo/reskit/deploykit.mspx.*

Objective 2.7 Review Lessons 1, 2, 3, and 5 in Chapter 4, "Planning a Name Resolution Strategy."

Microsoft Corporation. *Microsoft Windows Server 2003 Deployment Kit.* Volume: *Deploying Network Services.* Redmond, Washington: Microsoft Press, 2003. Review Chapter 3, "Deploying Domain Name System (DNS)." This volume can also be found on Microsoft's Web site at *http://www.microsoft.com/windowsserver2003 /techinfo/reskit/deploykit.mspx.*

Objective 2.8 Review Lesson 4 in Chapter 4, "Planning a Name Resolution Strategy."

Microsoft Corporation. *Microsoft Windows Server 2003 Deployment Kit.*

Microsoft Corporation. *Microsoft Windows Server 2003 Deployment Kit.* Volume: *Deploying Network Services.* Redmond, Washington: Microsoft Press, 2003. Review Chapter 4, "Deploying WINS." This volume can also be found on Microsoft's Web site at *http://www.microsoft.com/windowsserver2003/techinfo /reskit/deploykit.mspx.*

Objective 2.9 Review Lesson 6 in Chapter 4, "Planning a Name Resolution Strategy."

Microsoft Corporation. Windows Server 2003 Online Help. Review the "Troubleshooting DNS Clients" and "Troubleshooting DNS Servers" pages.

Plan a TCP/IP Network Infrastructure Strategy

IP addresses are the core of TCP/IP communications, and assigning proper IP addresses to your computers is an essential part of planning the network infrastructure. The first decision to make when determining your network's IP addressing requirements is whether you are going to use registered or unregistered IP addresses. **Registered addresses** are public IP addresses that you have obtained from the **Internet Assigned Numbers Authority (IANA)** or from an Internet service provider (ISP). Registered addresses are accessible from the Internet and are essential for computers that provide Internet services, such as World Wide Web servers. This Internet accessibility also makes the computers more vulnerable to attacks. You should always protect computers with registered addresses by installing a firewall on your network. **Unregistered addresses** fall within designated ranges allocated by the IANA for use by private networks. Because unregistered addresses are not associated with any particular organization, they are not accessible from the Internet and are therefore not vulnerable to many (but not all) types of attacks. To provide computers with unregistered addresses with access to the Internet, you must use a **network address translation (NAT) router** or a **proxy server**. The designated private IP address ranges are as follows:

- 10.0.0.0 through 10.255.255.255

- 172.16.0.0 through 172.31.255.255

- 192.168.0.0 through 192.168.255.255

Before you can assign IP addresses to your computers, you must know how many networks you will have and how many computers will be on each network. You can connect individual local area networks (LANs) in two ways, using routers or switches. A **router** is a network-layer device that connects two networks and forwards only the traffic destined for the other network. A **switch** is a data-link-layer device that connects separate LANs into one big network. The difference between a switch and a hub is that switches forward incoming data out through only the port providing access to the destination system but hubs forward incoming data out through all their ports. Switches, therefore, make it possible to connect LANs without causing inordinate amounts of network traffic.

To assign IP addresses to your network, you first must obtain a network address. You can either select one from the private IP address ranges or request one from your ISP.

Network addresses are sometimes expressed in the following format: 192.168.54.0/24, where the value after the slash represents the total number of bits used for the network identifier.

Once you obtain a network address, either registered or unregistered, it is often necessary to subnet it. An IP address consists of network identifier bits and host identifier bits. To subnet an address, you borrow some of the host bits and use them to create a subnet identifier. The number of bits you borrow determines how many subnets you can create, and the remaining number of host bits determines how many hosts you can have in each subnet. To calculate the subnet mask for a subnetted address, you assign a binary value of 1 to all the network and subnet bits and a value of 0 to the remaining host bits, and then convert the binary value to a decimal. To calculate the IP addresses, you increment the subnet bits and the remaining host bits separately and convert the entire value to decimal form.

Objectives 2.1 Questions

1. You are designing a new TCP/IP network and you request a Class B network address from your ISP. The ISP gives you the following address: 131.107.0.0/16. You want to be able to create as many as 50 subnets of 1,000 hosts each on your new network, so you decide to allocate 6 bits to be used as the subnet identifier. Which of the following subnet masks should you use for the computers on your network?

   A. 255.192.0.0

   B. 255.252.0.0

   C. 255.255.252.0

   D. 255.255.192.0

2. You are designing the LAN for a new branch office of a large corporation. The IT director at company headquarters has assigned you the network address 10.24.0.0/20 for your subnet. What is the maximum number of host addresses you can create?

   A. 4094

   B. 4096

   C. 1,048,574

   D. 1,048,576

3. Your company is expanding and has purchased a new ten-story office building. You are responsible for designing the network for the Sales department, which takes up the entire sixth floor. Your primary goal is to create a single subnet for the entire sixth floor, which consists of 78 TCP/IP computers and other devices. Your secondary goal is to give the users in the Sales department Internet access; the company has installed a NAT router and a T-1 connection to an Internet service provider for this purpose. The new IT director for the company has assigned you the network address 157.54.86.0/25 for the sixth floor subnet. Which of your goals does this address assignment satisfy?

   A. This address assignment satisfies both the primary and secondary goals by enabling you to create a single subnet on the sixth floor and to provide Internet access using the NAT router.

   B. This address assignment satisfies the primary goal by enabling you to create a single subnet on the sixth floor, but it does not satisfy the secondary goal.

   C. This address assignment satisfies the secondary goal by enabling you to give users Internet access using the NAT router, but it does not satisfy the primary goal.

   D. This address assignment satisfies neither the primary nor the secondary goal.

4.   Which of the following network addresses enable you to support a network consisting of 60 subnets with up to 300 hosts on each subnet? (Choose all that apply.)

   A. 10.48.0.0/14

   B. 192.168.98.0/24

   C. 172.30.0.0/25

   D. 10.236.128.0/21

Objective 2.1 Answers

1. **Correct Answers: C**

   A. Incorrect: This subnet mask indicates that the IP address has 10 network bits and 22 host bits, which would be the result if you subtracted 6 bits from the existing network identifier instead of adding 6 bits to it.

   B. Incorrect: This subnet mask indicates that the IP address has 14 network bits and 18 host bits. This mask would be the result if you used a 6-bit subnet identifier with a Class A address instead of a Class B address.

   C. Correct: Adding a 6-bit subnet identifier to the 16-bit network identifier of a Class B address results in 22 network bits and 10 host bits, yielding this subnet mask value.

   D. Incorrect: This subnet mask indicates that the IP address has 18 network bits and 14 host bits. This mask would be the result if you subtracted 6 bits from the 24-bit network identifier of a Class C address.

2. **Correct Answers: A**

   A. Correct: A network address of 10.24.0.0/20 leaves 12 bits for the host identifier. To calculate the number of hosts, you use the formula $2^x - 2$, and $2^{12} - 2 = 4,094$.

   B. Incorrect: If you calculate the number of possible hosts with a 12-bit host identifier, you get 4,096 only if you forget to subtract 2, because you cannot use all zeroes or all ones for a host identifier value.

   C. Incorrect: This value is the result if you calculate the number of possible hosts with a 20-bit host identifier. The number 20 in the network address represents the total number of bits in the network identifier, not in the host identifier.

   D. Incorrect: This value is the result if you calculate the number of possible hosts with a 20-bit host identifier and forget to subtract 2 from 220.

3. **Correct Answers: B**

   A. Incorrect: The address assignment satisfies the primary goal, but it does not satisfy the secondary goal because the address does not fall within the designated ranges for private addresses.

   B. Correct: The address assignment satisfies the primary goal because a 25-bit network identifier leaves 7 bits for the host identifier, which supports up to 126 hosts per subnet. However, this address does not satisfy the second goal because 157.54.86.0 is a registered address, and you must use unregistered addresses to access the Internet through a NAT router.

C. **Incorrect:** The supplied address cannot provide users with Internet access using a NAT router because the address is registered and NAT requires unregistered addresses. Therefore, it is not true that the address satisfies the secondary goal. The address does satisfy the primary goal, however, because the host identifier is large enough to support up to 126 hosts.

D. **Incorrect:** Although the supplied address does not satisfy the secondary goal because the address is registered, it does satisfy the primary goal.

4.   **Correct Answers: A and D**

A. **Correct:** This answer is correct because it is a Class A address with 14 network identifier bits. Class A addresses have 8 network identifier bits, which leaves 6 bits for the subnet identifier and 18 bits for the host identifier. The 6 bits are sufficient to support 60 subnets, and each subnet can have up to 26,142 hosts.

B. **Incorrect:** This answer is incorrect because this is an unsubnetted Class C address, which supports only one subnet with up to 254 hosts.

C. **Incorrect:** This answer is incorrect because, although a Class B address with 25 network identifier bits leaves 9 bits for the subnet identifier, which easily supports 60 subnets, only 7 bits are left for the host identifier. With only 7 bits for the host identifier, you can only have up to 126 hosts on each subnet.

D. **Correct:** This answer is correct because a Class A address with 21 network identifier bits leaves 13 bits for the subnet identifier, which supports over 8,000 subnets and over 2,000 hosts per subnet.

Plan and Modify a Network Topology

When creating a network infrastructure plan, deciding what protocols the network will use and selecting locations for your networking equipment are important parts of the process. These two tasks are related because the protocol selection can dictate how far apart your components can be.

The majority of LANs today use the **Ethernet** protocol at the data-link layer of the **Open Systems Interconnection (OSI) reference model**. When you design an Ethernet network, you can use any one of several network media and run the network at any one of three speeds. The most common network media that Ethernet supports are as follows:

■ **Unshielded twisted pair (UTP)**   A UTP cable consists of four separate pairs of copper wires in a single sheath, with each pair twisted at a different rate to avoid interference between the signals on the different wires. UTP cables are graded using categories; Category 5 (or CAT5) UTP is the most commonly used cable for Ethernet networks today. The connectors for UTP cables are called RJ-45, and are similar in appearance to standard telephone connectors (called RJ-11). When you build an Ethernet network with UTP cable, you use a star topology, with each computer connected to a central cable nexus called a hub. For most forms of UTP Ethernet, the distance between a computer and the hub can be no more than 100 meters. The speed of the network determines how many hubs you are allowed to use on a single LAN.

■ **Fiber optic**   Fiber-optic cables use strands of glass or plastic to carry signals in the form of light pulses. Because the signals are not electrical, fiber-optic cables are not affected by electromagnetic interference and are much less susceptible to signal weakening caused by attenuation. Fiber-optic cables can therefore span longer distances than copper-based cables. Fiber optic is also a more secure medium because it is difficult to tap into the cables. The drawbacks of using fiber-optic cables are its higher price and the specialized skills needed to install, maintain, and troubleshoot them.

■ **Wireless**   The **802.11b, 802.11g,** and **802.11a** wireless LAN standards published by the Institute of Electrical and Electronics Engineers (IEEE) provide reliable wireless network communications at speeds of up to 11 Mbps (802.11b) and 54 Mbps (802.11g and 802.11a). Wireless networks can use two topologies: ad hoc and infrastructure. An **ad hoc** network is one in which two or more computers equipped with wireless network adapters communicate directly with each other. An **infrastructure** network consists of a standard cabled network with a wireless **access point** connected to it. Wireless-equipped computers can then interact with the cabled network by communicating with the access point.

There are several Ethernet variants that run at different speeds, use different media, and have their own special cabling guidelines. These variants are listed in the following table:

Ethernet Type	Designation	Cable Type	Speed	Maximum Segment Length
Standard Ethernet	10Base-T	Category 3 UTP	10 Mbps	100 meters
Fast Ethernet	100Base-TX	Category 5 UTP	100 Mbps	100 meters
Fast Ethernet	100Base-FX	62.5/125 multimode fiber optic	100 Mbps	412 meters at half duplex and 2,000 meters at full duplex
Gigabit Ethernet	1000Base-LX	9/125 single-mode fiber optic	1000 Mbps	3 kilometers
Gigabit Ethernet	1000Base-LX	50/125 or 62.5/125 multimode fiber optic	1000 Mbps	550 meters
Gigabit Ethernet	1000Base-SX	50/125 multimode fiber optic (400 MHz)	1000 Mbps	500 meters
Gigabit Ethernet	1000Base-SX	62.5/125 multimode fiber optic (160 MHz)	1000 Mbps	220 meters
Gigabit Ethernet	1000Base-T	Category 5 (or 5E) UTP	1000 Mbps	100 meters

Selecting protocols for the network and transport layers of the OSI reference model depends more on the applications you will be running than on your network's physical layout. The possible choices you can make are as follows:

- **TCP/IP**   TCP/IP is a suite of protocols that encompasses the entire OSI reference model except for the physical layer, but which is associated primarily with the network and transport layers. TCP/IP is the industry standard for networking today, and is required for Internet communications. Most operating systems use TCP/IP by default, including Microsoft Windows and all versions of UNIX and Linux.

- **Internetwork Packet Exchange (IPX)**   IPX is a suite of protocols developed by Novell specifically for their NetWare operating system. Until NetWare version 5, the operating system only supported IPX. NetWare versions 5 and higher contain native support for TCP/IP as well. Windows operating systems have their own version of IPX, called NWLink, which enables them to communicate with NetWare servers. IPX is designed for use only on LANs, and does not have an independent addressing system, as TCP/IP does.

- **NetBEUI**   NetBIOS Extended User Interface (NetBEUI) is a network-layer protocol that was the original default for the Windows NT 3.1 and Windows for Workgroups operating systems. Because NetBEUI requires no configuration or maintenance, it is simple to install and use. However, NetBEUI is intended only for use on small single-segment networks, both because it relies on broadcast transmissions for name resolution and because it is not routable.

Objective 2.2 Questions

1. You are a network administrator installing new workstations, running Windows XP, on an existing network. The workstations must be able to access NetWare 3.11 servers for their file and print services, and they also use a NAT router to access the Internet. Which of the following protocols must you install on the workstations to accomplish these goals? (Choose all that apply.)

    A. NetBEUI

    B. NWLink

    C. IEEE 802.11b

    D. TCP/IP

2. You are installing a new Ethernet network in a building with a data center located at the far end of the west wing. You plan to install your Ethernet hubs in the data center, but some of the workstation locations you have selected are as much as 500 meters from the hubs. Which of the following Ethernet variants can you use to connect all the workstations to the hubs in the data center?

    A. 10Base-T

    B. 100Base-TX

    C. 100Base-FX

    D. 1000Base-T

3. Which of the following network media should you use to build a network in a factory containing equipment that generates enormous amounts of electromagnetic interference?

    A. Unshielded twisted pair (UTP)

    B. Fiber-optic

    C. IEEE 802.11b, using an ad hoc topology

    D. IEEE 802.11g, using an infrastructure topology

Objective 2.2 Answers

1.   Correct Answers: B and D

   A. Incorrect: You cannot use NetBEUI to access NetWare servers or the Internet, so it is not required for these workstations.

   B. Correct: To access NetWare 3.11 servers from a workstation running Windows, you must install the NWLink protocol, which provides IPX connectivity.

   C. Incorrect: IEEE 802.11b is a standard for a wireless data-link layer protocol, and is not applicable in this case.

   D. Correct: To access the Internet from any computer, you must install the TCP/IP protocols.

2.   Correct Answers: C

   A. Incorrect: 10Base-T calls for Category 5 unshielded twisted pair cable, which can extend no longer than 100 meters, so it cannot support workstations 500 meters from the hub.

   B. Incorrect: 100Base-TX calls for Category 5 unshielded twisted pair cable, which can extend no longer than 100 meters, so it cannot support workstations 500 meters from the hub.

   C. Correct: 100Base-FX calls for 62.5/125 multimode fiber-optic cable, which can span distances of up to 412 meters at half duplex and 2000 meters at full duplex easily enough to support workstations 500 meters away.

   D. Incorrect: 1000Base-T calls for Category 5 unshielded twisted pair cable, which can extend no longer than 100 meters, so it cannot support workstations 500 meters from the hub.

3.   Correct Answers: B

   A. Incorrect: UTP cables use copper conductors to carry electrical signals, and electromagnetic interference can affect the quality of the signals.

   B. Correct: Fiber-optic cable is completely resistant to electromagnetic interference because it uses light pulses instead of electrical charges for signaling.

   C. Incorrect: IEEE 802.11b is a wireless networking protocol, but it is still affected by electromagnetic interference, whether it uses the ad hoc topology or the infrastructure topology.

   D. Incorrect: IEEE 802.11g is a wireless networking protocol, but it is still affected by electromagnetic interference, whether it uses the ad hoc topology or the infrastructure topology.

Plan an Internet Connectivity Strategy

Planning an Internet connectivity strategy for your network is a matter of deciding how much bandwidth you need and how you are going to supply it in a secure manner. To estimate the bandwidth you need, you determine what Internet applications your network computers will be running, how many of the computers will be running them, and how many computers there are. It is also important to pinpoint the times of day when the need for Internet bandwidth is greatest, and to identify seasonal changes in Internet bandwidth usage. When estimating bandwidth, you should also try to anticipate future changes in your bandwidth requirements. You might have to add more clients to the network, or the company Web servers might experience a significant traffic increase.

Once you have decided how much bandwidth you need, you can select a wide area network (WAN) technology that provides sufficient bandwidth. Some of the WAN technologies most commonly used for Internet access are as follows:

- **Dial-up modem**   Operating at a maximum speed of only 53 Kbps, the dial-up modem is the slowest Internet access technology, but it is also the most flexible. Changing to a different Internet service provider is simply a matter of dialing a different number. You can share a dial-up connection among network users, but the bandwidth it provides is severely limited, and suitable only for a few users requiring minimal access.

- **Integrated Services Digital Network (ISDN)**   ISDN is a digital dial-up service that uses standard telephone lines to provide high-speed data communications. The ISDN service commonly found in the United States is called the **Basic Rate Interface (BRI)**. This service, also known as 2B+D, provides up to 128 Kbps of usable bandwidth. ISDN is relatively costly for the bandwidth it provides, but it has the same advantages as any dial-up service. You can disconnect from the ISP when no one is using the connection, and you can change ISPs by dialing a different number.

- **Cable television (CATV) networks**   Many cable television companies provide Internet access to subscribers through their private networks, using the same medium that supplies the television signals. CATV connections are asymmetrical, meaning that the upstream and downstream traffic run at different speeds. Downstream traffic (from the Internet to the CATV client) can run at speeds of 512 Kbps or more, but providers typically cap the upstream speed at 64 or 128 Kbps, because the bandwidth running in this direction is limited. Because of this asymmetry, CATV connections are typically not satisfactory for hosting Internet services, such as Web servers. A CATV connection can support multiple Internet clients, but because you must share the network medium with other local subscribers, the amount of bandwidth available at any given time is unpredictable.

- **Digital Subscriber Line (DSL)** DSL is a digital service provided by telephone carriers, using their standard telephone cables to provide a high-speed dedicated link between two points. There are many different types of DSL connections, targeted at applications ranging from home Internet use to long distance, high-speed backbones. The most common form of DSL for Internet access is **Asymmetrical Digital Subscriber Line (ADSL)**, which can run at speeds up to 8 Mbps. Like CATV connections, ADSL runs at different upstream and downstream speeds, but because it doesn't use a shared medium, the amount of bandwidth available is consistent and predictable. Both CATV and ADSL are targeted primarily at home Internet users, but it is possible to share one of these connections with an entire network.

- **Leased lines** A leased line is a permanent digital telephone connection between two points, running at a specified, consistent speed. The most common type of leased line for shared Internet connections is the **T-1**, running at 1.544 Mbps. Many service providers also make **fractional T-1** service available, which enables you to lease any part of a T-1 connection, in 64 Kbps increments. For ISPs and other organizations requiring an enormous amount of bandwidth, a **T-3** connection runs at 44.736 Mbps. The advantages of a leased line are also its drawbacks. You cannot change ISPs without performing a costly reinstallation of the line, you cannot increase or decrease the amount of bandwidth available to you without a costly reinstallation, and you pay for the bandwidth 24 hours a day, whether you are using it or not.

- **Frame relay** In a frame relay installation, you use a leased line to connect to a service provider, which provides access to a frame relay **cloud**. Your network then accesses your ISP's network through the cloud. The advantage of frame relay is that the cloud can provide you with a variable amount of bandwidth, so you can pay only for the bandwidth you use. You contract for a specific **committed information rate (CIR)** with your ISP, but you can exceed that rate (within limits) during periods of high activity. When you are not using the connection, you can disconnect and save on ISP charges.

In most cases, networks requiring Internet access using unregistered IP addresses and either a **network address translation (NAT)** router or a proxy server. A NAT router is a network layer device that enables client computers with unregistered addresses to access Internet services using the router's registered address. When a client computer sends a request to an Internet server, the NAT router substitutes its own registered IP address for the client's unregistered address before forwarding the message. The Internet server then replies to the NAT router, which relays the response to the client.

A **proxy server** is an application layer device that functions as an intermediary between private network clients and Internet servers, much as a NAT router does. The difference between the two is that proxy servers function only for specific applications, and you must configure the clients to use the proxy server. Because they are application-specific, proxy servers also provide administrators with more control over clients' Internet access. You can configure a proxy server to block client access to specific sites, to limit access to specific times of day, and to log all Internet activities. Proxy servers can also cache Internet data, so that the server can satisfy repeated requests for the same Internet resources using the cached information rather than repeatedly querying the same servers.

Objective 2.3 Questions

1. You are designing an Internet access solution for an accounting firm whose workers require constant access to Web sites and e-mail during business hours. The company also maintains a Web site that receives heavy traffic from clients. The company works extremely long hours during tax season, which runs from January through April, but drops back to a standard eight-hour work day after April 15. Which of the following wide area networking (WAN) technologies would provide the most flexible bandwidth service for this network?

   A. T-1 leased line

   B. BRI ISDN

   C. ADSL

   D. Frame relay

2. You are assigned the task of deploying an Internet access strategy for your company's new branch office. The IT director, never having supplied users with Internet access before, has two main concerns. One concern is that the company network be safe from Internet intruders. The director is also concerned about network users spending too much time viewing Web sites that are not related to work. The two primary goals for the project are therefore to implement some sort of security mechanism and to regulate the users' Internet access. To achieve these goals, the director has hired a network consultant who submitted a plan containing the following elements:

- Configure the client computers on the network with unregistered IP addresses.

- Install a T-1 leased line connecting the network site to an Internet service provider.

- Install a NAT router to connect the T-1 line to the company network.

Which of the stated goals does this plan satisfy?

   A. The plan satisfies both of the stated goals.

   B. The plan satisfies the goal of securing the network, but it does not regulate Internet activity.

   C. The plan satisfies the goal of regulating Internet activity, but it does not secure the network from Internet intrusion.

   D. The plan satisfies neither of the stated goals.

3.   Which of the following wide area network (WAN) connections commonly used for Internet access are asymmetrical? (Choose all that apply.)

   A. T-1

   B. Frame relay

   C. CATV

   D. ADSL

Objective 2.3 Answers

1. **Correct Answers: D**

   A. **Incorrect:** A T-1 leased line provides 1.544 Mbps of bandwidth at all times, whether the network is in use or not. If a T-1 is sufficient for the company's needs during its peak usage periods, then much of the bandwidth is wasted at non-peak times.

   B. **Incorrect:** A Basic Rate Interface ISDN connection provides 128 Kbps of bandwidth, and can be disconnected when the network is not in use. However, while the connection time can be controlled by the user, the amount of bandwidth cannot. Therefore, this is not the most flexible option.

   C. **Incorrect:** An Asymmetrical Digital Subscriber Line connection provides a fixed amount of bandwidth and uses a permanent connection, so there is no flexibility in connection time or bandwidth amount. In addition, ADSL connections are asymmetrical, which limits the amount of upstream bandwidth and makes this option unsuitable for an installation running busy Web servers.

   D. **Correct:** With a frame relay connection, you pay ISP charges only for the bandwidth you use and you can exceed your contracted allotment of bandwidth during peak usage periods. Frame relay is therefore the most flexible option.

2. **Correct Answers: B**

   A. **Incorrect:** While the combination of using unregistered IP addresses and a NAT router does secure the network from many types of Internet intrusion, it does not enable administrators to regulate users' Internet access.

   B. **Correct:** The NAT router enables clients with unregistered IP addresses to access the Internet with security, but because NAT is a network-layer process, it does not read the application layer information in the packets and therefore cannot regulate the client traffic to the Internet based on that information.

   C. **Incorrect:** This answer is doubly incorrect, in that NAT does not regulate Internet activity, but it does secure the network from Internet intrusion.

   D. **Incorrect:** While it is true that NAT does not enable administrators to regulate clients' Internet access, it does provide security by enabling the clients to use unregistered IP addresses.

3. **Correct Answers: C and D**

    A. Incorrect: A T-1 leased line provides 1.544 Mbps of symmetrical bandwidth.

    B. Incorrect: Frame relay connections are adjustable in terms of the amount of bandwidth they provide, but they run at the same speed in both directions.

    C. Correct: The Internet connections that cable television networks provide are asymmetrical because the networks were designed primarily to deliver television signals to subscribers. As a result, relatively little upstream bandwidth is available.

    D. Correct: ADSL stands for Asymmetrical Digital Subscriber Line, which means that the connections always run faster downstream than upstream.

Plan Network Traffic Monitoring

The Windows Server 2003 operating system includes powerful tools that you can use to monitor the traffic on your network. The two most important of these tools are the Performance console and Network Monitor.

The Performance console consists of two Microsoft Management Console (MMC) snap-ins called **System Monitor** and **Performance Logs And Alerts**. System Monitor is a performance monitoring tool that enables you to select certain aspects of specific system components and view their status in real time. In System Monitor, the computer's components are represented by **performance objects**, which in turn contain **performance counters**. When you select a performance object, such as Network Interface, System Monitor displays a list of counters for that object. After you select the counters you want to monitor, the snap-in adds them to a real-time line graph that continually updates itself. You can also display the information in histogram or report form.

While System Monitor is designed for real-time viewing, Performance Logs And Alerts enables you to track system performance over an extended period of time and save it to a log, or it can notify you when counter values reach a certain level. The Performance Logs And Alerts snap-in has the following three capabilities:

- **Counter logs** Using the same performance counters as System Monitor, a counter log saves the information to a log file in any one of several formats. You can then replay the log later using System Monitor.

- **Trace logs** Trace logs record information about specific system events, such as disk I/O operation or a page fault. When the specified event occurs, the snap-in records information about it to a log file for later study.

- **Alerts** Alerts are instances of a particular performance counter that the snap-in monitors continually, but instead of displaying the counter value in a graph or logging it to a file, the snap-in compares the counter's value to a threshold value specified by an administrator. If the counter reaches that threshold, the snap-in performs a specified action, such as sending a message to a particular computer or executing a certain program.

Network Monitor is an application that captures network traffic, interprets the information in the packets, and displays the information for the user. With Network Monitor, you can view the entire contents of a network packet, including all the protocol header fields and the payload inside. You can use Network Monitor to examine trends in network traffic, detect certain types of attacks, such as denial-of-service (DoS) events, and analyze message contents. To simplify the process of looking at specific groups of packets, Network Monitor enables you to create filters that specify which types of traffic you want to analyze. **Capture filters** control which packets the program saves to its buffers, and **display filters** control which buffered packets appear in the user interface.

Objective 2.4 Questions

1. You are reviewing the network help desk calls that your company has received during the past week, and you notice that for several isolated periods of time, multiple users were reporting an inability to access Internet Web sites. In each case, support personnel determined that the problem was caused by Domain Name System (DNS) name resolution failures, but they could find nothing wrong with the company's Windows Server 2003 DNS server. You suspect that the DNS server is experiencing intermittent denial-of-service attacks from the Internet. Which of the following procedures can you use to find out when such an attack occurs again? (Choose all that apply.)

A. Create a trace log in the Performance Logs And Alerts snap-in on the DNS server, using the DNS Trace provider.

B. Create a System Monitor graph on the DNS server using the Total Query Received counter in the DNS performance object.

C. Use Network Monitor to capture all the DNS server's traffic, then create a display filter to isolate the Transmission Control Protocol (TCP) traffic.

D. Create an alert with the Performance Logs And Alerts snap-in on the DNS server using the Datagrams Received/Sec counter in the UDPv4 performance object.

2. Which of the following can you use to view the IP address offered to a client by a DHCP server in a DHCPOFFER message?

A. Network Monitor

B. A trace log

C. System Monitor

D. A counter log

3. You are a network administrator trying to perform a detailed analysis of the DNS server traffic on a computer running Windows Server 2003 over a long time. To do this, you start Network Monitor to capture traffic, then leave it alone for 24 hours. When you return the next day, you determine that the capture buffer is full, but it contains only a few minutes' worth of traffic. Which of the following solutions can enable you to capture DNS server traffic over a longer time?

A. Increase the size of the capture buffer.

B. Create a display filter causing Network Monitor to display DNS traffic only.

C. Create a capture filter causing Network Monitor to capture only DNS traffic to the buffer.

D. Clear out some disk space on the computer.

4.   Which of the following network services has its own log in the Event Viewer console?

   A. DHCP Server

   B. WINS

   C. DNS Server

   D. RRAS

Objective 2.4 Answers

1.   **Correct Answers: B and D**

   A. Incorrect: You use trace logs to monitor conditions caused by specific system events, not particular network traffic patterns.

   B. Correct: This counter indicates the number of name resolution queries that the DNS server receives at any one time. If the value of this counter rises precipitously at a particular time, it is possible that the server is experiencing a denial-of-service attack.

   C. Incorrect: Most DNS traffic uses the UDP protocol, not TCP, so this procedure is not likely to detect a denial-of-service attack.

   D. Correct: Creating an alert using the Datagrams Received/Sec counter can inform you when the server experiences an increase in the number of incoming UDP messages, which could indicate that a denial-of-service attack is in progress.

2.   **Correct Answers: A**

   A. Correct: Network Monitor can capture network packets and display their contents, including the contents of a DHCPOFFER message, which contains the IP supplied to a client by a DHCP server.

   B. Incorrect: Trace logs capture information about certain system events, but they cannot read the contents of network packets.

   C. Incorrect: System Monitor can track the number of DHCPOFFER messages that a DHCP server transmits, but it cannot view the contents of those messages.

   D. Incorrect: Counter logs track the same information as System Monitor, but save it in a permanent form instead of displaying it in real time. Like System Monitor, counter logs can monitor the number of network packets transmitted, but they cannot read their contents.

3.   **Correct Answers: A**

   A. Correct: By default, Network Monitor's capture buffer is only 1 MB but you can increase it to any size, as long as the computer has sufficient disk space.

   B. Incorrect: Creating a display filter does not affect the amount of data in the capture buffer, but only the kind of data Network Monitor displays.

C. Incorrect: You cannot create a capture filter that restricts a capture to packets containing a specific application-layer protocol such as DNS. Capture filters can only filter protocols that use a SAP (service access point) or an Etype.

D. Incorrect: Just clearing disk space does not increase the amount of traffic that Network Monitor can capture. To do this, you must increase the size of the capture buffer.

4.   Correct Answers: C

A. Incorrect: The DHCP Server service does not have a separate log in the Event Viewer console. You can view DHCP Server information in the System log, in the DHCP console, and in the service's own text log.

B. Incorrect: The WINS service does not have a separate log in the Event Viewer console. You can view WINS information in the System log and in the WINS console.

C. Correct: The DNS Server service has its own log in the Event Viewer console, as well as an optional debugging log.

D. Incorrect: The RRAS service does not have a separate log in the Event Viewer console. You can view RRAS information in the Routing And Remote Access console.

Troubleshoot Connectivity to the Internet

When network users are unable to access Internet resources through a shared connection, the cause of the problem can lie anywhere between the client computer and the Internet server. To troubleshoot Internet connectivity problems, the first task is to isolate the exact location of the fault and determine how many users are affected. In many cases, the problem might be beyond your control, and the only solution is to call your ISP or the carrier that provides the connection to your ISP.

Determining the scope of an Internet connectivity problem is generally a matter of trying to recreate the problem on different computers. Depending on whether you can recreate the problem on computers connected to the same hub, to the same LAN, to different LANs, or throughout the enterprise, you can isolate the problem as being located in the client computer, in a hub, in a router, or in the Internet connection itself.

Client connectivity problems can be caused by hardware, such as a disconnected cable or a malfunctioning network interface adapter, but the most common cause of Internet connection failures in a single client is incorrect configuration. An incorrect **default gateway** address prevents the computer from accessing resources on other networks (including the Internet) but does not prevent the computer from accessing the local network. An incorrect **Domain Name Service (DNS)** server address (or a malfunctioning DNS server) can prevent a client from resolving Internet server names, therefore preventing it from accessing the server by using its name.

DNS servers are also subject to problems caused by incorrect cache information. If a DNS server has outdated or incorrect information in its cache, it might supply the wrong IP address to a client requesting the resolution of a particular Internet server name. The DNS server cache is sometimes a target for Internet attackers, who attempt to pollute its contents using unauthorized dynamic updates. You can prevent cache pollution on a Windows Server 2003 DNS server by using only secure dynamic updates and by activating the Secure Cache Against Pollution option that you select on the Advanced tab in the DNS server's Properties dialog box.

A problem with a **NAT router** or **proxy server** affects all clients who use that device to access the Internet. To determine whether the NAT router or proxy server is the cause of the problem, you can try to access the Internet using a computer with a registered IP address, which bypasses the router or server, and accesses the Internet directly using the same ISP connection. If the NAT router or proxy server is at fault, you should begin by checking the TCP/IP configuration parameters for all the device's network interfaces. Routers and servers are subject to the same configuration problems as a client, because they too must access the Internet through your ISP connection.

If all these factors turn out not to be the cause of your Internet connectivity problem, the difficulty might lie in your connection to the Internet or in the Internet itself. If this is the case, you generally have no recourse other than to contact your ISP or the provider of the WAN service that connects your network to the ISP.

Objective 2.5 Questions

1. You are working at the network help desk at your company and you receive a call from a user complaining that she cannot access any Internet Web sites. The company network has a T-1 connection to a local ISP, which all the network clients share, using a NAT router. All the network users rely on a single DNS server, which has a registered IP address, for name resolution services. After checking with other users on the network, you determine that everyone on the user's local area network (LAN) is experiencing the same Internet access problem. The other LANs are functioning properly. Which of the following could be the cause of the difficulty?

   A. The DNS server is down.

   B. The NAT router is malfunctioning.

   C. The user's default gateway is malfunctioning.

   D. The user's computer has an incorrect default gateway address.

2. A user calls the network help desk complaining that he can access some Internet Web sites but not others. Which of the following could conceivably be the cause of this problem? (Choose all that apply.)

   A. DNS cache pollution

   B. An Internet routing problem

   C. A malfunctioning NAT router

   D. An incorrect DNS server address

3. Which of the following indicates that an Internet connectivity problem is being caused by a malfunctioning NAT router?

   A. Some users can access the Internet while others cannot.

   B. A computer with a registered IP address can access the Internet, while computers with unregistered addresses cannot.

   C. Users can access some Internet servers but not others.

   D. Users can access the Internet using IP addresses but not server names.

4. A computer on your network with an unregistered IP address is unable to access a specific Internet Web site. After reproducing the problem on the computer several times, you try the same task on another computer connected to the same LAN and find that you can access the Web site. You then ping the Web server from the second computer to determine the Web site's IP address and try to connect from the malfunctioning computer by using the Web site's address instead of the server name. You can connect successfully using the IP address. Which of the following TCP/IP configuration parameters on the malfunctioning computer is probably incorrect?

A. IP Address

B. Subnet Mask

C. Default Gateway

D. Preferred DNS Server

5. You are working at the network help desk at your company and you receive a call from a user complaining that he cannot access Internet Web sites. After some investigation, you suspect a DNS (Domain Name System) name resolution problem. Which of the following procedures should you perform to gather information about the interaction between that user's computer and the DNS server?

A. Enable debug logging in the DNS console and create a filter with the user's IP address.

B. Open the System Monitor snap-in in the Performance console and create a graph using counters from the DNS performance object.

C. Open the Event Viewer console and study the contents of the DNS Server log.

D. Open the DNS console and display the DNS Server Statistics window.

Objective 2.5 Answers

1.   Correct Answers: C

   A. Incorrect: If the DNS server were not functioning, all the users on the network would be experiencing the same problem, not just the users on one LAN.

   B. Incorrect: If the NAT router were malfunctioning, no one on the network would be able to access the Internet. The fact that only one LAN is experiencing the problem points to a more specific cause.

   C. Correct: The user's default gateway is a router that connects the LAN to the rest of the network. If the default gateway router malfunctions, none of the users on that LAN can access the Internet or any other resource outside the local network.

   D. Incorrect: An incorrect default gateway address would affect only the single user's computer, not all the other users on the LAN.

2.   Correct Answers: A and B

   A. Correct: If a DNS server has a cache that has been polluted, it might supply clients with incorrect IP addresses for requested Internet server names. This could cause the user to be able to access some Internet servers but not others.

   B. Correct: It is common for Internet backbone problems, ISP network problems, and other conditions to cause temporary service interruptions for parts of the Internet. These problems are beyond the control of the individual network administrator, but they can cause users to experience service outages for some sites and not others.

   C. Incorrect: A malfunctioning NAT router would interrupt all the user's Internet communications, not just connections to certain sites.

   D. Incorrect: An incorrect DNS server address would prevent the user from accessing any Internet services using DNS names.

3.   Correct Answers: B

   A. Incorrect: A malfunctioning NAT router would prevent all users relying on that router from accessing the Internet.

   B. Correct: Computers with unregistered IP addresses must use the NAT router to access the Internet, while computers with registered addresses can access the Internet directly. Testing the Internet connection with a registered computer means that you are bypassing the NAT router, so a successful connection points to the NAT router as the source of the problem.

C. **Incorrect:** The ability to access some Internet sites but not others is typically an indication of an Internet routing or server problem, not a NAT router problem. A NAT router malfunction interrupts all Internet access.

D. **Incorrect:** The ability to access Internet sites with IP addresses but not names is an indication of a name resolution problem, such as a DNS server failure. A NAT router malfunction interrupts all Internet access.

4.   Correct Answers: D

A. **Incorrect:** An incorrect IP address would either have no effect at all on the computer (if the address were not already in use and on the same subnet) or it would interrupt all TCP/IP communications.

B. **Incorrect:** An incorrect subnet mask value would interrupt all TCP/IP communications.

C. **Incorrect:** An incorrect default gateway address would prevent the computer from accessing all resources except those on the local network.

D. **Correct:** An incorrect DNS server address would prevent the computer from resolving the names of Web servers into IP addresses. You can therefore connect to the server using the address, but not the name.

5.   Correct Answers: A

A. **Correct:** The debug logging feature of the Windows Server 2003 DNS Server service has a filtering capability that enables you to log only the interaction of a single IP address with the server.

B. **Incorrect:** The DNS performance counters enable you to display a great deal of information about the DNS Server service, not about the activities of a single client computer.

C. **Incorrect:** The DNS Server log contains information about the state of the DNS Server service, but not about the activities of a single client computer.

D. **Incorrect:** The DNS console does not have a DNS Server Statistics window.

Objective 2.6

Troubleshoot TCP/IP Addressing

One of the drawbacks of using TCP/IP on your network is that each computer must have a unique IP address and correct settings for several other TCP/IP configuration parameters. Even a minor configuration error can cause a partial or complete interruption of the computer's network communications and can even interfere with other computers on the network.

The primary TCP/IP configuration parameters on a client computer and their effects when someone configures them incorrectly are as follows:

- **IP Address**   An IP address that duplicates another address on the network can prevent both computers from communicating. The Microsoft Windows operating systems check for duplicate addresses each time the computer starts, then shut down the TCP/IP client if they detect one. An incorrect IP address that is on a different subnet prevents the computer from communicating with any of the systems on the local network (including routers that provide access to other networks).

- **Subnet Mask**   An incorrect subnet mask causes a computer to misinterpret its IP address by treating network bits as host bits or host bits as network bits. The system therefore interprets the address as being on a different subnet, interrupting all TCP/IP communications.

- **Default Gateway**   An incorrect default gateway address prevents the client computer from accessing resources on other networks. Communications with systems on the local network are not interrupted because the computer can send packets directly to them. To reach a system on another network, the packets must pass through a router such as the default gateway, which is inaccessible when the value of the Default Gateway parameter is incorrect.

- **Preferred DNS Server**   An incorrect DNS server address prevents the client computer from resolving DNS names into IP addresses. This interrupts all Internet communication that uses names, and might also interfere with internal communications, depending on the configuration of the private network. To determine whether name resolution failure is causing a communications problem, try connecting to a resource using its IP address instead of its name.

When you use a **DHCP** server to assign IP addresses and other TCP/IP configuration parameters to clients automatically, it is still possible for TCP/IP configuration problems to occur. The most obvious problem is if a DHCP client is unable to connect to a DHCP server. When this happens, the client cannot request an IP address, and in the case of a Windows client, a feature called **Automatic Private IP Addressing (APIPA)** takes over. APIPA enables a DHCP client to assign itself an IP address when it cannot obtain one from a DHCP server. If you find that a DHCP client has an IP address beginning with 169.254, it is because APIPA has assigned the address.

It is also possible for a DHCP client not to obtain an IP address from a DHCP server because the server is configured incorrectly or is configured to provide addresses for clients on a different subnet. If the scope you create on the DHCP server does not use the same network address as the interface connecting the server to the network, then clients on the same subnet as the DHCP server cannot obtain addresses from that scope. You should also make sure that the DHCP options you create are properly associated with either your scopes or the server.

Objective 2.6 Questions

1. After installing a DHCP server on your network, you create a scope to assign your computers IP addresses in the 192.168.86.0/24 network. You then configure all your workstations to function as DHCP clients and restart them. All the workstations are then able to communicate with the network except one. When you execute the IPCONFIG /all command on that workstation, you see that the computer's IP address is 169.254.0.1. Which of the following is a possible cause of the problem?

    A. The DHCP server is down.

    B. The client computer is configured with an incorrect DHCP server address.

    C. The scope on the DHCP server does not match the network address of the server's network interface.

    D. The client computer's network cable is unplugged.

2. Which of the following is a symptom of a client computer having an incorrect default gateway address?

    A. The computer can communicate with the local network but not with other networks.

    B. The computer can access Internet Web sites using IP addresses, but not names.

    C. The computer is not able to communicate with the network at all.

    D. The computer can access Web sites using names, but not IP addresses.

3. Which of the following TCP/IP parameters do you typically have to configure with DHCP scope option?

    A. IP Address

    B. Subnet Mask

    C. Default Gateway

    D. Preferred DNS Server

4. Which of the following tools can you use to monitor the DHCP Server service? (Choose all that apply.)

    A. The DHCP Server log in the Event Viewer console

    B. The DHCP Server performance object counters in System Monitor

    C. The DHCP log file

    D. The DHCP Server Statistics dialog box

Objective 2.6 Answers

1.   Correct Answers: D

   A. Incorrect: If the DHCP server were not functioning, none of the workstations on the network would have obtained functioning IP addresses.

   B. Incorrect: DHCP client computers locate DHCP servers by transmitting DHCP-DISCOVER broadcast messages. You cannot configure a client with the address of a specific DHCP server.

   C. Incorrect: If the scope were incorrect, none of the workstations on the network would be able to obtain IP addresses from the DHCP server.

   D. Correct: If the client computer is unable to communicate with the network for any reason, such as a disconnected cable, it cannot contact the DHCP server and obtain an IP address. The client would then fall back to using APIPA to assign itself an address.

2.   Correct Answers: A

   A. Correct: The default gateway is a router that a computer uses to access resources on other networks. If the computer has an incorrect default gateway address, it cannot access other networks, but local network traffic is not affected.

   B. Incorrect: The inability to access Internet Web sites using their names is a sign of a name resolution failure, possibly caused by an incorrect DNS server address, not an incorrect default gateway address.

   C. Incorrect: An incorrect default gateway address would not have any effect on local network communications, because the computer can transmit directly to other systems on the local network without using a router.

   D. Incorrect: TCP/IP computers always use IP addresses when communicating with other computers. There is no possible way for communication to occur with names and without addresses.

3.   Correct Answers: C

   A. Incorrect: DHCP servers assign IP addresses to clients using the scope itself, not a DHCP option.

   B. Incorrect: DHCP servers assign a Subnet Mask value along with an IP Address value, not as a DHCP option.

   C. Correct: The Default Gateway parameter specifies the address on a router on the client computer's local network. Therefore, the default gateway address must be different for each scope. To supply a different parameter value for each scope, you use a scope option, not a server option.

D. Incorrect: A computer can use any DNS server to resolve names into IP addresses, so it is typical for a single DNS server to service multiple scopes. Because the DNS server address is not specific to a subnet, you can use a server option to assign the same value to all your DHCP clients.

4.   **Correct Answers: B, C, and D**

A. Incorrect: There is no DHCP Server log in the Event Viewer console.

B. Correct: The DHCP Server performance object in System Monitor contains counters that enable you to display information about the numbers and types of DHCP messages transmitted and received by the server.

C. Correct: The DHCP Server service has its own log file, which appears as a text file on the computer's local drive.

D. Correct: The DHCP console has a DHCP Server Statistics dialog box that displays information about the various DHCP messages transmitted by the server and about the number of IP addresses the server has assigned to DHCP clients.

Plan a Host Name Resolution Strategy

Name resolution is the process of converting a computer's name into an IP address. All TCP/IP systems communicate using IP addresses; the names are just a convenience for the user. Networks running Windows Server 2003 can use several different name resolution mechanisms, but the primary one is the **Domain Name System (DNS)**. Windows Server 2003 includes a DNS Server service that is compatible with virtually all the other DNS implementations used on the Internet. Your computers need access to a DNS server if they are connected to the Internet or if you use the Active Directory directory service. Active Directory networks nearly always have their own DNS servers, but for Internet access, you can use your own DNS servers or those supplied by your ISP.

To resolve Internet names, no special effort is needed beyond installing a DNS server and configuring your computers to use it. The server interacts with other DNS servers on the Internet to resolve the name of any Internet computer. To resolve your own computers' names, you must create your own DNS namespace. The DNS namespace is a hierarchy of **domains**, with each domain containing a number of **hosts**. To create your own public DNS namespace, you must register a second-level domain name in one of the existing Internet top-level domains (such as .com or .net). Then, you can create as many subdomains as you need beneath that second-level domain. The primary reason for creating subdomains is to delegate administrative responsibility for certain parts of the namespace. For example, if your organization has several offices and you want each one to manage its own DNS names, you can create a subdomain for each office.

In many cases, organizations have both internal (that is, private) and external (Internet) networks, which they must keep separated. To design a DNS namespace for this type of situation, you have three alternatives:

- **Use the same domain name** By using the same domain name for your internal and external networks, you stand the risk of having computers with the same name on both networks. Microsoft strongly recommends against this option.

- **Use two domain names** Having two different domain names for your internal and external networks eliminates the possibility of name conflicts, but you must pay a registration fee for the external, publicly available, domain name and it can cause confusion for users having to distinguish between internal and external resources.

■ **Create a subdomain** The solution that Microsoft recommends is to register a second-level domain name for your external network, and then create a subdomain beneath that second-level domain for the internal network. This solution requires only one registration fee, avoids naming conflicts, and enables you to delegate authority across the internal and external domains.

To register host names in your domain, you must create a **zone** on your DNS server. A zone is an administrative element that contains all or part of your DNS namespace. To ensure that your zones are always available, it is a good idea to have primary and secondary zones on two separate DNS servers. A **secondary zone** is a copy of a primary zone. The DNS servers replicate the zone database automatically, using a process called a zone transfer. If you create Active Directory-integrated zones on a Windows Server 2003 DNS server, there is no need for zone transfers because Active Directory replicates the database automatically.

A **forwarder** is a DNS server that receives queries sent to it by other DNS servers that you explicitly configure to send them. You can use forwarders in a variety of ways to regulate the flow of DNS traffic on your network.

To ensure that your DNS services are always available, you should create at least one redundant server, with a copy of your zones on each redundant server. You can also protect your DNS data by securing your zone transfers. The Windows Server 2003 DNS server enables you to specify the IP addresses of the servers that you allow to participate in zone transfers. You can also use IPSec to encrypt the zone data as the servers transmit it over the network. **Dynamic update** is a feature that enables computers to update their DNS resource records when their IP addresses change. You can configure a DNS server to permit only **secure dynamic updates**; in this configuration, the server authenticates the computers before they can update their resource records.

Objective 2.7 Questions

1. You are designing a network running Windows Server 2003 for a new company called Fourth Coffee, which has two offices, one in New York and one in San Francisco. The company uses e-commerce Web servers to take orders from customers and has registered the fourthcoffee.com second-level domain for this purpose. Your customer does not want to register any additional domain names. At the moment, you are designing the DNS namespace for the company's internal and external networks. Because each office is going to maintain its own DNS server, you want to create a separate subdomain for each site. In accordance with the domain naming practices recommended by Microsoft, you are going to create a subdomain for the internal network, and then another level of subdomains for the individual offices. Based on this information, which of the following domain names would you use for the internal network at the New York office?

   A. fourthcoffee.com

   B. fourthcoffee.ny.com

   C. int.fourthcoffee.com

   D. ny.int.fourthcoffee.com

2. Which of the following enables you to keep a copy of your DNS database files on another server?

   A. IPSec

   B. Secured dynamic updates

   C. Zone transfers

   D. A forwarder

3. You are the designer of the new network for a large company that wants no connections to the Internet whatsoever. You have created an extensive DNS namespace for the company, with multiple DNS servers at different locations. Now that the network is up and running, users are experiencing name resolution failures when they try to resolve names of computers in other offices. Which of the following options would be likely to solve the problem? (Choose all that apply.)

   A. Create an internal root.

   B. Create a secondary copy of each zone in the namespace on every DNS server.

    C. Use conditional forwarding to send the queries for each domain in the namespace to the DNS server hosting that domain.

    D. Enable secure dynamic updates to prevent DNS resource records from being corrupted.

4. Which of the following DNS server features do you *not* need to use when you create Active Directory-integrated zones? (Choose all that apply.)

    A. Primary zones

    B. Secondary zones

    C. Zone transfers

    D. Dynamic updates

Objective 2.7 Answers

1. **Correct Answers: D**

   A. **Incorrect:** Because fourthcoffee.com is the registered second-level domain name, Internet users will expect to use this to reach the company's Web site. Although it is possible to use the same domain name for your internal and external networks, Microsoft strongly recommends against this practice.

   B. **Incorrect:** This domain name would require you to register the ny.com second-level domain, which goes against the customer's wishes. The name ny.com is also already taken.

   C. **Incorrect:** The plan calls for you to create a subdomain for the internal network, and int.fourthcoffe.com would be an appropriate choice. However, the plan also states that you are going to create another level of subdomains for the individual offices. This additional level is not reflected in this name.

   D. **Correct:** To create this domain name, you create a subdomain called int, beneath fourthcoffee.com, to represent the internal network. You then create fourth-level domains to represent the offices, with names such as ny.int.fourthcoffee.com and sf.int.fourthcoffee.com.

2. **Correct Answers: C**

   A. **Incorrect:** IPSec is a series of extensions to the Internet Protocol that protects data as it is transmitted over the network. Although you can secure your DNS traffic with IPSec, you cannot use it by itself to replicate the DNS database.

   B. **Incorrect:** Secured dynamic updates enable DNS client computers to modify their resource records on a DNS server when their information changes. Dynamic updates do not replicate the DNS database.

   C. **Correct:** A zone transfer is the process by which one DNS server copies its zone database to another DNS server on the network. Zone transfers enable you to maintain redundant DNS servers on your network without having to modify each copy of the DNS database separately.

   D. **Incorrect:** A forwarder is a DNS server that receives queries from another DNS server. Forwarding has nothing to do with DNS database replication.

3. **Correct Answers: A, B, and C**

   A. **Correct:** The name resolution failures are occurring because DNS servers are attempting to send queries to the root name servers on the Internet, which are inaccessible. By creating an internal root, the servers send their queries to an internal DNS server instead.

B. Correct: By creating a secondary zone on every server for each of the other zones in the namespace, each DNS server is able to resolve any name in any domain, eliminating the need to send queries to the root name servers on the Internet.

C. Correct: Conditional forwarding enables you to send queries for names in specific domains to specific DNS servers. Because each server can forward queries directly to the authoritative server for the requested domain, there is no need to send queries to the root name servers on the Internet.

D. Incorrect: Dynamic updates, whether secured or not, enable DNS clients to modify their resource records on a DNS server. Using secured dynamic updates would not prevent DNS servers from sending queries for names in other domains to the root name servers on the Internet.

4.   **Correct Answers: B and C**

A. Incorrect: You must still create primary zones to host your domains, even if they are Active Directory-integrated zones.

B. Correct: When you create Active Directory-integrated zones, there is no need to create secondary zones, because Active Directory takes on the responsibility of replicating the DNS data.

C. Correct: Zone transfers replicate DNS data from primary to secondary zones. When you create Active Directory-integrated zones, the directory service replicates the DNS data automatically, and there is no need for secondary zones or zone transfers.

D. Incorrect: The integration of a zone into Active Directory has no effect on the need for dynamic updates. Dynamic update can still modify a computer's DNS resource record, whether the resource record is stored in a standard zone database file or in the Active Directory database.

Plan a NetBIOS Name Resolution Strategy

Up until the release of Microsoft Windows 2000, the Microsoft Windows operating systems relied on the **NetBIOS** namespace to provide friendly names for the computers on the network. NetBIOS names are 16 characters long, with the Windows operating system reserving the sixteenth character for code specifying the type of resource the name represents. Beginning with Windows 2000 Server, the Active Directory directory service replaces the NetBIOS namespace with the DNS namespace. However, Windows 2000 Server and Windows Server 2003 both continue to support NetBIOS names so that the computers can interact with the older Windows operating systems.

The Windows operating system includes several mechanisms that it can use to resolve NetBIOS names into IP addresses, such as the following:

- **NetBIOS name cache**   Whenever a computer running a Windows operating system resolves a NetBIOS name, it stores the name and its IP address in a memory cache for later use. All Windows NetBIOS name resolution mechanisms check the cache before doing anything else, because the cache is the fastest way of resolving a name. You can preload the cache with frequently used names by using the #PRE tag in an LMHOSTS file.

- **Broadcast name resolution**   On a network that doesn't use WINS, computers running Windows operating systems resolve NetBIOS names by transmitting broadcast messages containing the name they need to resolve. The computer using that name then must reply with a message containing its IP address. The drawbacks of the broadcast method are the amount of network traffic it generates and the fact that broadcast transmissions are limited to the local network. To resolve names of computers on other networks, the Windows operating system must use another name resolution mechanism, such as Lmhosts.

- **Windows Internet Name Service (WINS)**   WINS is a NetBIOS name server that enables computers to transmit their name resolution requests as unicasts to the WINS server. This reduces the amount of network traffic generated by the name resolution process and also enables clients to access WINS servers on other networks. To use WINS, you must configure your workstations with the IP address of a WINS server on the network. WINS servers automatically register clients' NetBIOS names and IP address when the computers start up. When you use multiple WINS servers on a network, for fault tolerance and load balancing, you configure them to replicate their databases with each other, so that each server has a complete listing of the NetBIOS names, and their IP addresses, on its network. To configure replication on a WINS server, you create replication partners and designate them as **push partners** or **pull partners**. A push partner sends messages to all its pull partners whenever the database changes, causing the pull partners to request an update. A pull partner issues requests to its push partners for database records with version numbers higher than the number of the last record it received during the previous replication.

■ **Lmhosts**   Lmhosts is a text file containing NetBIOS names and their equivalent IP addresses stored on a computer's local drive, much as a HOSTS file contains DNS names and IP addresses. Lmhosts name resolution is fast because it requires no network communication, but to register the names, you must add them to the Lmhosts file manually. Administrators typically use Lmhosts files to enable their computers to resolve names on other networks, which they cannot resolve with broadcasts. When you use WINS, Lmhosts files are not necessary.

Objective 2.8 Questions

1. Which of the following NetBIOS name resolution mechanisms can resolve only the names of computers on the local network?

    A. NetBIOS name cache

    B. Broadcast name resolution

    C. Lmhosts

    D. WINS

2. When a computer running a Windows operating system is not configured to use WINS, in what order does it use the NetBIOS name resolution mechanisms during its attempt to resolve a name?

    A. NetBIOS name cache, Lmhosts, then broadcast name resolution

    B. Broadcast name resolution, Lmhosts, then NetBIOS name cache

    C. Lmhosts, broadcast name resolution, then NetBIOS name cache

    D. NetBIOS name cache, broadcast name resolution, then Lmhosts

3. You are planning a WINS NetBIOS name resolution strategy for a company with headquarters in New York and ten branch offices located in different cities all over the world. Each office has its own WINS servers and, because the users of the company network frequently have to access computers in other branches, it is essential that all the servers have a complete database of all the network's NetBIOS names. The branch offices are all connected to the headquarters using T-1 leased lines, but these lines are heavily trafficked, and you want to keep WINS traffic to a minimum. Which of the following replication strategies will provide satisfactory replication performance with a minimum of wide area network (WAN) traffic?

    A. Configure the WINS servers in the New York office to pull WINS data from the server in each of the ten branch offices.

    B. Configure one WINS server in each office as a push partner with the WINS server in its nearest neighboring office to the east and a pull partner with its nearest neighbor to the west.

    C. On each WINS server, create a separate push/pull partnership with each of the other WINS servers on the network.

    D. Configure the WINS clients in all branches with the IP addresses of all the WINS servers on the enterprise network.

4. You are designing the NetBIOS name resolution strategy for a multisegment network running Windows Server 2003 but that still includes some Windows NT servers and Windows 95 workstations. You have decided that you don't want to run a WINS server, but you have a Windows NT 4.0 print server that all users must be able to access. Which of the following strategies would make this possible? (Choose all that apply.)

A. Do nothing. The computers will be able to resolve the name of the server running Windows NT name automatically using broadcast name resolution.

B. Create an Lmhosts file on each computer with an entry containing the NetBIOS name and IP address of the server running Windows NT.

C. Preload the NetBIOS name and IP address of the server running Windows NT into the NetBIOS name cache.

D. It can't be done. You must run a WINS server for computers to be able to resolve the NetBIOS names of computers on other networks.

Objective 2.8 Answers

1.   Correct Answers: B

   A. Incorrect: The NetBIOS name cache contains all the NetBIOS names that the computer has recently resolved by any means, whether the resolved names are for computers on the local network or another network.

   B. Correct: Broadcast transmissions are limited to the local network, so the broadcast method can only resolve the name of a computer on the local network.

   C. Incorrect: You can create entries in an Lmhosts file for the NetBIOS name of any computer on any network. In fact, the primary reason for using Lmhosts files is to resolve the names of computers on other networks.

   D. Incorrect: WINS can resolve the NetBIOS names of any computer on any network.

2.   Correct Answers: D

   A. Incorrect: A computer running a Windows operating system always checks the NetBIOS name cache before using any other NetBIOS name resolution method, but it uses Lmhosts only after broadcast name resolution has failed.

   B. Incorrect: A computer running a Windows operating system always checks the NetBIOS name cache before using any other NetBIOS name resolution method, then uses broadcasts and, failing that, Lmhosts.

   C. Incorrect: Computers running Windows operating systems try to resolve NetBIOS names using broadcast transmissions before they try using Lmhosts, and they always check the NetBIOS name cache before any other mechanism.

   D. Correct: A computer running a Windows operating system that is not a WINS client always checks the NetBIOS name cache first when trying to resolve a NetBIOS name, then tries the broadcast transmission method. If the broadcast method fails, the computer tries to look up the name in the Lmhosts file.

3.   Correct Answers: B

   A. Incorrect: This replication topology would result in only the New York WINS servers having complete replicas of the database, because all replication traffic is traveling in one direction.

   B. Correct: This solution is called a ring replication topology, because each site is sending its data to the east and receiving data from the west. This enables every server to have a complete replica of the WINS database without creating a large amount of redundant WAN traffic.

    C. Incorrect: While this option does provide satisfactory replication performance, it also generates much more WAN traffic than a ring topology.

    D. Incorrect: The WINS client enables you to specify multiple WINS server addresses only as fallbacks in case of a server failure. Adding all the WINS server addresses to each client does not cause the client to register its NetBIOS name with all the servers.

4.   **Correct Answers: B and C**

    A. Incorrect: Only the client computers on the same local area network as the server running Windows NT would be able to resolve its name using broadcast transmissions.

    B. Correct: Lmhosts functions as a backup to the broadcast name resolution method, because it is able to resolve NetBIOS names of computers on other networks.

    C. Correct: Preloading the name of the server running Windows NT into the cache using an Lmhosts file enables the computer to resolve the name without using the broadcast method.

    D. Incorrect: An Lmhosts file can resolve any NetBIOS name, regardless of whether it is on the local network or not.

Troubleshoot Host Name Resolution

Name resolution failures can often appear to users as complete TCP/IP communications failures, but that is not the case. When a client computer is unable to resolve a name, it cannot obtain the IP address it needs to initiate communication with the named computer. However, if you already have the named computer's IP address, you can connect to it directly by using the address in place of the name. This is the best way to determine if a failure to connect to a TCP/IP system is due to a name resolution problem. Once you have determined that a name resolution problem is causing your communications failure, you can begin to isolate the location of the problem.

Name resolution failures can be the result of a problem on the client or on the computer running the DNS server. At the client, the problem is typically an incorrect DNS server address. Either the Preferred DNS Server or the Alternate DNS Server field in the Windows Internet Protocol (TCP/IP) Properties dialog box must contain the IP address of a valid and operating DNS server.

If the client contains valid DNS server addresses, the servers themselves might be malfunctioning. The most obvious problem is that the DNS server is not functioning at all, because it is suffering from its own TCP/IP communications failure. Like any other computer, the DNS server must have the correct TCP/IP configuration parameters, including a valid IP address and subnet mask, plus a default gateway address. Malfunctioning hardware can also inhibit the server's communications. If you cannot successfully ping a DNS server address, it is suffering from some sort of TCP/IP communications failure.

If you can ping the DNS server computer, you should then check to see if the DNS Server service is running. You might find that someone has shut down the service, or that the service never started when the computer booted, or that the service has stopped. You can check the Event Viewer console for error messages that might explain the stoppage or just try restarting the service yourself.

In some cases, a DNS server might successfully resolve a name, but supply the wrong IP address to the client. This could be due to any one of the following reasons:

- **Incorrect resource records**   Administrators frequently type DNS resource records by hand, and typographic errors can result. If a resource record contains an incorrect IP address, the only solution is to correct it manually.

- **Dynamic update failures**   If dynamic updates fail for any reason, the DNS server's resource records could contain incorrect or outdated IP addresses. In this event, you can correct the resource records manually, or trigger a new dynamic update by traveling to the computer whose resource record is wrong and typing IPCONFIG / registerdns at a command prompt. If dynamic updates still fail to occur, check to see whether the server supports them and is configured to accept them.

- **Zone transfer failures**   If the DNS server is supplying incorrect IP addresses from a secondary zone, it is possible that a zone transfer has failed to occur, leaving outdated information in the secondary zone database file. Try to manually trigger a zone transfer. If the zone transfer still does not occur, the problem might be due to the incompatibility of different DNS server implementations, such as different compression formats or unsupported resource record types. If this is the case, you might have to update the secondary zone's resource records manually until you can update one or both servers to compatible DNS software implementations.

Objective 2.9 Questions

1. Which of the following sets of symptoms could indicate that the DNS server service has shut down?

    A. You are unable to ping the DNS server from the client computer or any other computer.

    B. You are unable to ping the DNS server from the client computer, but you can ping it from other computers.

    C. You can successfully ping the DNS server from any computer, but you cannot resolve a name using NSLOOKUP.EXE with that server.

    D. You can successfully resolve a name using NSLOOKUP.EXE with the DNS server, but the IP address it supplies is outdated.

2. Which of the following symptoms indicates that a DNS server has incorrect root hints?

    A. The server can resolve names of computers on the local network, but it cannot resolve names of computers on other networks.

    B. The server can resolve all names, but the IP addresses for computers on the local network are incorrect.

    C. The server can resolve names into IP addresses, but it cannot resolve IP addresses into names.

    D. The server can resolve names for which it is authoritative, but it cannot resolve any other names.

3. When troubleshooting an Internet connection problem on a client running the Windows operating system, which of the following actions should you take to determine if name resolution failures are the cause of the problem?

    A. Connect to an Internet server using its IP address.

    B. Ping the client's preferred DNS server address.

    C. Execute the IPCONFIG /registerdns command on the client.

    D. Trigger a manual zone transfer on the client's DNS.

Objective 2.9 Answers

1.   Correct Answers: C

   A. Incorrect: This symptom is an indication that either the client or the DNS server is suffering from a complete TCP/IP communications failure, not just the failure of the DNS service.

   B. Incorrect: Because the server is operational, this symptom indicates that the client computer is experiencing a TCP/IP communications failure.

   C. Correct: The fact that the client can ping the DNS server indicates that the server computer is operational, but the failure of the server to resolve names indicates that the DNS Server service is not running or is not functioning properly.

   D. Incorrect: A non-functioning DNS Server service would not supply any IP addresses in response to client requests.

2.   Correct Answers: D

   A. Incorrect: DNS servers do not use broadcast transmissions during the name resolution process, so there is no way that they can be limited to resolving names on the local network only.

   B. Incorrect: Incorrect IP addresses could be a symptom of typographical errors in resource records, dynamic update failures, or zone transfer failures. They are not a symptom of incorrect root hints.

   C. Incorrect: DNS servers perform reverse name resolutions (from addresses to names) the same way they perform standard name resolutions. Incorrect root hints would affect both of these processes.

   D. Correct: The names for which a DNS server is authoritative are those stored in its own zone database files. The inability to resolve other names indicates that the server is having problems sending queries to other servers, which could be caused by incorrect root hints.

3.   Correct Answers: A

   A. Correct: The ability to connect to an Internet server using its IP address when the client cannot connect to the same server using its name is a definitive indication of a name resolution problem.

B. Incorrect: The fact that the client computer cannot successfully ping the preferred DNS server address does not establish that name resolution is the cause of the client's Internet connection problem. The client could be using the alternate DNS server to resolve names and could actually be suffering from another problem.

C. Incorrect: This command causes the client computer to reregister its name with the DNS server using dynamic update. While this action does verify that the client can communicate with the DNS server, it does not definitively identify name resolution failure as the source of the Internet connection problem.

D. Incorrect: Triggering a zone transfer initiates a replication process between two DNS servers. This action cannot determine anything about DNS clients.

16 Planning, Implementing, and Maintaining Routing and Remote Access (3.0)

The Routing and Remote Access service in the Microsoft Windows Server 2003 family of operating systems can route traffic in several ways, enabling you to configure a server to route traffic between local area networks (LANs), between a LAN and a wide area network (WAN), or a LAN and remote users who access the network using modems or virtual private network (VPN) connections. Remote access servers present unusual problems because of potential security hazards they represent. Users connecting to a private network using the Internet or an open dial-up telephone line must be authenticated before they receive access, and in many cases, must have their access limited to specific resources. To create an effective routing and remote access strategy, you must consider the security ramifications of the access you grant to your users and take steps to prevent access by unauthorized users.

Tested Skills and Suggested Practices

The skills that you need to successfully master the Planning, Implementing, and Maintaining Routing and Remote Access objective domain on the 70-293 exam include:

- Plan a routing strategy.

    - Practice 1: Configure a computer running Windows Server 2003 to function as a router and install the Routing Information Protocol (RIP) and Open Shortest Path First (OSPF) routing protocols. Then, examine the configuration parameters available for each protocol and use the online help to determine their functions.

    - Practice 2: Configure the Routing and Remote Access service on a computer running Windows Server 2003 four times, using the four preset configurations provided by the Routing And Remote Access Server Setup Wizard. For each configuration, list the components that the service installs by default and examine the default configuration settings for each component.

- Plan security for remote access users.

    - Practice 1: Configure a computer running Windows Server 2003 on a network to function as a VPN remote access server. Then, configure a workstation running Microsoft Windows XP or Microsoft Windows 2000 Professional to function as a VPN client and use it to connect to the server.

❑ Practice 2: Using the Routing And Remote Access console, practice creating remote access policies using various combinations of conditions and remote access profile elements.

■ Implement secure access between private networks.

❑ Practice 1: Configure a server running Windows Server 2003 to use the Secure Server (Require Security) IPSec policy and a workstation running Windows XP Professional to use the Client (Respond Only) IPSec policy. Then, connect to the server from the workstation and, using the IP Security Monitor snap-in, examine the statistics of the IPSec connection.

❑ Practice 2: Use the Network Monitor application included with Windows Server 2003 to capture a sample of the traffic between two computers configured to use IPSec and examine the internal structure of the packets.

■ Troubleshoot TCP/IP routing. Tools might include the ROUTE, TRACERT, PING, PATHPING, and NETSH commands and Network Monitor.

❑ Practice 1: Open a Command Prompt window on a computer running Windows Server 2003 and examine the online help screens for the ROUTE, TRACERT, PING, PATHPING, and NETSH commands. Then, experiment with the various functions of these tools.

❑ Practice 2: Configure a computer running Windows Server 2003 to function as a router. Then, install Network Monitor on the computer and use it to capture traffic on both network interfaces and examine the changes the router makes to the IP headers in the captured packets.

Further Reading

This section lists supplemental readings by objective. We recommend that you study these sources thoroughly before taking exam 70-293.

Objective 3.1   Review Lesson 2 in Chapter 2, "Planning a TCP/IP Network Infrastructure," and Lessons 1 and 2 in Chapter 5, "Using Routing and Remote Access."

Microsoft Corporation. *Microsoft Windows Server 2003 Deployment Kit*. Volume: *Deploying Network Services*. Redmond, Washington: Microsoft Press, 2003. Review Chapter 1, "Designing a TCP/IP Network." This volume can also be found on the Microsoft Web site at *http://www.microsoft.com/windowsserver2003/techinfo/reskit /deploykit.mspx*.

Objective 3.2   Review Lesson 3 in Chapter 5, "Using Routing and Remote Access."

Microsoft Corporation. *Microsoft Windows Server 2003 Deployment Kit*. Volume: *Deploying Network Services*. Redmond, Washington: Microsoft Press, 2003. Review Chapter 8, "Deploying Dial-up and VPN Remote Access Servers." This volume can also be found on the Microsoft Web site at *http://www.microsoft.com/windowsserver2003/techinfo/reskit/deploykit.mspx.*

Objective 3.3   Review Lessons 2 and 3 in Chapter 12, "Securing Network Communications Using IPSec."

Microsoft Corporation. *Microsoft Windows Server 2003 Deployment Kit.* Volume: *Deploying Network Services.* Redmond, Washington: Microsoft Press, 2003. Review Chapter 6, "Deploying IPSec." This volume can also be found on the Microsoft Web site at *http://www.microsoft.com/windowsserver2003/techinfo/reskit/deploykit.mspx.*

Objective 3.4   Review Lesson 4 in Chapter 5, "Using Routing and Remote Access."

Microsoft Corporation. Windows Server 2003 Online Help. Review the "Using the Route Command," "Using the Tracert Command," "Using the Ping Command," "Using the Pathping Command," and "The Netsh Command-Line Utility" pages in the Windows Server 2003 Help and Support Center.

Objective 3.1

Plan a Routing Strategy

A **router** is a device that connects two networks, either two local area networks (LANs) or a LAN and a wide area network (WAN), and forwards traffic between the networks. A router can be a dedicated hardware device or a computer with two network interfaces. Windows Server 2003 includes the **Routing and Remote Access Service** (RRAS), which enables the computer to function as a router, using any one of several configurations.

Routers forward packets using information stored in a **routing table**. The routing table consists of entries for specific network destinations, each entry specifying the interface and the gateway that the router should use to send traffic to that destination. (**Gateway** is the TCP/IP term for a router.) To reach a particular destination on a large network, a router typically has to send packets to another router, which forwards them in the same way, handing off the packets until they reach their final destinations. On the route from the source to the destination computer, each router that processes a packet is referred to as a **hop**. For example, a destination can be said to be four hops away from the source.

One of the most important tasks in the operation of a router is adding information to the routing table. Routers must have current and complete information to forward traffic properly. On a large installation, the network configuration can change frequently, and the routing table must keep up with the changes. There are two methods for inserting information into a routing table: static routing and dynamic routing.

Static routing is a manual process in which an administrator creates or modifies routing table entries using a tool like the Windows Server 2003 Routing And Remote Access console or the ROUTE.EXE command-line utility. Although static routing has the advantage of not generating any additional network traffic, it suffers from several disadvantages, including the possibility of typographical errors and the inability to automatically compensate for changes in the network. Static routing is suitable only for small networks that do not often change.

Dynamic routing uses a specialized **routing protocol** to gather information from other routers on the network and automatically add it to the routing table. Routers are able to create their own routing table entries for destinations on the networks to which they are directly attached, but they have no direct knowledge of more distant networks. Dynamic routing protocols enable routers to share their routing table information with other routers, enabling each router to build a composite routing table compiled from many sources and containing an overall picture of the network.

Each entry in a routing table contains a value called a **metric**, which specifies the relative efficiency of the route. When a router is processing a packet and there is more than one route to the packet's destination, the router always chooses the route with the lowest metric value. Routing protocols determine their metric values in one of two ways. **Distance vector routing** uses the number of hops between the router and the destination for the metric value, while **link state routing** uses a more complex (and more accurate) calculation that accounts for additional factors such as the transmission speeds of the networks involved and network congestion.

Windows Server 2003 supports two routing protocols: **Routing Information Protocol (RIP)** and **Open Shortest Path First (OSPF)**. RIP is a simple distance vector routing protocol that enables a router to broadcast or multicast the contents of its routing table at regular intervals. RIP is intended for relatively small networks, because it generates large amounts of traffic and because distance vector routing is generally not suitable for large installations with networks running at different speeds. OSPF is a more complex protocol that uses link state routing, does not use broadcast or multicast transmissions, and has the ability to split a network into distinct **areas**, so that routers only have to share their information with other routers in the immediate vicinity. OSPF has more features and is more efficient than RIP, but it is also more difficult to implement. You must plan an OSPF deployment carefully, while deploying RIP is simply a matter of installing the protocol on a network's routers.

Multicasting is a one-to-many communications technique that enables systems to transmit messages to designated groups of recipients. Multicast transmissions use a single destination IP address that identifies a group of systems on the network, called a **host group**. Multicasts use Class D addresses, as assigned by the Internet Assigned Numbers Authority (IANA), which can range from 224.0.0.0 to 239.255.255.255.

For a multicast transmission to reach an entire multicast group with members on different LANs, the routers on the network must know which hosts are members of the group, so that they can forward the messages to them. Computers that are to be members of a particular multicast host group must register themselves with the routers on the local network, using the **Internet Group Management Protocol (IGMP)**. To support multicasting, all the members of the host group and all the routers providing access to the members of the host group must have support for IGMP.

Objective 3.1 Questions

1. You are the new administrator of the corporate internetwork for an Internet technology company, which consists of approximately 500 nodes, located in several buildings on a campus, and all connected using Fast Ethernet. Each building on the campus contains one or more separate LANs, and the LANs are all connected by routers. The routers were installed several years ago and are currently running RIP version 1 as their routing protocol. To get an idea of the network's performance, you use a protocol analyzer to capture a representative sample of network traffic. While examining the sample, you notice that a significant amount of the network's bandwidth is being consumed by RIP broadcast traffic. You want to reduce the amount of traffic generated by RIP, but you cannot reduce its functionality, as changes to the network infrastructure are frequent and the routers must be able to keep up with them. You also do not want to increase the current administrative burden of routing table maintenance. Which of the following solutions can achieve all these goals?

   A. Upgrade the routers to RIP version 2 and configure them to use multicast transmissions instead of broadcasts.

   B. Increase the RIP Periodic Announcement Interval settings on all the routers.

   C. Configure all the routers to use OSPF instead of RIP.

   D. Stop using RIP on all the routers and use static routing instead.

2. Which of the following are valid reasons for using a link state routing protocol on a computer running Windows Server 2003 instead of a distance vector routing protocol? (Choose all that apply.)

   A. Link state routing protocols are easier to implement and configure than distance vector routing protocols.

   B. Link state routing protocols generate less network traffic than distance vector routing protocols.

   C. Link state routing protocols support multicast transmissions, while distance vector routing protocols do not.

   D. Link state protocols use metrics that account for conditions such as network speed and congestion, while distance vector routing protocols do not.

3. Which of the following protocols does a router need to support multicasting?

   A. Routing Information Protocol (RIP)

   B. Internet Control Message Protocol (ICMP)

C. Open Shortest Path First (OSPF)

D. Internet Group Management Protocol (IGMP)

4. Which of the following are RIP version 2 features that are not found in RIP version 1? (Choose all that apply.)

    A. Support for multicast transmissions

    B. A Netmask value in the RIP message format

    C. Support for unicast transmissions

    D. A Gateway value in the RIP message format

Objective 3.1 Answers

1. **Correct Answers: A**

   A. **Correct:** RIP version 1 always uses broadcasts to transmit routing table informa-tion to other routers. Because all systems on the network must process incoming broadcasts, the amount of traffic generated by the frequent update messages can negatively affect network performance. By upgrading the routers to RIP version 2, you can use multicast transmissions instead of broadcasts. Multicast RIP messages are processed only by other routers.

   B. **Incorrect:** Increasing the Periodic Announcement Interval setting on a RIP router causes the system to transmit its routing table update messages less frequently, reducing the amount of traffic that RIP generates. However, this also reduces the functionality of RIP by causing it to compensate for network configuration changes more slowly.

   C. **Incorrect:** OSPF uses unicast transmissions instead of broadcasts, so it generates less network traffic than RIP. However, OSPF requires more administrative atten-tion than RIP.

   D. **Incorrect:** Static routing generates no network traffic at all, but requires a great deal more administration than RIP.

2. **Correct Answers: B and D**

   A. **Incorrect:** Implementing OSPF, the link state routing protocol included with Windows Server 2003, requires careful planning and configuration, while RIP, a distance vector routing protocol, requires virtually no planning or configuration.

   B. **Correct:** OSPF uses unicast transmissions to communicate with other routers, while RIP can use only broadcast or multicast transmissions. Unicasts generate less traffic because each packet is processed by only one destination computer.

   C. **Incorrect:** OSPF, a link state routing protocol, uses only unicast transmissions; it does not support multicasting. RIP, a distance vector routing protocol, does sup-port multicasting.

   D. **Correct:** OSPF, a link state routing protocol, computes its metrics based on a vari-ety of factors, while RIP, a distance vector routing protocol, uses only the number of hops for its metrics.

3. **Correct Answers: D**

   A. **Incorrect:** RIP is a dynamic routing protocol. Although it can use multicast trans-missions to send its messages, it does not facilitate multicasting.

B. Incorrect: ICMP is a TCP/IP protocol that routers use to send error messages back to end systems. ICMP has nothing to do with multicasting.

C. Incorrect: OSPF is a dynamic routing protocol that does not provide support for multicasting.

D. Correct: IGMP is the protocol that makes multicasting possible by enabling members of a host group to register themselves with routers.

4.   **Correct Answers: A, B, and D**

A. Correct: RIP version 1 supports only broadcast transmissions, while version 2 supports multicasting as well, enabling you to reduce the amount of network traffic that RIP generates.

B. Correct: RIP version 1 cannot supply a Netmask (or subnet mask) value in its routes. The RIP version 2 message format contains a Netmask field.

C. Incorrect: RIP versions 1 and 2 both support the use of broadcast transmissions.

D. Correct: RIP version 1 cannot supply a Gateway value in its routes; RIP routers use the transmitting router's IP address instead when creating routing table entries from RIP messages. The RIP version 2 message format contains a Gateway field.

Plan Security for Remote Access Users

A **remote access server** enables users at distant locations to connect to a network using a dial-up telephone line or an Internet connection. The remote users establish a connection with the remote access server, which then functions as a router, providing them with access to network resources. The Routing and Remote Access service (RRAS) in Windows Server 2003 is capable of functioning as a remote access server for multiple clients simultaneously. RRAS supports remote access clients using standard dial-up modems and **virtual private network (VPN)** connections. A VPN connection is a secured conduit through the Internet that connects the remote access client and server. The client dials in to a local Internet service provider (ISP) and establishes a connection to the server using the Internet as a medium.

Having your network accessible through standard telephone lines and the Internet is convenient for your users, but it also opens up your network to any potential intruder with a modem or an Internet connection. Planning security is therefore a major part of implementing a remote access server. Windows Server 2003 RRAS includes a variety of security mechanisms that can protect the server and the network from unauthorized access, including dial-in properties, authentication protocols, and remote access policies.

Dial-in properties are configuration settings that you find on the Dial-In tab of the Properties dialog box for every user object in the Active Directory database. These properties are as follows:

- Remote Access Permission (Dial-in Or VPN)—Specifies whether the individual user is allowed or denied remote access. You can also specify that remote access be controlled using group memberships, as indicated in remote access policies.

- Verify Caller ID—Enables you to specify the user's telephone number, which the system will verify using caller ID during the connection process. If the number the user calls from does not match the number supplied, the system denies the connection.

- Callback Options—Causes the RRAS server to break the connection after it authenticates a user, then dial the user to reconnect. This mechanism saves on long distance expenses by having the remote access calls originate at the server's location, but it can also function as a security mechanism if you furnish a specific callback number in this box. The user must be dialing in from the location you specify to connect to the server.

The most basic method for securing a remote access server is to perform an authentication that verifies the user's identity. In most cases, users authenticate themselves by supplying an account name and password after connecting to the server. The nature of the authentication messages is controlled by an authentication protocol. RRAS supports the following authentication protocol options:

- **Extensible Authentication Protocol (EAP)**—An open-ended system that makes it possible for RRAS to use third-party authentication protocols as well as those supplied with Windows 2000. EAP is the only authentication protocol supported by Windows Server 2003 RRAS that enables you to use mechanisms other than passwords (such as digital certificates stored on smart cards) to verify a user's identity.

- Microsoft Encrypted Authentication Version 2 **(MS-CHAP v2)**—Version 2 of the **Microsoft Challenge Handshake Authentication Protocol** is a password-based protocol that enables the client and the server to mutually authenticate each other using encrypted passwords. MS-CHAP v2 is the simplest and most secure option to use when your remote access clients are running Microsoft Windows 98 or a later version of the Windows operating system.

- Microsoft Encrypted Authentication **(MS-CHAP)**—The original version of the MS-CHAP protocol uses one-way authentication and a single encryption key for transmitted and received messages. The security that MS-CHAP version 1 provides is inferior to that of version 2, but RRAS includes it to support remote access clients running Microsoft Windows 95 and Microsoft Windows NT 3.51, which cannot use MS-CHAP v2.

- Encrypted Authentication **(CHAP)**—An industry standard authentication protocol that is included in RRAS to support non-Microsoft remote access clients that cannot use MS-CHAP or EAP. CHAP is less secure than either version of MS-CHAP because CHAP requires using a reversibly encrypted password.

- **Shiva Password Authentication Protocol (SPAP)**—Shiva Password Authentication Protocol is a relatively insecure authentication protocol designed for use with Shiva remote access products. SPAP uses a reversible encryption mechanism for authentication.

- Unencrypted Password **(PAP)**—The **Password Authentication Protocol** is a password-based authentication protocol that transmits passwords in clear text, leaving them open to interception by packet captures.

- Allow Remote Systems To Connect Without Authentication—Enables remote access clients to connect to the RRAS server with no authentication at all, enabling anyone to access the network. The use of this option is strongly discouraged.

RRAS also supports the use of **Remote Authentication Dial-In User Service (RADIUS)**, a standard defining a service that provides authentication, authorization, and accounting for remote access installations. A RADIUS server stores the user accounts and passwords for all remote access users, and can provide authentication services for multiple remote access servers.

Remote access policies are sets of conditions that users must meet before RRAS authorizes them to access the server or the network. You can create policies that limit user access based on group memberships, day and time restrictions, and many other criteria. Remote access policies can also specify which authentication protocol and what type of encryption clients must use. Using the Routing And Remote Access console, you can create different policies for different types of connections, such as dial-up, virtual private network (VPN), and wireless connections.

Remote access policies consist of three elements, which are as follows:

- **Conditions**—Specific attributes that the policy uses to grant or deny authorization to a user. If there is more than one condition, the user must meet all the conditions before the server can grant access. Some of the conditions that RRAS remote access policies can use include day and time restrictions and the use of a specific authentication protocol, data-link layer protocol, or tunnel type, and membership in a specific group set up using the Windows operating system.

- **Remote access permission**—Clients receive permission to access the remote network either by satisfying the conditions of the RRAS server's remote policies, or by an administrator explicitly granting them the permission on the Dial-in tab of each user's Properties dialog box.

- **Remote access profile**—A set of attributes associated with a remote access policy that the RRAS server applies to a client once it has authenticated and authorized it. The profile can consist of elements such as time limits for the connection or specific IP addresses, authentication protocols, and types of encryption.

Remote access connections only validate the credentials of the remote access user. Therefore, the computer used to connect to a private network can often access network resources even when its configuration does not comply with organization network policy. For example, a remote access user with valid credentials could connect to a network with a computer that does not have the latest service pack or security patches installed, or does not have the most updated signature files downloaded for virus protection. **Network Access Quarantine Control**, a new feature in Windows Server 2003 with Service Pack 1, delays full remote access to a private network until the configuration of the remote access computer has been examined and validated by an administrator-provided script. When a remote access computer initiates a connection to a remote access server, the user is authenticated and the remote access computer is assigned an IP address. However, the connection is placed in **quarantine mode**, which provides limited network access. The administrator-provided script is run on the remote access computer. When the script notifies the remote access server that it has successfully run and the remote access computer complies with current network policies, quarantine mode is removed and the remote access computer is granted normal remote access.

Objective 3.2 Questions

1. Which of the following authentication protocols requires you to modify the way that Active Directory encrypts user passwords?

    A. PAP

    B. CHAP

    C. MS-CHAP

    D. MS-CHAP v2

2. You are a network administrator designing a remote access security strategy for your company. You want users accessing the network with VPN connections to be able to connect to the server during business hours only, and you intend to require that users authenticate themselves using smart cards. To accomplish these goals, you configure RRAS to use the MS-CHAP v2 authentication protocol and you create a remote access policy with a condition specifying the hours during which the users can connect. Specify which of the stated goals are accomplished by this solution.

    A. This solution can accomplish neither of the stated goals: it will neither limit the users' logon hours nor enable smart card authentication.

    B. This solution accomplishes only one of the stated goals: it will not limit the users' logon hours, but it will enable smart card authentication.

    C. This solution accomplishes only one of the stated goals: it will limit the users' logon hours, but it will not enable smart card authentication.

    D. This solution accomplishes both stated goals: it will limit the users' logon hours and enable smart card authentication.

3. Which of the following Windows Server 2003 remote access configurations would enable an attacker running Network Monitor to read user passwords from captured packets in unencrypted form?

    A. You configure RRAS to use CHAP for its authentication protocol and enable the Store Password Using Reversible Encryption password policy for all remote access users.

    B. You configure RRAS to use PAP for its authentication protocol, and issue a smart card to each user.

    C. You configure the Allow Remote Systems To Connect Without Authentication option on the RRAS server, and create a remote policy with a profile specifying the use of the strongest encryption method available.

D. You configure RRAS to use MS-CHAP for its authentication protocol and set up the callback options so the server reconnects to the client at a predetermined telephone number.

4. Which of the following procedures can you use to limit client access to a remote access server based on group membership?

A. Modify the properties of the clients' user objects in the Active Directory Users And Computers console.

B. Configure RRAS to use the EAP authentication protocol in the Routing And Remote Access console.

C. Configure RRAS to use a RADIUS server to authenticate incoming client connections.

D. Use the Routing And Remote Access console to create a remote access policy.

Objective 3.2 Answers

1. **Correct Answers: B**

    A. Incorrect: The Password Authentication Protocol transmits passwords in clear text, so it has no encryption requirements.

    B. Correct: The Challenge Handshake Authentication Protocol requires access to the users' passwords, and by default, Windows Server 2003 does not store the passwords in a form that CHAP can use. To authenticate users with CHAP, you must open the group policy governing the users and enable the Store Password Using Reversible Encryption password policy mechanism.

    C. Incorrect: Version 1 of the Microsoft Challenge Handshake Authentication Protocol uses one-way authentication and a single encryption key for transmitted and received messages, but it requires no modification of Active Directory's password storage method.

    D. Incorrect: Version 2 of the Microsoft Challenge Handshake Authentication Protocol enables clients and servers to mutually authenticate each other using encrypted passwords, but requires no modification to Active Directory.

2. **Correct Answers: C**

    A. Incorrect: You can successfully limit remote access users' logon hours using a remote access policy, so the solution does accomplish one of the stated goals.

    B. Incorrect: Remote access policies can limit users' logon hours, but the MS-CHAP v2 authentication protocol does not support smart cards.

    C. Correct: The remote access policy can limit users' logon hours, but to enable smart card authentication, you must use the Extensible Authentication Protocol (EAP).

    D. Incorrect: While the solution can successfully limit users' logon hours, you cannot authenticate users with smart cards using MS-CHAP v2.

3. **Correct Answers: B**

    A. Incorrect: Storing passwords using a reversible encryption method, as required for the Challenge Handshake Authentication Protocol, does not alter the fact that the passwords are encrypted when the clients transmit them over the remote access connection. An attacker capturing the packets using Network Monitor would not be able to read the encrypted passwords.

    B. Correct: The Password Authentication Protocol transmits user passwords in clear text, so that anyone capturing the packets with a protocol analyzer such as Network Monitor would be able to read the passwords.

C. **Incorrect:** Although enabling the Allow Remote Systems To Connect Without Authentication option is a grave security risk, there is no danger of passwords being compromised, because the clients do not transmit any passwords at all.

D. **Incorrect:** The Microsoft Challenge Handshake Authentication Protocol always transmits passwords in encrypted form, so there is no danger of passwords being compromised by Network Monitor, regardless of the callback options in effect.

4.   Correct Answers: D

A. **Incorrect:** You can grant or deny users remote access and set caller ID and callback options by modifying the properties of user objects, but you cannot limit their access based on group membership.

B. **Incorrect:** Authentication protocols do not limit users' access based on group memberships or any other criteria. They simply specify the format for the message exchanges that the clients and server will use when authenticating.

C. **Incorrect:** Using RADIUS offloads the authentication process from the RRAS service to an external RADIUS service, but RRAS is still responsible for server access control.

D. **Correct:** Remote access policies enable you to limit user access based on group memberships, day and time restrictions, and various other criteria.

Objective 3.3

Implement Secure Access Between Private Networks

The Routing and Remote Access service in Windows Server 2003 can route traffic between networks at remote locations, using a wide area networking (WAN) link. To do this, you must connect the two sites using any functional WAN technology, such as a dial-up telephone line, leased line, or VPN, and install a router at each site to connect the private network to the WAN. However, one of the problems in implementing a connection between private networks is securing the traffic passing over the WAN link. Depending on the nature of the WAN technology you choose and the sensitivity of your data, you might choose to encrypt the traffic passing between the networks. To do this with routers running Windows Server 2003, you use the **IP Security extensions (IPSec)**.

IPSec is a set of extensions to the Internet Protocol (IP) that enable systems to digitally sign and encrypt data before it is transmitted over the network. With the transmitted data protected in this way, attackers capturing packets cannot read the information inside, nor can they modify the contents of the packet without the modifications being detected by the recipient.

To define when and how computers running Windows Server 2003 use IPSec, you use **IPSec policies**, which you manage using the IP Security Policies snap-in for Microsoft Management Console (MMC). Windows Server 2003 has three default IPSec policies, which are as follows:

- **Client (Respond Only)**—Configures the computer to use IPSec only when another computer requests its use. The computer using this policy never initiates an IPSec negotiation; it only responds to requests from other computers for secured communications.

- **Secure Server (Require Security)**—Configures the computer to require IPSec security for all communications. If the computer attempts to communicate with another computer and discovers that it does not support IPSec, the computer terminates the connection.

- **Server (Request Security)**—Configures the computer to request the use of IPSec when communicating with another computer. If the other computer supports IPSec, the IPSec negotiation begins. If the other computer does not support IPSec, the systems establish a standard, unsecured IP connection.

You can use these policies as they are, modify them, or create your own. An IPSec policy consists of the following elements:

- Rules—A rule is a combination of an IP filter list and a filter action that specifies when and how the computer should use IPSec. An IPSec policy can consist of multiple rules.

- IP filter lists—A collection of filters that specifies what traffic the system should secure with IPSec, based on IP addresses, protocols, or port numbers. You can also create filters using a combination of these criteria.

- Filter actions—Configuration parameters that specify exactly how IPSec should secure the filtered packets. Filter actions specify whether IPSec should use the IP Authentication Header protocol, the IP Encapsulating Security Payload protocol, or both, as well as what data integrity and encryption algorithms the system should use.

To implement an IPSec policy, you can apply it to an individual computer, using local policies, but for network installations it is more common for administrators to deploy IPSec policies by assigning them to Active Directory objects using group policies. Once you have created IPSec policies in the appropriate places, you must then activate them by selecting Assign from the Action menu in the IP Security Policies snap-in.

Objective 3.3 Questions

1. You are a network administrator for a company with headquarters in New York and a branch office in Chicago. You have installed a T-1 leased line connecting the two offices and you are using computers running Windows Server 2003 as the routers at each end of the WAN connection. There is a database server at headquarters that hosts confidential company information, and users in the Chicago office must be able to access the information on that server. The workstations in the Chicago office are using a variety of operating systems, not all of which support IPSec. You want to use IPSec to encrypt only the database information, and only as it is passing over the T-1 connection. Which of the following solutions can accomplish this goal?

    A. Configure both routers running Windows Server 2003 to use the Secure Server (Require Security) IPSec policy.

    B. Configure the database server to use the Secure Server (Require Security) IPSec policy and the clients in the Chicago office to use the Client (Respond Only) policy.

    C. Create a new IPSec policy for the two routers with a tunnel mode rule and a filter list containing the port numbers used by the database application.

    D. Modify the Secure Server (Require Security) policy by adding a filter list containing the port numbers used by the database application and configure the database server and the Chicago clients to use it.

2. Which of the following IPSec policies should you use for an e-mail server that you want to use IPSec encryption whenever possible, when some of the clients that must access the server are running operating systems that do not support IPSec?

    A. Client (Respond Only)

    B. Server (Request Security)

    C. Secure Server (Require Security)

    D. None of the above. You must create a new IPSec policy.

3. When creating IPSec policies using tunnel mode, which of the following configuration elements must the policies contain? (Choose all that apply.)

    A. The IP addresses of the tunnel endpoints

    B. The port numbers of all applications that will use the tunnel

    C. The name of the algorithm that the systems will use to encrypt the traffic passing through the tunnel

    D. The IP addresses of the clients and servers using the tunnel

4.   You are the network administrator for a large corporation in Phoenix that has recently acquired a small company in Albuquerque. Both companies are running networks based on Windows Server 2003, but at this time, the company in Albuquerque is still running a separate network with its own Active Directory installation. Also, neither company has a public key infrastructure (PKI) implementation. You are in the process of creating an IPSec policy that will enable users on the Albuquerque network to access servers in the Phoenix office with complete security. Which of the following authentication methods should you specify in the policy?

   A. Kerberos V5

   B. Digital certificates

   C. Smart cards

   D. Preshared secret key

Objective 3.3 Answers

1.   Correct Answers: C

    A. Incorrect: Configuring the routers to use the Secure Server (Require Security) policy would encrypt all traffic generated by the routers, but it would not encrypt traffic passing through the routers that is generated by other computers.

    B. Incorrect: Configuring the database server and clients in this way would protect the traffic generated by the database application, but it would also protect all other application traffic. In addition, the IPSec encryption would not be limited to the T-1 line, but would be in effect for the entire route between the source and destination systems.

    C. Correct: IPSec in tunnel mode is designed specifically to protect traffic passing between two routers over a WAN link. In tunnel mode, a router receives normal (unencrypted) packets and protects them using IPSec before transmitting them to the router at the other end of the WAN. The other router then decrypts the data and forwards it to its destination. Specifying the port numbers that the database application uses enables the routers to encrypt only the database traffic.

    D. Incorrect: Even with a filter list that designates only the database server traffic for encryption, this IPSec policy would be in effect over the entire connection between the database server and the clients, not just the T-1 line.

2.   Correct Answers: B

    A. Incorrect: The Client (Respond Only) policy causes a system to use IPSec only when the other system it is communicating with requests it. This policy is not appropriate for a server that you want to use IPSec whenever it can.

    B. Correct: The Server (Request Security) policy enables the e-mail server to use IPSec whenever the client supports it, but still enables clients that do not support IPSec to access server resources.

    C. Incorrect: The Secure Server (Require Security) policy would deny clients not supporting IPSec access to the e-mail server.

    D. Incorrect: There is no need to create a new IPSec policy for this application, because the Server (Request Security) policy satisfies all the stated requirements.

3.   Correct Answers: A and C

    A. Correct: When creating a new IPSec policy, if you elect to use tunnel mode, you must specify the IP address of the system that will function as the endpoint of the tunnel. Typically, this router relays traffic between two private networks using a WAN link.

B. Incorrect: The filter list for a tunnel mode IPSec policy is no different from the list for a transport mode policy. You only have to specify port numbers if you want to filter traffic based on the applications generating the traffic.

C. Correct: All IPSec policies must specify the algorithm that the system will use to encrypt the protected data.

D. Incorrect: IPSec in tunnel mode is an arrangement between the two routers functioning as endpoints for the tunnel. The only requirement for the clients and servers making use of the tunnel is that they have access to the routers.

4.   Correct Answers: D

A. Incorrect: The Kerberos protocol is the default authentication method for Active Directory networks. However, as these two networks are running completely separate Active Directory installations, clients on one network cannot be authenticated by servers on the other.

B. Incorrect: Because neither network has a PKI in place, the use of digital certificates for IPSec authentication would not be practical.

C. Incorrect: Smart cards rely on digital certificates, which are stored on the cards. Without a PKI in place, using smart cards for IPSec authentication would not be practical.

D. Correct: Using a key that you have supplied to the administrators of the other network beforehand, IPSec systems can authenticate each other without the need for additional infrastructure.

Troubleshoot TCP/IP Routing

Windows Server 2003 includes a variety of tools that you can use to troubleshoot TCP/IP routing problems. Most of the following tools are command-line utilities, which you run from a command prompt window. The tools are as follows:

- **ROUTE** Route.exe is a command-line program that you can use to view and manage the routing table on a computer running Windows Server 2003. Whether you are using static or dynamic routing, TCP/IP routing problems are often caused by missing or incorrect information in the routing table, and working directly with the routing table can help you isolate the source of the problem.

- **PING** PING is the standard TCP/IP tool for testing connectivity, which takes the form of a command-line program called Ping.exe in Windows Server 2003. By typing **ping** plus an IP address on the command line, you can test any TCP/IP system's connectivity with any other system. PING functions by transmitting a series of Echo Request messages containing a sample of random data to the destination you specify, using the Internet Control Message Protocol (ICMP). The system receiving the Echo Request messages must generate an Echo Reply message for each request containing the same data sample, and then return them to the sender.

  Compared with other tools, PING has relatively limited utility when you are trying to locate a malfunctioning router. You might be able to ping a router's IP address successfully, even when it is not routing traffic properly. However, as part of your initial troubleshooting efforts, you can use PING to test for routing problems by pinging various computers on different LANs to determine which router is not functioning properly.

- **TRACERT** Tracert.exe is the Windows Server 2003 command-line implementation of the UNIX traceroute program. TRACERT enables you to view the path that packets take from a computer to a specific destination. When you type **tracert** and an IP address at the Windows operating system's command prompt, the program displays a list of the hops to the destination, including the IP address and DNS name (where available) of each router along the way. If the program fails to trace the entire route to the specified destination, you can assume that the problem occurs immediately after the last router listed in the tracing.

- **PATHPING** PathPing.Exe is a Windows Server 2003 command-line tool that is similar to TRACERT in that it traces a path through the network to a particular destination and displays the names and addresses of the routers along the path. PATHPING is different, however, because it is designed to report packet loss rates at each router on the path. After displaying the path to the destination, PATHPING sends 100 packets (by default) to each router on the path and computes the packet loss rate in the form of a percentage. TRACERT is the preferred tool for locating a router failure that completely interrupts communications, while PATH-PING is more useful when you can connect to a destination, but you are experiencing data loss or transmission delays.

- **NETSH** NETSH.EXE is a Windows Server 2003 command-line utility that enables you to display or modify the network configuration of any computer on the network. NETSH also provides a scripting feature that allows you to run a group of commands in batch mode against a specified computer. You can use NETSH in a variety of contexts, but for routing purposes, NETSH essentially functions as a command-line equivalent for the Routing And Remote Access console.

- **Network Monitor** A graphical utility included with Windows Server 2003 that can capture and analyze packets transmitted to or from any of the network interfaces on the computer where the program is running. Once the program has captured the packets, it uses built-in parsers for the various network protocols to display the packet contents in decoded form. You can use Network Monitor to examine the values of packet header fields, which can help locate and diagnose TCP/IP routing problems.

1. You are the sole network administrator for a small company with an internetwork consisting of five local area networks (LANs) connected by routers. You are currently using static routing because the network configuration does not often change. You are in the process of adding a sixth LAN to the internetwork, and you must create new static routes to give all the computers on the network access to the new LAN. Which of the following programs can you use to create the new static routes? (Choose all that apply.)

   A. Network Monitor

   B. Route.exe

   C. Pathping.exe

   D. Netsh.exe

2. You are at the network help desk for your company and, in the past hour, have received several complaints from users that they cannot access certain servers on the network. The servers that the users cannot contact are different, but you determine that they are all located on the same local area network (LAN). You suspect that the router providing access to that LAN has experienced a hardware failure. Which of the following tools can you use from your workstation to determine whether the router is up and running? (Choose all that apply.)

   A. PING

   B. TRACERT

   C. ROUTE

   D. PATHPING

3. When you run the Tracert.exe program on Windows Server 2003 with the IP address of a computer on another LAN, the output display lists several IP addresses and computer names, but stops well before the packets reach the destination system. Which of the following problems could this indicate? (Choose all that apply.)

   A. One of the routers on the way to the destination is not functioning.

   B. The destination system is not functioning.

   C. The network interface on the computer you are using is malfunctioning.

   D. The computer you are using has an incorrect default gateway address.

4.   You are able to successfully ping computers on your local network, but you cannot ping computers on other networks. However, when you try to ping the IP address of the computer running Windows Server 2003 that is your default gateway, the test is successful. Based on this information, which of the following statements is definitely *not* true?

   A. Your computer has an incorrect default gateway address.

   B. The default gateway has incorrect or missing routing table entries.

   C. The Routing and Remote Access service on the default gateway has shut down.

   D. The default gateway system is not running.

Objective 3.4 Answers

1. **Correct Answers: B and D**

    A. **Incorrect:** Network Monitor is capable only of capturing and analyzing network traffic; it cannot create static routes.

    B. **Correct:** Route.exe enables you to view a computer's routing table as well as create, modify, and delete static routes.

    C. **Incorrect:** Pathping.exe is a diagnostic tool that can help you to determine whether a router is functioning properly, but you cannot use it to create static routes.

    D. **Correct:** Netsh.exe is a comprehensive configuration and scripting tool that enables you to perform a multitude of network-related functions, including creating static routes on a RRAS server.

2. **Correct Answers: A, B, and D**

    A. **Correct:** You can use PING to test whether a TCP/ IP system, including a router, is up and running. Any computer with an operational TCP/IP stack and network interface can receive and return the Internet Control Message Protocol (ICMP) messages generated by the PING program.

    B. **Correct:** TRACERT displays the path packets take through an internetwork to reach a particular destination, listing all the routers on the way. If a router appears in the list of hops produced by TRACERT, you know the router is functioning.

    C. **Incorrect:** The ROUTE command enables you to manage the routing table on the local computer only. You cannot connect to a router elsewhere on the network and manage it using ROUTE.

    D. **Correct:** PATHPING, like TRACERT, displays the path packets take through an internetwork. If a router is listed in the PATHPING output, the router is functioning properly.

3. **Correct Answers: A and C**

    A. **Correct:** When a router is malfunctioning, it does not return the appropriate messages to the TRACERT program, and the path through the network displayed by TRACERT stops at that point.

    B. **Incorrect:** When TRACERT fails to create a complete trace through the network, it does not indicate a fault in the destination computer, but rather in one of the routers on the path to that destination.

C. Correct: Although unlikely, it is possible for the network interface in the computer running TRACERT to malfunction in the middle of a test, preventing the system from completing the trace.

D. Incorrect: If the computer has an incorrect default gateway address, the TRACERT program would not display even one router entry in its output. Because the program does list several router addresses, you know that the default gateway address is correct.

4. Correct Answers: D

A. Incorrect: If your computer is configured with an incorrect default gateway address, you might be able to ping the computer using that address successfully, even though the computer is not a router. Therefore, this statement could be true.

B. Incorrect: If the default gateway has incorrect routing table entries, it might be unable to forward packets to other networks, even though its TCP/IP stack is functioning properly, enabling it to pass a PING test. Therefore, this statement could be true.

C. Incorrect: If RRAS on the default gateway shuts down, the system is unable to route traffic, even though it can still participate on a TCP/IP network. Therefore, this statement could be true.

D. Correct: If the default gateway system were not running at all, your attempt to ping it would fail. Therefore, it is not possible for this statement to be true.

17 Planning, Implementing, and Maintaining Server Availability (4.0)

Servers are an essential component on most networks, and keeping them running whenever clients need them is a daunting task. Server performance can be interrupted by any number of factors, including hardware problems, software incompatibilities, accidents, theft, and natural disasters. Keeping servers available requires careful planning and continual monitoring.

Microsoft Windows Server 2003 includes tools and services that you can use to ensure that servers remain available to users. For example, Windows Server 2003 supports **clusters**, which are groups of connected servers that function as a single resource, sharing the performance load and providing fault tolerance. Regular backups keep servers available by enabling administrators to restore data that is lost due to a drive erasure or failure. Windows Server 2003 includes a Backup program that enables you to protect all your server files, including key elements such as the registry, Active Directory directory service databases, and cluster configuration data.

Keeping servers available is often a matter of anticipating problems that could cause a server failure. Tools such as Network Monitor and the Performance console enable you to track the performance of specific server components, to locate system bottlenecks, and to detect network service failures.

Tested Skills and Suggested Practices

The skills that you need to successfully master the Planning, Implementing, and Maintaining Server Availability objective domain on the 70-293 exam include:

- Plan services for high availability.
    - ❏ Practice 1: Using information from vendors' World Wide Web sites, catalogs, or manufacturers' product collateral, research the hardware products currently on the market that you can use to build large Network Load Balancing (NLB) and server clusters.
    - ❏ Practice 2: Design two 10-node clusters: a 10-node server cluster for a database application and a 10-node Web server NLB cluster. Your design should include diagrams of the networks and a list of all the hardware products required to build the clusters.

- Identify system bottlenecks, including memory, processor, disk, and network related bottlenecks.

  ❏ Practice 1: On a computer running Windows Server 2003, open the Performance console and use System Monitor to examine the performance counters for the system's various hardware components. Using the explanation that System Monitor provides for each counter, create a list of counters that you think could help you detect performance bottlenecks on a server.

  ❏ Practice 2: Using the list of counters you created in Practice 1, open the Performance console, create a counter log in the Performance Logs And Alerts snap-in and use it to establish a performance baseline for the computer running Windows Server 2003. Then, create a series of alerts to inform you when system performance parameters reach unacceptable levels.

- Implement a cluster server.

  ❏ Practice 1: Use the Cluster Administrator application to create a 1-node server cluster on a computer running Windows Server 2003, Enterprise Edition. Study the hardware requirements for creating server clusters and determine what components you would need to add more nodes to the cluster you have created.

  ❏ Practice 2: On a lab network, install Microsoft Internet Information Services (IIS) on a computer running Windows Server 2003 and use the Network Load Balancing Manager application to create a 1-node NLB cluster.

  ❏ Practice 3: Study the components that the Windows Server 2003 Backup program protects when you back up the System State element and determine which of these elements can help you restore a cluster node that has suffered a complete hard drive failure.

  ❏ Practice 4: On a lab network, create a 2-node Web server NLB cluster and monitor the log messages in Network Load Balancing Manager as you disable one of the nodes.

- Manage Network Load Balancing. Tools might include the Network Load Balancing Manager and the WLBS cluster control utility.

  ❏ Practice 1: Use Network Load Balancing Manager to add additional nodes to your NLB cluster and monitor the messages displayed in the Manager's log pane.

  ❏ Practice 2: Use NLB.EXE or WLBS.EXE to control your NLB cluster, using parameters such as START, STOP, SUSPEND, RESUME, ENABLE, DISABLE, and DRAINSTOP.

■ Plan a backup and recovery strategy.

□ Practice 1: Using the Windows Server 2003 Backup program, create backup jobs to perform differential or incremental jobs six days a week and a normal job on the seventh day.

□ Practice 2: Perform a full system backup using the Windows Server 2003 Backup program, then practice restoring individual files, multiple files, and folders, both to their original locations and to an alternate location, using the various file overwrite options.

Further Reading

This section lists supplemental readings by objective. We recommend that you study these sources thoroughly before taking exam 70-293.

Objective 4.1   Review Lessons 1, 2, and 3 in Chapter 7, "Clustering Servers."

Microsoft Corporation. *Microsoft Windows Server 2003 Deployment Kit.* Volume: *Planning Server Deployments.* Redmond, Washington: Microsoft Press, 2003. Review Chapter 6, "Planning for High Availability and Scalability." This volume can also be found on Microsoft's Web site at *http://www.microsoft.com/windowsserver2003 /techinfo/reskit/deploykit.mspx.*

Microsoft Corporation. *Microsoft Encyclopedia of Networking,* 2d ed. Redmond, Washington: Microsoft Press, 2002. See entries for "clustering."

Objective 4.2   Review Lesson 2 in Chapter 6, "Maintaining Server Availability."

Microsoft Corporation. *Microsoft Windows 2000 Server Resource Kit.* Volume: *Windows 2000 Server Operations Guide.* Redmond, Washington: Microsoft Press, 2000. Review Chapters 5 to 9. (The performance monitoring principles outlined in these chapters are applicable to Windows Server 2003.)

Objective 4.3   Review Lesson 3 in Chapter 6, "Maintaining Server Availability" and Lessons 1, 2, and 3 in Chapter 7, "Clustering Servers."

Microsoft Corporation. *Microsoft Windows Server 2003 Deployment Kit.* Volume: *Planning Server Deployments.* Redmond, Washington: Microsoft Press, 2003. Review Chapter 7, "Designing and Deploying Server Clusters." This volume can also be found on Microsoft's Web site at *http://www.microsoft.com/windowsserver2003 /techinfo/reskit/deploykit.mspx.*

Microsoft Corporation. *Microsoft SQL Server 2000 High Availability Series.* Review the article on "Implementing Failover Clustering" on Microsoft's Web site at *http://www.microsoft.com/technet/prodtechnol/sql/2000/deploy/hasog01.mspx.*

Microsoft Corporation. Windows Server 2003 Help and Support Center. Review the "Backing Up and Restoring Server Clusters" pages.

Objective 4.4   Review Lesson 2 in Chapter 7, "Clustering Servers."

Microsoft Corporation. Windows Server 2003 Help and Support Center. Review the "Nlb: Command-line reference" page for syntax and parameters for the NLB cluster control program (NLB.EXE).

Objective 4.5   Review Lesson 3 in Chapter 6, "Maintaining Server Availability."

Microsoft Corporation. Windows Server 2003 Help and Support Center. Review the "Understanding Backup" pages.

Objective 4.1

Plan Services for High Availability

Servers must be available to perform their functions, and depending on how critical those functions are to your organization, you might want to take steps to ensure that your servers are up and running as much of the time as possible. One way of ensuring the high availability of your servers is to create **clusters**, which are groups of servers that function as a single entity. Clients access the server applications using a specially assigned cluster name and cluster Internet Protocol (IP) address, and one or more of the servers in the cluster are responsible for responding to each client request. If a server in the cluster should go offline, another server in the cluster takes over its processes, a procedure called **failover**. When the malfunctioning server comes back online, it can begin to perform its regular processes again, which is called **failback**. There are three basic types of clusters: **server clusters**, Component Load Balancing (CLB) clusters, and **Network Load Balancing (NLB)** clusters. The properties of these cluster types are specified in the following table:

	Server Cluster	**CLB Cluster**	**NLB Cluster**
Supported Applications	Stateful applications (database and e-mail servers)	COM+ components	Stateless applications (Web servers)
Number of nodes supported in Windows Server 2003, Standard Edition	0	Not supported	32
Number of nodes supported in Windows Server 2003, Enterprise Edition	8	Not supported	32
Number of nodes supported in Windows Server 2003, Datacenter Edition	8	Not supported	32
Special hardware required in Windows Server 2003	Shared storage infrastructure	N/A	None

Objective 4.1 Questions

1. A rapidly expanding company has recently extended its operations to three shifts, and as a result, the IT department must keep the company's intranet Web and Microsoft SQL Server database servers running 24 hours a day. The network administrators have decided to use Windows Server 2003 clustering to keep the servers available at all times, and have purchased two additional computers for this purpose, bringing the total number of servers to four. Which of the following clustering deployments is best suited to this company's needs?

    A. A single 4-node server cluster running the Web and database applications on all four servers

    B. A single 4-node Network Load Balancing cluster running the Web and database applications on all four servers

    C. Two separate 2-node clusters: a server cluster to run the database application and a Network Load Balancing cluster to run the Web server application

    D. A single 4-node cluster, with the database application running on two of the nodes and the Web server application running on the other two

2. A server administrator for a company with a number of different clusters is told by his superiors that the 4-node Network Load Balancing cluster running the company's Internet Web servers is running at peak capacity nearly all the time, and that he should design a plan to scale up the cluster to support more traffic. Which of the following actions would you be likely to see in the administrator's plan? (Choose all that apply.)

    A. Add two more servers to the cluster, bringing the total number to six.

    B. Install additional memory in all the cluster servers.

    C. Convert the Network Load Balancing cluster to a server cluster.

    D. Install a second processor in each cluster server.

3. Which of the following operating system versions is capable of hosting an 8-node Network Load Balancing cluster? (Choose all that apply.)

    A. Microsoft Windows XP Professional

    B. Windows Server 2003, Standard Edition

    C. Windows Server 2003, Enterprise Edition

    D. Windows Server 2003, Datacenter Edition

Objective 4.1 Answers

1.   Correct Answers: C

    A. Incorrect: A Web server is a stateless application that you cannot deploy on a server cluster. Instead, you should use a Network Load Balancing cluster for the Web server.

    B. Incorrect: A database server is a stateful application that you cannot deploy on a Network Load Balancing cluster. Instead, you should use a server cluster for the database server.

    C. Correct: You should create a server cluster to run stateful applications, such as database servers, and a Network Load Balancing cluster to run stateless applications, such as Web servers.

    D. Incorrect: Although you can deploy multiple applications on a single cluster, all the applications must be either stateful or stateless, which dictates the types of cluster you should create. In this case, the database application is stateful and the Web server is stateless.

2.   Correct Answers: B and D

    A. Incorrect: Scaling up a cluster is the process of increasing the existing servers' capabilities, usually by upgrading their hardware. Adding new servers to a cluster is called scaling out.

    B. Correct: Adding memory is a method of scaling up cluster servers that is likely to make them perform more efficiently and increase their overall throughput.

    C. Incorrect: Server clusters are not suitable for running stateless applications like Web servers. Server clusters and Network Load Balancing clusters are parallel technologies; changing an NLB cluster to a server cluster is not necessarily an upgrade.

    D. Correct: Assuming that the servers in the cluster support multiple processors, adding a second processor is a valid method of scaling up their performance levels.

3. **Correct Answers: B, C, and D**

   A. **Incorrect:** Windows XP is not capable of any type of clustering.

   B. **Correct:** Windows Server 2003, Standard Edition, does not support server clusters, but like all Windows Server 2003 versions, it can support Network Load Balancing clusters of up to 32 nodes.

   C. **Correct:** Windows Server 2003, Enterprise Edition, can support 8-node server clusters and Network Load Balancing clusters of up to 32 nodes.

   D. **Correct:** Windows Server 2003, Datacenter Edition, can support 8-node server clusters and up to 32-node Network Load Balancing clusters.

Identify System Bottlenecks

Server performance can be affected by many different factors, ranging from the hardware components in the server through the software running on the server to the network carrying the traffic between the server and clients. In most cases, degraded performance is caused by a single component that slows down the entire system. This single component is said to be functioning as a **bottleneck** that prevents the server from achieving optimum performance.

Locating the bottleneck that is affecting server performance can be a difficult task. The best tool for locating the bottleneck in a computer running Windows Server 2003 is the **Performance console.** The Performance console consists of two Microsoft Management Console (MMC) snap-ins, called **System Monitor** and **Performance Logs And Alerts**. Both of these snap-ins enable you to monitor the ongoing performance of specific hardware and software components in the computer. The components are represented in the console as **performance counters**, which are grouped in categories called **performance objects**. Installing Windows Server 2003 software components such as the WINS and DNS Server services adds new performance objects to the console, as do some third-party software products.

The best way to detect a bottleneck is to use the Performance console to establish a baseline reading of particular performance counter levels under normal conditions, and then to continue to monitor the same counters for a substantial deviation from the baseline.

In most cases, a bottleneck affecting server performance is located in one of the computer's four primary subsystems, which are as follows:

- Processor—If the server's processor is unable to keep up with the rest of the components, incoming client requests might have to be queued for extended periods, slowing down the server's response time. To determine whether the processor is the bottleneck, monitor the **% Processor Time** counter in the Processor performance object and the **Processor Queue Length** counter in the System performance object. A % Processor Time value close to 100% and an increase in the Processor Queue Length value are both indicators of a processor bottleneck.

- Memory—Insufficient memory can cause a server to store more information on the disk in the form of paging files, slowing down the responses to client requests. To check a server for a memory bottleneck, monitor the **Pages/Sec, Page Reads/ Sec,** and **Available MBytes** counters in the Memory performance object. If you detect a trend in which the Pages/Sec and Page Reads/Sec values go up and the Available MBytes values go down, you should consider installing additional memory in the computer.

■ Storage—As the number of requests to a server for disk reads and writes increases, the heads in the disk drives move to new locations more frequently and eventually the overall performance of the disk subsystem degrades. To check for a bottleneck in the storage subsystem, you can monitor the **% Disk Time** and **Avg. Disk Queue Length** counters in the PhysicalDisk performance object. If you notice these values increasing, you should consider installing a drive array using a redundant array of independent disks (RAID) or adding more drives to your existing array.

■ Network—A slowdown in network performance can be the result of increased traffic levels, whether legitimate or not. To check for a network bottleneck, you can monitor the **Output Queue Length** counter in the Network Interface performance object, which can tell you if packets are waiting to be transmitted because the network is busy, or you can monitor the various protocols and services that generate network traffic to determine the source of the increased traffic levels. If your network is being overwhelmed by its own traffic, you should consider either upgrading to a faster network or creating a larger number of local area networks (LANs), each with a smaller number of computers.

Objective 4.2 Questions

1. You are the network administrator for a company that has recently landed a lucrative new contract and is planning to hire a number of new employees to handle the extra work. You are not sure that your database server can keep up with the increased load, so you decide to implement a plan to monitor the server for bottlenecks. As the first step in the plan, you establish a baseline by using the Performance Logs And Alerts snap-in to create a counter log that will track the values for critical counters in the Processor, Memory, PhysicalDisk, and Network Interface performance objects. After establishing the normal operational values for the counters, what should you do next to configure the Performance console to detect a bottleneck?

    A. Leave the counter log running at all times and check the values of the counters at regular intervals.

    B. Using System Monitor, create a graph of the same counters and configure the snap-in to sound an alarm when any counter value exceeds the maximum baseline value.

    C. In the Performance Logs And Alerts snap-in, create a series of alerts that send a message to your workstation when any baseline counter exceeds a certain value.

    D. In the Performance Logs And Alerts snap-in, create a trace log using the same counters as the baseline.

2. Which of the following performance counters could you use to detect a bottleneck in a server's processor subsystem? (Choose all that apply.)

    A. Processor Queue Length

    B. Interrupts/Sec

    C. % User Time

    D. % Processor Time

3. You are a network administrator who has been given the task of determining why the Windows Server 2003 file and print server on a particular local area network is performing poorly. You must also implement a remedy for the problem. After monitoring server performance counters using the Performance console, you have determined that the network itself is the bottleneck preventing peak performance. Which of the following solutions would enable you to achieve the goal of increasing the performance level of the file and print server? (Choose all that apply.)

A. Install a second network interface adapter in the server and connect it to the same network.

B. Increase the speed of the network by replacing the 10Base-T network interface adapters in the computers on the network and on the hub to which the computers are connected with 100Base-TX equipment.

C. Split the network into two separate LANs with an equal number of computers on each. Then, install a second network interface adapter in the file and print server and connect the server to both LANs.

D. Replace the network interface adapter in the file and print server with a model that has a larger memory buffer.

4. A server on your network is experiencing a slowdown in performance due to a bottle-neck in the storage subsystem. The three hard drives in the computer are running independently and are all approximately three-quarters full. Which of the following procedures would eliminate the storage bottleneck? (Choose all that apply.)

A. Install a fourth hard drive in the server.

B. Install a fourth hard drive in the server and move some of the data from the other drives to the new drive, so that each drive contains approximately the same amount of data.

C. Determine which of the three drives is receiving the largest number of access requests and replace it with a drive that has twice the capacity.

D. Install a fourth hard drive in the server and convert all four drives into a RAID array.

Objective 4.2 Answers

1.   Correct Answers: C

   A. Incorrect: Although leaving the counter log running will collect the data needed to detect a bottleneck, the task of monitoring and evaluating that data is the administrator's responsibility. The Performance console only collects the data; it is incapable of monitoring and evaluating the data.

   B. Incorrect: Although you can monitor the values of the performance counters in real time using System Monitor, you cannot configure the snap-in to sound alarms.

   C. Correct: The Alerts feature in the Performance Logs And Alerts snap-in enables you to specify values for particular performance counters and configure the program to perform an action, such as generating a message on a computer, if any counter reaches its specified value.

   D. Incorrect: Trace logs do not monitor performance counters, so you cannot use them to detect bottlenecks. Instead, trace logs record the particular system application events that you specify.

2.   Correct Answers: A and D

   A. Correct: The Processor Queue Length counter in the System performance object indicates the number of threads that are currently waiting for processor time. If the value of this counter increases over time, it indicates that the processor cannot keep up with the tasks demanded of it. In other words, the processor is functioning as a bottleneck and is degrading system performance.

   B. Incorrect: The Interrupts/Sec counter in the Processor performance object specifies the number of hardware interrupts the processor is receiving. This counter does not measure the processor's overall load, nor can its value identify the processor as a system bottleneck.

   C. Incorrect: The % User Time counter in the Processor performance object specifies the amount of time that the processor is spending in user mode. This counter value cannot indicate the presence of a system bottleneck.

   D. Correct: The % Processor Time counter in the Processor performance object is the primary indicator of processor activity. Consistently high values for this counter indicate that the processor is operating at peak capacity much of the time and might be a bottleneck preventing the system from achieving superior performance.

3.   Correct Answers: B and C

   A. Incorrect: If the network itself is the bottleneck, a second connection to the same network would not enable any more traffic to reach the server, and therefore would not eliminate the bottleneck.

   B. Correct: Speeding up the network would enable it to carry more traffic, eliminating the bottleneck.

   C. Correct: Creating two LANs out of one reduces the amount of traffic on each network by half, and connecting the server to each of those networks enables more traffic to reach the server.

   D. Incorrect: When the network itself is the bottleneck, the amount of traffic actually reaching the server is limited, and buffering a larger amount of data would not eliminate the bottleneck.

4.   Correct Answers: B and D

   A. Incorrect: Simply installing another drive in the server would do nothing to eliminate the bottleneck because the existing drives would be receiving the same number of access requests as before.

   B. Correct: Spreading the data among a larger number of drives reduces the number of access requests that each drive receives. Reducing the burden on each drive enables them all to operate more efficiently and eliminates the bottleneck.

   C. Incorrect: Adding capacity to one of the drives does nothing to reduce the number of access requests that the drive receives and therefore does nothing to eliminate the bottleneck.

   D. Correct: A RAID array can store redundant data on multiple drives and distribute incoming access requests evenly among the drives, lessening the burden on each drive and eliminating the bottleneck.

Implement a Cluster Server

To implement a cluster on your network, you use Cluster Administrator to create server clusters, or Network Load Balancing Manager to create NLB clusters. However, before you actually create the cluster, you must plan the deployment carefully to meet the availability needs of your network. You must decide on the hardware and configuration options you want to use for the cluster.

NLB clusters do not require special hardware, but they can benefit from having a second network interface adapter in each cluster server. This second adapter enables you to keep all cluster-related traffic separate while allowing the cluster servers to communicate with each other in the normal manner.

In addition to deciding whether to install the second adapter, you must decide whether to run the NLB servers in unicast or multicast mode. In **unicast** mode, the virtual network adapter created by the Clustering service takes over the physical network interface adapter, preventing it from using its original Media Access Control (MAC) address and IP address. If there is only one network interface adapter in the computer, running in unicast mode means that the servers cannot exchange normal network communications. In **multicast** mode, the clustering servers enable the network interface adapter to use the cluster MAC and IP addresses as well as the adapter's original addresses. The servers in the cluster can therefore communicate with each other normally. However, some routers are not capable of handling multicast MAC addresses.

You must configure all the servers in your cluster to run in either unicast or multicast mode, and you can install either one or two network interface adapters in each server. Using two network interface adapters supports larger amounts of traffic than using one adapter in multicast mode.

For a server cluster deployment, you must install a shared storage solution, so that all the servers in the cluster can access the same application data. Windows Server 2003 server clusters support three shared storage hardware solutions:

- **Small Computer System Interface (SCSI)**—To create a shared SCSI bus, you install a SCSI host adapter in each cluster server and connect the adapters to the same storage devices. Windows Server 2003 supports shared SCSI only on 2-node server clusters running the 32-bit version of Windows Server 2003, Enterprise Edition.

- **Fibre Channel arbitrated loop (FC-AL)**—In an FC-AL deployment, you install a Fibre Channel host adapter in each cluster server and connect the servers to the external storage devices using a ring topology. FC-AL support in Windows Server

2003 is limited to 2-node server clusters, but you can connect up to 124 storage devices to the loop. The disadvantage of FC-AL is that it uses a shared network medium, so that packets must pass through one device to get to the others on the loop.

■ **Fibre Channel switched fabric (FC-SW)**—In an FC-SW deployment, you install a Fibre Channel host adapter in each cluster server and connect them, along with the external storage devices, to a Fibre Channel switch. Because the Fibre Channel connections between the devices are switched, there is no shared network medium and each pair of devices has what amounts to a dedicated connection running at the full bandwidth of the network. FC-SW is the only shared storage solution supported by Windows Server 2003 server clustering that can host more than two cluster servers.

The servers in a cluster communicate with each other using **heartbeat** messages, generated at the rate of one per second. The servers use these messages to keep track of the other servers in the cluster. If a cluster server fails, the other servers notice the lack of heartbeat messages from that server. After five missed heartbeats, the other servers begin to compensate for the failed server's absence, a process called **convergence**. The same convergence process occurs in reverse when you add a new server to the cluster and the other servers detect a new heartbeat.

Server clusters and Network Load Balancing clusters are capable of detecting a node failure and of compensating for the node's loss through the convergence process. However, depending on the reason for the node failure, you might have to perform repairs and restore data from your backups before you can bring the server back online. It is therefore crucial that you consider the special needs of your cluster servers when you plan your backup strategy. There are four elements to consider when you are planning backups for a cluster node, which are as follows:

■ **Cluster disk signatures** and partitions—If you have to perform a complete recovery of a server cluster node, you might have to restore the signature of the quorum disk. To back up the cluster disk signatures and partitions, you must perform an Automated System Recovery (ASR) backup.

■ Quorum data—A cluster's quorum contains the cluster's configuration data, which nodes use to update their registries during the failback process. The quorum is included as part of the **System State** object as long as the Clustering service is running on the computer.

■ Cluster disk data—The data stored on cluster disks consists of standard application data, and is not included in the System State object or in an ASR backup. You can back up the cluster disk data from any node owning those disks by performing a standard full backup job.

- Cluster node data—You only have to back up the quorum data and the cluster disk data once to protect the cluster, but there is still important information on each cluster server that you should back up. This information can include the clustering software, the Cluster Administrator application, and any other applications and data that might be on the computer's local, or unshared, drives. Therefore, you should always perform regular full, incremental, or differential backups of each cluster server's local drives, including the System State object.

Objective 4.3 Questions

1. Which of the following diagrams depict a correctly configured server cluster using a Fibre Channel arbitrated loop shared storage solution? (Choose all that apply.)

A.

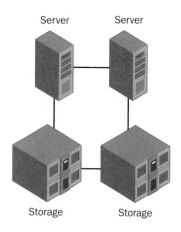

B.

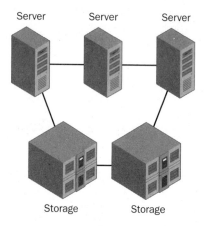

C.

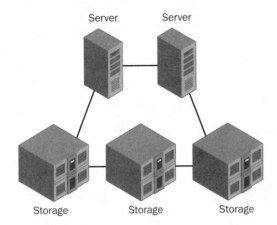

D.

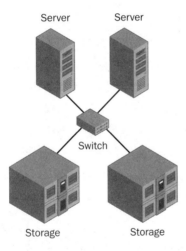

2.   Your team is responsible for designing a Network Load Balancing cluster solution for your company's Internet Web servers. The cluster will consist of six servers, one of which also functions as the network backup server. Because of the need to perform daily backups, the cluster servers must be capable of exchanging data with each other. You have also determined that the routers on your network do not support the use of multicast MAC addresses. Your team has come up with three plans for consideration by the department manager:

■   Plan A calls for replacing the network's routers with models that support multicast MAC addresses and configuring all the cluster servers to use multicast mode.

■   Plan B calls for configuring all the cluster servers to use unicast mode and installing a second network interface adapter on each computer for cluster-related traffic.

■ Plan C calls for configuring the cluster server that also functions as a backup server to use multicast mode, and all the other servers to use unicast mode.

Which of these plans is capable of achieving the stated goals for the project? (Choose all that apply.)

   A. Plan A achieves the stated goals.

   B. Plan B achieves the stated goals.

   C. Plan C achieves the stated goals.

   D. None of the three plans achieves the stated goals.

3. Which of the following terms describes the messages that cluster servers use to determine when a server in the cluster has gone offline?

   A. Convergence messages

   B. Arbitrated loop messages

   C. Multicast messages

   D. Heartbeat messages

4. You are designing a 4-node Windows Server 2003 server cluster. Which of the following additional hardware components are required for the cluster to function? (Choose all that apply.)

   A. A SCSI host adapter for each server in the cluster

   B. A Fibre Channel host adapter for each server in the cluster

   C. A second network interface adapter for each server in the cluster

   D. A Fibre Channel switch

5. Backing up the System State object with the Windows Server 2003 Backup program protects which of the following system elements? (Choose all that apply.)

   A. Cluster disk signatures

   B. The Active Directory database

   C. Cluster quorum data

   D. Cluster disk data

   E. The system registry

6. Which of the following backup types protects cluster disk signatures?

   A. Volume shadow copy

   B. ASR

   C. A full backup

   D. A differential or incremental backup, including the System State object

7. Which of the following conditions must be met for the Windows Server 2003 Backup program to protect a cluster quorum? (Choose all that apply.)

   A. You must select the System State object in the backup job.

   B. The Cluster Administrator application must be running on the server performing the backup.

   C. The Clustering service must be running on the computer you are backing up.

   D. You must perform a full backup, not an incremental or differential backup.

Objective 4.3 Answers

1. **Correct Answers: A and C**

   A. Correct: A Windows Server 2003 server cluster using Fibre Channel arbitrated loop can have up to two servers and up to 124 storage devices, connected using a ring topology.

   B. Incorrect: A Windows Server 2003 server cluster using Fibre Channel arbitrated loop can have no more than two servers. Therefore, this diagram, which contains three servers, is incorrect.

   C. Correct: A Fibre Channel arbitrated loop installation supports up to 126 devices, of which only two can be cluster servers. Therefore, a loop with three storage devices is a valid configuration.

   D. Incorrect: In a Fibre Channel arbitrated loop installation, you must connect the devices using a ring topology. This diagram indicates the use of a switch, which would be a Fibre Channel switched fabric network.

2. **Correct Answers: A and B**

   A. Correct: Once you replace the routers with models supporting multicast addresses, you can configure the cluster servers to use multicast mode with no fear of problems. While operating in multicast mode, the cluster servers can communicate with each other and perform daily backups.

   B. Correct: Installing a second network interface adapter in each cluster server enables you to keep all cluster-related traffic on a separate network connection, leaving the other adapter free for normal network communications, such as daily backups.

   C. Incorrect: You must configure all the servers in a cluster to use either unicast mode or multicast mode. You cannot mix modes in the same cluster.

   D. Incorrect: Operating the cluster servers in multicast mode or installing a second network interface adapter in each server are both viable plans that achieve the stated goals for the project.

3. **Correct Answers: D**

   A. Incorrect: Convergence is the process by which cluster servers adjust their performance when a server is added to or removed from the cluster. Convergence doesn't begin until the other servers in the cluster detect the absence of the malfunctioning server.

B. Incorrect: An arbitrated loop is a type of Fibre Channel connection used to create a shared storage solution for a server cluster; it has nothing to do with detecting offline cluster servers.

C. Incorrect: Multicast is an operational mode for Network Load Balancing clusters and a type of Transmission Control Protocol/Internet Protocol (TCP/IP) message that uses a single address to represent a group of hosts. Neither of these definitions is related to the process of detecting offline cluster servers.

D. Correct: All the servers in a cluster transmit a heartbeat message once a second to the other cluster servers. If the heartbeats from a particular server stop, the other servers assume it is offline and begin the convergence process, to compensate for losing a server.

4.   **Correct Answers: B and D**

A. Incorrect: A Windows Server 2003 server cluster that uses a shared SCSI storage solution can have no more than 2 nodes.

B. Correct: A 4-node Windows Server 2003 server cluster can only use Fibre Channel for its shared storage solution.

C. Incorrect: Although the cluster servers would benefit from the installation of a second network interface adapter for cluster-related traffic, it is not a requirement.

D. Correct: A 4-node Windows Server 2003 server cluster must use a Fibre Channel switched fabric network as its shared storage solution, which requires the installation of a Fibre Channel switch.

5.   **Correct Answers: B, C, and E**

A. Incorrect: To back up cluster disk signatures, you must use the Automated System Recovery (ASR) feature in the Backup program.

B. Correct: The System State object includes the Active Directory database as well as boot files and other important system elements.

C. Correct: Backing up the System State element protects the cluster quorum on any server on which the Cluster service is running.

D. Incorrect: The System State element does not include the data stored on cluster disks. To back up this data, you must use a standard backup job, such as a full backup.

E. Correct: The System State element includes the registry, as well as boot files and other important system elements.

6.   **Correct Answers: B**

   A. **Incorrect:** The volume shadow copy feature in the Windows Server 2003 Backup program enables the program to back up files that are locked open by other processes; it does not protect cluster disk signatures.

   B. **Correct:** An Automated System Recovery (ASR) backup includes cluster disk signatures, as well as other vital operating system files.

   C. **Incorrect:** A full backup does not protect the cluster disk signatures, as they are considered part of the operating system and require special treatment.

   D. **Incorrect:** Differential or incremental backup jobs are no different from full backups in the resources that they protect, and they do not protect cluster disk signatures, even when you include the System State object.

7.   **Correct Answers: A and C**

   A. **Correct:** On a cluster server, the System State object includes the quorum data, along with other important system elements.

   B. **Incorrect:** Server Clustering runs as a separate service, unrelated to the Cluster Administrator application. You don't have to have Cluster Administrator running to back up the quorum.

   C. **Correct:** The quorum data is only included as part of the System State object on servers on which the Clustering service is actually running.

   D. **Incorrect:** Any of the standard backup jobs, full, incremental, or differential, can back up the quorum data, as long as you select the System State object.

Manage Network Load Balancing

In Windows Server 2003, by default, the Network Load Balancing Manager application displays the ongoing activities of the cluster to which you are connected in its log pane. However, the program does not save this information to a permanent log, unless you enable logging by selecting Log Settings from the Options menu. Also, the Manager only displays information related to the activities you have performed in the Manager application. To display log information about the Network Load Balancing service itself, you must open the System log in the Event Viewer console. System log entries pertaining to the NLB service are labeled WLBS (which stands for Windows Load Balancing Service).

The other primary application for managing Network Load Balancing clusters in Windows Server 2003 is the WLBS cluster control utility, which is a command-line program called **NLB.EXE**. In earlier versions of the Microsoft Windows operating system, the program was called **WLBS.EXE**. Windows Server 2003 includes the program using both names, so that you can still use command lines and scripts developed for earlier versions of the service. The cluster control utility is a powerful program that you can use to control many of the NLB service's functions. Some of the command-line parameters you can use are as follows:

- DISPLAY *cluster*—For the cluster specified by the *cluster* variable, displays the configuration parameters that are stored in the registry, plus the most recent System log entries related to the cluster, the computer's IP configuration, and the cluster's current status.

- DRAIN *port*—Prevents a specified cluster from handling any new traffic conforming to the rule that contains the port specified by the *port* variable.

- DRAINSTOP *cluster*—Disables all cluster traffic handling after completing the transactions currently in process. If the *cluster* variable is not specified, this command applies to the local host.

- PARAMS *cluster*—Displays all the current configuration parameters for the cluster specified by the variable *cluster*.

- QUERY *cluster*—Displays the current state of all hosts in the cluster specified by the *cluster* variable.

- QUERYPORT *port*—Displays the current status of the rule containing the port specified by the variable *port*.

Objective 4.4 Questions

1. Which of the following parameters for the WLBS cluster control utility should you use when you want to bring a cluster server down for maintenance?

   A. DRAIN

   B. PARAMS

   C. QUERYPORT

   D. DRAINSTOP

2. Which of the following functions can you perform using the WLBS cluster control utility? (Choose all that apply.)

   A. Create a new NLB cluster

   B. Suspend all cluster operations

   C. Add a host to an existing NLB cluster

   D. Shut down cluster operations on a specified host

3. You are responsible for the day-to-day administration of a Network Load Balancing cluster that is critical to your company's operation, and a user has just reported that she cannot access the cluster. Which of the following utilities should you use on each cluster server to find out if the NLB service has stopped running, and why should you use it?

   A. NBTSTAT.EXE

   B. Event Viewer

   C. NET.EXE

   D. Performance console

Objective 4.4 Answers

1.   Correct Answers: D

A. Incorrect: The DRAIN parameter stops the NLB service from handling new traffic on a specific port, but it does not disable all cluster traffic handling.

B. Incorrect: The PARAMS parameter only displays the current configuration parameters for the cluster; it does not affect the functionality of the NLB service.

C. Incorrect: The QUERYPORT parameter displays status information about the rule containing a specified port, but does not modify the functionality of that port.

D. Correct: The DRAINSTOP parameter causes the NLB service to wait until all transactions currently in progress are completed, then disables all cluster operations on that server. This enables you to shut down the server without interrupting client connections to the cluster.

2.   Correct Answers: B and D

A. Incorrect: To create a new cluster, you must use the Network Load Balancing Manager application. You cannot create a new cluster with the WLBS cluster control utility.

B. Correct: You can use the WLBS cluster control utility to suspend cluster operations for an entire cluster by running NLB.EXE or WLBS.EXE with the SUSPEND parameter.

C. Incorrect: You cannot add a host to a cluster using the WLBS cluster control utility. You must use the Network Load Balancing Manager application.

D. Correct: You can use the WLBS cluster control utility to suspend cluster operations for an entire cluster by running NLB.EXE or WLBS.EXE with the STOP parameter and the name of the host.

3.   Correct Answers: B

A. Incorrect: NBTSTAT.EXE displays statistics about NetBIOS Over TCP/IP operations on the computer. This program cannot tell you why the NLB service has stopped.

B. Correct: When the NLB service stops or malfunctions, error messages appear in the System log, found in the Event Viewer console.

C. Incorrect: You can use NET.EXE to start and stop services, but you cannot use it to determine why they have stopped.

D. Incorrect: The Performance console enables you to display statistics for selected system components in real time, but it cannot display error messages regarding service failures.

Objective 4.5

Plan a Backup and Recovery Strategy

A network backup strategy typically consists of one or more backup drives connected to a server running a network backup software program. You configure the program to execute backup jobs at times when the network is not in use, so that it can protect data stored on computers all over the network without affecting normal operations. The most common storage medium used by backup drives is magnetic tape, which is available in a variety of formats that differ in capacity, data transmission speed, and the price of the drive and media. When selecting a backup medium, you should take into account the amount of data you have to back up on a daily basis. The object is typically to select a backup drive that fits all the data you must back up every day on a single tape, so that you can configure the jobs to run unattended.

To prevent having to back up all the data on your network every day, all backup software products provide a number of different backup jobs, the most common of which are as follows:

- **Full backup**—Copies all the selected files to the backup medium and resets the archive bits for all the copied files

- **Incremental backup**—Copies only the selected files that have archive bits and then resets those archive bits

- **Differential backup**—Copies only the selected files that have archive bits without resetting those archive bits

The basic premise of incremental and differential backups is that there is no need to back up the same files every day if they have not changed. Backup software uses the **archive bit** stored as part of every file to determine whether that file has changed recently. Performing a full backup job copies all your files to the backup drive and resets all their archive bits to a value of 0. When an application on the computer modifies a file, the file system changes the value of the archive bit to 1. When you perform an incremental or differential backup, the backup software copies only the files with archive bit values of 1. The difference between an incremental and a differential backup is whether the backup software resets the archive bits of the files it has copied. With incremental jobs, the software does reset the archive bits; with differential jobs, it does not. Incremental backups use less storage space than differential backups, but the process of restoring an entire drive is longer and more complicated.

Windows Server 2003 includes a Backup program that enables you to protect all the files on the computer by copying them to a backup drive or to a disk file that you can move to a safe location. The version of Backup in Windows Server 2003 includes a new feature called **volume shadow copy** that enables the Backup program to protect files that are currently open and in use. This feature also has another function that can simplify the job of the administrator. You can configure Windows Server 2003 to automatically maintain shadow copies of the files on a specific volume. Shadow copies capture a frequently changed file's state at one point in time. The server creates these copies on a regular schedule you specify. By default, the volume shadow copy feature creates shadow copies of each changed file twice a day, and users can access any of the previous versions of their files still stored in the shadow copy area. A user who accidentally modifies or deletes an important file can access a previous version of the file from the shadow copy area, rather than asking the backup administrator to restore a previous version from tape. You must enable the volume shadow copy feature for an entire volume and you must specify the amount of disk space to be allotted to the shadow copies. When the disk space is full, the system automatically purges the oldest copies.

Automated System Recovery (ASR), another feature of the Windows Server 2003 Backup program, enables you to restore an entire system drive without reinstalling the operating system. With a standard backup, you can't restore a computer whose drive has been completely erased from a backup until you reinstall the operating system, because you must be able to run the backup program to perform the restore. ASR is a disaster recovery feature that enables you to create a backup of your operating system with a boot disk that enables you to perform a restore immediately. When you use the ASR feature to create a backup, the program prompts you for a standard backup device, such as a tape, and a floppy disk. After the backup is complete, if your system drive fails, you can simply replace the drive, insert the backup tape in it, start the computer from the floppy disk, and let the restoration of the operating system proceed automatically.

Objective 4.5 Questions

1. You are the backup administrator for a corporate network, and you are in the process of creating and scheduling your backup jobs. The company you work for has purchased a backup tape drive that uses very expensive media, and you have been ordered to keep the amount of tape used for backups to an absolute minimum. Which of the following strategies best achieves your goals?

   A. Perform a full backup every Friday night and a differential backup every Monday night through Thursday night.

   B. Perform a full backup every Friday night and an incremental backup every Monday night through Thursday night.

   C. Perform a full backup every Friday night and a volume shadow copy every Monday night through Thursday night.

   D. Perform a full backup every night.

2. Your company has recently expanded to three shifts, meaning that the network is in use 24 hours a day, seven days a week. Your current backup strategy consists of a full backup job every Sunday and incremental jobs on Monday through Saturday. Which of the following Windows Server 2003 Backup features should you use to ensure that the system backs up all open files every day?

   A. ASR

   B. Differential backups instead of incremental backups

   C. Volume shadow copy

   D. Full backups every night, instead of incrementals

3. Which of the following magnetic tape drive types offers the greatest tape capacity and the fastest data transfer rates?

   A. Linear Tape-Open (LTO)

   B. 8mm

   C. Digital audio tape (DAT)

   D. Digital linear tape (DLT)

4. You have recently been named administrator of backups for your company, and you are in the process of developing a backup strategy. Your goals for this strategy are to schedule a backup job to run each night that will back up all the files modified during that day's work, and to create the fastest possible recovery solution in the event of a

complete server system disk failure. Which of the following strategies would enable you to achieve all these goals?

A. Perform a full backup every Friday and an incremental backup every Monday night through Thursday night.

B. Perform an ASR backup every night.

C. Perform an ASR backup once a month and perform a full backup every Friday and a differential backup every Monday night through Thursday night.

D. Perform a full backup every night.

Objective 4.5 Answers

1. **Correct Answers: B**

   A. **Incorrect:** While this strategy would adequately protect the network, it does not achieve the goal of using the minimum amount of tape because differential jobs back up some of the same files every night.

   B. **Correct:** Incremental backup jobs use the least amount of tape because they back up only the files that have changed since the last backup.

   C. **Incorrect:** Volume shadow copy is not a type of backup job, although it is a feature you can use for your backup jobs. Creating shadow copies of the files on your volumes is not a substitute for regular backups, because the system still stores them on the same hard drive, which can fail.

   D. **Incorrect:** Performing a full backup every night is an effective solution, but it does not fulfill the goal of using the minimum amount of tape.

2. **Correct Answers: C**

   A. **Incorrect:** Automated System Recovery is a feature that enables you to create a bootable operating system backup; it does not protect open files.

   B. **Incorrect:** Changing the incremental backups to differentials would not enable the system to back up open files. A differential backup only differs from an incremental in its treatment of the archive bits.

   C. **Correct:** Volume shadow copy enables the Windows Server 2003 Backup program to back up files that are locked open by other applications.

   D. **Incorrect:** Performing full backups instead of incrementals does nothing to enhance the backup of open files.

3. **Correct Answers: A**

   A. **Correct:** Linear Tape-Open drives support tape capacities of up to 200 gigabytes (uncompressed) and data transfer speeds of up to 3,600 megabytes per minute.

   B. **Incorrect:** 8mm drives support tape capacities of up to 100 gigabytes (uncompressed) and data transfer speeds of up to 1,400 megabytes per minute, which are exceeded by DLT and LTO drives.

   C. **Incorrect:** Digital audio tape drives support tape capacities of up to 20 gigabytes (uncompressed) and data transfer speeds of up to 360 megabytes per minute. These figures are exceeded by 8mm, DLT, and LTO drives.

D. Incorrect: DLT drives support tape capacities of up to 160 gigabytes (uncompressed) and data transfer speeds of up to 960 megabytes per minute. LTO drives have greater capacities, and LTO and 8mm drives offer faster data transfer speeds.

4.   Correct Answers: C

A. Incorrect: This solution does back up all the files that have changed each day, but it does not provide the fastest possible recovery solution. Incremental jobs take longer to restore than differential jobs, and the lack of an ASR backup means that you must first reinstall the operating system in the event of a server system disk failure.

B. Incorrect: ASR backups provide for a fast recovery of the operating system in the event of a server system disk failure, but they only back up operating system files, and are therefore not a substitute for standard backup jobs.

C. Correct: An ASR backup, in combination with daily differential backups, protects all the files changed during each day's work and also provides the fastest possible recovery. In the event of a server system disk failure, you only have to restore from the ASR backup, the most recent full backup, and the most recent differential backup.

D. Incorrect: Performing a full backup every night protects all the files that users change each day, but it does not provide the fastest recovery, since you must reinstall the operating system before you can restore files from the backup.

18 Planning and Maintaining Network Security (5.0)

Security is an essential part of the network administrator's function in almost every enterprise. As businesses become increasingly dependent on their computer networks, the threats they face become more dangerous and the attackers more ingenious. The Microsoft Windows Server 2003 family of operating systems includes a wide array of security mechanisms that can protect the network against these threats, and a competent network administrator must know how to use them properly. This domain examines the protocols you can use to secure data as computers transmit it over the network, and the tools that Windows Server 2003 provides for implementing and managing these protocols.

Tested Skills and Suggested Practices

The skills that you need to successfully master the Planning and Maintaining Network Security objective domain on the 70-293 exam include:

- Configure network protocol security.
    - ❏ Practice 1: Compile a list of the workstation operating systems most commonly used for business networking and, using product literature or the World Wide Web sites of the operating system manufacturers, determine whether the products include support for Internet Protocol Security (IPSec).
    - ❏ Practice 2: Create a new IPSec policy that will digitally sign all traffic to a particular server using the Internet Protocol (IP) Authentication Header (AH) protocol.
- Configure security for data transmission.
    - ❏ Practice 1: In the Windows Server 2003 IP Security Policies snap-in, open the Properties dialog box for each default IPSec policy. List the types of traffic the policy is designed to protect and the degree of protection the policy calls for, including the IPSec protocols and encryption algorithms it uses.
    - ❏ Practice 2: Using the IP Security Policies snap-in, create a series of filter lists that you can use in IPSec policies to protect the traffic generated by the DNS, DHCP, and WINS services.

■ Plan for network protocol security.

❑ Practice 1: Examine the well-known port numbers in the Internet Assigned Numbers Authority (IANA) Port Numbers online database (available at *http://www.iana.org/assignments/port-numbers*) and make a list of the ports that you suspect are used most on a typical business network.

❑ Practice 2: On a computer running Windows Server 2003, configure the Transmission Control Protocol/Internet Protocol (TCP/IP) Filtering option in the TCP/IP client to block all Web traffic using the well-known port 80. Then, if you have a computer running Windows Server 2003 with Service Pack 1 (SP1), enable the Windows Firewall service and configure a port exception for port 23 to allow inbound Telnet access.

■ Plan secure network administration methods.

❑ Practice 1: Using the System Properties dialog box, configure a computer running Windows Server 2003 to use Remote Desktop, specifying the names of the remote users that you want to be able to access this server.

❑ Practice 2: Using group policies, configure a computer running Windows Server 2003 to use Remote Assistance.

■ Plan security for wireless networks.

❑ Practice 1: Examine the Web sites or product literature of companies manufacturing wireless LAN products. Make a list of network interface adapters and access points, specifying the wireless networking and security standards they support.

❑ Practice 2: Design a wireless networking infrastructure for an office building that uses multiple access points and list the steps you would take to provide maximum security for the wireless transmissions.

■ Plan security for data transmission.

❑ Practice 1: Install Network Monitor on a computer running Windows Server 2003 and use it to capture a representative sampling of the network traffic generated by all the applications you commonly use. Examine the captured packets and make a list of the protocols and port numbers the applications use.

❑ Practice 2: Using the IP Security Policies snap-in, create a new IPSec policy to encrypt all the traffic using the protocols and port numbers you listed in Practice 1.

- Troubleshoot security for data transmission. Tools might include the IP Security Monitor MMC snap-in and the Resultant Set of Policy (RSoP) MMC snap-in.

  ❑ Practice 1: On a computer running Windows Server 2003, open Microsoft Management Console and create a new console containing the IP Security Monitor and Resultant Set of Policy snap-ins.

  ❑ Practice 2: Use the Resultant Set of Policy snap-in to view the effective policies on your computer.

Further Reading

This section lists supplemental readings by objective. We recommend that you study these sources thoroughly before taking exam 70-293.

Objective 5.1   Review Lessons 2 and 3 in Chapter 12, "Securing Network Communications Using IPSec."

Microsoft Corporation. *Microsoft Windows Server 2003 Deployment Kit.* Volume: *Deploying Network Services.* Redmond, Washington: Microsoft Press, 2003. Review Chapter 6, "Deploying IPSec." This volume can also be found on Microsoft's Web site at *http://www.microsoft.com/windowsserver2003/techinfo/reskit/deploykit.mspx.*

Microsoft Corporation. *Windows Server 2003 Technical Reference.* Collection: *Windows Security Collection.* Review "Data Security Technologies: IPSec Technical Reference." This volume can be found on Microsoft's Web site at *http://technet2.microsoft.com/WindowsServer/en/Library/fa2c6e21-a693-4a7c-bc0f-c171477928de1033.mspx.*

Objective 5.2   Review Lessons 2 and 3 in Chapter 12, "Securing Network Communications Using IPSec."

Microsoft Corporation. Windows Server 2003 Online Help. Review the "Define IPSec Policies" pages in the Internet Protocol Security (IPSec) help file, accessible from the IP Security Policies snap-in.

Objective 5.3   Review Lessons 1, 2, and 3 in Chapter 12, "Securing Network Communications Using IPSec."

Microsoft Corporation. *Microsoft Windows Server 2003 Deployment Kit.* Volume: *Deploying Network Services.* Redmond, Washington: Microsoft Press, 2003. Review Chapter 6, "Deploying IPSec." This volume can also be found on Microsoft's Web site at *http://www.microsoft.com/windowsserver2003/techinfo/reskit/deploykit.mspx.*

Objective 5.4   Review Lesson 3 in Chapter 13, "Designing a Security Infrastructure."

Microsoft Corporation. *Microsoft Windows Server 2003 Deployment Kit.* Volume: *Planning Server Deployments.* Redmond, Washington: Microsoft Press, 2003. Review Chapter 4, "Hosting Applications with Terminal Server." This volume can also be found on Microsoft's Web site at *http://www.microsoft.com/windowsserver2003 /techinfo/reskit/deploykit.mspx.*

Microsoft Corporation. Windows Server 2003 Online Help. Review the "I Am Managing The Use Of Remote Assistance" pages in the Remote Assistance help file, accessible from the Remote tab of the System Properties dialog box.

Objective 5.5   Review Lesson 2 in Chapter 13, "Designing a Security Infrastructure."

Microsoft Corporation. *Microsoft Windows Server 2003 Deployment Kit.* Volume: *Deploying Network Services.* Redmond, Washington: Microsoft Press, 2003. Review "Deploying a Wireless LAN." This volume can also be found on Microsoft's Web site at *http://www.microsoft.com/windowsserver2003/techinfo/reskit/deploykit.mspx.*

Objective 5.6   Review Lessons 2 and 3 in Chapter 12, "Securing Network Communications Using IPSec."

Microsoft Corporation. *Microsoft Windows Server 2003 Deployment Kit.* Volume: *Deploying Network Services.* Redmond, Washington: Microsoft Press, 2003. Review Chapter 6, "Deploying IPSec." This volume can also be found on Microsoft's Web site at *http://www.microsoft.com/windowsserver2003/techinfo/reskit/deploykit.mspx.*

Microsoft Corporation. *Windows Server 2003 Technical Reference.* Collection: *Windows Security Collection.* Review "Data Security Technologies: IPSec Technical Reference." This volume can be found on Microsoft's Web site at *http: //technet2.microsoft.com/WindowsServer/en/Library/fa2c6e21-a693-4a7c-bc0f-c171477928de1033.mspx.*

Objective 5.7   Review Lesson 4 in Chapter 12, "Securing Network Communications Using IPSec."

Microsoft Corporation. Windows Server 2003 Online Help. Review the Resultant Set of Policy help file, accessible from the Resultant Set of Policy snap-in, and the "Monitor IPSec Activity" pages of the Internet Protocol Security (IPSec) help file, accessible from the IP Security Monitor snap-in.

Microsoft Corporation. *Microsoft Windows Server 2003 Deployment Kit.* Volume: *Deploying Network Services.* Redmond, Washington: Microsoft Press, 2003. Review Chapter 6, "Deploying IPSec." This volume can also be found on Microsoft's Web site at *http://www.microsoft.com/windowsserver2003/techinfo/reskit/deploykit.mspx.*

Configure Network Protocol Security

Most of the file encryption mechanisms used on computers today are designed to protect data as it is stored on a hard drive or other storage device. For example, the Encrypting File System (EFS) in Windows Server 2003 can prevent intruders from viewing the files stored on your computer, but when you transmit those files over the network, EFS decrypts them first. Protecting data as it is transmitted over the network is a more complex proposition, especially on a network with computers running different operating systems. The **IP Security extensions (IPSec)** are industry standard protocols that you can use to digitally sign and encrypt data before transmitting it over the network. The receiving system then checks the signature and decrypts the data.

- **Key generation**—For two computers to communicate over the network using encrypted IP datagrams, both must have access to a shared encryption key. This key enables each computer to encrypt its data and the other computer to decrypt it. However, the key cannot be transmitted over the network without compromising the security of the system. Therefore, computers preparing to communicate with each other using IPSec both use a technique called the Diffie-Hellman algorithm to compute identical encryption keys. The computers publicly exchange information about the calculations that enable them to arrive at the same result, but they do not exchange the key themselves or information that would enable a third party to calculate the key.

- **Cryptographic checksums**—In addition to encrypting the data transmitted over the network, IPSec uses its cryptographic keys to calculate a checksum for the data in each packet, called a **hash message authentication code (HMAC)**, and transmits it with the data. If anyone modifies the packet while it is in transit, the HMAC calculated by the receiving computer will be different from the one in the packet. This prevents attackers from modifying the information in a packet or adding information to it (such as a virus).

- **Mutual authentication**—Before two computers can communicate using IPSec, they must authenticate each other to establish a trust relationship. Windows Server 2003 IPSec can use Kerberos, digital certificates, or a preshared key for authentication. Once the computers have authenticated each other, the cryptographic checksum in each packet functions as a digital signature, preventing anyone from spoofing or impersonating one of the computers.

- **Replay prevention**—In some cases, it is possible for attackers to use data from captured packets against you, even when the data in the packets is encrypted. Using traffic analysis, it is possible to determine the function of some encrypted packets. For example, the first few packets that two computers exchange during a secured transaction are likely to be authentication messages. Sometimes, by retransmitting these same packets, still in their encrypted form, attackers can use them to gain access to secured resources. IPSec prevents packet replays from being effective by assigning a sequence number to each packet. An IPSec system will not accept a packet that has an incorrect sequence number.

- **IP packet filtering**—IPSec includes its own independent packet filtering mechanism that enables you to prevent denial-of-service (DoS) attacks by blocking specific types of traffic using IP addresses, protocols, ports, or any combination of the three.

IPSec is based on a series of public domain standards published by the Internet Engineering Task Force (IETF). This means that any IPSec implementation that is compliant with the standards should be able to interact with any other compliant implementation.

To implement IPSec on a network running Windows operating systems, you use **IPSec policies**, which specify what type of protection IPSec should provide and what traffic it should protect. To deploy IPSec policies on your network, you can assign them to Group Policy Objects (GPO) in Active Directory or assign them to an individual computer's local policy settings.

Objective 5.1 Questions

1. After an incident in which an intruder compromised a wide area network (WAN) link and intercepted data, a financial company has engaged you as a network consultant to secure all communications between the corporate headquarters and the company's five branch offices. The various locations have servers and workstations running a variety of operating systems, including Microsoft Windows NT Server, Microsoft Windows 2000 Server, Windows Server 2003, several varieties of UNIX, Microsoft Windows 98, Microsoft Windows 2000 Professional, and Microsoft Windows XP Professional. The branch offices are connected to the headquarters using T-1 leased lines as WAN links. The routers connecting the T-1 lines to the individual private networks are all computers running Windows 2000 Server or Windows Server 2003. Which of the following solutions can protect the traffic running between the offices with the least expense?

    A. Configure every computer in every office to use the Encrypting File System (EFS), upgrading operating systems that do not support EFS in the process.

    B. Configure every computer in every office to use the IPSec Secure Server (Require Security) policy.

    C. Configure the WAN routers at all locations to use IPSec in transport mode, creating a new IPSec policy to secure only the WAN traffic.

    D. Configure the WAN routers at all locations to use IPSec in tunnel mode, creating a new IPSec policy to secure the WAN traffic.

2. Which of the following IPSec features prevents attackers from replaying encrypted packets?

    A. IP packet filtering

    B. Sequence numbers

    C. Hash message authentication codes (HMACs)

    D. Diffie-Hellman key generation

3. You are the administrator of a network that uses Active Directory and consists of 200 computers, of which 175 are workstations, running various versions of the Microsoft Windows operating system, all of which support IPSec. You have already configured the network servers to use an IPSec policy you created, which encrypts all traffic

generated by a specific application. Now you want to configure all the workstations to use the Client (Respond Only) IPSec policy supplied with the Windows operating system. Which of the following procedures most easily accomplishes this task?

A. Assign the Client (Respond Only) policy to the Default Domain Policy GPO.

B. Assign the Client (Respond Only) IPSec policy to each workstation individually using its Local Security Policy console.

C. Create a new organizational unit object in Active Directory for the workstations and assign the Client (Respond Only) IPSec policy to the default Group Policy Object for that organizational unit.

D. Create a new Active Directory domain for the workstations, subordinate to the existing domain, and assign the Client (Respond Only) IPSec policy to the Default Domain Policy GPO for the new domain.

4. You are in the process of designing an IPSec implementation for a network containing mostly computers running Windows 2000, Windows XP, and Windows Server 2003, but with a few servers running UNIX. How can you tell whether the IPSec implementations in the UNIX operating systems are compatible with Microsoft Windows IPSec?

A. You cannot tell until the computers are configured to use IPSec and attempt to communicate.

B. Check the names of the IPSec policies included with the UNIX implementation. If they have the same names as the Windows operating system's default policies, the two implementations are compatible.

C. Use a protocol analyzer to capture IPSec packets from the UNIX and Windows operating systems and compare the structures of their protocol headers.

D. Check to see if the UNIX implementation of IPSec conforms to the standards published by the IETF.

Objective 5.1 Answers

1.   Correct Answers: D

    A.   Incorrect: EFS is designed to protect data only while it is stored on a computer. When a computer using EFS transmits the data over the network, the operating system decrypts it before transmitting.

    B.   Incorrect: The network has computers running operating systems that do not support IPSec, such as Windows 98. In addition, configuring all the computers to use the Secure Server (Require Security) policy would encrypt all network traffic, not just the traffic passing over the WAN links.

    C.   Incorrect: Configuring the routers to use transport mode would protect only the packets generated by the routers themselves, but not the packets generated by the local computers using the routers to access the WAN.

    D.   Correct: IPSec tunnel mode is intended to protect WAN traffic. Because only the routers have to support IPSec, all the workstations receive the benefits of the IPSec protection, regardless of whether they themselves support it.

2.   Correct Answers: B

    A.   Incorrect: Packet filtering enables IPSec to apply its protection to specific types of traffic; it does nothing to prevent attackers from replaying packets.

    B.   Correct: An IPSec computer transmitting protected data assigns a sequence number value to each packet in a particular transaction. If the destination system receives a packet with an incorrect sequence number, it discards the packet immediately.

    C.   Incorrect: HMACs are used to protect IPSec traffic from being modified while en route to its destination. A destination computer performs the same HMAC calculations as the sender, and compares the results to those in the packet. If the two results do not match, the packet is discarded.

    D.   Incorrect: Windows Server 2003 IPSec uses the Diffie-Hellman algorithm to calculate encryption keys; this algorithm does not perform an anti-replay function.

3.   Correct Answers: C

    A.   Incorrect: Assigning an IPSec policy to the Default Domain Policy GPO will cause all the computers in the domain to use that policy, including the servers, which you want to use a different policy.

    B.   Incorrect: Although you can assign an IPSec policy to individual computers, this is certainly not the easiest method for deploying IPSec, especially when Active Directory is available.

C. **Correct:** Creating a new organizational unit and assigning the Client (Respond Only) policy to it enables you to keep the workstations separate from the servers, so that each role can use a different IPSec policy.

D. **Incorrect:** Creating a new domain would force you to have additional domain controllers, which would receive the same IPSec policy as the workstations.

4. **Correct Answers: D**

A. **Incorrect:** You can usually tell if two IPSec implementations are compatible before you actually implement them by checking to see if they are compliant with the IPSec standards published by the IETF.

B. **Incorrect:** IPSec policies are a feature of the Microsoft Windows IPSec implementation, and are not necessarily present in other implementations of IPSec.

C. **Incorrect:** Two implementations of IPSec might use the same protocol header format but still be incompatible. For example, if the two implementations use different encryption algorithms, computers using them would not be able to communicate.

D. **Correct:** The Internet Engineering Task Force (IETF) has published the standards on which IPSec is based in the public domain, so that anyone can use them. Compliance with the same standards usually means that two implementations are compatible.

Configure Security for Data Transmission

In Windows Server 2003, you use the **IP Security Policies snap-in** to create and manage **IPSec policies**. IPSec policies consist of rules, filter lists, and filter actions. When you create a new policy, you design each of these three elements in combinations appropriate to your security needs. The IP Security Policies snap-in provides wizards that can walk you through the process of creating rules, filter lists, and filter actions, or you can create them manually, using standard dialog boxes.

A **rule** is a combination of filter lists and filter actions, both of which define what traffic IPSec should protect and how it should protect it. When you create a rule, you specify whether IPSec should operate in **transport mode** or **tunnel mode**; what authentication protocol the computers should use to verify each other's identities; and what filter lists and filter actions to use. An IPSec policy can have multiple rules, which the IPSec driver applies to the computer in order, beginning with the rule having the most specific filter list and proceeding to the one with the least specific filter list. There is no way to specify the order in which IPSec applies the rules, but you can enable or disable specific rules in a policy by selecting or clearing the corresponding check boxes in the IP Security Rules list.

Filter lists specify what types of traffic IPSec should protect. Creating a filter list is similar to implementing the IP packet filtering feature in the Windows Server 2003 Routing and Remote Access service, except that instead of specifying which packets can have access to the computer, IPSec filter lists specify what traffic IPSec should protect. When creating a filter list, you can specify the IP addresses of source and destination systems, IP subnet addresses, specific protocols, and well-known port numbers that use those protocols. Combining these filtering criteria enables you to selectively protect traffic generated by or destined for specific systems, or traffic generated by specific applications running on those systems. For example, if you have a server that runs a database application hosting confidential company information, but which is also the company DNS server, you can create an IPSec policy containing a filter list that specifies the IP addresses of the clients that need access to the database and the port numbers of the database application. IPSec would then encrypt the confidential database information, while still giving everyone on the network access to the DNS server. Once you create a filter list in the IP Security Policies snap-in, it becomes available to all the other policies on the computer.

Filter actions specify what steps IPSec should take to secure the traffic specified by a filter list. When you create a filter action, you specify whether you want to permit or block the traffic specified by the filter list, or if you want the transmitting computer to negotiate security terms with the destination computer. When you choose the latter (enabling IPSec's security capabilities), you can choose to require security or let the computers fall back to unsecured communications if they are unable to negotiate a common security configuration. Next, you specify what type of security you want IPSec to provide. You can select the Integrity Only option (causing the system to use the **IP Authentication Header** protocol only) or the Integrity And Encryption option, which adds the **IP Encapsulating Security Payload** protocol. If you choose, you can also customize the protocol settings, configuring them to use specific integrity and encryption algorithms, and specifying how often the systems should generate new keys.

Objective 5.2 Questions

1.   You are creating a new IPSec policy, and you have configured the following filter list parameters:

■ The Mirrored option is disabled

■ Source Address: Any IP Address

■ Destination Address: My IP Address

■ Protocol: TCP

■ From This Port: 110

■ To Any Port

The filter action in the policy specifies that all traffic conforming to the filters be protected with both integrity and encryption. Which of the following types of packets will be protected using IPSec?

A. All e-mail messages transmitted by the computer

B. All e-mail messages received by the computer

C. All incoming traffic from the Internet

D. All outgoing traffic to the Internet

2.   You are the network administrator for a company that has recently implemented IPSec on all their computers. To provide the maximum possible protection, you have assigned the Secure Server (Require Security) IPSec policy to the Default Domain Policy GPO, so that all the computers on the network must use IPSec for all communications. However, it has come to your attention that one of the company's critical client/server applications is not functioning properly while IPSec is in use. Therefore, you want to configure the Secure Server (Require Security) policy to permit all traffic generated by that application to be transmitted without protection. Which of the following procedures must you perform to accomplish this goal? (Choose all that apply.)

A. Create a new IPSec policy and assign it to the Default Domain Policy GPO along with the Secure Server (Require Security) policy.

B. Create a new rule in the Secure Server (Require Security) policy.

C. Create a new filter list specifying the port number used by the application.

D. Create a new filter action that permits the computer to transmit certain traffic without IPSec security.

3. You want to create an IPSec policy to protect all the traffic generated by a specific application passing over a WAN link connecting two offices in different cities. The routers connecting the private networks to the WAN in both locations are running Windows Server 2003, and the workstations on the two networks are running various versions of Microsoft Windows, including Windows 98, Windows 2000 Professional, and Windows XP Professional. Which of the following tasks must you perform while creating this policy? (Choose all that apply.)

   A. Create a rule with a tunnel endpoint IP address.

   B. Create a filter list specifying the port number used by the application.

   C. Create a filter list specifying the IP addresses of the two routers connected to the WAN link.

   D. Create a filter action with the Permit option.

4. A filter action that is configured to provide only integrity causes IPSec to use which of the following components? (Choose all that apply.)

   A. AH

   B. ESP

   C. 3DES

   D. SHA1

Objective 5.2 Answers

1. **Correct Answers: B**

   A. **Incorrect:** Because the Destination Address selector value is My IP Address and the Mirrored option is disabled, this filter list is designed to isolate only traffic inbound to the computer.

   B. **Correct:** The well-known TCP port number 110 is used by Post Office Protocol, version 3 (POP3), which clients use to retrieve their messages from e-mail servers. The fact that the Mirrored option is disabled and the Destination Address is My IP Address means that this filter list isolates only the incoming traffic from the POP3 server.

   C. **Incorrect:** The fact that the Mirrored option is disabled and the Destination Address is My IP Address means that this filter list is designed to isolate the incoming traffic, but the specification of the TCP protocol and a port number means that the filter list isolates the traffic of a single application, not all Internet traffic.

   D. **Incorrect:** Because the Destination Address value is My IP Address and the Mirrored option is disabled, this filter list is designed to isolate only traffic inbound to the computer.

2. **Correct Answers: B and C**

   A. **Incorrect:** You can only assign a single IPSec policy in a particular Group Policy Object.

   B. **Correct:** You must create a new rule in the Secure Server (Require Security) policy to create an exception that allows the computers to transmit the packets generated by a particular application without IPSec protection.

   C. **Correct:** To specify that the traffic generated by a particular application be excluded from the protection provided by the Secure Server (Require Security) policy, you must create a filter list isolating that traffic.

   D. **Incorrect:** To modify the Secure Server (Require Security) policy so that it permits the transmission of a certain application's traffic without IPSec security, you must use a filter action configured with the Permit option, which disables all IPSec negotiation between the computers for the traffic specified by the associated filter list. However, because the Windows Server 2003 implementation of IPSec includes a Permit filter action by default, there is no need to create a new one.

3. Correct Answers: A and B

A. Correct: To protect data passing over a WAN connection when there are clients on the connected networks that do not support IPSec (such as Windows 98), you specify the use of tunnel mode when creating a rule for the IPSec policy. When you use tunnel mode, you must also specify the IP address of the tunnel endpoint, that is, the router connecting the local network to the WAN.

B. Correct: To configure IPSec to secure only the traffic generated by a particular application, you must create a filter list isolating that traffic.

C. Incorrect: Filter lists identify the types of traffic that IPSec will secure, but in the case of a tunnel mode policy, you specify the IP addresses of the routers when you configure the endpoints of the tunnel.

D. Incorrect: The Permit option allows the computer to transmit packets conforming to the filter list without any security negotiation or IPSec protection. You do not need a filter action using this option when you want to secure the traffic generated by an application.

4. Correct Answers: B and D

A. Incorrect: IPSec does not use the IP Authentication Header protocol with either of the two default filter action settings (Integrity Only and Integrity And Encryption). To configure IPSec to use AH, you must create custom filter action settings.

B. Correct: IPSec uses the IP Encapsulating Security Payload protocol for both default filter action settings (Integrity Only and Integrity And Encryption).

C. Incorrect: The ESP protocol uses the Triple-Data Encryption Standard (3DES) algorithm to encrypt data only. This algorithm is not needed when you select the Integrity Only option, because no encryption occurs.

D. Correct: ESP uses Secure Hash Algorithm 1 (SHA1) to provide data integrity and authentication when you select either the Integrity Only option or the Integrity And Encryption option.

Plan for Network Protocol Security

The data encapsulation method used by the protocols operating at the various layers of the **Open Systems Interconnection (OSI) reference model** requires that each layer be informed of the protocol operating at the next layer. For example, the network layer protocol header of a packet must specify what transport layer protocol generated the information inside the packet, and the transport layer protocol header must specify an application transport layer protocol. This method ensures that a receiving computer running more than one protocol at a particular layer knows where to send each packet as it travels up through the protocol stack.

The **Internet Protocol (IP)** has a Protocol field in its header that identifies the protocol that generated the information in the datagram. In most cases, the Protocol field specifies a transport layer protocol, such as the **Transmission Control Protocol (TCP)** or the **User Datagram Protocol (UDP)**, but it can also specify another network layer protocol, the **Internet Control Message Protocol (ICMP)**. In the same way, the TCP and UDP protocols have header fields called Source Port and Destination Port, which specify the application or service that generated and will receive the message in the packet. The transport layer protocols contain separate source and destination port numbers because the client and server parts of a particular application frequently use different port numbers.

The values that IP, TCP, and UDP use in the Protocol, Source Port, and Destination Port fields use numerical codes that are standardized by the **Internet Assigned Numbers Authority (IANA)** and published online in the IANA Port Numbers online database (this database replaces RFC 1700, "Assigned Numbers"). The protocol values are relatively few, and on TCP/IP systems, the value of the Protocol field in an IP packet is nearly always 6 (for TCP), 17 (for UDP), or 1 (for ICMP). Port numbers are much more numerous, because there are many applications registered with the IANA. There are two types of port numbers: well-known port numbers and ephemeral port numbers.

A **well-known port number** is a permanently assigned number representing a specific application or service. Most well-known port numbers represent the server side of a client/server application. Every TCP/IP system has a file called Services, which contains a list of the most commonly used well-known port numbers. Some of these well-known port numbers are shown in the following table:

Application	Abbreviation	Protocol	Port Number
File Transfer Protocol [Default Data]	ftp-default data	TCP	20
File Transfer Protocol [Control]	ftp-control	TCP	21
Telnet	telnet	TCP	23
Simple Mail Transfer Protocol	smtp	TCP	25
Domain Name System	domain	TCP/UDP	53
Dynamic Host Configuration Protocol (Server) Bootstrap Protocol Server (nondynamic)	dhcpsbootps	UDP	67
Dynamic Host Configuration Protocol (Client) Bootstrap Protocol Client (nondynamic)	dhcpcbootpc	UDP	68
World Wide Web HTTP	http	TCP	80
Post Office Protocol version 3	pop3	TCP	110
Simple Network Management Protocol	snmp	UDP	161
Simple Network Management Protocol Trap	snmp-trap	UDP	162

An **ephemeral port number** is chosen at random by a client when it initiates a transaction with a server. The numbers that clients use for their ephemeral ports are outside the range of values that the IANA uses for well-known port number assignments. The client uses the selected port number only for the duration of that transaction. This enables the client to open multiple connections with the same type of server and still differentiate the response messages from the server.

Protocol and port numbers provide the primary method that TCP/IP systems use to differentiate network traffic types for the purpose of packet filtering. The packet filtering mechanisms in both the Windows operating system's TCP/IP client and the Windows Server 2003 Routing and Remote Access service enable you to use protocol and port numbers to limit the traffic that can reach the computer. The filter lists in IPSec function in much the same way as packet filters, except that they use protocols and port numbers to specify which types of traffic IPSec should protect.

Objective 5.3 Questions

1.   Which of the following fields in an Internet Protocol (IP) header specifies the protocol that generated the information carried in the datagram?

   A. Protocol

   B. Source Port

   C. Destination Port

   D. Next Header

2.   Which of the following elements does not use code numbers assigned by the Internet Assigned Numbers Authority (IANA)?

   A. Protocol codes

   B. Well-known port numbers

   C. Ephemeral port numbers

   D. Ethertypes

3.   You are creating a new IPSec policy to encrypt the e-mail traffic on your network. The network has a Post Office Protocol, version 3 (POP3) server from which clients retrieve incoming mail and a Simple Mail Transfer Protocol (SMTP) server to which they send their outgoing mail. Which of the following well-known port numbers should you specify in the policy's filter list? (Choose all that apply.)

   A. 80

   B. 110

   C. 25

   D. 53

4. You are the administrator of a network that includes five Web servers, all located on a perimeter LAN in a locked data center, which is separated from the rest of the company network by a firewall. You want to be able to manage these servers by connecting with a Windows XP Telnet client on the company network, but you want to secure the Telnet traffic so that no one can capture the packets and read the passwords and other information inside. Which of the following tasks must you perform to make this possible? (Choose all that apply.)

A. Open up port number 23 on the firewall separating the perimeter LAN from the rest of the network.

B. Create a packet filter on the Web servers, blocking all traffic except that using port number 23.

C. Create a packet filter on the Telnet client workstation, allowing it to transmit traffic using port number 23.

D. Create an IPSec policy containing a filter list that specifies port number 23.

Objective 5.3 Answers

1. **Correct Answers: A**

    A. Correct: The Protocol field in the IP header contains a code that specifies the protocol that generated the information in the packet, usually Transmission Control Protocol (TCP), User Datagram Protocol (UDP), or Internet Control Message Protocol (ICMP).

    B. Incorrect: The Source Port field is found in the TCP and UDP headers, not in the IP header.

    C. Incorrect: The Destination Port field is found in the TCP and UDP headers, not in the IP header.

    D. Incorrect: The Next Header field is found in the IP Authentication Header (AH) and IP Encapsulating Security Payload (ESP) protocol headers, not in the IP header.

2. **Correct Answers: C**

    A. Incorrect: The IANA Port Numbers online database contains a list of the codes used in the Protocol field of the Internet Protocol (IP) header.

    B. Incorrect: The IANA Port Numbers online database contains a list of the well-known port numbers used in the Source Port and Destination Port fields of the Transmission Control Protocol (TCP) and User Datagram Protocol (UDP).

    C. Correct: Ephemeral port numbers are chosen at random by client computers, and therefore do not have to be registered with or documented by the IANA.

    D. Incorrect: The IANA Port Numbers online database contains a list of the Ether-type values used by data-link layer protocols to specify the network layer protocol that generated the information carried in the frame.

3. **Correct Answers: B and C**

    A. Incorrect: The Internet Assigned Numbers Authority (IANA) has assigned port number 80 to the World Wide Web HTTP protocol, not to POP3 or SMTP.

    B. Correct: The IANA has assigned port number 110 to Post Office Protocol, version 3.

    C. Correct: The IANA has assigned port number 25 to SMTP.

    D. Incorrect: The IANA has assigned port number 53 to the Domain Name System (DNS), not to POP3 or SMTP.

4.   Correct Answers: A and D

A. Correct: For the Telnet traffic to reach the Web servers from a workstation on the company network, you must configure the firewall to allow traffic using port number 23 (the well-known port for Telnet) to pass onto the perimeter network.

B. Incorrect: If you configure the Web servers to allow in only traffic using port number 23, the Web clients would be unable to connect to the servers using the World Wide Web HTTP, which uses port 80.

C. Incorrect: There is no need to create a packet filter permitting the workstation to transmit traffic using port number 23, because this port is open by default in Windows XP.

D. Correct: To encrypt the Telnet traffic exchanged by the workstation and the Web servers, you must create an IPSec policy that secures only the traffic using port number 23. To do this, you must create a filter list specifying that port number.

Plan Secure Network Administration Methods

Many of the administration tools included with Windows Server 2003 are capable of managing services on remote computers as well as on the local system. For example, most MMC snap-ins have this capability, enabling administrators to work with systems throughout the enterprise without traveling. These are specialized tools, however, that can perform only a limited number of tasks. For comprehensive administrative access to a remote computer, Windows Server 2003 includes two tools that are extremely useful to the network administrator, called Remote Assistance and Remote Desktop.

Remote Assistance enables a user at a distant location (such as technical support or help desk personnel) to connect to another user's computer and either view all the local user's activities or take over the system entirely. With Remote Assistance, users can request help from specific individuals (referred to as experts or helpers by the Windows Server 2003 software) and receive it on their own computers without requiring an expert to travel to a user's location. To use Remote Assistance, both computers involved must be running Windows XP Professional or Windows Server 2003, and the host computer must be configured to allow remote users to access the system.

Because an expert offering assistance to another user can perform virtually any activity on the remote computer that the local user can, this feature can conceivably be a security hazard. An unauthorized user who takes control of a computer using Remote Assistance can cause practically unlimited damage. However, the Remote Assistance feature is designed to minimize the dangers and includes features that enable administrators to regulate the remote assistance process. Some of these features are as follows:

- **Invitations**—To obtain remote assistance, a user must issue an invitation and send it to an expert using either e-mail or Microsoft Windows Messenger. An expert can also offer help to a user, but the user must accept it before the expert can connect. The local user also maintains control over the Remote Assistance connection. Even when the expert has the ability to perform tasks on the remote computer, the user can terminate the connection at any time.

- **Configuration**—By default, Windows XP and Windows Server 2003 have Remote Assistance turned off. Before users can send invitations for remote assistance, they must turn on the feature from the Remote tab of the System Properties dialog box. By clicking Advanced on this tab, users can also specify whether the connected expert can perform tasks on the user's computer or merely observe the user's activities, and can define the maximum amount of time that invitations remain open.

- **Group policies**—Rather than configure Remote Assistance on each computer individually, network administrators can use group policies to control the Remote Assistance settings throughout the network. In the Group Policy Object Editor console, the Computer Configuration\Administrative Templates\System\Remote Assistance folder contains two policies. The **Solicited Remote Assistance** policy controls whether users can issue Remote Assistance invitations; whether experts can view the client computer or perform tasks remotely; specifies the maximum ticket time; and specifies the method for sending invitations. The **Offer Remote Assistance** policy enables you to specify the names of users or groups that can function as experts and to specify whether those experts can perform tasks or just observe.

- **Firewalls**—Remote Assistance uses TCP port number 3389 for all its network communications. For networks that use Remote Assistance internally and are connected to the Internet, it is recommended that network administrators block this port in their firewalls to prevent users outside the network from taking control of computers requesting remote assistance. It is also possible to provide remote assistance over the Internet, which would require port 3389 to be left open.

Remote Desktop, a feature similar to Remote Assistance, is designed to give administrators access to a computer at a remote location. Remote Desktop For Administration is essentially an application of the **Terminal Services** service supplied with Windows Server 2003. A desktop version called Remote Desktop is included with Windows XP Professional. Windows Server 2003 allows up to two simultaneous remote desktop connections without the need for a separate license. Administrators can use Remote Desktop to manage computers that are at distant locations or are secured in a server closet or data center. Unlike Remote Assistance, Remote Desktop is designed to give a remote user complete control of a computer, with no interaction at the client end. There are no invitations and no read-only capabilities. When you connect to a system using Remote Desktop, you see a separate session on the host computer, independent of the console session. You must log on to the system in the normal manner, meaning that the remote user must have a user account and the appropriate permissions to access the host system. Windows Server 2003 and Windows XP Professional also include a Remote Desktop Connection client, which you can install on a computer running an earlier version of the Windows operating system.

Objective 5.4 Questions

1. You are a network administrator who has been instructed to create a Remote Assistance strategy that will enable help desk personnel to connect to computers on the company network to provide technical support to end users. The network uses Active Directory and consists of Windows XP Professional workstations and servers running Windows Server 2003. You have already created an organizational unit called Workstations, containing all the computer objects that represent the computers running Windows XP. The network is also connected to the Internet using a T-1 line. The goals of the project are to activate Remote Assistance on all the workstations without having to configure them individually and to prevent unauthorized users on the Internet from taking control of workstations on the company network. To achieve these goals, you decide to perform the following procedure:

   1. Create a security group in Active Directory called Remote Experts and add all the help desk operators to it.

   2. Enable the Solicited Remote Assistance policy in the GPO for the Workstations organizational unit.

   3. Enable the Offer Remote Assistance policy in the GPO for the Workstations organizational unit and add the Remote Experts group to the Helpers list.

How many of the stated goals does this procedure accomplish?

   A. The procedure accomplishes none of the stated goals.

   B. The procedure will successfully configure the workstations to use Remote Assistance, but it does not protect the workstations from unauthorized Internet connections.

   C. The procedure will successfully protect the workstations from unauthorized Internet connections, but it will not configure the workstations to use Remote Assistance.

   D. The procedure accomplishes both stated goals.

2. Which of the following procedures can prevent users on the local network from making unauthorized use of the Remote Assistance feature? (Choose all that apply.)

    A. Blocking TCP port 3389 in the network's Internet firewall.

    B. Specifying the names of authorized helpers in the Offered Remote Assistance policy for Default Domain Policy GPO.

    C. Leaving the Solicited Remote Assistance policy unconfigured in the Default Domain Policy GPO.

    D. Configuring the TCP/IP client on each workstation to filter out traffic using TCP port 3389.

3. You are a network administrator who wants to be able to manage a member server at a branch office using Remote Desktop For Administration. The server is running Windows Server 2003 and your workstation is running Windows 2000 Professional. You have not been given Administrator access to the server. Which of the following tasks must you perform before you can successfully connect to the server? (Choose all that apply.)

    A. Install the Remote Desktop Connection program on the server.

    B. Install the Remote Desktop Connection program on the workstation.

    C. Add your user object to the Remote Desktop Users local group on the server.

    D. Enable Remote Assistance in the System Properties dialog box on the server.

4. Which of the following operating systems is *not* capable of receiving remote assistance from an expert? (Choose all that apply.)

    A. Windows XP Home Edition

    B. Windows 2000 Server

    C. Windows XP Professional

    D. Windows 2000 Professional

    E. Windows Server 2003

Objective 5.4 Answers

1. **Correct Answers: D**

    A. Incorrect: Applying the two Remote Assistance policies in this way would successfully accomplish both stated goals.

    B. Incorrect: Applying the two Remote Assistance policies as specified here would enable Remote Assistance on all the workstations without needing to configure them individually, and specifying the authorized Helpers would prevent unauthorized access by Internet users.

    C. Incorrect: Applying the two Remote Assistance policies in this way would successfully enable Remote Assistance on all the network workstations.

    D. Correct: Applying the two Remote Assistance policies as specified here would enable Remote Assistance on all the workstations without needing to configure them individually, and specifying the authorized Helpers would prevent unauthorized access by Internet users.

2. **Correct Answers: B and D**

    A. Incorrect: Configuring the firewall to block TCP port 3389 would prevent users on the Internet from using Remote Assistance to connect to computers on the private network, but it would do nothing to prevent two computers on the private network from connecting to each other using Remote Assistance.

    B. Correct: By specifying the names of the users or groups that can function as experts in the Helpers list, you prevent others not on the list from connecting to a client using Remote Assistance.

    C. Incorrect: Leaving a policy unconfigured means that the GPO does not modify the local computer settings. Individual users would therefore be able to activate the Remote Assistance feature on their computers.

    D. Correct: All the network traffic generated by the Remote Assistance feature uses TCP port 3389. Using packet filtering to block that port would prevent users from establishing any Remote Assistance connections.

3. **Correct Answers: B and C**

    A. Incorrect: The Remote Desktop Connection program is a client that enables a computer running an earlier version of the Windows operating system to manage a computer running Windows XP or Windows Server 2003.

    B. Correct: Windows 2000 Professional does not include support for Remote Desktop. Therefore, you must install the Remote Desktop Connection client supplied with Windows XP and Windows Server 2003.

    C. Correct: When a user is not a member of the Administrators group on a computer to be managed with Remote Desktop, the user must be a member of the Remote Desktop Users local group on the computer.

    D. Incorrect: Remote Assistance is a separate feature that is not associated with and not required to use Remote Desktop.

4.   **Correct Answers: B and D**

    A. Incorrect: Windows XP Home Edition includes the Remote Assistance client.

    B. Correct: Windows 2000 Server does not include support for Remote Assistance.

    C. Incorrect: Windows XP Professional includes the Remote Assistance client.

    D. Correct: Windows 2000 Professional does not include support for Remote Assistance.

    E. Incorrect: Windows Server 2003 includes the Remote Assistance client.

Plan Security for Wireless Networks

Wireless networking has existed for many years, but it is only recently, with the publication of the 802.11 series of standards by the Institute of Electrical and Electronic Engineers (IEEE), that **wireless local area networking (WLAN)** technologies have become mainstream products. The 802.11b standard defines a WLAN technology running at speeds up to 11 megabits per second (Mbps). This was the first affordable wireless standard to provide performance comparable to that of a cabled LAN. The 802.11a and 802.11g standards provide wireless networking at greater speeds, up to 54 Mbps.

WLANs can use two topologies: ad hoc and infrastructure. An **ad hoc topology** consists of two or more computers equipped with wireless network interface adapters that communicate directly with each other. An **infrastructure topology** consists of wireless computers that communicate with an **access point**, which provides a connection to a standard cabled network. An access point is a WLAN transceiver that is also attached to the cabled network, using a standard Ethernet (or other data-link layer protocol) connection. Wireless systems in an infrastructure topology can communicate with each other, but they do so through the access point; they cannot communicate directly.

Because WLAN network interface adapters and access points transmit their network packets using radio signals, they present a significant natural security risk. WLAN signals are omnidirectional, extending to the specified range of the equipment. Any compatible device within transmission range can therefore transmit and receive the WLAN signals, enabling an unauthorized user to connect to the network or capture the packets transmitted by other users, compromising the data inside. Depending on the range of your equipment and where you locate your access points, unauthorized users might even be able to access your WLAN from outside the building, unless you take steps to protect the network.

To provide security for a wireless network, you must first create an environment in which users are authenticated and authorized before they are able to send data to and receive it from an access point. Authentication and authorization prevent unknown users from connecting to the wireless network, but they do not prevent eavesdroppers from capturing the data packets transmitted by wireless systems. To do this, you must configure the wireless devices to encrypt all the data they transmit. The most commonly used security mechanisms on WLANs are the following:

- **IEEE 802.11 authentication**—The 802.11 standard defines two types of authentication. **Open System authentication** is not really an authentication at all, but rather an exchange of messages between a wireless client and an access point that specifies the identity of the user. In **Shared Key authentication**, a wireless client verifies its identity to an access point by demonstrating its knowledge of a secret key that the access point shared with the client earlier using a secure channel. Shared key encryption is not a particularly secure system, because the access point shares the same key with all the wireless clients.

- **IEEE 802.1X authentication**—For authentication and authorization, Windows Server 2003 and Windows XP Service Pack 1 include a wireless client that is compliant with the IEEE 802.1X standard. IEEE 802.1X provides support for centralized user identification using a Remote Authentication Dial-In User Service (RADIUS) server, such as the Internet Authentication Service (IAS) included with Windows Server 2003. With this combination in place, the access points send the connection requests they receive from wireless clients to the RADIUS server, which authenticates them using an authentication protocol such as Extensible Authentication Protocol-Transport Level Security (EAP-TLS) or Protected EAP-Microsoft Challenge Handshake Authentication Protocol version 2 (PEAP-MS-CHAP v2), both of which are supported by ISA. The RADIUS server then uses remote access policies to authorize the authenticated clients. To use 802.1X on a network running the Windows operating system and using an infrastructure topology, your access points must support 802.1X and RADIUS authentication.

- **Wired Equivalent Privacy (WEP) encryption**—Included in the 802.11 standard, WEP encrypts the data transmitted on a wireless network using an encryption key that is either 40 or 104 bits long and an algorithm called RC4. When the authentication that precedes the encryption process uses EAP-TLS or PEAP-MS-CHAP v2, WEP is provided with strong cryptographic keys for each communications session, EAP-TLS using smart cards or digital certificates, and PEAP-MS-CHAP v2 using passwords only.

- **Wireless Network (IEEE 802.11) policies**—The Group Policy Object Editor console contains a subheading where you can create a policy that enables you to limit a computer's wireless networking capabilities. You can restrict computers to infrastructure or ad hoc networks, and also specify the networks to which the computer can connect.

Objective 5.5 Questions

1. Which of the following protocol standards defines the mechanism that Windows XP and Windows Server 2003 use to authenticate and authorize wireless network clients?

   A. IEEE 802.11a

   B. IEEE 802.11b

   C. IEEE 802.1X

   D. WEP

2. You are adding wireless network clients to your Ethernet network, in the form of laptop computers that will be deployed to the sales staff. To secure the wireless connections, you intend to use 802.1X and WEP. The laptops are also equipped with card readers, and you plan to issue smart cards to the salespeople. Which of the following authentication protocols must you use to support this security solution?

   A. PEAP-MS-CHAP v2

   B. RADIUS

   C. RC4

   D. EAP-TLS

3. You are a network consultant who has been called in to troubleshoot a wireless networking problem. The company has a large wireless presence, with multiple access points scattered throughout a building. The access points are located so as to provide an unbroken field of coverage throughout the building, but in practice this has proven not to be so. When a wireless computer moves out of the transmission range of its native access point, it moves into the range of another access point, but it cannot connect. No matter which access point the computer starts at, it cannot connect to any of the other access points on the network. Which of the following reasons could possibly explain why this is happening? (Choose all that apply.)

   A. The wireless devices are configured to use Shared Key authentication.

   B. The construction of the building is inhibiting the wireless transmissions.

   C. The Wireless Network (IEEE 802.11) policy does not have the correct entries in the Preferred Networks list.

   D. The wireless devices are configured to use certificates for authentication, and the certificates are configured incorrectly.

4.   You have recently installed a WLAN access point on your network and equipped a number of laptop computers with wireless network interface adapters. You want all the wireless clients to be able to connect only to the access point, but not directly to each other, so that your security infrastructure will remain in effect. Which of the following steps can you use to limit the clients' connectivity in this way?

A. Configure the wireless devices to use IEEE 802.1X and authenticate using the EAP-TLS protocol with smart cards.

B. Configure the wireless devices to use Open System authentication.

C. Create a Wireless Network (IEEE 802.11) policy, configure it to allow ad hoc networking only, and apply it to the computers.

D. Create a Wireless Network (IEEE 802.11) policy, configure it to allow infrastructure networking only, and apply it to the computers.

Objective 5.5 Answers

1. **Correct Answers: C**

   A. Incorrect: The IEEE 802.11a standard defines a physical layer implementation that transmits signals at 5 gigahertz (GHz) and sends data at up to 54 Mbps using Orthogonal Frequency Division Multiplexing (OFDM). IEEE 802.11a is not used to authenticate and authorize wireless clients.

   B. Incorrect: The IEEE 802.11b standard defines a physical layer implementation that transmits signals at 2.4 GHz and sends data at up to 11 Mbps using direct sequence spread spectrum modulation. IEEE 802.11b is not used to authenticate and authorize wireless clients.

   C. Correct: IEEE 802.1X is a standard for authentication for wired Ethernet networks and wireless 802.11 networks. Windows XP and Windows Server 2003 can use IEEE 802.1X in conjunction with a RADIUS server to authenticate wireless clients using any one of several authentication protocols, including EAP-TLS and PEAP-MS-CHAP v2.

   D. Incorrect: Wired Equivalent Privacy (WEP), part of the IEEE 802.11 standard, defines the encryption that WLAN systems use to secure their transmissions. WEP is not used for authentication and authorization.

2. **Correct Answers: D**

   A. Incorrect: Protected Extensible Authentication Protocol-Microsoft-Challenge Handshake Authentication Protocol version 2 (PEAP-MS-CHAP v2) is an authentication protocol for wireless networks that do not have access to a public key infrastructure (PKI). Without a PKI, the network cannot use certificates, and without certificates, the network cannot use smart cards for authentication.

   B. Incorrect: Remote Authentication Dial-In User Service (RADIUS) is not an authentication protocol; it is a service that provides centralized authentication for other servers on the network, using any one of several authentication protocols.

   C. Incorrect: RC4 is not an authentication protocol; it is an encryption algorithm that wireless systems use as part of their WEP implementations.

   D. Correct: Extensible Authentication Protocol-Transport Level Security (EAP-TLS) is the only authentication protocol supported by Windows Server 2003 that enables users to authenticate with smart cards.

3. **Correct Answers: A and C**

   A. **Correct:** When you use Shared Key authentication, each client's network key is unique to its initial access point. Connecting to other access points requires a different key, which is one possible explanation for the clients' failure to connect to multiple access points.

   B. **Incorrect:** Environmental factors, including the construction of the building, can affect wireless transmission ranges, but the effect would not be as consistent as it is in this case. The fact that each computer can successfully connect to its initial access point, but not to any other access points, indicates that the source of the problem lies elsewhere.

   C. **Correct:** If the network administrator has created a Wireless Network (IEEE 802.11) policy that specifies only the native access point in the Preferred Networks list, the clients cannot connect to the other networks using different access points.

   D. **Incorrect:** If the certificates were configured incorrectly, the computers would not be able to authenticate themselves to any wireless network.

4. **Correct Answers: D**

   A. **Incorrect:** The authentication mechanism you use does not affect which topology the computers are able to use. In this case, the client must use a smart card for authentication to the infrastructure network, but it can still connect to the other wireless computers on an ad hoc basis.

   B. **Incorrect:** The authentication mechanism you use does not affect which topology the computers are able to use. Despite the use of Open System authentication, the client can still connect to the other wireless computers on an ad hoc basis.

   C. **Incorrect:** An ad hoc network is one in which wireless computers communicate directly with each other, which is precisely what you are trying to avoid in this case.

   D. **Correct:** When you create a Wireless Network (IEEE 802.11) policy, you can limit the computers receiving the policy to ad hoc or infrastructure networking. By limiting the computers to infrastructure networking, you prevent them from communicating directly with each other.

Plan Security for Data Transmission

Windows Server 2003 and Windows XP Professional include three default IPSec policies, which are as follows:

- **Client (Respond Only)** Configures the computer to use IPSec only when another computer requests its use. The computer using this policy never initiates an IPSec negotiation; it only responds to requests from other computers for secured communications.

- **Secure Server (Require Security)** Configures the computer to require IPSec security for all communications. If the computer attempts to communicate with another computer and discovers that the second computer does not support IPSec, the computer terminates the connection.

- **Server (Request Security)** Configures the computer to request the use of IPSec when communicating with another computer. If the other computer supports IPSec, the IPSec negotiation begins. If the other computer does not support IPSec, the systems establish a standard, unsecured IP connection.

The default IPSec policies included with Windows Server 2003 define security specifications for client and server roles that might not be appropriate for your network installation. Although a computer is not running a server operating system, the computer may actually be functioning as a server. The Client (Respond Only) IPSec policy enables computers to use IPSec in response to another computer that requests it, but they cannot initiate IPSec communications themselves. When implementing IPSec on your network, you must first examine the traffic patterns and the roles of your computers to determine which computers communicate with each other and for what reasons. Then, you either assign the default IPSec policies based on this communications analysis or create IPSec policies that are better suited to your network's security requirements.

Objective 5.6 Questions

1. You are a network administrator who has recently implemented IPSec on your network, which consists of servers running Windows Server 2003 and client workstations running Windows XP Professional. You have created separate organizational units in Active Directory for the servers and the workstations, and assigned the Secure Server (Require Security) IPSec policy to the Servers organizational unit and the Client (Respond Only) policy to the Workstations organizational unit. On examining the network traffic with a protocol analyzer, you notice that the users on some workstations are sharing files with each other directly without first copying the files to a server, and that none of this traffic is being protected by IPSec. Which of the following steps can you take to secure the communications between the clients as well as the communications between clients and servers? (Choose all that apply.)

A. Configure the Workstations organizational unit to use the Secure Server (Require Security) IPSec policy instead of the Client (Respond Only) policy.

B. Modify the default response rule in the Clients (Respond Only) IPSec policy to include the IP addresses of the workstations.

C. Modify the filter list in the Secure Server (Require Security) IPSec policy to include the IP addresses of the workstations.

D. Move the computer objects from the Workstations organizational unit to the Servers organizational unit.

2. Which of the following types of traffic is *not* secured by the default Secure Server (Require Security) IPSec policy?

A. TCP

B. UDP

C. ICMP

D. IP

3. You are the administrator of a network that has a number of servers running Windows Server 2003 that host a variety of data file types, some of which contain classified information needed by specific company officers and many of which do not. You have already stored the classified documents in directories that are protected using the Encrypting File System, but you also want to ensure their protection when they are transmitted over the network. You have decided to implement IPSec on the network for this purpose, but your testing has determined that encrypting all the network traffic causes a severe degradation in server performance, and there is no money in the budget for server upgrades at this time. Which of the following IPSec solutions will enable you to protect the sensitive files without encrypting all your network traffic?

A. Configure the servers to use the Secure Server (Require Security) IPSec policy, the company officers' computers to use the Server (Request Security) policy, and the other users' computers to use the Client (Respond Only) policy.

B. Configure the servers to use the Server (Request Security) IPSec policy and the company officers' computers to use the Secure Server (Require Security) policy.

C. Configure the servers to use the Secure Server (Require Security) IPSec policy and the company officers' computers to use the Client (Respond Only) policy.

D. Configure the servers and the company officers' computers to use the Client (Respond Only) IPSec policy.

Objective 5.6 Answers

1.   Correct Answers: A and D

A. Correct: Configuring the Workstations organizational unit to use the Secure Server (Require Security) policy instead of the client (Respond Only) policy would ensure that all communications between the client workstations are secured.

B. Incorrect: The default response rule in an IPSec policy uses a dynamic filter list that you cannot modify.

C. Incorrect: Modifying the Secure Server (Require Security) policy would have no effect on the client workstations when they are communicating with each other, because the workstations are using the Client (Respond Only) policy.

D. Correct: Moving the workstations' computer objects to the Servers organizational unit would cause them to use the Secure Server (Require Security) policy instead of the Client (Respond Only) policy, causing all workstation traffic to be protected by IPSec.

2.   Correct Answers: C

A. Incorrect: The Secure Server (Require Security) policy protects all IP traffic, which includes TCP traffic, because TCP messages are carried in IP datagrams.

B. Incorrect: The Secure Server (Require Security) policy protects all IP traffic, which includes UDP traffic, because UDP messages are carried in IP datagrams.

C. Correct: The Secure Server (Require Security) policy permits systems to transmit all ICMP traffic without any IPSec negotiation or protection.

D. Incorrect: The Secure Server (Require Security) policy protects all IP traffic.

3.   Correct Answers: B

A. Incorrect: Configuring the servers to use the Secure Server (Require Security) policy would cause them to encrypt all traffic, not just the traffic containing the sensitive information.

B. Correct: Configuring the servers to use the Server (Request Security) policy would cause them to initiate IPSec communications when the client computer supports IPSec. Configuring the company officers' computers to require IPSec communications ensures that all sensitive information will be encrypted.

C. Incorrect: Configuring the servers to use the Secure Server (Require Security) policy would cause them to encrypt all traffic, not just the traffic containing the sensitive information.

D. Incorrect: Configuring both the servers and the company officers' computers to use the Client (Respond Only) policy would result in no encryption at all, because the Client (Respond Only) policy never initiates IPSec negotiations.

Objective 5.7

Troubleshoot Security for Data Transmission

When network communications fail to occur because of IPSec problems, the most common cause of the difficulty is a mistake in the configuration of the IPSec components on one or both of the systems trying to communicate. This is particularly true when you create your own IPSec policies. For example, one of your computers might require IPSec for a particular port, while the other computer is not configured to use IPSec for that port. It is also possible for two computers to be configured to use IPSec for a particular type of traffic but have incompatible filter action settings, such as different authentication methods or encryption algorithms. This prevents the computers from negotiating a common IPSec configuration, and communications fail.

To determine if a policy mismatch is the cause of a communications problem, you should examine the Security logs in the Event Viewer console. The Security log should contain a warning message if the system attempted to perform an Internet Key Exchange (IKE) negotiation that failed. Windows Server 2003 also includes tools that you can use to monitor and troubleshoot IPSec and other policy-based security mechanisms, including the IPSec Security Monitor and Resultant Set of Policy (RSoP) snapins for Microsoft Management Console.

IP Security Monitor is a tool that you can use to view the currently active policy on any network computer, plus other detailed information, including IPSec statistics, filter details, security associations, and so on. When you open IP Security Monitor, the Active Policy folder specifies the policy that is currently in effect on the computer, where the policy is stored, and what Group Policy Object applied it. In some cases, you might discover that a policy mismatch is being caused by a computer that is running a different policy than you thought. If you have IPSec policies deployed by Group Policy Objects at different levels of the Active Directory tree, the IPSec policy that is closest to the computer object is the one that takes effect. For example, if you assign the Client (Respond Only) policy to your domain object and the Secure Server (Require Security) policy to an organizational unit, Secure Server (Require Security) will be the effective policy for the computers in that organizational unit.

If you have recently made changes to IPSec policies that you deploy using Group Policy Objects, it is possible that your computers have not yet received the new policy settings from a domain controller. You can use IP Security Monitor to examine the details of a computer's currently effective policy, such as the details of the IP filter lists. If you determine that the computer's policy settings are outdated, you can wait for the system to refresh its group policy settings or reboot the computer to force an update from the domain controller.

The Resultant Set of Policy (RSoP) snap-in is a more comprehensive tool than IP Security Monitor. You can use RSoP to view all the effective group policy settings for a computer or user, including the IPSec policies. To use RSoP, you must first load the snap-in into an MMC console, and then perform a query on a specific computer, specifying what information you want to gather. The result is a display containing the group policy settings the selected computer is using, similar to the display of the Group Policy Object Editor console.

When you expand the Windows Settings and Security Settings headers in RSoP and click the IP Security Policies On Local Computer heading, the details pane contains a list of the computer's assigned policies. The display specifies the Group Policy Object from which the computer received the policy (something the IP Security Monitor snap-in cannot do) and enables you to open a read-only Properties dialog box for the IPSec policy, so you can review its settings.

Objective 5.7 Questions

1.   You have recently taken over as network administrator for a company whose previous administrator departed suddenly, leaving no documentation for the network running Windows Server 2003. When you examine the Active Directory installation, you see a complex hierarchy of organizational unit objects, five layers deep in some cases. As you examine the organizational units, you notice that most of them have Group Policy Objects applied to them, creating complicated security policy inheritance relationships for the objects at the various levels. Which of the following tools can you use to view the currently effective security policies for a particular computer? (Choose all that apply.)

   A. Security Configuration And Analysis snap-in

   B. Microsoft Baseline Security Analyzer

   C. Resultant Set of Policy snap-in

   D. Security Templates

2.   Which of the following types of information is not displayed by the IP Security Monitor snap-in?

   A. The computer's currently active IPSec policy

   B. The amount of IPSec tunnel mode traffic sent and received by the computer

   C. The number of IPSec transmission failures the computer has experienced

   D. The Group Policy Object from which the computer received the currently effective IPSec policy

3.   Which of the following audit policies must you enable to capture information about IPSec events in the Windows Server 2003 Event Viewer console logs? (Choose all that apply.)

   A. Audit Logon Events

   B. Audit Policy Change

   C. Audit System Events

   D. Audit Account Management

Objective 5.7 Answers

1.   Correct Answers: A and C

   A. Correct: The Security Configuration And Analysis snap-in can compare a computer's current security policy settings with those in a specified security template and display the differences between them.

   B. Incorrect: Microsoft Baseline Security Analyzer examines a computer for common security lapses, such as improper passwords; it does not display the computer's currently effective security policies.

   C. Correct: The RSoP snap-in displays the currently effective policy settings for a computer, no matter how the system received them.

   D. Incorrect: The Security Templates console is only capable of displaying the security policy settings that have been saved to a template, not the policies that are actually in effect on a computer.

2.   Correct Answers: D

   A. Incorrect: The IP Security Monitor snap-in displays the IPSec policy that is currently active on the computer.

   B. Incorrect: The IP Security Monitor snap-in displays the amount of incoming and outgoing tunnel mode traffic in the Bytes Sent In Tunnels and Bytes Received In Tunnels counters in the Quick Mode\Statistics folder.

   C. Incorrect: The Main Mode\Statistics folder in the IP Security Monitor snap-in contains counters that display the number of transmission failures that have occurred.

   D. Correct: The IP Security Monitor snap-in cannot display the name of the Group Policy Object from which the computer received its currently effective IPSec policy. To display this information, you must use the Resultant Set of Policy snap-in.

3.   Correct Answers: A and B

   A. Correct: The Audit Logon Events policy causes Windows Server 2003 to capture events related to IPSec to the Event Viewer console logs.

   B. Correct: The Audit Policy Change policy causes Windows Server 2003 to capture events related to IPSec to the Event Viewer console logs.

   C. Incorrect: The Audit System events policy does not capture IPSec information to the Event Viewer logs.

   D. Incorrect: The Audit Account Management policy does not capture IPSec information to the Event Viewer logs.

19 Planning, Implementing, and Maintaining Security Infrastructure (6.0)

More than ever before, security is a major element of network administration. From the very first planning stages, you must consider how security concerns affect the hardware products you purchase, the software you install, and the network services you deploy. Microsoft Windows Server 2003 includes a robust collection of security features that you can use to protect your data in a variety of ways.

However, network infrastructure security is as much an administrative concern as a technological one. Proper security planning, implementation, and maintenance require input from representatives throughout the organization as well as from IT people. To create an effective security infrastructure, you must understand what resources need to be protected, what threatens these resources, and what steps you can take to provide protection.

Tested Skills and Suggested Practices

The skills that you need to successfully master the Planning, Implementing, and Maintaining Security Infrastructure objective domain on the 70-293 exam include:

- Configure Active Directory directory service for certificate publication.

  - ❏ Practice 1: Install Certificate Services on a computer running Windows Server 2003 and create an enterprise root certificate authority (CA).

  - ❏ Practice 2: Use the Certificates snap-in for Microsoft Management Console (MMC) to request certificates from an enterprise root CA.

- Plan a public key infrastructure (PKI) that uses Certificate Services.

  - ❏ Practice 1: Design a Windows Server 2003 PKI for a large multinational corporation, using a single root CA and enabling users in every branch office to obtain certificates automatically, from a local CA. All the corporation's internal users must be able to send and receive digitally signed and encrypted e-mail, and Internet users must be able to obtain digitally signed software from the company's World Wide Web servers. For each CA in the infrastructure, specify its type and its role in the PKI.

❑ Practice 2: Open the Certificate Templates snap-in in Microsoft Management Console, create a duplicate of the Administrator template, display the Properties dialog box for the new template and study the properties you can set.

■ Plan a framework for planning and implementing security.

❑ Practice 1: Make a list of resources that need protection in a typical corporation and specify what Windows Server 2003 features you could use to provide this protection.

❑ Practice 2: Make a list of the Windows Server 2003 tools you can use to monitor a network's security and, for each tool, indicate what types of threats it can detect.

■ Plan a security update infrastructure. Tools might include Microsoft Baseline Security Analyzer and Microsoft Windows Server Update Services (WSUS).

❑ Practice 1: Download the Microsoft Baseline Security Analyzer tool from the Microsoft Web site at *http://www.microsoft.com/technet/security/tools /mbsahome.msp* and use it to examine the security configuration of your computer.

❑ Practice 2: Examine the materials provided on the WSUS home page (*http: //www.microsoft.com/windowsserversystem/updateservices/default.mspx*) and make a list of the tasks that WSUS can perform, which network administrators would otherwise have to perform manually.

Further Reading

This section lists supplemental readings by objective. We recommend that you study these sources thoroughly before taking exam 70-293.

Objective 6.1 Review Lessons 1, 2, and 3 in Chapter 11, "Creating and Managing Digital Certificates."

Microsoft Corporation. "PKI Enhancements in Windows XP Professional and Windows Server 2003." This article is available on the Microsoft Web site at *http: //www.microsoft.com/technet/prodtechnol/winxppro/plan/pkienh.mspx*.

Objective 6.2 Review Lessons 1, 2, and 3 in Chapter 11, "Creating and Managing Digital Certificates."

Microsoft Corporation. "Designing a Public Key Infrastructure." This article is available on the Microsoft Web site at *http://technet2.microsoft.com/WindowsServer /en/Library/4b9e6078-6b7d-4cc1-a927-77c1eab7c1341033.mspx*.

Objective 6.3 Review Lesson 2 in Chapter 8, "Planning a Secure Baseline Installation."

Microsoft Corporation. *Securing Windows 2000 Server.* Review Chapter 2, "Defining the Security Landscape." Although written for the Microsoft Windows 2000 Server operating systems, this article discusses many concepts that are equally applicable to Windows Server 2003. This content is available on the Microsoft Web site at *http: //www.microsoft.com/technet/security/prodtech/windows2000/secwin2k/default .mspx.*

Objective 6.4   Review Lesson 1 in Chapter 13, "Designing a Security Infrastructure."

Microsoft Corporation. "Software Update Services Overview White Paper." This white paper is available on the Microsoft Web site at *http://www.microsoft.com /windowsserversystem/updateservices/evaluation/previous/susoverview.mspx.*

Objective 6.1

Configure Active Directory Directory Service for Certificate Publication

Windows Server 2003 Certificate Services is a flexible application that can provide many different types of certificates to clients both inside and outside an organization. For internal clients, the best practice is to publish and store certificates in the **Active Directory** database. Because of its replicated architecture, Active Directory is available to all clients at all times and easy to protect with regular backups.

To use Active Directory to publish and store certificates, you must configure Certificate Services to function as an **enterprise certification authority**. Enterprise CAs provide a number of advantages over the alternative, **stand-alone CAs**, including the following:

- **Active Directory storage**   When an enterprise CA issues certificates, it publishes them in the Active Directory database, where they are protected from accidental loss and are always available.

- **Auto-enrollment**   When an enterprise CA receives a certificate enrollment request from a client, it consults the information about the client stored in Active Directory and automatically determines whether to issue or deny the certificate. Stand-alone CAs, by contrast, store incoming requests in a queue, and an administrator must manually evaluate, then issue or deny, the certificates.

- **Certificate templates**   A certificate template contains the properties that a CA uses to create a particular type of certificate, including the provider of cryptographic services and the key length. Enterprise CAs can automatically enroll clients because they use certificate templates to obtain all the settings needed to create certificates. Stand-alone CAs cannot use templates, and therefore all the settings for certificates must be included in requests. To receive a certificate from an enterprise CA, a client must have the appropriate permissions for the template for the requested certificate type.

1. Which of the following conditions must a user on a Windows Server 2003 network meet to obtain an IPSec certificate from an enterprise CA? (Choose all that apply.)

    A. The user must have an account in Active Directory.

    B. The user must have access to the Certification Authority console.

    C. The user must have the Enroll permission for the IPSec certificate template.

    D. An administrator must manually process the user's certificate enrollment request.

2. You are a user on a network running Windows Server 2003 Active Directory with an enterprise CA, and you need a certificate to encrypt your data files using Encrypting File System (EFS). Which of the following procedures can you use to obtain the certificate?

    A. Open the Certificates snap-in in Microsoft Management Console and request a certificate from the CA.

    B. Display the Command Prompt window and use the Certutil.exe program to request a certificate from the CA.

    C. Open the Certificate Templates snap-in in Microsoft Management Console, select the Basic EFS template, and request a certificate.

    D. Open Microsoft Internet Explorer, connect to the Certificate Services Web Enrollment Support page on the CA, and generate a certificate request.

3. You are a network administrator for a company with an Active Directory network using servers running Windows Server 2003. The network's PKI consists of multiple enterprise CAs in various offices throughout the enterprise. After checking the security logs on the CAs at the branch offices, you discover that an unauthorized user gained access to the Administrator account and has compromised one of the CAs. As a result, you must make sure that no certificates issued by that CA are ever used again. Which of the following tools can you use to revoke the certificates issued by the CA? (Choose all that apply.)

    A. The Certificate Templates snap-in

    B. The Certificates snap-in

    C. Certutil.exe

    D. The Certification Authority console

4. You are designing a PKI for a small network installation. You want users to be able to obtain certificates for EFS, IPSec, and smart card logons immediately, with no administrative intervention. You have decided to deploy only one CA on the network. Which of the following CA types should you use?

   A. Enterprise root

   B. Enterprise subordinate

   C. Stand-alone root

   D. Stand-alone subordinate

Objective 6.1 Answers

1. **Correct Answers: A and C**

   A. Correct: Enterprise CAs are intended for internal users on Active Directory networks. Because an enterprise CA stores certificates in the Active Directory database and uses Active Directory information to decide whether to issue a certificate, a user must be an Active Directory client.

   B. Incorrect: Administrators use the Certification Authority console to manage CAs and the certificates they issue. Users do not require access to this tool.

   C. Correct: Enterprise CAs use certificate templates to create specific types of certificates, and for users to receive certificates from the CA, they must have the Enroll permission for the template representing the particular type of certificate they need.

   D. Incorrect: Enterprise CAs support auto-enrollment, which enables a CA to autonomously decide whether to issue or deny a certificate.

2. **Correct Answers: A**

   A. Correct: The Certificates snap-in enables users to view their certificates and to request certificates from an enterprise CA.

   B. Incorrect: The Certutil.exe program is a command-line alternative to the Certification Authority console that administrators use to manage a CA. Users do not employ the Certutil.exe program to request certificates.

   C. Incorrect: The Certificate Templates snap-in is a tool that PKI administrators use to create and configure certificate templates. Although the CA uses the templates to create certificates, users do not use this snap-in to request them.

   D. Incorrect: The Web Enrollment Support interface for Certificate Services enables users to request certificates from stand-alone CAs. Users on a network running enterprise CAs would have to use the Certificates snap-in to manually request certificates.

3. **Correct Answers: C and D**

   A. Incorrect: The Certificate Templates snap-in enables PKI administrators to create and manage certificate templates. You cannot use this tool to access, manage, or revoke the certificates that a CA creates using the templates.

   B. Incorrect: The Certificates snap-in enables users to view their certificates and request new certificates from an enterprise CA. Users cannot revoke their own certificates using this tool.

C. **Correct:** The Certutil.exe program is a command-line utility that can perform the same tasks as the Certification Authority console. To revoke a certificate using Certutil.exe, you use the Revoke parameter.

D. **Correct:** The Certification Authority console enables PKI administrators to manage the activities of a CA by viewing the certificates that it has created, processing certificate requests, and revoking certificates.

4.   Correct Answers: A

A. **Correct:** Enterprise CAs support auto-enrollment and are capable of issuing the specified certificate types. When deploying enterprise CAs, you must always create a root CA first.

B. **Incorrect:** Although an enterprise subordinate CA is capable of issuing the specified certificate types using auto-enrollment, you cannot create an enterprise subordinate CA without having an enterprise root CA first.

C. **Incorrect:** Stand-alone CAs do not support auto-enrollment and are not capable of issuing smart card logon certificates.

D. **Incorrect:** In addition to not supporting auto-enrollment or the required certificate types, a stand-alone subordinate CA cannot be created until a stand-alone root CA exists.

Plan a Public Key Infrastructure (PKI) That Uses Certificate Services

To implement a PKI using Windows Server 2003 Certificate Services, you must install at least one **certification authority (CA)**. For a relatively small organization, a single CA might be sufficient, but for larger organizations, or if you want to provide fault tolerance and load balancing for your CAs, you can create a hierarchy of certification authorities.

The correct type of CA is an essential part of an effective PKI design. Certificate Services supports two types of CA, which are as follows:

- **Enterprise CAs**   Enterprise CAs store their certificates, certificate revocation lists (CRLs), and other information in the Active Directory database. Because the CA's clients must have access to Active Directory, enterprise CAs are intended for an organization's internal users. Enterprise CAs also support auto-enrollment through the use of certificate templates, eliminating the need for administrators to manually issue or deny certificates.

- **Stand-alone CAs**   Stand-alone CAs store their certificates and other information as standard files on the computer's hard drive, and are therefore intended for users external to the enterprise, such as clients connecting to the company's Web servers. Stand-alone CAs do not support auto-enrollment and cannot use certificate templates, which means that the CA queues incoming certificate enrollment requests until an administrator decides whether the clients should receive the requested certificates.

For both enterprise and stand-alone CAs, you can elect to create either a **root CA** or a **subordinate CA**. The standard trust model for a PKI is called a **rooted hierarchy**. The root CA is at the top of the hierarchy and issues certificates to the subordinate CAs beneath it. These certificates grant the subordinate CAs the same degree of trustworthiness as the root CA. In large installations, the CA hierarchy consists of three layers, beginning with a root CA at the top. The second layer consists of subordinate CAs that represent different geographic locations or different types of certificates; these are also called **intermediate CAs**. The third layer consists of subordinate CAs that actually issue the end-user certificates to clients; these are called **issuing CAs**. Every certificate that an issuing CA supplies to a client contains a certificate chain leading up through the CA hierarchy to a root CA, confirming the trustworthiness of the certificate.

The process by which clients of the PKI request certificates from a CA is called **enrollment**. Enrollment can occur automatically, for example, when an application sends a certificate request to an enterprise CA and immediately receives a certificate in return, or manually, when a user explicitly requests a certificate from a CA. To send enrollment requests to an enterprise CA, you use the Certificates snap-in for Microsoft Management Console. To send enrollment requests to a stand-alone CA, you use the Web Enrollment Support interface provided with Windows Server 2003 Certificate Services.

A **smart card** is a portable data storage device, approximately the size of a credit card, that contains memory and, in some cases, an integrated circuit. Windows Server 2003 can use smart cards as authentication devices by storing a user's certificate and private key on the card. This enables users to log on to the network from any computer with their full privileges, as granted by the PKI. Because smart card logons are intended only for internal users with access to Active Directory, only enterprise CAs can issue smart card certificates.

Objective 6.2 Questions

1.   On a network using a PKI with a three-level rooted hierarchy, which of the following types of CAs issue smart card certificates to end users?

    A. Stand-alone root

    B. Stand-alone subordinate

    C. Enterprise root

    D. Enterprise subordinate

2.   You are a network consultant who has been hired to design a Windows Server 2003 PKI for a company with offices in different cities throughout the United States. The goals of the project, as specified by the client, are as follows:

    1. Provide encrypted and digitally signed e-mail communications for all company employees

    2. Provide key-based authentication for clients connecting to a company extranet from remote locations using the Internet

    3. Provide key-based authentication for roaming company employees accessing the company's wireless LAN using laptops

    4. Provide fault tolerance, so that the failure of a single CA anywhere in the enterprise cannot prevent users from requesting and receiving certificates

To address these goals, you design a PKI in the form of a rooted hierarchy, which consists of a single enterprise root CA located at the company's home office, and three enterprise subordinate CAs at each of the company's branch offices. At each branch, one of the three servers functions as an intermediate CA and the other two as issuing CAs.

Which of the following statements about this PKI design is true?

    A. This design satisfies all the goals specified by the client.

    B. This design satisfies all the goals specified by the client except number 2, because enterprise CAs cannot support external users.

    C. This design satisfies all the goals specified by the client except number 3, because Windows Server 2003 Certificate Services does not support certificates for wireless network authentication.

    D. This design satisfies all the goals specified by the client except number 4, because the use of a single root CA prevents the PKI from being fault tolerant.

3. You are a junior network administrator who has been given the task of setting up a workstation for the company's new CFO. All high-level officers of the company are required to encrypt all their network storage and communications using EFS, IPSec, and encrypted e-mail. The company runs a number of enterprise CAs to provide certificates for these purposes. After installing Microsoft Windows XP on the workstation, you determine that you must request a Basic EFS certificate for the new user, and to do so, you log on to the computer with the new user's account, open Internet Explorer, and connect to one of the CAs using the Web Enrollment Support interface. When you attempt to request a Basic EFS certificate, the Web interface informs you that the user does not have the permissions needed. Which of the following steps can you take to resolve this problem?

   A. Use the Certificates snap-in instead of the Web Enrollment Support interface to request the certificate.

   B. Log off the new user's account and log on as Administrator, then request the certificate again.

   C. Install a stand-alone CA on the network, because enterprise CAs do not support Basic EFS certificates.

   D. Use the Certificate Templates snap-in to grant the new user the Read and Autoenroll permissions for the Basic EFS template.

4. When a PKI uses a three-level rooted hierarchy with enterprise CAs, to what clients do intermediate CAs issue certificates?

   A. To the root CA

   B. To other intermediate CAs

   C. To issuing CAs

   D. To end users

Objective 6.2 Answers

1.   Correct Answers: D

A. Incorrect: Stand-alone root CAs cannot issue smart card logon certificates, because this type of CA does not use Active Directory, which is required for a smart card logon.

B. Incorrect: Stand-alone subordinate CAs cannot issue smart card logon certificates, because this type of CA does not use Active Directory, which is required for a smart card logon.

C. Incorrect: In a root hierarchy, enterprise root CAs only issue certificates to other CAs, not to end users.

D. Correct: The issuing CAs in a rooted hierarchy are always subordinate CAs, and because only enterprise CAs use Active Directory, they are the only ones that can issue smart card logons.

2.   Correct Answers: B

A. Incorrect: Although the design does satisfy three of the four goals, it does not satisfy goal number 2, because enterprise CAs cannot support external clients.

B. Correct: External users cannot obtain certificates from enterprise CAs because these users do not have access to Active Directory. Therefore, because this PKI design contains only enterprise CAs, it cannot support external users, as goal number 2 requires.

C. Incorrect: Windows Server 2003 Certificate Services is capable of issuing certificates for wireless network authentication, so the PKI design does satisfy goal number 3.

D. Incorrect: In a rooted hierarchy, the root CA only issues certificates to the subordinate CAs at the next lower level. Once it has done this, a failure of the root CA server would not prevent end users from requesting and receiving certificates.

3.   Correct Answers: D

A. Incorrect: When you are working with enterprise CAs, the Certificates snap-in provides the same basic functionality as the Web Enrollment Support interface. If the user lacks the permissions to obtain a certificate from the Web interface, a request from the Certificates snap-in would fail as well.

B. Incorrect: You must request the certificate with the new user's account for that user to be able to access and use the certificate in Active directory. Logging on as Administrator would request a certificate in the name of the Administrator account, which would be useless to the CFO.

C. Incorrect: Enterprise CAs do support Basic EFS certificates, as do stand-alone CAs.

D. Correct: For users to request certificates from an enterprise CA, they must have permission to use the templates corresponding to the certificates they need. Granting the new user account the Read and Autoenroll permissions for the Basic EFS template would make it possible for you to request and receive a certificate in the CFO's name.

4.   Correct Answers: C

A. Incorrect: CAs always issue certificates to entities that are below them in the PKI hierarchy. Therefore, an intermediate CA would never issue a certificate to a root CA, which is above it in the hierarchy.

B. Incorrect: In a rooted hierarchy, intermediate CAs always receive their certificates from root CAs, never from other intermediate CAs.

C. Correct: The function of an intermediate CA in a three-level rooted hierarchy is to issue certificates to the issuing CAs at the third level of the hierarchy. This provides the issuing CAs with a certificate chain that extends all the way up to the root CA.

D. Incorrect: In a rooted hierarchy, intermediate CAs are located at the second level, between the root CA and the issuing CAs. Intermediate CAs do not issue certificates to end users, only to the issuing CAs on the level directly below them.

Plan a Framework for Planning and Implementing Security

You must begin the security strategy for a data network long before you purchase or install any technology. Planning a security strategy for an enterprise network requires a framework of policies and procedures that dictate how your organization performs tasks such as the following:

- Estimating security risks

- Specifying security requirements

- Selecting security features

- Implementing security policies

- Designing security deployments

- Specifying security management policies

The creation of a security framework for a large organization requires input from people throughout the enterprise, not just IT personnel. The object of the security planning process is to answer questions such as the following:

- What are your organization's most valuable resources?

- What are the potential threats to your organization's resources?

- Which resources are most at risk?

- What are the consequences if specific resources are compromised?

- What security features are available to the organization?

- Which security features are best able to protect specific resources?

- How secure is secure enough?

- What is involved in implementing specific security features?

- What maintenance do the security features require?

- How will implementing specific security features affect users, administrators, and managers?

Creating a security framework is not a one-time project that ends when you have finished designing the initial security plan for your network. Security is an ongoing concern, and the responsibilities of the security design team are also ongoing. A security life cycle typically consists of three basic phases:

■ Designing a security infrastructure—The initial planning phase consists of evaluating the organization's resources and the threats to them, selecting the security features you intend to implement, and creating an implementation plan. Windows Server 2003 security features are based on security principles such as authentication, encryption, access control, firewalls, and auditing.

■ Implementing security features—Implementing the security features you have selected should include a phase of lab testing and a pilot deployment before you proceed with the full enterprise-wide implementation. At this time, you should also create security policies that govern the use of the security features and ways to ensure compliance with those policies.

■ Ongoing security management—Once your security features and policies are in place, the project is not over. You must also consider what maintenance your security framework requires. Many security features are designed to gather information about network processes, and administrators must monitor them regularly to determine if a security-related incident has occurred. Auditing, for example, is a major element of Windows Server 2003 security that requires the network administrator's constant vigilance. Security strategies also must evolve over time to deal with new threats and accommodate new capabilities. Your security framework should include policies and procedures for evaluating new security information and acting on it in an organized manner.

Objective 6.3 Questions

1. Which of the following phases are part of a properly planned implementation of a security feature? (Choose all that apply.)

    A. Pilot deployment

    B. Performance simulation

    C. Lab testing

    D. Enterprise deployment

2. You are a new network administrator for a financial firm running a large Windows Server 2003 network that is spread out among buildings all over the corporate campus. Your supervisor has assigned you the task of checking the auditing information gathered by all the domain controllers on the network on a daily basis, to make sure that their security has not been penetrated. There are 12 domain controllers on the network, located in eight different buildings. Which of the following procedures will enable you to accomplish your task?

    A. Travel to each domain controller every morning and examine the auditing keys in the Microsoft Windows registry.

    B. Access each domain controller from your own workstation every morning, using the C$ administrative share, and use Notepad to view the latest entries in the audit logs.

    C. Create an MMC console containing an instance of the Event Viewer snap-in for each domain controller and use it to examine the Security logs each morning.

    D. Open the Active Directory Users And Computers console on your workstation each morning and examine the auditing logs in each domain controller's computer object.

3. To protect the users on a network running Windows Server 2003 from having their data files intercepted during transmission, you have implemented IPSec on all the network's computers. Now you want to monitor the network to make sure that all the network transmissions are actually using IPSec. Which of the following Windows Server 2003 tools can you use to do this?

    A. Network Monitor

    B. IP Security Monitor

    C. System Monitor

    D. Performance Monitor

Objective 6.3 Answers

1.   Correct Answers: A, C, and D

   A. Correct: A pilot deployment is a limited implementation of a particular technology, using selected users on the live network. You should always perform a pilot deployment of a security feature before you proceed with a mass deployment on the entire network.

   B. Incorrect: A performance simulation is not part of a standard technology deployment. Instead of using simulations, it is preferable to test a technology on actual equipment under conditions as near to those of the real world as possible.

   C. Correct: Before implementing any new technology on a live network, you should always test it thoroughly in a lab environment first. A test lab is a network environment that is kept wholly separate from the organization's actual production network, and that is used to test specific network elements.

   D. Correct: The final stage of a technology implementation, after lab testing and the pilot deployment, is a full deployment throughout the enterprise.

2.   Correct Answers: C

   A. Incorrect: Auditing information is not stored in the Windows registry.

   B. Incorrect: Auditing information is not stored in a text file, so you cannot use Notepad to view it.

   C. Correct: Windows Server 2003 stores auditing information in the Security log, which you can access using the Event Viewer console. To simplify the process of monitoring the logs on multiple computers, you can create a custom MMC console containing multiple instances of the Event Viewer snap-in, each focused on a different computer.

   D. Incorrect: You cannot view auditing information in the Active Directory object for a particular computer.

3.   Correct Answers: B

   A. Incorrect: By using Network Monitor to capture packets and view their contents, you can tell when IPSec has encrypted the data within the packets. However, the version of Network Monitor included with Windows Server 2003 can only capture packets that the computer running the Network Monitor program has transmitted or received, so Network Monitor can't check whether IPSec has encrypted all network transmissions.

   B. Correct: The IP Security Monitor snap-in for MMC enables you to view the currently active IPSec policy on a computer and information such as whether computers are using a secure channel for their communications.

C. Incorrect: The System Monitor tool contains IPSec performance objects and can display statistics about IPSec operations, such as the total number of bytes sent and received using transport mode, but it cannot tell you whether all network transmissions are using IPSec.

D. Incorrect: The tool that is now called System Monitor in Windows Server 2003 was called Performance Monitor in Windows 2000. System Monitor is part of the Performance console, but there is no tool called Performance Monitor in Windows Server 2003.

Objective 6.4

Plan a Security Update Infrastructure

Security technologies are constantly changing, and network administrators must be vigilant to stay ahead of potential intruders who are continually developing new ways to exploit the weaknesses of other people's networks. Microsoft regularly releases updates and patches for its operating systems to address new security issues and eliminate potential hazards. To keep computers using Windows Server 2003 running securely, you must apply new service pack and hot fix releases as needed.

When you are administering a large network, applying security updates is far more complicated than it is on a single computer. Not only must you install each update on hundreds or thousands of systems, you must also test each release carefully beforehand to ensure that it does not cause a problem that could cost you a great deal of time and production.

When planning a security update infrastructure for a medium to large network, you must address a number of problems, including the following:

- Determining when updates are released—Microsoft frequently releases security updates that might or might not be applicable to the systems on your network. Network administrators must be aware of new releases when they occur, and of the specific issues each release addresses.

- Determining which computers need to be updated—In some cases, a new security update might apply only to computers performing a specific function or using a specific application or feature. Network administrators must understand each release's specific function and determine which of their computers require the update.

- Testing update releases on multiple system configurations—A security update that causes a malfunction might be just an annoyance on a single computer, but on a large network, it could be a catastrophe. Network administrators must perform their own tests of all security updates before deploying them on the entire network.

- Deploying update releases on large fleets—Manually installing security updates on hundreds or thousands of computers requires enormous amounts of time, effort, and expense. To deploy updates on a large network efficiently, the process must be automated.

There is a variety of tools that network administrators can use to address these problems. Some of these tools are as follows:

- Microsoft Baseline Security Analyzer (MBSA)—A graphical tool that can scan multiple computers running Microsoft Windows operating systems for common security misconfigurations, such as unsuitable passwords, important security updates that have not been installed, file system and account weaknesses, and insufficient auditing policies. MBSA is useful for determining what security updates systems need, but it cannot download or deploy the actual updates themselves.

- Microsoft Windows Server Update Services (WSUS) or Microsoft Software Update Services (SUS) —Server-based tools that enable network administrators to receive notifications when new security updates are available, download the updates, and then deploy them to the computers on the network. WSUS (or SUS) receives notification of critical updates so that administrators do not have to check for new releases. Administrators then download the updates to the server, where they remain offline (presumably while being tested) until the administrator chooses to deploy them. When it is time to deploy the updates to the network computers, WSUS (or SUS) provides a local Microsoft Update or Windows Update server, from which the other computers can download the updates without having to access the Internet.

Objective 6.4 Questions

1.   Which of the following functions is Microsoft Baseline Security Analyzer able to perform?

   A. Download security updates from the Internet

   B. Specify which security updates have not been installed on a computer

   C. Install security updates on computers that need them

   D. Identify users with non-expiring passwords

2.   You are a network security consultant under contract to a corporation with a 700-node network running Windows Server 2003 and Windows XP Professional. The computers on the network are in various states of configuration because their operating systems were installed by the different vendors who supplied them. Your job is to examine the security configuration of all the computers on the network and determine whether any of them constitute a security risk. Which of the following procedures can achieve this goal most efficiently?

   A. Install Microsoft Baseline Security Analyzer on each computer and scan it for possible security breaches.

   B. Install Microsoft Baseline Security Analyzer on one computer and use it to scan all the computers on the network.

   C. Install Microsoft Software Update Services on one computer and use it to deploy the latest security updates to all the other computers on the network.

   D. Install Windows Server Update Services on each computer and use it to download the latest security updates.

3.   Which of the following tools can inform you when new security updates are released, download them from the Internet, and then install them on your workstation?

   A. Windows Update

   B. Microsoft Baseline Security Analyzer

   C. Windows Server Update Services

   D. Security Configuration And Analysis snap-in

Objective 6.4 Answers

1.   Correct Answers: B and D

   A.   Incorrect: Microsoft Baseline Security Analyzer can scan computers for security breaches, such as missing security updates, but it cannot download the required updates from the Internet.

   B.   Correct: Microsoft Baseline Security Analyzer scans computers for security updates, compares the list of installed updates to a list of available updates, and displays the results.

   C.   Incorrect: Microsoft Baseline Security Analyzer can only diagnose security problems on computers; it cannot remedy them by installing missing security updates.

   D.   Correct: Microsoft Baseline Security Analyzer examines the user accounts on a computer and specifies the number of users with passwords that do not expire. Non-expiring passwords are a security hazard because the users are not compelled to change their passwords, increasing the risk that the passwords will eventually be compromised.

2.   Correct Answers: B

   A.   Incorrect: Although Microsoft Baseline Security Analyzer is the correct tool for this purpose, there is no need to install it on every computer, because a single copy of the program on one computer can scan an entire network for security hazards.

   B.   Correct: A copy of Microsoft Baseline Security Analyzer installed on a single computer can scan all the Windows operating systems on a network and analyze them for a variety of common security lapses.

   C.   Incorrect: Microsoft Software Update Services can notify you when security updates are released, and can download and install those releases, but it cannot scan a computer for security hazards.

   D.   Incorrect: Windows Server Update Services is designed to download security updates from the Internet and deploy them to an entire network, eliminating the need to perform a manual operation on each computer. There is, therefore, no need to install the program on every computer.

3.   Correct Answers: C

   A.   Incorrect: Windows Update is a Web page from which you can download and install security updates, but it does not notify you when new updates are released.

B. Incorrect: Microsoft Baseline Security Analyzer can examine a computer and list the security updates that have not been applied to it, but it cannot download or install those updates.

C. Correct: Windows Server Update Services is designed to inform administrators of new security update releases, download the new releases, and deploy them through the network.

D. Incorrect: Security Configuration And Analysis is a tool that can compare a computer's current security policy settings to those stored in a security template and display the results. You cannot use this tool to modify the computer's security configuration in any way, including installing new security updates.

Glossary

Numbers

10Base-T   Shorthand name for an Ethernet physical layer specification that uses unshielded twisted-pair (UTP) cables in a star topology. The "10" refers to the network's speed of 10 Mbps, the "base" refers to the network's baseband transmissions, and the "T" refers to the use of twisted-pair cable. The maximum cable segment length for a 10Base-T network is 100 meters.

100Base-FX   Shorthand name for a 100-Mbps Fast Ethernet physical layer specification, defined in the Institute of Electrical and Electronic Engineers (IEEE) 802.3u standard document, that uses 62.5/125 multimode fiber-optic cable in a star topology, with a maximum segment length of 412 meters at half duplex and 2,000 meters at full duplex.

100Base-TX   Shorthand name for a 100-Mbps Fast Ethernet physical layer specification, defined in the Institute of Electrical and Electronic Engineers (IEEE) 802.3u standard document, that uses Category 5 or better unshielded twisted-pair (UTP) cable in a star topology, with a maximum segment length of 100 meters. 100Base-TX achieves its high speed using only two pairs of the wires in the cable because the specification insists on the use of high-quality cable. 100Base-TX is the most popular Fast Ethernet specification.

1000Base-LX   Shorthand name for a 1000-Mbps gigabit Ethernet physical layer specification, defined in the Institute of Electrical and Electronic Engineers (IEEE) 802.3z standard document, that runs over either 9/125 single-mode fiber-optic cable, with a maximum segment length of 3 kilometers, or 50/125 or 62.5/125 multimode fiber-optic cable with a maximum segment length of 550 meters.

1000Base-SX   Shorthand name for a 1000-Mbps gigabit Ethernet physical layer specification, defined in the Institute of Electrical and Electronic Engineers (IEEE) 802.3z standard document, that runs over 50/125 multimode fiber-optic cable with a maximum segment length of 500 meters or 62.5/125 multimode fiber-optic cable with a maximum segment length of 220 meters.

1000Base-T   Shorthand name for a 1000-Mbps gigabit Ethernet network, defined in the Institute of Electrical and Electronic Engineers (IEEE) 802.3ab standard document, that uses Category 5 or 5E unshielded twisted-pair (UTP) cable in a star topology, with a maximum segment length of 100 meters.

5-4-3 rule   An Ethernet cabling guideline stating that an Ethernet local area network (LAN) can consist of up to five cable segments, connected by four repeaters, with up to three of those cable segments being mixing segments.

A

abstract syntax   The native format used by a computer to encode information generated by an application or process. The presentation layer of the Open Systems Interconnection (OSI) reference model receives data from the application in the system's abstract syntax and is responsible for converting it to a common transfer syntax understood by both communicating systems. *See also* transfer syntax.

access control list (ACL)   The mechanism for limiting access to certain items of information or certain controls based on users' identity and their membership in various predefined groups. Access control is typically used by system administrators to control user access to network resources such as servers, directories, and files and is typically implemented by granting permissions to users and groups for access to specific objects.

access permissions   Features that control access to shares in the Microsoft Windows Server 2003 family of operating systems. Permissions can be set for the following access levels: No Access—prevents access to the shared directory, its subdirectories, and its files; Read—allows viewing of file and subdirectory names, moving to a shared directory's subdirectory, viewing data in files, and running applications; Change—allows viewing of file and subdirectory names, moving to a shared directory's subdirectories, viewing data in files and running application files, adding files and subdirectories to a shared directory, changing data in files, and deleting subdirectories and files; Full Control—includes the same permissions as Change, plus changing permissions and taking ownership of the NTFS files and directories only.

access point   A hardware device, used on wireless local area networks (LANs) that use the infrastructure topology, that provides an interface between a cabled network and wireless devices. The access point is connected to a standard network using a cable and also has a transceiver enabling it to communicate with wireless computers and other devices. *See also* infrastructure topology.

account   *See* user account.

account lockout   A Windows Server 2003 security feature that locks a user account if a number of failed logon attempts occur within a specified amount of time, based on security policy lockout settings. After an account is locked, users cannot use it to log on.

ACL   *See* access control list (ACL).

Active Directory   The enterprise directory service included with the Windows Server 2003 operating system. The Active Directory service is a hierarchical directory service that consists of objects that represent users, computers, groups, and other network resources. The objects are arranged in a tree display that consists of hierarchical layers ranging upward from organizational units, to domains, to trees, and to forests. Objects are composed of attributes that contain information about the resource the object represents. When users log on to the network, their user names and passwords are authenticated against the Active Directory database by a computer that has been designated as a domain controller. This single logon can grant them access to resources anywhere on the network. *See also* directory service.

Active Directory Domains And Trusts console   An administrative tool that enables you to manage trust relationships between domains. These domains can be Microsoft Windows Server 2003 domains in the same forest, Windows Server 2003 domains in different forests, domains set up with operating systems earlier than Windows Server 2003, and even Kerberos v5 realms.

Active Directory Sites And Services console   An administrative tool that contains information about the physical structure of your network. Active Directory uses this information to determine how to replicate directory information and handle service requests.

Active Directory Users And Computers console   An administrative tool designed to perform day-to-day Active Directory administration tasks. These tasks include creating, deleting, modifying, moving, and setting permissions on objects stored in the directory. These objects include organizational units, users, contacts, groups, and computers.

ad hoc topology   A type of communication used on wireless local area networks (LANs) in which devices equipped with wireless network interface adapters communicate with each other at will. Compare with infrastructure topology.

Address Resolution Protocol (ARP)   A Transmission Control Procotol/Internet Protocol (TCP/IP) protocol used to resolve the Internet Protocol (IP) addresses of computers on a local area network (LAN) into the hardware (or media access control [MAC]) addresses needed to transmit data-link layer frames to them. Before transmitting an IP datagram, TCP/IP clients broadcast an ARP request message containing the IP address of the destination computer to the local network. The computer using that IP address must then respond with an ARP reply message containing its hardware address. With the information in the reply message, the computer can encapsulate the IP datagram in the appropriate data-link layer frame and transmit it to the destination system.

administrator   A person responsible for setting up and managing domain controllers, servers, and local computers, their services, user and group accounts, password and permission assignments, and for helping users with networking issues.

ADSL   *See* Asymmetrical Digital Subscriber Line (ADSL).

agent   A program that performs a background task for a user and reports to the user when the task is done or when some expected event has taken place.

AH   *See* IP Authentication Header (AH).

analog   Related to a continuously variable physical property, such as voltage, pressure, or rotation. An analog device can represent an infinite number of values within the range the device can handle. *See also* digital.

APIPA   *See* Automatic Private IP Addressing (APIPA).

application   A complete, self-contained set of computer instructions that you use to perform a specific task, such as word processing, accounting, or data management. An application is also called a program.

application layer   The top layer of the Open Systems Interconnection (OSI) reference model, which provides the entrance point used by applications to access the networking protocol stack. Some of the protocols operating at the application layer include the Hypertext Transfer Protocol (HTTP), the Simple Mail Transfer Protocol (SMTP), the Dynamic Host Configuration Protocol (DHCP), the File Transfer Protocol (FTP), and the Simple Network Management Protocol (SNMP).

application programming interface (API)   A set of routines that an application program uses to request and carry out lower level services performed by the operating system.

ARP   *See* Address Resolution Protocol (ARP).

ARPANET (Advanced Research Projects Agency Network)   A pioneering wide area network (WAN) commissioned by the Department of Defense, ARPANET was designed to facilitate the exchange of information between universities and other research organizations. ARPANET, which became operational in the 1960s, is the network from which the Internet evolved.

ARP.EXE   A command-line utility provided by the Transmission Control Protocol/Internet Protocol (TCP/IP) client included with the Microsoft Windows operating systems, which enables you to display and manipulate the information stored in the cache created by the Address Resolution Protocol (ARP). By preloading the ARP cache, you can save time and network traffic by eliminating the ARP transaction of resolving an IP address into a hardware address that the TCP/IP client for every system it transmits to. *See also* Address Resolution Protocol (ARP).

ASCII (American Standard Code for Information Interchange)   A coding scheme that assigns numeric values to letters, numbers, punctuation marks, and certain other characters. By standardizing the values used for these characters, ASCII enables computers and computer programs to exchange information.

ASR   *See* Automated System Recovery (ASR).

Asymmetrical Digital Subscriber Line (ADSL)   A point-to-point, digital wide area network (WAN) technology that uses standard telephone lines to provide consumers with high-speed Internet access, remote local area network (LAN) access, and other services. The term asymmetrical refers to the fact that the service provides a higher transmission rate for downstream than for upstream traffic. Downstream transmission rates can be up to 8.448 Mbps, whereas upstream rates range up to 640 Kbps. *See also* Digital Subscriber Line (DSL).

asynchronous transmission A form of data transmission in which information is sent one character at a time, with variable time intervals between characters. Asynchronous transmission does not rely on a shared timer that allows the sending and receiving units to separate characters by specific time periods. Therefore, each transmitted character consists of a number of data bits (which compose the character itself), preceded by a start bit and ending in an optional parity bit followed by a 1-stop, 1.5-stop, or 2-stop bit.

attenuation The tendency of a signal to weaken in strength as it travels along a medium. Different types of network media have different attenuation rates, which is one of the main factors contributing to their respective distance limitations.

attribute A unit of information that makes up an object in a directory service such as Active Directory.

auditing A process that tracks network activities by user accounts, and a routine element of network security. Auditing can produce records of list users who have accessed—or attempted to access—specific resources; help administrators identify unauthorized activity; and track activities such as logon attempts, connection and disconnection from designated resources, changes made to files and directories, server events and modifications, password changes, and logon parameter changes.

authentication Verification typically based on user name, password, and time and account restrictions.

authoritative server A Domain Name System (DNS) server that has been designated as the definitive source of information about the computers in a particular domain. When resolving a computer's DNS name into its Internet Protocol (IP) address, DNS servers consult the authoritative server for the domain in which that computer is located. Whatever information the authoritative server provides about that domain is understood by all DNS servers to be correct. *See also* Domain Name System (DNS).

authorization A process that verifies that the user has the correct rights or permissions to access a resource.

autochanger A hardware device consisting of one or more backup drives, a media array, and a robotic mechanism that inserts media into and removes it from the drives. Used to perform automated backups of large amounts of data.

autoenrollment The process by which a computer automatically requests and receives a digital certificate from a certification authority, with no manual interaction from the user.

Automated System Recovery (ASR)   A feature that helps to recover a system that won't start. It backs up only the operating system partition; you must back up other partitions using Backup or other means.

automatic allocation   An operational mode of Dynamic Host Configuration Protocol (DHCP) servers in which the server permanently assigns an Internet Protocol (IP) address and other Transmission Control Protocol/Internet Protocol (TCP/IP) configuration settings to a client from a pool of addresses. Compare with dynamic allocation, which assigns addresses in the same way but reclaims them when a lease of a given duration expires, and manual allocation, which permanently assigns specific addresses to clients. *See also* Dynamic Host Configuration Protocol (DHCP).

Automatic Private IP Addressing (APIPA)   A Transmission Control Protocol/ Internet Protocol (TCP/IP) feature in Microsoft Windows 2000 and later versions that automatically configures a unique IP address from the range of 169.254.0.1 through 169.254.255.254 and a subnet mask of 255.255.0.0 when the protocol is configured for dynamic addressing and a Dynamic Host Configuration Protocol (DHCP) server is not available.

AXFR   *See* full zone transfer (AXFR).

B

backbone network   A network that connects a series of other networks, using routers to relay traffic between them.

bandwidth   In communications, the difference between the highest and lowest frequencies in a given range. For example, a telephone accommodates a bandwidth of 3000 Hz, or the difference between the lowest (300 Hz) and highest (3300 Hz) frequencies it can carry. In computer networks, greater bandwidth indicates faster or greater data-transfer capability.

Bandwidth Allocation Protocol (BAP)   A Point-to-Point Protocol (PPP) control protocol that is used on a multiprocessing connection to dynamically add and remove links.

BAP   *See* Bandwidth Allocation Protocol (BAP).

basic service area (BSA)   The operational range of a group of wireless networking devices.

basic service set (BSS)   A group of wireless networking devices within operational range of each other.

bind   To associate two pieces of information with one another.

bit   Short for binary digit: either 1 or 0 in the binary number system. In processing and storage, a bit is the smallest unit of information handled by a computer. It is represented physically by an element such as a single pulse sent through a circuit or small spot on a magnetic disk capable of storing either a 1 or 0. Eight bits make a byte.

bits per second (bps)   A measure of the speed at which a device can transfer data.

BOOTP   *See* Bootstrap Protocol (BOOTP).

Bootstrap Protocol (BOOTP)   A server application that can supply client computers with Internet Protocol (IP) addresses, other Transmission Control Protocol/ Internet Protocol (TCP/IP) configuration parameters, and executable boot files. As the progenitor to the Dynamic Host Configuration Protocol (DHCP), BOOTP provides the same basic functions, except that it does not allocate IP addresses from a pool and reclaim them after a specified length of time. Administrators must supply the IP address and other settings for each computer to be configured by the BOOTP server. *See also* Dynamic Host Configuration Protocol (DHCP).

bottleneck   The limiting factor when analyzing performance of a system or network. Poor performance results when a device uses noticeably more CPU time than it should, consumes too much of a resource, or lacks the capacity to handle the load. Potential bottlenecks can be found in the CPU, memory, network interface adapter, and other components.

bounded media   A type of network medium in which the signals are confined to a restricted space, such as the inside of a cable. Compare with unbounded media.

bps   *See* bits per second (bps).

broadcast   A message transmitted to all the other computers on the local network. Data-link layer protocols have special addresses designated as broadcast addresses, which means that every computer that receives the message will read it into memory and process it. Local area networks (LANs) use broadcasts for a variety of tasks, such as to discover information about other computers on the network.

broadcast domain   A group of computers connected in such a way that if one computer transmits a broadcast message, all the other computers will receive it.

BSA   *See* basic service area (BSA).

BSS   *See* basic service set (BSS).

byte   A unit of information consisting of eight bits. In computer processing or storage, a byte is equivalent to a single character, such as a letter, numeral, or punctuation mark. Because a byte represents only a small amount of information, amounts of computer memory are usually given in kilobytes (1,024 bytes or 2 raised to the 10th power), megabytes (1,048,576 bytes or 2 raised to the 20th power), gigabytes (1,024 megabytes), terabytes (1,024 gigabytes), petabytes (1,024 terabytes), or exabytes (1,024 petabytes).

C

CA   *See* certification authority (CA).

cache   For Domain Name System (DNS) and Windows Internet Name Service (WINS), a local information store of resource records for recently resolved names of remote hosts. Typically, the cache is built dynamically as the computer queries and resolves names. It also helps optimize the time required to resolve queried names.

Carrier Sense Multiple Access with Collision Detection (CSMA/CD)   The Media Access Control (MAC) mechanism used by Ethernet networks to regulate access to the network. Before they can transmit data, CSMA/CD systems listen to the network to determine if it is in use. If the network is free, the system transmits its data. However, sometimes another computer transmits at precisely the same time, causing a signal quality error or collision. Collisions are normal occurrences on Ethernet networks, and network interface adapters are capable of detecting them and compensating for them by discarding the collided packets and retransmitting them in a controlled manner.

certificate   A collection of data used for authentication and secure exchange of information on nonsecured networks, such as the Internet. A certificate securely binds a public key to the entity that holds the corresponding private key. Certificates are digitally signed by the issuing certification authority (CA) and can be managed for a user, computer, or service. The most widely accepted format for certificates is defined by the Telecommunication Standards Section of the International Telecommunications Union (ITU-T) X.509 international standard.

certificate revocation list (CRL)   A list of certificates that have been revoked, rendering them unusable. Certification authorities publish their CRLs at regular intervals, so that authenticating systems can check the validity of certificates.

Certificate Services   A Microsoft Windows Server 2003 service that enables the computer to act as a certification authority that issues, renews, manages, and revokes digital certificates for an organization. Digital certificates have many uses including secure e-mail, Web-based authentication, and smart card authentication.

certification authority (CA)   An entity responsible for establishing the authenticity of public keys belonging to users or other CAs. Activities of a CA can include binding public keys to distinguished names through signed certificates, managing certificate serial numbers, and revoking certificates.

Challenge Handshake Authentication Protocol (CHAP)   A challenge-response authentication protocol for Point-to-Point Protocol (PPP) connections. It uses the Message Digest 5 (MD5) hashing algorithm to hash the combination of a challenge string issued by the authentication server and the user's password in the response.

channel service unit/data service unit (CSU/DSU)   A hardware device at either end of a leased telephone line that provides the connection to the network.

CHAP   *See* Challenge Handshake Authentication Protocol (CHAP).

child domain   For a Domain Name System (DNS), a domain located in the name space tree directly beneath another directory name (the parent domain). For example, sales.microsoft.com would be a child domain of the microsoft.com parent domain. A child domain is also called a subdomain.

CIR   *See* committed information rate (CIR).

client   A program designed to communicate with a server program on another computer, usually to request and receive information. The client provides the interface with which the user can view and manipulate the server data. A client can be a module in an operating system, which enables the user to access resources on the network's other computers, or a separate application, such as a World Wide Web browser or e-mail reader.

client/server networking   A computing model in which data processing tasks are distributed between clients, which request, display, and manipulate information, and servers, which supply and store information. When each client is responsible for displaying and manipulating its own data, the server is relieved of a large part of the processing burden. The alternative is a mainframe or minicomputer system in which one computer performs all the processing for all the users, who work with terminals that do not have processors (dumb terminals).

clustering   A group of two or more servers functioning as a single entity, to provide fault tolerance and load balancing to applications.

collision   In local area networking, a condition that occurs when two computers transmit data at precisely the same time and their signals occupy the same cable, causing data loss. On some types of networks, such as Ethernet, collisions are a normal occurrence, whereas on Token Ring networks, they are an indication of a serious problem. Also called a signal quality error.

collision domain   A group of computers connected in such a way that if any two transmit a message at exactly the same time, a collision occurs.

COM+   *See* Component Object Model (COM+).

command   A word or phrase, usually found on a menu, that you click to carry out an action. You click a command on a menu or type a command at the command prompt. You can also type a command in the Run dialog box, which you open from the Start menu by clicking Run.

Command Prompt window   A window that appears on the Microsoft Windows desktop, used to interface with the operating system's command line.

committed information rate (CIR)   In a frame relay connection, the base data transmission rate agreed upon by the client and the service provider. Frame relay connections can exceed the CIR to a certain degree during periods of heavy traffic.

Component Object Model (COM+)   An object-based programming model that allows two or more applications or components to easily cooperate with one another, even if the applications or components are written by different vendors.

computer account   An account that is created by a domain administrator and that uniquely identifies the computer on the domain. The Microsoft Windows Server 2003 computer account matches the name of the computer joining the domain.

connectionless   A type of protocol that transmits messages to a destination without first establishing a connection with the destination system. Connectionless protocols have very little overhead and are used primarily for transactions that consist of a single request and reply. The Internet Protocol (IP) and the User Datagram Protocol (UDP) are both connectionless protocols.

connection-oriented   A type of protocol that transmits a series of messages to a destination to establish a connection before sending any application data. Establishing the connection ensures that the destination system is active and ready to receive data. Connection-oriented protocols are typically used to send large amounts of data, such as entire files, which must be split into multiple packets and which are useless unless every packet arrives at the destination without error. The Transmission Control Protocol (TCP) is a connection-oriented protocol.

console   A collection of administrative tools.

console tree   The left pane in a Microsoft Management Console (MMC) display, which lists the items in the console. By default, the console tree appears in the left pane of a console window, but it can be hidden. The items in the console tree and their hierarchical organization determine the capabilities of a console. Also called the *scope pane*.

contention   Competition among stations on a network for the opportunity to use a communication line or network resource. Two or more computers attempt to transmit over the same cable at the same time, causing a collision on the cable. This kind of system needs regulation to eliminate data collisions that can destroy data and bring network traffic to a halt. *See also* Carrier Sense Multiple Access with Collision Detection (CSMA/CD).

convergence   1. The process by which dynamic routers update their routing tables to reflect the current state of the internetwork. The primary advantage of dynamic routing is that it enables routers to modify their routing information automatically as the configuration of the network changes. For example, should a router malfunction, the nearby routers, after failing to receive regular updates from it, will eventually remove it from their routing tables, thus preventing computers on the network from using that router. The elapsed time between the failure of the router and its removal from the other routers' routing tables is the convergence period. 2. In clustering, the process by which cluster servers recalculate their traffic distribution algorithm to compensate for a missing server.

counter log   Collects performance counter data in a comma-separated or tab-separated format for easy import to spreadsheet programs. You can view logged counter data using System Monitor or by exporting the data to spreadsheet programs or databases for analysis and report generation.

counters   The individual system attributes or processes monitored by the Performance console in Microsoft Windows Server 2003.

CRC   *See* cyclical redundancy check (CRC).

CRL   *See* certificate revocation list (CRL).

cryptography   The processes, art, and science of keeping messages and data secure. Cryptography is used to enable and ensure confidentiality, data integrity, authentication (entity and data origin), and nonrepudiation.

CSMA/CD   *See* Carrier Sense Multiple Access with Collision Detection (CSMA/CD).

CSU/DSU   *See* channel service unit/data service unit (CSU/DSU).

cyclical redundancy check (CRC)   An error detection mechanism in which a computer performs a calculation on a data sample with a specific algorithm, and then transmits the data and the results of the calculation to another computer. The receiving computer then performs the same calculation and compares its results to those supplied by the sender. If the results match, the data has been transmitted successfully. If the results do not match, the data has been damaged in transit.

D

daemon   UNIX term for a computer program or process that runs continuously in the background and performs tasks at predetermined intervals or in response to specific events. Called a service by Microsoft Windows operating systems, a daemon typically performs server tasks, such as spooling print jobs, handling e-mail, and transmitting Web files.

data encapsulation   The process by which information generated by an application is packaged for transmission over a network by successive protocols operating at the various layers of the Open Systems Interconnection (OSI) reference model. A protocol packages the data it receives from the layer above by adding a header (and sometimes a footer) containing protocol-specific information used to ensure that the data arrives at its destination intact.

data encryption   *See* encryption.

Data Encryption Standard (DES)   A commonly used, highly sophisticated algorithm developed by the U.S. National Bureau of Standards for encrypting and decoding data. *See also* encryption.

datagram   A term for the unit of data used by the Internet Protocol (IP) and other network layer protocols. Network layer protocols accept data from transport layer protocols and package it into datagrams by adding their own protocol headers. The protocol then passes the datagrams down to a data-link layer protocol for further packaging before they are transmitted over the network.

data-link layer   The second layer from the bottom of the Open Systems Interconnection (OSI) reference model. Protocols operating at the data-link layer are responsible for packaging network layer data, addressing it to its next destination, and transmitting it over the network. Some of the local area network (LAN) protocols operating at the data-link layer are Ethernet, Token Ring, and the Fiber Distributed Data Interface (FDDI). Wide area network (WAN) protocols operating at the data-link layer include the Point-to-Point Protocol (PPP) and the Serial Line Internet Protocol (SLIP).

default gateway   The router on the local network used by a Transmission Control Protocol/Internet Protocol (TCP/IP) client computer to transmit messages to computers on other networks. To communicate with other networks, TCP/IP computers consult their routing tables for the address of the destination network. If they locate the address, they send their packets to the router specified in the table entry, which relays them to the desired network. If no specific entry for the network exists, the computer sends the packets to the router specified in the default gateway entry, which the user (or a Dynamic Host Configuration Protocol [DHCP] server) supplies as one of the basic configuration parameters of the TCP/IP client.

DES   *See* Data Encryption Standard (DES).

Destination Address   A 48-bit field in data-link layer protocol headers that contains a hexadecimal sequence used to identify the network interface to which a frame will be transmitted.

Destination IP Address   A 32-bit field in the Internet Protocol (IP) header that contains a value used to identify the network interface to which a packet will be transmitted.

details pane   The pane on the right side of the Microsoft Management Console (MMC) that displays the details for the selected item in the scope pane. The details can be a list of items or they can be administrative properties, services, and events that are acted on by a console or snap-in.

device driver   A program that enables a specific device, such as a modem, network interface adapter, or printer, to communicate with an operating system such as Microsoft Windows Server 2003. For example, without a device driver, a network interface adapter cannot communicate with the computer's operating system. Although a device might be installed on your system, Windows Server 2003 cannot use the device until you have installed and configured the appropriate driver. If a device is listed in the Hardware Compatibility List (HCL), a driver is usually included with Windows Server 2003. Device drivers load automatically for all enabled devices when a computer is started, and thereafter run invisibly.

DHCP   *See* Dynamic Host Configuration Protocol (DHCP).

DHCP client   Any network-enabled device that supports the ability to communicate with a Dynamic Host Configuration Protocol (DHCP) server for the purpose of obtaining a dynamically leased Internet Protocol (IP) address and other Transmission Control Protocol/Internet Protocol (TCP/IP) configuration settings.

DHCP relay agent   A Dynamic Host Configuration Protocol (DHCP) server feature that forwards Internet Protocol (IP) address allocation requests from DHCP clients to a specific DHCP server on another network. This enables a DHCP server to provide addresses to clients anywhere on the internetwork.

DHCP scope   A range of Internet Protocol (IP) addresses that are available to be leased or assigned to Dynamic Host Configuration Protocol (DHCP) clients by the DHCP service.

DHCP server   In Microsoft Windows Server 2003, a computer running the Microsoft DHCP Server service that offers dynamic configuration of Internet Protocol (IP) addresses and related information to Dynamic Host Configuration Protocol (DHCP)-enabled clients.

dial-up connection   A communications link to a remote system or network that is created by a device that uses the Public Switched Telephone Network (PSTN). This includes modems with standard phone lines, ISDN cards with high-speed ISDN lines, or X.25 networks. If you are a typical user, you might have one or two dial-up connections, perhaps to the Internet and to your corporate network. In a more complex server situation, multiple network modem connections might be used to implement an advanced routing configuration.

differential backup   A type of backup job that uses a filter that causes it to back up only the files that have changed since the last full backup job. The filter evaluates the state of each file's archive bit, which a full backup job clears. Creating or modifying a file sets its archive bit, and the differential job backs up only the files that have their archive bit set. The differential job does not modify the state of the bits, so the next differential job will also back up only the files that have changed since the last full backup. Differential jobs use more tape or other media than incremental jobs, because they repeatedly back up the same files, but they're easier to restore in the event of a disaster. You only have to restore the last full backup and the most recent differential to completely restore a drive. Compare with incremental backup.

Diffie-Hellman algorithm   A method used by IP Security (IPSec) systems to securely compute identical encryption keys based on shared information that does not compromise the key generation process.

digital   A system that encodes information numerically, by using digits such as 0 and 1, in a binary context. Computers use digital encoding to process data. A digital signal is a discrete binary state, either on or off. *See also* analog.

digital line   A communication line that carries information only in binary-encoded (digital) form. To minimize distortion and noise interference, a digital line uses repeaters to regenerate the signal periodically during transmission.

digital signature   A means for originators of a message, file, or other digitally encoded information to bind their identity to the information. The process of signing information entails transforming the information, as well as some secret information held by the sender, into a tag called a signature. Digital signatures are used in public key environments and they provide nonrepudiation and integrity services.

Digital Subscriber Line (DSL)   A type of point-to-point, digital wide area network (WAN) connection that uses standard telephone lines to provide high-speed communications. DSL is available in many different forms, including Asymmetrical Digital Subscriber Line (ADSL) and High-bit-rate Digital Subscriber Line (HDSL). The various DSL technologies differ greatly in their speeds and in the maximum possible distance between the installation site and the telephone company's nearest central office. DSL connections are used for many applications, ranging from local area network (LAN) and Private Branch Exchange (PBX) interconnections to consumer Internet access. *See also* Asymmetrical Digital Subscriber Line (ADSL).

direct route   An Internet Protocol (IP) transmission to a destination on the local network, in which the Destination IP Address and the data-link layer protocol's Destination Address identify the same computer. Compare with indirect route, in which the IP destination is on another network and the data-link layer Destination Address identifies a router on the local network that is used to access the destination network.

directory   An information source (for example, a telephone directory) that contains information about people, computer files, or other objects. In a file system, a directory stores information about files. In a distributed computing environment (such as a Microsoft Windows Server 2003 domain), the directory stores information about objects such as printers, fax servers, applications, databases, and other users.

directory database   The physical storage for each replica of the Active Directory service. The directory database is also called the data store.

directory service   A database containing information about network entities and resources, used as a guide to the network and as an authentication resource by multiple users. Early network operating systems included basic flat file directory services, such as Microsoft Windows NT domains and the Novell NetWare bindery. Today's directory services, such as Microsoft's Active Directory and Novell Directory Services (NDS) tend to be hierarchical and designed to support large enterprise networks. *See also* Active Directory.

distance vector protocol   A dynamic routing protocol that rates the relative efficiency of network routes by the number of hops to the destination. This is not necessarily an efficient method because with networks of different speeds a route with fewer hops can take longer to transmit data than one requiring more hops. The most common distance vector routing protocol is the Routing Information Protocol (RIP). Compare with link state protocol.

DMZ   *See* perimeter network.

DNS   *See* Domain Name System (DNS).

DNS name server   In the Domain Name System (DNS) client/server model, the server containing information about a portion of the DNS database that makes computer names available to client resolvers querying for name resolution across the Internet.

domain   A group of computers and other devices on a network that are administered as a single unit. On the Internet, domain names are hierarchical constructions (such as microsoft.com) that form the basis for the Domain Name System (DNS). On a Microsoft Windows Server 2003 network, a domain is a group of users, computers, and other resources for which information is stored in a directory service on a server called a domain controller.

domain controller   A computer running Microsoft Windows Server 2003, Microsoft Windows 2000, or Microsoft Windows NT that has been designated to store and process directory service information. Windows NT domains and the Windows Active Directory service store their directory service databases on domain controllers, which also authenticate users accessing network resources.

domain model   A grouping of one or more domains that have administration and communication links between them, set up to manage users and resources.

Domain Name System (DNS)   A distributed, hierarchical namespace designed to provide Transmission Control Protocol/Internet Protocol (TCP/IP) networks (such as the Internet) with friendly names for computers and users. Although TCP/IP computers use numerical IP addresses to identify each other, people work better with names. DNS provides a naming system for network resources and a service for resolving those names into IP addresses. TCP/IP computers frequently access DNS servers to send them the names of the computers they want to access. The DNS server communicates with other DNS servers on the network to find out the IP address associated with the requested name, and then sends it back to the client computer, which initiates communications with the destination system using its IP address.

domain namespace   The database structure used by the Domain Name System (DNS).

driver   *See* device driver.

DSL   *See* Digital Subscriber Line (DSL).

dynamic allocation   An operational mode of Dynamic Host Configuration Protocol (DHCP) servers in which the server assigns an IP address and other Transmission Control Protocol/Internet Protocol (TCP/IP) configuration settings to a client from a pool of addresses and then reclaims them when a lease of a given duration expires. This enables you to move computers to different subnets without having to manually release the previously allocated IP addresses from the other subnets. Compare with automatic allocation, manual allocation. *See also* Dynamic Host Configuration Protocol (DHCP).

Dynamic Host Configuration Protocol (DHCP) A service that automatically configures the Transmission Control Protocol/Internet Protocol (TCP/IP) client computers on a network by assigning them unique IP addresses and other configuration parameters. DHCP servers can assign IP addresses to clients from a pool and reclaim them when a lease of a set duration expires. Virtually all operating systems include a DHCP client, and most of the major server operating systems, such as Microsoft Windows Server 2003, Microsoft Windows 2000 Server, Microsoft Windows NT Server, Novell NetWare, and many forms of UNIX, include DHCP server software. DHCP is a cross-platform service that can support various operating systems with a single server. *See also* automatic allocation, dynamic allocation, manual allocation.

dynamic routing A system in which routers automatically build their own routing tables using specialized protocols to communicate with other nearby routers. By sharing information in this way, a router builds up a composite picture of the internetwork on which it resides, enabling it to route traffic more efficiently. The two basic types of routing protocols are distance vector routing protocols, like the Routing Information Protocol (RIP), and link state routing protocols, like the Open Shortest Path First (OSPF) protocol.

dynamic update Enables clients with dynamically assigned Internet Protocol (IP) addresses to register directly with a server running the Domain Name System (DNS) service and update their DNS resource records automatically. Dynamic updates eliminate the need for other Internet naming services, such as Windows Internet Name Service (WINS), in a homogeneous environment.

E

EAP *See* Extensible Authentication Protocol (EAP).

e-mail A service that transmits messages in electronic form to specific users on a network.

EFS *See* encrypting file system (EFS).

encrypting file system (EFS) A Microsoft Windows Server 2003 feature that enables users to encrypt files and folders on an NTFS volume to keep them safe from intruders who have physical access to the disk.

encryption The process of making information indecipherable in order to protect it from unauthorized viewing or use, especially during transmission or when the data is stored on a transportable magnetic medium. A key is required to decode the information. *See also* data encryption standard (DES).

end system   On a Transmission Control Protocol/Internet Protocol (TCP/IP) network, a computer or other device that is the original sender or ultimate recipient of a transmission. The end systems in a TCP/IP transmission are identified by the Source IP Address and Destination IP Address fields in the IP header. All the other systems (that is, routers) involved in the transmission are known as intermediate systems.

enrollment   The process by which a user or computer obtains a certificate from a certification authority.

ephemeral port   A Transmission Control Protocol (TCP) or User Datagram Protocol (UDP) port number of 1024 or higher, chosen at random by a Transmission Control Protocol/Internet Protocol (TCP/IP) client computer during the initiation of a transaction with a server. Because the client initiates the communication with the server, it can use any port number beyond the range of the well-known port numbers (which run up to 1023). The server reads the ephemeral port number from the transport layer protocol header's Source Port field and uses it to address its replies to the client. Compare with well-known port.

ESP   *See* IP Encapsulating Security Payload (ESP).

Ethernet   Common term used to describe Institute of Electrical and Electronic Engineers (IEEE) 802.3, a data-link layer local area network (LAN) protocol developed in the 1970s, which is now the most popular protocol of its kind in the world. Ethernet runs at 10 Mbps, is based on the Carrier Sense Multiple Access with Collision Detection (CSMA/CD) Media Access Control (MAC) mechanism, and supports a variety of physical layer options, including coaxial, unshielded twisted pair (UTP), and fiber-optic cables. More recent revisions of the protocol support speeds of 100 Mbps (Fast Ethernet) and 1,000 Mbps (gigabit Ethernet). *See also* Carrier Sense Multiple Access with Collision Detection (CSMA/CD).

event   An action or occurrence to which a program might respond. Examples of events are mouse clicks, key presses, and mouse movements. Also, any significant occurrence in the system or in a program that requires users to be notified or an entry to be added to a log.

event logging   The Microsoft Windows Server 2003 process of recording an audit entry in the audit trail whenever certain events occur, such as services starting and stopping or users logging on and off and accessing resources. You can use Event Viewer to review Windows Server 2003 events.

Event Viewer   A Microsoft Management Console (MMC) snap-in that maintains and displays logs about application, security, and system events on your computer.

expand   To show hidden directory levels in a directory or console tree.

Extensible Authentication Protocol (EAP)   An extension to the Point-to-Point Protocol (PPP) that permits arbitrary authentication mechanisms to be used to validate a PPP connection.

F

failback   The ability of a cluster to redistribute its application load when a failed node is restored to the cluster.

failover   In server clustering, the ability of one or more cluster nodes to assume the tasks of a node that has failed.

fault tolerance   The ability of a computer or an operating system to respond to an event such as a power outage or a hardware failure in such a way that no data is lost and no work in progress is interrupted.

FDDI   *See* Fiber Distributed Data Interface (FDDI).

Fiber Distributed Data Interface (FDDI)   A data-link layer local area network (LAN) protocol running at 100 Mbps and designed for use with fiber-optic cable. Typically used for backbone networks, FDDI uses the token-passing Media Access Control (MAC) mechanism and supports a double ring topology that provides fault tolerance in the event of a system disconnection or cable failure. Originally the principal 100-Mbps LAN protocol, FDDI has since largely been replaced by the Fast Ethernet and gigabit Ethernet fiber-optic options.

fiber optic   A type of network medium that uses cables made of glass or plastic that transmit signals in the form of light pulses. Compared to copper-based cables, which use electrical signals, fiber optic is less susceptible to attenuation and immune to electromagnetic interference. Fiber-optic cables are also considerably more expensive to purchase, install, and maintain than copper-based cables.

Fibre Channel   A high-speed serial networking technology used primarily for connections between computers and storage devices. "Fibre" is deliberately misspelled to distinguish the term from "fiber optic."

File Transfer Protocol (FTP)   An application layer Transmission Control Protocol/ Internet Protocol (TCP/IP) protocol designed to perform file transfers and basic file management tasks on remote computers. FTP is a mainstay of Internet communications. FTP client support is integrated into most Web browsers and FTP server support is integrated into many Web server products. FTP is also an important UNIX tool; all UNIX systems support both FTP client and server functions. FTP is unique among TCP/IP protocols in that it uses two simultaneous TCP connections. One, a control connection, remains open during the entire life of the session between the FTP client and the FTP server. When the client initiates a file transfer, a second connection is opened between the two computers to carry the transferred data. This connection closes when the data transfer concludes.

firewall   A hardware or software product designed to isolate part of an internetwork to protect it against intrusion by outside processes. Typically used to protect a private network from intrusion from the Internet, firewalls use a number of techniques to provide this protection, while still allowing certain types of traffic through. Some of these techniques include packet filtering and network address translation (NAT). Once intended only for large network installations, firewall products now come in smaller versions designed to protect small networks and individual computers from Internet intruders.

folder   A grouping of files or other folders, graphically represented by a folder icon, in both Microsoft Windows Server 2003 and Macintosh environments. Also called a directory.

forward lookup   In Domain Name System (DNS), a query process in which the friendly DNS domain name of a host computer is searched to find its Internet Protocol (IP) address.

forwarder   In Domain Name System (DNS), a server that receives queries from other DNS servers that are specifically configured to send them.

FQDN   *See* fully qualified domain name (FQDN).

frame   Unit of data constructed, transmitted, and received by data-link layer protocols such as Ethernet and Token Ring. Data-link layer protocols create frames by packaging the data they receive from network layer protocols inside a header and footer. Frames can be different sizes, depending on the protocol used to create them.

frame relay   A type of wide area networking technology in which two or more locations install their own leased lines to connect to a service provider's frame relay network, called a cloud. The devices connected to the cloud can then establish connections with the other connected systems. The advantage of frame relay over a standard leased line is that the amount of bandwidth is variable, and can accommodate periods of increased traffic.

FTP   *See* File Transfer Protocol (FTP).

full duplex communications   Any type of network communication in which traffic moves over the medium in both directions simultaneously.

full zone transfer (AXFR)   The standard query type supported by all Domain Name System (DNS) servers to update and synchronize zone data when the zone has been changed. When a DNS query is made using AXFR as the specified query type, the entire zone is transferred as the response.

fully qualified domain name (FQDN)   An unambiguous DNS domain name that indicates its location in the domain namespace with absolute certainty. Fully qualified domain names differ from relative names in that they can be stated with a trailing period (.)—for example, host.example.microsoft.com.—to qualify their position in relation to the root of the name space.

G

gateway   On a Transmission Control Protocol/Internet Protocol (TCP/IP) network, the term gateway is often used synonymously with the term router, referring to a network layer device that connects two networks and relays traffic between them as needed, such as the default gateway specified in a TCP/IP client configuration. However, gateway is also used to refer to an application layer device that relays data between two different services, such as an e-mail gateway that enables two separate e-mail services to communicate with each other.

GB   Gigabyte, equal to 1000 megabytes, 1,000,000 kilobytes, or 1,000,000,000 bytes.

GBps   Gigabytes per second, a unit of measurement typically used to measure the speed of data storage devices.

Gbps   Gigabits per second, a unit of measurement typically used to measure network transmission speed.

group   In networking, an account containing other accounts that are called members. The permissions and rights granted to a group are also provided to its members; thus, groups offer a convenient way to grant common capabilities to collections of user accounts.

group account   A collection of user accounts. By making a user account a member of a group, you give the related user all the rights and permissions granted to the group.

group memberships   The groups to which a user account belongs. Permissions and rights granted to a group are also provided to its members. In most cases, the actions a user can perform in Microsoft Windows Server 2003 are determined by the group memberships of the account with which the user is logged on to the network.

group policy   The Microsoft Windows Server 2003 Microsoft Management Console (MMC) snap-in used to specify the behavior of users' desktops. A Group Policy Object (GPO), which an administrator creates using the Group Policy snap-in, is the mechanism for configuring desktop settings.

Group Policy Object (GPO)   A collection of group policy settings. GPOs are essentially the documents created by the Group Policy snap-in. GPOs are stored at the domain level and affect users and computers contained in sites, domains, and organizational units. In addition, each computer running Microsoft Windows Server 2003 has exactly one group of settings stored locally, called the local GPO.

H

handshaking   A term applied to network communications. Refers to the process by which information is transmitted between the sending and receiving devices to maintain and coordinate data flow between them. Proper handshaking ensures that the receiving device will be ready to accept data before the sending device transmits.

hash message authentication code (HMAC)   A type of checksum calculation used by IP Security (IPSec) systems to ensure that data is not modified during transmission over the network.

hierarchical name space   A namespace, such as the Domain Name System (DNS) and Active Directory service, that has a tiered structure that allows names and objects to be nested inside each other.

histogram   A chart consisting of horizontal or vertical bars, the widths or heights of which represent the values of certain data.

hop   A unit of measurement used to quantify the length of a route between two computers on an internetwork, indicated by the number of routers that packets must pass through to reach the destination end system. For example, if packets must be forwarded by four routers in their journey from end system to end system, the destination is said to be four hops from the source. Distance vector routing protocols like the Routing Information Protocol (RIP) use the number of hops as a way to compare the relative efficiency of routes.

horizontal network   A network that connects multiple computers and is itself connected to a backbone network. *See* backbone network.

host name   The name of a device on a network. For a device on a Microsoft Windows Server 2003 network, this can be the same as the computer name.

Hosts   An ASCII text file used by Transmission Control Protocol/Internet Protocol (TCP/IP) computers to resolve host names into IP addresses. The Hosts file is a simple list of the host names used by TCP/IP computers and their equivalent IP addresses. When a user or an application refers to a computer using a host name, the TCP/IP client looks it up in the Hosts file to determine its IP address. The Hosts file was the original name resolution method for what later became the Internet until the number of computers on the network grew too large to manage using this technique. Eventually, the Domain Name System (DNS) was created to perform the same function in a more efficient and manageable way. TCP/IP computers still have the ability to use a Hosts file for name resolution, but because the names and addresses of each computer must be added manually, this method is rarely used today.

hotfix   A small Microsoft software update, released between service packs, that is designed to address a specific issue.

HTTP   *See* Hypertext Transfer Protocol (HTTP).

hub   A hardware component to which cables running from computers and other devices are connected, joining all the devices into a network. In most cases, the term hub refers to an Ethernet multiport repeater, a device that amplifies the signals received from each connected device and forwards them to all the other devices simultaneously. *See also* multiport repeater.

Hypertext Transfer Protocol (HTTP)   Application layer protocol that is the basis for World Wide Web communications. Web browsers generate HTTP GET request messages containing Uniform Resource Locators (URLs) and transmit them to Web servers, which reply with one or more HTTP Response messages containing the requested files. HTTP traffic is encapsulated using the Transmission Control Protocol (TCP) at the transport layer and the Internet Protocol (IP) at the network layer. Each HTTP transaction requires a separate TCP connection.

IANA   *See* Internet Assigned Numbers Authority (IANA).

IAS   *See* Internet Authentication Services (IAS).

ICMP   *See* Internet Control Message Protocol (ICMP).

IEEE   *See* Institute of Electrical and Electronic Engineers (IEEE).

IEEE 802.1X   A standard that defines a method of authenticating and authorizing users connecting to a local area network (LAN) conforming to the Institute of Electrical and Electronic Engineers (IEEE) 802 standards, and blocking access to the LAN by those users should the authentication fail. IEEE 802.1X can authenticate users connecting to any type of LAN, such as Ethernet or Token Ring, but it is particularly valuable in the case of IEEE 802.11 wireless LANs.

IEEE 802.11   Standard document published by the Institute of Electrical and Electronic Engineers (IEEE) defining a wireless local area network (LAN) technology using any one of three physical layer technologies: direct sequence spread spectrum (DSSS), frequency hopping spread spectrum (FHSS), and infrared.

IEEE 802.11a   Standard document published by the Institute of Electrical and Electronic Engineers (IEEE) defining an IEEE 802.11 wireless local area network (LAN) using the 5 GHz band.

IEEE 802.11b   Standard document published by the Institute of Electrical and Electronic Engineers (IEEE) defining an IEEE 802.11 wireless local area network (LAN) running using the 2.4 GHz band and running at speeds of up to 11 Mbps. Most wireless local area network (WLAN) technology used today conforms to this standard.

IEEE 802.2   Standard document published by the Institute of Electrical and Electronic Engineers (IEEE) defining the Logical Link Control (LLC) sublayer used by the IEEE 802.3, IEEE 802.5, and other protocols.

IEEE 802.3   Standard document published by the Institute of Electrical and Electronic Engineers (IEEE) defining what is commonly referred to as the Ethernet protocol. Although there are slight differences from the original Ethernet standards, such as the omission of the Ethertype field and the separation of the data-link layer into two sublayers, the Media Access Control (MAC) sublayer and the Logical Link Control (LLC) sublayer, IEEE 802.3 retains the defining characteristics of Ethernet, including the Carrier Sense Multiple Access with Collision Detection (CSMA/CD) MAC mechanism. IEEE 802.3 also adds to the physical layer options defined in the DIX Ethernet standards by including support for unshielded twisted-pair (UTP) cable.

IETF   *See* Internet Engineering Task Force (IETF).

IGMP   *See* Internet Group Management Protocol (IGMP).

IIS   *See* Internet Information Services (IIS).

IMAP   *See* Internet Message Access Protocol (IMAP).

in-addr.arpa domain   A special top-level Domain Name System (DNS) domain reserved for reverse mapping of Internet Protocol (IP) addresses to DNS host names.

incremental backup   A type of backup job that employs a filter that causes it to back up only the files that have changed since the last backup job. The filter evaluates the state of each file's archive bit, which a full backup job or an incremental backup job clears. Creating or modifying a file sets its archive bit, and the incremental job backs up only the files with an archive bit that is set. It then resets the archive bits (unlike a differential job, which does not reset the bits). Incremental jobs use the least amount of tape or other medium, but are more difficult to restore in the event of a disaster. You must restore the last full backup job and all the incremental jobs performed since that last full backup, in the correct chronological order, to fully restore a drive. Compare with differential backup.

incremental zone transfer (IXFR)   An alternate query type that some Domain Name System (DNS) servers can use to update and synchronize zone data when a zone is changed. When IXFR is supported between DNS servers, servers can keep track of and transfer only incremental changes of resource records between each version of the zone.

indirect route   An Internet Protocol (IP) transmission to a destination on a different network, in which the Destination IP Address and the data-link layer protocol's Destination Address identify different computers. Compare with direct route, in which the IP destination is on the same network and the data-link layer Destination Address identifies the same computer as the Destination IP Address.

infrastructure server   A computer that runs network services such as DNS server, DHCP server, or Windows Internet Name Service (WINS).

infrastructure topology   A type of communication used on wireless local area networks (LANs) in which devices equipped with wireless network interface adapters communicate with a standard cabled network using a network access point. Compare with ad hoc topology. *See also* access point.

Institute of Electrical and Electronic Engineers (IEEE)   An organization, founded in 1963, dedicated to the development and publication of standards for the computer and electronics industries. Best known in computer networking for the IEEE 802 series of documents defining the data-link layer local area network (LAN) protocols commonly known as Ethernet and Token Ring.

Integrated Services Digital Network (ISDN)   A dial-up communications service that uses standard telephone lines to provide high-speed digital communications. Originally conceived as a replacement for the existing analog telephone service, it never achieved its anticipated popularity, Today, ISDN is used in the United States primarily as an Internet access technology, although it is more commonly used for wide area network (WAN) connections in Europe and Japan. The two most common ISDN services are the Basic Rate Interface (BRI), which provides two 64-kilobits per second (Kbps) B channels and one 16-Kbps D (control) channel, and the Primary Rate Interface (PRI), which provides 23 64-Kbps B channels and one 64-Kbps D channel.

intermediate system   On a Transmission Control Protocol/Internet Protocol (TCP/IP) network, a router that relays traffic generated by an end system from one network to another. The end systems in a TCP/IP transmission are identified by the Source IP Address and Destination IP Address fields in the IP header. All the other systems (that is, routers) involved in the transmission are known as intermediate systems.

International Organization for Standardization (ISO)   An organization, founded in 1946, that consists of standards bodies from over 75 countries, such as the American National Standards Institute (ANSI) from the United States. The ISO is responsible for the publication of many computer-related standards, the best known of which is "The Basic Reference Model for Open Systems Interconnection," commonly known as the OSI reference model. (ISO is not merely an acronym; it's a name derived from the Greek word isos, meaning "equal.")

International Telecommunications Union (ITU)   An organization, founded in 1865, devoted to the development of treaties, regulations, and standards governing telecommunications. Since 1992 it has included the standards development organization formerly known as the Comité Consultatif International Téléphonique et Télégraphique (CCITT), which was responsible for the creation of modem communication, compression, and error correction standards.

International Telecommunications Union-Telecommunication (ITU-T)   The Telecommunication Standards Section of the International Telecommunications Union (ITU) responsible for telecommunication standards. Its responsibilities include standardizing modem design and operations and standardizing protocols for networks and facsimile transmission. ITU is an international organization within which governments and the private sector coordinate global telecom networks and services.

internet   *See* internetwork.

Internet   A packet-switching internetwork that consists of thousands of individual networks and millions of computers around the world. No central managing body owns or administers the Internet; all administration chores are distributed among users all over the network.

Internet Assigned Numbers Authority (IANA)   The organization responsible for the assignment of unique parameter values for the Transmission Control Protocol/Internet Protocol (TCP/IP) protocols, including IP address assignments for networks and protocol number assignments. The "Assigned Numbers" Requests for Comments (RFC) document (currently RFC 1700) lists all the protocol number assignments and many other unique parameters regulated by the IANA.

Internet Authentication Services (IAS)   A service included with Microsoft Windows Server 2003 that provides centralized authentication and authorization services. *See* Remote Authentication Dial-In User Service (RADIUS).

Internet Control Message Protocol (ICMP)   A network layer Transmission Control Protocol/Internet Protocol (TCP/IP) protocol that carries administrative messages, particularly error messages and informational queries. ICMP error messages are primarily generated by intermediate systems that, because the packets they route travel no higher than the network layer, have no other means of signaling errors to the end system that transmitted the packet. Typical ICMP error messages inform the sender that the network or host to which a packet is addressed could not be found, or that the Time to Live value for a packet has expired. ICMP query messages request information (or simply a response) from other computers, and are the basis for TCP/IP utilities like Ping, which is used to test the ability of one computer on a network to communicate with another.

Internet Engineering Task Force (IETF)   The primary standards ratification body for the Transmission Control Protocol/Internet Protocol (TCP/IP) protocol and the Internet. The IETF publishes Requests for Comments (RFCs), which are the working documents for what eventually become Internet standards. The IETF is an international body of network designers, operators, software programmers, and other technicians, all of whom devote part of their time to the development of Internet protocols and technologies.

Internet Group Management Protocol (IGMP)   A protocol that enables network devices to support Internet Protocol (IP) multicasting by registering hosts in specific multicast groups.

Internet Information Services (IIS)   Software services that support Web site creation, configuration, and management, along with other Internet functions. Microsoft Internet Information Services include Network News Transfer Protocol (NNTP), File Transfer Protocol (FTP), and Simple Mail Transfer Protocol (SMTP).

Internet Message Access Protocol (IMAP) An application layer Transmission Control Protocol/Internet Protocol (TCP/IP) protocol used by e-mail clients to download mail messages from a server. E-mail traffic between servers and outgoing e-mail traffic from clients to servers use the Simple Mail Transfer Protocol (SMTP). *See also* Post Office Protocol 3 (POP3).

Internet Protocol (IP) The primary network layer protocol in the Transmission Control Protocol/Internet Protocol (TCP/IP) suite. IP is the protocol that is ultimately responsible for end-to-end communications on a TCP/IP internetwork, and it includes functions such as addressing, routing, and fragmentation. IP packages data that it receives from transport layer protocols into data units called datagrams by applying a header containing the information needed to transmit the data to its destination. The IP addressing system uses 32-bit addresses to uniquely identify the computers on a network and specifies the address of the destination system as part of the IP header. IP is also responsible for routing packets to their destinations on other networks by forwarding them to other routers on the network. When a datagram is too large to be transmitted over a particular network, IP breaks it into fragments and transmits each in a separate packet.

Internet service provider (ISP) A company whose business is supplying consumers or businesses with Internet access. At the consumer level, an ISP provides users with dial-up access to the ISP's networks, which are connected to the Internet, as well as other end-user services, such as access to Domain Name System (DNS), e-mail, and news servers. At the business level, ISPs provide high-bandwidth Internet connections using leased telephone lines or other technologies and sometimes provide other services, such as registered IP addresses, Web site hosting, and DNS domain hosting.

internetwork A group of interconnected local area networks (LANs) or wide area networks (WANs), or both, that are connected so that any computer can transmit data to any other computer. The networks are connected by routers, which are responsible for relaying packets from one network to another. The largest example of an internetwork is the Internet, which is composed of thousands of networks around the world. Private internetworks consist of a smaller number of LANs, often at various locations and connected by WAN links.

Internetwork Packet Exchange (IPX) A network layer protocol used by Novell NetWare networks. IPX performs many of the same functions as the Internet Protocol (IP), but instead of being a self-contained addressing system like IP, IPX is designed for use on local area networks (LANs) only and uses a network identifier assigned by the network administrator plus the network interface adapter's hardware address to identify individual computers on the network. Unlike IP, IPX is not based on an open standard. Novell owns all rights to the protocols of the IPX protocol suite, although Microsoft has developed its own IPX-compatible protocol for inclusion in Microsoft Windows operating systems.

intranet   A Transmission Control Protocol/Internet Protocol (TCP/IP) network owned by a private organization that provides services such as Web sites only to that organization's users.

IP   See Internet Protocol (IP).

IP address   A 32-bit address assigned to Transmission Control Protocol/Internet Protocol (TCP/IP) client computers and other network equipment that uniquely identifies that device on the network. The IP uses IP addresses to transmit packets to their destinations. Expressed as four 8-bit decimal values separated by periods (for example, 192.168.71.19), the IP address consists of a network identifier (which specifies the network that the device is located on) and a host identifier (which identifies the particular device on that network). The sizes of the network and host identifiers can vary depending on the address class. For a computer to be accessible from the Internet, it must have an IP address containing a network identifier registered with the Internet Assigned Numbers Authority (IANA).

IP Authentication Header (AH)   One of the two protocols used by IPSec to protect data as it is transmitted over the network. AH provides authentication, anti-replay, and data integrity services, but it does not encrypt the data. *See* IP Encapsulating Security Payload (ESP).

IP Encapsulating Security Payload (ESP)   One of the two protocols used by IP Security (IPSec) to protect data as it is transmitted over the network. ESP provides encryption, authentication, anti-replay, and data integrity services. *See* IP Authentication Header (AH).

IP Security protocol (IPSec)   A set of Transmission Control Protocol/Internet Protocol (TCP/IP) protocol extensions designed to provide encrypted network layer communications. For computers to communicate using IPSec, they must share a public key.

IPCONFIG.EXE   A Microsoft Windows Server 2003 command-line utility used to view the Transmission Control Protocol/Internet Protocol (TCP/IP) configuration parameters for a particular computer. A graphical version of the tool, called Winipcfg.exe, is included with Microsoft Windows 95, Microsoft Windows 98, and Microsoft Windows Me. Ipconfig.exe is most useful on computers with TCP/IP clients configured automatically by a Dynamic Host Configuration Protocol (DHCP) server because it is the easiest way to view the assigned settings for the client system. You can also use Ipconfig.exe to release and renew TCP/IP configuration parameters assigned by DHCP.

IPSec   *See* IP Security protocol (IPSec).

IPSec policy   A collection of configuration settings containing rules, filter lists, and filter actions, which defined what network traffic IP Security (IPSec) should secure and how IPSec should secure it.

IPv6   New version of the Internet Protocol (IP) that expands the IP address space from 32 to 128 bits. *See also* Internet Protocol (IP).

IPX   *See* Internetwork Packet Exchange (IPX).

ISDN   *See* Integrated Services Digital Network (ISDN).

ISO   *See* International Organization for Standardization (ISO).

ISP   *See* Internet service provider (ISP).

iterative query   In Domain Name System (DNS), a name resolution request query to which a server is expected to respond immediately with whatever information it has on the name.

ITU   *See* International Telecommunications Union (ITU).

ITU-T   *See* International Telecommunications Union-Telecommunication (ITU-T).

IXFR   *See* incremental zone transfer (IXFR).

K

KB   Kilobyte, equal to 1,000 bytes.

Kbps   Kilobits per second, a unit of measurement typically used to measure network transmission speed.

KBps   Kilobytes per second, a unit of measurement typically used to measure network transmission speed.

KDC   *See* Key Distribution Center (KDC).

Kerberos V5   An Internet standard security protocol for handling authentication of user or system identity. With Kerberos V5, passwords that are sent across network lines are encrypted, not sent as plain text. Kerberos V5 also includes other security features.

Key Distribution Center (KDC)   A network service that supplies session tickets and temporary session keys used in the Kerberos V5 authentication protocol.

L

LAN   *See* local area network (LAN).

Layer 2 Tunneling Protocol (L2TP)   A protocol used to establish virtual private network connections across the Internet. *See also* virtual private network (VPN).

layering   The coordination of various protocols in a specific architecture that enables the protocols to work together to ensure that the data is prepared, transferred, received, and acted on as intended.

LDAP   *See* Lightweight Directory Access Protocol (LDAP).

lease identification cookie   A string that consists of a computer's Internet Protocol (IP) address and its hardware address, which a Dynamic Host Configuration Protocol (DHCP) server uses to uniquely identify a client in its database. *See also* Dynamic Host Configuration Protocol (DHCP).

Lightweight Directory Access Protocol (LDAP)   The primary access protocol for the Active Directory service. LDAP version 3 is defined by a set of proposed standard documents published by the Internet Engineering Task Force (IETF), including RFC 2251.

link state protocol   A dynamic routing protocol that rates the relative efficiency of network routes by the properties of the connections providing access to the destination. Compare with distance vector protocols, which use the number of hops to rate the efficiency of a network. The most common link state protocol is the Open Shortest Path First (OSPF) protocol.

LLC   *See* Logical Link Control sublayer (LLC).

Lmhosts   An ASCII text file used by Transmission Control Protocol/Internet Protocol (TCP/IP) computers running Microsoft Windows operating systems to resolve Network Basic Input/Output System (NetBIOS) names into IP addresses. Like the Hosts file used to resolve host names into IP addresses, an Lmhosts file is a list of the NetBIOS names assigned to computers on the network and their corresponding IP addresses. Lmhosts files can also contain special entries used to preload the computer's NetBIOS name cache or to identify the domain controllers on the network. Systems running the Windows operating system can use individual Lmhosts files for NetBIOS name resolution, but they more commonly use either network broadcast transmissions or the Windows Internet Name Service (WINS).

load balancing   A technique used to scale the performance of a server-based program (such as a Web server) by distributing its client requests across multiple servers within the cluster. Typically, each host can specify the load percentage that it will handle, or the load can be equally distributed across all the hosts. If a host fails, the load is dynamically redistributed among the remaining hosts.

local area network (LAN)   A collection of computers that are connected to each other using a shared medium. The computers communicate with each other using a common set of protocols. Compare with wide area network (WAN), metropolitan area network (MAN).

local computer   A computer that you can access directly without using a communications line or a communications device such as a network interface adapter or a modem.

local group   For computers running Microsoft Windows operating systems that function as workstations and member servers, a group that can be granted permissions and rights from its own computer and (if the computer participates in a domain) user accounts and global groups both from its own domain and from trusted domains.

local user account   For Microsoft Windows Server 2003, a user account a domain provides for a user whose global account is not in a trusted domain. A local account is not required where trust relationships exist between domains.

log file   A file that stores messages generated by an application, service, or operating system. These messages are used to track the operations performed. Log files are usually plain text (ASCII) files and often have a .log extension.

Logical Link Control (LLC) sublayer   One of the two sublayers of the data-link layer defined by the Institute of Electrical and Electronic Engineers (IEEE) 802 standards. The LLC standard (IEEE 802.2) defines additional fields carried within the data field of data-link layer protocol headers. *See also* Media Access Control (MAC) sublayer.

M

MAC   *See* Media Access Control (MAC).

MAN   *See* metropolitan area network (MAN).

manual allocation   An operational mode of Dynamic Host Configuration Protocol (DHCP) servers in which the server assigns clients IP addresses and other Transmission Control Protocol/Internet Protocol (TCP/IP) configuration settings that the the server administrator specifies for each computer. The IP addresses are not assigned randomly from a pool, as in the automatic and dynamic allocation modes. The end result is no different from configuring the TCP/IP clients by hand, but using the manual allocation mode of a DHCP server saves the administrator from having to travel to the client computer and prevents other computers on the network from being assigned duplicate addresses. Manual allocation is typically used for clients that must have a specific IP address, such as a Web server that must be accessible from the Internet using a Domain Name System (DNS) name. *See also* Dynamic Host Configuration Protocol (DHCP).

master server   An authoritative Domain Name System (DNS) server for a zone. Master servers can vary and are either primary or secondary masters, depending on how the server obtains its zone data.

MB   Megabyte, equal to 1000 kilobytes or 1,000,000 bytes.

Mbps   Megabits per second, a unit of measurement typically used to measure network transmission speed.

MBps   Megabytes per second, a unit of measurement typically used to measure the speed of data storage devices.

MD5   *See* Message Digest 5 (MD5).

media   In networking, a term used to describe the hardware mechanism for carrying data that computers and other network devices use to send information to each other. In computers, a term used to describe a means of storing data permanently, such as a hard or floppy disk.

Media Access Control (MAC)   A method by which computers determine when they can transmit data over a shared network medium. When multiple computers are connected to a single network segment, two computers transmitting data at the same time cause a collision, which destroys the data. The MAC mechanism implemented in the data-link layer protocol prevents these collisions from occurring or permits them to occur in a controlled manner. The MAC mechanism is the defining characteristic of a data-link layer local area network (LAN) protocol. The two most common MAC mechanisms in use today are Carrier Sense Multiple Access with Collision Detection (CSMA/CD), which is used by Ethernet networks, and token passing, which is used by Token Ring and Fiber Distributed Data Interface (FDDI) networks, among others.

Media Access Control (MAC) sublayer   One of the two sublayers of the data-link layer defined by the Institute of Electrical and Electronic Engineers (IEEE) 802 standards. The MAC sublayer defines the mechanism used to regulate access to the network medium. *See also* Logical Link Control (LLC) sublayer.

member server   A computer that runs Microsoft Windows Server 2003 but is not a domain controller of a Windows Server 2003 domain. Member servers participate in a domain but do not store a copy of the directory database. For a member server, permissions can be set on resources that allow users to connect to the server and use its resources. Resource permissions can be granted for domain global groups and users as well as for local groups and users.

Message Digest 5 (MD5)   A 128-bit hashing scheme developed by RSA Security Inc. and used by various Point-to-Point (PPP) vendors for encrypted authentication.

Metric   A field in a Transmission Control Protocol/Internet Protocol (TCP/IP) computer's routing table that contains a value rating the relative efficiency of a particular route. When routing packets, a router scans its routing table for the desired destination, and if two routes to that destination are listed in the table, the router chooses the one with the lowest metric value. Depending on how the routing information is inserted into the table, the metric can represent the number of hops needed to reach the destination network, or it can contain a value that reflects the actual time needed to reach the destination.

metropolitan area network (MAN)   A data network that services an area larger than a local area network (LAN) and smaller than a wide area network (WAN). Most MANs today service communities, towns, or cities and are operated by cable television companies using fiber-optic cable.

Microsoft Baseline Security Analyzer A graphical tool that can check a single computer or multiple computers running various versions of the Windows operating system for common security lapses, such as missing security updates and improper passwords.

Microsoft Management Console (MMC) A framework for hosting administrative tools, called consoles. A console may contain tools, folders, or other containers, World Wide Web pages, and other administrative items. These items are displayed in the left pane of the console, called a console tree. A console has one or more windows that can provide views of the console tree. The main MMC window provides commands and tools for authoring consoles. The authoring features of MMC and the console tree itself may be hidden when a console is in User Mode.

Microsoft Software Update Services (SUS) An intranet version of the Microsoft Windows Update Web site that notifies administrators when new software updates are released and deploys them to the computers on the internal network.

minimal routing The process of routing Internet Protocol (IP) using only the default routing table entries created by the operating system. Compare with static routing, dynamic routing.

MMC *See* Microsoft Management Console (MMC).

modem Short for modulator/demodulator, a hardware device that converts the digital signals generated by computers into analog signals suitable for transmission over a telephone line, and back again. A dial-up connection between two computers requires a modem at each end, both of which support the same communication protocols. Modems take the form of internal devices that plug into one of a computer's expansion slots or external devices that connect to one of the computer's serial ports. The term modem is also used. incorrectly in many cases, to describe any device that provides a connection to a wide area communications service, such as a cable television or Digital Subscriber Line (DSL) connection. These devices are not actually modems because the service is digital, and no analog/digital conversion takes place.

multicast A network transmission with a destination address that represents a group of computers on the network. Transmission Control Protocol/Internet Protocol (TCP/IP) multicast addresses are defined by the Internet Assigned Numbers Authority (IANA) and represent groups of computers with similar functions, such as all the routers on a network. Compare with broadcast and unicast.

multihomed A computer with two or more network interfaces, whether they take the form of network interface adapters, dial-up connections using modems, or other technologies. On a Transmission Control Protocol/Internet Protocol (TCP/IP) network, each network interface in a multihomed computer must have its own IP address.

multiple master replication   A technique usually associated with a directory service, in which identical copies of a database are maintained on various computers scattered throughout a network. In multiple master replication, users can make changes to any copy of the database, and the changes to that copy are replicated to all the other copies. This is a complex technique because it is possible for different users to make changes to the same record on different masters. The system must therefore have a mechanism for reconciling data conflicts among the various masters, such as using time stamps or version numbers to assign priorities to data modifications. The Microsoft Active Directory service uses multiple master replication. Compare with single master replication.

multiplexing   Any one of several techniques used to simultaneously transmit multiple signals over a single cable or other network medium. Multiplexing works by separating the available bandwidth of the network medium into separate bands, by frequency, wavelength, time, or other criteria, and transmitting a different signal in each band. Local area network (LAN) media carry only one signal and therefore do not use multiplexing, but some networks, such as cable television and telephone networks, do.

multiport repeater   A network connection device used primarily on Ethernet networks that propagates signals received through any of its ports out through all its other ports and amplifies the signals to travel greater distances. Also called a hub.

N

name resolution   The process of converting a computer or other device's name into an address. Computers communicate using numeric addresses, but people work better with names. To be able to send data to a particular destination identified by name in the user interface, the computer must first resolve that name into an address. On Transmission Control Protocol/Internet Protocol (TCP/IP) networks, for example, Domain Name System (DNS) names and Network Basic Input/Output System (NetBIOS) names must be resolved into IP addresses. Computers can use several name resolution methods, depending on the type of name and type of address involved, including table lookups using text files such as Hosts and Lmhosts; independent processes, such as broadcast message generation; and network services, such as DNS and the Windows Internet Name Service (WINS). Compare with Address Resolution Protocol (ARP).

namespace   A set of unique names for resources or items used in a shared computing environment. For MMC, the namespace is represented by the console tree, which displays all the snap-ins and resources that are accessible to a console. For DNS, namespace is the vertical or hierarchical structure of the domain name tree. For example, each domain label, such as host1 or example, used in a fully qualified domain name, such as host1.example.microsoft.com, indicates a branch in the domain namespace tree.

NAT   *See* network address translation (NAT).

native mode   The condition in which all domain controllers in the domain have been upgraded to Microsoft Windows 2000 and an administrator has enabled native mode operation (through the Active Directory Domains And Trusts console).

NetBEUI   *See* NetBIOS Extended User Interface (NetBEUI).

NetBIOS   An application programming interface (API) that provides computers with a namespace and other local area networking functions.

NetBIOS Extended User Interface (NetBEUI)   Transport protocol sometimes used by the Microsoft Windows operating systems for local area networking. NetBEUI was the default protocol in the first version of Microsoft Windows NT and in Microsoft Windows for Workgroups; it has since been replaced as the default Windows protocol by Transmission Control Protocol/Internet Protocol (TCP/IP). NetBEUI is a simplified networking protocol that requires no configuration and is self-adjusting. However, the protocol is suitable only for small networks because it is not routable. NetBEUI identifies computers by the Network Basic Input/Output System (NetBIOS) names (or computer names) assigned during the installation of the Windows operating system. Because NetBIOS uses no network identifier, there is no way for the protocol to route traffic to systems on another network.

Network Address Translation (NAT)   A firewall technique that enables Transmission Control Protocol/Internet Protocol (TCP/IP) client computers using unregistered IP addresses to access the Internet. Client computers send their Internet service requests to a router equipped with NAT, which substitutes its own registered IP address for the client's unregistered address and forwards the request to the specified server. The server sends its reply to the NAT router, which then relays it back to the original client. This renders the unregistered clients invisible to the Internet, preventing direct access to them. *See also* firewall.

network interface adapter   A hardware device that provides a computer with access to a local area network (LAN). Network interface adapters can be integrated into a computer's motherboard or take the form of an expansion card, in which case they are called network interface cards (NICs). The adapter, along with its driver, implements the data-link layer protocol on the computer. The adapter has one or more connectors for network cables or some other interface to the network medium. The network interface adapter and its driver are responsible for functions such as the encapsulation of network layer protocol data into data-link layer protocol frames, the encoding and decoding of data into the signals used by the network medium, and the implementation of the protocol's Media Access Control (MAC) mechanism.

network layer   The third layer from the bottom of the Open Systems Interconnection (OSI) reference model. Protocols operating at the network layer are responsible for packaging transport layer data into datagrams, addressing them to its final destination, routing them across the internetwork, and fragmenting the datagrams as needed. The Internet Protocol (IP) is the most common protocol operating at the network layer, although Novell NetWare networks use a proprietary network layer protocol called Internetwork Packet Exchange (IPX).

Network Load Balancing (NLB)   A type of clustering designed for stateless applications, such as Web servers, in which each node has a duplicate copy of the server data and incoming client requests are distributed among the cluster nodes.

Network Monitor   A network troubleshooting tool included with Microsoft Windows Server 2003 and Microsoft Windows 2000 Server that performs real-time network traffic analysis and captures packets for decoding and analysis. Network Monitor can also generate statistics based on network traffic to help create a picture of the network's cabling, software, file server, clients, and network interface adapters. Also called a protocol analyzer.

NIC   *See* network interface adapter.

NLB   See network load balancing (NLB).

node   Any uniquely addressable device on a network, such as a computer, router, or printer.

notify list   A list maintained by the primary master for a zone of other Domain Name System (DNS) servers that should be notified when zone changes occur. The notify list consists of Internet Protocol (IP) addresses for DNS servers configured as secondary masters for the zone. When the listed servers are notified of a change to the zone, they initiate a zone transfer with another DNS server and update the zone.

Novell NetWare   One of the leading network operating systems.

NSLOOKUP.EXE   A command-line utility that enables you to generate Domain Name System (DNS) queries and send them to specific name servers for testing and troubleshooting your DNS installation.

NTFS   One of the file systems included with the Microsoft Windows Server 2003, Microsoft Windows XP, Microsoft Windows 2000, and Microsoft Windows NT operating systems. Compared to the file allocation table (FAT) file system also supported by Windows operating systems, NTFS supports larger volumes, includes transaction logs to help in recovery from disk failures, and enables network administrators to control access to specific directories and files. The main drawback to NTFS is that the drives are not accessible by any other operating systems. If you boot the computer with an MS-DOS disk, for example, the NTFS drives are invisible.

Nwlink IPX/SPX/NetBIOS Compatible Transport Protocol   Microsoft Windows implementation of the Internetwork Packet Exchange (IPX) protocol suite, providing computers running Windows operating systems with Novell NetWare connectivity.

O

object   An entity such as a file, folder, shared folder, printer, or Active Directory object described by a distinct, named set of attributes. For example, the attributes of a file object include its name, location, and size; the attributes of an Active Directory user object might include the user's first name, last name, and e-mail address.

octet   A data unit consisting of eight bits. *See also* byte.

Open Shortest Path First (OSPF)   A dynamic routing protocol that exchanges information with other routers on the network to update the system's routing table with current information about the configuration of the internetwork. OSPF is a link state protocol that evaluates routes based on their actual performance, rather than using a less accurate measurement such as the number of hops needed to reach a particular destination. Compare with distance vector protocols, in general, and the Routing Information Protocol (RIP), in particular.

Open System authentication   A null authentication method used by wireless local area networks (WLANs) using the Institute of Electrical and Electronic Engineers (IEEE) 802.11 standard that consists solely of messages in which one system identifies itself to another and the other system replies. There is no exchange of passwords, keys, or any other type of credential, and there is no way for a device configured to use Open System authentication to refuse authentication to another system.

Open Systems Interconnection (OSI) reference model   A theoretical model defined in documents published by the International Organization for Standardization (ISO) and the Telecommunication Standards Section of the International Telecommunication Union (ITU-T), used for reference and teaching, that divides the computer networking functions into seven layers: from top to bottom, application, presentation, session, transport, network, data-link, and physical. However, the layers do not correspond exactly to any of the currently used networking protocol stacks.

operating system   The primary program running on a computer, which processes input and output, runs other programs, and provides access to the computer's hardware.

organizational unit (OU)   A type of Active Directory container object used within domains. OUs are logical containers into which you can place users, groups, computers, and other OUs. An OU can contain objects only from its parent domain. An OU is the smallest scope to which you can apply a group policy or delegate authority.

OSI   *See* Open Systems Interconnection (OSI) reference model.

OSPF   *See* Open Shortest Path First (OSPF).

OU   *See* organizational unit (OU).

owner   In Microsoft Windows Server 2003, the person who controls how permissions are set on objects and grants permissions to others.

P

packet   The largest unit of data that can be transmitted over a data network at any one time. Messages generated by applications are split into pieces and packaged into individual packets for transmission over the network. Each packet is transmitted separately and can take a different route to the destination. When all the packets arrive at the destination, the receiving computer reassembles them into the original message. This is the basic functionality of a packet switching network.

packet filtering   A firewall technique in which a router is configured to prevent certain packets from entering a network. Packet filters can be created based on hardware addresses, Internet Protocol (IP) addresses, port numbers, or other criteria. For example, you can configure a router to allow only certain computers to access the network from the Internet, or you can allow your network users access to Internet e-mail but deny them access to Internet Web servers. Although typically used to prevent intrusion into a private network from the Internet, packet filtering can also be used to limit access to one of the local area networks (LANs) on a private internetwork.

parent domain   In the Domain Name System (DNS), a domain that is located in the namespace tree directly above other derivative domain names (child domains). For example, microsoft.com would be the parent domain of example.microsoft.com, a child domain.

password   A security measure used to restrict logon names to user accounts and access to computer systems and resources. A password is a unique string of characters that must be provided before a logon name or an access is authorized.

path   A sequence of directory (or folder) names that specifies the location of a directory, file, or folder within the directory tree. Each directory name and file name within the path (except the first) must be preceded by a backslash (\).

PATHPING.EXE   A Microsoft Windows Server 2003 command-line utility that displays the path through an internetwork to a particular destination and computes packet loss percentages for each hop on the path.

PDC   *See* primary domain controller (PDC).

PDU   *See* protocol data unit (PDU).

PEAP   *See* Protected Extensible Authentication Protocol (PEAP).

performance alert   A Microsoft Windows Server 2003 feature that detects when a predefined counter value rises above or falls below the configured threshold and notifies a user by means of the Messenger service.

performance counter In System Monitor, a data item associated with a performance object. For each counter selected, System Monitor presents a value corresponding to a particular aspect of the performance defined for the performance object.

Performance Logs And Alerts A tool that give you the ability to create counter logs, trace logs, and system alerts automatically from local or remote computers.

performance object In System Monitor, a logical collection of counters that is associated with a resource or service that can be monitored.

performance object instance In System Monitor, a term used to distinguish between multiple performance objects of the same type on a computer.

perimeter network A network separated from an organization's primary production network by a firewall, to prevent outside traffic from infiltrating the private network. Also known as a DMZ.

physical layer The bottom layer of the Open Systems Interconnection (OSI) reference model, which defines the nature of the network medium itself, how it should be installed, and what types of signals it should carry. In the case of local area networking, the physical layer is closely related to the data-link layer immediately above it because the data-link layer protocol includes the physical layer specifications.

PING.EXE A Transmission Control Protocol/Internet Protocol (TCP/IP) command-line utility used to test whether a computer can communicate with another computer on the network. Ping generates Internet Control Message Protocol (ICMP) Echo Request messages and transmits them to the computer specified on the command line. The target computer, on receiving the messages, transmits them back to the sender as ICMP Echo Replies. The system running Ping then displays the elapsed times between the transmission of the requests and the receipt of the replies. Almost every TCP/IP client implementation includes a version of Ping.

PKI *See* public key infrastructure (PKI).

Plain Old Telephone Service (POTS) Common phrase referring to the Public Switched Telephone Network (PSTN), the standard copper-cable telephone network used for analog voice communications around the world. *See* Public Switched Telephone Network.

pointer (PTR) resource record A resource record used in a reverse lookup zone created within the in-addr.arpa domain to designate a reverse mapping of a host Internet Protocol (IP) address to a host Domain Name System (DNS) domain name.

Point-to-Point Protocol (PPP) A data-link layer Transmission Control Protocol/Internet Protocol (TCP/IP) protocol used for wide area network (WAN) connections, especially dial-up connections to the Internet and other service providers. Unlike its progenitor, the Serial Line Internet Protocol (SLIP), PPP includes support for multiple network layer protocols, link quality monitoring protocols, and authentication protocols. PPP is used for connections between two computers only, and therefore does not need many of the features found in local area network (LAN) protocols, such as address fields for each packet and a Media Access Control (MAC) mechanism.

Point-to-Point Tunneling Protocol (PPTP)   A data-link layer protocol used to provide secured communications for virtual private network (VPN) connections. VPNs are private network connections that use the Internet as a network medium. To secure data as it is transmitted across the Internet, the computers use a process called tunneling, in which the entire data-link layer frame generated by an application process is encapsulated within an Internet Protocol (IP) datagram. This arrangement violates the rules of the Open Systems Interconnection (OSI) reference model, but it enables the entire PPP frame generated by the user application to be encrypted inside an IP datagram.

policy   The mechanism by which computer settings are configured automatically, as defined by the administrator. Depending on context, this can refer to a Microsoft Windows Server 2003 group policy, a remote access server (RAS) policy, a Microsoft Windows NT 4 system policy, or a specific setting in a Group Policy Object (GPO).

POP3   *See* Post Office Protocol 3 (POP3).

port   A code number identifying a process running on a Transmission Control Protocol/Internet Protocol (TCP/IP) computer. Transport layer protocols, such as the Transmission Control Protocol (TCP) and the User Datagram Protocol (UDP), specify the port number of the source and destination application processes in the header of each message they create. The combination of an IP address and a port number is called a socket; it identifies a specific application on a specific computer on a specific network. Port numbers lower than 1024 are called well-known port numbers, which the Internet Assigned Numbers Authority (IANA) assigns to common applications. The TCP port number 80, for example, is the well-known port number for Web servers. Port numbers 1024 and above are ephemeral port numbers, which are selected at random by clients for each transaction they initiate with a server. Because of tremendous growth in network applications, many of these high port numbers have been put to use. For example, Microsoft Terminal Services uses TCP port 3389. Alternatively, a port is a hardware connector in a computer or other network device that is used to attach cables that run to other devices.

Post Office Protocol 3 (POP3)   An application layer Transmission Control Protocol/Internet Protocol (TCP/IP) protocol used by e-mail clients to download messages from an e-mail server. E-mail traffic between servers and outgoing e-mail traffic from clients to servers uses the Simple Mail Transfer Protocol (SMTP). *See also* Internet Message Access Protocol (IMAP).

POTS   *See* Plain Old Telephone Service (POTS).

PPP   *See* Point-to-Point Protocol (PPP).

PPTP   *See* Point-to-Point Tunneling Protocol (PPTP).

presentation layer   The second layer from the top of the Open Systems Interconnection (OSI) reference model, which is responsible for translating the syntaxes used by different types of computers on a network. A computer translates the data generated by its applications from its own abstract syntax to a common transfer syntax suitable for transmission over the network. When the data arrives at its destination, the presentation layer on the receiving system translates the transfer syntax into the computer's own native abstract syntax.

primary master   An authoritative Domain Name System (DNS) server for a zone that can be used as a point of update for the zone. Only primary masters can be updated directly to process zone updates, which include adding, removing, or modifying resource records that are stored as zone data. Primary masters are also the first sources used for replicating the zone to other DNS servers.

primary zone database file   The master zone database file. Changes to a zone, such as adding domains or hosts, are performed on the server that contains the primary zone database file.

private key   The secret half of a cryptographic key pair that is used with a public key algorithm. Private keys are typically used to decrypt a symmetric session key, digitally sign data, or decrypt data that has been encrypted with the corresponding public key.

promiscuous mode   Operational mode available in some network interface adapters that causes the adapter to read and process all packets transmitted over the local area network (LAN), not just the packets addressed to it. Protocol analyzers use promiscuous mode to capture comprehensive samples of network traffic for later analysis.

Protected Extensible Authentication Protocol (PEAP)   A standards-based authentication method, used by Microsoft Windows 2000 and later versions of the operating system, that uses digitial certificates to verify the user's identity.

protocol   A documented format for the transmission of data between two networked devices. A protocol is essentially a "language" that a computer uses to communicate, and the other computer to which it is connected must use the same language for communication to take place. In most cases, network communication protocols are defined by open standards created by bipartisan committees. However, there are still a few proprietary protocols in use. Computers use many different protocols to communicate, which has given rise to the Open Systems Interconnection (OSI) reference model, which defines the layers at which different protocols operate.

Protocol   An ASCII text file found on Transmission Control Protocol/Internet Protocol (TCP/IP) systems that lists the codes used in the Protocol field of the IP header. This field identifies the transport layer protocol that generated the data carried within the datagram, ensuring that the data reaches the appropriate process on the receiving computer. The protocol numbers are registered by the Internet Assigned Numbers Authority (IANA) and are derived from the "Assigned Numbers" Request for Comments document.

protocol data unit (PDU)   A generic term for the data constructions created by the protocols operating at the various layers of the Open Systems Interconnection (OSI) reference model. For example, the PDUs created by data-link layer protocols are called frames, and network layer PDUs are called datagrams.

protocol driver   The driver responsible for offering four or five basic services to other layers in the network, while "hiding" the details of how the services are implemented. Services performed include session management, datagram service, data segmentation and sequencing, acknowledgment, and possibly routing across a wide area network (WAN).

protocol stack   The multilayered arrangement of communications protocols that provides a data path ranging from the user application to the network medium. Although based on the Open Systems Interconnection (OSI) reference model, not every layer in the model is represented by a separate protocol. On a computer connected to a local area network (LAN), for example, the protocol stack generally consists of protocols at the application, transport, network, and data-link layers, the last of which includes a physical layer specification.

proxy server   An application layer firewall technique that enables Transmission Control Protocol/Internet Protocol (TCP/IP) client systems to access Internet resources without being susceptible to intrusion from outside the network. A proxy server is an application that runs on a computer with a registered IP address, whereas the clients use unregistered IP addresses, making them invisible from the Internet. Client applications are configured to send their Internet service requests to the proxy server instead of directly to the Internet, and, using its own registered address, the proxy server relays the requests to the appropriate Internet server. On receiving a response from the Internet server, the proxy server relays it back to the original client. Proxy servers are designed for specific applications, and the client must be configured with the address of the proxy server. Administrators can also configure the proxy server to cache Internet information for later use and to restrict access to particular Internet sites. Compare with network address translation (NAT). *See also* firewall.

PSTN   *See* Public Switched Telephone Network (PSTN).

public key   The nonsecret half of a cryptographic key pair that is used with a public key algorithm. Public keys are typically used when encrypting a session key, verifying a digital signature, or encrypting data that can be decrypted with the corresponding private key.

public key cryptography   A method of cryptography in which two different keys are used: a public key for encrypting data and a private key for decrypting data.

public key infrastructure (PKI)   The term generally used to describe the laws, policies, standards, and software that regulate or manipulate certificates and public and private keys. In practice, it is a system of digital certificates, certification authorities, and other registration authorities that verify and authenticate the validity of each party involved in an electronic transaction. Standards for PKI are still evolving, even though they are being widely implemented as a necessary element of electronic commerce.

Public Switched Telephone Network (PSTN)   The standard copper-cable telephone network used for analog voice communications around the world. Also known as Plain Old Telephone Service (POTS).

Q

quad   A data unit consisting of eight bits. *See also* byte.

query   A specific request for data retrieval, modification, or deletion.

quorum   A storage resource in a cluster that contains all the configuration data needed for the recovery of the cluster. To create a cluster, the first node must be able to take control of the quorum resource, so that it can save the quorum data there.

R

RADIUS   *See* Remote Authentication Dial-In User Service (RADIUS).

RAS   *See* Remote Access Server (RAS).

recursive query   In Domain Name System (DNS), a query in which a server is expected to take full responsibility for resolving the requested name, including issuing its own queries to other servers.

redirector   A network client component that determines whether a resource requested by an application is located on the network or on the local system, and then sends the request either to the local input/output system or to the networking protocol stack. A computer can have multiple redirectors to support different networks, such as a network running Microsoft Windows and a network running Novell NetWare.

refresh   To update displayed information with current data.

refresh interval   A period of time used by secondary masters of a zone to determine how often to check to see if their zone data needs to be refreshed. When the refresh interval expires, the secondary master checks with its source for the zone to see whether its zone data is still current or needs to be updated using a zone transfer. This interval is set in the SOA (start-of-authority) resource record for each zone.

remote access   Part of the integrated Microsoft Windows Server 2003 Routing and Remote Access service that provides remote networking for telecommuters, mobile workers, and system administrators who monitor and manage servers at multiple branch offices.

Remote Access Server (RAS)   Any computer running Microsoft Windows Server 2003 that is configured to accept remote access connections.

Remote Assistance   A Microsoft Windows Server 2003 and Microsoft Windows XP feature that enables users to request help from a designated expert, who can then connect to their computers, view their activities, and take control of the console.

Remote Authentication Dial-In User Service (RADIUS)   A security authentication protocol based on clients and servers and widely used by Internet service providers (ISPs) on remote servers that do not run Microsoft operating systems. RADIUS is the most popular means of authenticating and authorizing dial-up and tunneled network users today.

remote computer   A computer that can be accessed only by using a communications line or a communications device, such as a network interface adapter or a modem.

Remote Desktop   A Microsoft Windows Server 2003 and Microsoft Windows XP feature that enables an administrator to connect to a computer at a distant location and remotely operate the console.

remote user   A user who dials in to the server over modems and telephone lines from a remote location.

replication   The process of copying data from a data store or file system to multiple computers to synchronize the data. The Active Directory service provides multiple master replication of the directory between domain controllers within a given domain. The replicas of the directory on each domain controller can be written to, enabling administrators to apply updates to any replica of a given domain. The replication service automatically copies the changes from a given replica to all other replicas. *See also* multiple master.

Request for Comments (RFC)   A document published by the Internet Engineering Task Force (IETF) that contains information about a topic related to the Internet or to the Transmission Control Protocol/Internet Protocol (TCP/IP) suite. For example, all TCP/IP protocols have been documented and published as RFCs and eventually might be ratified as Internet standards. Some RFCs are only informational or historical, however, and are not submitted for ratification as a standard. After they are published and assigned numbers, RFCs are never changed. If a new version of an RFC document is published, it is assigned a new number and cross-indexed to indicate that it renders the old version obsolete.

requester (LAN requester)   Software that resides in a computer and forwards requests for network services from the computer's application programs to the appropriate server. *See also* redirector.

resolver   Another name for the Domain Name System (DNS) client found on every Transmission Control Protocol/Internet Protocol (TCP/IP) computer. Whenever the computer attempts to access a TCP/IP system using a DNS name, the resolver generates a DNS Request message and sends it to the DNS server specified in the computer's TCP/IP client configuration. The DNS server then takes the necessary steps to resolve the requested name into an IP address and returns the address to the resolver in the client computer. The resolver can then furnish the IP address to the TCP/IP client, which uses it to transmit a message to the desired destination. *See also* Domain Name System (DNS).

resource   Any part of a computer system. Users on a network can share computer resources such as hard disks, printers, modems, CD-ROM drives, and even the processor.

resource record   The unit in which a Domain Name System (DNS) server stores information about a particular computer. The information stored in a resource record depends on the type of record it is, but a typical resource record includes the host name of a computer and its equivalent IP address. In most cases, administrators must manually create the resource records on a DNS server, but recent additions to the DNS standards define a method for dynamically updating resource records. This capability is central to the DNS functionality required by the Active Directory service. *See also* Domain Name System (DNS).

Resultant Set of Policy (RSoP)   A Microsoft Management Console snap-in that displays all the effective group policy settings for a computer or user.

reverse lookup   In Domain Name System (DNS), a query process by which the Internet Protocol (IP) address of a host computer is searched to find its friendly DNS domain name.

reverse name resolution   The process of resolving an Internet Protocol (IP) address into a Domain Name System (DNS) name, which is the opposite of the normal name-to-address resolution performed by DNS servers. Reverse DNS name resolution is accomplished using an extension to the DNS namespace consisting of a domain called in-addr.arpa, which contains four levels of subdomains named using the numbers 0 through 255. These subdomains contain resource records called pointers; each pointer contains an IP address and its equivalent DNS name. A DNS server looks up an IP address by locating the domain name equivalent to the address. For example, the IP address 192.168.1.15 becomes the domain name 15.1.168.192.in-addr.arpa.

RFC   *See* Request for Comments (RFC).

RJ-45   Short for Registered Jack 45, an eight-pin modular connector that is used in telephone and data networking. The majority of local area networks (LANs) today use RJ-45 connectors with unshielded twisted-pair (UTP) cables.

RIP   *See* Routing Information Protocol (RIP).

root domain   The domain at the top of the DNS namespace hierarchy, represented as a period (.).

root name server   One of a handful of servers that represent the top of the Domain Name System (DNS) namespace by supplying other DNS servers with the Internet Protocol (IP) addresses of the authoritative servers for all the top-level domains in the DNS. When resolving a DNS name into an IP address, a DNS server that is unable to resolve the name itself sends a DNS request to one of the root name servers identified in the server's configuration. The root name server reads the top-level domain (that is, the last word, such as com in www.microsoft.com) from the requested name and supplies the requesting server with the IP address for that top-level domain. The requesting server then transmits the same request to the top-level domain server that the root name server supplied. The root name servers are also the authoritative servers for some of the top-level domains, so they can eliminate a step from the process and supply the address of the second-level domain's authoritative server. *See also* Domain Name System (DNS), authoritative server.

routed   A UNIX daemon, pronounced "route-dee," that was the original implementation of the Routing Information Protocol (RIP), the most popular of the distance vector routing protocols. *See also* distance vector protocol, dynamic routing.

router   A network layer hardware or software device that connects two networks and relays traffic between them as needed. Using a table containing information about the other routers on the network, a router examines the Destination Address of each packet it receives, selects the most efficient route to that destination, and forwards the packet to the router or computer that is the next step in its path. Routers can connect two local area networks (LANs) or provide access to remote resources by connecting a LAN to a distant network using a wide area network (WAN) link. One of the most common scenarios involves using routers to connect a LAN to the network of an Internet service provider (ISP), thus providing Internet access to all the LAN's users.

Routing and Remote Access   A Windows Server 2003 service that enables the computer to function as a router, connecting two local area networks (LANs) together, or connecting a LAN to a wide area network (WAN) The Routing and Remote Access service (RRAS) also includes additional features, such as network address translation (NAT), Routing Information Protocol (RIP), and Open Shortest Path First (OSPF).

Routing Information Protocol (RIP)   A dynamic routing protocol that enables routers to receive information about the other routers on the network, which enables them to keep their routing tables updated with the latest information. RIP works by generating frequent broadcast messages that convey the contents of the router's routing table. Other routers use this information to update their own tables, thus spreading the routing information all over the network. For routers the absence of RIP messages from a particular router is a sign that it's not functioning so they remove that router from their tables after a given interval. RIP is frequently criticized for the large amount of broadcast traffic that it generates on the network and for the limitations of its distance vector routing method, which evaluates routes based solely on the number of hops between the source and the destination. *See also* distance vector protocol, dynamic routing.

routing table   A list maintained in every Transmission Control Protocol/Internet Protocol (TCP/IP) computer of network destinations and the routers and interfaces that the computer should use to transmit to them. In a computer that is not a router, the routing table contains only a few entries; the most frequently used is the default gateway entry. On a router, the routing table can contain a great many entries that are either manually added by a network administrator or automatically created by a dynamic routing protocol. When there is more than one routing table entry for a specific destination, the computer selects the best route based on a metric, which is a rating of the route's relative efficiency.

RRAS   *See* Routing and Remote Access service (RRAS).

RSoP   *See* Resultant Set of Policy (RSoP).

S

SAN   *See* storage area network (SAN).

scope   The pool of Internet Protocol (IP) addresses on a given subnet that a Dynamic Host Configuration Protocol (DHCP) server is configured to assign to clients when using the automatic or dynamic allocation method. *See also* Dynamic Host Configuration Protocol (DHCP), automatic allocation, dynamic allocation.

SCSI   *See* Small Computer System Interface (SCSI).

SECEDIT.EXE   A Microsoft Windows Server 2003 command-line utility that can perform the same functions as the Security Configuration And Analysis snap-in. *See also* Security Configuration and Analysis.

secondary master   An authoritative Domain Name System (DNS) server for a zone that is used as a source for replicating the zone to other servers. Secondary masters update their zone data only by transferring zone data from other DNS servers. They do not have the ability to perform zone updates.

second-level domains   Domain names that are rooted hierarchically at the second tier of the domain name space directly beneath the top-level domain names such as .com and .org. When Domain Name System (DNS) is used on the Internet, second-level domains are names, such as microsoft.com, that are registered and delegated to individual organizations and businesses according to their top-level classification. The organization then assumes further responsibility for managing parenting and the growth of its name into additional subdomains.

security   Making computers and data stored on them safe from harm or unauthorized access.

Security Configuration and Analysis   A Microsoft Windows Server 2003 Microsoft Management Console (MMC) snap-in that can analyze the current system security configuration and compare it to a baseline saved as a security template.

security log   An event log containing information about security events that are specified in the audit policy.

security template   A collection of group policy configuration settings that is stored as a text file with the .inf extension.

segment   A section of a network that is bounded by hubs, bridges, routers, or switches. Depending on the data-link layer protocol and type of cable, a segment may consist of more than one length of cable. For example, a thin Ethernet network uses separate pieces of coaxial cable to connect each computer to the next one on the bus, but all those pieces of cable constitute a segment.

Sequenced Packet Exchange (SPX)   A connection-oriented transport-layer protocol that is part of Novell's IPX protocol suite. *See also* Internetwork Packet Exchange (IPX).

Serial Line Internet Protocol (SLIP)   A data-link layer Transmission Control Protocol/Internet Protocol (TCP/IP) protocol used for wide area network (WAN) connections, especially dial-up connections to the Internet and other service providers. Because it is used only for connections between two computers, SLIP does not need many of the features found in local area network (LAN) protocols, such as address fields for each packet and a Media Access Control (MAC) mechanism. SLIP is the simplest of protocols, consisting only of a single End Delimiter byte that is transmitted after each IP datagram. Unlike its successor, the Point-to-Point Protocol (PPP), SLIP has no inherent security capabilities or any other additional services. For this reason, it is rarely used today.

server   A computer that provides shared resources to network users.

server cluster   A type of clustering in which two or more servers are joined together to service stateful applications, such as database servers. In a server cluster, the nodes are all connected to a shared data storage device, and the application load can be distributed among the servers using a variety of criteria.

server message block (SMB)   The protocol developed by Microsoft, Intel, and IBM that defines a series of commands used to pass information between network computers. The redirector packages SMB requests into a network control block

(NCB) structure that can be sent over the network to a remote device. The network provider listens for SMB messages destined for it and removes the data portion of the SMB request so that it can be processed by a local device.

service   Microsoft Windows term for a computer program or process that runs continuously in the background and performs tasks at predetermined intervals or in response to specific events. Called daemons by UNIX operating systems, services typically perform server tasks, such as sharing files and printers, handling e-mail, and transmitting Web files.

service-dependent filtering   A type of packet filtering used in firewalls that limits access to a network based on the port numbers specified in packets' transport layer protocol headers. The port number identifies the application that generated the packet or that is destined to receive it. With this technique, network administrators can limit access to a network to specific applications or prevent users from accessing specific applications outside the network. *See also* firewall, port, packet filtering.

service pack   A software update package provided by Microsoft for one of its products. A service pack contains a collection of fixes and enhancements packaged into a single self-installing archive file.

service (SRV) resource record   A resource record used in a zone to register and locate well-known Transmission Control Protocol/Internet Protocol (TCP/IP) services. The SRV resource record is specified in RFC 2052 and is used in the Microsoft Windows 2000 operating system and later versions to locate domain controllers for Active Directory service.

Services   An ASCII text file found on Transmission Control Protocol/Internet Protocol (TCP/IP) systems that lists the codes used in the Source Port and Destination Port fields of the TCP and User Datagram Protocol (UDP) headers. These fields identify the application process that generated the data carried within the packet, or the process for which it is destined. The port numbers are registered by the Internet Assigned Numbers Authority (IANA) and derived from the "Assigned Numbers" online database at *http://www.iana.org/assignments/port-numbers.*

session layer   The third layer from the top of the Open Systems Interconnection (OSI) reference model. There are no protocols specific to the session layer, but the session layer performs 22 services, which are incorporated into various application layer protocols. The most important functions are dialog control and dialog separation. Dialog control provides two modes for communicating systems—two-way alternate (TWA) mode or two-way simultaneous (TWS) mode—and dialog separation controls the process of inserting checkpoints in the data stream to synchronize functions on the two computers.

share   To make resources, such as folders and printers, available to other users on the network. Also used as a noun to refer to a shared resource.

shared folder   A folder on a computer that has been made available to other users on the network.

shared folder permissions   Permissions that restrict a shared resource's availability over the network to specific users.

Shared Key authentication   An authentication method, used by wireless local area networks (WLANs) using the Institute of Electrical and Electronic Engineers (IEEE) 802.11 standard, that is based on a security key that an external process shares with both systems.

shared resource   Any device, data, or program that is used by more than one other device or program. For Microsoft Windows Server 2003, shared resources refer to any resource that is made available to network users, such as folders, files, and printers.

Simple Mail Transfer Protocol (SMTP)   An application layer Transmission Control Protocol/Internet Protocol (TCP/IP) protocol used to carry e-mail messages between servers and from clients to servers. To retrieve e-mail from mail servers, clients typically use the Post Office Protocol 3 (POP3) or the Internet Message Access Protocol (IMAP).

Simple Network Management Protocol (SNMP)   An application layer Transmission Control Protocol/Internet Protocol (TCP/IP) protocol and query language used to transmit information about the status of network components to a central network management console. Components embedded in network hardware and software products, called SNMP agents, are responsible for collecting data about the activities of the products they service, storing the data in a management information base (MIB), and transmitting that data to the console at regular intervals using SNMP messages.

single master replication   A technique usually associated with a directory service in which identical copies of a database are maintained on various computers scattered throughout a network. In single master replication, users can make changes on only one copy of the database (the master), and the master replicates those changes to all the other copies. This is a relatively simple technique compared to multiple master replication because data only travels in one direction. However, the system is limited because users might have to connect to a master located at another site to make changes to the database.

sliding window   A technique used to implement flow control in a network communications protocol. By acknowledging the number of bytes that have been successfully transmitted and specifying the number of bytes that it is capable of receiving, a computer on the receiving end of a data connection creates a "window" that consists of the number of bytes the sender is authorized to transmit. As the transmission progresses, the window slides along the byte stream, and might change its size, until all data has been transmitted and received successfully.

SLIP   *See* Serial Line Internet Protocol (SLIP).

Small Computer System Interface (SCSI)   A bus architecture used to connect storage devices and other peripherals to personal computers. SCSI implementations typically take the form of a host adapter in the computer, and a number of internal or external devices that you connect to the card, using appropriate SCSI cables.

smart card   A credit card-size device used to securely store public and private keys, passwords, and other types of personal information. To use a smart card, you need a smart card reader attached to the computer and a personal identification number for the smart card. In Microsoft Windows Server 2003, smart cards can be used to enable certificate-based authentication and single sign-on to the enterprise.

SMB   *See* server message block (SMB).

SMTP   *See* Simple Mail Transfer Protocol (SMTP).

snap-in   A type of tool you can add to a console supported by Microsoft Management Console (MMC). A stand-alone snap-in can be added by itself; an extension snap-in can only be added to extend the function of another snap-in.

SNMP   *See* Simple Network Management Protocol (SNMP).

socket   On a Transmission Control Protocol/Internet Protocol (TCP/IP) network, the combination of an IP address and a port number, which together identify a specific application process running on a specific computer. The Uniform Resource Locators (URLs) used in Internet client applications express a socket as the IP address followed by the port number, separated by a colon, as in 192.168.1.17:80.

Source IP Address   A 32-bit field in the Internet Protocol (IP) header that contains a value used to identify the particular network interface from which a packet originated.

SPX   *See* Sequenced Packet Exchange (SPX).

stand-alone server   A computer that runs Microsoft Windows Server 2003 Server but does not participate in a domain. A stand-alone server has only its own database of users, and it processes logon requests by itself. It does not share account information with any other computer and cannot provide access to domain accounts.

start-of-authority (SOA) resource record   A record that indicates the starting point or original point of authority for information stored in a zone. The SOA resource record is the first resource record created when adding a new zone. It also contains several parameters used by other computers that use Domain Name System (DNS) to determine how long they will use information for the zone and how often updates are required.

stateful application   An application that has long-running in-memory states or large, frequently changing data sets, such as a database server, making it suitable for server clustering.

stateless application   An application with relatively small data sets that rarely change (or may even be read-only), and that does not have long-running in-memory states, such as a Web or FTP server, which is suitable for Network Load Balancing.

static routing   A method for creating a Transmission Control Protocol/Internet Protocol (TCP/IP) router's routing table, in which a network administrator manually creates the table entries. Compare with dynamic routing, in which routing table entries are automatically created by specialized routing protocols that exchange information with the other routers on the network.

storage area network (SAN)   A dedicated local area network (LAN) that connects servers with storage devices, often using the Fibre Channel protocol, reducing the storage-related traffic on the user network.

subdirectory   A directory within a directory. Also called a folder within a folder.

subnet   A group of computers on a Transmission Control Protocol/Internet Protocol (TCP/IP) network that share a common network identifier. In some cases, a TCP/IP network is divided into multiple subnets by modifying the subnet mask and designating some of the host identifier bits as subnet identifier bits. This enables the administrator to divide a network address of a particular class into multiple subnets, each of which contains a group of the hosts supported by the class.

subnet mask   A Transmission Control Protocol/Internet Protocol (TCP/IP) configuration parameter that specifies which bits of the IP address identify the host and which bits identify the network on which the host resides. When the subnet mask is viewed in binary form, the bits with a value of 1 are the network identifier and the bits with a value of 0 are the host identifier.

SUS   *See* Microsoft Software Update Services (SUS).

switch   A data-link layer network connection device that looks like a hub, but forwards incoming packets only to the computers for which they are destined. Switches essentially eliminate the need to share the medium on Ethernet networks by providing each computer with a dedicated connection to its destination. Using switches, you can build larger network segments, because there is no contention for the network medium and no increase in collisions as the number of computers connected to the network rises. Contrast with a hub, which forwards incoming packets through all its ports.

synchronous   A form of communication that relies on a timing scheme coordinated between two devices to separate groups of bits and transmit them in blocks called frames. Special characters are used to begin the synchronization and periodically check its accuracy. Because the bits are sent and received in a timed, controlled (synchronized) fashion, start and stop bits are not required. Transmission stops at the end of one transmission and starts again with a new one. It is a start/stop approach and is more efficient than asynchronous transmission. If an error occurs, the synchronous error detection and correction scheme implements a retransmission. However, because more sophisticated technology and equipment are required to transmit synchronously, it is more expensive than asynchronous transmission.

syntax   The order in which you must type a command and the elements that follow the command.

System Monitor   A tool that enables you to collect and view extensive data about the usage of hardware resources and the activity of system services on computers you administer.

systemroot   The path and folder name where the Microsoft Windows Server 2003 system files are located. Typically, this is C:\Winnt, although you can designate a different drive or folder when you install Windows Server 2003. You can use the value *%systemroot%* to replace the actual location of the folder that contains the Windows Server 2003 system files. To identify your systemroot folder, click Start, select Run, and then type **%systemroot%**.

T

T-1   A dedicated telephone connection, also called a leased line, running at 1.544 Mbps. A T-1 line consists of 24 64-Kbps channels, which can be used separately, in combinations, or as a single data pipe. Large companies use T-1 lines for both voice and data traffic; smaller companies can lease part of a T-1, which is called fractional T-1 service. Although it uses the telephone network, a T-1 used for data networking does not use a dial-up connection; it is permanently connected to a specific location.

T-3   A dedicated telephone connection, also called a leased line, running at 44.736 Mbps.

TCP   *See* Transmission Control Protocol (TCP).

TCP/IP   *See* Transmission Control Protocol/Internet Protocol (TCP/IP).

Telecommunications Network Protocol (Telnet)   An application layer Transmission Control Protocol/Internet Protocol (TCP/IP) client/server protocol used to remotely control a computer at another location. A mainstay of UNIX networking, Telnet is a true remote control application. When you access another computer and run a program, it is the processor in the remote computer that executes that program. The Telnet service is command-line-based, making it relatively useless on computers running Microsoft Windows operating systems, which rely on a graphical interface. However, all versions of the Windows operating system include a Telnet client. Windows Server 2003 also includes a Telnet server, but compared to a UNIX Telnet implementation, it has relatively few functions. This is because the primary user interface in a UNIX operating system is character-based, while the Windows interface is primarily graphical.

Telnet   *See* Telecommunications Network Protocol (Telnet).

Time to Live (TTL)   A timer value included in packets sent over networks based on Transmission Control Protocol/Internet Protocol (TCP/IP) that tells routers when a packet has been forwarded too many times. For Domain Name System (DNS), TTL values are used in resource records within a zone to determine how long requesting clients should cache and use this information when it appears in a query response answered by a DNS server for the zone.

TLS   *See* Transport Layer Security (TLS).

token passing   A Media Access Control (MAC) mechanism used on ring topology networks that uses a separate frame type called a token, which circulates around the network from computer to computer. Only the computer in possession of the token is permitted to transmit its data, which prevents computers from transmitting at the same time, causing collisions. On receipt of the token, a computer transmits a packet and either regenerates a new token immediately or waits for the packet to circulate around the network and return to its source, at which time the computer removes the packet and transmits the token frame. Unlike the Carrier Sense Multiple Access with Collision Detection (CSMA/CD) MAC mechanism, no collisions occur on a properly functioning token passing network. Token passing is used by several different data-link layer protocols, including Token Ring and Fiber Distributed Data Interface (FDDI).

Token Ring   A data-link layer protocol originally developed by IBM that is used on local area networks (LANs) with a ring topology. Running at 4 Mbps or 16 Mbps, Token Ring networks use the token passing Media Access Control (MAC) mechanism. Although they use a logical ring topology, Token Ring networks are physically cabled like a star, using a hub called a multistation access unit (MAU) that transmits incoming packets through each successive port in turn. Early Token Ring networks used a shielded twisted-pair (STP) cable known as IBM Type 1, but today most Token Ring networks use unshielded twisted-pair (UTP) cable.

top-level domain   The highest level in the Domain Name System (DNS) namespace and the rightmost word in a DNS name. For example, in the DNS name www.microsoft.com, com is the top-level domain. Domain names that are rooted hierarchically at the first tier of the domain namespace directly beneath the root (.) of the Domain Name System (DNS) namespace. On the Internet, top-level domain names such as .com and .org are used to classify and assign second-level domain names (such as microsoft.com) to individual organizations and businesses according to their organizational purpose.

topology   The method used to install network cabling and connect the network computers to the cable, which is determined by the data-link layer protocol and cable type you choose. The three basic network topologies are the bus, in which one computer is connected to the next in daisy-chain fashion; the star, in which all the computers are connected to a central hub; and the ring, in which the computers are logically connected to each other with the ends joined. Wireless networks also use topologies to determine how the computers communicate, although there are no cables. *See also* ad hoc topology, infrastructure topology.

TRACERT.EXE   A Transmission Control Protocol/Internet Protocol (TCP/IP) command-line utility that displays the path that packets are taking to a specific destination. Tracert.exe uses Internet Control Message Protocol (ICMP) Echo Request and Echo Reply messages with varying Time to Live (TTL) values in the IP header. This causes packets to time out at each successive router on the way to the destination, and the error messages generated by the timeouts enable the Tracert.exe program to display a list of the routers forming the path to the destination.

transfer syntax   A format used to encode application information for transmission over a network. The presentation layer of the Open Systems Interconnection (OSI) reference model is responsible for converting application data from its native abstract syntax to a common transfer syntax understood by both communicating systems. *See also* abstract syntax.

Transmission Control Protocol (TCP)   A Transmission Control Protocol/Internet Protocol (TCP/IP) transport layer protocol used to transmit large amounts of data generated by applications, such as entire files. TCP is a connection-oriented protocol that provides guaranteed delivery service, packet acknowledgment, flow control, and error detection. The two computers involved in the TCP transaction must exchange a specific series of messages called a three-way handshake to establish a connection before any application is transmitted. The receiving computer also transmits periodic acknowledgment messages to verify the receipt of the data packets, and the two computers perform a connection termination procedure after the data is transmitted. These additional messages, plus the large 20-byte TCP header in every packet, greatly increase the protocol's control overhead.

Transmission Control Protocol/Internet Protocol (TCP/IP)   A set of networking protocols used on the Internet that provide communications across interconnected networks that consist of computers with diverse hardware architectures and various operating systems. TCP/IP includes standards for how computers communicate and conventions for connecting networks and routing traffic.

transport layer   The middle (fourth) layer of the Open Systems Interconnection (OSI) reference model, which contains protocols providing services that are complementary to the network layer protocol. A protocol suite typically has both connection-oriented and connectionless protocols at the transport layer, providing different types of service to suit the needs of different applications. In the Transmission Control Protocol/Internet Protocol (TCP/IP) suite, the transport layer protocols are the TCP and the User Datagram Protocol (UDP).

Transport Layer Security (TLS)   The most secure version of the Secure Sockets Layer (SSL) protocol that is used to provide secure Web communications on the Internet or on intranets by enabling servers to authenticate clients or clients to authenticate servers.

transport mode   An IPSec operational mode that protects data transmissions from end system to end system. *See also* tunnel mode.

trap   A message generated by a Simple Network Management Protocol (SNMP) agent and transmitted immediately to the network management console, indicating that an event requiring immediate attention has taken place.

TTL   *See* Time to Live (TTL).

tunnel   A logical connection over which data is encapsulated. Typically, both encapsulation and encryption are performed and the tunnel is a private, secure link between a remote user or host and a private network.

tunnel mode   An IPSec operational mode designed to secure wide area network (WAN) communications by protecting data transmissions from gateway to gateway. *See also* transport mode.

tunneling   A technique for transmitting data over a network by encapsulating it within another protocol. For example, Novell NetWare networks at one time supported Transmission Control Protocol/Internet Protocol (TCP/IP) only by encapsulating IP datagrams within NetWare's native Internetwork Packet Exchange (IPX) protocol. The Point-to-Point Tunneling Protocol (PPTP) also uses tunneling to carry PPP frames inside IP datagrams.

U

UDP   *See* User Datagram Protocol (UDP).

unbounded media   A type of network medium in which the signals are not confined to a restricted space, such as wireless radio signals. Compare with bounded media.

UNC   *See* Universal Naming Convention (UNC).

unicast   A network transmission addressed to a single computer. Compare with broadcast, multicast.

Uniform Resource Locator (URL)   Provides the hypertext links between documents on the World Wide Web (WWW). Every resource on the Internet has its own location identifier, or URL, that specifies the server to access as well as the access method and the location. URLs can use various protocols, including File Transfer Protocol (FTP) and Hypertext Transfer Protocol (HTTP).

Universal Naming Convention (UNC)   The standard used for a full Microsoft Windows Server 2003 name of a resource on a network. It conforms to the syntax \\servername\share, where servername is the name of the server and sharename is the name of the shared resource. UNC names of directories or files can also include the directory path under the share name, with the following syntax: \\servername\share\directory\filename.

unqualified name   An incomplete Domain Name System (DNS) name that identifies only the host and not the domain in which the host resides. Some Transmission Control Protocol/Internet Protocol (TCP/IP) clients can handle unqualified names by automatically appending to them the name of the domain in which the computer is located or by appending user-specified domain names.

unshielded twisted pair (UTP)   A type of cable used for data and telephone networking that consists of eight copper wires twisted into four pairs with different twist rates, encased in a protective sheath. The twisting of the wire pairs reduces the crosstalk generated by signals traveling over the wires and minimizes their susceptibility to electromagnetic interference. UTP cables are graded by the Electronics Industry Association/Telecommunications Industry Association (EIA/TIA) using a series of categories. Most UTP cable installed today is Category 5, although Enhanced Category 5 (or Category 5e) cable is also available.

user account   A record that consists of all the information that defines a user to Microsoft Windows Server 2003. This includes the user name and password required to log on, the groups in which the user account has membership, and the user's rights and permissions for using the computer and network and accessing their resources. For workstation running a Windows operating system and member servers, user accounts are managed with the Local Users And Groups console. For domain controllers, user accounts are managed with the Active Directory Users And Computers console.

User Datagram Protocol (UDP)   A connectionless Transmission Control Protocol/Internet Protocol (TCP/IP) transport layer protocol used for short transactions, usually consisting of a single request and reply. UDP keeps overhead low by supplying almost none of the services provided by its connection-oriented transport layer counterpart, the TCP, such as packet acknowledgment and flow control. UDP does offer an error detection service, however. Because it is connectionless, UDP generates no additional handshake messages, and its header is only eight bytes long.

user name   A unique name identifying a user account to Microsoft Windows Server 2003. An account's user name must be unique among the group names and user names within its own domain or workgroup.

UTP   *See* unshielded twisted pair (UTP).

V

virtual LAN (VLAN)   A technique often used on switched networks to make a group of computers behave as though they are connected to the same local area network (LAN), even though they are physically connected to different network segments. Computers can remain in the same VLAN even when they're physically moved to a different segment.

virtual private network (VPN)   A technique for connecting to a network at a remote location using the Internet as a network medium. A user can dial in to a local Internet service provider (ISP) and connect through the Internet to a private network at a distant location, using a protocol like the Point-to-Point Tunneling Protocol (PPTP) to secure the private traffic.

VLAN   *See* virtual LAN (VLAN).

volume shadow copy   A Microsoft Windows Server 2003 feature that provides multiple copies of files in a shared folder, made at specific times, enabling users to retrieve copies of files as they existed at a previous time. This enables users to recover files that they accidentally deleted or overwrote.

VPN   *See* virtual private network (VPN).

W

WAN   *See* wide area network (WAN).

Web server   A computer that is maintained by a system administrator or Internet service provider (ISP) and that responds to requests from a user's Web browser.

well-known port   Transmission Control Protocol/Internet Protocol (TCP/IP) port numbers that have been permanently assigned to specific applications and services by the Internet Assigned Numbers Authority (IANA). Well-known ports make it possible for client programs to access services without having to specify a port number. For example, when you type a Uniform Resource Locator (URL) into a Web browser, the port number 80 is assumed because this is the port associated with Web servers.

WEP   *See* Wired Equivalent Privacy (WEP).

Wi-Fi   Another name for wireless networking technologies defined by the Institute for Electrical and Electronic Engineers (IEEE) 802.11 standards.

wide area network (WAN)   A network that spans a large geographical area using long-distance point-to-point connections, rather than shared network media as with a local area network (LAN). WANs can use a variety of communication technologies for their connections, such as leased telephone lines, dial-up telephone lines, and Integrated Services Digital Network (ISDN) or Digital Subscriber Line (DSL) connections. The Internet is the ultimate example of a WAN. Compare with local area network (LAN).

Windows Internet Name Service (WINS)   A service supplied with Microsoft Windows server operating systems that registers the Network Basic Input/Output System (NetBIOS) names and Internet Protocol (IP) addresses of the computers on a local area network (LAN) and resolves NetBIOS names into IP addresses for its clients as needed. WINS is the most efficient name resolution method for NetBIOS-based networks because it uses only unicast transmissions. Other methods rely on the repeated transmission of broadcast messages, which can generate large amounts of network traffic.

WINS   *See* Windows Internet Name Service (WINS).

Wired Equivalent Privacy (WEP)   A feature of the Institute of Electrical and Electronic Engineers (IEEE) 802.11 wireless networking standard that defines a method for encrypting data transmitted by wireless devices.

wireless local area network (WLAN)   A local area networking technology that uses radio signals, rather than cables, as a network medium.

WLAN   *See* wireless local area network (WLAN).

X

X.509   A document published by the International Telecommunications Union (ITU) that defines the structure of digital certificates.

Z

zone   In a Domain Name System (DNS) database, a zone is a subtree of the DNS database that is administered as a single, separate entity. This administrative unit can consist of a single domain or a domain with subdomains. A DNS zone administrator sets up one or more name servers for the zone.

zone database file   The file where name-to-IP-address mappings for a zone are stored.

zone transfer   The process by which Domain Name System (DNS) servers interact to maintain and synchronize authoritative name data. When a DNS server is configured as a secondary master for a zone, it periodically queries another DNS server configured as its source for the zone. If the version of the zone kept by the source is different, the secondary master server will pull zone data from its source DNS server to synchronize zone data.

Index

U

Prepare for Certification with Self-Paced Training Kits

Official Exam Prep Guides—
Plus Practice Tests

Ace your preparation for the skills measured by the MCP exams—and on the job. With official *Self-Paced Training Kits* from Microsoft, you'll work at your own pace through a system of lessons, hands-on exercises, troubleshooting labs, and review questions. Then test yourself with the Readiness Review Suite on CD, which provides hundreds of challenging questions for in-depth self-assessment and practice.

- **MCSE Self-Paced Training Kit (Exams 70-290, 70-291, 70-293, 70-294): Microsoft® Windows Server™ 2003 Core Requirements.** 4-Volume Boxed Set. ISBN: 0-7356-1953-0. (Individual volumes are available separately.)

- **MCSA/MCSE Self-Paced Training Kit (Exam 70-270): Installing, Configuring, and Administering Microsoft Windows® XP Professional, Second Edition.** ISBN: 0-7356-2152-7.

- **MCSE Self-Paced Training Kit (Exam 70-298): Designing Security for a Microsoft Windows Server 2003 Network.** ISBN: 0-7356-1969-7.

- **MCSA/MCSE Self-Paced Training Kit (Exam 70-350): Implementing Microsoft Internet Security and Acceleration Server 2004.** ISBN: 0-7356-2169-1.

- **MCSA/MCSE Self-Paced Training Kit (Exam 70-284): Implementing and Managing Microsoft Exchange Server 2003.** ISBN: 0-7356-1899-2.

For more information about Microsoft Press® books, visit: **www.microsoft.com/mspress**

For more information about learning tools such as online assessments, e-learning, and certification, visit: **www.microsoft.com/mspress** *and* **www.microsoft.com/learning**

Additional Windows (R2) Resources for Administrators

Published and Forthcoming Titles from Microsoft Press

Microsoft® Windows Server™ 2003 Administrator's Pocket Consultant, Second Edition

William R. Stanek • ISBN 0-7356-2245-0

Here's the practical, pocket-sized reference for IT professionals supporting Microsoft Windows Server 2003—fully updated for Service Pack 1 and Release 2. Designed for quick referencing, this portable guide covers all the essentials for performing everyday system administration tasks. Topics include managing workstations and servers, using Active Directory® directory service, creating and administering user and group accounts, managing files and directories, performing data security and auditing tasks, handling data back-up and recovery, and administering networks using TCP/IP, WINS, and DNS, and more.

MCSE Self-Paced Training Kit (Exams 70-290, 70-291, 70-293, 70-294): Microsoft Windows Server 2003 Core Requirements, Second Edition

Holme, Thomas, Mackin, McLean, Zacker, Spealman, Hudson, and Craft • ISBN 0-7356-2290-6

The Microsoft Certified Systems Engineer (MCSE) credential is the premier certification for professionals who analyze the business requirements and design and implement the infrastructure for business solutions based on the Microsoft Windows Server 2003 platform and Microsoft Windows Server System—now updated for Windows Server 2003 Service Pack 1 and R2. This all-in-one set provides in-depth preparation for the four required networking system exams. Work at your own pace through the lessons, hands-on exercises, troubleshooting labs, and review questions. You get expert exam tips plus a full review section covering all objectives and sub-objectives in each study guide. Then use the Microsoft Practice Tests on the CD to challenge yourself with more than 1500 questions for self-assessment and practice!

Microsoft Windows® Small Business Server 2003 R2 Administrator's Companion

Charlie Russel, Sharon Crawford, and Jason Gerend • ISBN 0-7356-2280-9

Get your small-business network, messaging, and collaboration systems up and running quickly with the essential guide to administering Windows Small Business Server 2003 R2. This reference details the features, capabilities, and technologies for both the standard and premium editions—including Microsoft Windows Server 2003 R2, Exchange Server 2003 with Service Pack 1, Windows SharePoint® Services, SQL Server™ 2005 Workgroup Edition, and Internet Information Services. Discover how to install, upgrade, or migrate to Windows Small Business Server 2003 R2; plan and implement your network, Internet access, and security services; customize Microsoft Exchange Server for your e-mail needs; and administer user rights, shares, permissions, and Group Policy.

Microsoft Windows Small Business Server 2003 R2 Administrator's Companion

Charlie Russel, Sharon Crawford, and Jason Gerend • ISBN 0-7356-2280-9

Here's the ideal one-volume guide for the IT professional administering Windows Server 2003. Now fully updated for Windows Server 2003 Service Pack 1 and R2, this *Administrator's Companion* offers up-to-date information on core system administration topics for Microsoft Windows, including Active Directory services, security, scripting, disaster planning and recovery, and interoperability with UNIX. It also includes all-new sections on Service Pack 1 security updates and new features for R2. Featuring easy-to-use procedures and handy work-arounds, this book provides ready answers for on-the-job results.

MCSA/MCSE Self-Paced Training Kit (Exam 70-290): Managing and Maintaining a Microsoft Windows Server 2003 Environment, Second Edition
Dan Holme and Orin Thomas • ISBN 0-7356-2289-2

MCSA/MCSE Self-Paced Training Kit (Exam 70-291): Implementing, Managing, and Maintaining a Microsoft Windows Server 2003 Network Infrastructure, Second Edition
J.C. Mackin and Ian McLean • ISBN 0-7356-2288-4

MCSE Self-Paced Training Kit (Exam 70-293): Planning and Maintaining a Microsoft Windows Server 2003 Network Infrastructure, Second Edition
Craig Zacker • ISBN 0-7356-2287-6

MCSE Self-Paced Training Kit (Exam 70-294): Planning, Implementing, and Maintaining a Microsoft Windows Server 2003 Active Directory® Infrastructure, Second Ed.
Jill Spealman, Kurt Hudson, and Melissa Craft • ISBN 0-7356-2286-8

For more information about Microsoft Press® books and other learning products,
visit: **www.microsoft.com/mspress** *and* **www.microsoft.com/learning**

Microsoft Windows Server 2003 Resource Kit
The *definitive* resource
for Windows Server 2003!

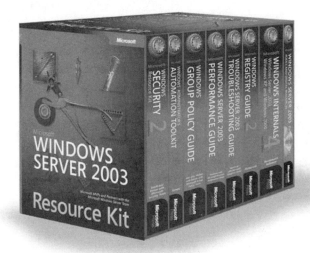

Get the in-depth technical information and tools you need to manage and optimize Microsoft® Windows Server™ 2003—with expert guidance and best practices from Microsoft MVPs, leading industry consultants, and the Microsoft Windows Server team. This official *Resource Kit* delivers seven comprehensive volumes, including:

- **Microsoft Windows® Security Resource Kit, Second Edition**
- **Microsoft Windows Administrator's Automation Toolkit**
- **Microsoft Windows Group Policy Guide**
- **Microsoft Windows Server 2003 Performance Guide**
- **Microsoft Windows Server 2003 Troubleshooting Guide**
- **Microsoft Windows Registry Guide, Second Edition**
- **Microsoft Windows Internals, Fourth Edition**

You'll find 300+ timesaving tools and scripts, an eBook of the entire *Resource Kit*, plus five bonus eBooks. It's everything you need to help maximize system performance and reliability—and help reduce ownership and support costs.

Microsoft Windows Server 2003 Resource Kit
Microsoft MVPs and Partners with the Microsoft Windows Server Team
ISBN: 0-7356-2232-9

For more information about Microsoft Press® books, visit: **www.microsoft.com/mspress**

For more information about learning tools such as online assessments,
e-learning, and certification, visit: **www.microsoft.com/learning**

Microsoft
Press

Additional SQL Server Resources for Administrators

Published and Forthcoming Titles from Microsoft Press

Microsoft® SQL Server™ 2005 Reporting Services *Step by Step*
Hitachi Consulting Services ● ISBN 0-7356-2250-7

SQL Server Reporting Services (SRS) is Microsoft's customizable reporting solution for business data analysis. It is one of the key value features of SQL Server 2005: functionality more advanced and much less expensive than its competition. SRS is powerful, so an understanding of how to architect a report, as well as how to install and program SRS, is key to harnessing the full functionality of SQL Server. This procedural tutorial shows how to use the Report Project Wizard, how to think about and access data, and how to build queries. It also walks the reader through the creation of charts and visual layouts to enable maximum visual understanding of the data analysis. Interactivity (enhanced in SQL Server 2005) and security are also covered in detail.

Microsoft SQL Server 2005 Administrator's Pocket Consultant
William R. Stanek ● ISBN 0-7356-2107-1

Here's the utterly practical, pocket-sized reference for IT professionals who need to administer, optimize, and maintain SQL Server 2005 in their organizations. This unique guide provides essential details for using SQL Server 2005 to help protect and manage your company's data—whether automating tasks; creating indexes and views; performing backups and recovery; replicating transactions; tuning performance; managing server activity; importing and exporting data; or performing other key tasks. Featuring quick-reference tables, lists, and step-by-step instructions, this handy, one-stop guide provides fast, accurate answers on the spot, whether you're at your desk or in the field!

Microsoft SQL Server 2005 Administrator's Companion
Marci Frohock Garcia, Edward Whalen, and Mitchell Schroeter ● ISBN 0-7356-2198-5

Microsoft SQL Server 2005 Administrator's Companion is the comprehensive, in-depth guide that saves time by providing all the technical information you need to deploy, administer, optimize, and support SQL Server 2005. Using a hands-on, example-rich approach, this authoritative, one-volume reference book provides expert advice, product information, detailed solutions, procedures, and real-world troubleshooting tips from experienced SQL Server 2005 professionals. This expert guide shows you how to design high-availability database systems, prepare for installation, install and configure SQL Server 2005, administer services and features, and maintain and troubleshoot your database system. It covers how to configure your system for your I/O system and model and optimize system capacity. The expert authors provide details on how to create and use defaults, constraints, rules, indexes, views, functions, stored procedures, and triggers. This guide shows you how to administer reporting services, analysis services, notification services, and integration services. It also provides a wealth of information on replication and the specifics of snapshot, transactional, and merge replication. Finally, there is expansive coverage of how to manage and tune your SQL Server system, including automating tasks, backup and restoration of databases, and management of users and security.

Microsoft SQL Server 2005 Analysis Services *Step by Step*
Hitachi Consulting Services ● ISBN 0-7356-2199-3

One of the key features of SQL Server 2005 is SQL Server Analysis Services—Microsoft's customizable analysis solution for business data modeling and interpretation. Just compare SQL Server Analysis Services to its competition to understand/grasp the great value of its enhanced features. One of the keys to harnessing the full functionality of SQL Server will be leveraging Analysis Services for the powerful tool that it is—including creating a cube, and deploying, customizing, and extending the basic calculations. This step-by-step tutorial discusses how to get started, how to build scalable analytical applications, and how to use and administer advanced features. Interactivity (which is enhanced in SQL Server 2005), data translation, and security are also covered in detail.

Microsoft SQL Server 2005 Express Edition
Step by Step
Jackie Goldstein ● ISBN 0-7356-2184-5

Inside Microsoft SQL Server 2005:
The Storage Engine
Kalen Delaney ● ISBN 0-7356-2105-5

Inside Microsoft SQL Server 2005:
T-SQL Programming
Itzik Ben-Gan ● ISBN 0-7356-2197-7

Inside Microsoft SQL Server 2005:
Query Processing and Optimization
Kalen Delaney ● ISBN 0-7356-2196-9

For more information about Microsoft Press® books and other learning products,
visit: **www.microsoft.com/mspress** *and* **www.microsoft.com/learning**

Microsoft *Press*

content•master

www.contentmaster.com
info@contentmaster.com

knowledge into understanding

Providing leading-edge content

Content Master is one of the world's leading technical authoring and consultancy organizations, working with key software vendors to provide leading-edge content to technical audiences. This content, combined with our business knowledge helps enable business decision makers, developers and IT Professionals to keep abreast of new initiatives, helping them build innovative enterprise solutions.

We also offer educational and content consultancy, identifying the most effective strategies for the development and deployment of materials. Our unique approach encompasses technical, business and educational requirements. This ensures that developed content not only offers the right level of specialist knowledge but that it addresses commercial requirements and is structured in the most effective way for the audience.

Microsoft
GOLD CERTIFIED
Partner